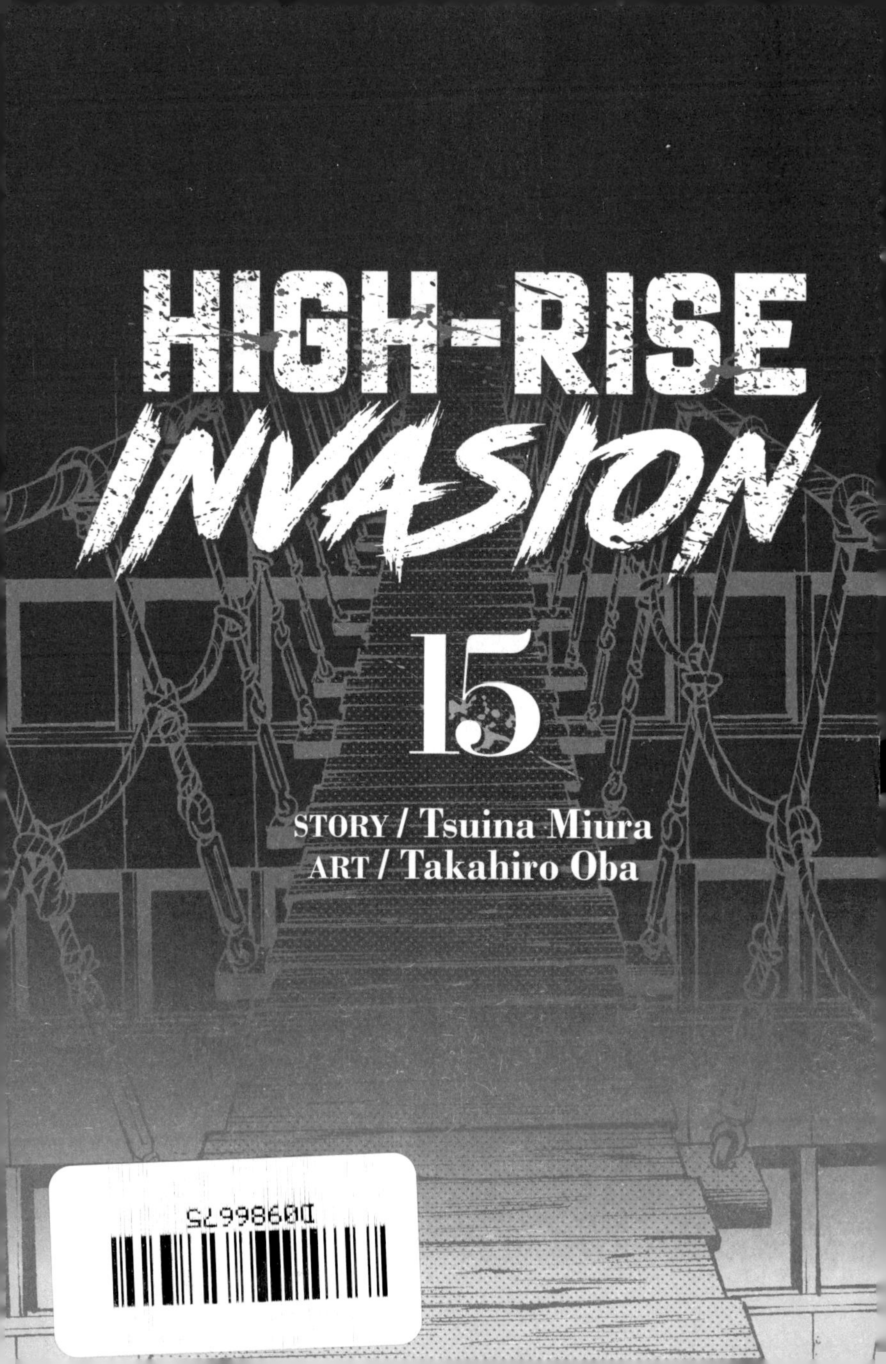

HIGH-RISE INVASION

15

STORY / Tsuina Miura
ART / Takahiro Oba

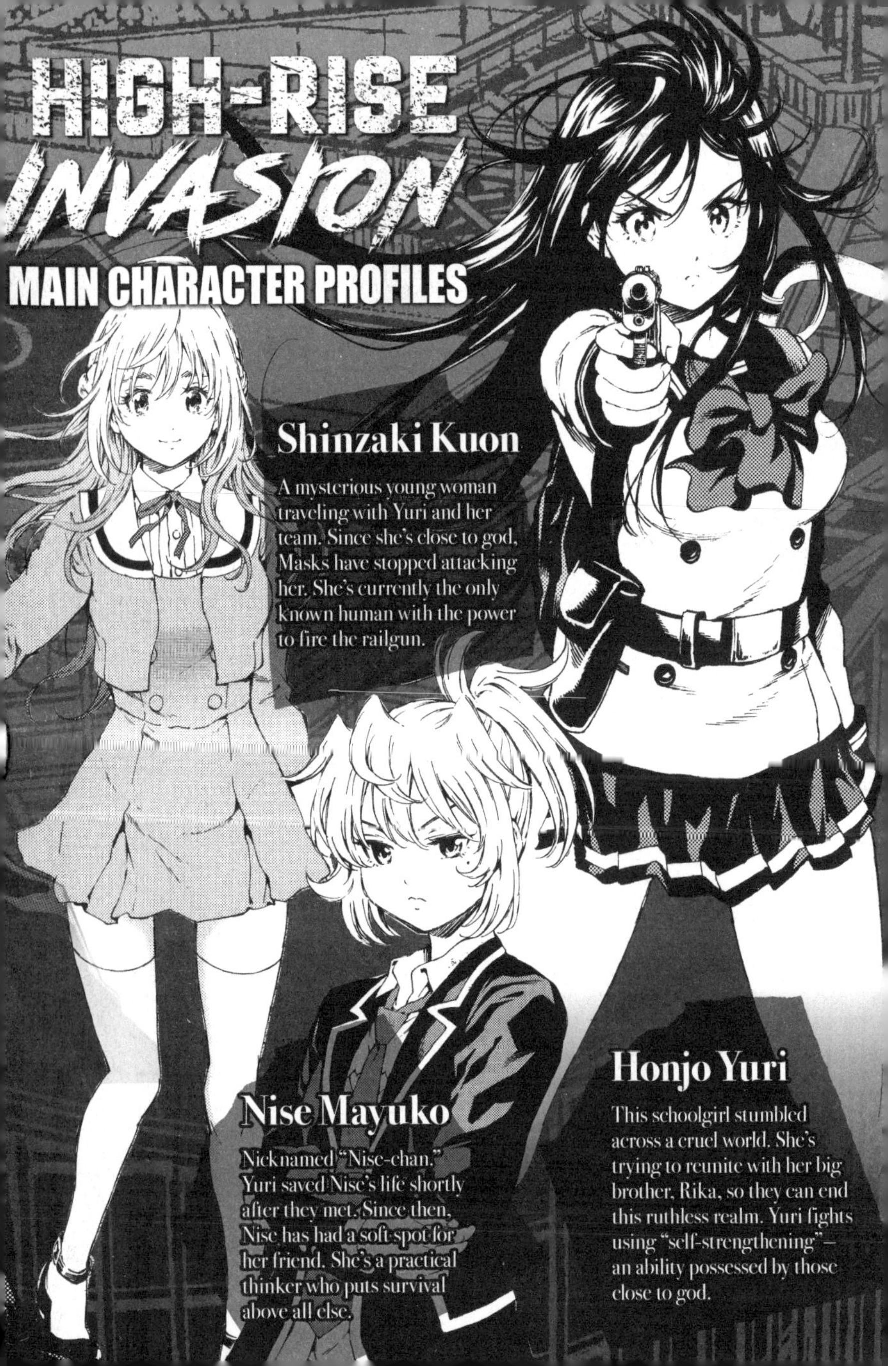
HIGH-RISE INVASION
MAIN CHARACTER PROFILES
Shinzaki Kuon
A mysterious young woman traveling with Yuri and her team. Since she's close to god, Masks have stopped attacking her. She's currently the only known human with the power to fire the railgun.
Honjo Yuri
This schoolgirl stumbled across a cruel world. She's trying to reunite with her big brother, Rika, so they can end this ruthless realm. Yuri fights using "self-strengthening"—an ability possessed by those close to god.
Nise Mayuko
Nicknamed "Nise-chan." Yuri saved Nise's life shortly after they met. Since then, Nise has had a soft spot for her friend. She's a practical thinker who puts survival above all else.

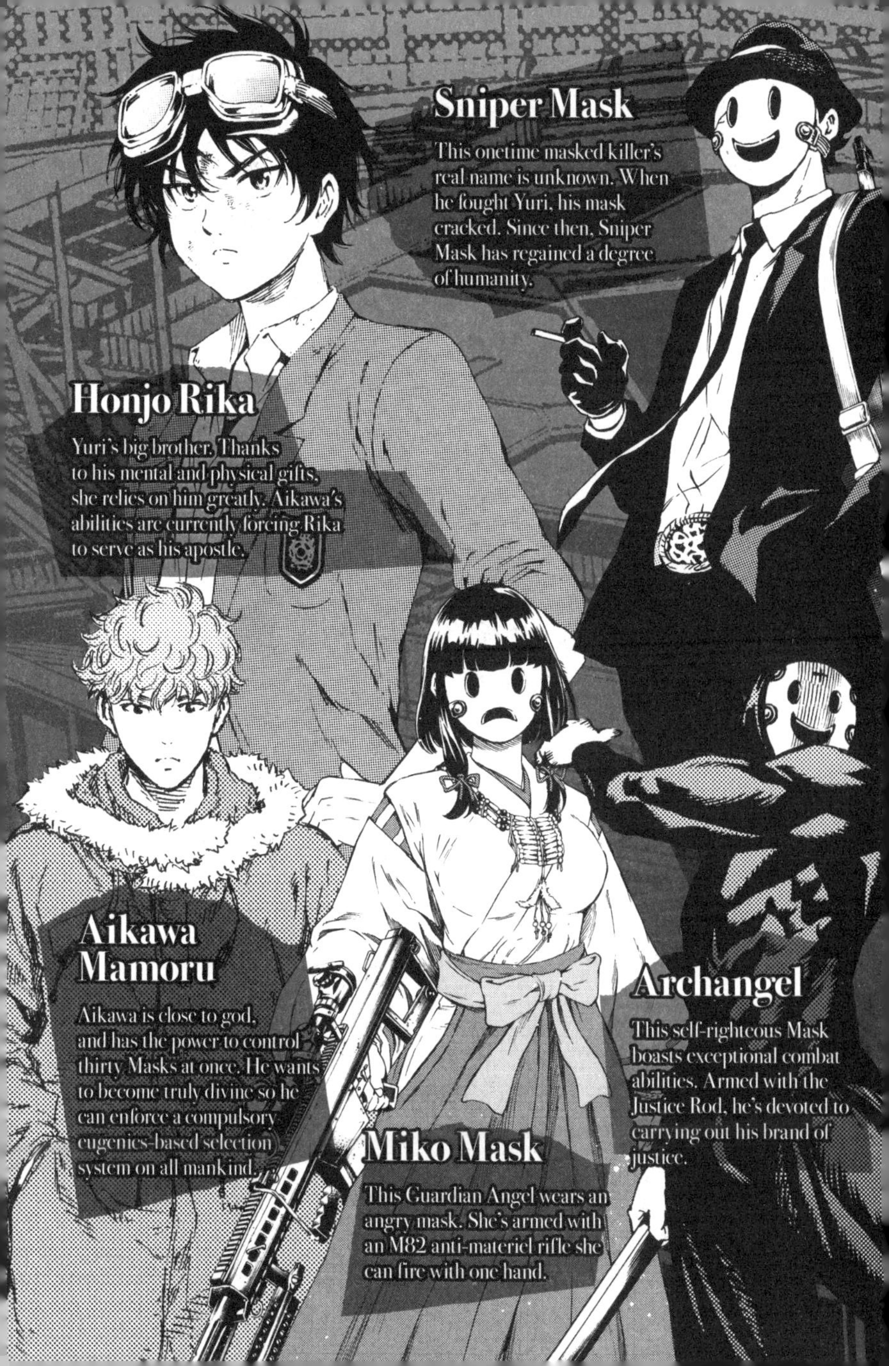
Sniper Mask
This onetime masked killer's real name is unknown. When he fought Yuri, his mask cracked. Since then, Sniper Mask has regained a degree of humanity.
Honjo Rika
Yuri's big brother. Thanks to his mental and physical gifts, she relies on him greatly. Aikawa's abilities are currently forcing Rika to serve as his apostle.
Archangel
This self-righteous Mask boasts exceptional combat abilities. Armed with the Justice Rod, he's devoted to carrying out his brand of justice.
Miko Mask
This Guardian Angel wears an angry mask. She's armed with an M82 anti-materiel rifle she can fire with one hand.
Aikawa Mamoru
Aikawa is close to god, and has the power to control thirty Masks at once. He wants to become truly divine so he can enforce a compulsory eugenics-based selection system on all mankind.

HIGH-RISE INVASION

15

CONTENTS

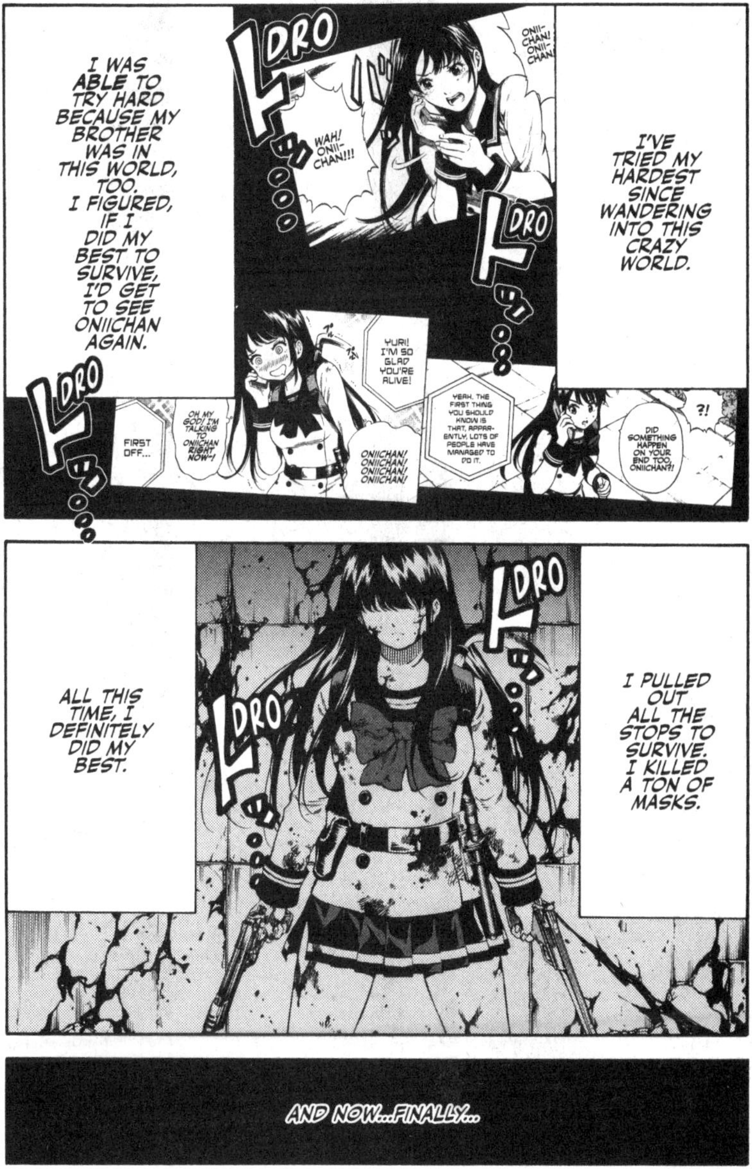
I'VE TRIED MY HARDEST SINCE WANDERING INTO THIS CRAZY WORLD.
DRO
ONII-CHAN! ONII-CHAN!
WAH! ONII-CHAN!!!
DRO
I WAS ABLE TO TRY HARD BECAUSE MY BROTHER WAS IN THIS WORLD, TOO. I FIGURED, IF I DID MY BEST TO SURVIVE, I'D GET TO SEE ONIICHAN AGAIN.
DRO
?!
DID SOMETHING HAPPEN ON YOUR END TOO, ONIICHAN?!
YEAH, THE FIRST THING YOU SHOULD KNOW IS THAT, APPARENTLY, LOTS OF PEOPLE HAVE MANAGED TO DO IT.
YURI! I'M SO GLAD YOU'RE ALIVE!
ONIICHAN! ONIICHAN! ONIICHAN! ONIICHAN!
OH MY GOD! I'M TALKING TO ONIICHAN RIGHT NOW~!
FIRST OFF...
DRO
I PULLED OUT ALL THE STOPS TO SURVIVE. I KILLED A TON OF MASKS.
DRO
DRO
ALL THIS TIME, I DEFINITELY DID MY BEST.
AND NOW...FINALLY...

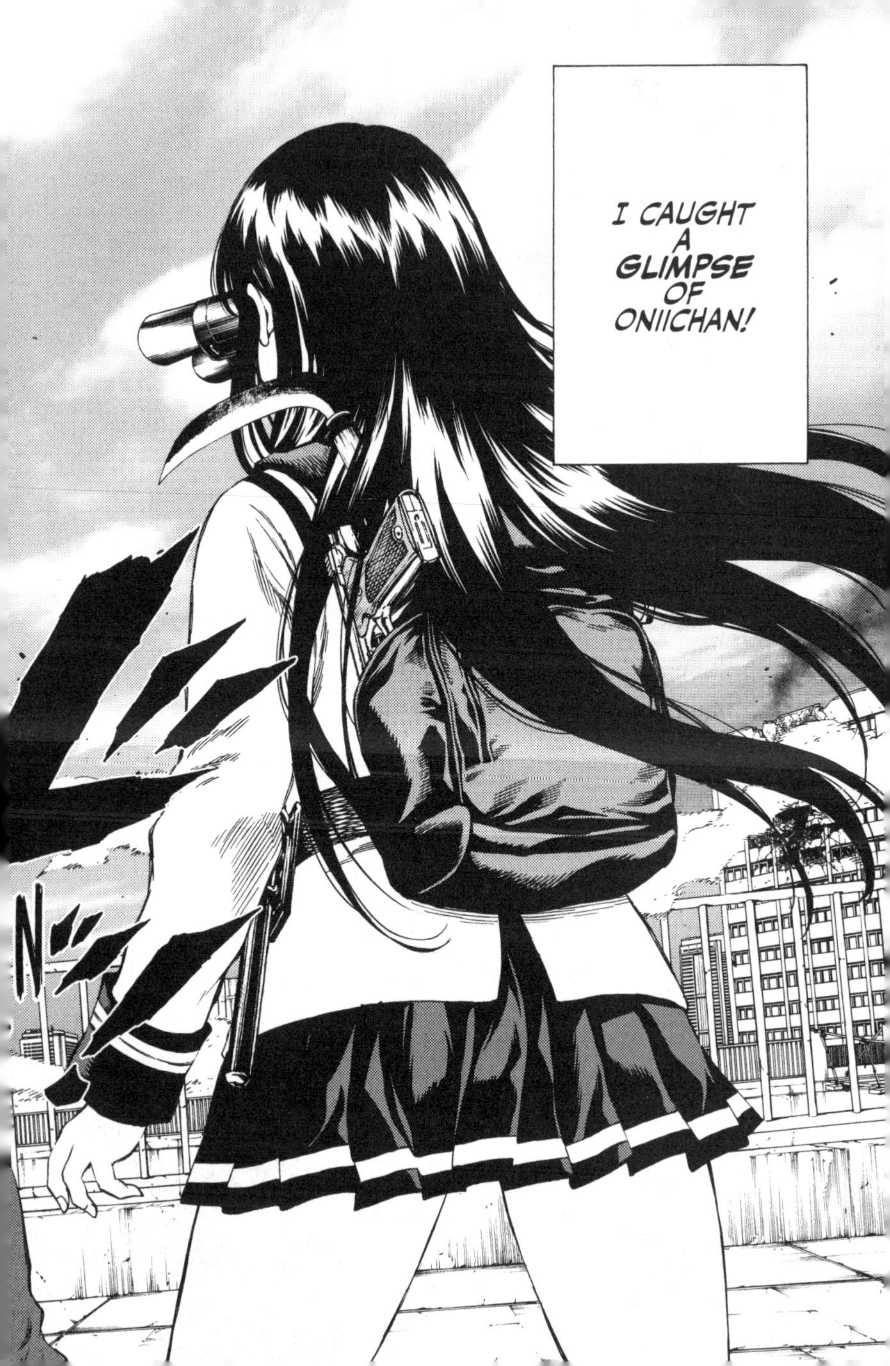
I CAUGHT A GLIMPSE OF ONIICHAN!
N

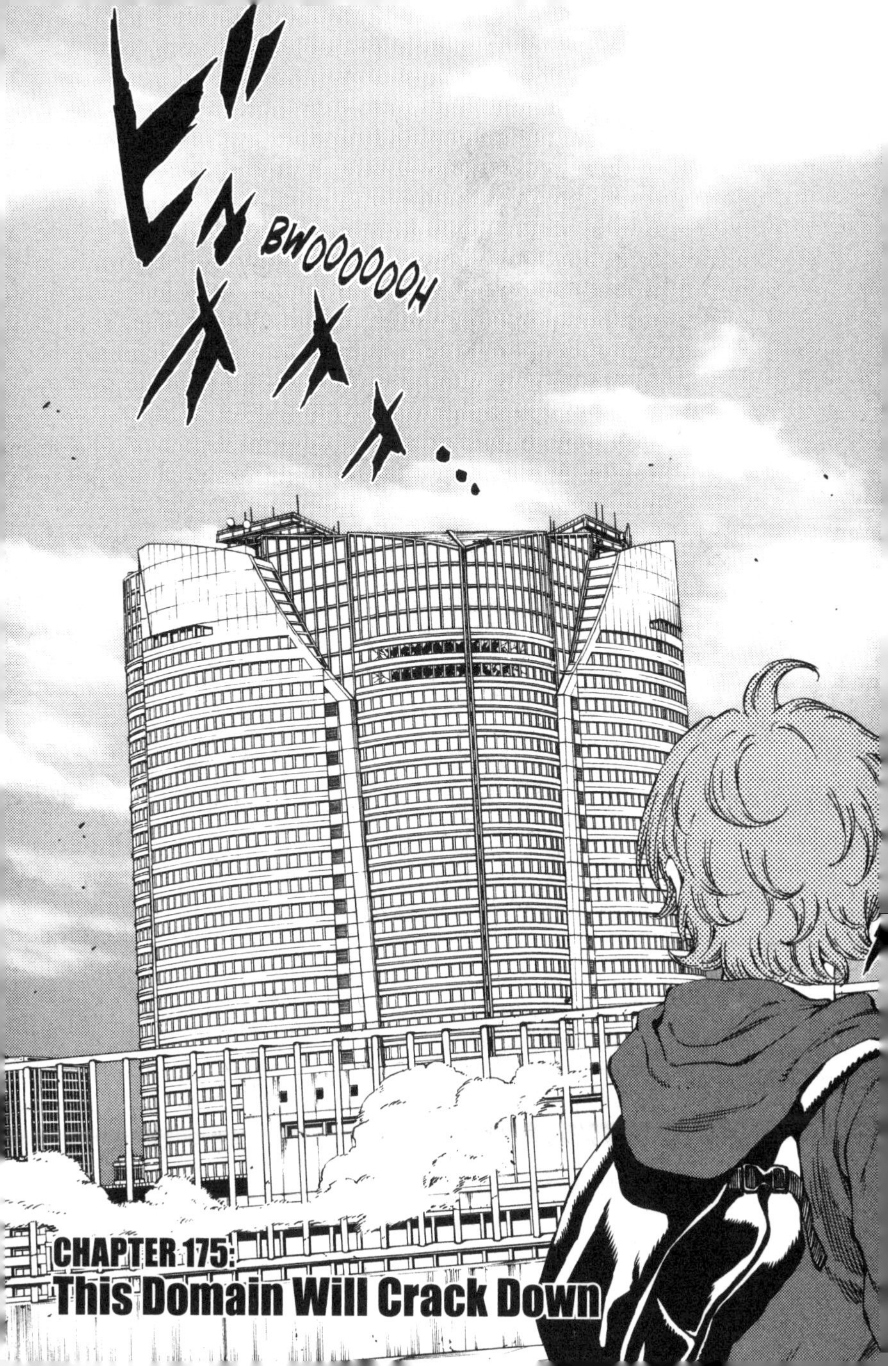
ビン オォォ…
BWOOOOOOH
CHAPTER 175:
This Domain Will Crack Down

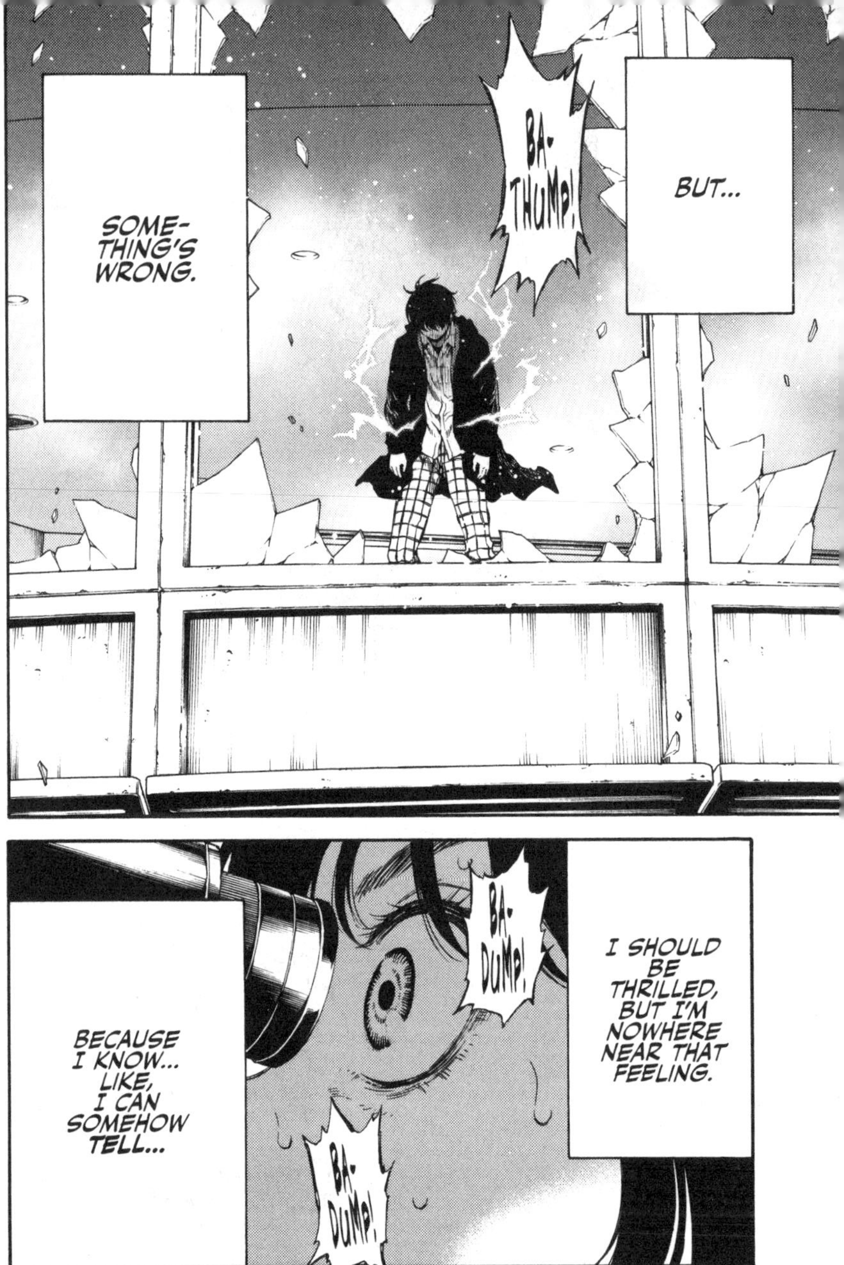
BUT...
BA-THUMP!
SOME-THING'S WRONG.
I SHOULD BE THRILLED, BUT I'M NOWHERE NEAR THAT FEELING.
BA-DUMP!
BA-DUMP!
BECAUSE I KNOW... LIKE, I CAN SOMEHOW TELL...

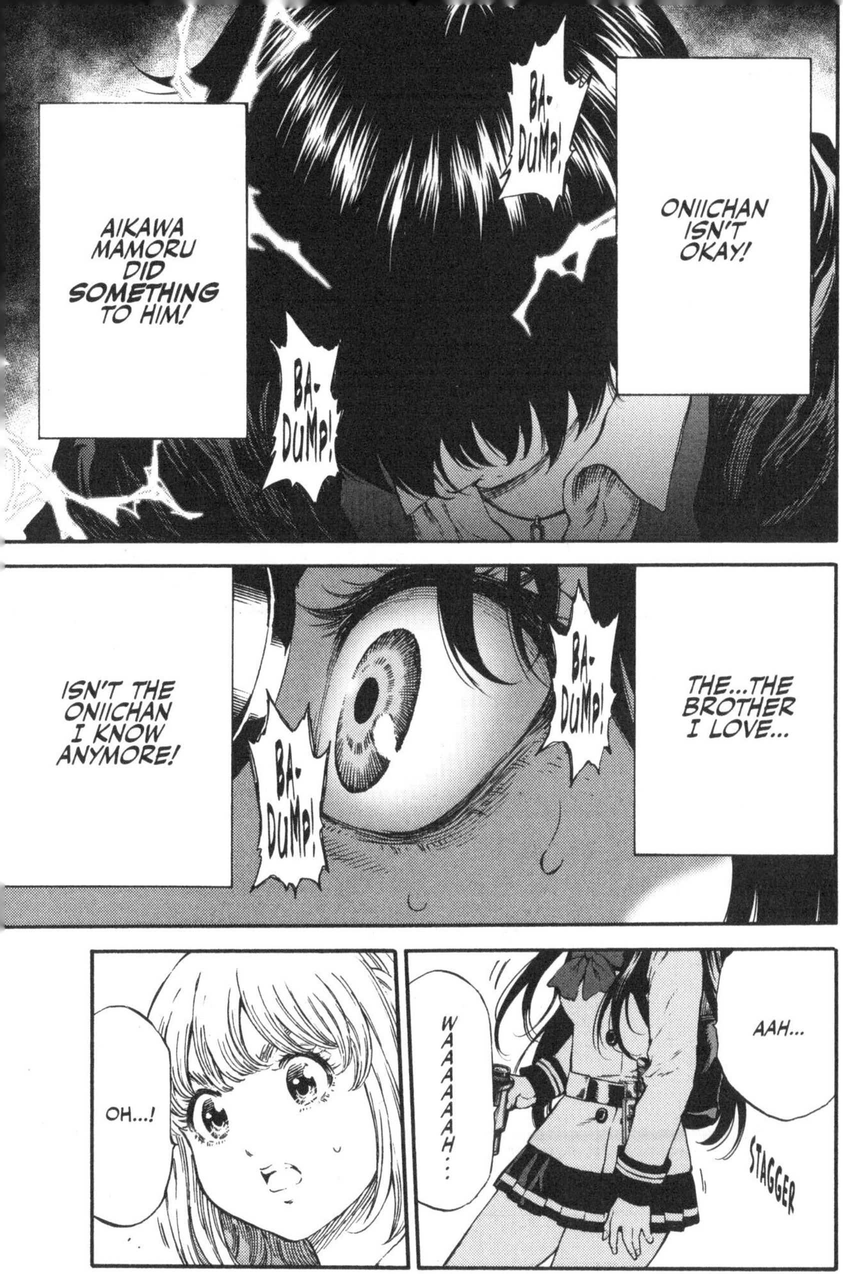
ONIICHAN ISN'T OKAY!
BA-DUMP!
AIKAWA MAMORU DID SOMETHING TO HIM!
BA-DUMP!
THE...THE BROTHER I LOVE...
BA-DUMP!
BA-DUMP!
ISN'T THE ONIICHAN I KNOW ANYMORE!
AAH...
STAGGER
WAAAAAAAH...
OH...!

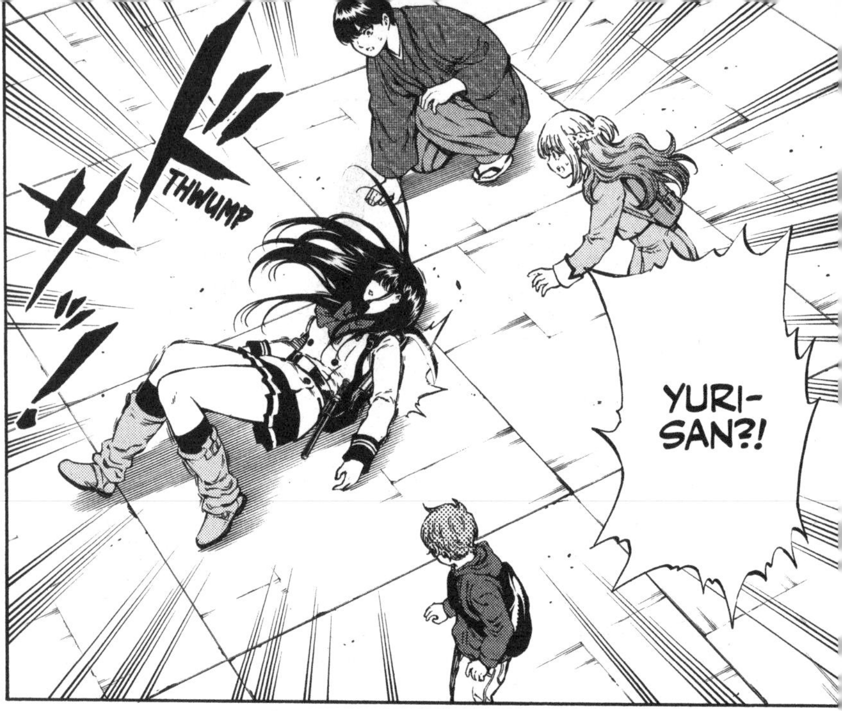
THWUMP
YURI-SAN?!
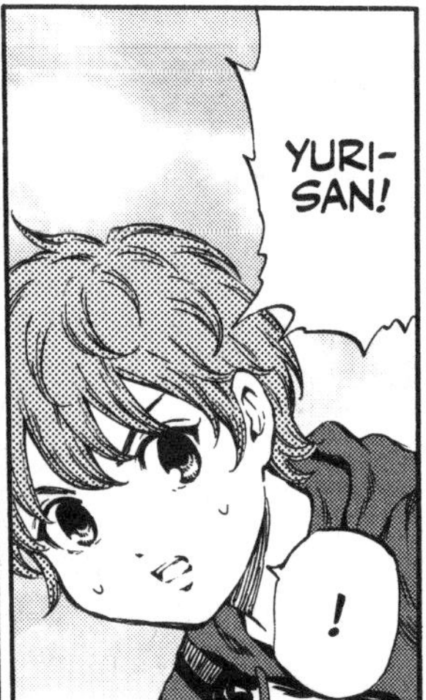
YURI-SAN!
!
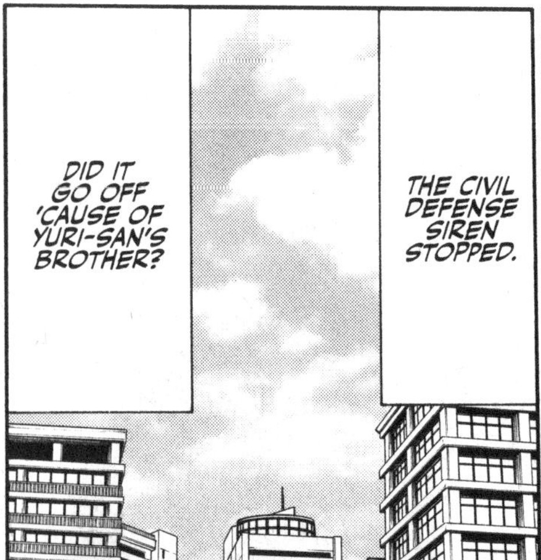
THE CIVIL DEFENSE SIREN STOPPED.
DID IT GO OFF 'CAUSE OF YURI-SAN'S BROTHER?

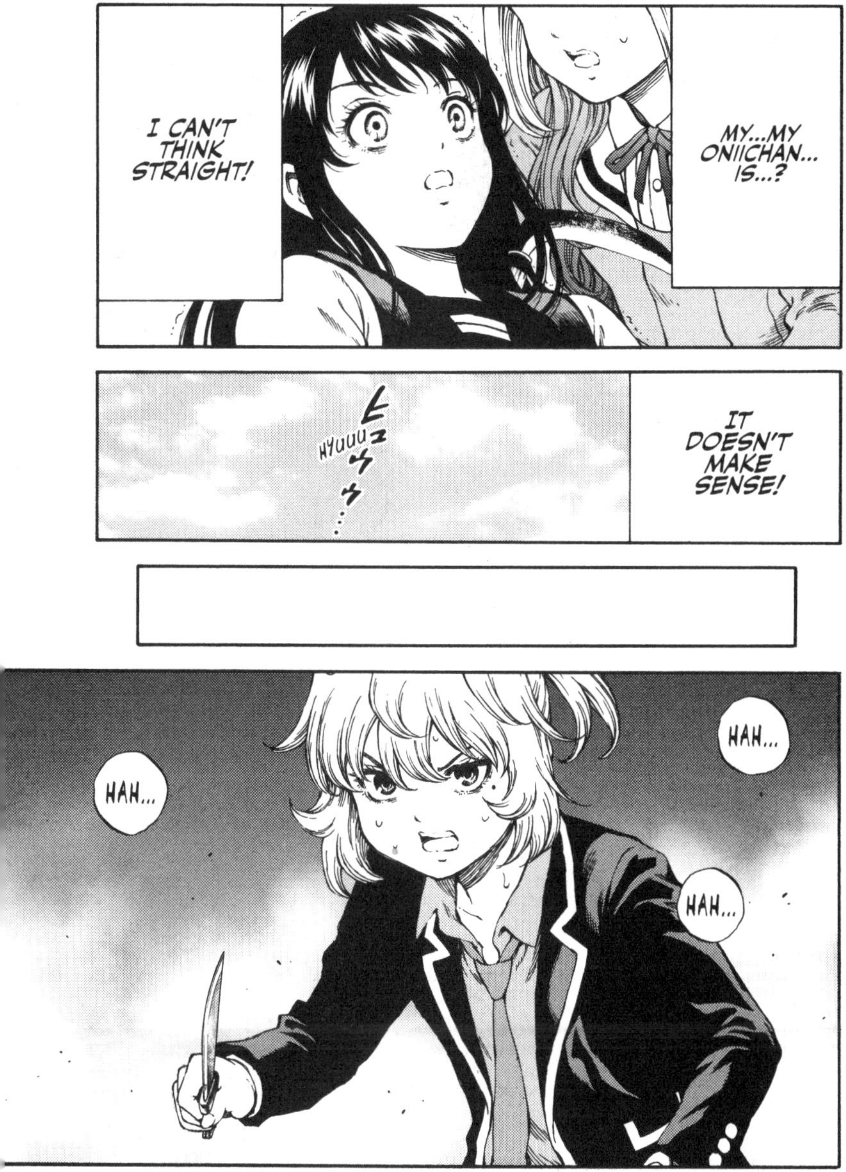
MY...MY ONIICHAN... IS...?
I CAN'T THINK STRAIGHT!
IT DOESN'T MAKE SENSE!
HYUUUU
HAH...
HAH...
HAH...

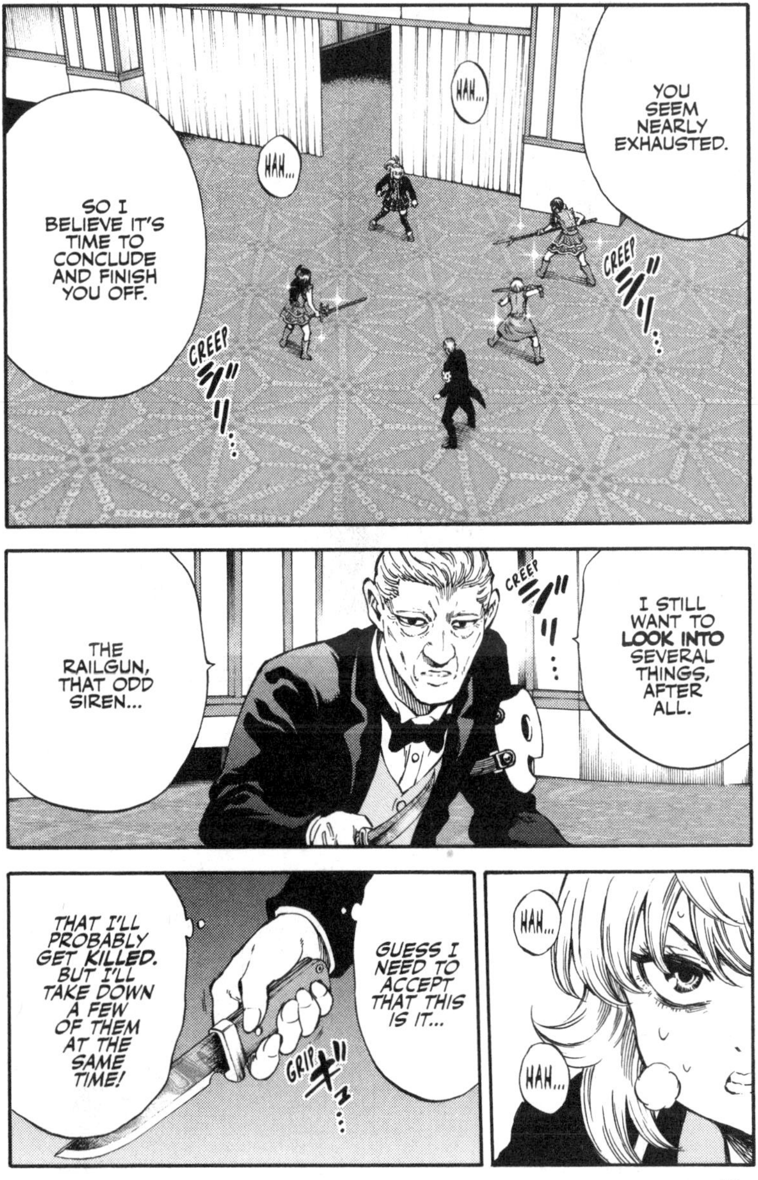
YOU SEEM NEARLY EXHAUSTED.
HAH...
HAH...
CREEP
SO I BELIEVE IT'S TIME TO CONCLUDE AND FINISH YOU OFF.
CREEP
I STILL WANT TO **LOOK INTO** SEVERAL THINGS, AFTER ALL.
CREEP
THE RAILGUN, THAT ODD SIREN...
HAH...
HAH...
GUESS I NEED TO ACCEPT THAT THIS IS IT...
GRIP
*THAT I'LL PROBABLY GET **KILLED**. BUT I'LL TAKE DOWN A FEW OF THEM AT THE SAME TIME!*

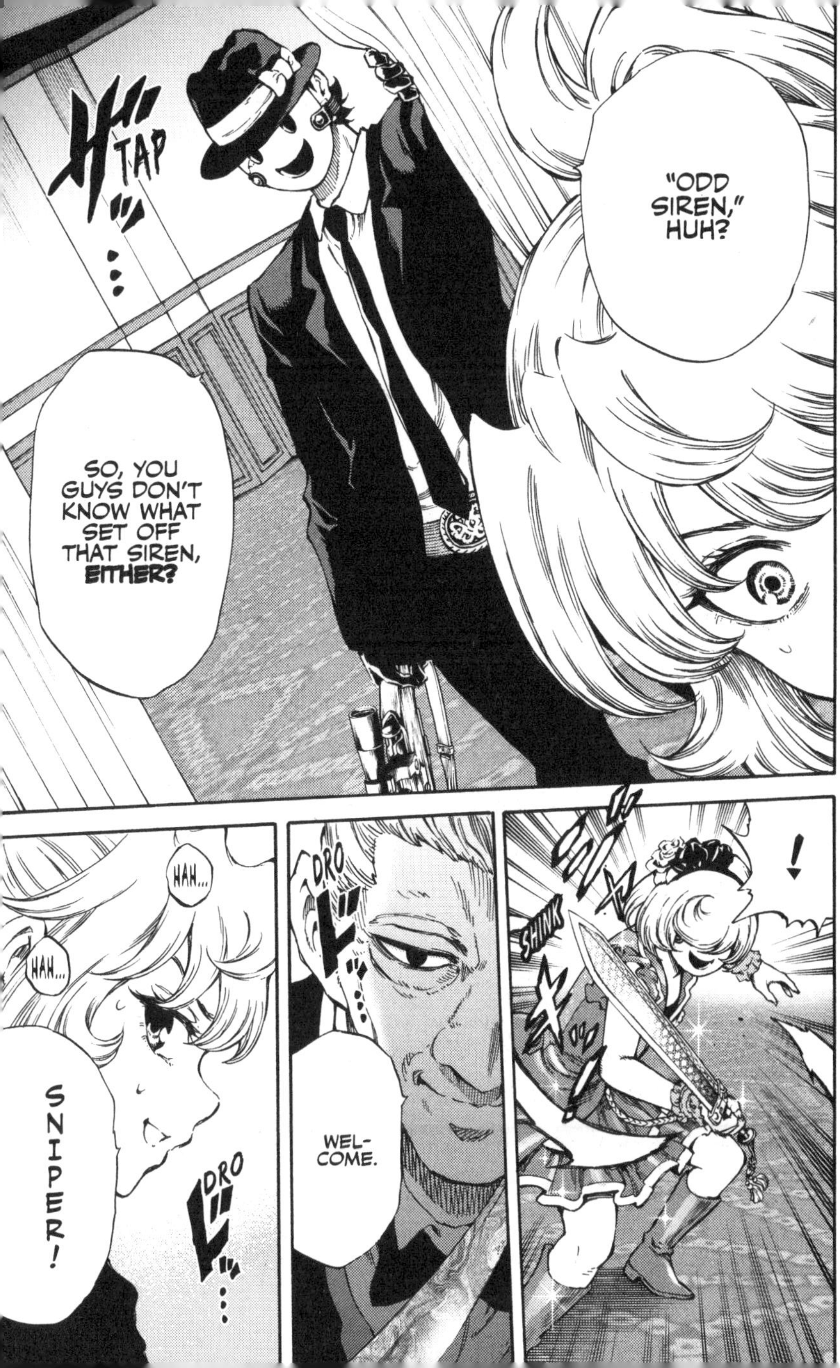
"ODD SIREN," HUH?
TAP
...
SO, YOU GUYS DON'T KNOW WHAT SET OFF THAT SIREN, **EITHER?**
!
SHINK
DRO
...
WEL-COME.
HAH...
HAH...
SNIPER!
DRO
...

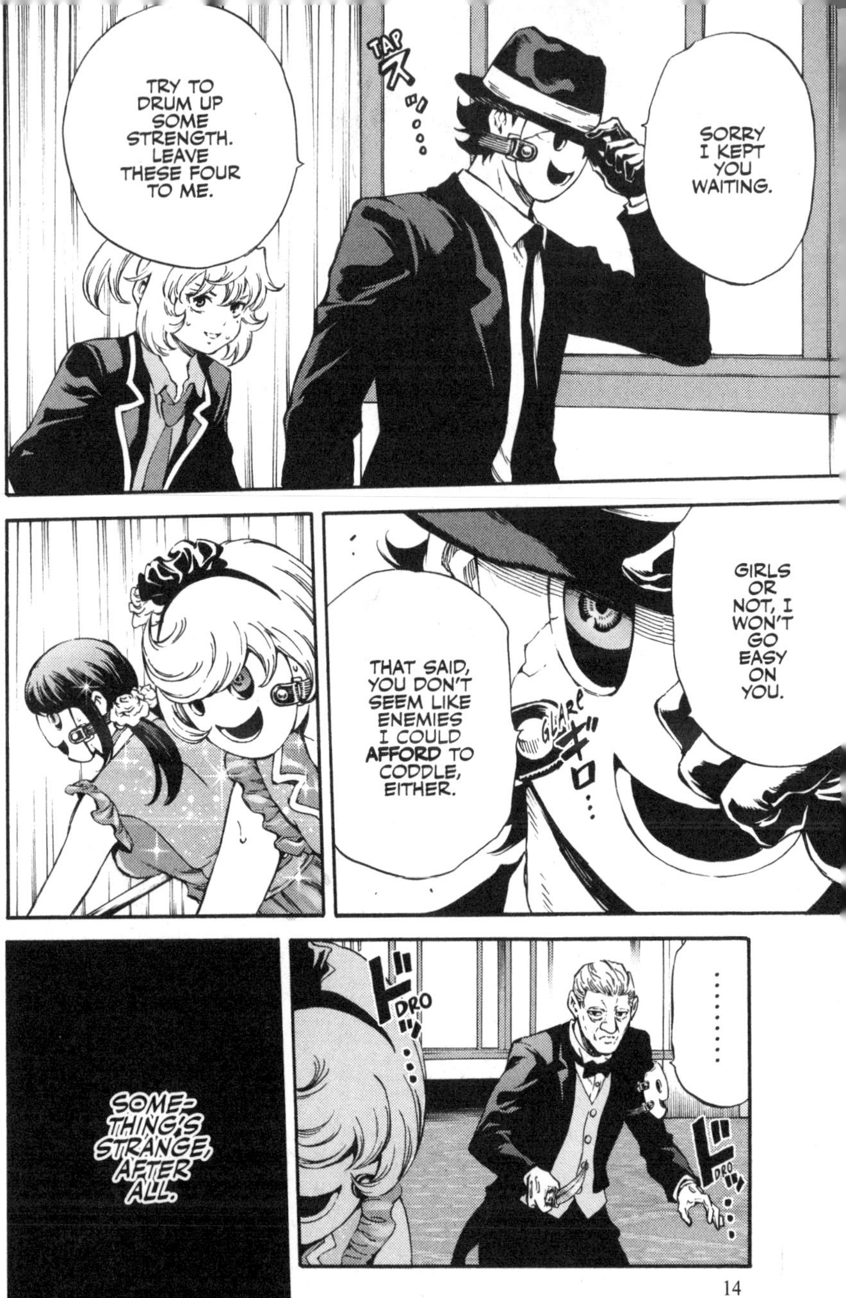
SORRY I KEPT YOU WAITING.
TAP
TRY TO DRUM UP SOME STRENGTH. LEAVE THESE FOUR TO ME.
GIRLS OR NOT, I WON'T GO EASY ON YOU.
GLARE
THAT SAID, YOU DON'T SEEM LIKE ENEMIES I COULD **AFFORD** TO CODDLE, EITHER.
....
DRO
DRO
SOME-THING'S STRANGE, AFTER ALL.

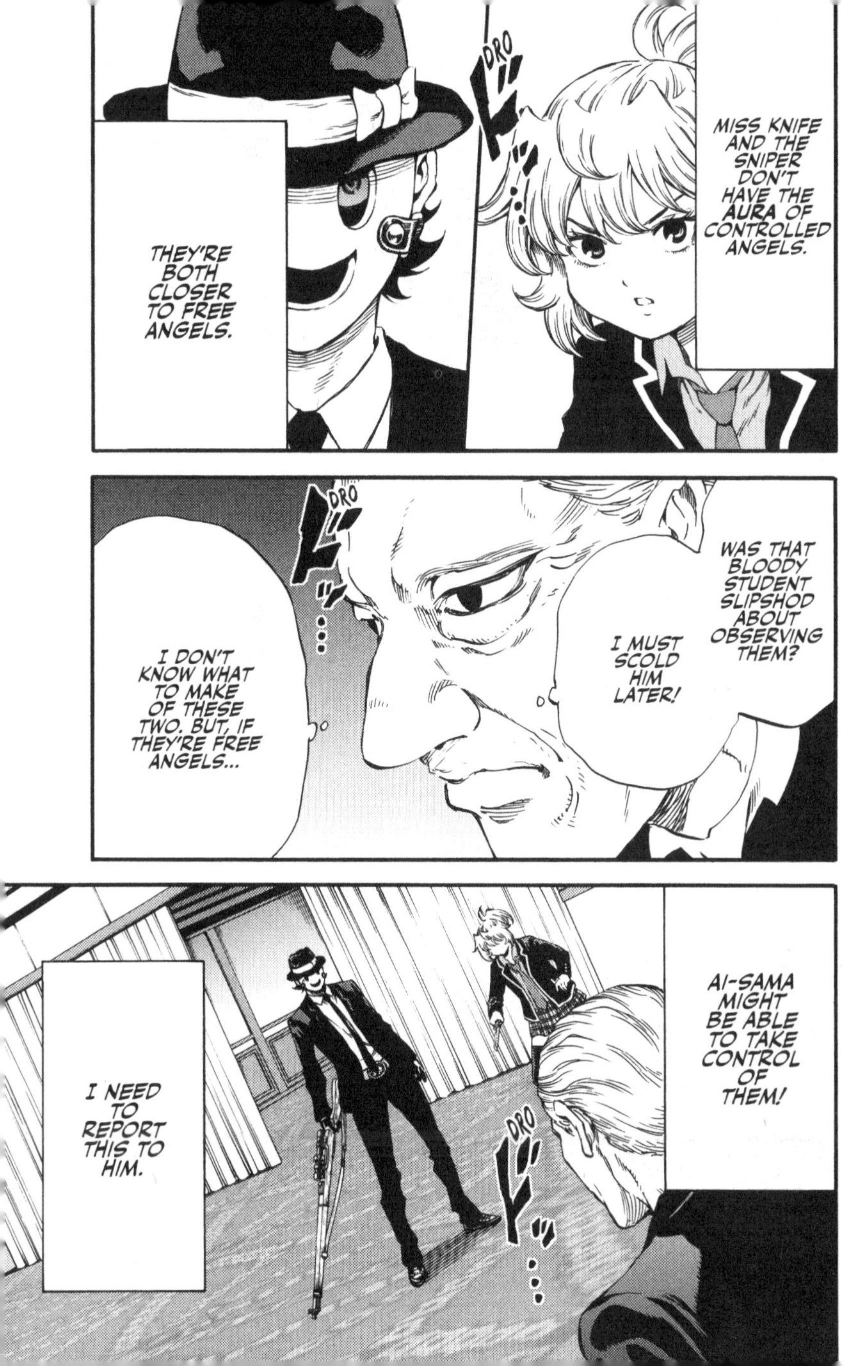
MISS KNIFE AND THE SNIPER DON'T HAVE THE AURA OF CONTROLLED ANGELS.
DRO
THEY'RE BOTH CLOSER TO FREE ANGELS.
DRO
WAS THAT BLOODY STUDENT SLIPSHOD ABOUT OBSERVING THEM?
I MUST SCOLD HIM LATER!
I DON'T KNOW WHAT TO MAKE OF THESE TWO. BUT, IF THEY'RE FREE ANGELS...
AI-SAMA MIGHT BE ABLE TO TAKE CONTROL OF THEM!
DRO
I NEED TO REPORT THIS TO HIM.

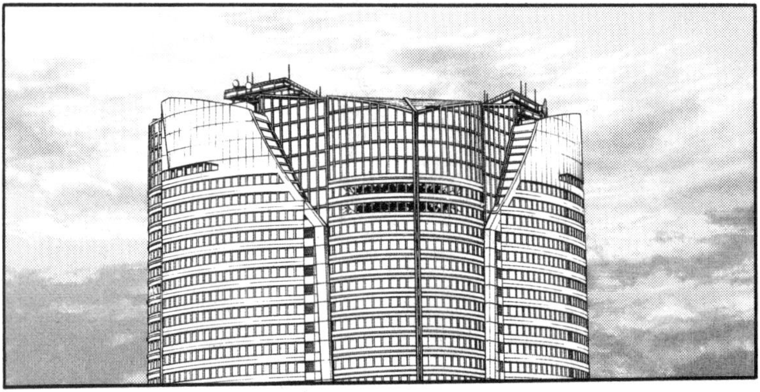

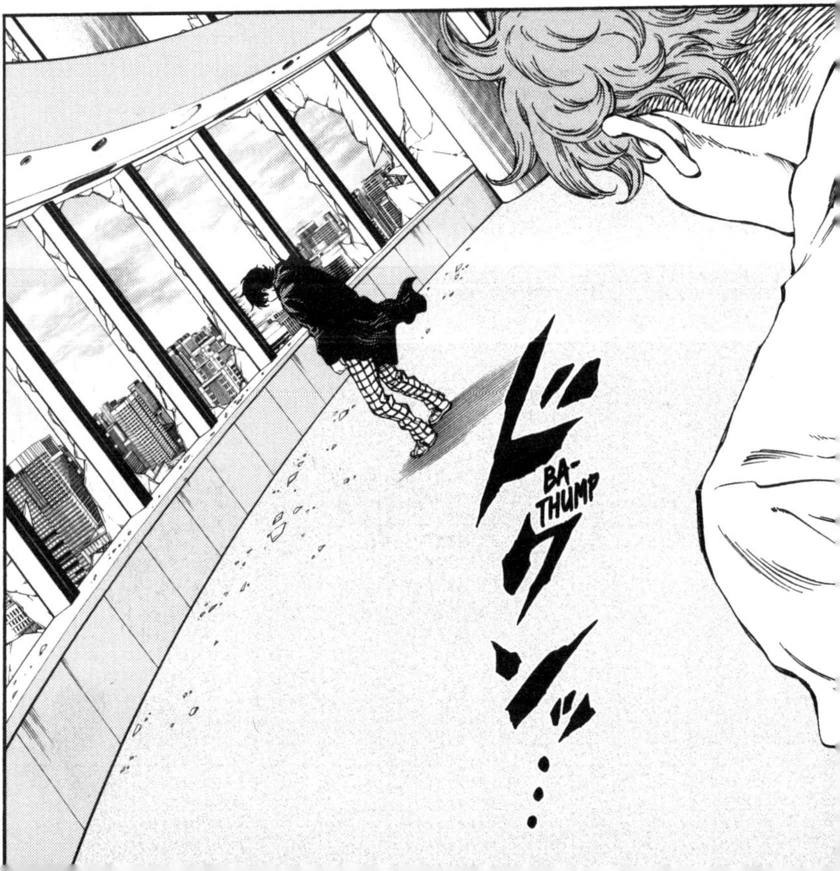
BA-
THUMP

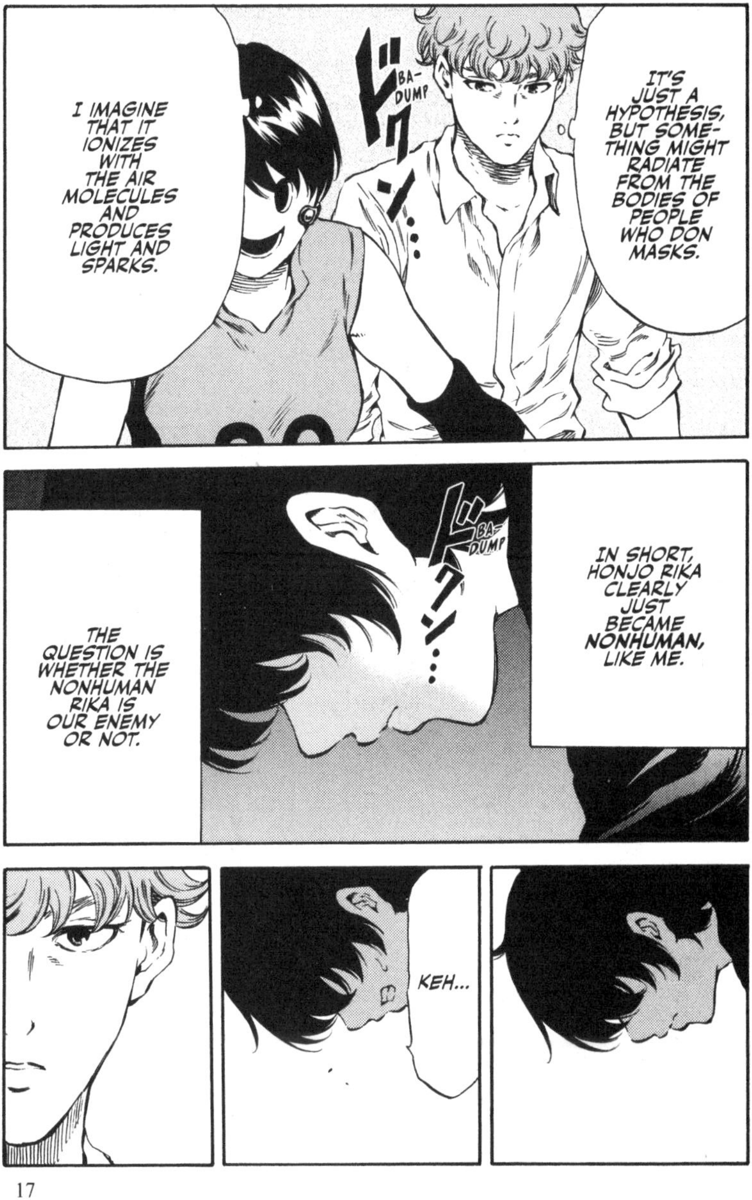
IT'S JUST A HYPOTHESIS, BUT SOME-THING MIGHT RADIATE FROM THE BODIES OF PEOPLE WHO DON MASKS.
BA-DUMP
I IMAGINE THAT IT IONIZES WITH THE AIR MOLECULES AND PRODUCES LIGHT AND SPARKS.
IN SHORT, HONJO RIKA CLEARLY JUST BECAME **NONHUMAN**, LIKE ME.
BA-DUMP
THE QUESTION IS WHETHER THE NONHUMAN RIKA IS OUR ENEMY OR NOT.
KEH...

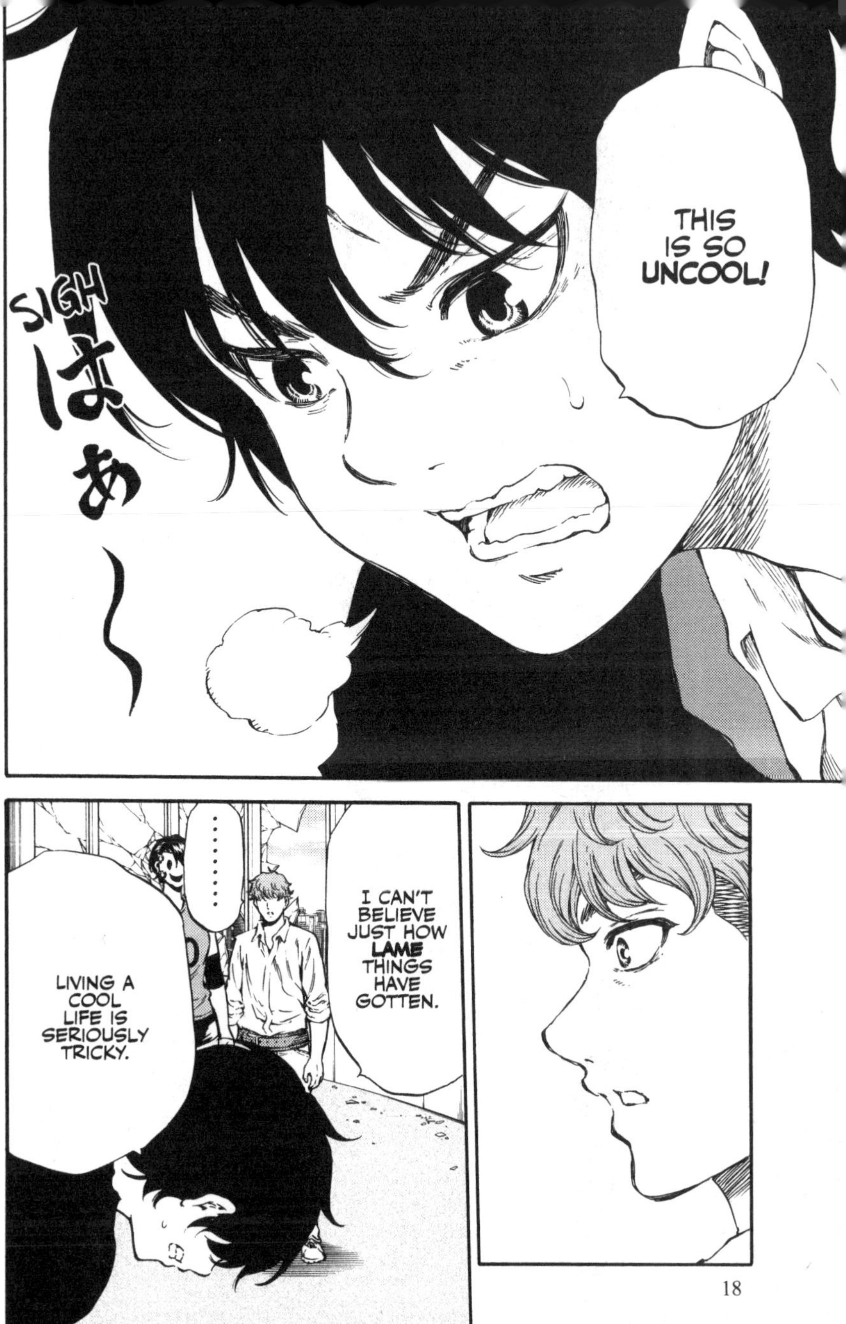
THIS IS SO UNCOOL!
SIGH
はぁ～
I CAN'T BELIEVE JUST HOW LAME THINGS HAVE GOTTEN.
....
LIVING A COOL LIFE IS SERIOUSLY TRICKY.

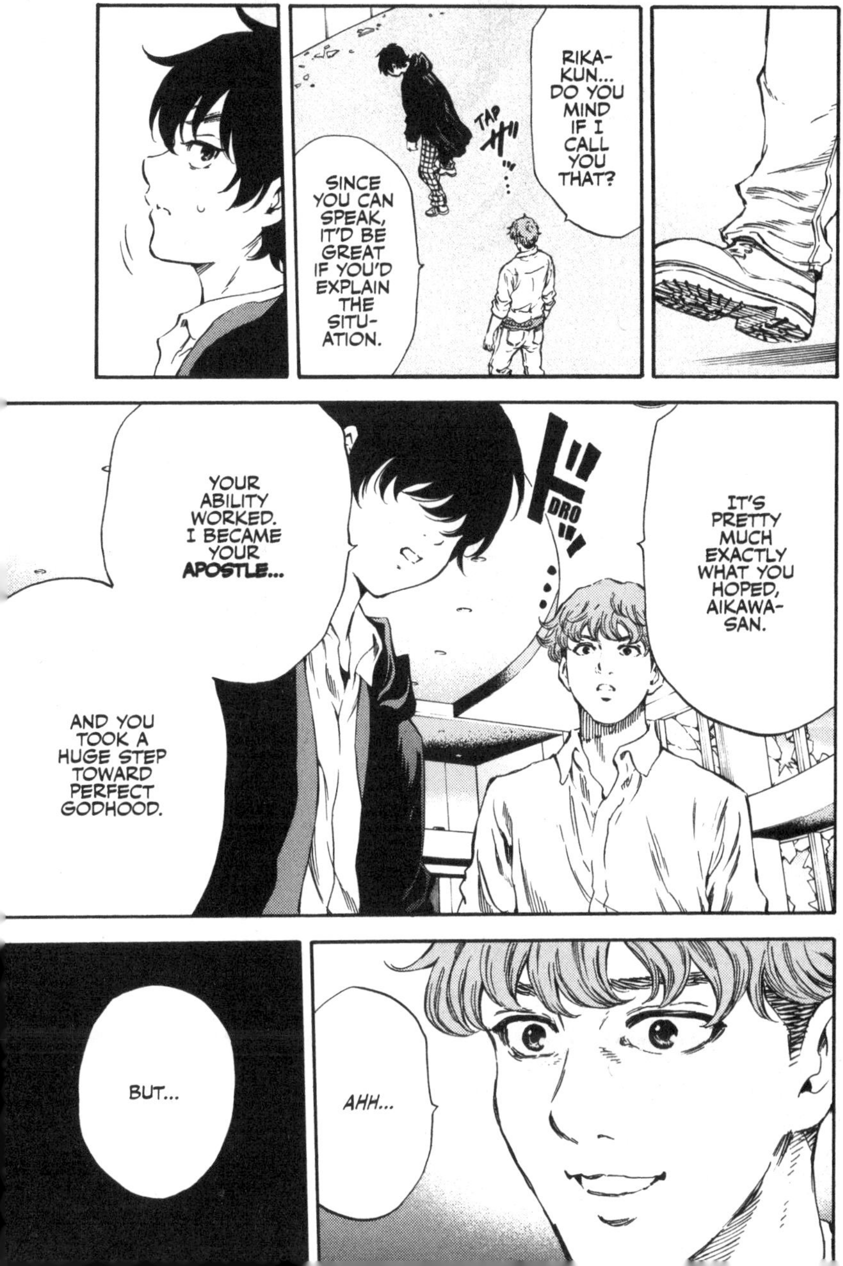
RIKA-KUN... DO YOU MIND IF I CALL YOU THAT?
TAP
SINCE YOU CAN SPEAK, IT'D BE GREAT IF YOU'D EXPLAIN THE SITUATION.
IT'S PRETTY MUCH EXACTLY WHAT YOU HOPED, AIKAWA-SAN.
DRO
YOUR ABILITY WORKED. I BECAME YOUR **APOSTLE...**
AND YOU TOOK A HUGE STEP TOWARD PERFECT GODHOOD.
AHH...
BUT...

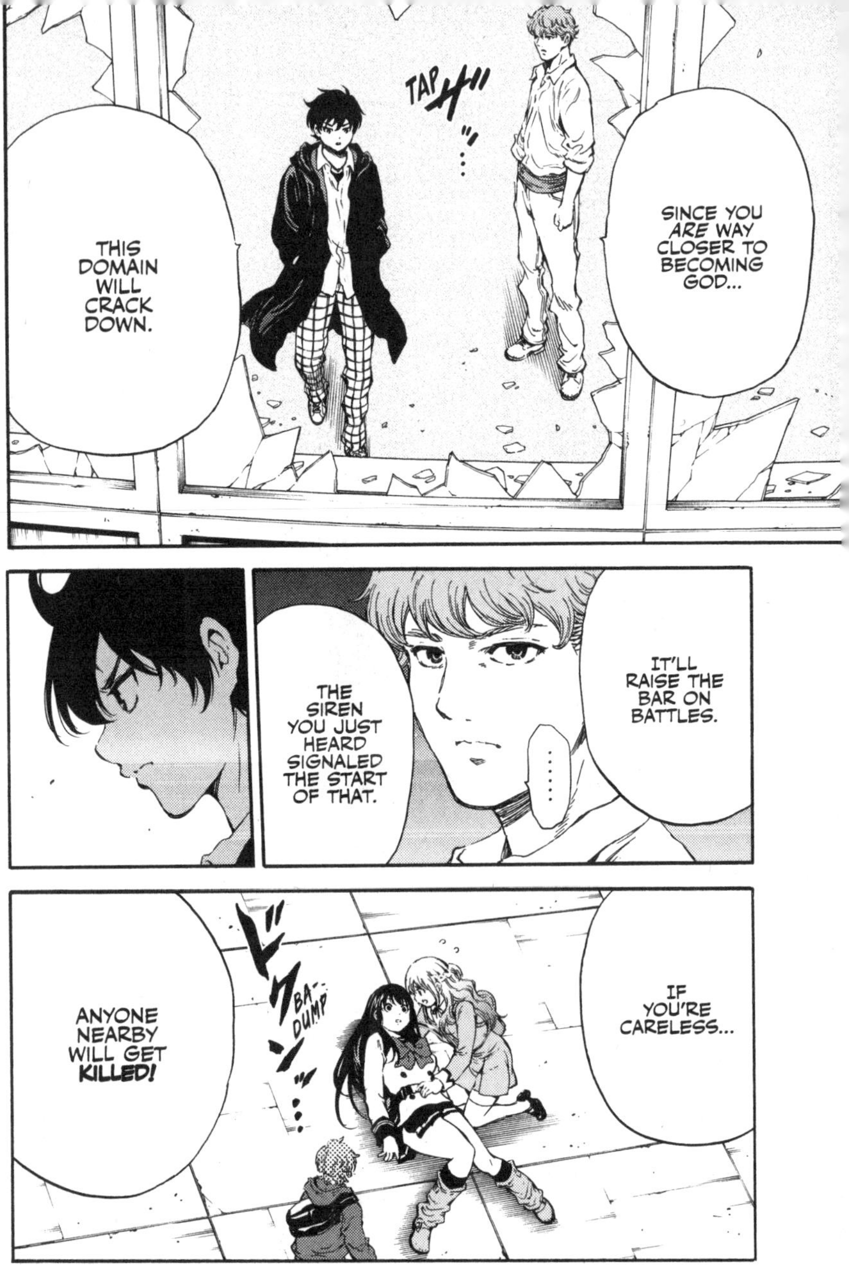
SINCE YOU *ARE* WAY CLOSER TO BECOMING GOD...
TAP
...
THIS DOMAIN WILL CRACK DOWN.
IT'LL RAISE THE BAR ON BATTLES.
......
THE SIREN YOU JUST HEARD SIGNALED THE START OF THAT.
IF YOU'RE CARELESS...
BA-DUMP
ANYONE NEARBY WILL GET **KILLED!**

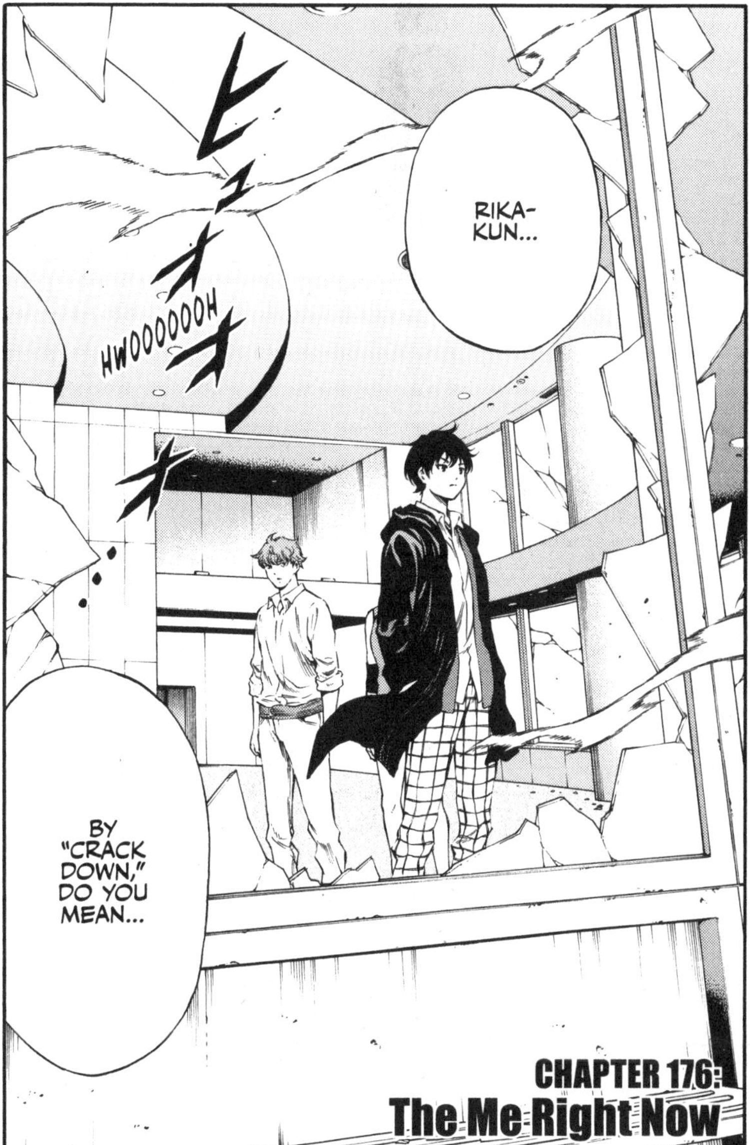
RIKA-KUN...
ヒュオオオ
HWOOOOOOH
BY "CRACK DOWN," DO YOU MEAN...

CHAPTER 176: The Me Right Now

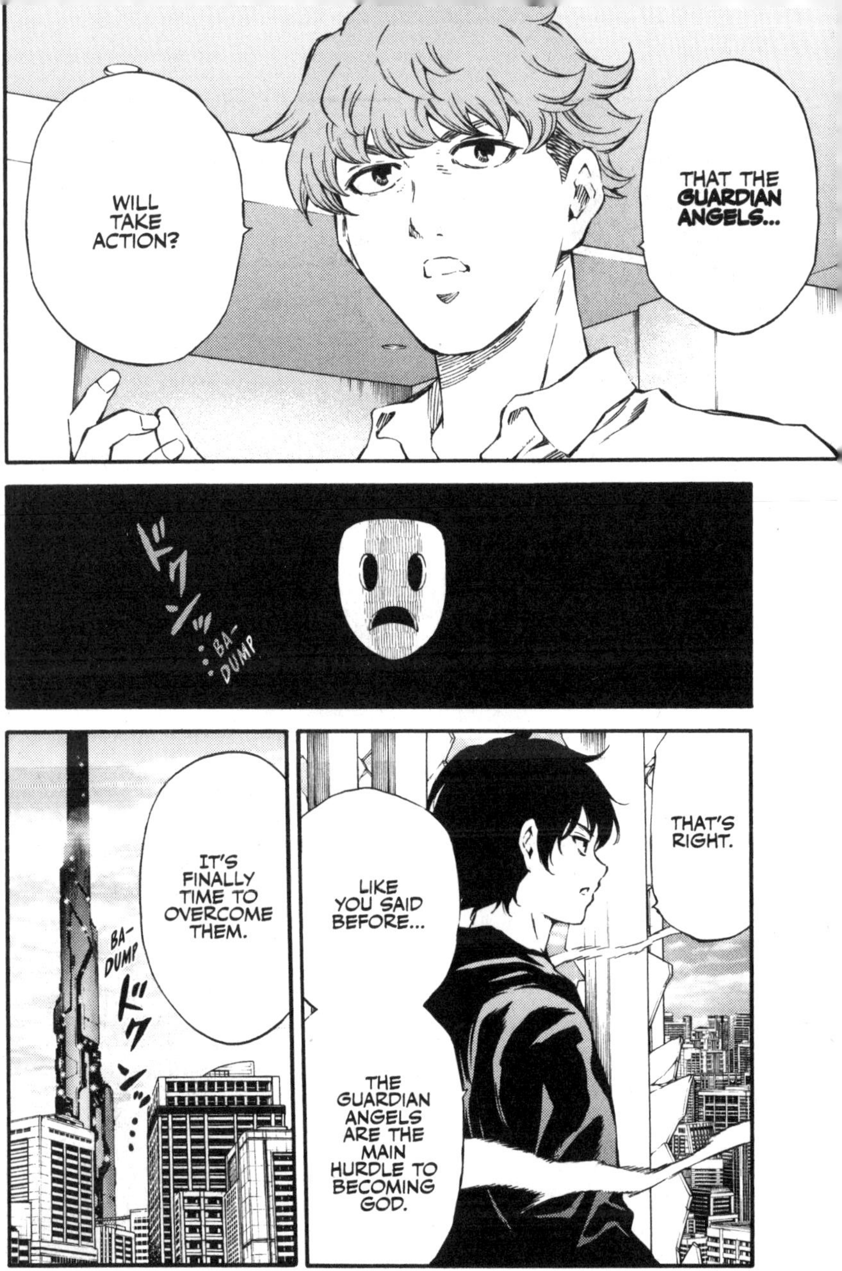
THAT THE GUARDIAN ANGELS...
WILL TAKE ACTION?
ドクンッ
BA-DUMP
THAT'S RIGHT.
LIKE YOU SAID BEFORE...
THE GUARDIAN ANGELS ARE THE MAIN HURDLE TO BECOMING GOD.
IT'S FINALLY TIME TO OVERCOME THEM.
BA-DUMP
ドクンッ

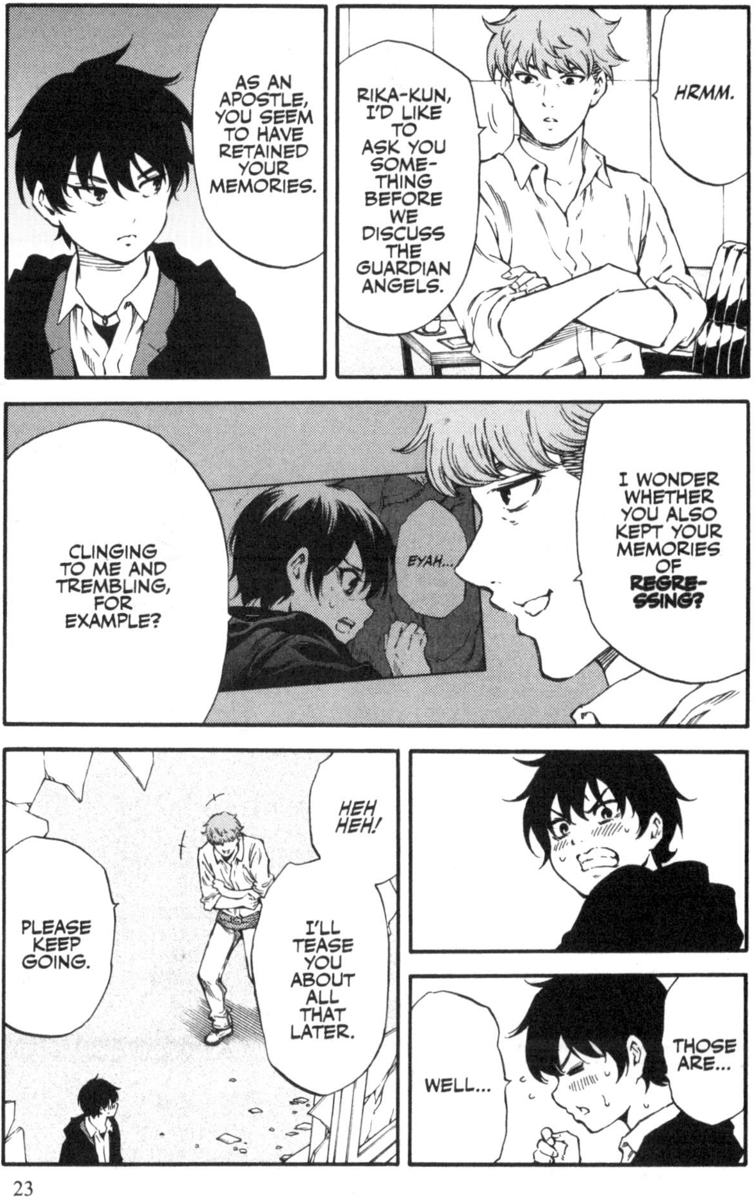
HRMM.
RIKA-KUN, I'D LIKE TO ASK YOU SOMETHING BEFORE WE DISCUSS THE GUARDIAN ANGELS.
AS AN APOSTLE, YOU SEEM TO HAVE RETAINED YOUR MEMORIES.
I WONDER WHETHER YOU ALSO KEPT YOUR MEMORIES OF **REGRESSING?**
EYAH...
CLINGING TO ME AND TREMBLING, FOR EXAMPLE?
THOSE ARE...
WELL...
HEH HEH!
I'LL TEASE YOU ABOUT ALL THAT LATER.
PLEASE KEEP GOING.

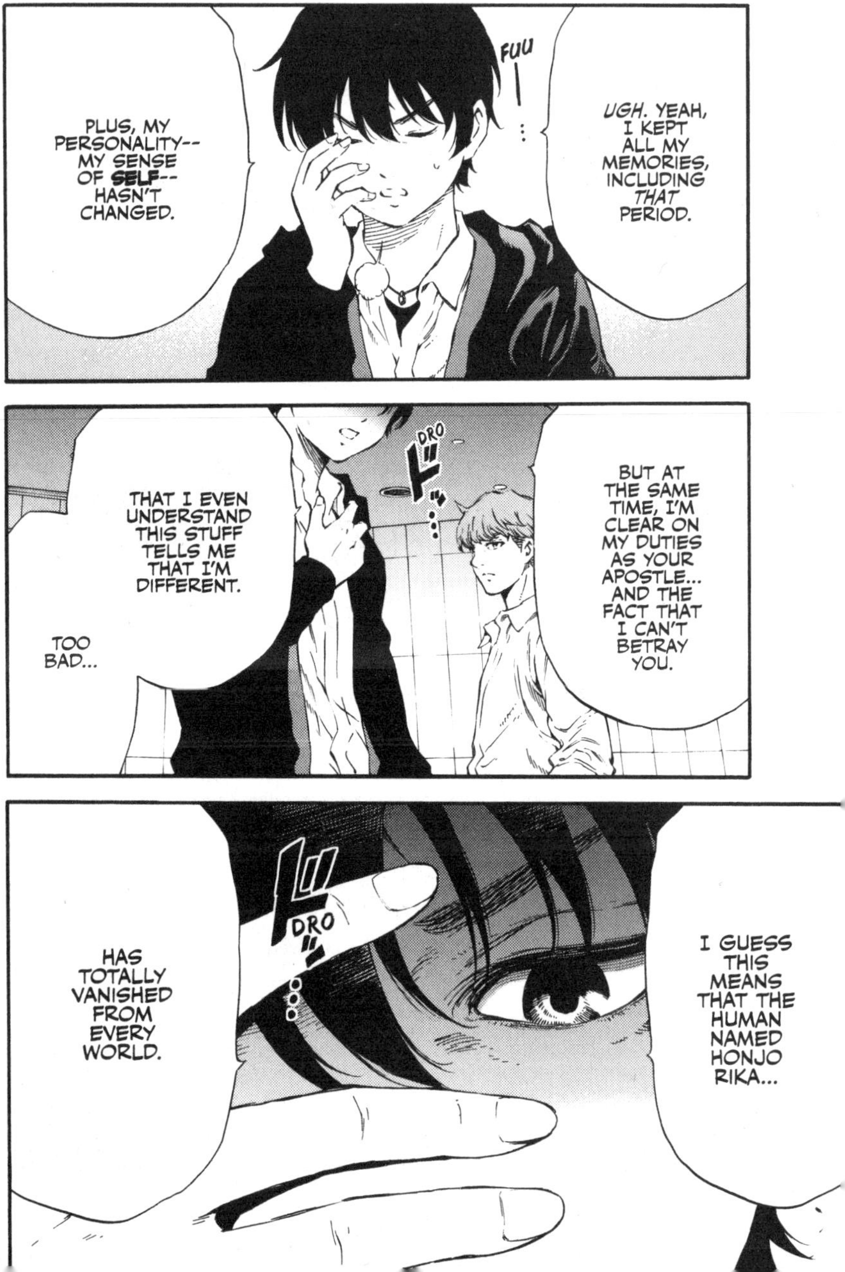
UGH. YEAH, I KEPT ALL MY MEMORIES, INCLUDING *THAT* PERIOD.
FUU
PLUS, MY PERSONALITY-- MY SENSE OF SELF-- HASN'T CHANGED.
BUT AT THE SAME TIME, I'M CLEAR ON MY DUTIES AS YOUR APOSTLE... AND THE FACT THAT I CAN'T BETRAY YOU.
DRO
THAT I EVEN UNDERSTAND THIS STUFF TELLS ME THAT I'M DIFFERENT.
TOO BAD...
I GUESS THIS MEANS THAT THE HUMAN NAMED HONJO RIKA...
DRO
HAS TOTALLY VANISHED FROM EVERY WORLD.

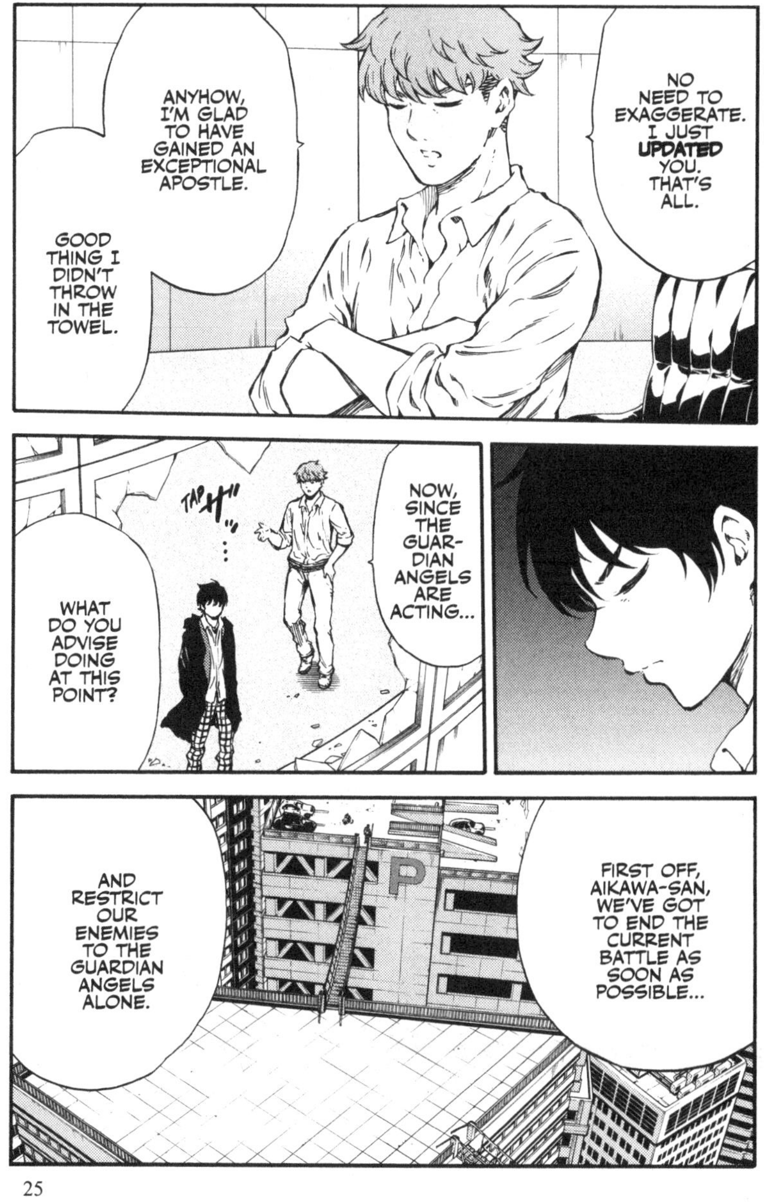
NO NEED TO EXAGGERATE. I JUST **UPDATED** YOU. THAT'S ALL.
ANYHOW, I'M GLAD TO HAVE GAINED AN EXCEPTIONAL APOSTLE.
GOOD THING I DIDN'T THROW IN THE TOWEL.
NOW, SINCE THE GUARDIAN ANGELS ARE ACTING...
TAP
...
WHAT DO YOU ADVISE DOING AT THIS POINT?
FIRST OFF, AIKAWA-SAN, WE'VE GOT TO END THE CURRENT BATTLE AS SOON AS POSSIBLE...
AND RESTRICT OUR ENEMIES TO THE GUARDIAN ANGELS ALONE.

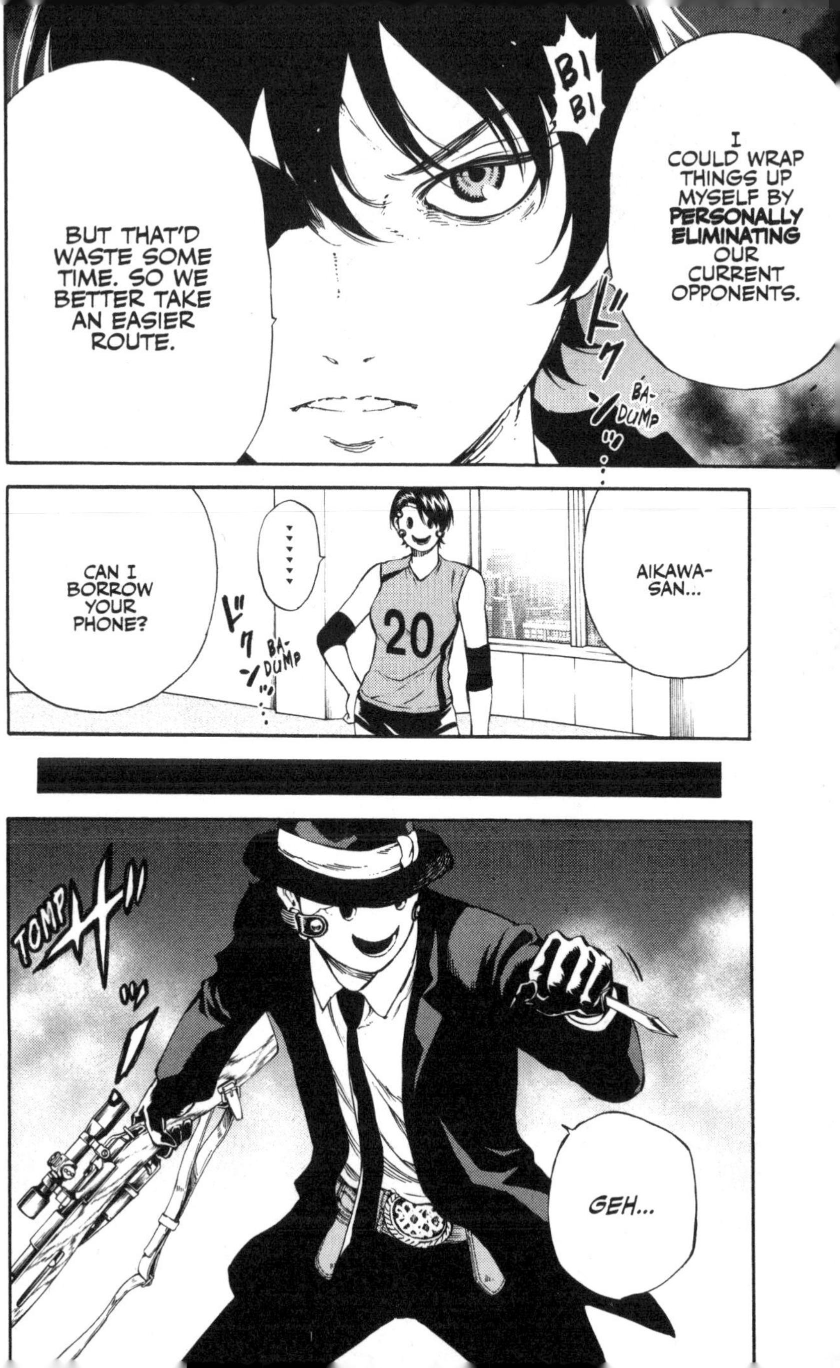
BI BI
I COULD WRAP THINGS UP MYSELF BY PERSONALLY ELIMINATING OUR CURRENT OPPONENTS.
BA-DUMP
BUT THAT'D WASTE SOME TIME. SO WE BETTER TAKE AN EASIER ROUTE.
AIKAWA-SAN...
......
BA-DUMP
CAN I BORROW YOUR PHONE?
TOMP
GEH...

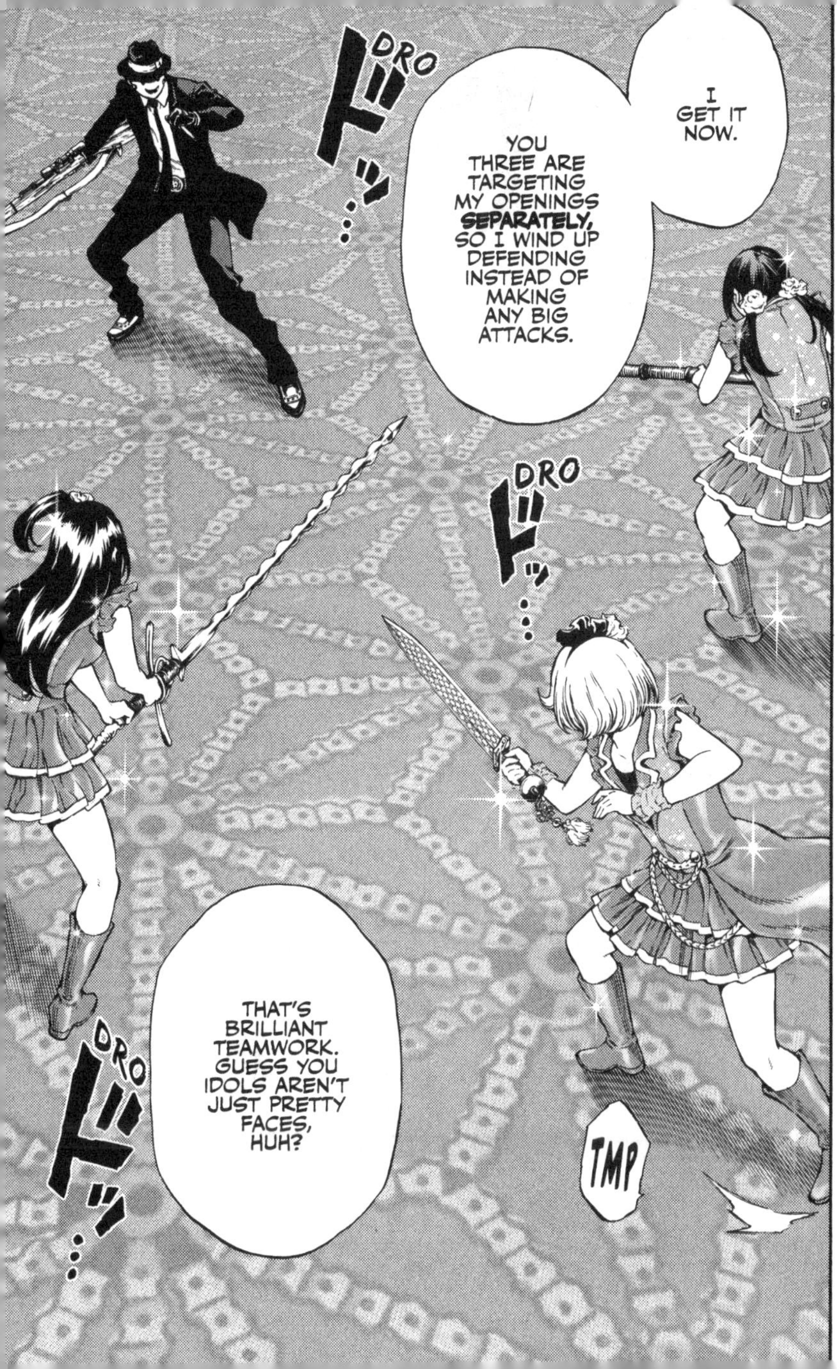

I GET IT NOW.
YOU THREE ARE TARGETING MY OPENINGS **SEPARATELY,** SO I WIND UP DEFENDING INSTEAD OF MAKING ANY BIG ATTACKS.
DRO
DRO
TMP
THAT'S BRILLIANT TEAMWORK. GUESS YOU IDOLS AREN'T JUST PRETTY FACES, HUH?
DRO

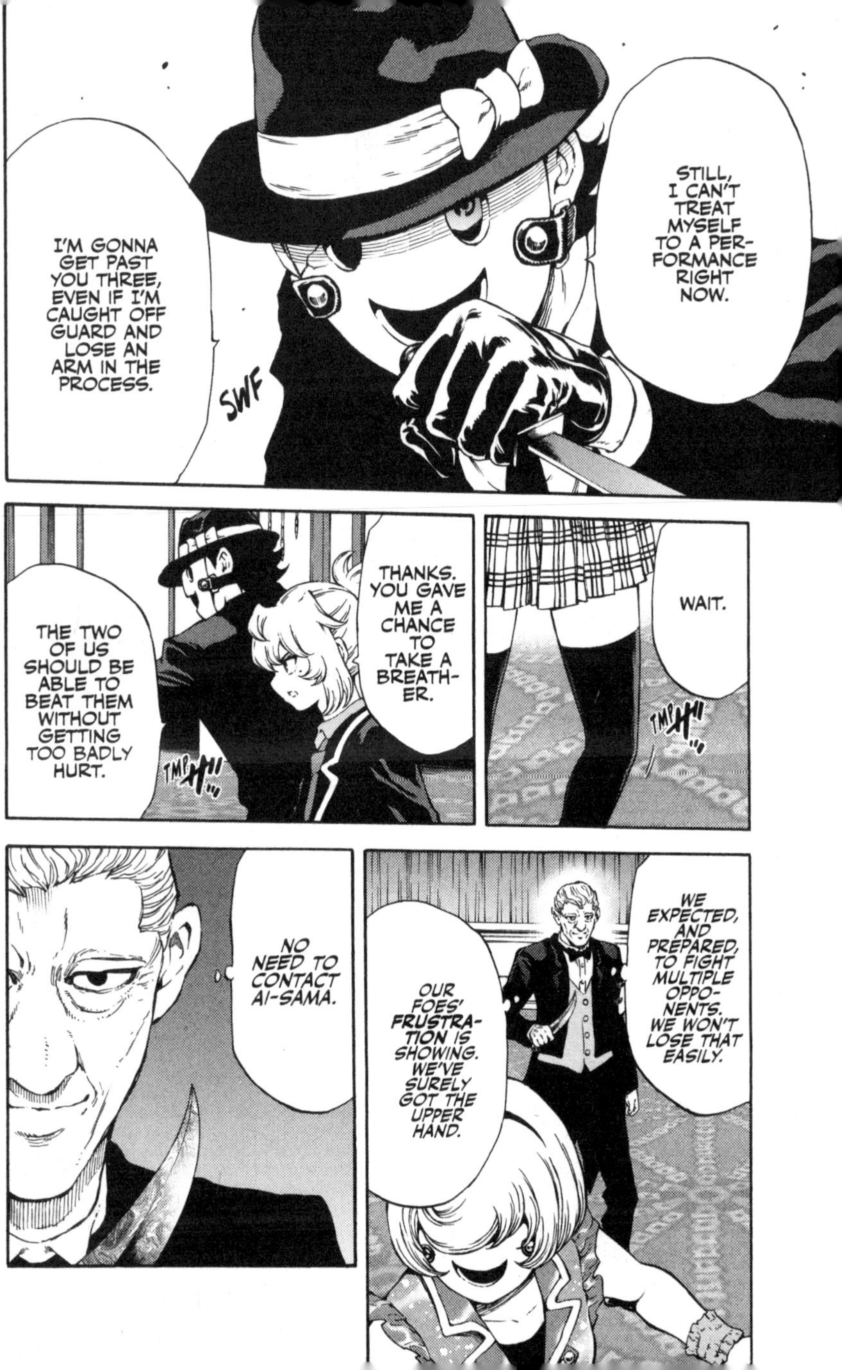
STILL, I CAN'T TREAT MYSELF TO A PER-FORMANCE RIGHT NOW.
I'M GONNA GET PAST YOU THREE, EVEN IF I'M CAUGHT OFF GUARD AND LOSE AN ARM IN THE PROCESS.
SWF
WAIT.
TMP
THANKS. YOU GAVE ME A CHANCE TO TAKE A BREATH-ER.
THE TWO OF US SHOULD BE ABLE TO BEAT THEM WITHOUT GETTING TOO BADLY HURT.
TMP
WE EXPECTED, AND PREPARED, TO FIGHT MULTIPLE OPPO-NENTS. WE WON'T LOSE THAT EASILY.
OUR FOES' FRUSTRA-TION IS SHOWING. WE'VE SURELY GOT THE UPPER HAND.
NO NEED TO CONTACT AI-SAMA.

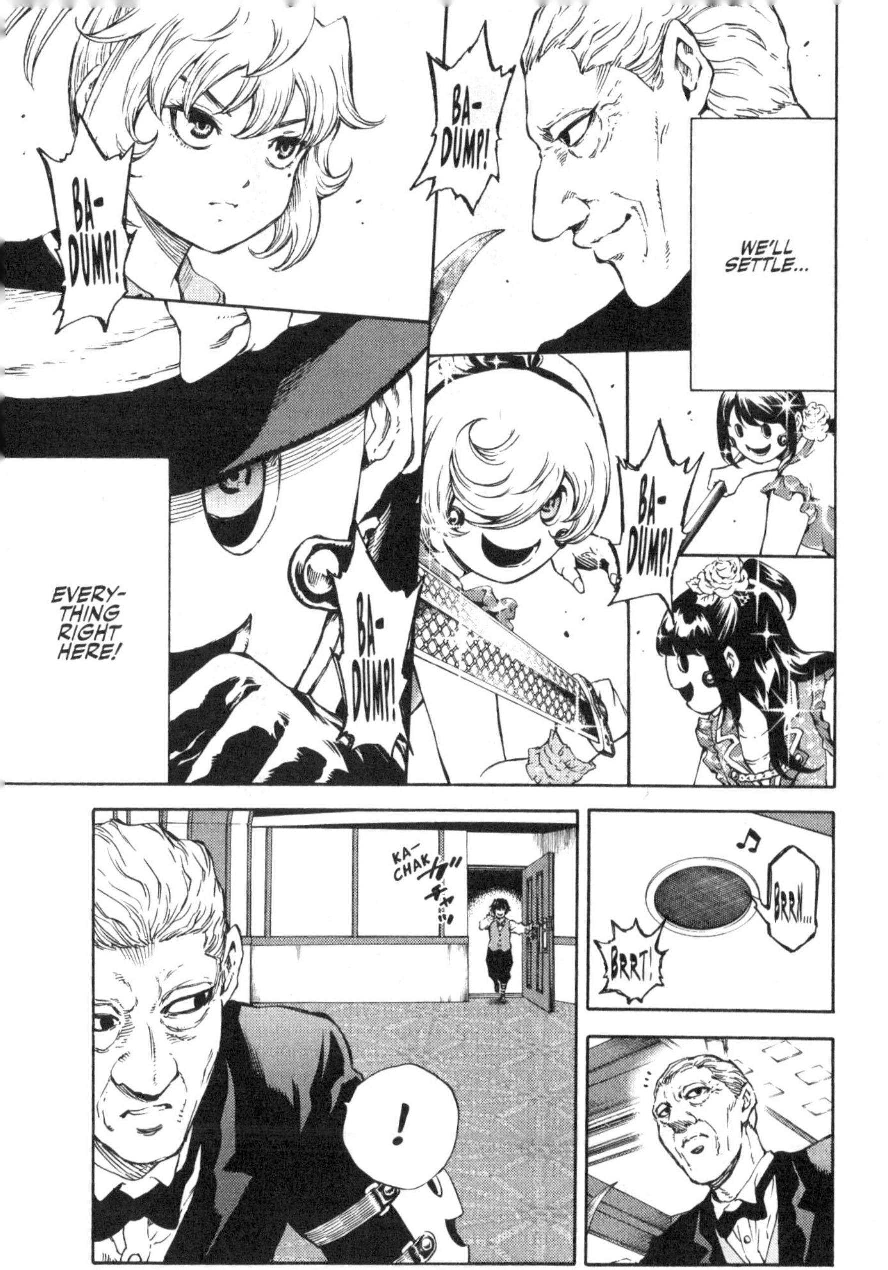
WE'LL SETTLE...
BA-DUMP!
BA-DUMP!
BA-DUMP!
BA-DUMP!
EVERYTHING RIGHT HERE!
BA-DUMP!
♪
BRRN...
BRRT!
KA-CHAK
!

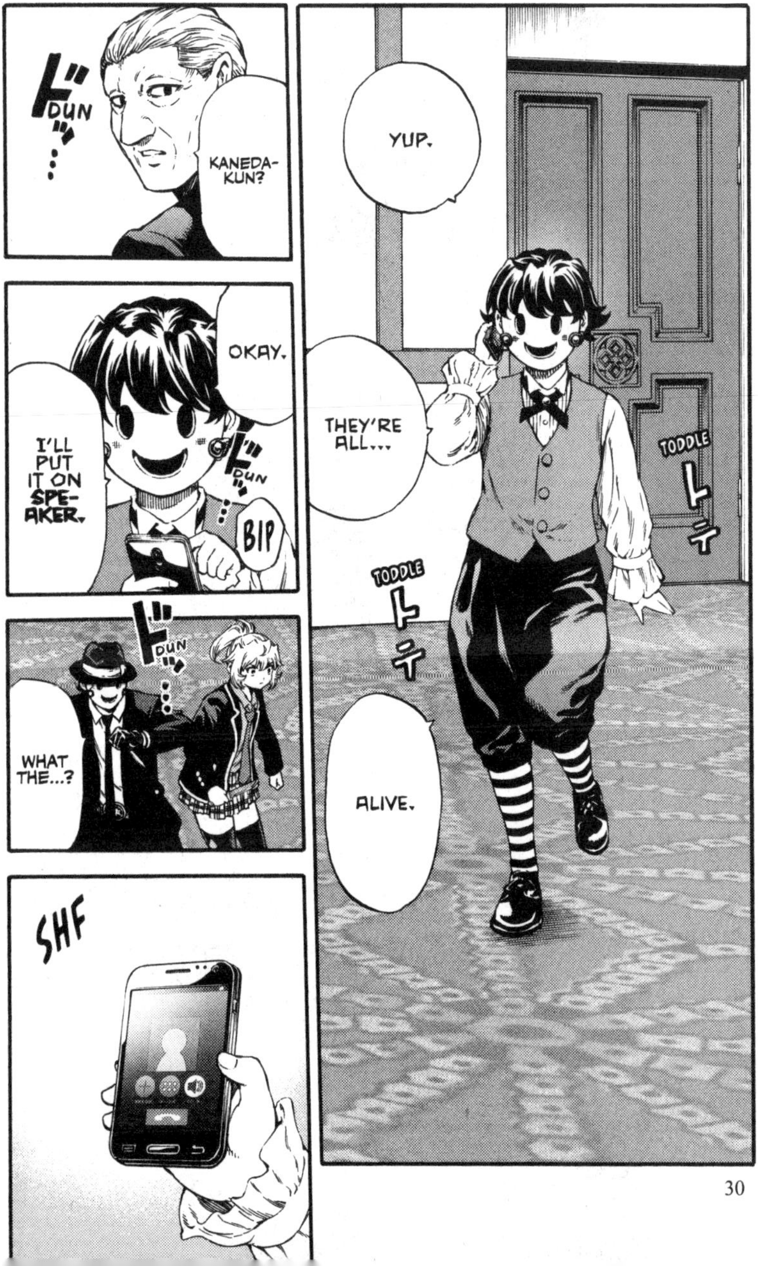
YUP.
THEY'RE ALL...
TODDLE トテ
TODDLE トテ
ALIVE.
ド DUN ...
KANEDA-KUN?
OKAY.
I'LL PUT IT ON SPEAKER.
ド DUN ...
BIP
ド DUN ...
WHAT THE...?
SHF

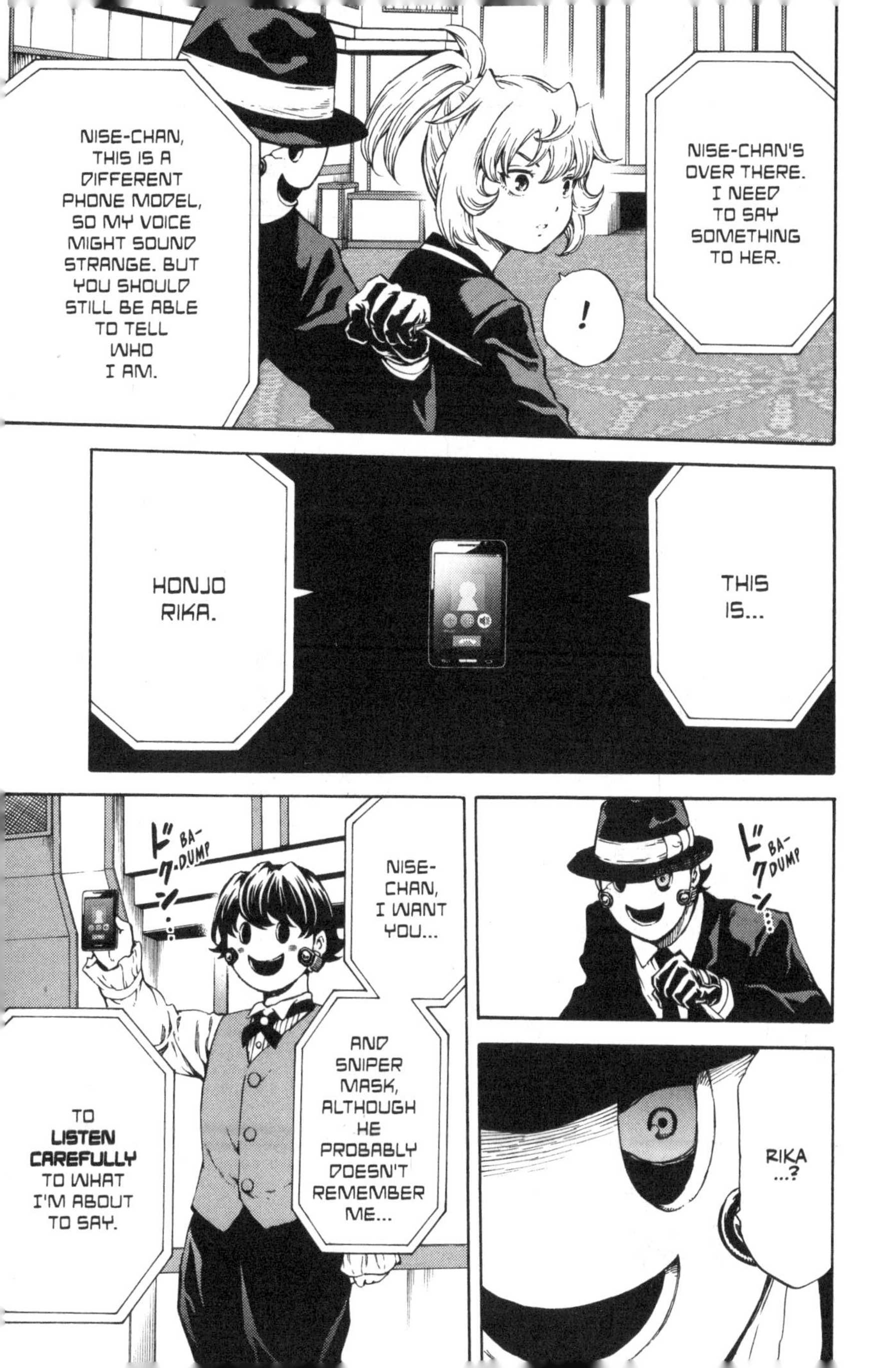
NISE-CHAN'S OVER THERE. I NEED TO SAY SOMETHING TO HER.
!
NISE-CHAN, THIS IS A DIFFERENT PHONE MODEL, SO MY VOICE MIGHT SOUND STRANGE. BUT YOU SHOULD STILL BE ABLE TO TELL WHO I AM.
THIS IS...
HONJO RIKA.
ドク BA-DUMP
RIKA ...?
NISE-CHAN, I WANT YOU...
AND SNIPER MASK, ALTHOUGH HE PROBABLY DOESN'T REMEMBER ME...
TO **LISTEN CAREFULLY** TO WHAT I'M ABOUT TO SAY.
ドク BA-DUMP

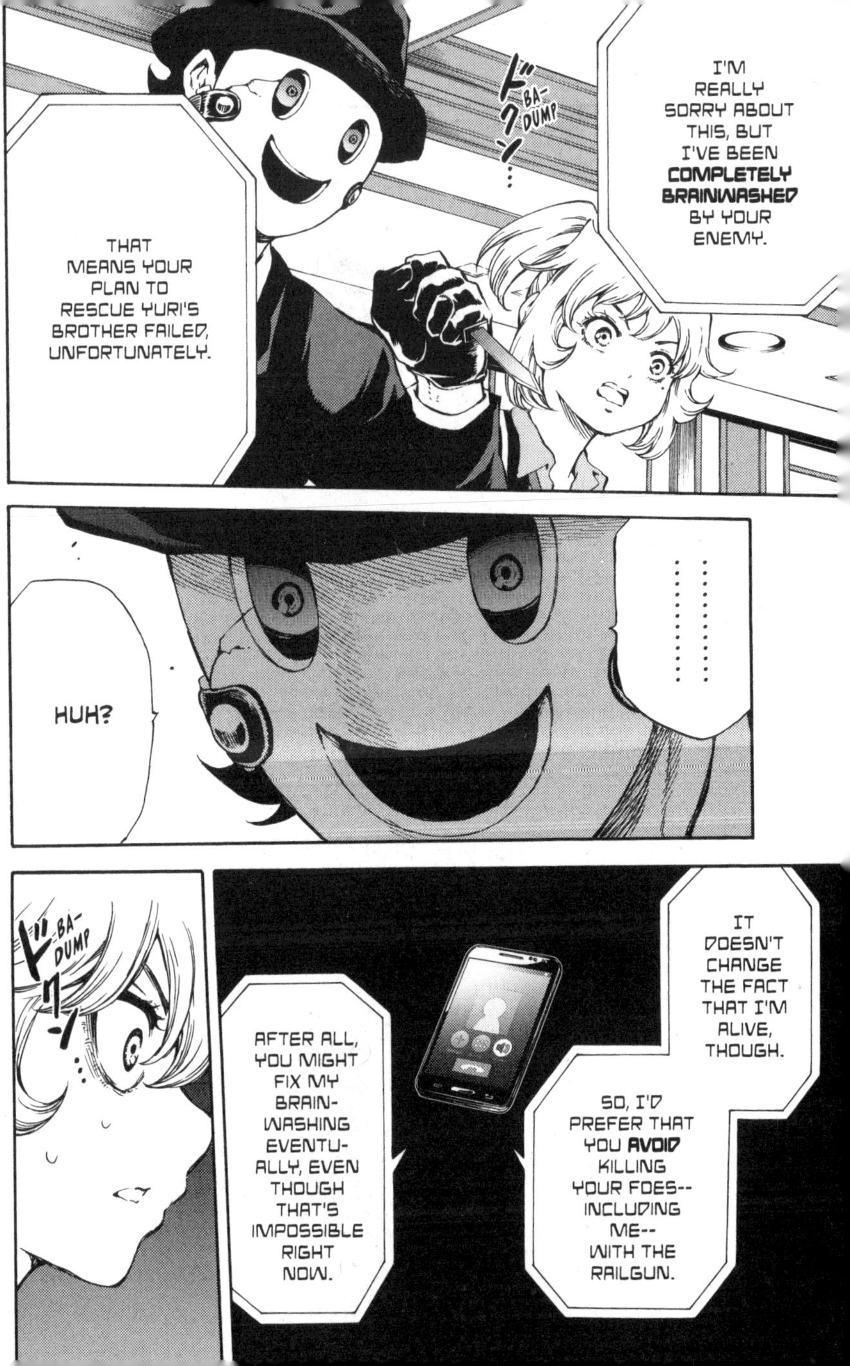
I'M REALLY SORRY ABOUT THIS, BUT I'VE BEEN **COMPLETELY BRAINWASHED** BY YOUR ENEMY.
BA-DUMP
THAT MEANS YOUR PLAN TO RESCUE YURI'S BROTHER FAILED, UNFORTUNATELY.
......
HUH?
IT DOESN'T CHANGE THE FACT THAT I'M ALIVE, THOUGH.
SO, I'D PREFER THAT YOU **AVOID** KILLING YOUR FOES--INCLUDING ME--WITH THE RAILGUN.
AFTER ALL, YOU MIGHT FIX MY BRAIN-WASHING EVENTU-ALLY, EVEN THOUGH THAT'S IMPOSSIBLE RIGHT NOW.
BA-DUMP

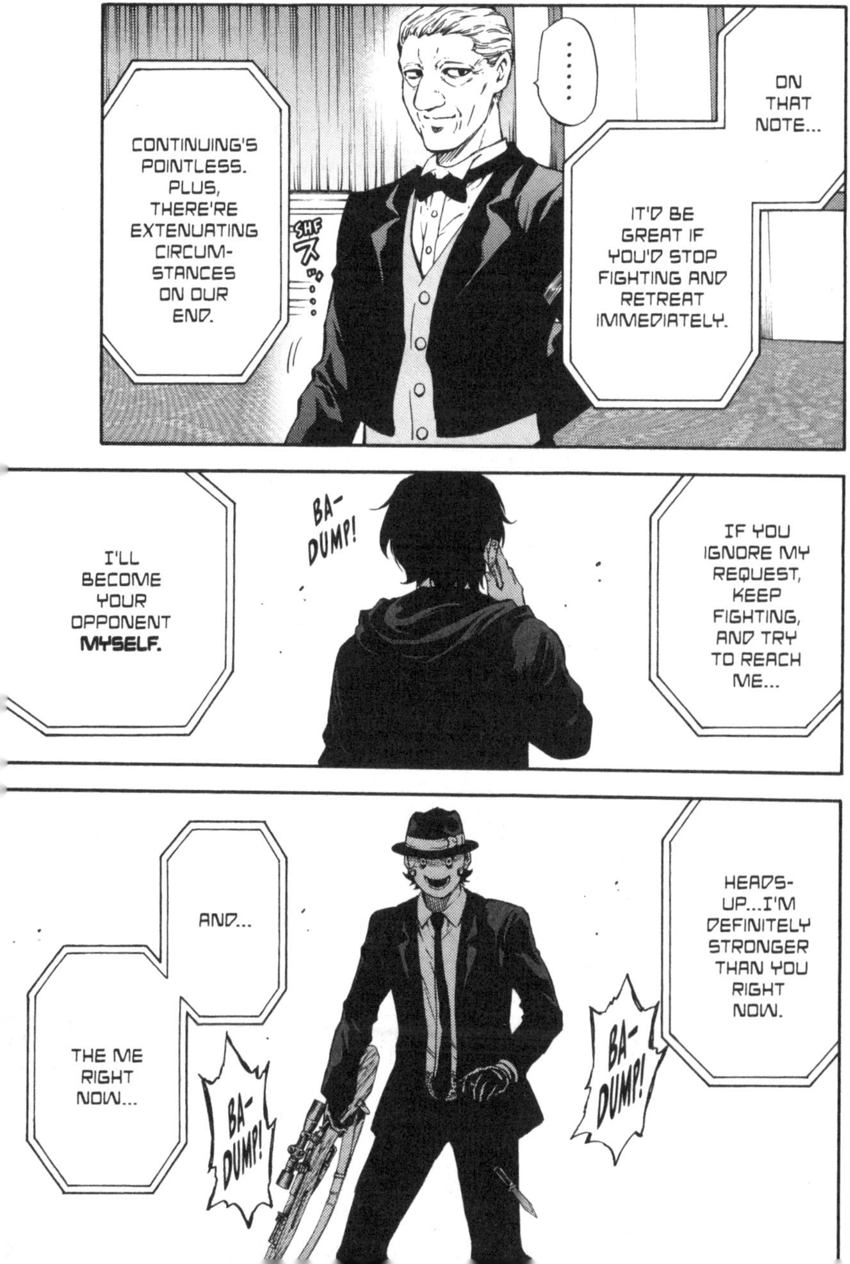

ON THAT NOTE...
......
IT'D BE GREAT IF YOU'D STOP FIGHTING AND RETREAT IMMEDIATELY.
SHF
CONTINUING'S POINTLESS. PLUS, THERE'RE EXTENUATING CIRCUMSTANCES ON OUR END.
IF YOU IGNORE MY REQUEST, KEEP FIGHTING, AND TRY TO REACH ME...
BA-DUMP!
I'LL BECOME YOUR OPPONENT **MYSELF.**
HEADS-UP...I'M DEFINITELY STRONGER THAN YOU RIGHT NOW.
BA-DUMP!
AND...
THE ME RIGHT NOW...
BA-DUMP!

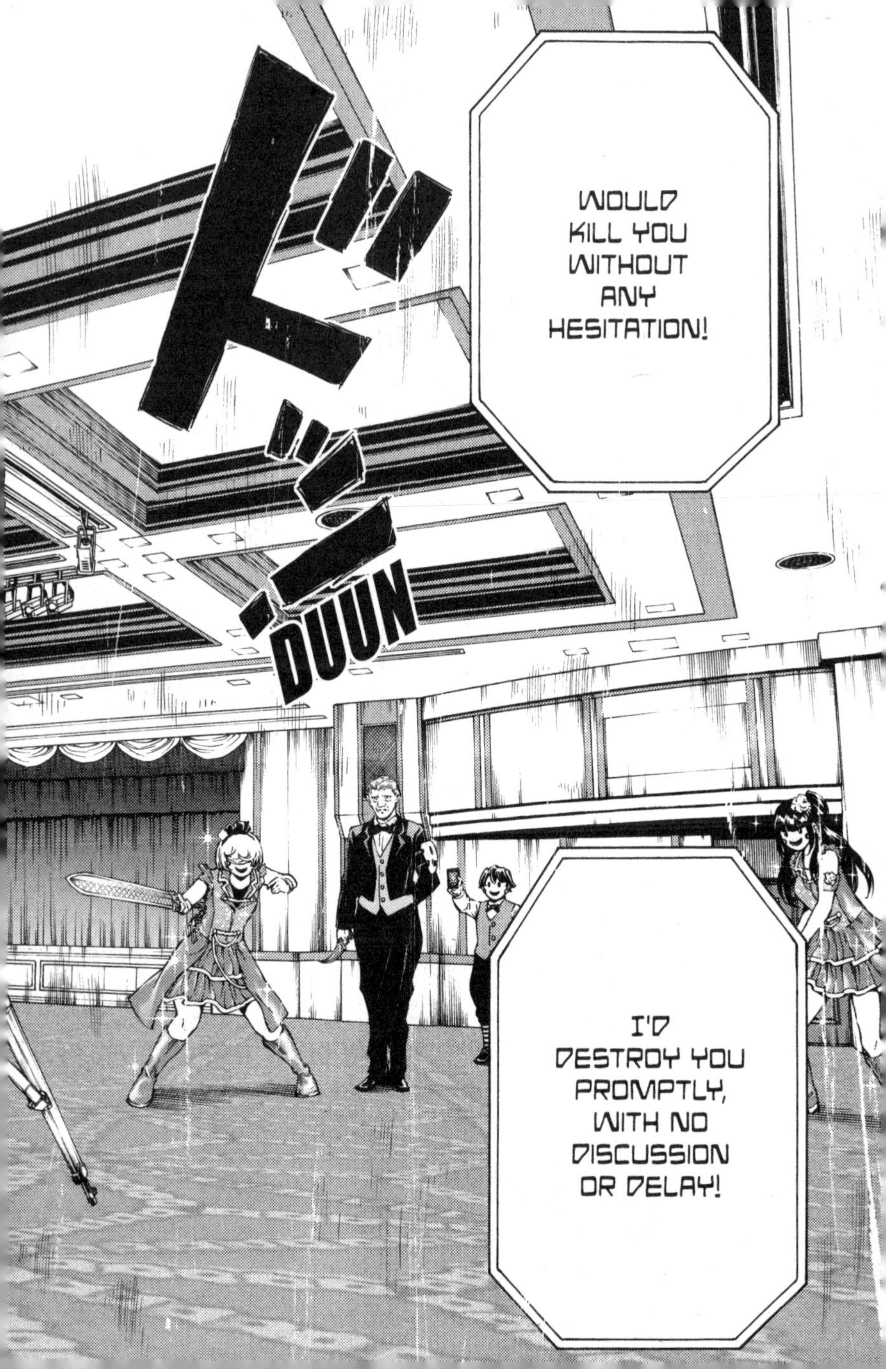
WOULD KILL YOU WITHOUT ANY HESITATION!
DUUN
I'D DESTROY YOU PROMPTLY, WITH NO DISCUSSION OR DELAY!

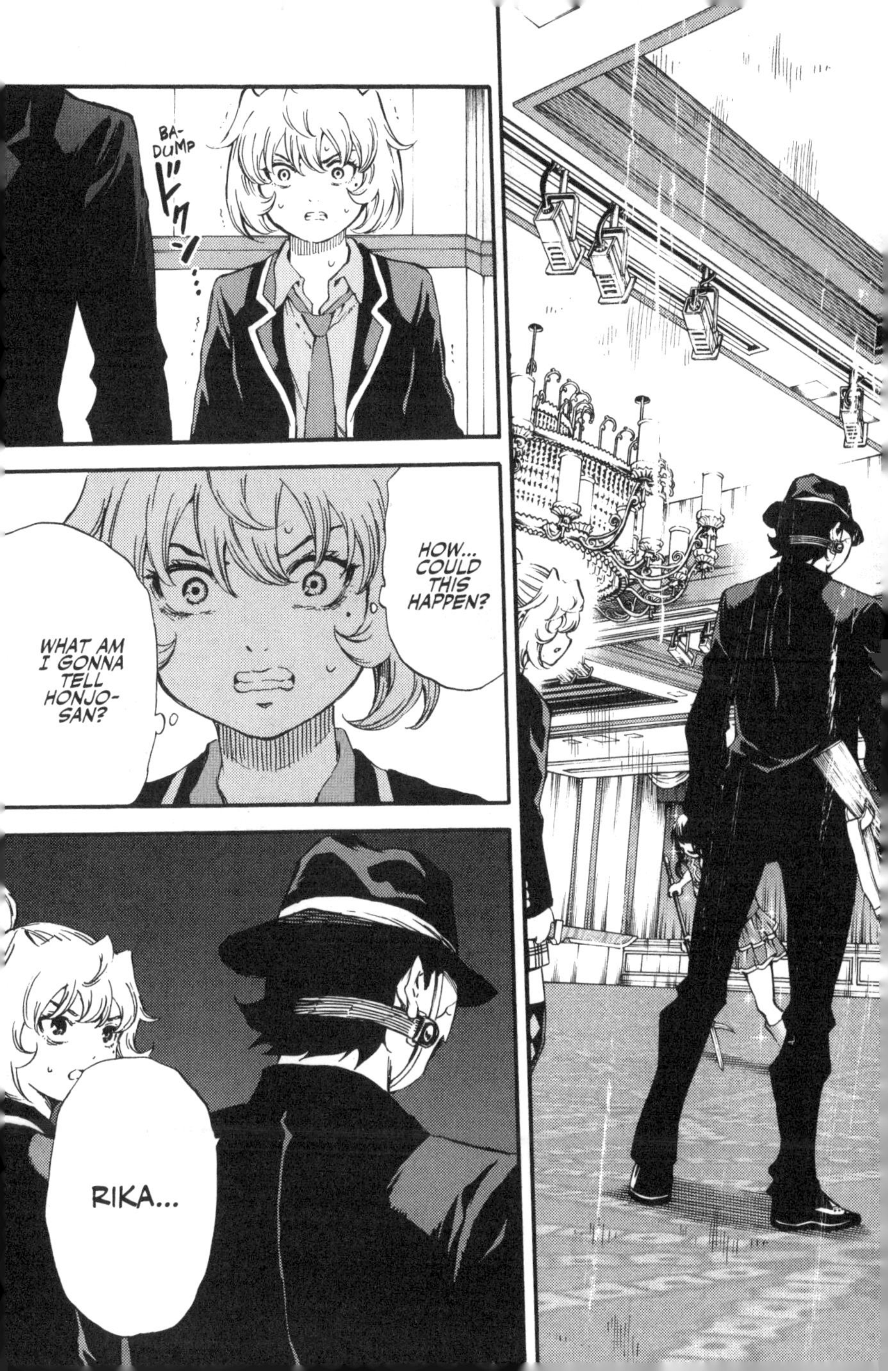
BA-DUMP
HOW... COULD THIS HAPPEN?
WHAT AM I GONNA TELL HONJO-SAN?
RIKA...

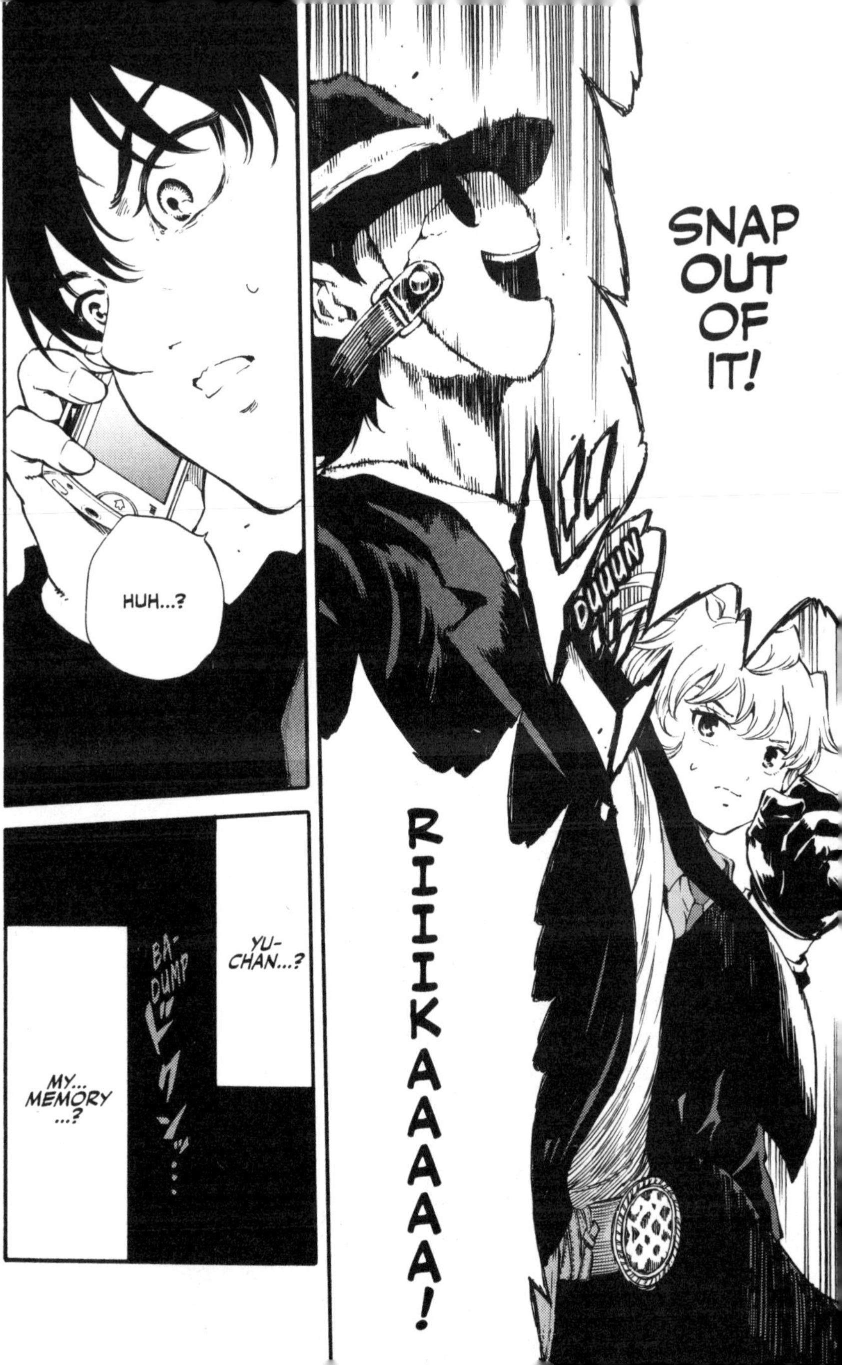
SNAP OUT OF IT!
DUUUN
RIIIIKAAAAAA!
HUH...?
YU-CHAN...?
BA-DUMP
MY... MEMORY ...?

Rejected rough
cover sketch.

HIGH-RISE INVASION

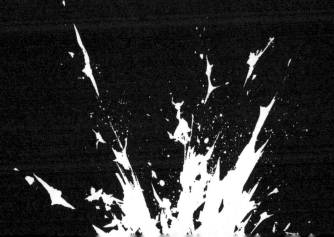

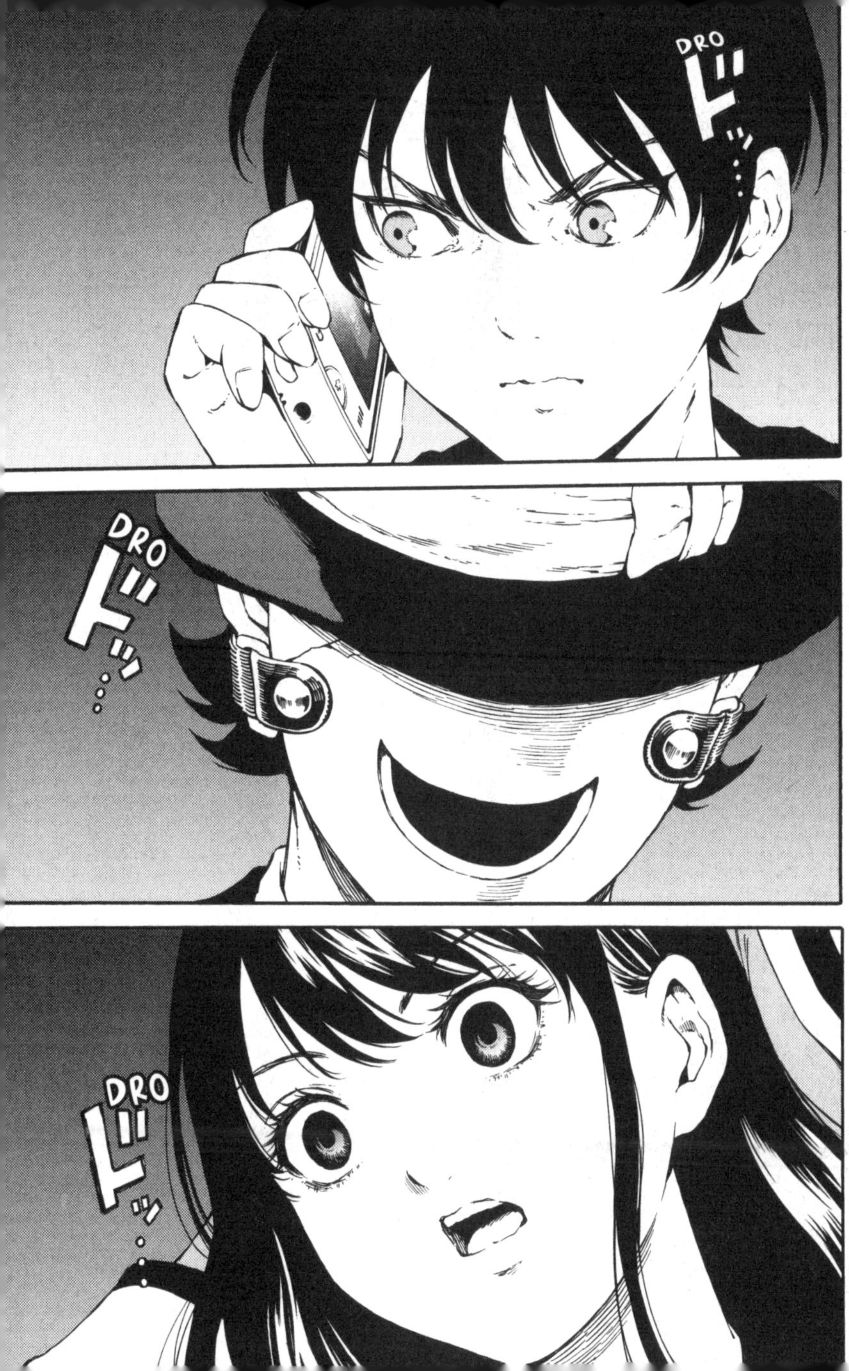
DRO
ドッ…
DRO
ドッ…
DRO
ドッ…

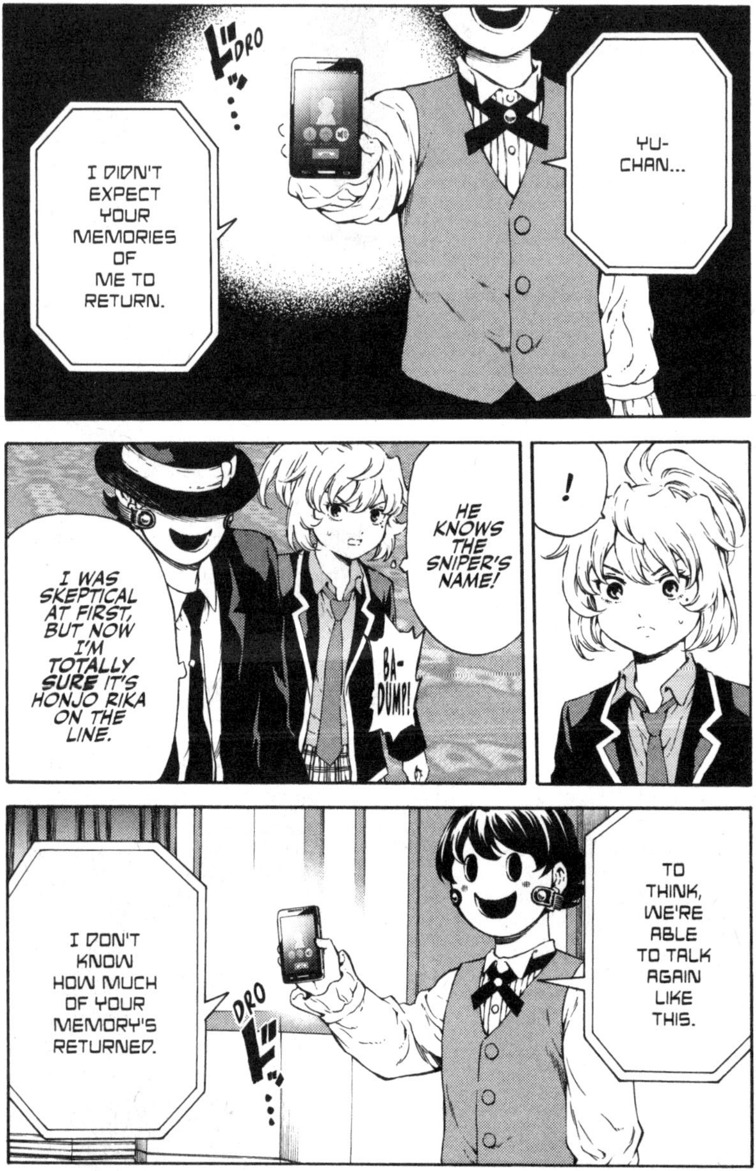
YU-CHAN...
DRO...
I DIDN'T EXPECT YOUR MEMORIES OF ME TO RETURN.
!
HE KNOWS THE SNIPER'S NAME!
BA-DUMP!
I WAS SKEPTICAL AT FIRST, BUT NOW I'M TOTALLY SURE IT'S HONJO RIKA ON THE LINE.
TO THINK, WE'RE ABLE TO TALK AGAIN LIKE THIS.
DRO...
I DON'T KNOW HOW MUCH OF YOUR MEMORY'S RETURNED.

CHAPTER 177: I'm an Avenging Angel

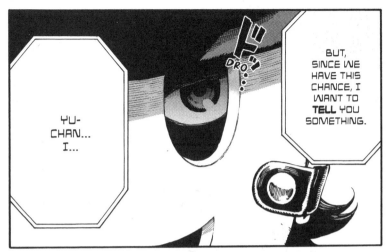

YU-
CHAN...
I...

BUT,
SINCE WE
HAVE THIS
CHANCE, I
WANT TO
TELL YOU
SOMETHING.

I...

BA-
DUMP!

BA-
DUMP!

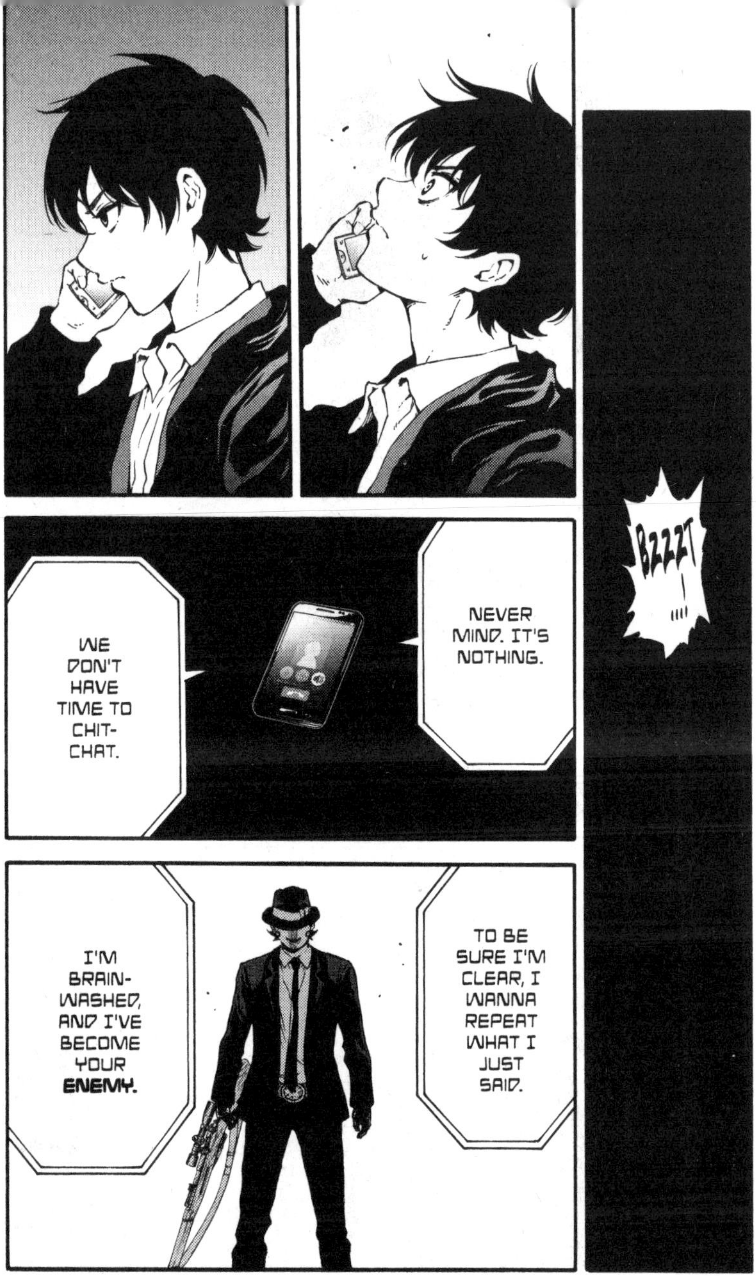
BZZZT!!
NEVER MIND. IT'S NOTHING.
WE DON'T HAVE TIME TO CHIT-CHAT.
TO BE SURE I'M CLEAR, I WANNA REPEAT WHAT I JUST SAID.
I'M BRAIN-WASHED, AND I'VE BECOME YOUR **ENEMY.**

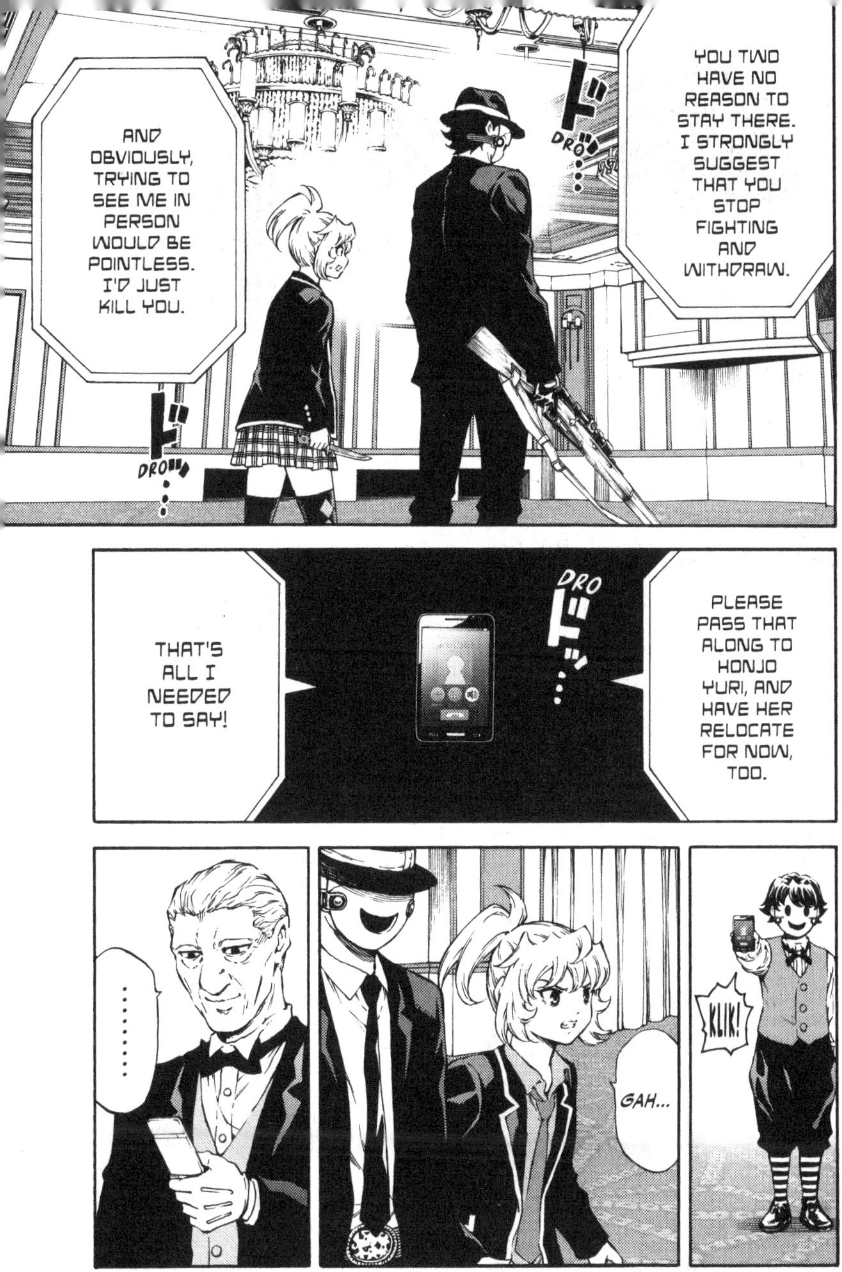
YOU TWO HAVE NO REASON TO STAY THERE. I STRONGLY SUGGEST THAT YOU STOP FIGHTING AND WITHDRAW.
DRO...
AND OBVIOUSLY, TRYING TO SEE ME IN PERSON WOULD BE POINTLESS. I'D JUST KILL YOU.
DRO...
PLEASE PASS THAT ALONG TO HONJO YURI, AND HAVE HER RELOCATE FOR NOW, TOO.
DRO...
THAT'S ALL I NEEDED TO SAY!
KLIK!
GAH...
....

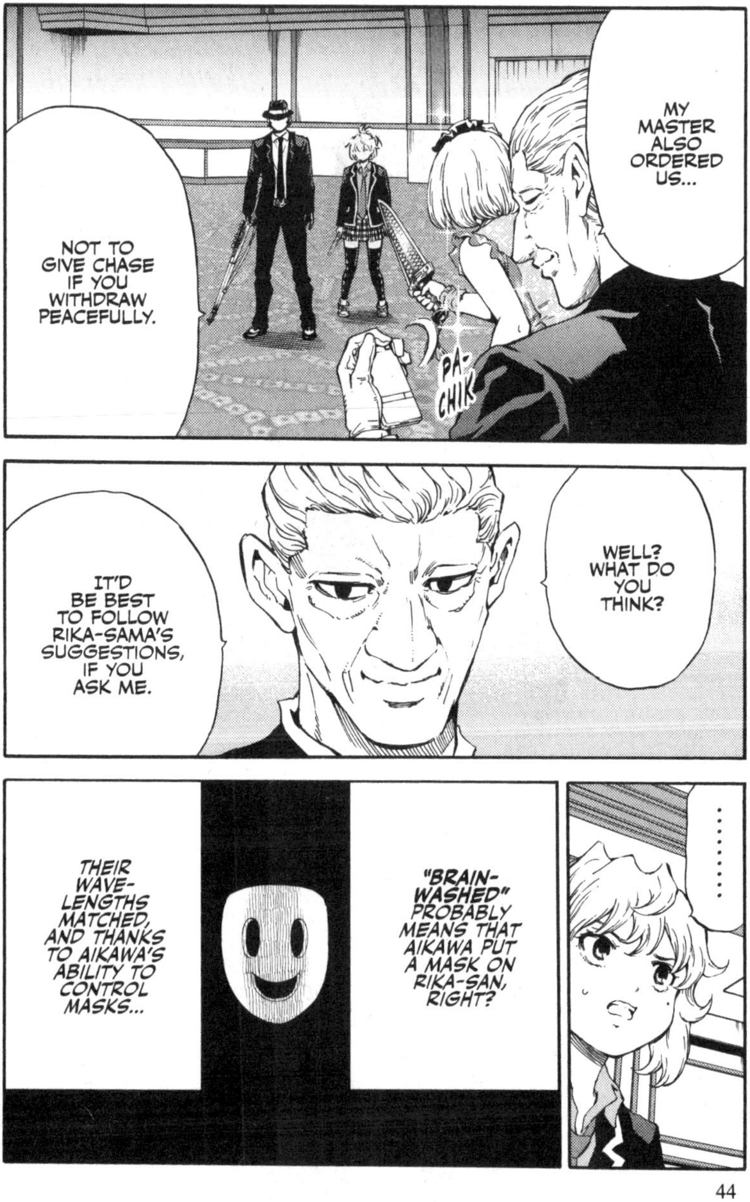
MY MASTER ALSO ORDERED US...
PA-CHIK
NOT TO GIVE CHASE IF YOU WITHDRAW PEACEFULLY.
WELL? WHAT DO YOU THINK?
IT'D BE BEST TO FOLLOW RIKA-SAMA'S SUGGESTIONS, IF YOU ASK ME.
....
"BRAIN-WASHED" PROBABLY MEANS THAT AIKAWA PUT A MASK ON RIKA-SAN, RIGHT?
THEIR WAVE-LENGTHS MATCHED, AND THANKS TO AIKAWA'S ABILITY TO CONTROL MASKS...

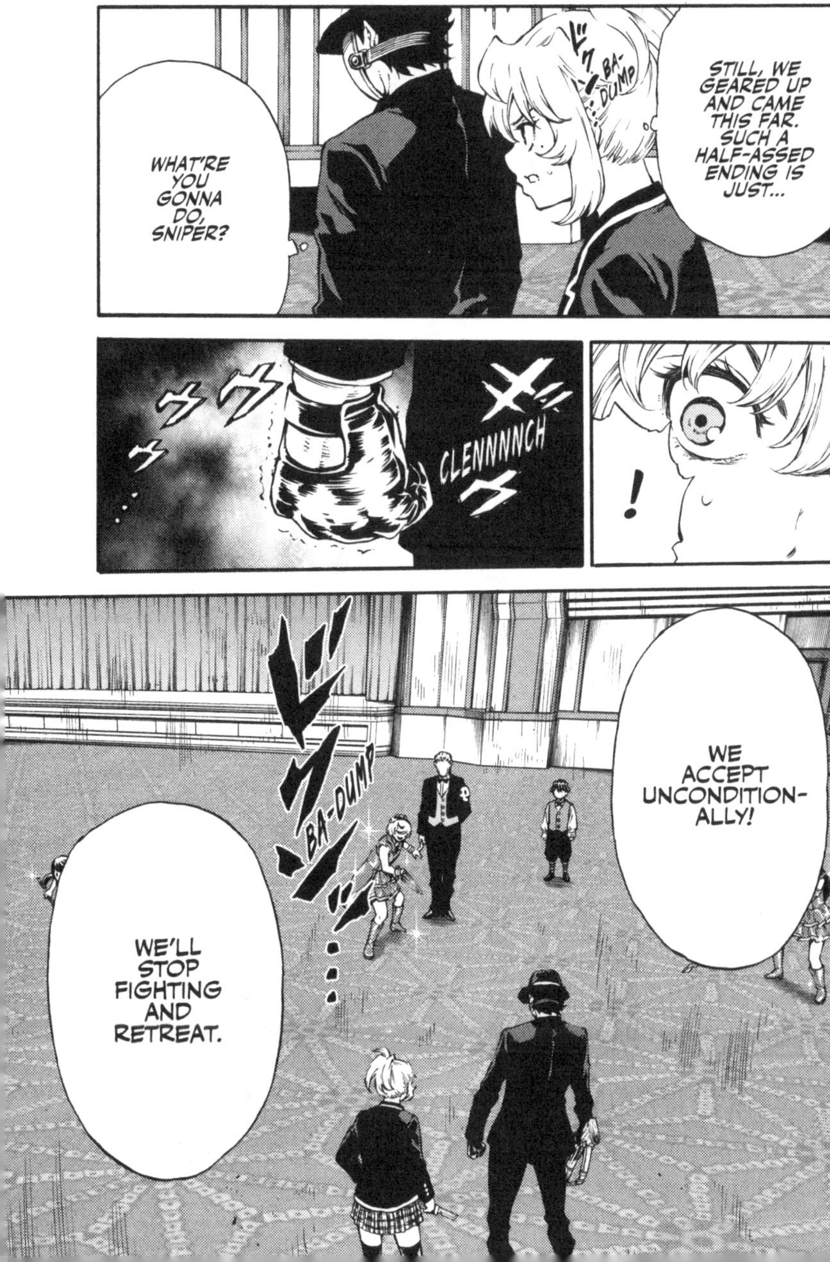
STILL, WE GEARED UP AND CAME THIS FAR. SUCH A HALF-ASSED ENDING IS JUST...
BA-DUMP
WHAT'RE YOU GONNA DO, SNIPER?
!
CLENNNNCH
WE ACCEPT UNCONDITION-ALLY!
BA-DUMP
WE'LL STOP FIGHTING AND RETREAT.

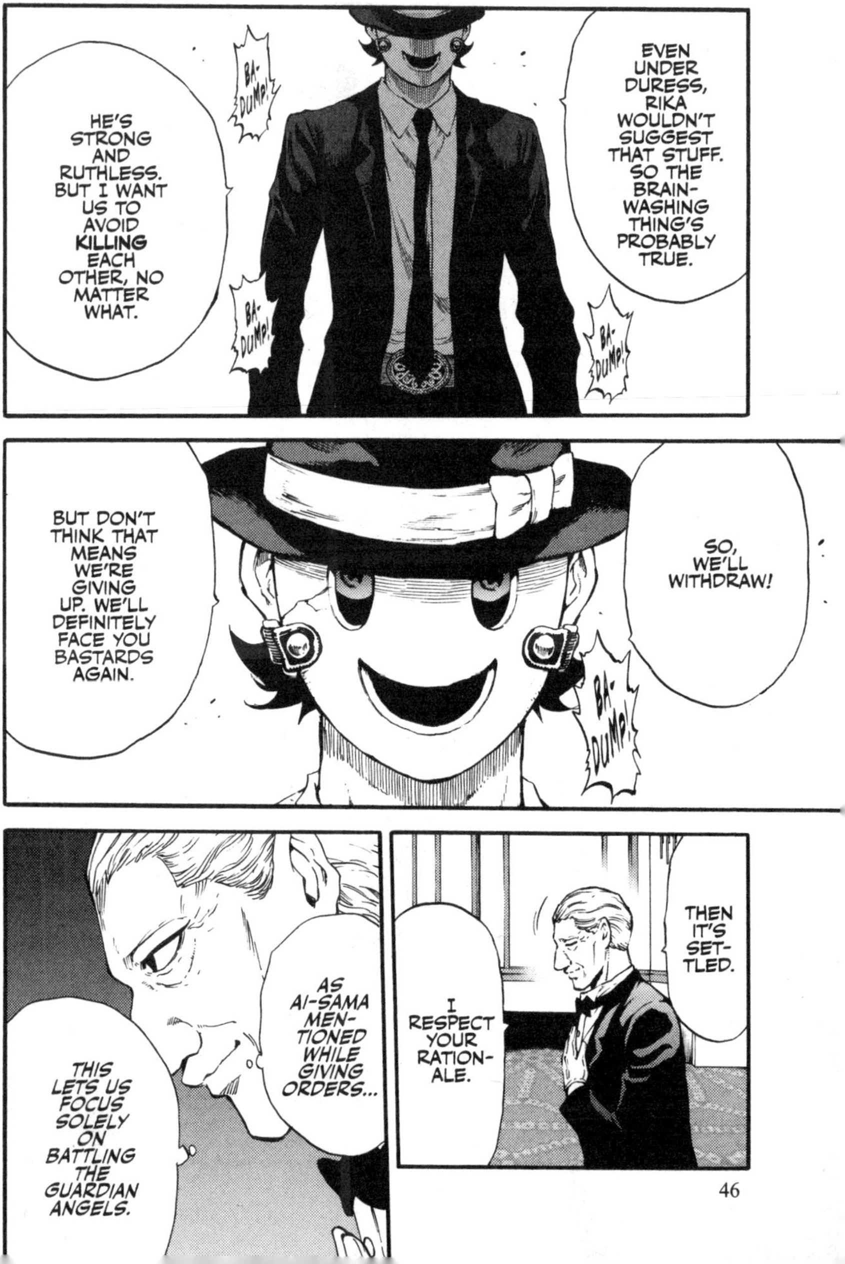
EVEN UNDER DURESS, RIKA WOULDN'T SUGGEST THAT STUFF. SO THE BRAIN-WASHING THING'S PROBABLY TRUE.
BA-DUMP!
HE'S STRONG AND RUTHLESS. BUT I WANT US TO AVOID **KILLING** EACH OTHER, NO MATTER WHAT.
BA-DUMP!
BA-DUMP!
SO, WE'LL WITHDRAW!
BA-DUMP!
BUT DON'T THINK THAT MEANS WE'RE GIVING UP. WE'LL DEFINITELY FACE YOU BASTARDS AGAIN.
THEN IT'S SET-TLED.
I RESPECT YOUR RATION-ALE.
AS AI-SAMA MEN-TIONED WHILE GIVING ORDERS...
THIS LETS US FOCUS SOLELY ON BATTLING THE GUARDIAN ANGELS.

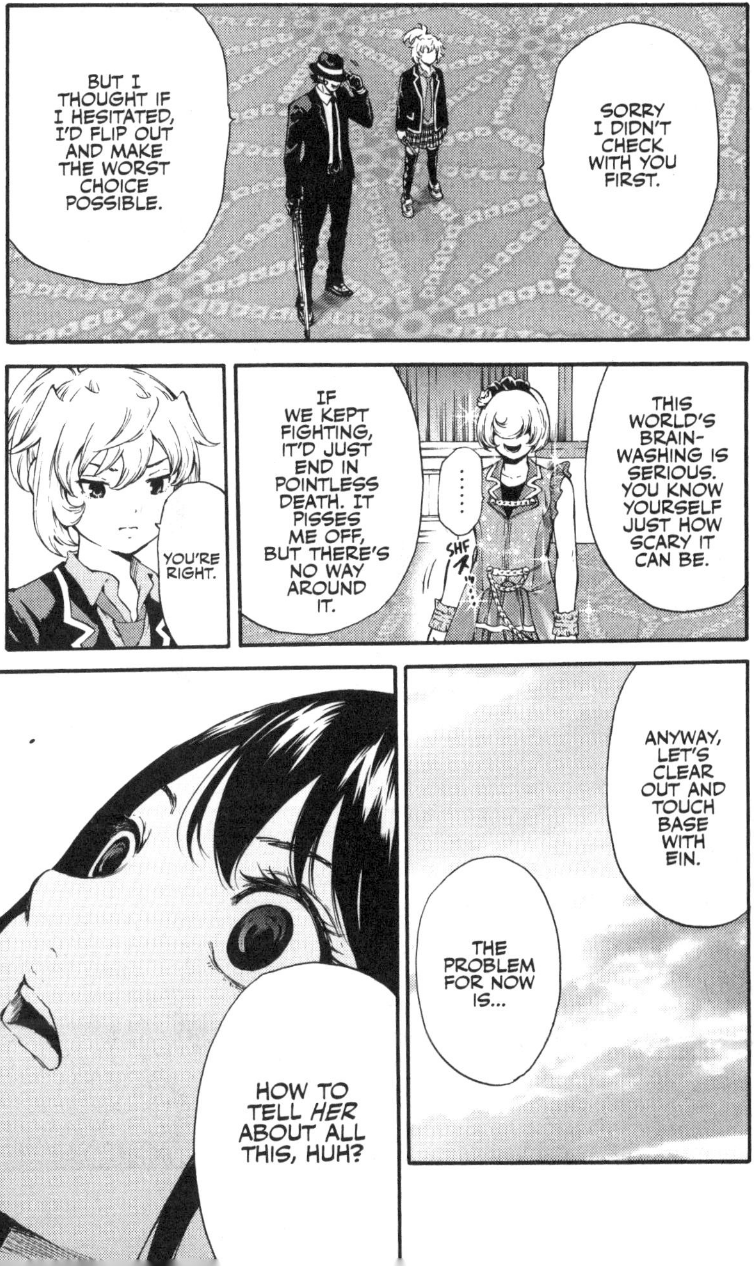
SORRY I DIDN'T CHECK WITH YOU FIRST.
BUT I THOUGHT IF I HESITATED, I'D FLIP OUT AND MAKE THE WORST CHOICE POSSIBLE.
THIS WORLD'S BRAIN-WASHING IS SERIOUS. YOU KNOW YOURSELF JUST HOW SCARY IT CAN BE.
IF WE KEPT FIGHTING, IT'D JUST END IN POINTLESS DEATH. IT PISSES ME OFF, BUT THERE'S NO WAY AROUND IT.
......
SHF
YOU'RE RIGHT.
ANYWAY, LET'S CLEAR OUT AND TOUCH BASE WITH EIN.
THE PROBLEM FOR NOW IS...
HOW TO TELL *HER* ABOUT ALL THIS, HUH?

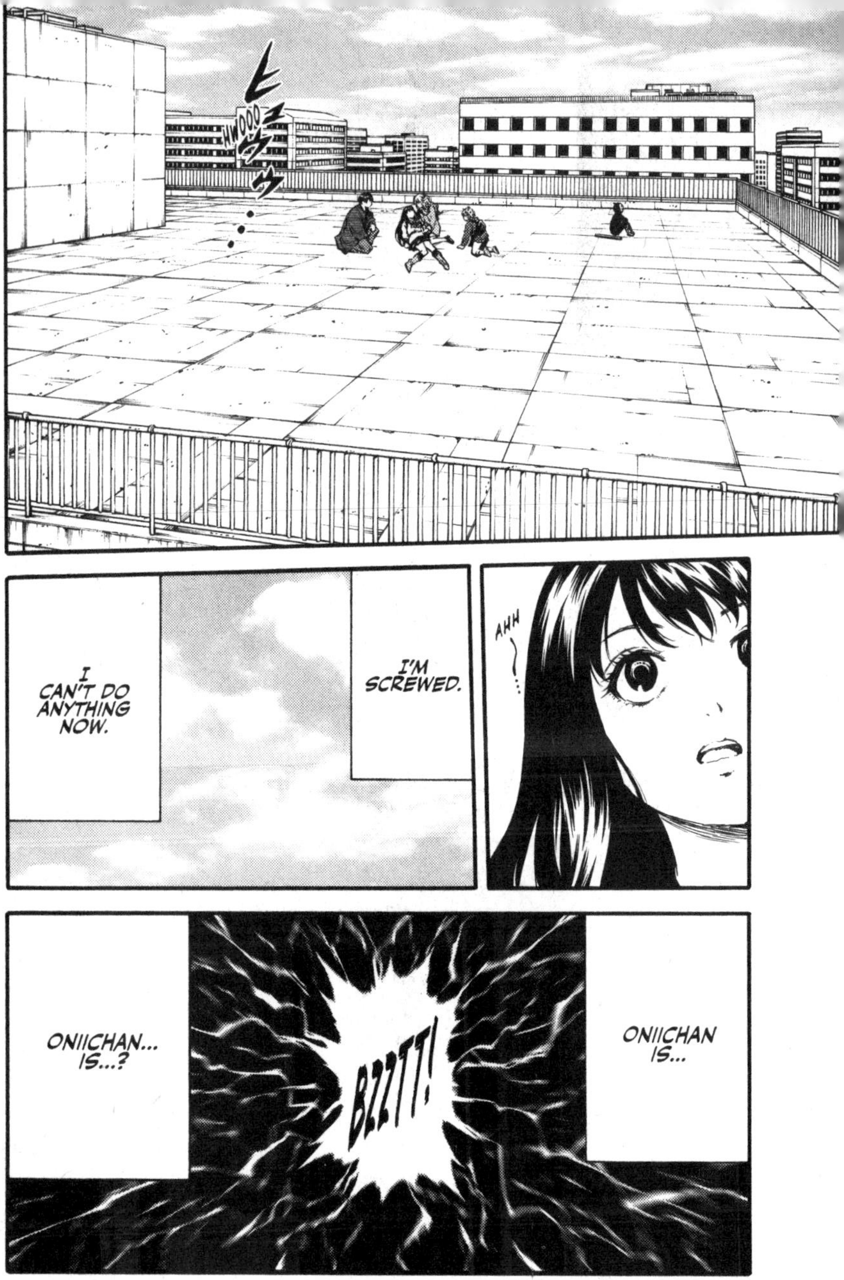
HWOOO
AHH...
I'M SCREWED.
I CAN'T DO ANYTHING NOW.
ONIICHAN IS...
BZZTT!
ONIICHAN... IS...?

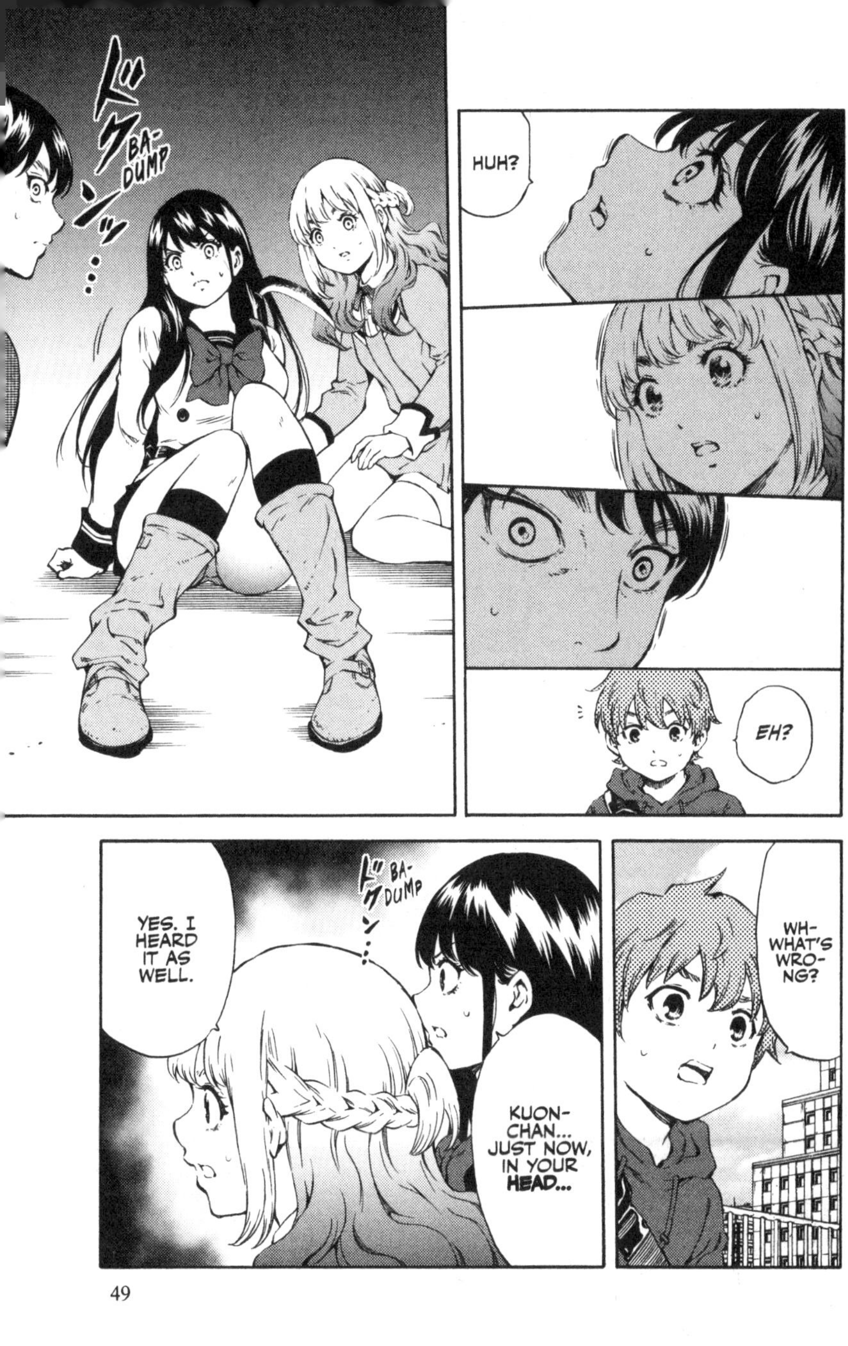
HUH?
EH?
BA-DUMP
WH-WHAT'S WRO-NG?
BA-DUMP
KUON-CHAN... JUST NOW, IN YOUR **HEAD...**
YES. I HEARD IT AS WELL.

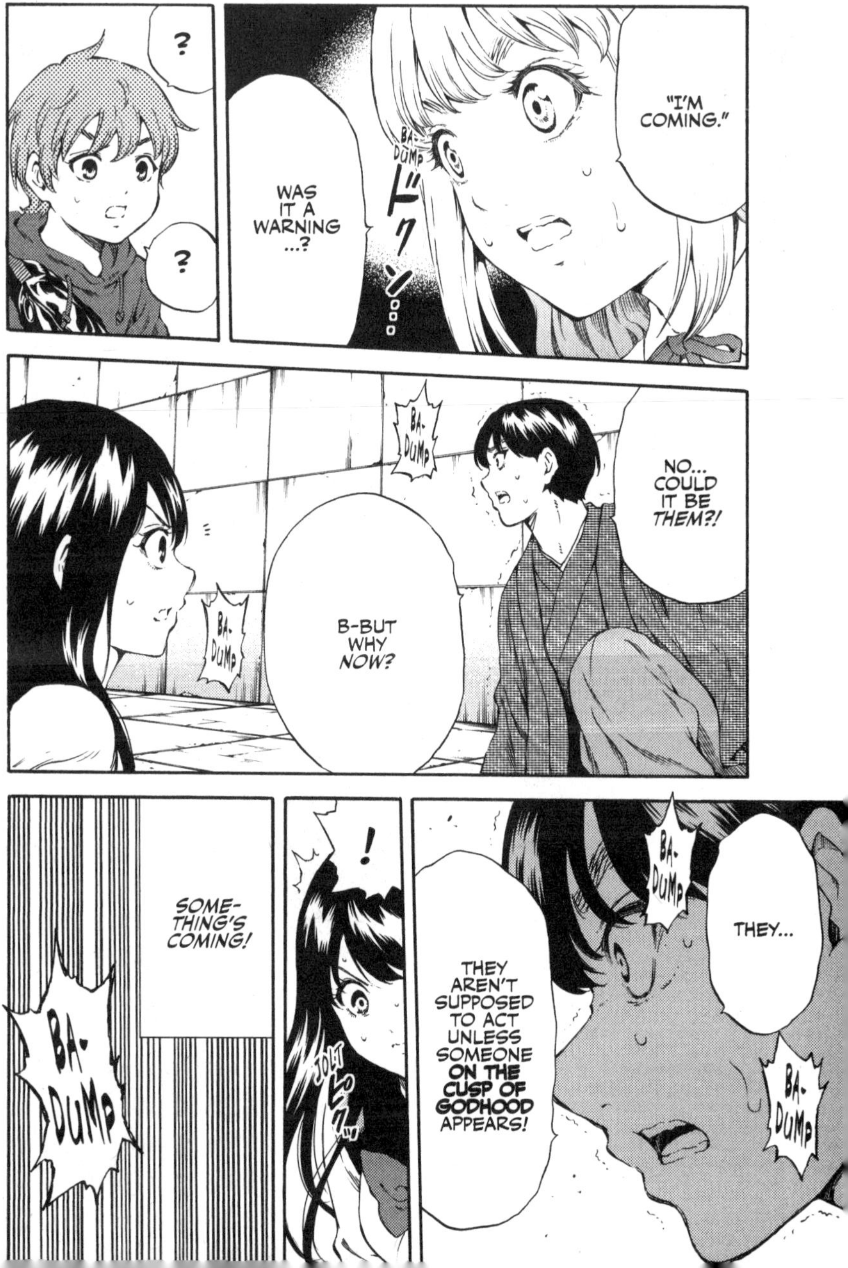
"I'M COMING."
WAS IT A WARNING ...?
BA-DUMP
?
?
NO... COULD IT BE *THEM?!*
BA-DUMP
B-BUT WHY *NOW?*
BA-DUMP
THEY...
BA-DUMP
THEY AREN'T SUPPOSED TO ACT UNLESS SOMEONE **ON THE CUSP OF GODHOOD** APPEARS!
BA-DUMP
!
JOLT
SOME-THING'S COMING!
BA-DUMP

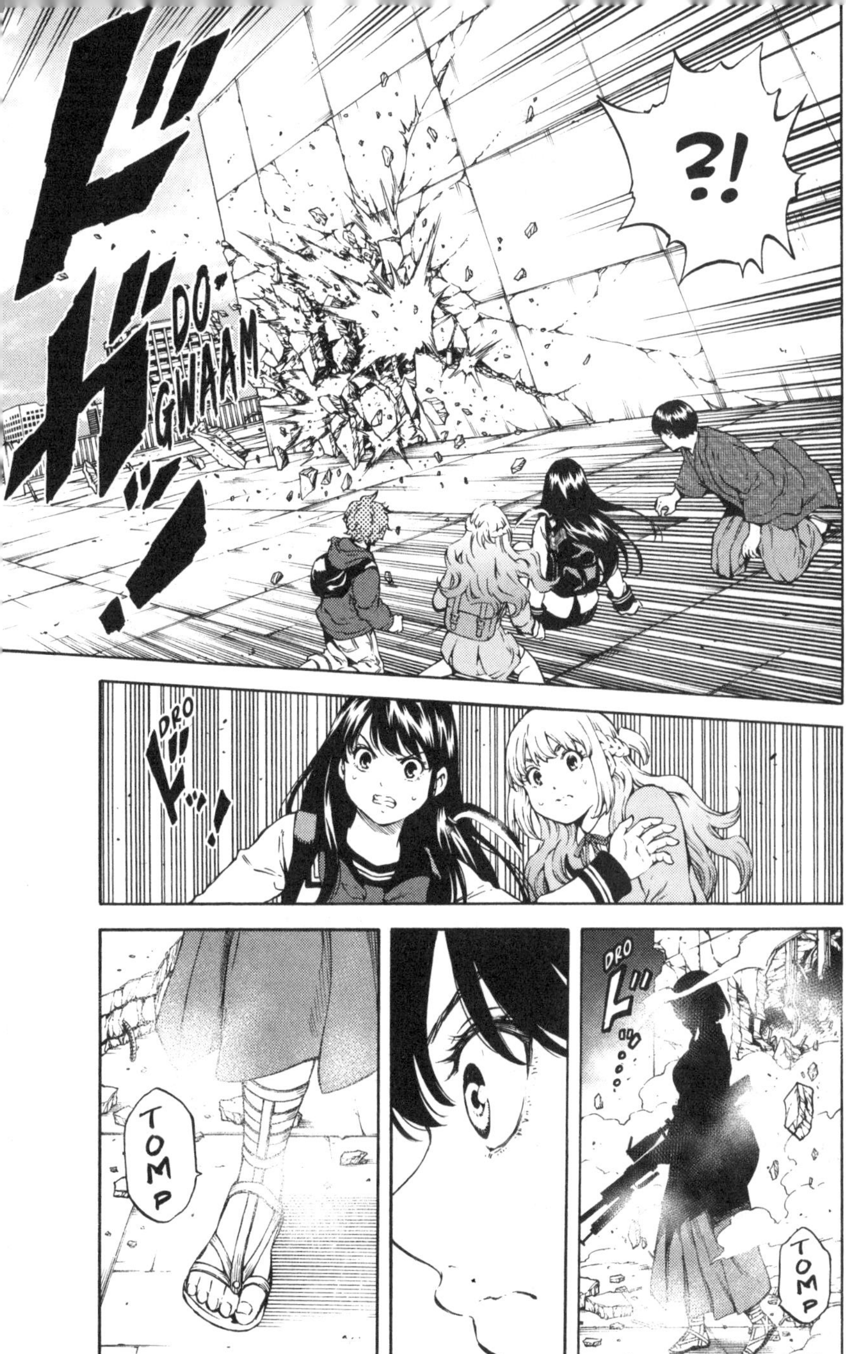
?!
DO GWAAM
DRO
DRO
TOMP
TOMP

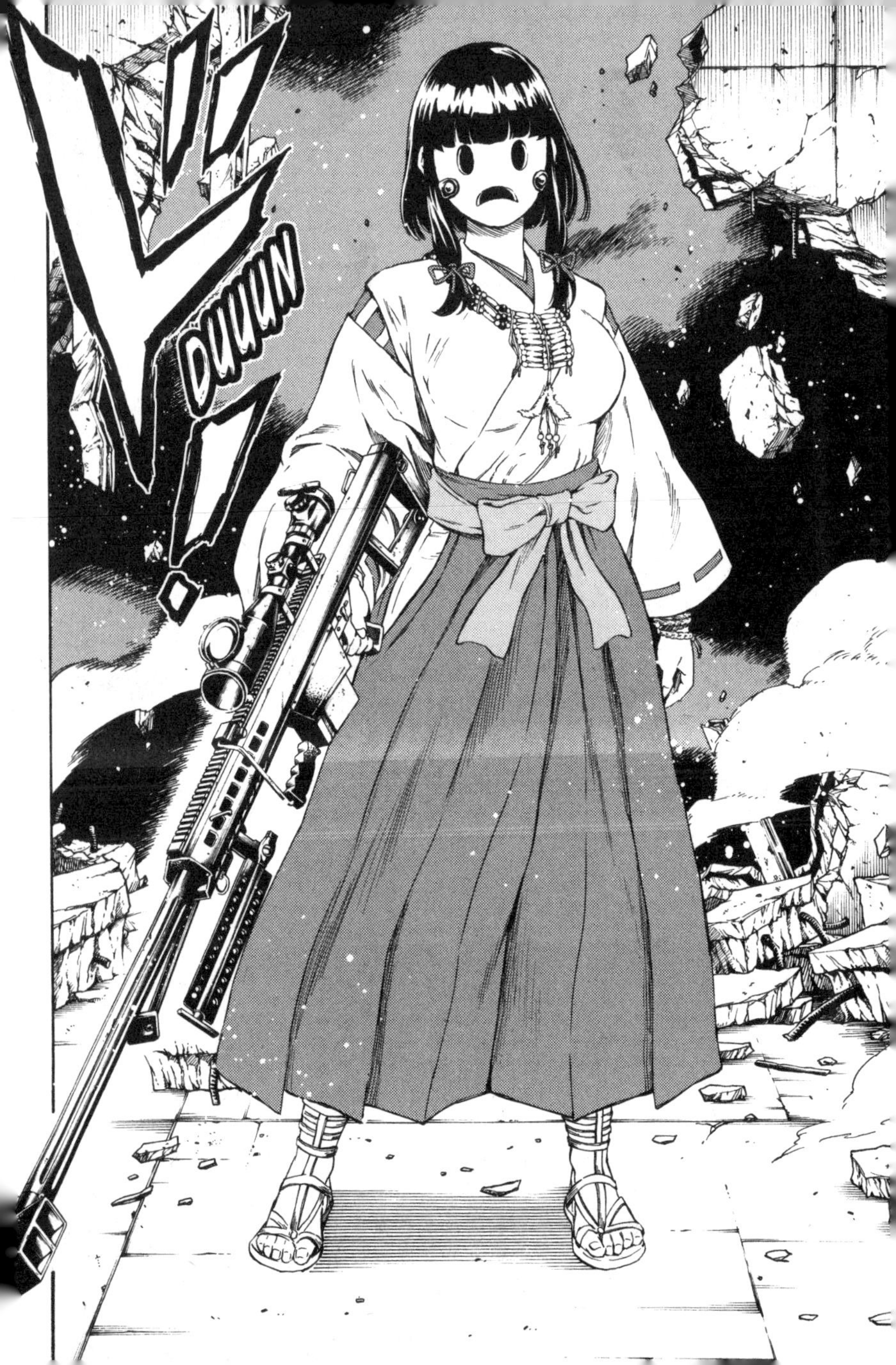
DUUUN

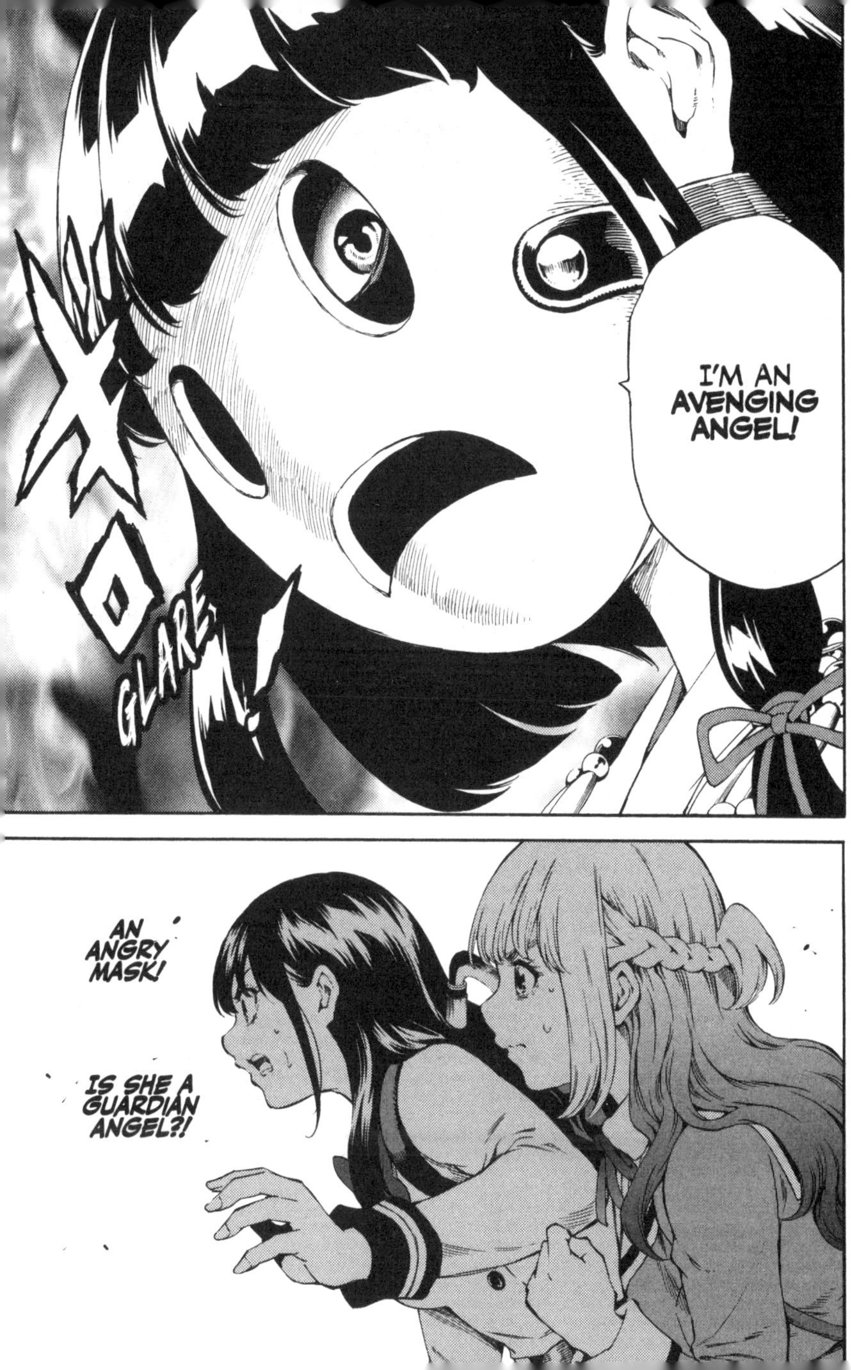
I'M AN AVENGING ANGEL!
GLARE
AN ANGRY MASK!
IS SHE A GUARDIAN ANGEL?!

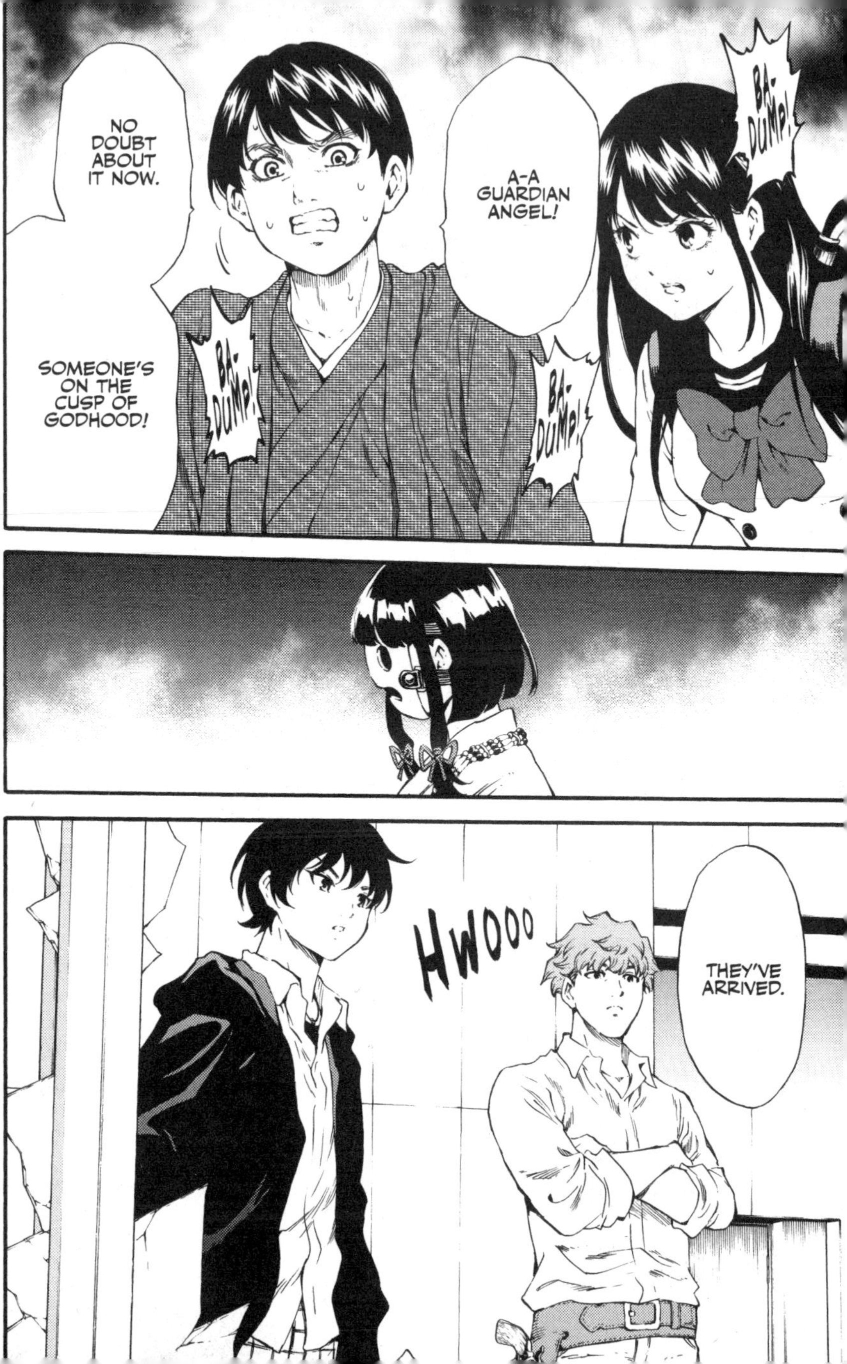
BA-DUMP!
A-A GUARDIAN ANGEL!
BA-DUMP!
NO DOUBT ABOUT IT NOW.
SOMEONE'S ON THE CUSP OF GODHOOD!
BA-DUMP!
THEY'VE ARRIVED.
HWOOO

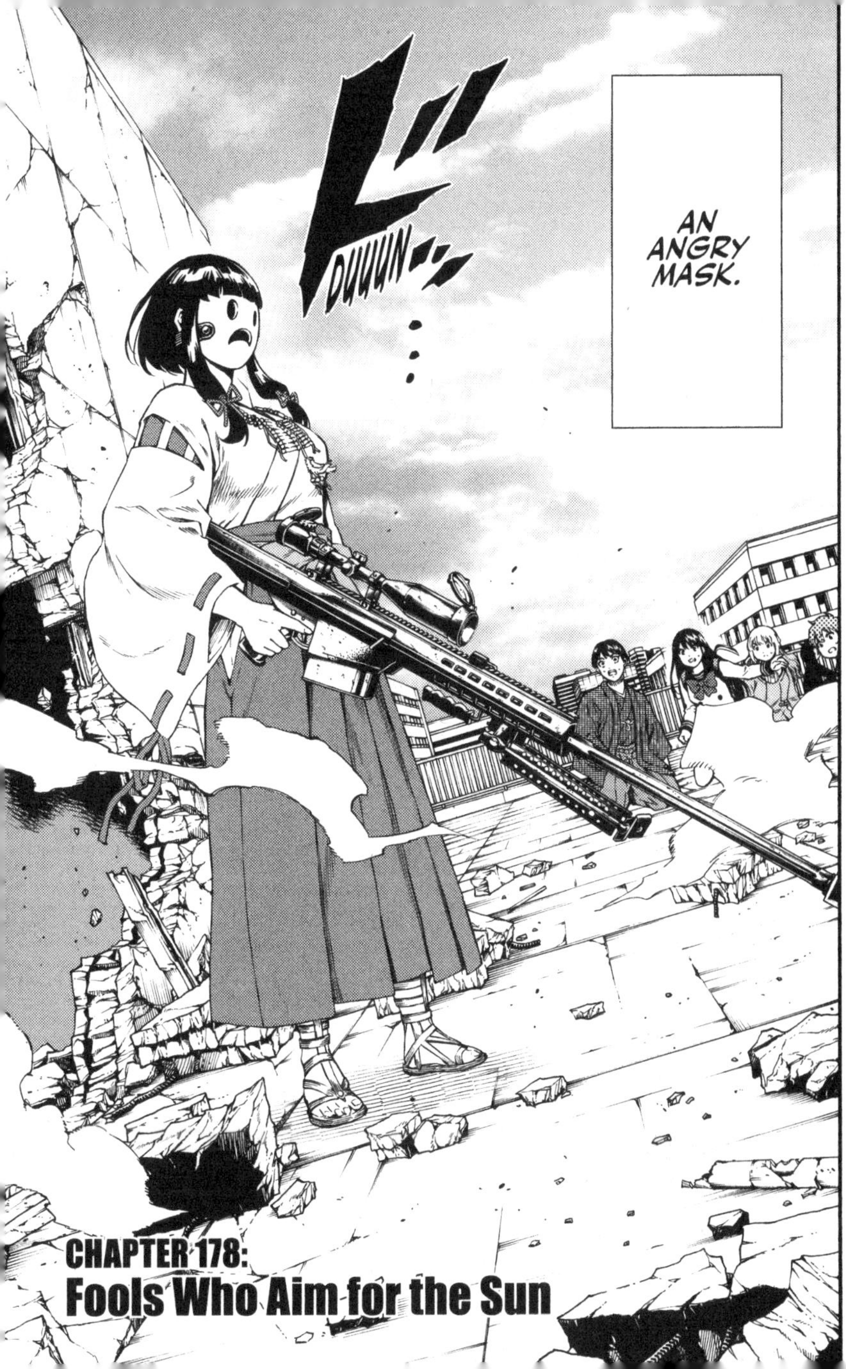
AN ANGRY MASK.
DUUUN
CHAPTER 178:
Fools Who Aim for the Sun

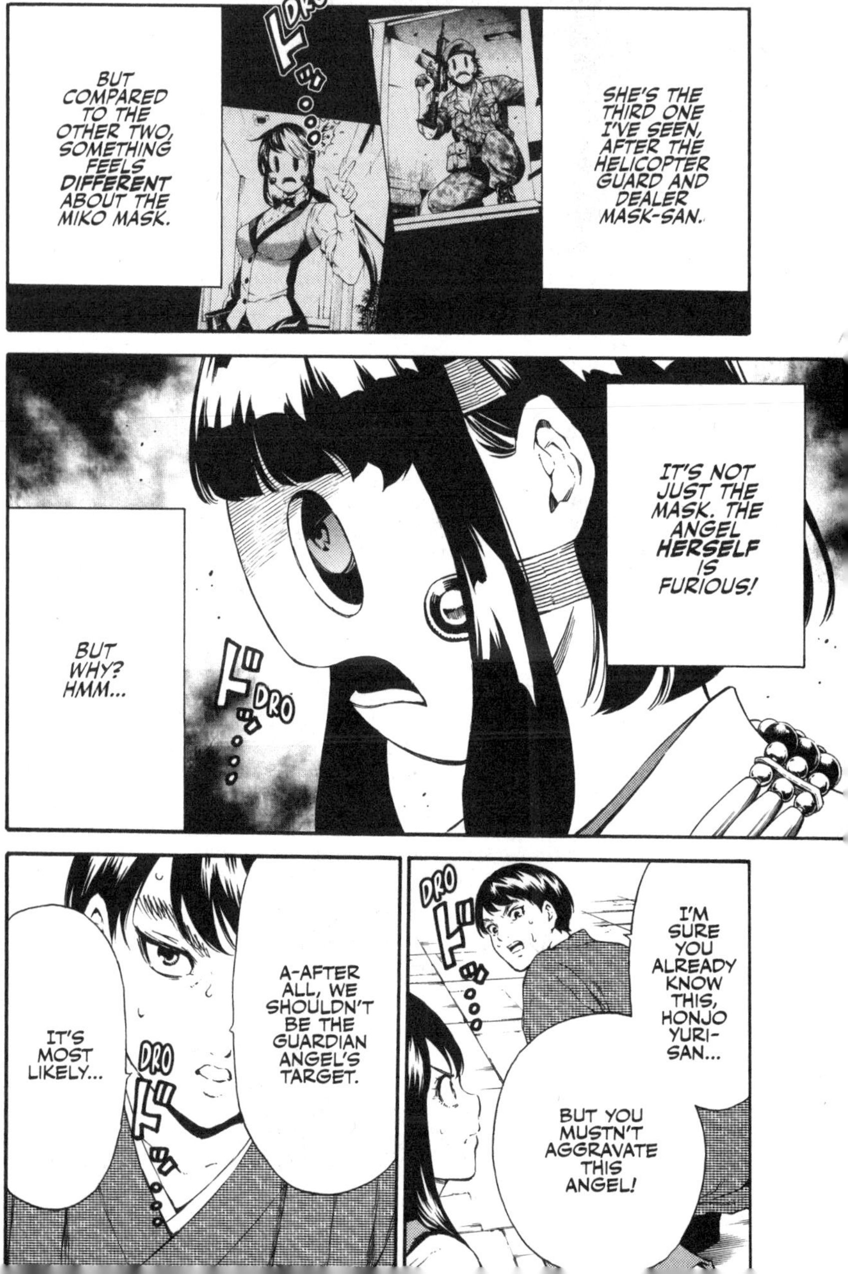
SHE'S THE THIRD ONE I'VE SEEN, AFTER THE HELICOPTER GUARD AND DEALER MASK-SAN.
DRO
BUT COMPARED TO THE OTHER TWO, SOMETHING FEELS DIFFERENT ABOUT THE MIKO MASK.
IT'S NOT JUST THE MASK. THE ANGEL HERSELF IS FURIOUS!
DRO
BUT WHY? HMM...
DRO
I'M SURE YOU ALREADY KNOW THIS, HONJO YURI-SAN...
BUT YOU MUSTN'T AGGRAVATE THIS ANGEL!
A-AFTER ALL, WE SHOULDN'T BE THE GUARDIAN ANGEL'S TARGET.
IT'S MOST LIKELY...
DRO

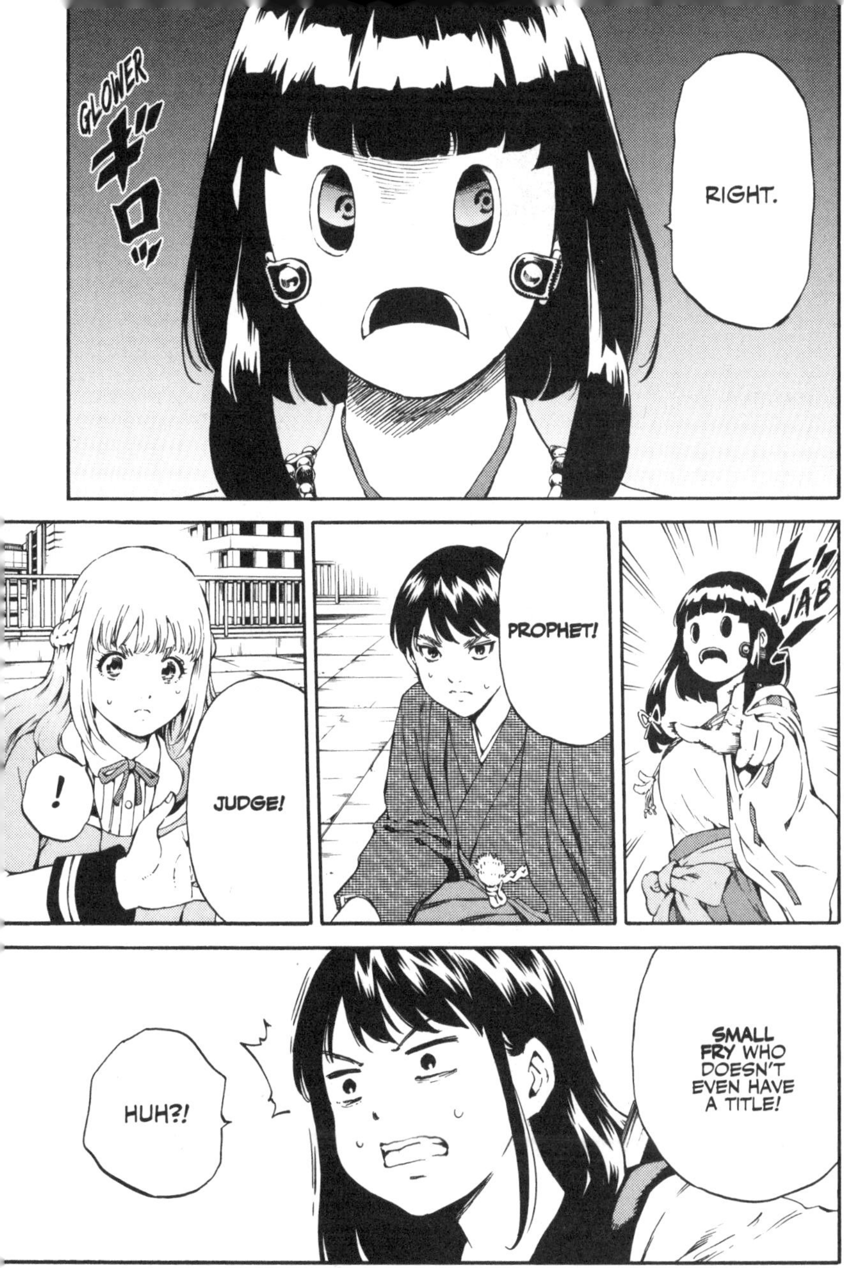
RIGHT.
GLOWER
ギロッ
ビッ
JAB
PROPHET!
JUDGE!
!
SMALL FRY WHO DOESN'T EVEN HAVE A TITLE!
HUH?!

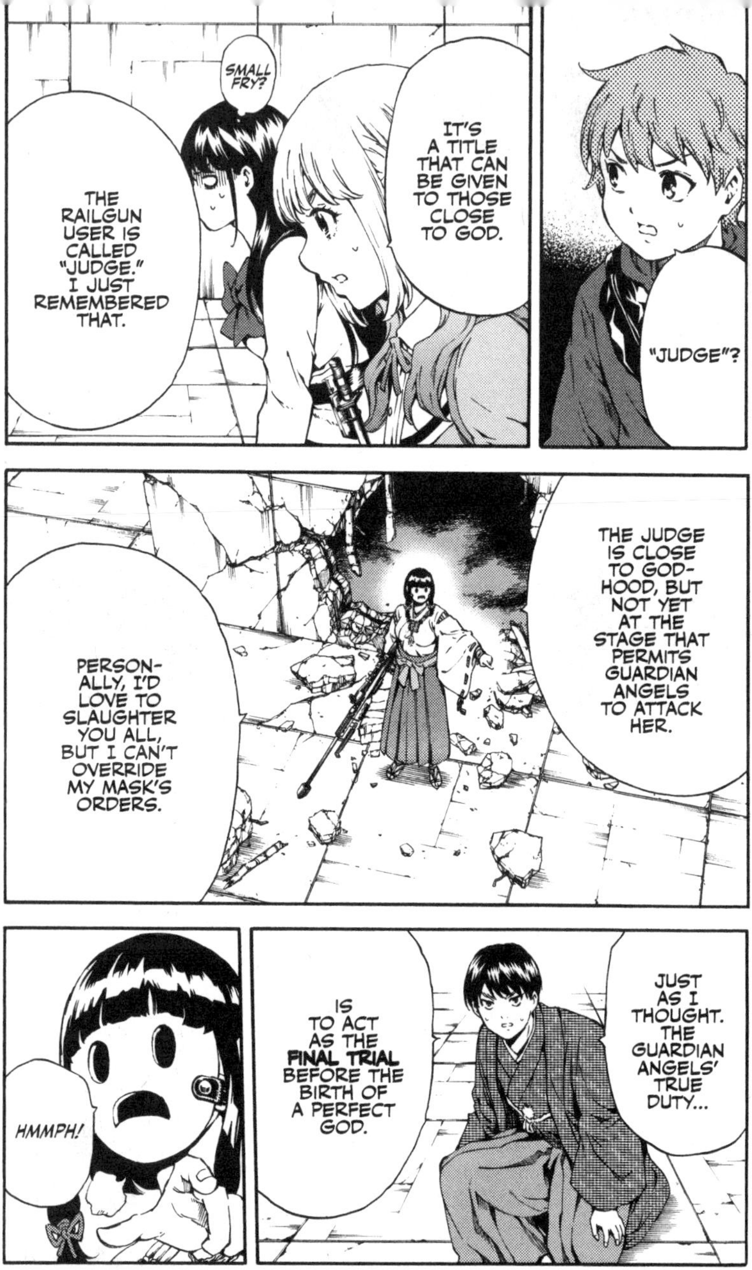
"JUDGE"?
IT'S A TITLE THAT CAN BE GIVEN TO THOSE CLOSE TO GOD.
SMALL FRY?
THE RAILGUN USER IS CALLED "JUDGE." I JUST REMEMBERED THAT.
THE JUDGE IS CLOSE TO GOD-HOOD, BUT NOT YET AT THE STAGE THAT PERMITS GUARDIAN ANGELS TO ATTACK HER.
PERSON-ALLY, I'D LOVE TO SLAUGHTER YOU ALL, BUT I CAN'T OVERRIDE MY MASK'S ORDERS.
JUST AS I THOUGHT. THE GUARDIAN ANGELS' TRUE DUTY...
IS TO ACT AS THE **FINAL TRIAL** BEFORE THE BIRTH OF A PERFECT GOD.
HMMPH!

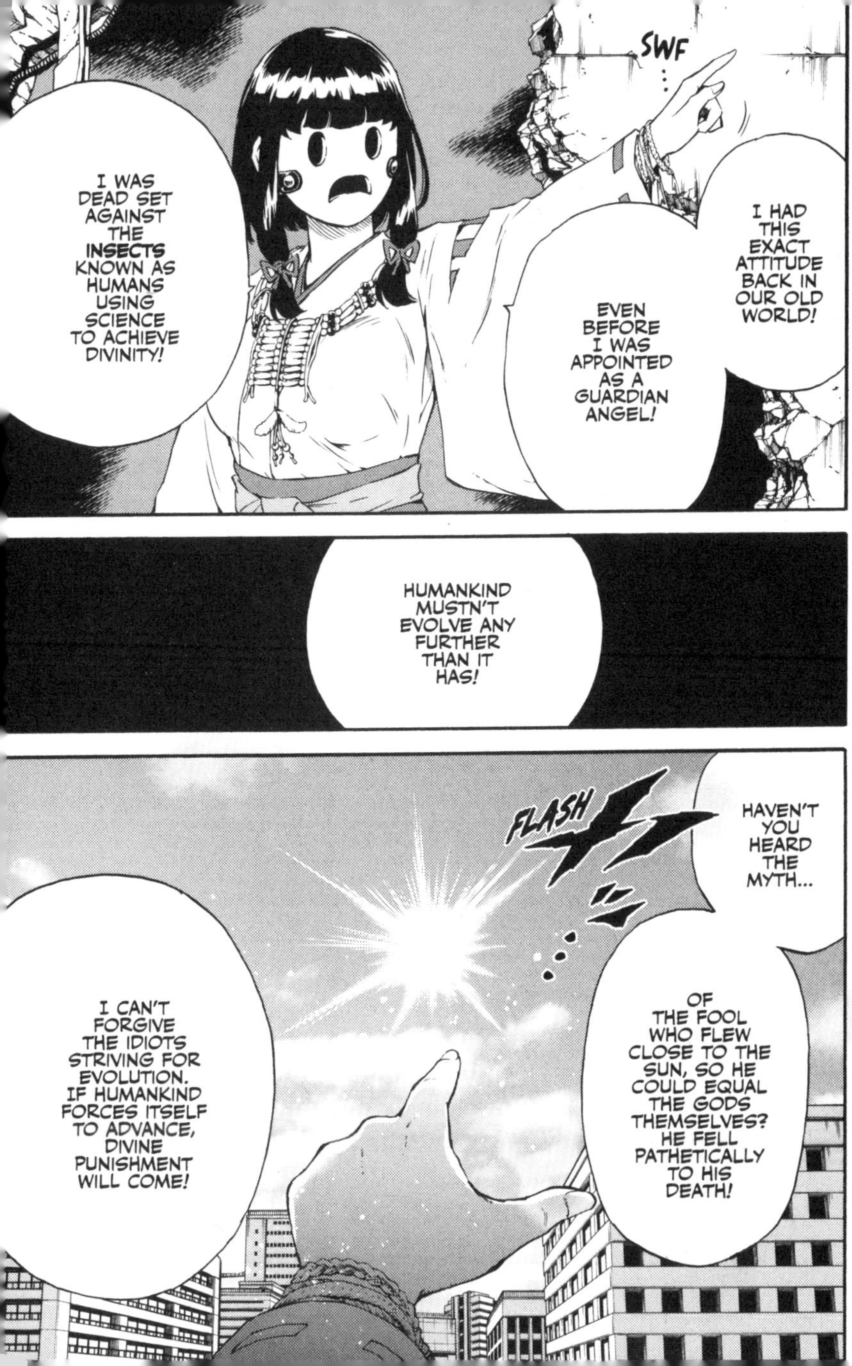
SWF
I HAD THIS EXACT ATTITUDE BACK IN OUR OLD WORLD!
EVEN BEFORE I WAS APPOINTED AS A GUARDIAN ANGEL!
I WAS DEAD SET AGAINST THE **INSECTS** KNOWN AS HUMANS USING SCIENCE TO ACHIEVE DIVINITY!
HUMANKIND MUSTN'T EVOLVE ANY FURTHER THAN IT HAS!
FLASH
HAVEN'T YOU HEARD THE MYTH...
OF THE FOOL WHO FLEW CLOSE TO THE SUN, SO HE COULD EQUAL THE GODS THEMSELVES? HE FELL PATHETICALLY TO HIS DEATH!
I CAN'T FORGIVE THE IDIOTS STRIVING FOR EVOLUTION. IF HUMANKIND FORCES ITSELF TO ADVANCE, DIVINE PUNISHMENT WILL COME!

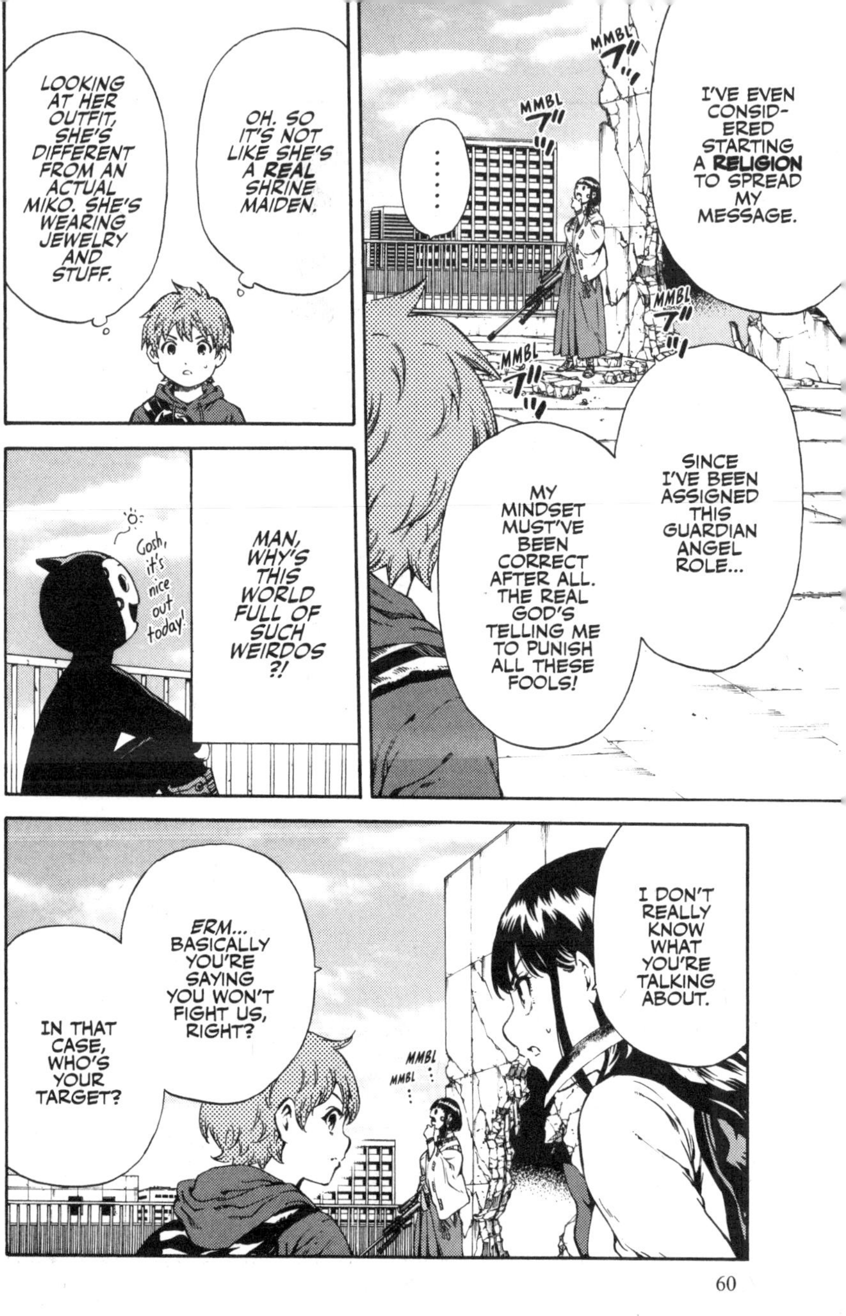
MMBL ブ"
MMBL ブ"
......
I'VE EVEN CONSIDERED STARTING A **RELIGION** TO SPREAD MY MESSAGE.
MMBL ブ"
MMBL ブ"
SINCE I'VE BEEN ASSIGNED THIS GUARDIAN ANGEL ROLE...
MY MINDSET MUST'VE BEEN CORRECT AFTER ALL. THE REAL GOD'S TELLING ME TO PUNISH ALL THESE FOOLS!
OH. SO IT'S NOT LIKE SHE'S A **REAL** SHRINE MAIDEN.
LOOKING AT HER OUTFIT, SHE'S DIFFERENT FROM AN ACTUAL MIKO. SHE'S WEARING JEWELRY AND STUFF.
MAN, WHY'S THIS WORLD FULL OF SUCH WEIRDOS?!
Gosh, it's nice out today!
I DON'T REALLY KNOW WHAT YOU'RE TALKING ABOUT.
MMBL MMBL...
ERM... BASICALLY YOU'RE SAYING YOU WON'T FIGHT US, RIGHT?
IN THAT CASE, WHO'S YOUR TARGET?

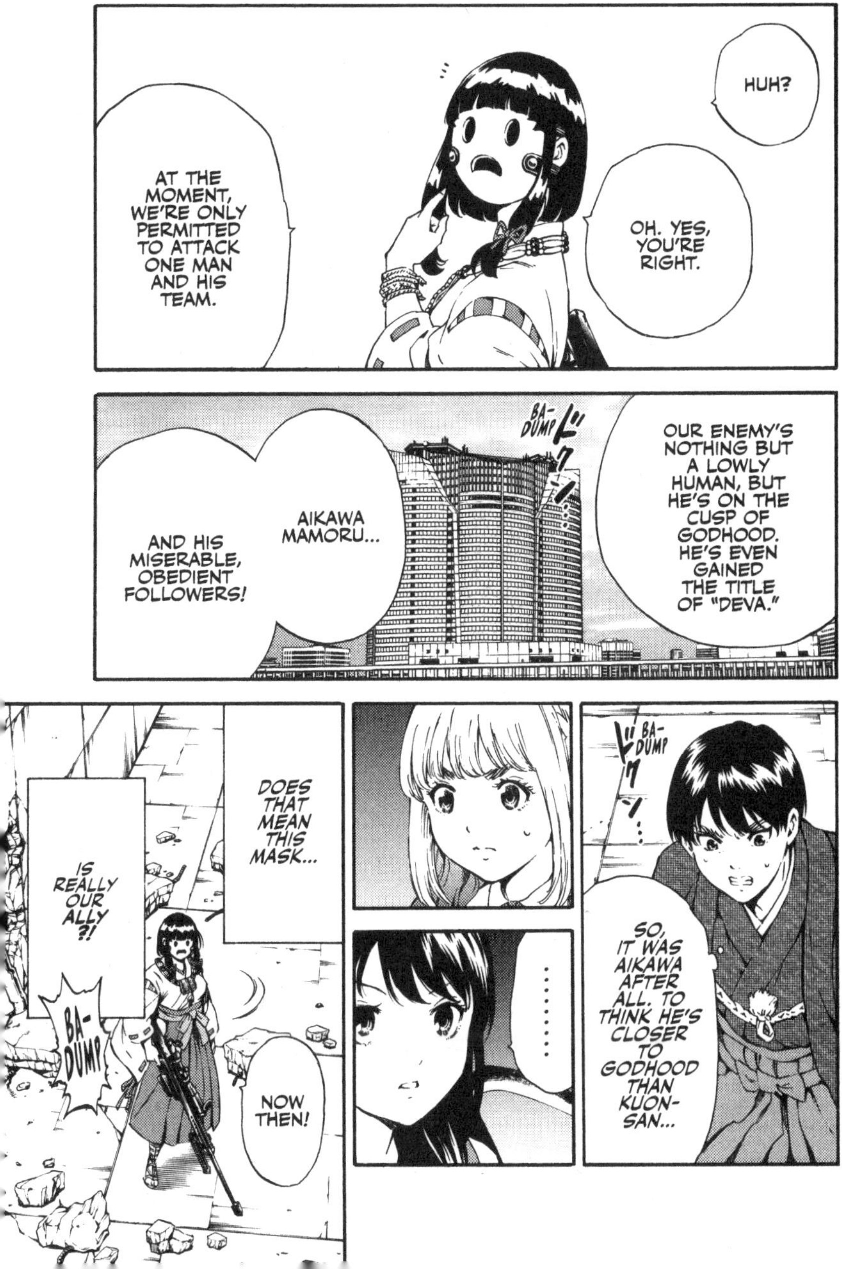
HUH?
OH. YES, YOU'RE RIGHT.
AT THE MOMENT, WE'RE ONLY PERMITTED TO ATTACK ONE MAN AND HIS TEAM.
BA-DUMP
OUR ENEMY'S NOTHING BUT A LOWLY HUMAN, BUT HE'S ON THE CUSP OF GODHOOD. HE'S EVEN GAINED THE TITLE OF "DEVA."
AIKAWA MAMORU...
AND HIS MISERABLE, OBEDIENT FOLLOWERS!
BA-DUMP
SO, IT WAS AIKAWA AFTER ALL. TO THINK HE'S CLOSER TO GODHOOD THAN KUON-SAN...
....
DOES THAT MEAN THIS MASK...
IS REALLY OUR ALLY?!
BA-DUMP
NOW THEN!

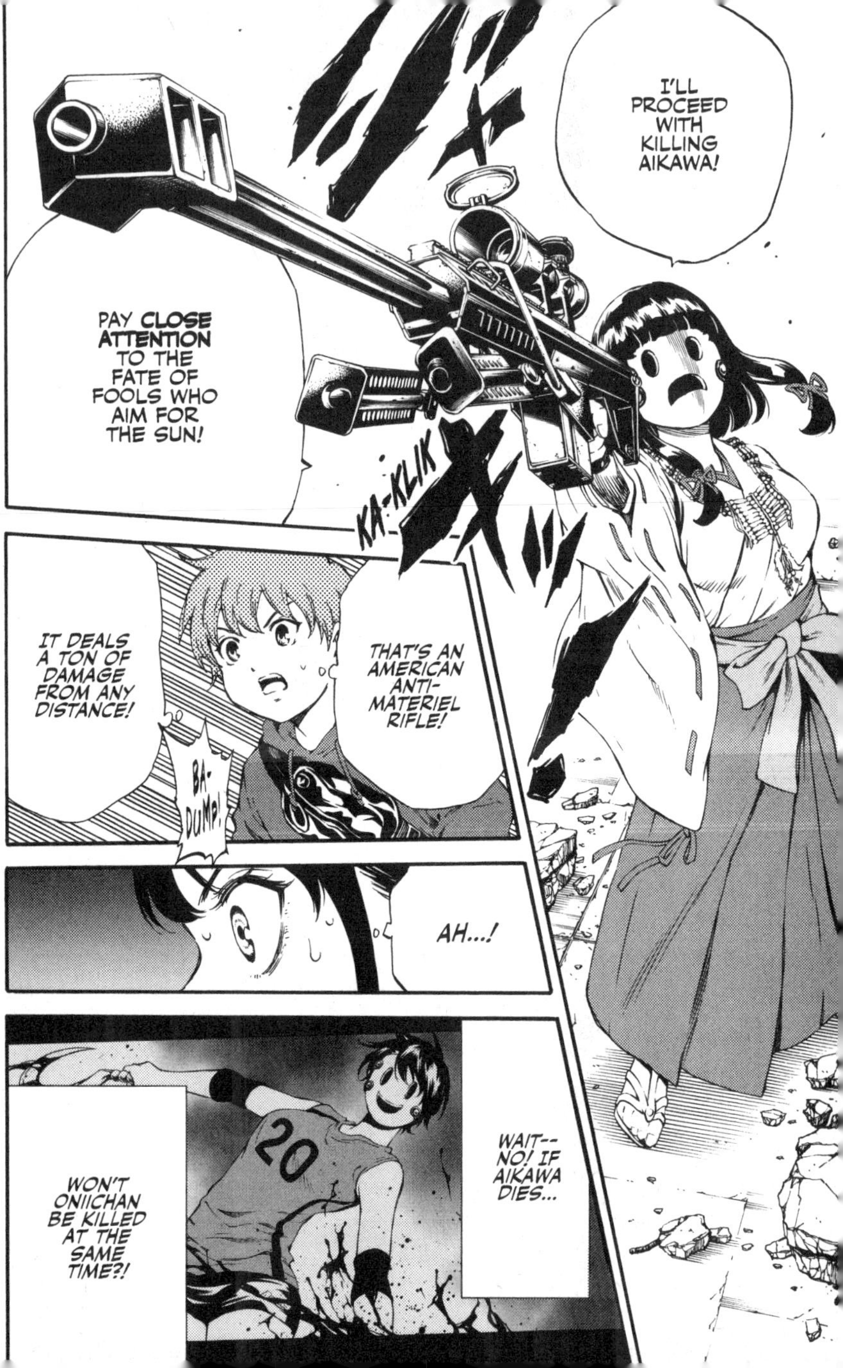
I'LL PROCEED WITH KILLING AIKAWA!
PAY **CLOSE ATTENTION** TO THE FATE OF FOOLS WHO AIM FOR THE SUN!
KA-KLIK
THAT'S AN AMERICAN ANTI-MATERIEL RIFLE!
IT DEALS A TON OF DAMAGE FROM ANY DISTANCE!
BA-DUMP!
AH...!
WAIT-- NO! IF AIKAWA DIES...
WON'T ONIICHAN BE KILLED AT THE SAME TIME?!

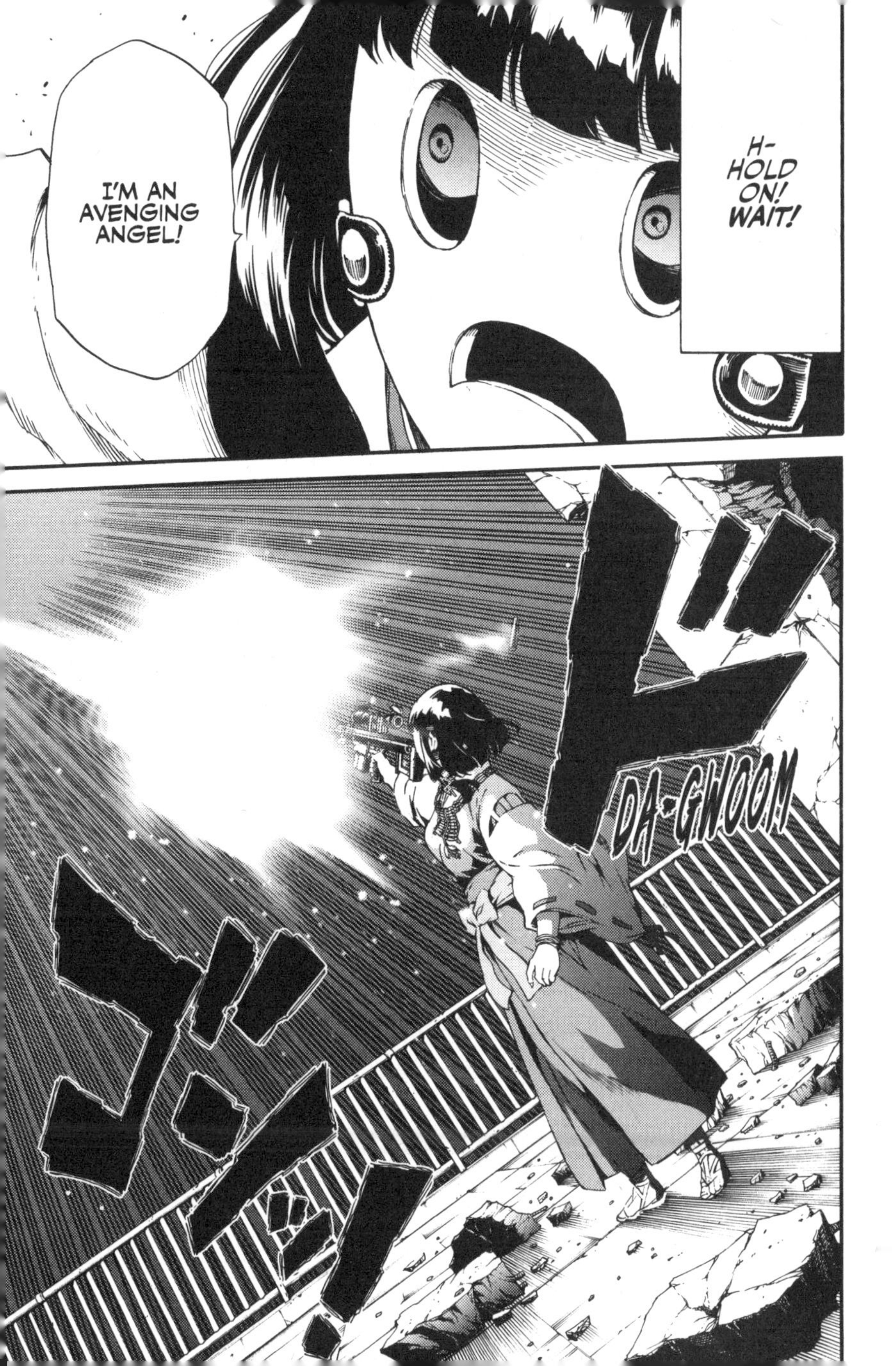
H-HOLD ON! WAIT!
I'M AN AVENGING ANGEL!
DA-GWOOM

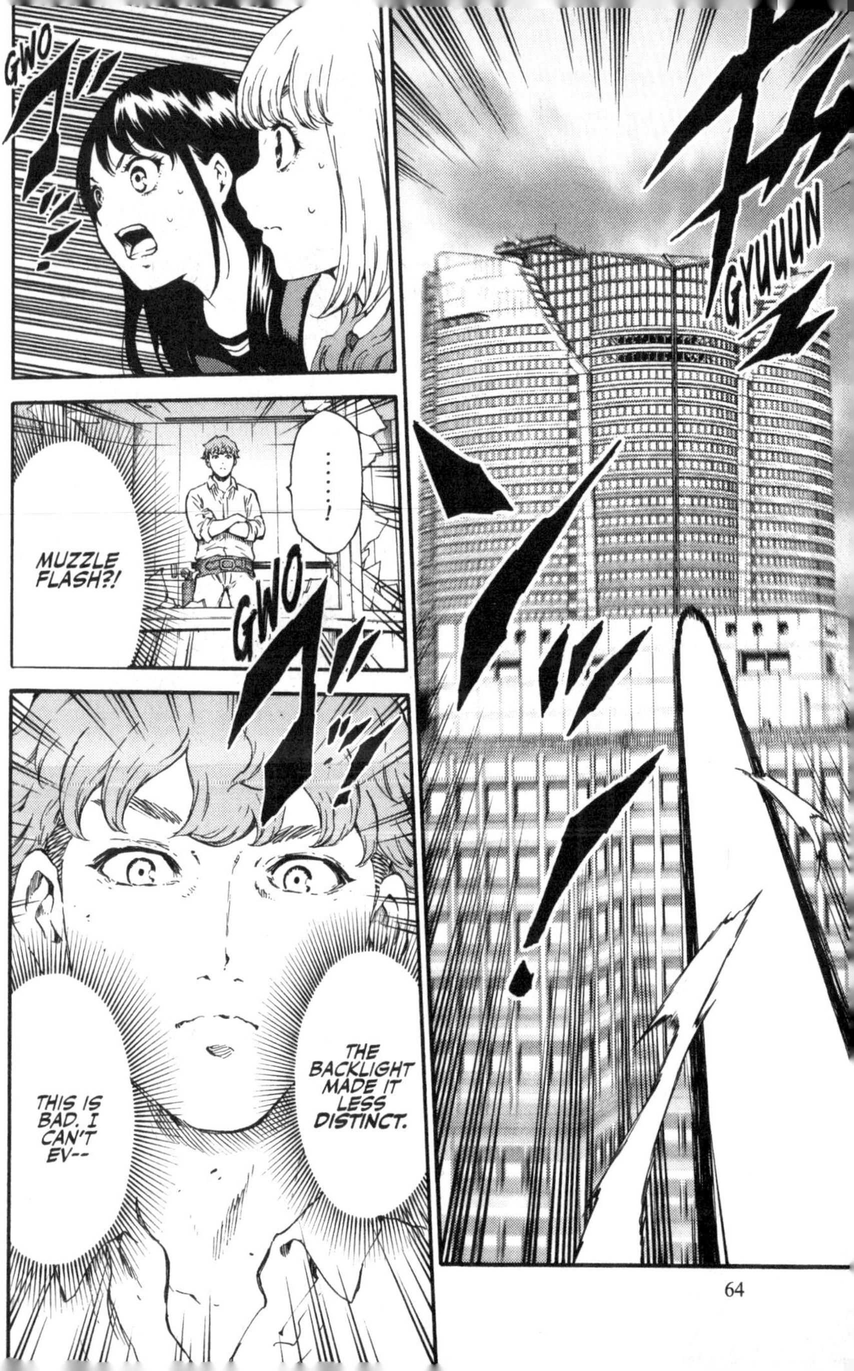
GYUUUN
GWO
......!
MUZZLE FLASH?!
GWO
THE BACKLIGHT MADE IT LESS DISTINCT.
THIS IS BAD. I CAN'T EV--

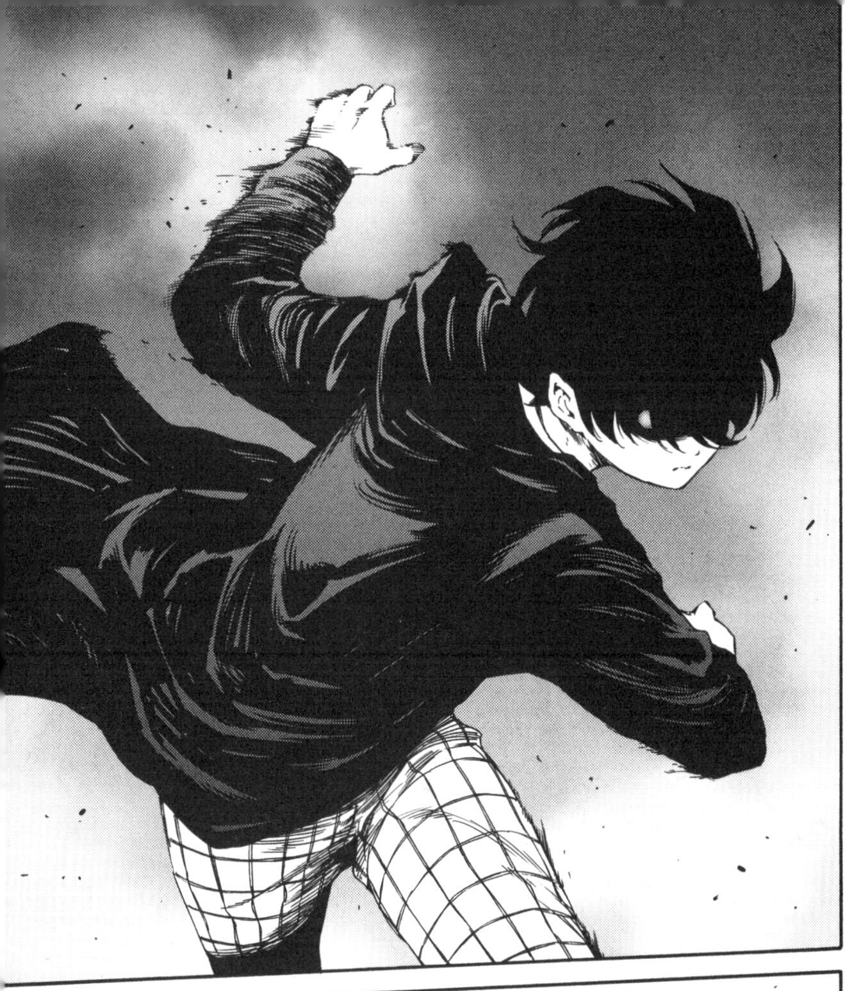
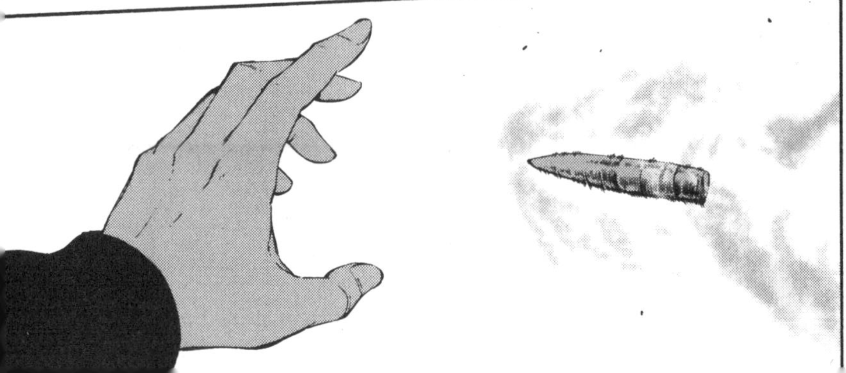

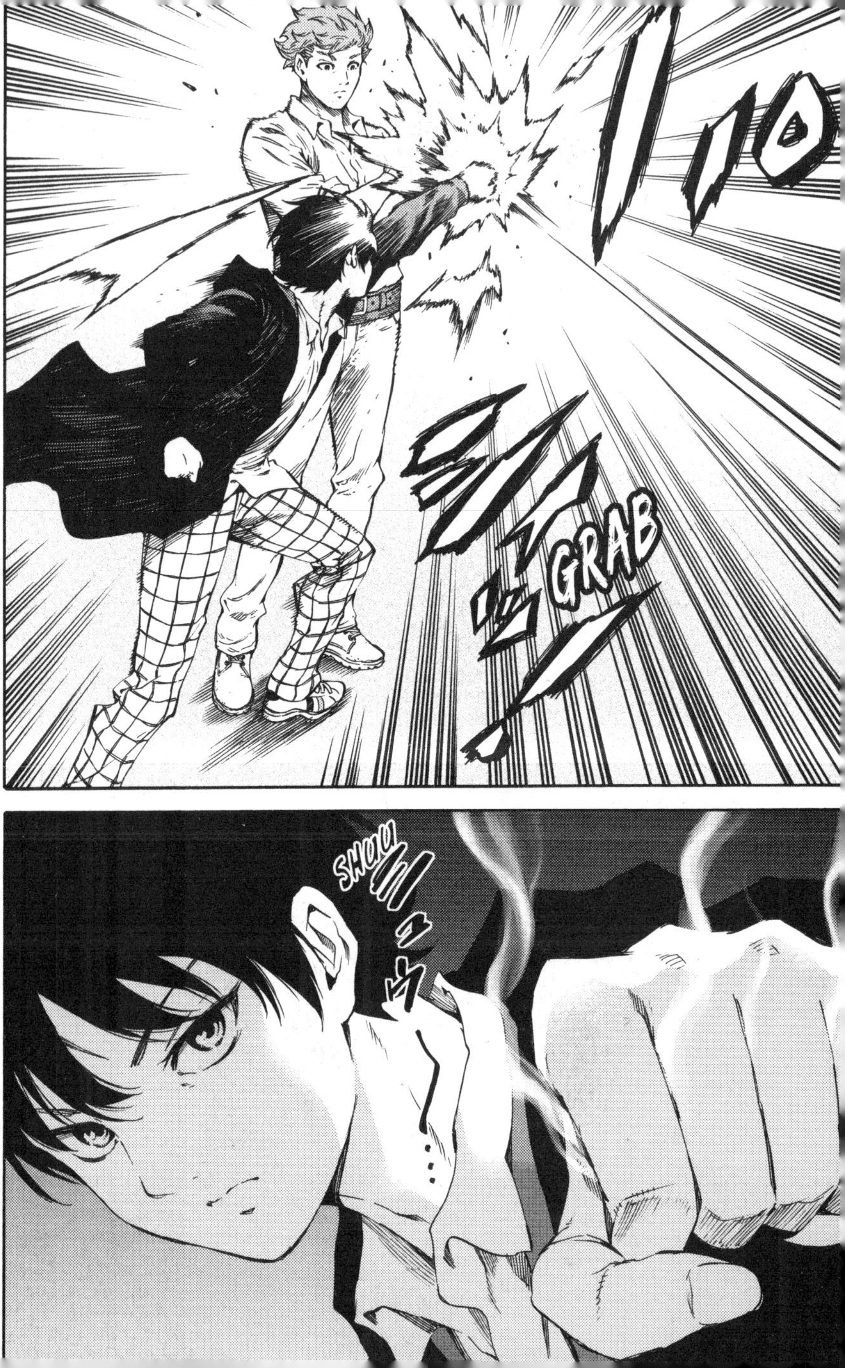
GRAB
SHUU

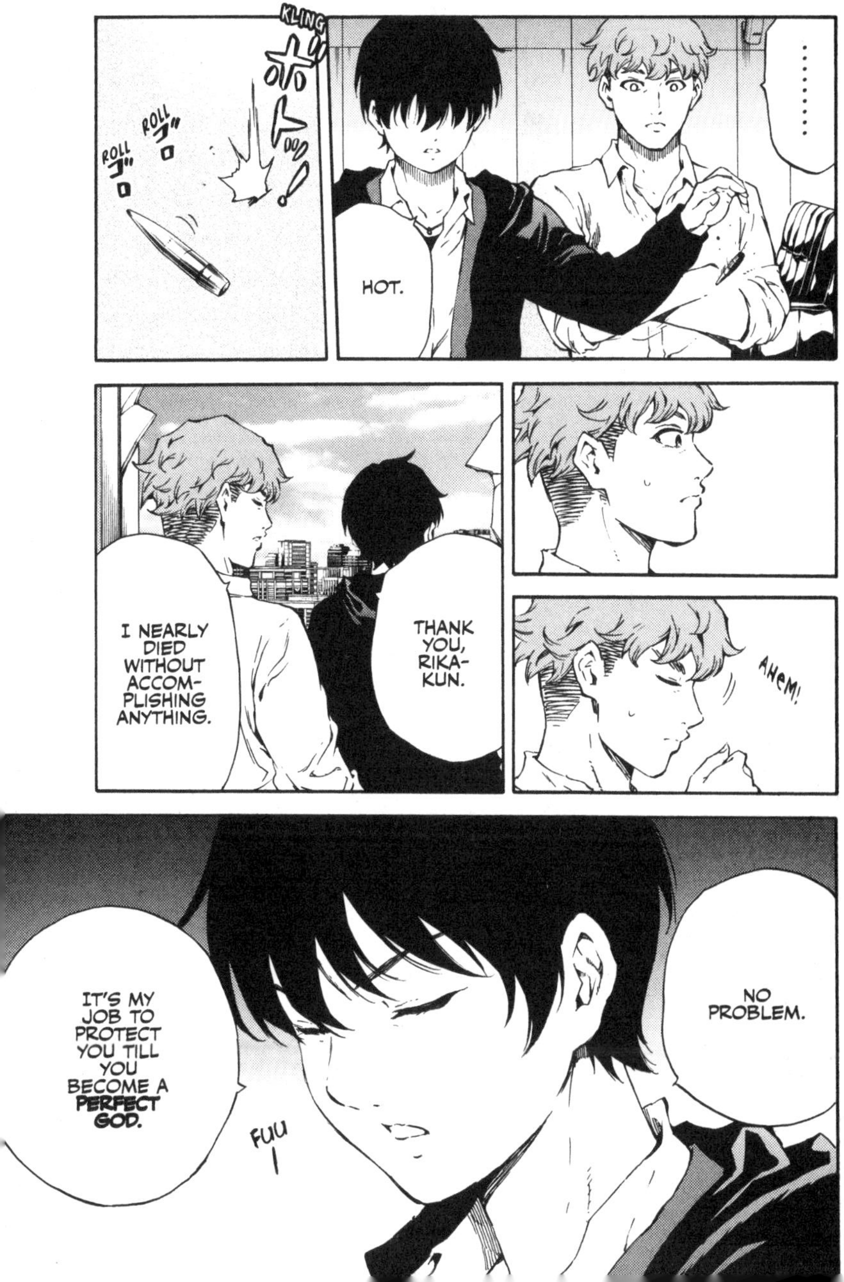
....
HOT.
KLING
ROLL
ROLL
AHEM!
THANK YOU, RIKA-KUN.
I NEARLY DIED WITHOUT ACCOMPLISHING ANYTHING.
NO PROBLEM.
FUU
IT'S MY JOB TO PROTECT YOU TILL YOU BECOME A **PERFECT GOD.**

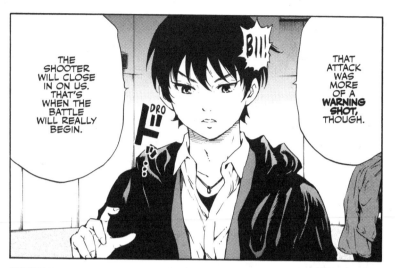

THAT ATTACK WAS MORE OF A **WARNING SHOT,** THOUGH.
BII!
DRO
THE SHOOTER WILL CLOSE IN ON US. THAT'S WHEN THE BATTLE WILL REALLY BEGIN.
I KNEW HE WOULD BE...
BUT AS AN APOSTLE, HONJO RIKA'S ON A LEVEL I'VE NEVER SEEN.
DRO
SNIPING AIKAWA FAILED.
DRO
THE APOSTLE HE CREATED POSSESSES STRENGTH RIVALING OURS!
CHAK

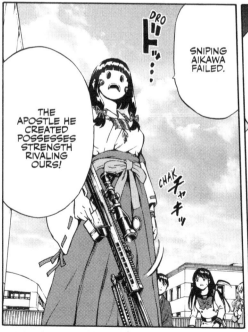

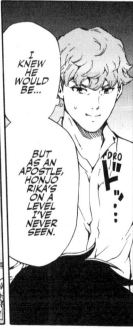

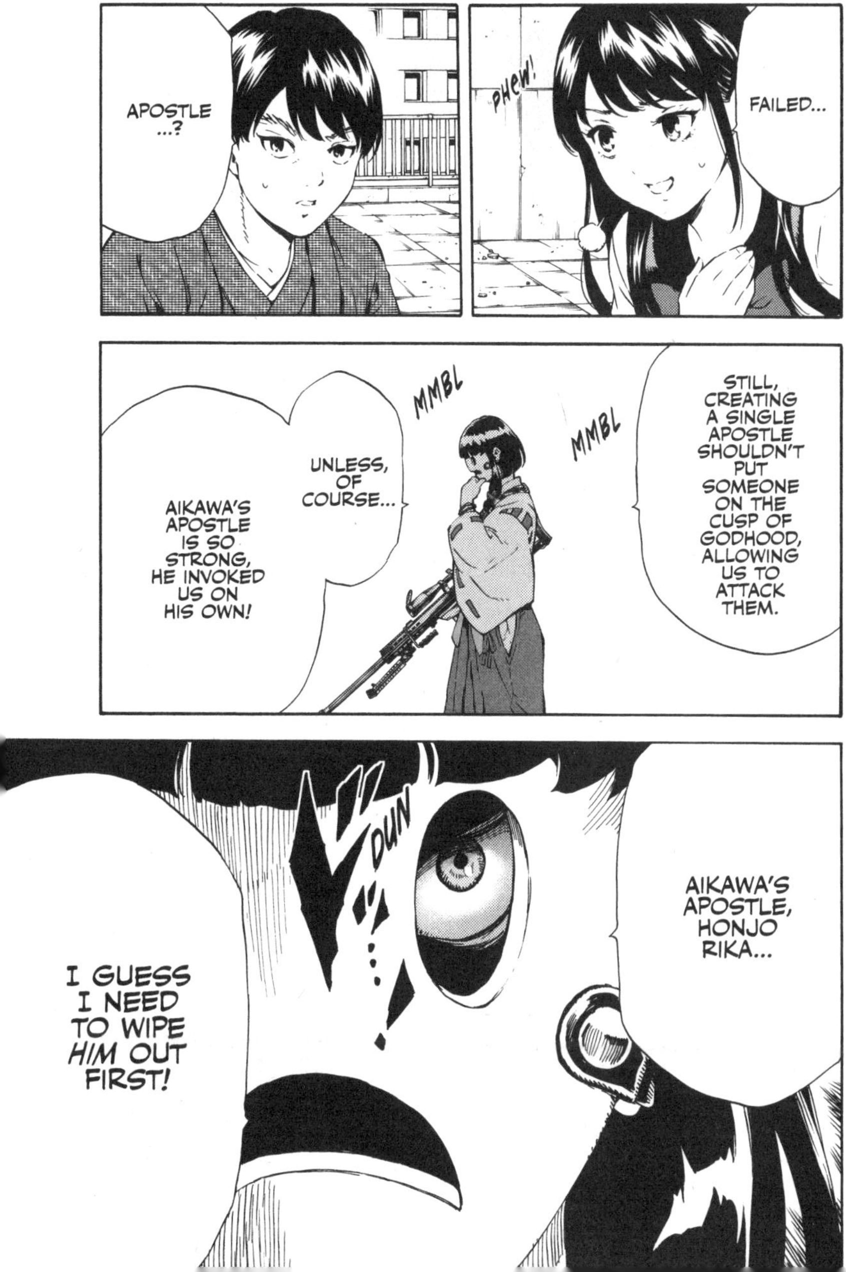
PHEW!
FAILED...
APOSTLE ...?
STILL, CREATING A SINGLE APOSTLE SHOULDN'T PUT SOMEONE ON THE CUSP OF GODHOOD, ALLOWING US TO ATTACK THEM.
MMBL
MMBL
UNLESS, OF COURSE...
AIKAWA'S APOSTLE IS SO STRONG, HE INVOKED US ON HIS OWN!
AIKAWA'S APOSTLE, HONJO RIKA...
DUN
I GUESS I NEED TO WIPE *HIM* OUT FIRST!

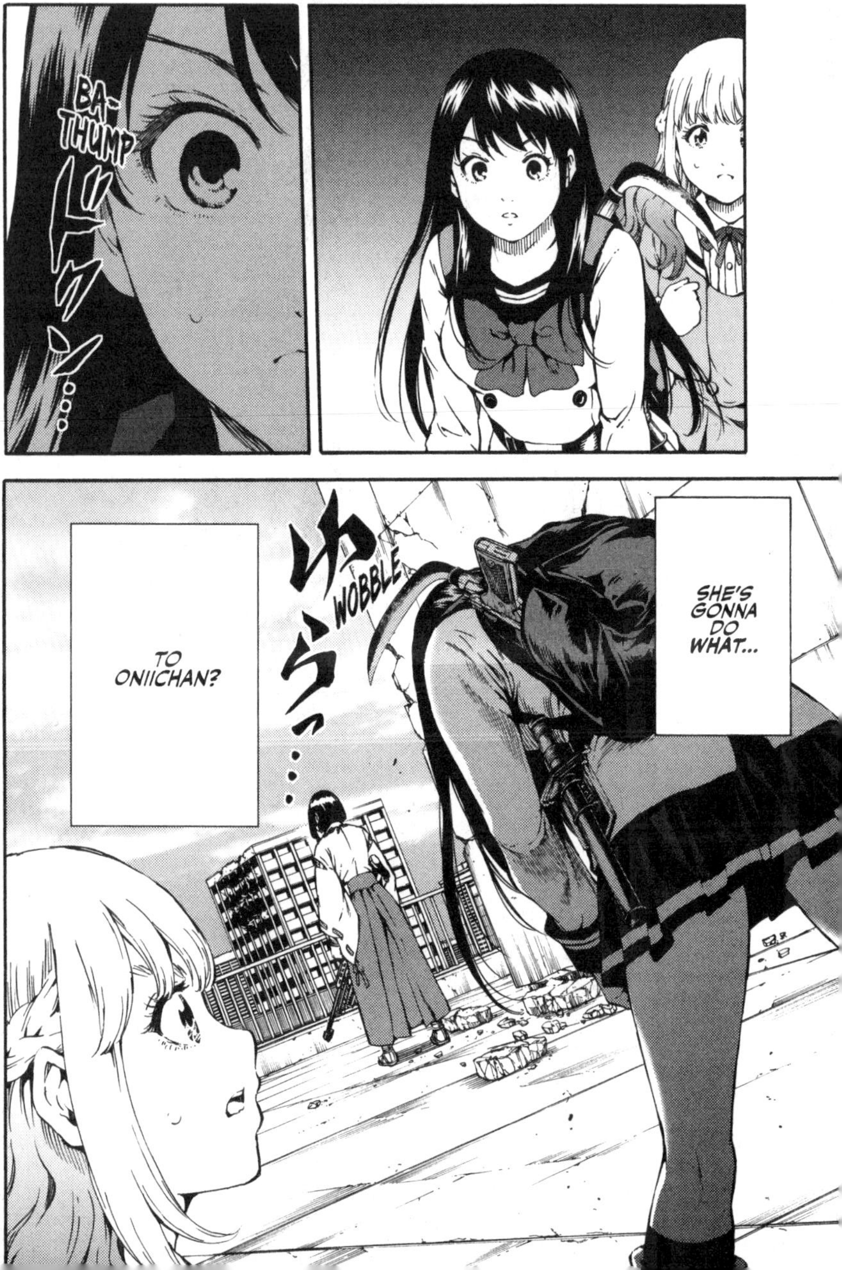
BA-THUMP
SHE'S GONNA DO WHAT...
WOBBLE
TO ONIICHAN?

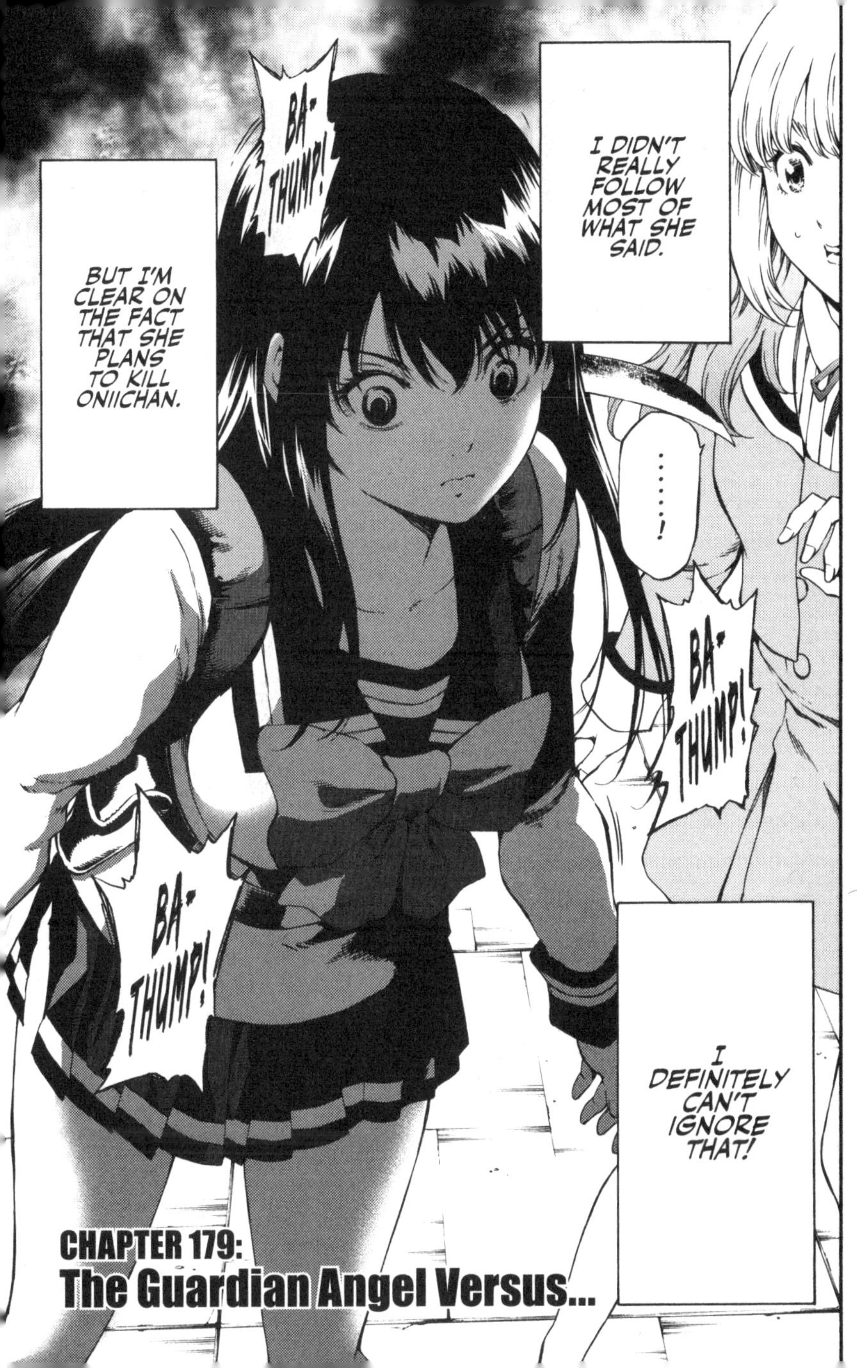
I DIDN'T REALLY FOLLOW MOST OF WHAT SHE SAID.
BA-THUMP!
BUT I'M CLEAR ON THE FACT THAT SHE PLANS TO KILL ONIICHAN.
......!
BA-THUMP!
BA-THUMP!
I DEFINITELY CAN'T IGNORE THAT!
CHAPTER 179:
The Guardian Angel Versus...

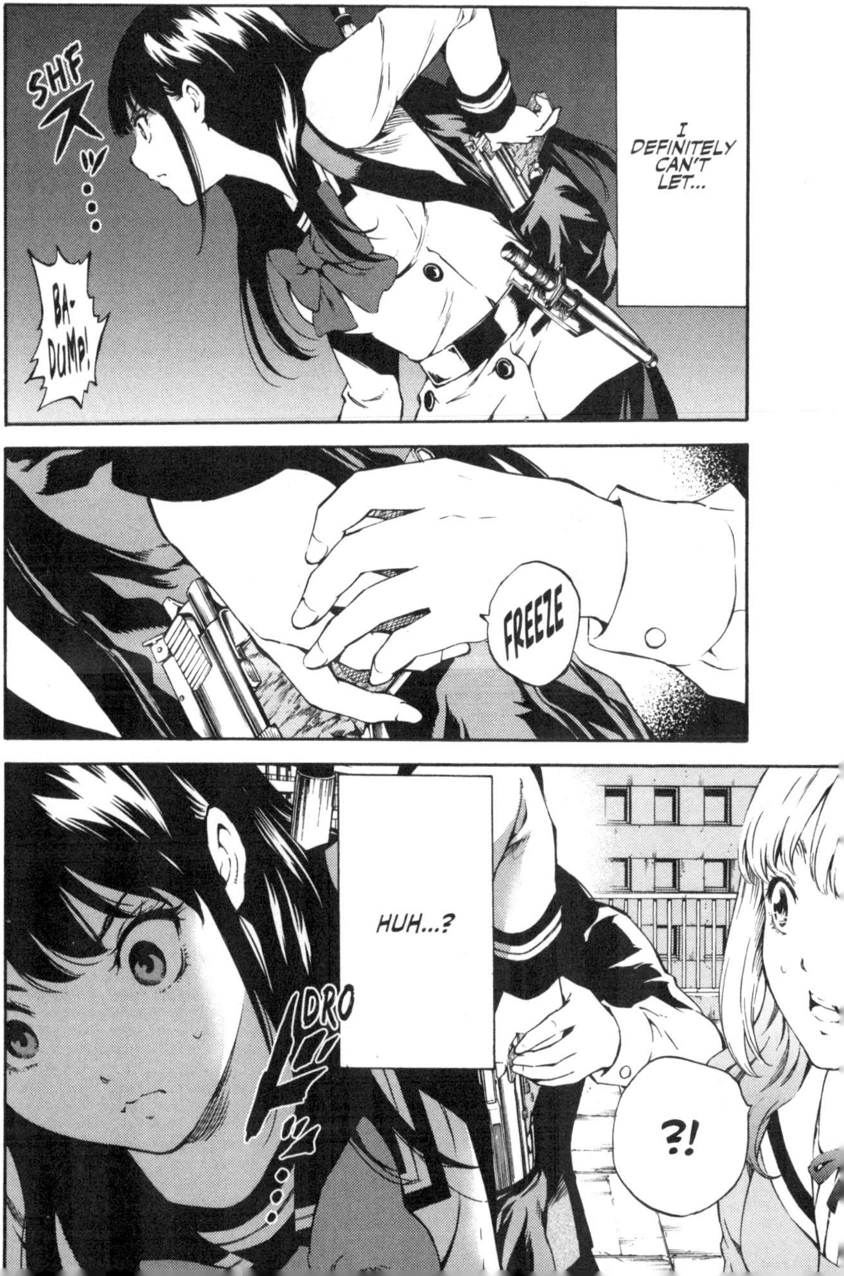
I DEFINITELY CAN'T LET...
SHF
BA-DUMP!
FREEZE
HUH...?
?!
DRO

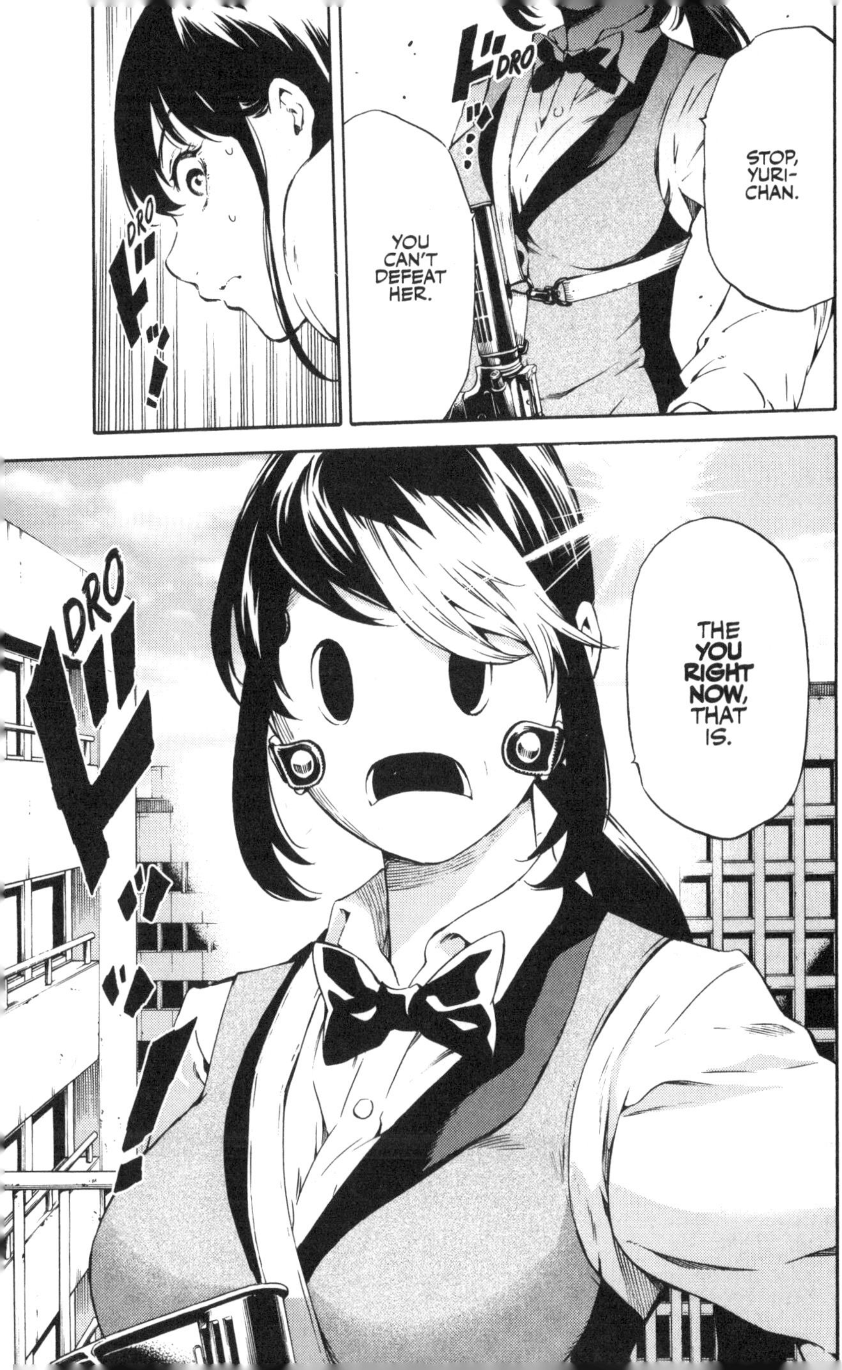
DRO
STOP, YURI-CHAN.
YOU CAN'T DEFEAT HER.
DRO
DRO
THE **YOU RIGHT NOW,** THAT IS.

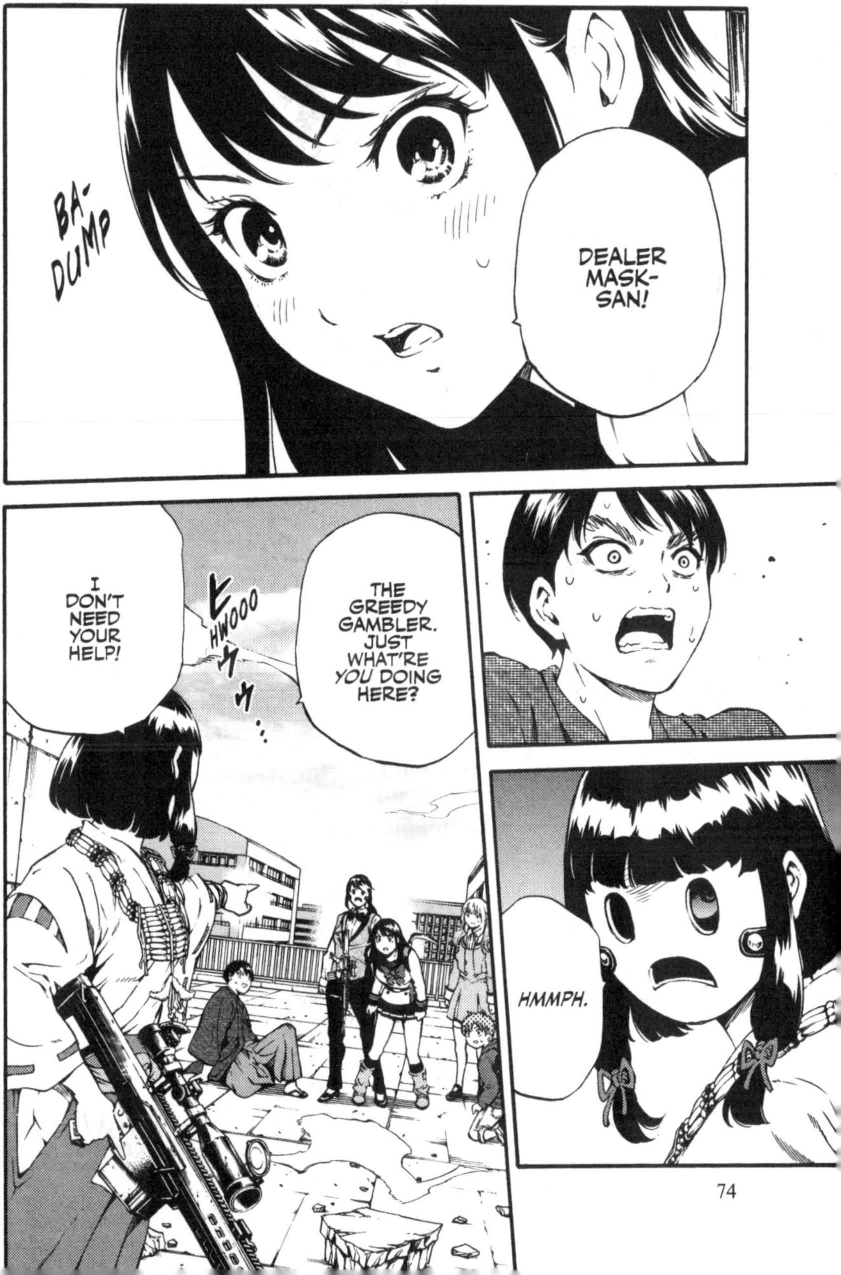
DEALER MASK-SAN!
BA-DUMP
HMMPH.
THE GREEDY GAMBLER. JUST WHAT'RE *YOU* DOING HERE?
HWOOO...
I DON'T NEED YOUR HELP!

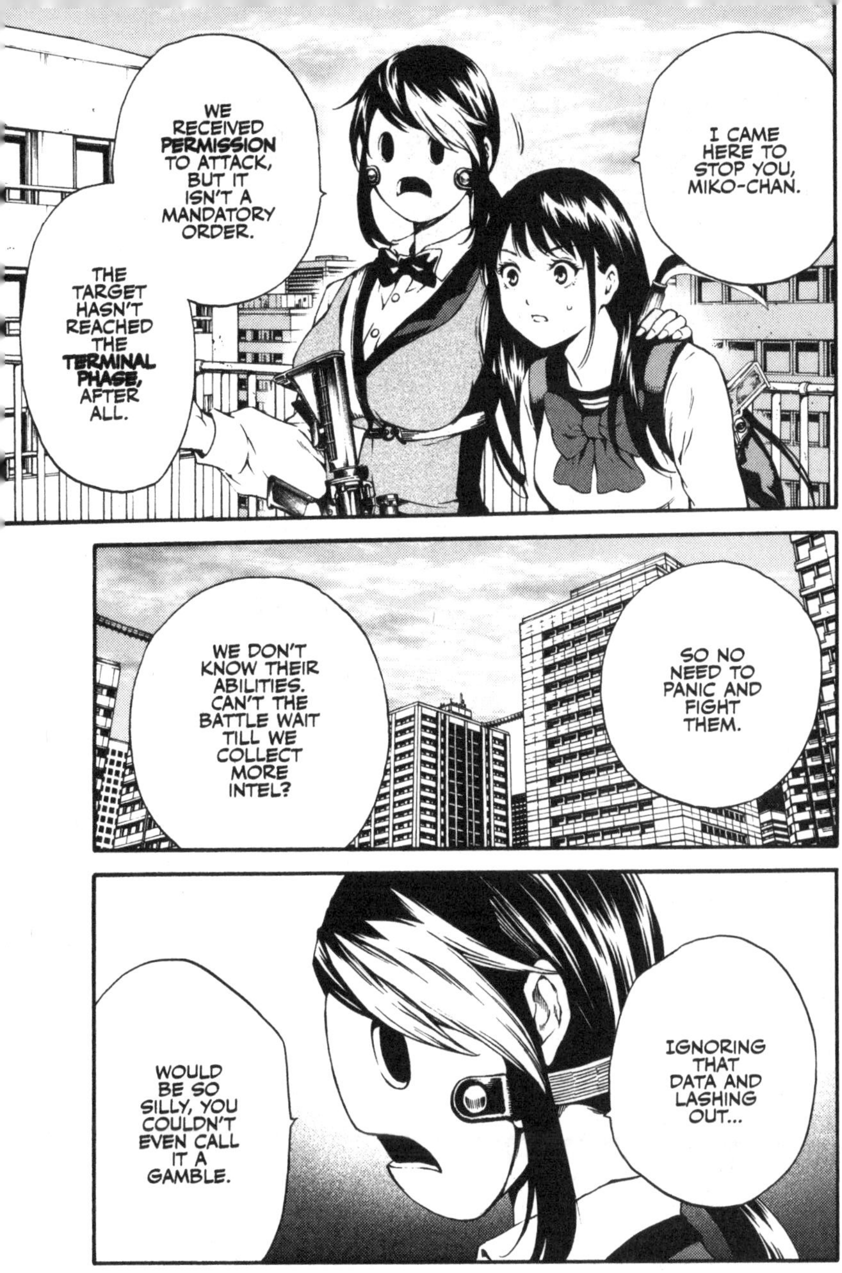
I CAME HERE TO STOP YOU, MIKO-CHAN.
WE RECEIVED **PERMISSION** TO ATTACK, BUT IT ISN'T A MANDATORY ORDER.
THE TARGET HASN'T REACHED THE **TERMINAL PHASE,** AFTER ALL.
SO NO NEED TO PANIC AND FIGHT THEM.
WE DON'T KNOW THEIR ABILITIES. CAN'T THE BATTLE WAIT TILL WE COLLECT MORE INTEL?
IGNORING THAT DATA AND LASHING OUT...
WOULD BE SO SILLY, YOU COULDN'T EVEN CALL IT A GAMBLE.

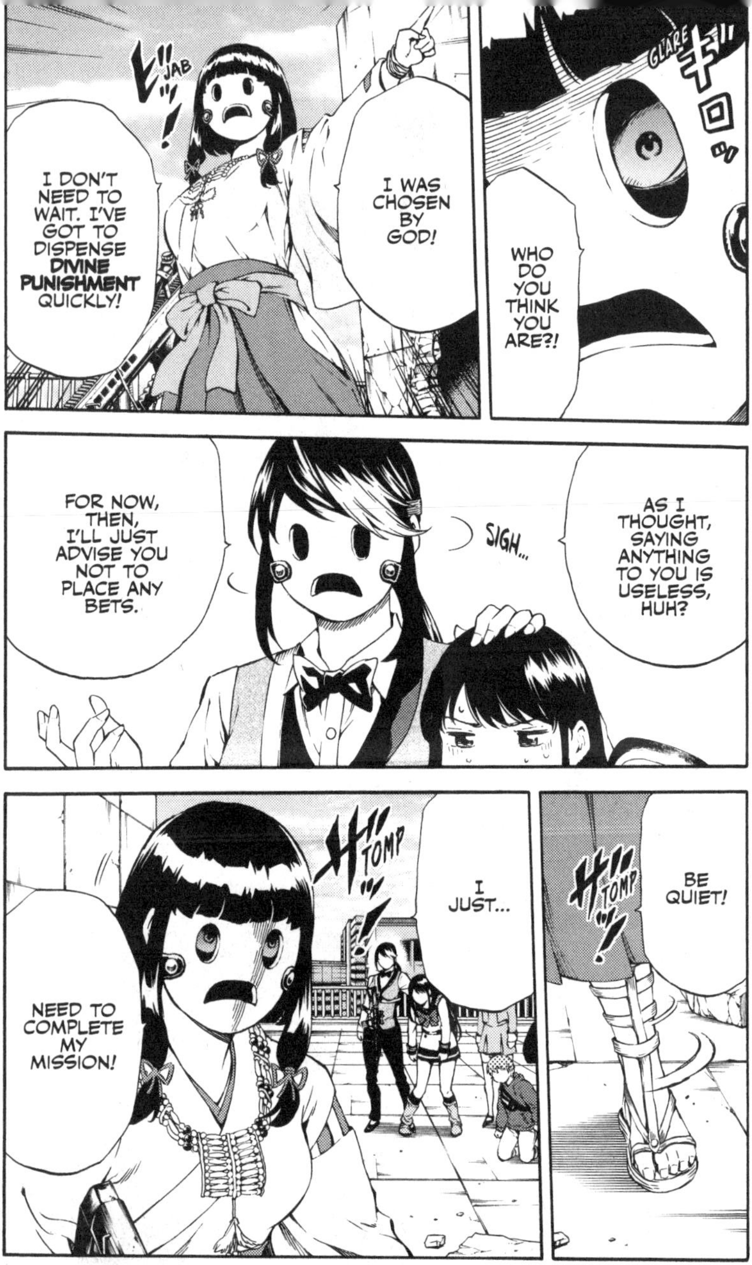
GLARE
WHO DO YOU THINK YOU ARE?!
I WAS CHOSEN BY GOD!
JAB
I DON'T NEED TO WAIT. I'VE GOT TO DISPENSE **DIVINE PUNISHMENT** QUICKLY!
AS I THOUGHT, SAYING ANYTHING TO YOU IS USELESS, HUH?
SIGH...
FOR NOW, THEN, I'LL JUST ADVISE YOU NOT TO PLACE ANY BETS.
BE QUIET!
TOMP
I JUST...
TOMP
NEED TO COMPLETE MY MISSION!

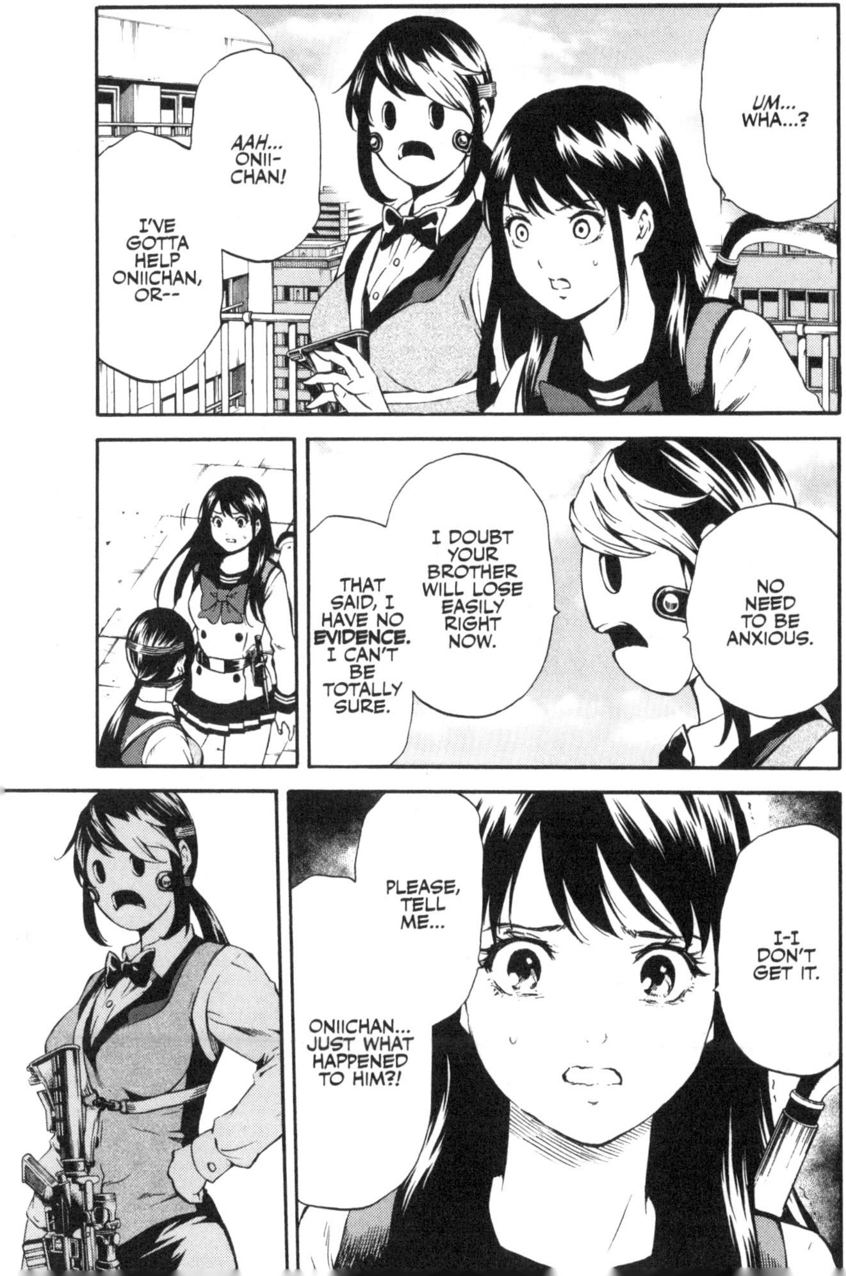
UM... WHA...?
AAH... ONII-CHAN!
I'VE GOTTA HELP ONIICHAN, OR--
NO NEED TO BE ANXIOUS.
I DOUBT YOUR BROTHER WILL LOSE EASILY RIGHT NOW.
THAT SAID, I HAVE NO EVIDENCE. I CAN'T BE TOTALLY SURE.
I-I DON'T GET IT.
PLEASE, TELL ME...
ONIICHAN... JUST WHAT HAPPENED TO HIM?!

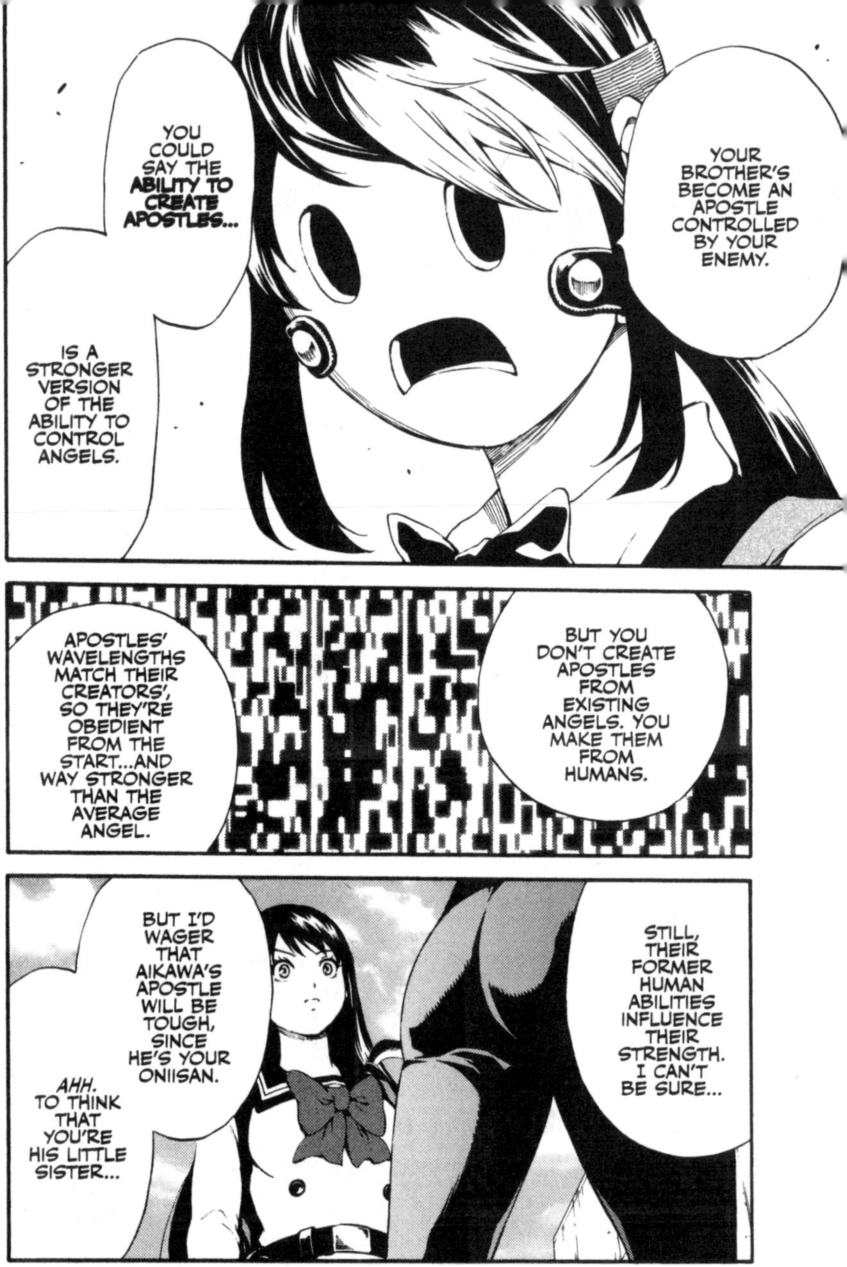

YOUR BROTHER'S BECOME AN APOSTLE CONTROLLED BY YOUR ENEMY.
YOU COULD SAY THE **ABILITY TO CREATE APOSTLES...**
IS A STRONGER VERSION OF THE ABILITY TO CONTROL ANGELS.
BUT YOU DON'T CREATE APOSTLES FROM EXISTING ANGELS. YOU MAKE THEM FROM HUMANS.
APOSTLES' WAVELENGTHS MATCH THEIR CREATORS', SO THEY'RE OBEDIENT FROM THE START...AND WAY STRONGER THAN THE AVERAGE ANGEL.
STILL, THEIR FORMER HUMAN ABILITIES INFLUENCE THEIR STRENGTH. I CAN'T BE SURE...
BUT I'D WAGER THAT AIKAWA'S APOSTLE WILL BE TOUGH, SINCE HE'S YOUR ONIISAN.
AHH. TO THINK THAT YOU'RE HIS LITTLE SISTER...

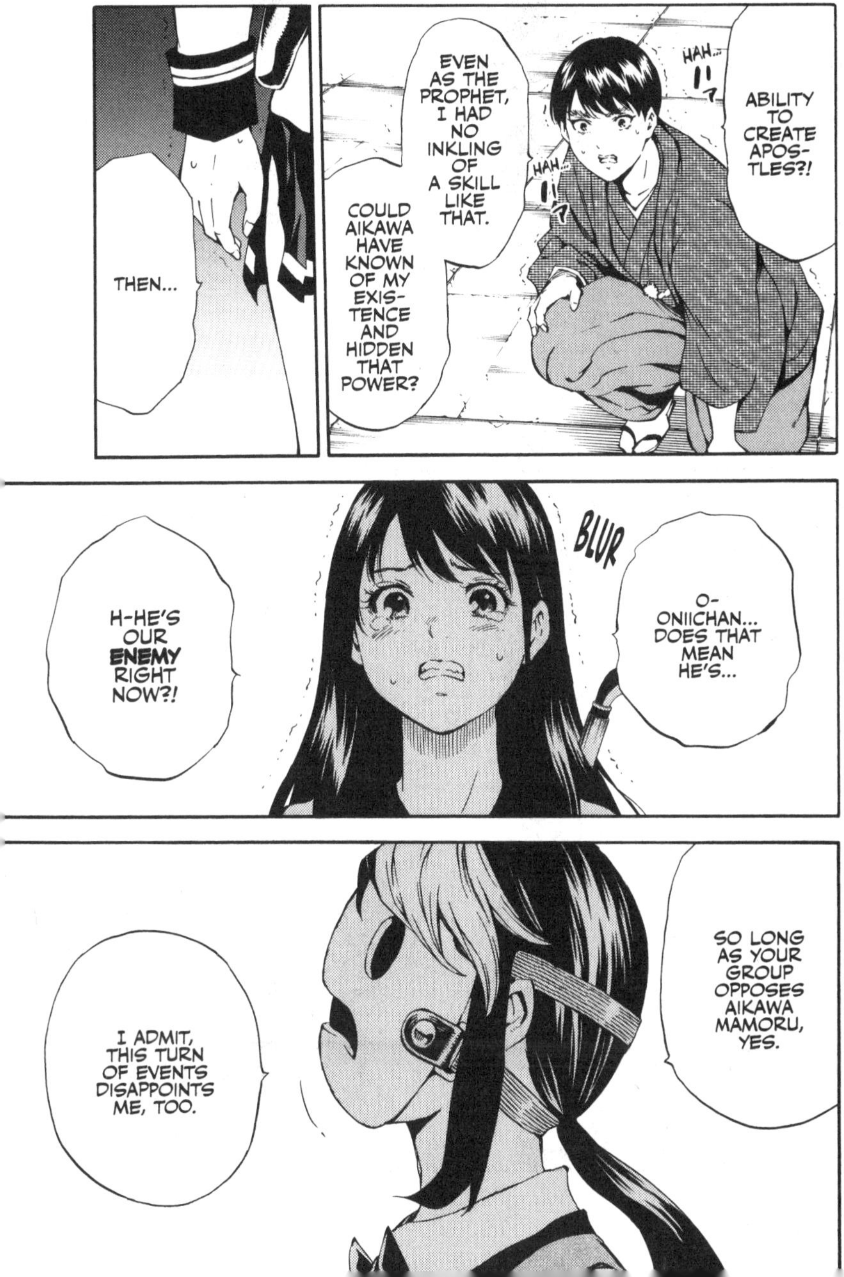

ABILITY TO CREATE APOS-TLES?!
HAH...
HAH...
EVEN AS THE PROPHET, I HAD NO INKLING OF A SKILL LIKE THAT.
COULD AIKAWA HAVE KNOWN OF MY EXIS-TENCE AND HIDDEN THAT POWER?
THEN...
BLUR
O-ONIICHAN... DOES THAT MEAN HE'S...
H-HE'S OUR **ENEMY** RIGHT NOW?!
SO LONG AS YOUR GROUP OPPOSES AIKAWA MAMORU, YES.
I ADMIT, THIS TURN OF EVENTS DISAPPOINTS ME, TOO.

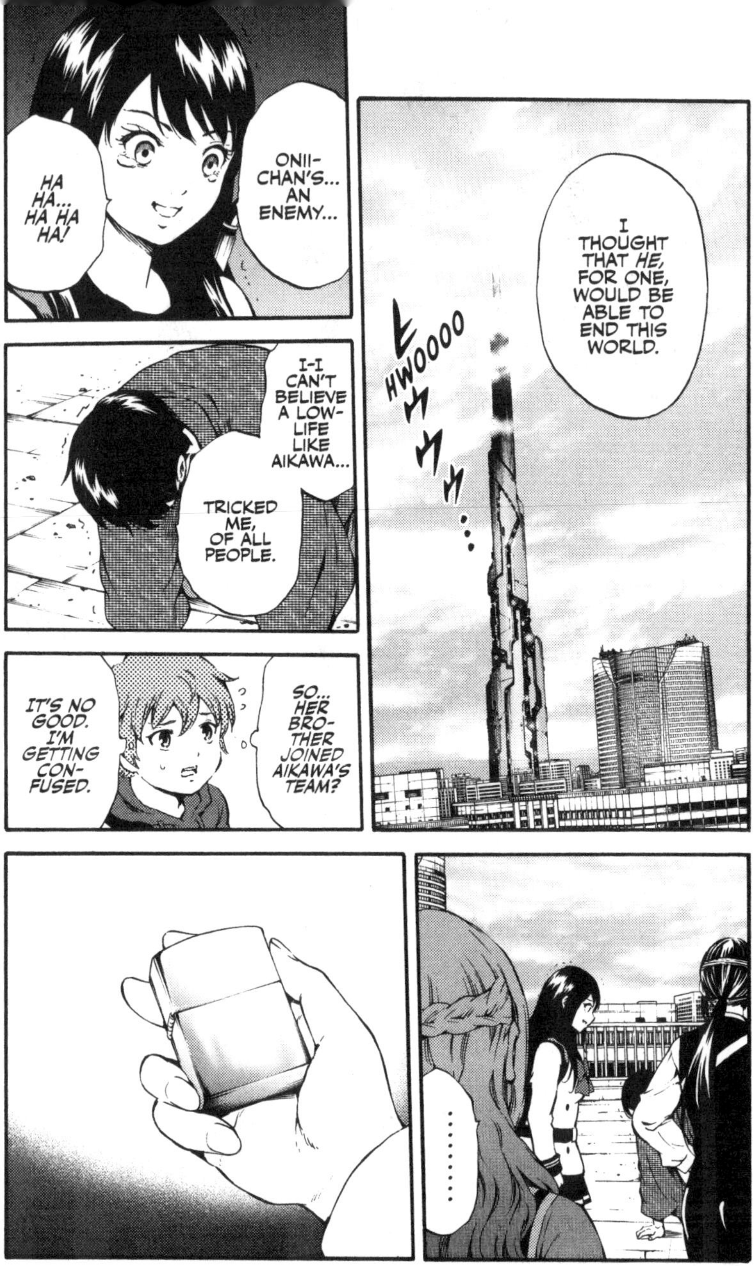
I THOUGHT THAT HE, FOR ONE, WOULD BE ABLE TO END THIS WORLD.
HWOOOO...
ONII-CHAN'S... AN ENEMY...
HA HA... HA HA HA!
I-I CAN'T BELIEVE A LOW-LIFE LIKE AIKAWA...
TRICKED ME, OF ALL PEOPLE.
SO... HER BROTHER JOINED AIKAWA'S TEAM?
IT'S NO GOOD. I'M GETTING CONFUSED.
....

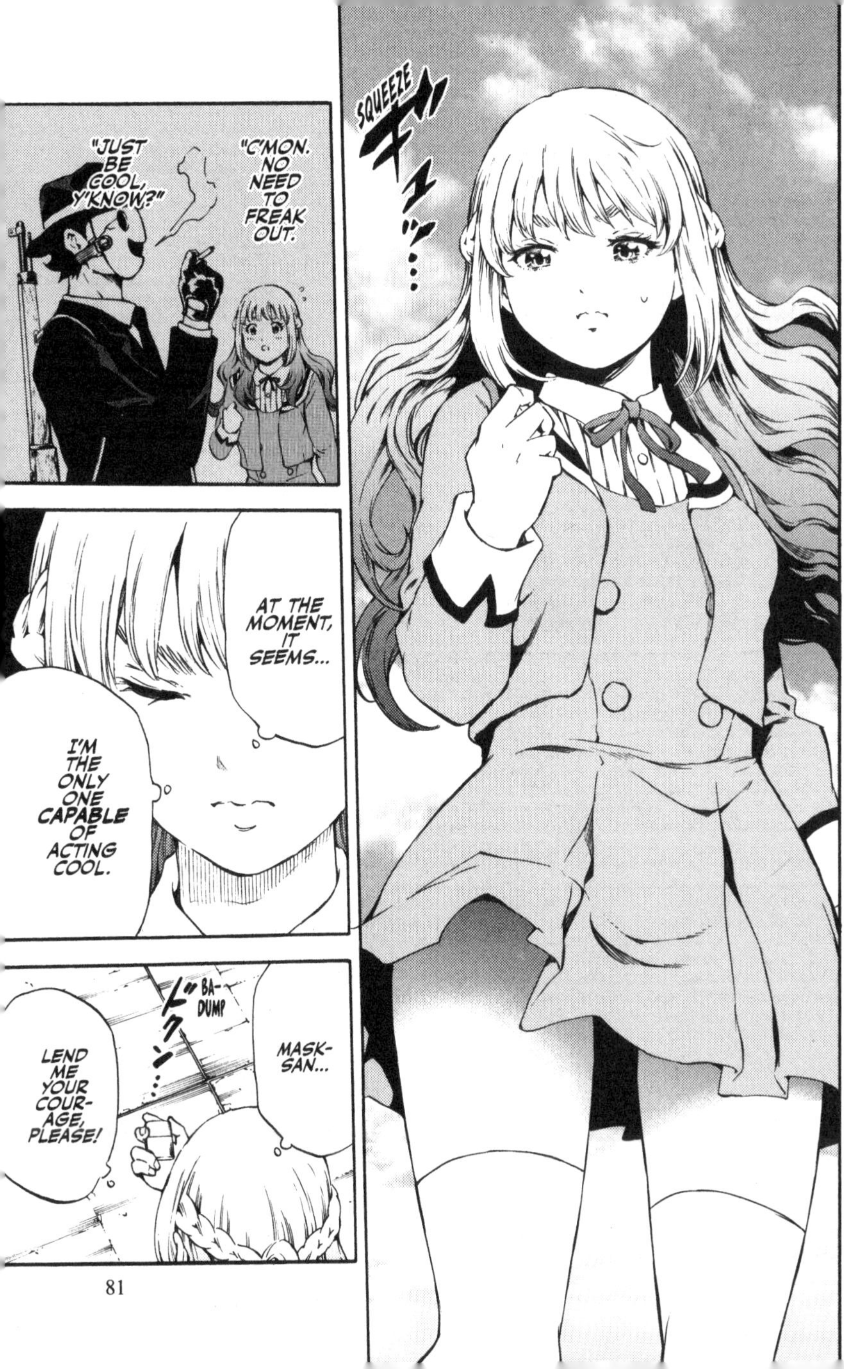
SQUEEZE
"C'MON. NO NEED TO FREAK OUT.
"JUST BE COOL, Y'KNOW?"
AT THE MOMENT, IT SEEMS...
I'M THE ONLY ONE CAPABLE OF ACTING COOL.
BA-DUMP
MASK-SAN...
LEND ME YOUR COURAGE, PLEASE!

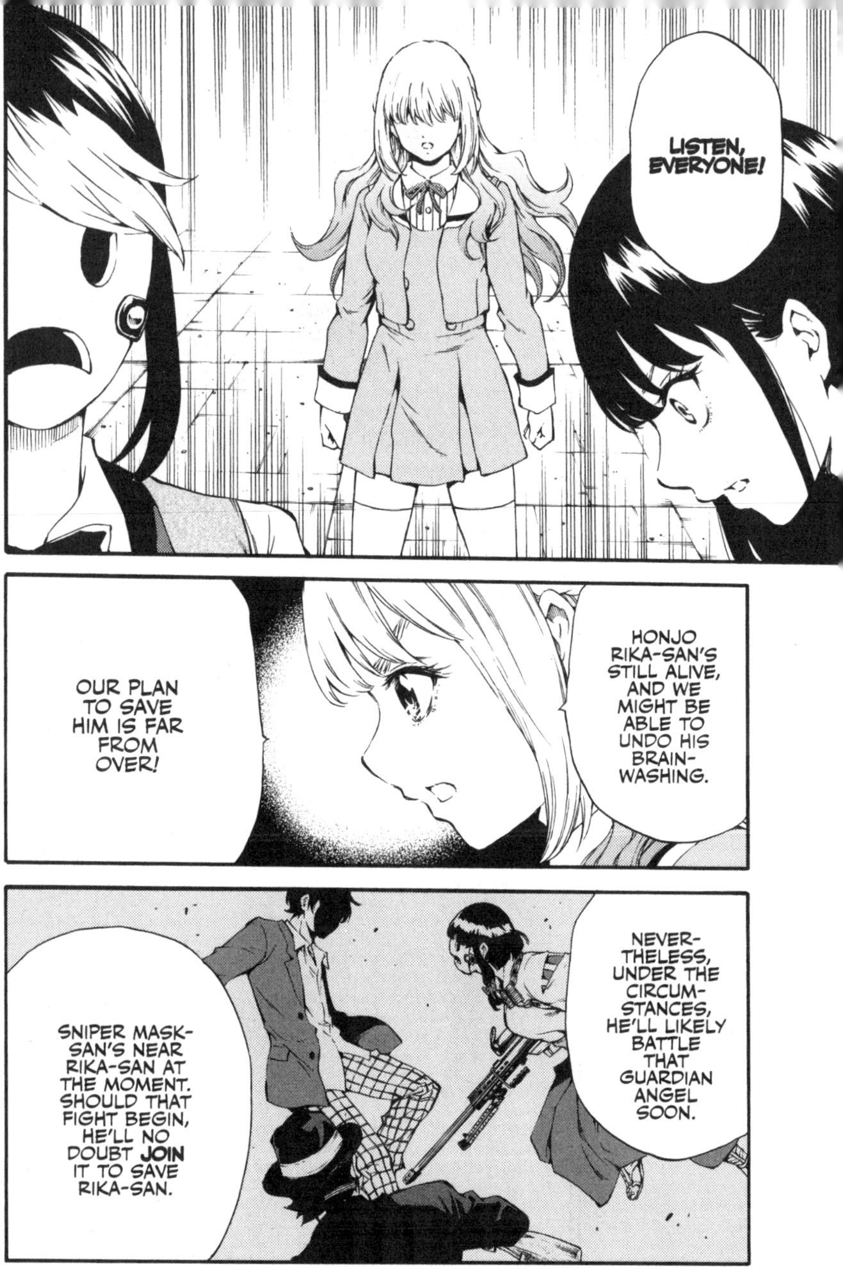
LISTEN, EVERYONE!
HONJO RIKA-SAN'S STILL ALIVE, AND WE MIGHT BE ABLE TO UNDO HIS BRAIN-WASHING.
OUR PLAN TO SAVE HIM IS FAR FROM OVER!
NEVER-THELESS, UNDER THE CIRCUM-STANCES, HE'LL LIKELY BATTLE THAT GUARDIAN ANGEL SOON.
SNIPER MASK-SAN'S NEAR RIKA-SAN AT THE MOMENT. SHOULD THAT FIGHT BEGIN, HE'LL NO DOUBT **JOIN** IT TO SAVE RIKA-SAN.

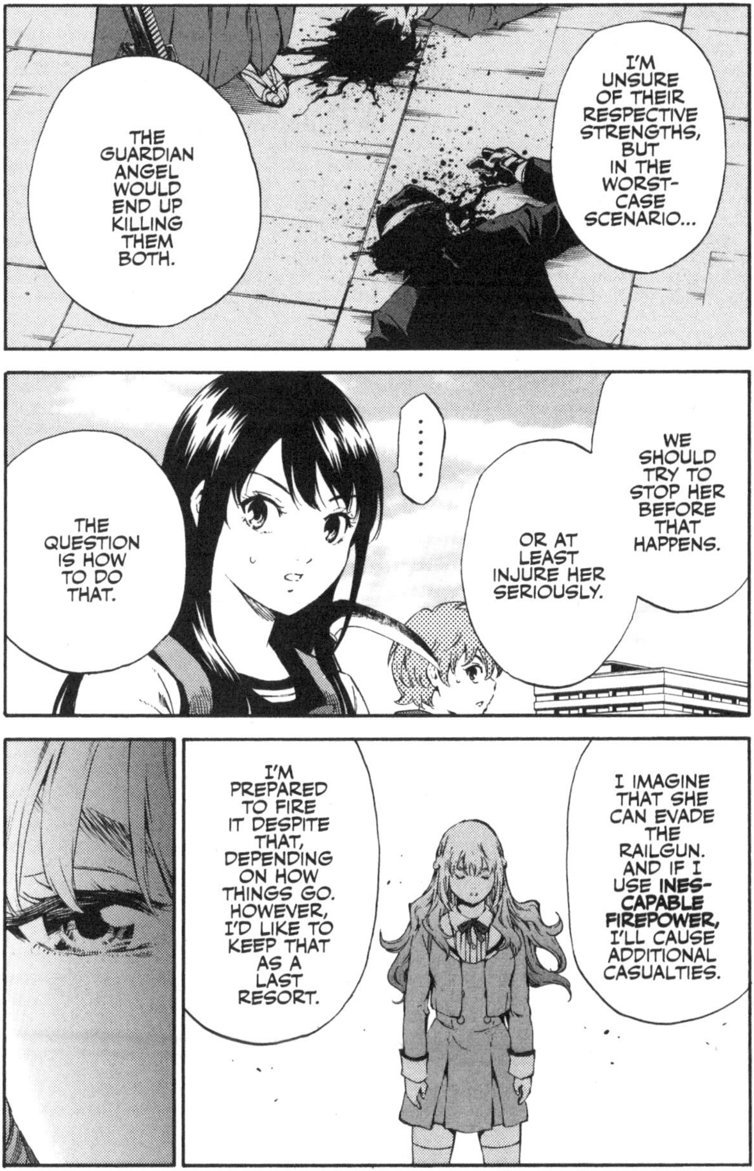
I'M UNSURE OF THEIR RESPECTIVE STRENGTHS, BUT IN THE WORST-CASE SCENARIO...
THE GUARDIAN ANGEL WOULD END UP KILLING THEM BOTH.
WE SHOULD TRY TO STOP HER BEFORE THAT HAPPENS.
OR AT LEAST INJURE HER SERIOUSLY.
......
THE QUESTION IS HOW TO DO THAT.
I IMAGINE THAT SHE CAN EVADE THE RAILGUN. AND IF I USE **INESCAPABLE FIREPOWER,** I'LL CAUSE ADDITIONAL CASUALTIES.
I'M PREPARED TO FIRE IT DESPITE THAT, DEPENDING ON HOW THINGS GO. HOWEVER, I'D LIKE TO KEEP THAT AS A LAST RESORT.

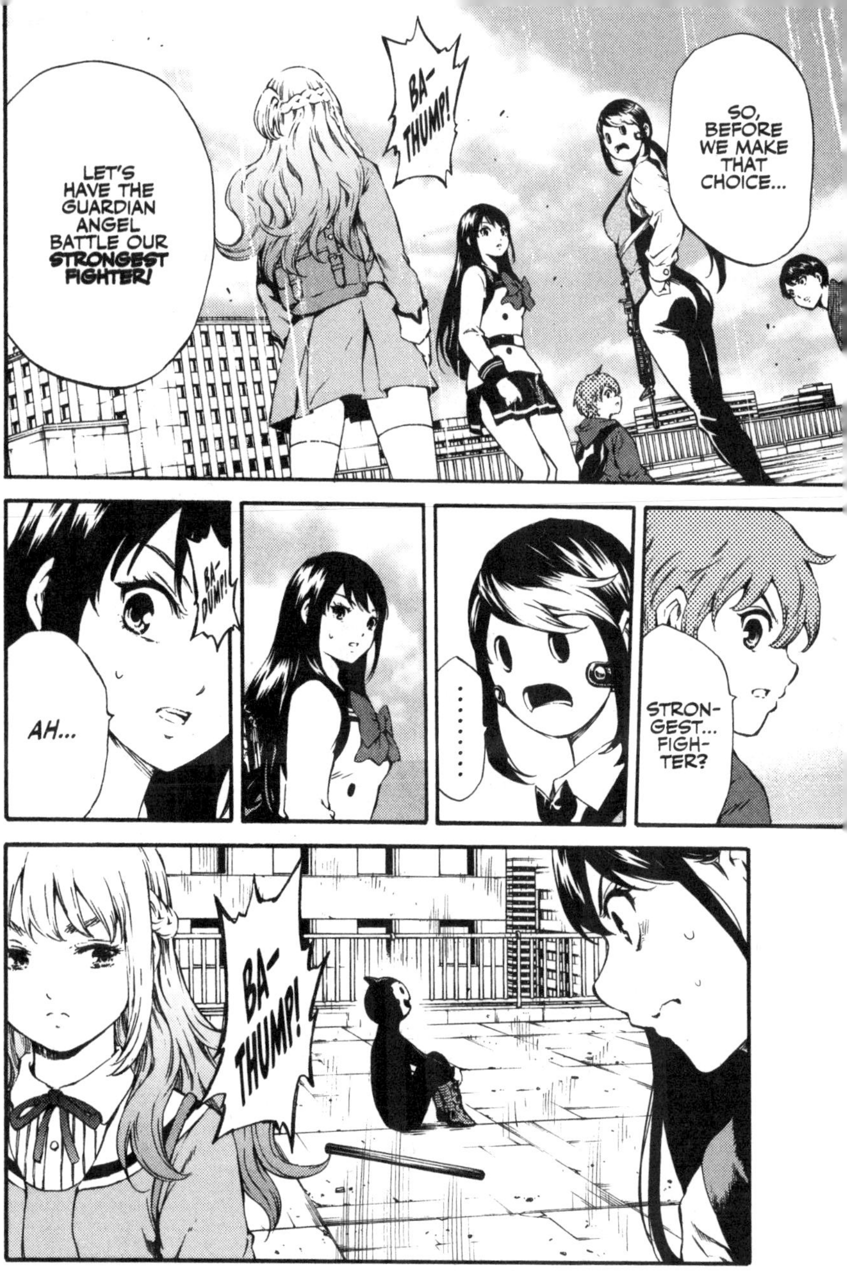
SO, BEFORE WE MAKE THAT CHOICE...
BA-THUMP!
LET'S HAVE THE GUARDIAN ANGEL BATTLE OUR STRONGEST FIGHTER!
STRONG-EST... FIGH-TER?
....
BA-DUMP!
AH...
BA-THUMP!

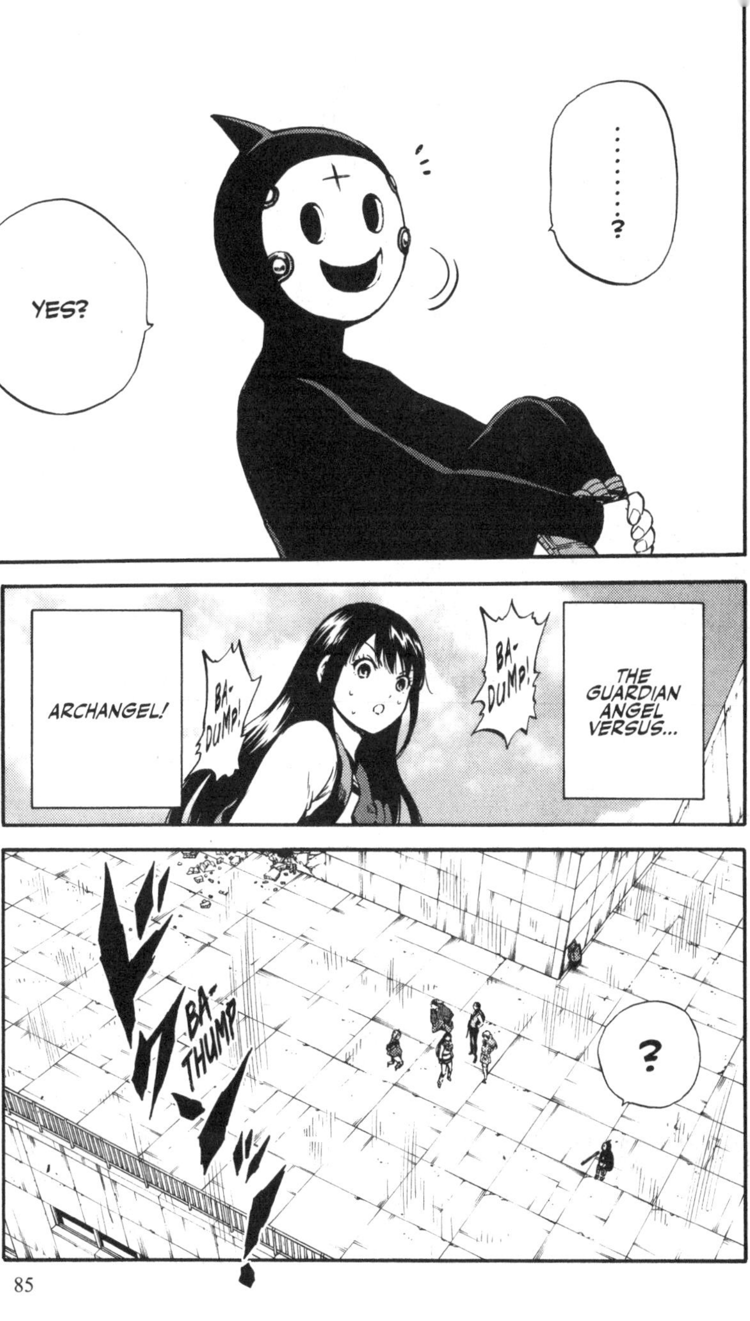

.........?
YES?
THE GUARDIAN ANGEL VERSUS...
BA-DUMP!
BA-DUMP!
ARCHANGEL!
?
BA-THUMP

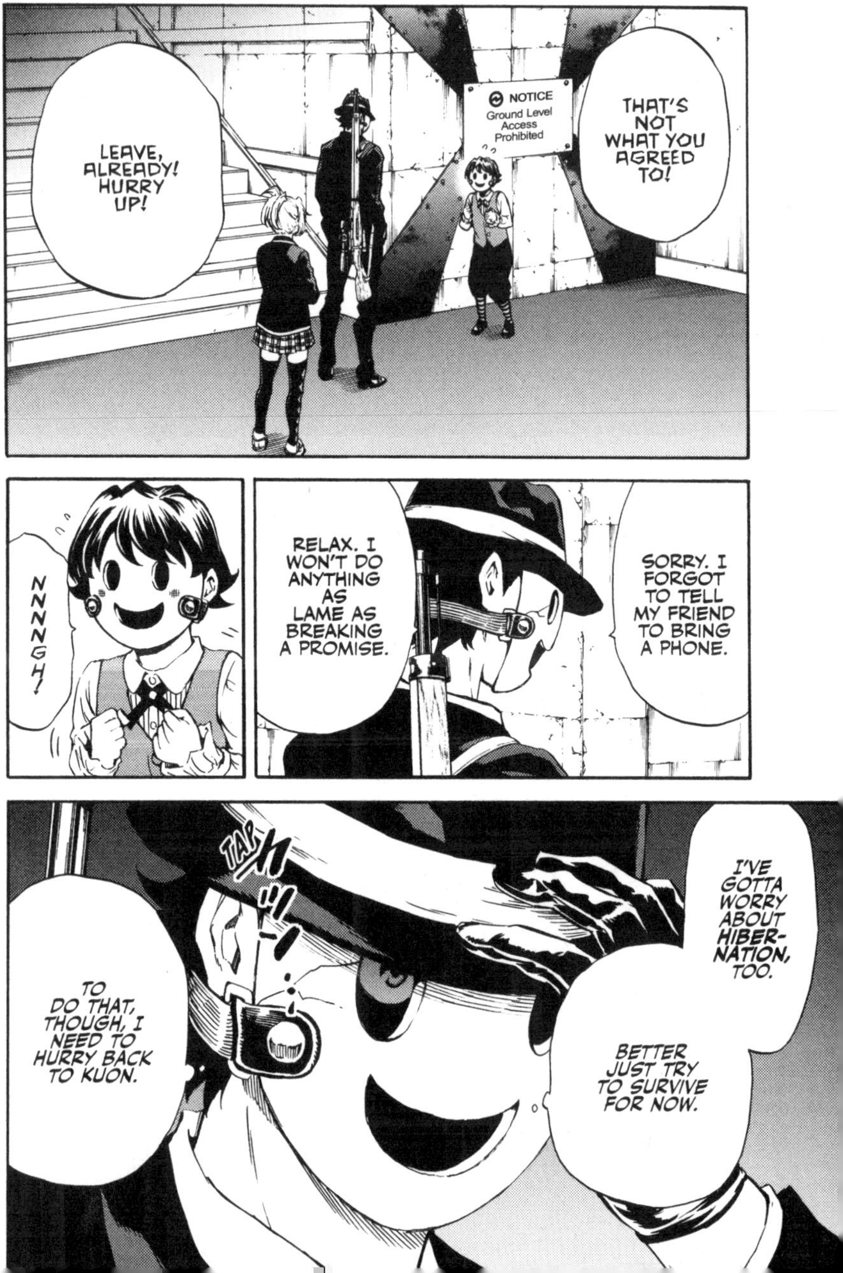
THAT'S NOT WHAT YOU AGREED TO!
NOTICE
Ground Level Access Prohibited
LEAVE, ALREADY! HURRY UP!
SORRY. I FORGOT TO TELL MY FRIEND TO BRING A PHONE.
RELAX. I WON'T DO ANYTHING AS LAME AS BREAKING A PROMISE.
NNNNGH!
I'VE GOTTA WORRY ABOUT HIBERNATION, TOO.
TAP
BETTER JUST TRY TO SURVIVE FOR NOW.
TO DO THAT, THOUGH, I NEED TO HURRY BACK TO KUON.

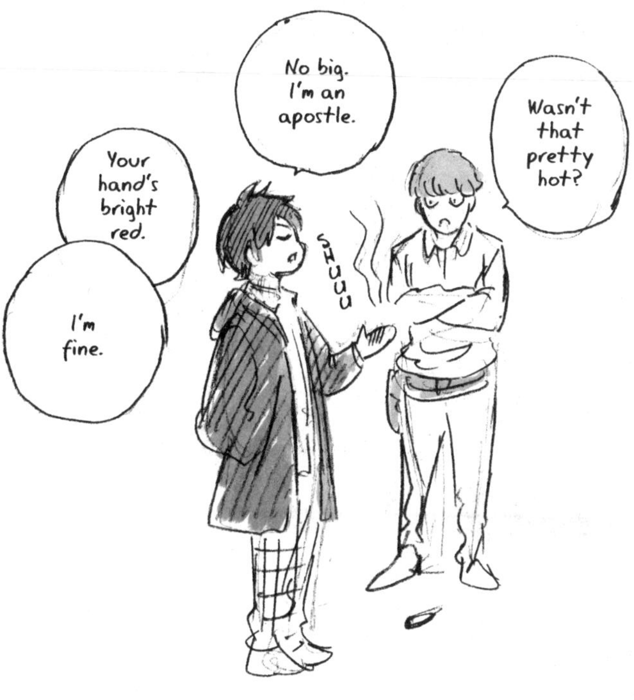
Wasn't that pretty hot?
No big. I'm an apostle.
SHUUU
Your hand's bright red.
I'm fine.

HIGH-RISE INVASION

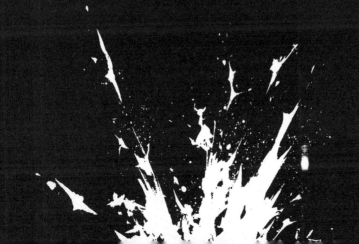

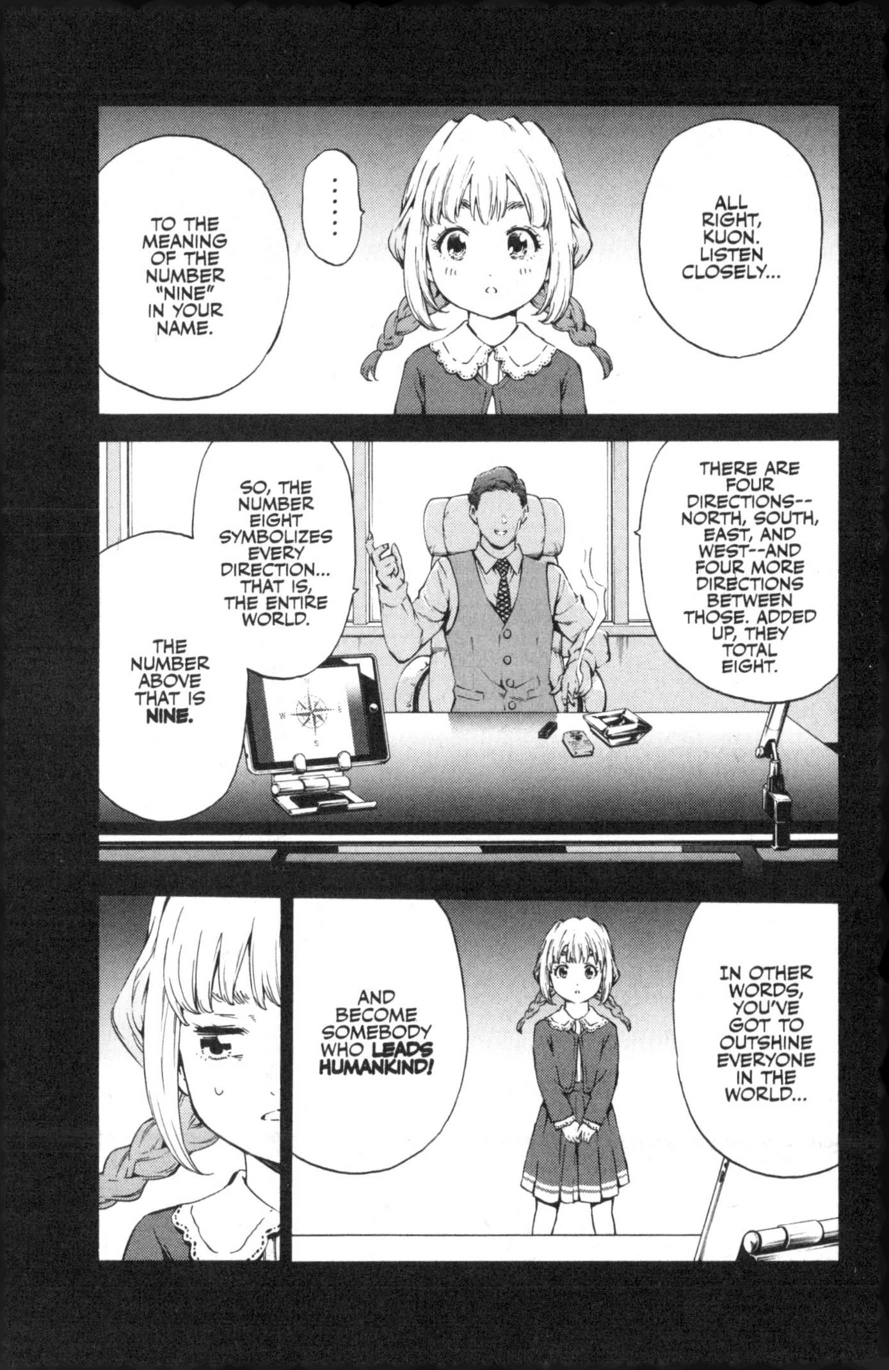
ALL RIGHT, KUON. LISTEN CLOSELY...
......
TO THE MEANING OF THE NUMBER "NINE" IN YOUR NAME.
THERE ARE FOUR DIRECTIONS--NORTH, SOUTH, EAST, AND WEST--AND FOUR MORE DIRECTIONS BETWEEN THOSE. ADDED UP, THEY TOTAL EIGHT.
SO, THE NUMBER EIGHT SYMBOLIZES EVERY DIRECTION... THAT IS, THE ENTIRE WORLD.
THE NUMBER ABOVE THAT IS **NINE.**
IN OTHER WORDS, YOU'VE GOT TO OUTSHINE EVERYONE IN THE WORLD...
AND BECOME SOMEBODY WHO **LEADS HUMANKIND!**

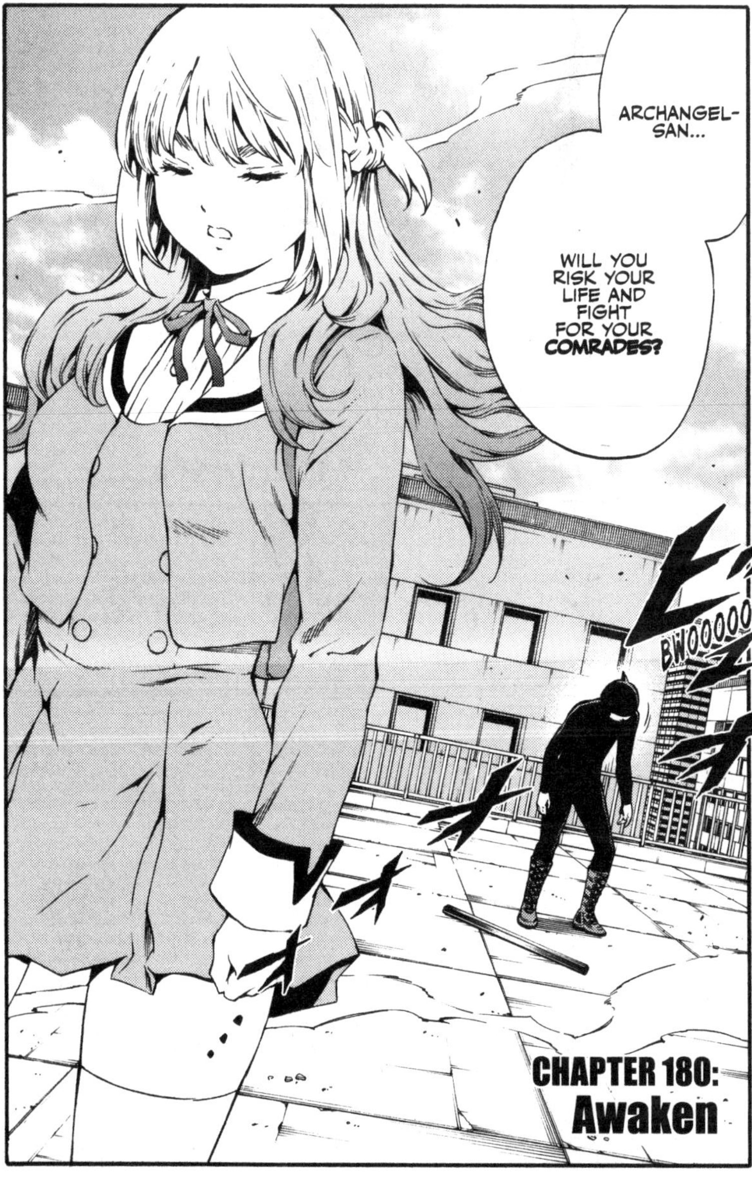
ARCHANGEL-SAN...
WILL YOU RISK YOUR LIFE AND FIGHT FOR YOUR **COMRADES?**
BWOOOOOOH
CHAPTER 180:
Awaken

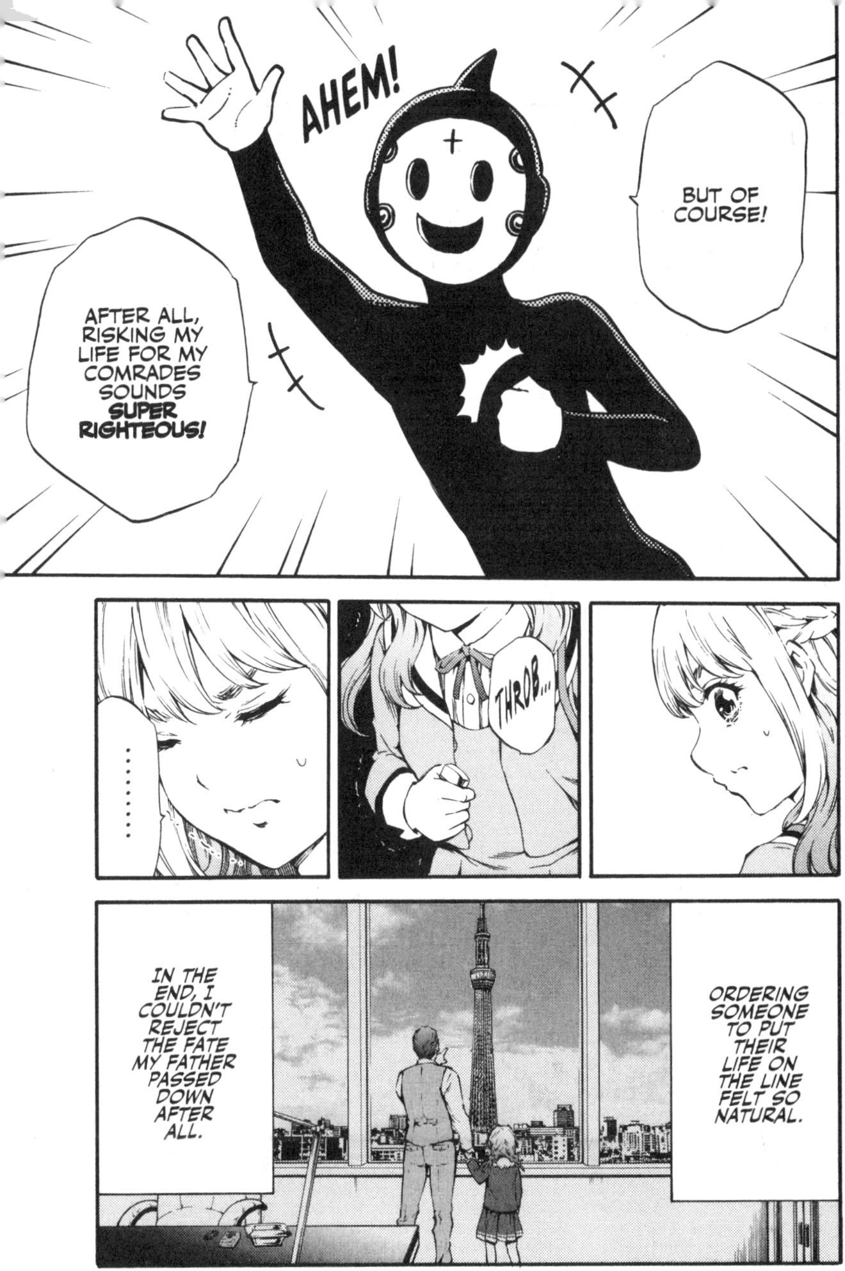

BUT OF COURSE!
AHEM!
AFTER ALL, RISKING MY LIFE FOR MY COMRADES SOUNDS **SUPER RIGHTEOUS!**
THROB...
....
ORDERING SOMEONE TO PUT THEIR LIFE ON THE LINE FELT SO NATURAL.
IN THE END, I COULDN'T REJECT THE FATE MY FATHER PASSED DOWN AFTER ALL.

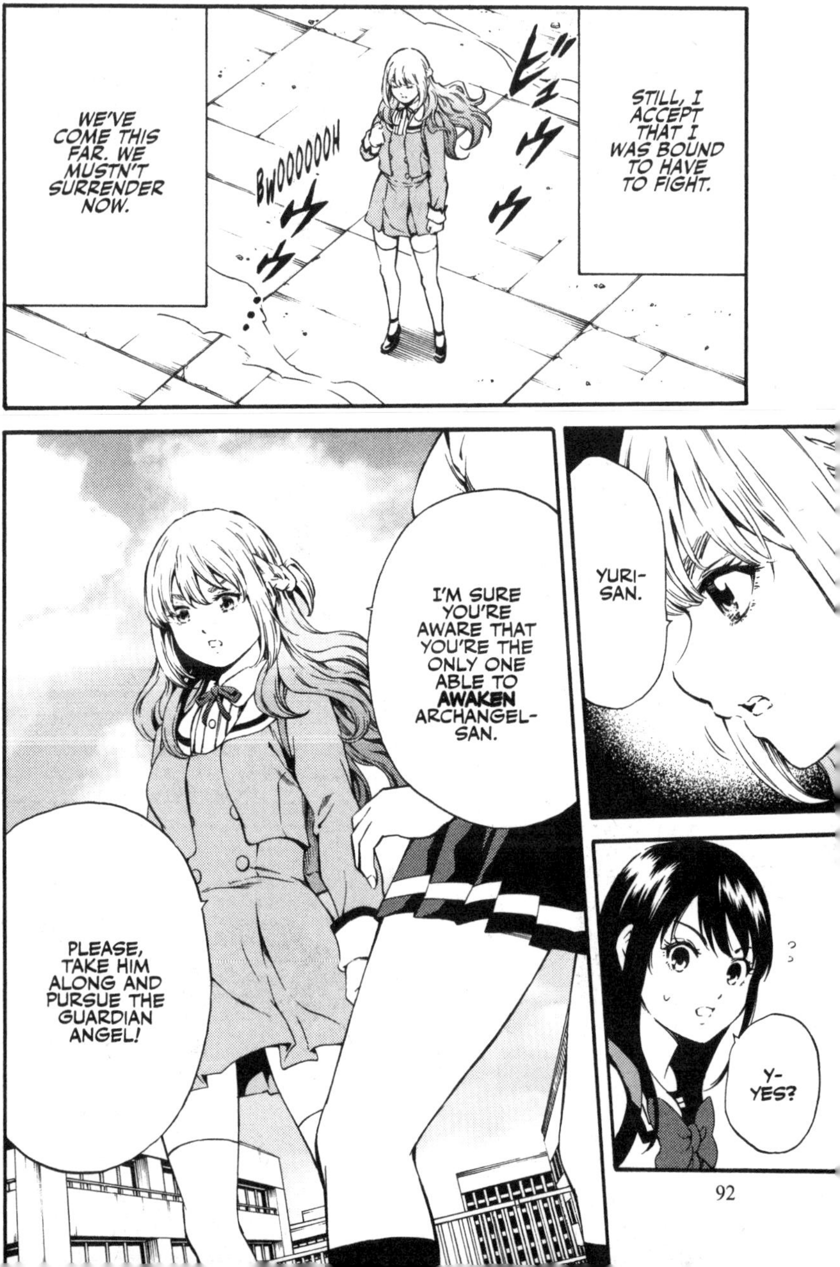
STILL, I ACCEPT THAT I WAS BOUND TO HAVE TO FIGHT.
BWOOOOOOH
WE'VE COME THIS FAR. WE MUSTN'T SURRENDER NOW.
YURI-SAN.
Y-YES?
I'M SURE YOU'RE AWARE THAT YOU'RE THE ONLY ONE ABLE TO **AWAKEN** ARCHANGEL-SAN.
PLEASE, TAKE HIM ALONG AND PURSUE THE GUARDIAN ANGEL!

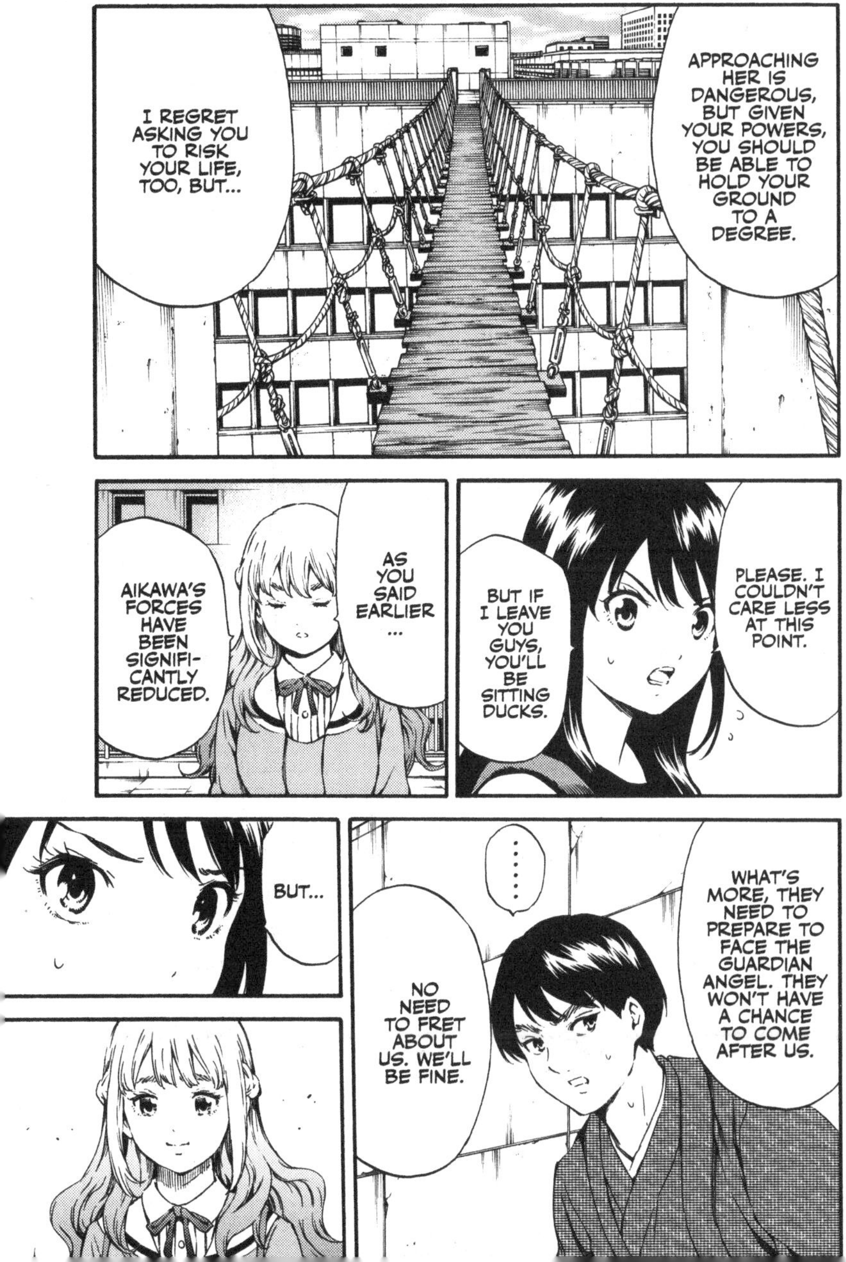
APPROACHING HER IS DANGEROUS, BUT GIVEN YOUR POWERS, YOU SHOULD BE ABLE TO HOLD YOUR GROUND TO A DEGREE.
I REGRET ASKING YOU TO RISK YOUR LIFE, TOO, BUT...
PLEASE. I COULDN'T CARE LESS AT THIS POINT.
BUT IF I LEAVE YOU GUYS, YOU'LL BE SITTING DUCKS.
AS YOU SAID EARLIER...
AIKAWA'S FORCES HAVE BEEN SIGNIFI-CANTLY REDUCED.
WHAT'S MORE, THEY NEED TO PREPARE TO FACE THE GUARDIAN ANGEL. THEY WON'T HAVE A CHANCE TO COME AFTER US.
......
NO NEED TO FRET ABOUT US. WE'LL BE FINE.
BUT...

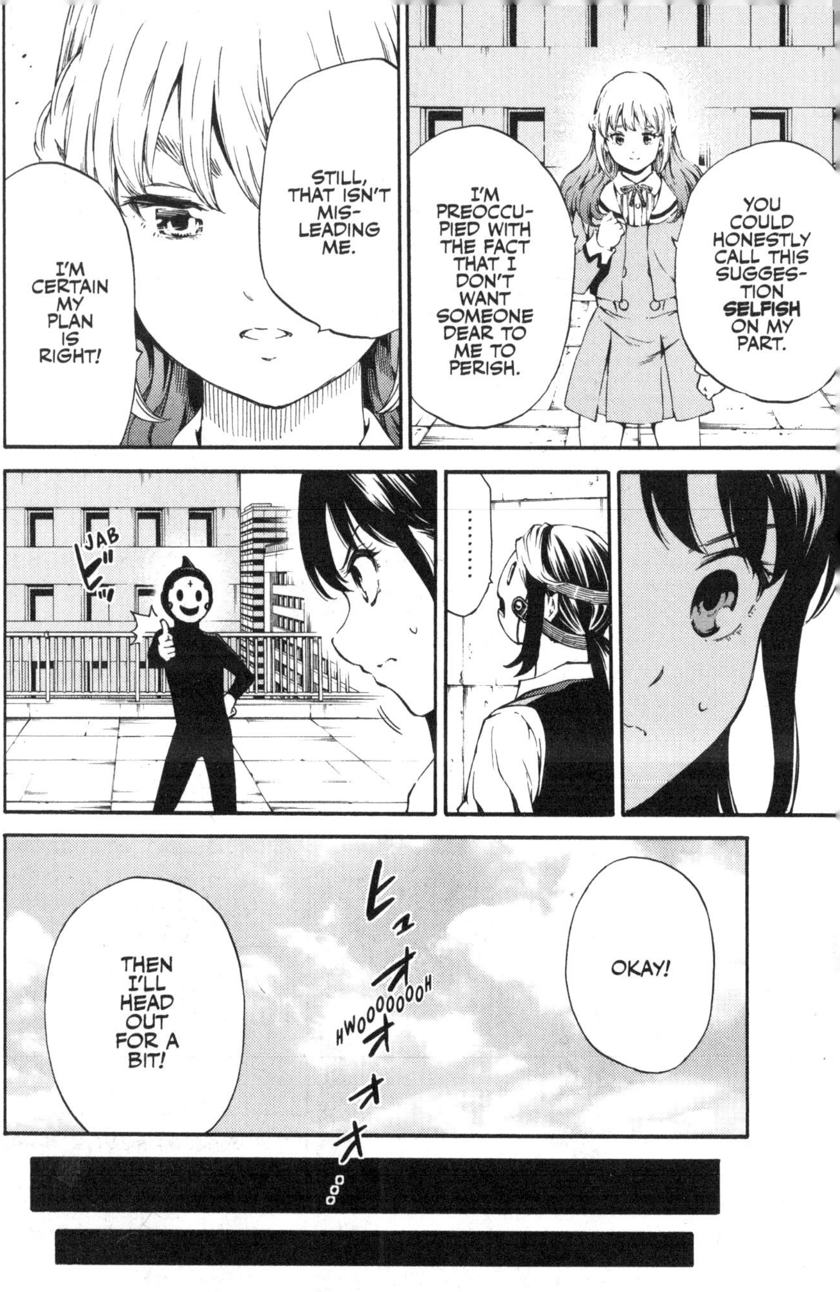
YOU COULD HONESTLY CALL THIS SUGGESTION SELFISH ON MY PART.
I'M PREOCCUPIED WITH THE FACT THAT I DON'T WANT SOMEONE DEAR TO ME TO PERISH.
STILL, THAT ISN'T MISLEADING ME.
I'M CERTAIN MY PLAN IS RIGHT!
......
JAB
OKAY!
HWOOOOOOOH
THEN I'LL HEAD OUT FOR A BIT!

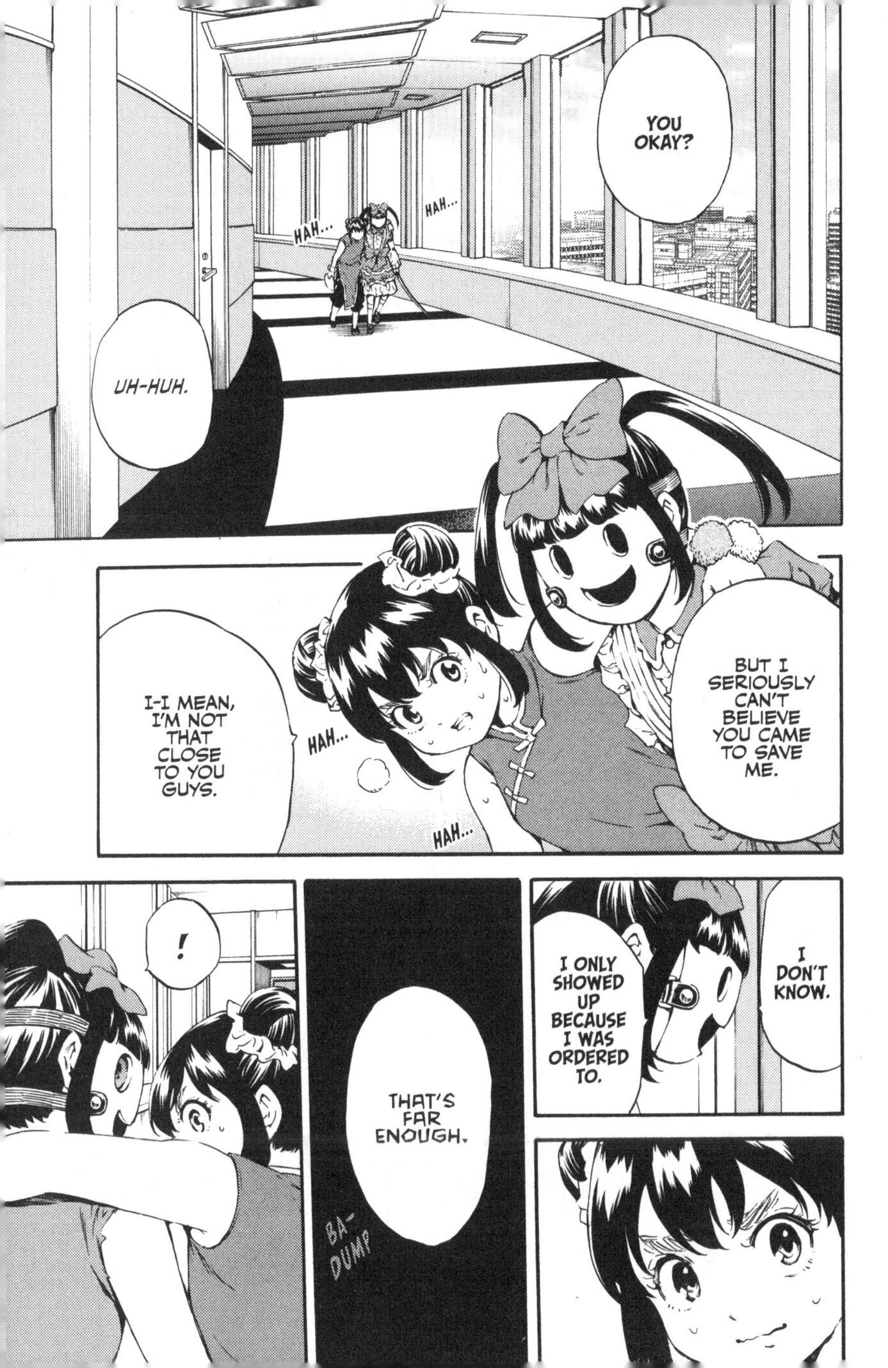
YOU OKAY?
HAH...
HAH...
UH-HUH.
BUT I SERIOUSLY CAN'T BELIEVE YOU CAME TO SAVE ME.
HAH...
I-I MEAN, I'M NOT THAT CLOSE TO YOU GUYS.
HAH...
I DON'T KNOW.
I ONLY SHOWED UP BECAUSE I WAS ORDERED TO.
THAT'S FAR ENOUGH.
BA-DUMP
!

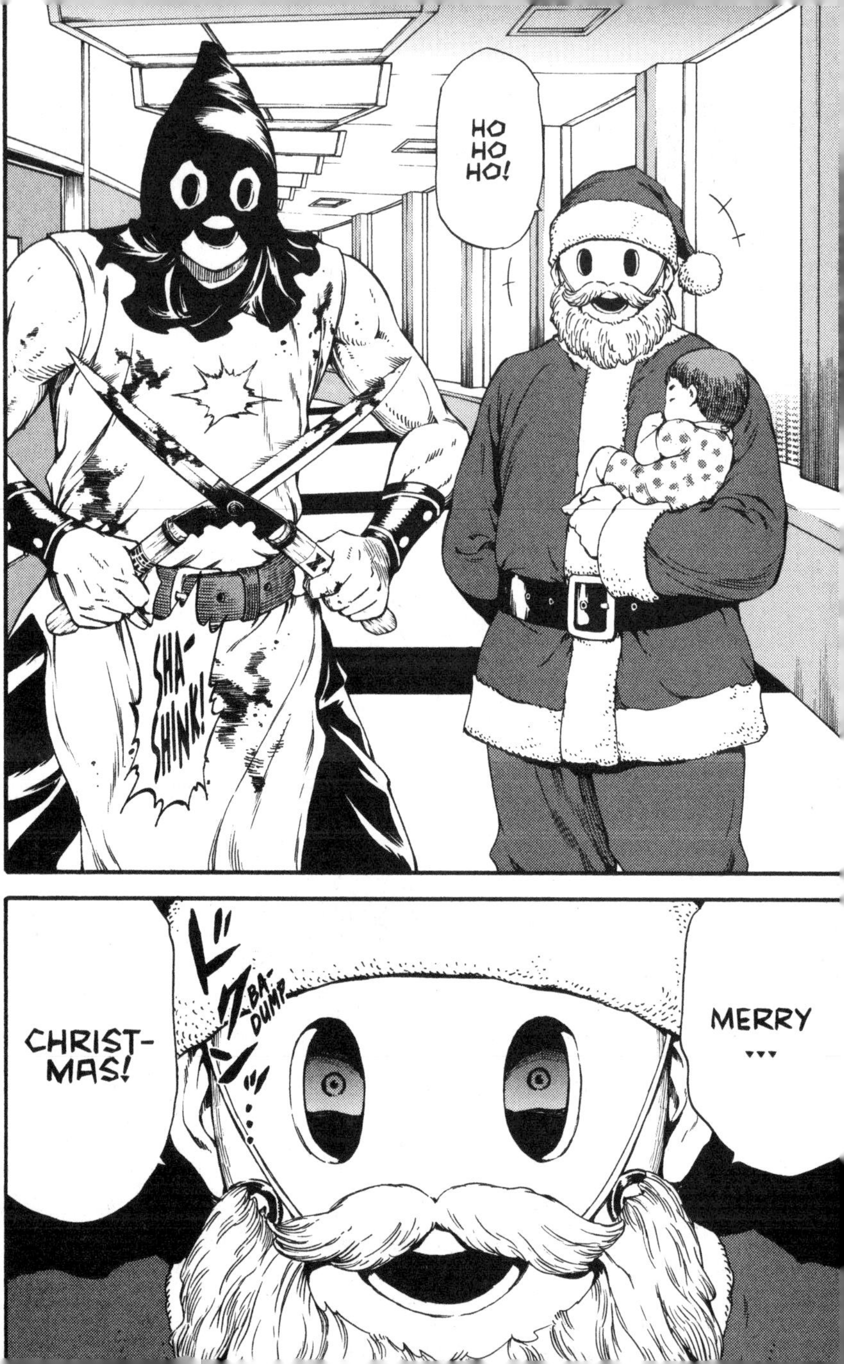
HO HO HO!
SHA-SHINK!
MERRY...
BA-DUMP
CHRIST-MAS!

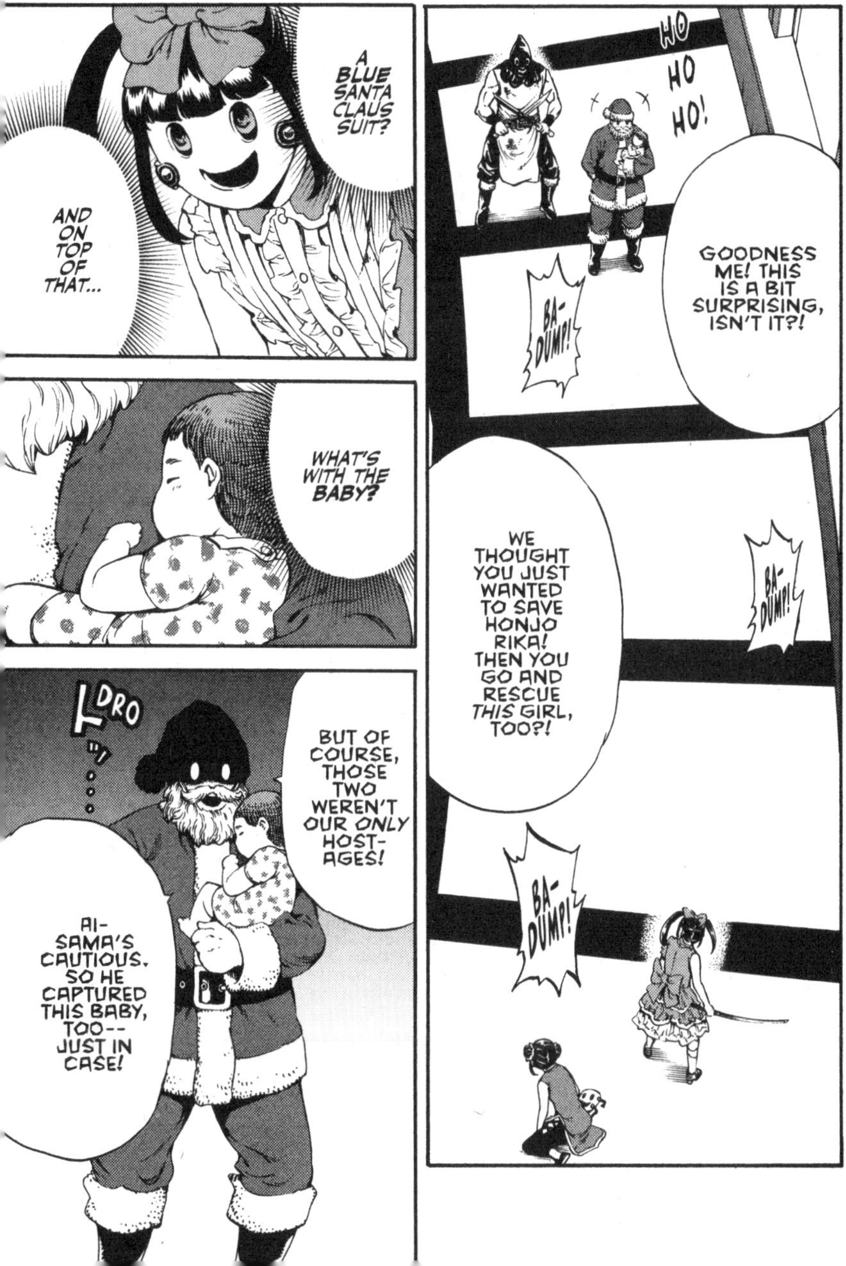
HO HO HO!
GOODNESS ME! THIS IS A BIT SURPRISING, ISN'T IT?!
BA-DUMP!
WE THOUGHT YOU JUST WANTED TO SAVE HONJO RIKA! THEN YOU GO AND RESCUE THIS GIRL, TOO?!
BA-DUMP!
BA-DUMP!
A BLUE SANTA CLAUS SUIT?
AND ON TOP OF THAT...
WHAT'S WITH THE BABY?
BUT OF COURSE, THOSE TWO WEREN'T OUR ONLY HOST-AGES!
トDRO
ッ...
AI-SAMA'S CAUTIOUS. SO HE CAPTURED THIS BABY, TOO-- JUST IN CASE!

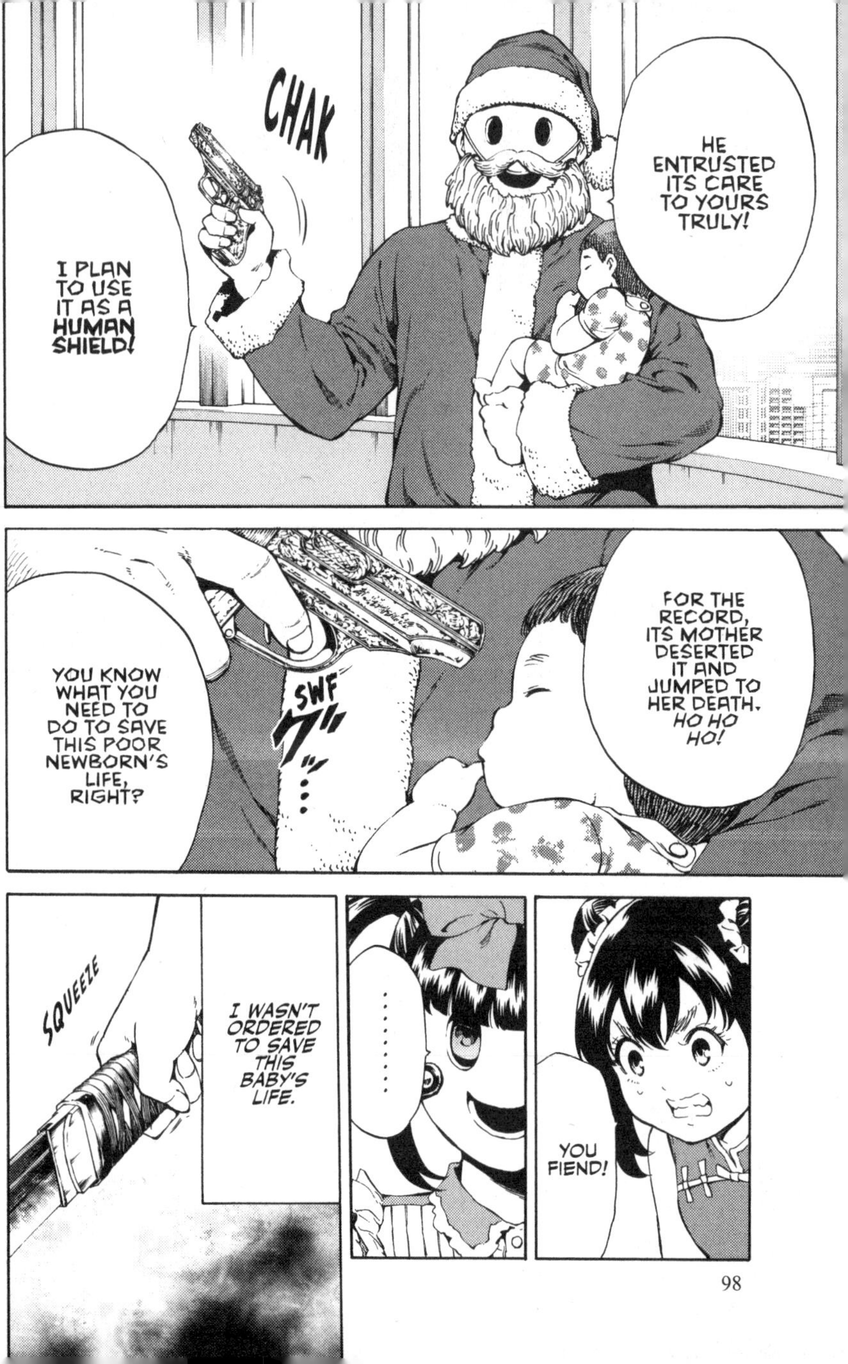
HE ENTRUSTED ITS CARE TO YOURS TRULY!
CHAK
I PLAN TO USE IT AS A **HUMAN SHIELD!**
FOR THE RECORD, ITS MOTHER DESERTED IT AND JUMPED TO HER DEATH. *HO HO HO!*
SWF
YOU KNOW WHAT YOU NEED TO DO TO SAVE THIS POOR NEWBORN'S LIFE, RIGHT?
YOU FIEND!
......
I WASN'T ORDERED TO SAVE THIS BABY'S LIFE.
SQUEEZE

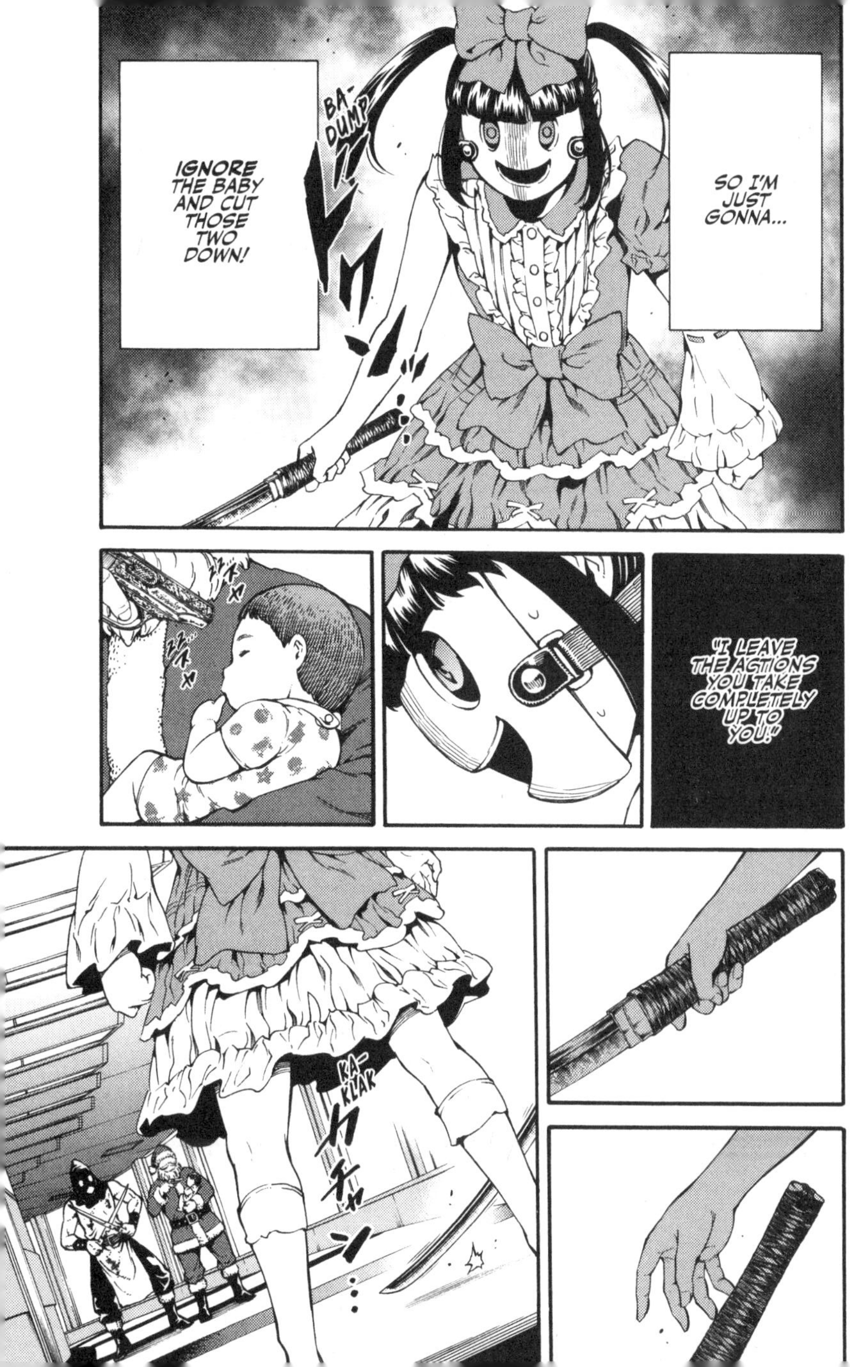
SO I'M JUST GONNA...
IGNORE THE BABY AND CUT THOSE TWO DOWN!
BA-DUMP
"I LEAVE THE ACTIONS YOU TAKE COMPLETELY UP TO YOU!"
KA-KLAK

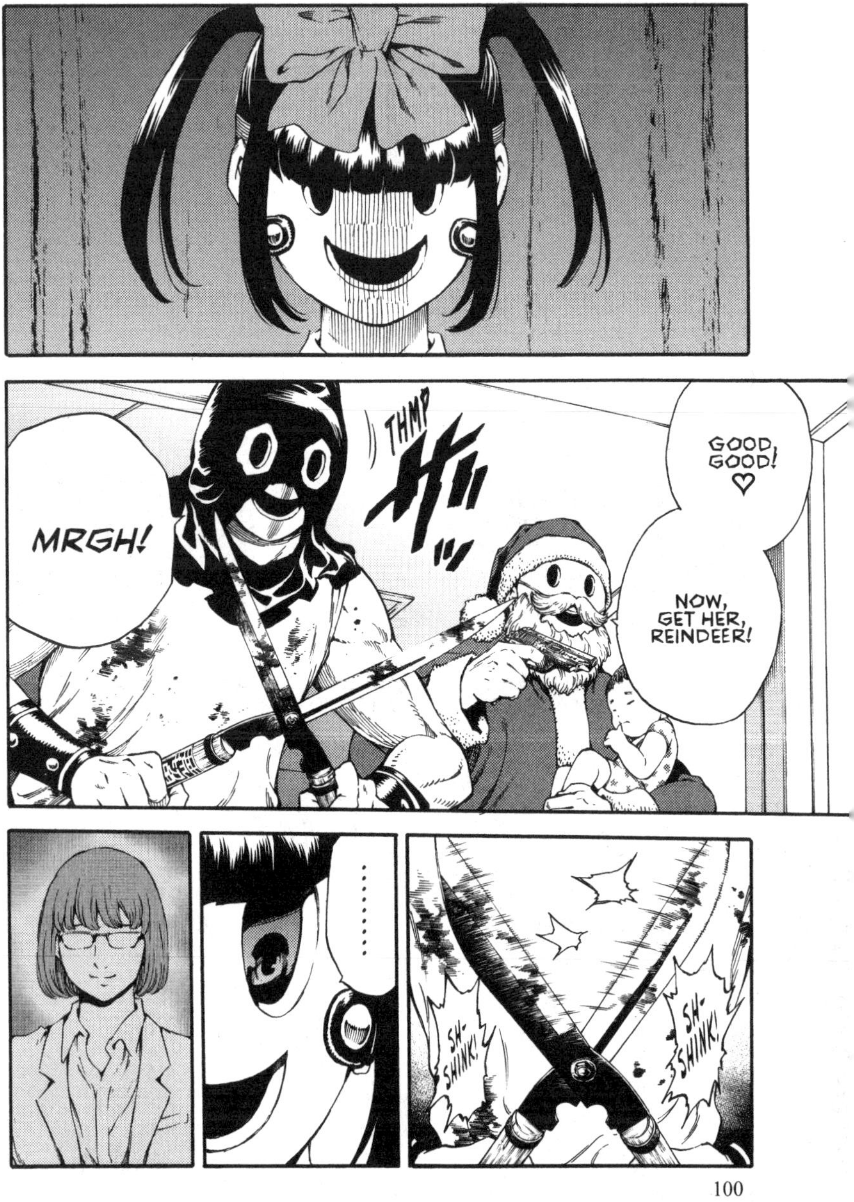
GOOD, GOOD! ♡
NOW, GET HER, REINDEER!
THMP
MRGH!
SH-SHINK!
SH-SHINK!
....

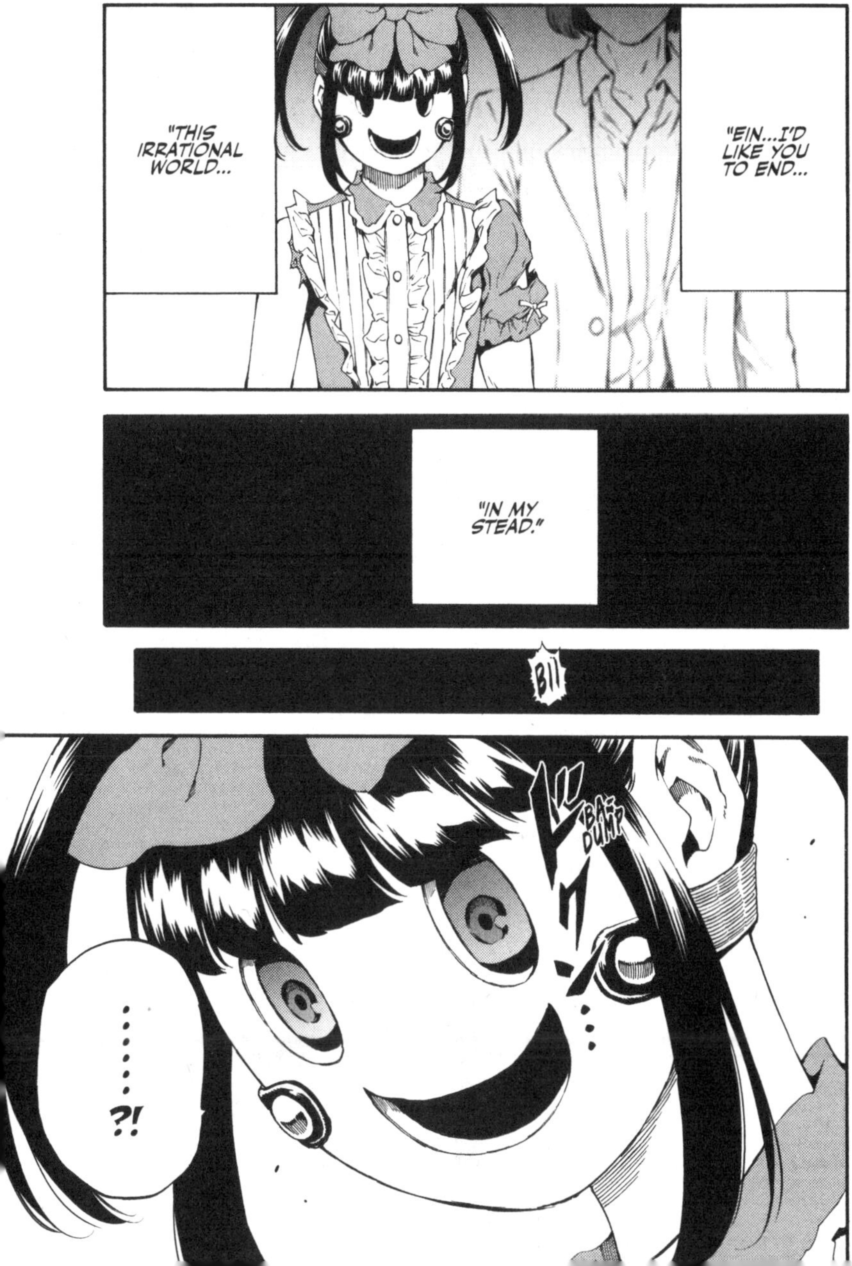
"EIN...I'D LIKE YOU TO END...
"THIS IRRATIONAL WORLD...
"IN MY STEAD."
BI!
BA-DUMP
...
......?!

HO HO HO!

NO DICE! ♥

HOW 'BOUT YOU TAKE *ME* HOSTAGE AGAIN, INSTEAD OF THAT BABY?

H-HANG ON A SEC!

HUH?

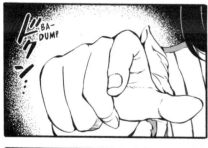

BA-DUMP

BA-DUMP

......?

BA-DUMP

JAB

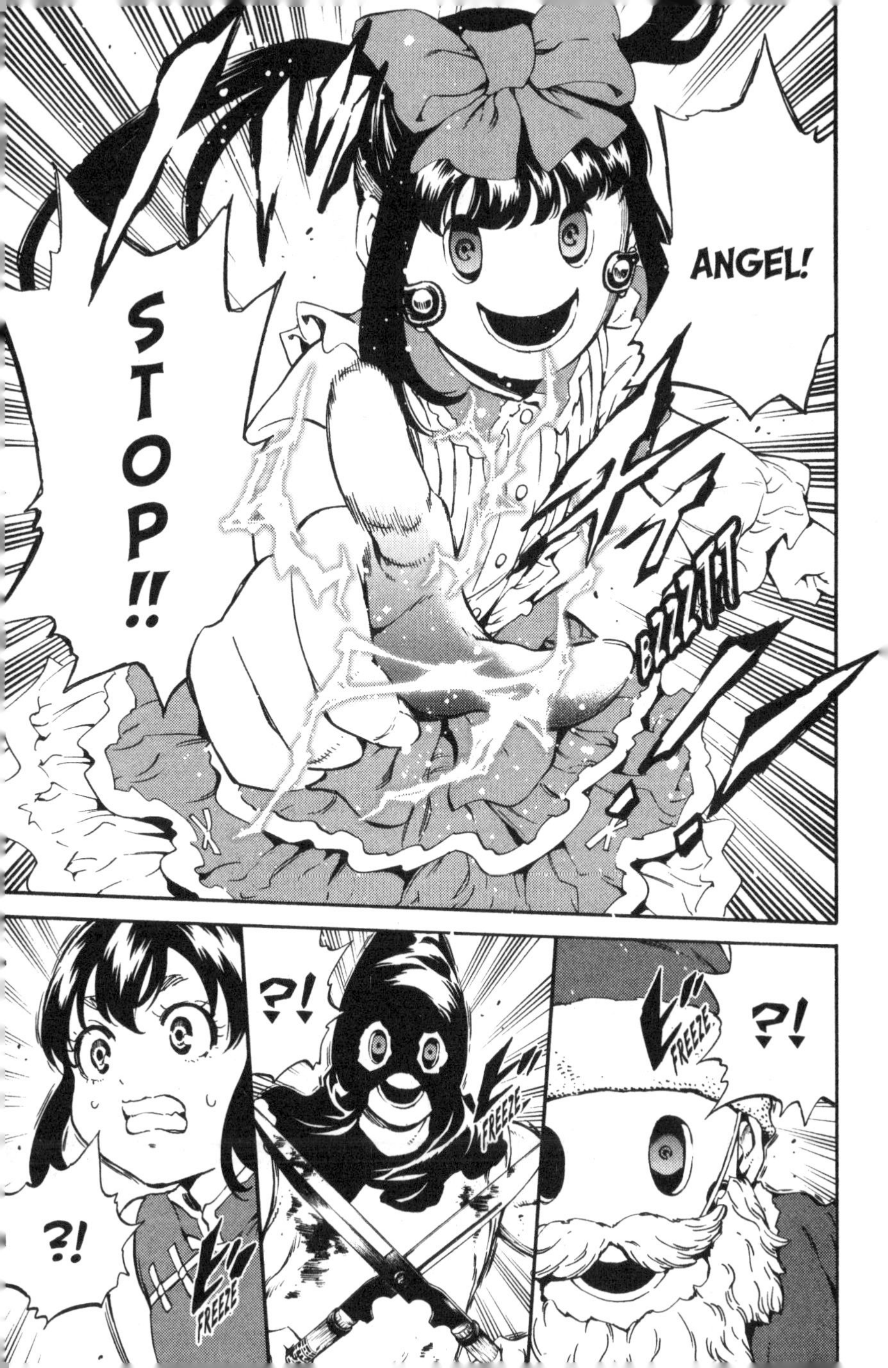
ANGEL!
STOP!!
BZZZTTT
?!
FREEZE
?!
FREEZE
?!
FREEZE

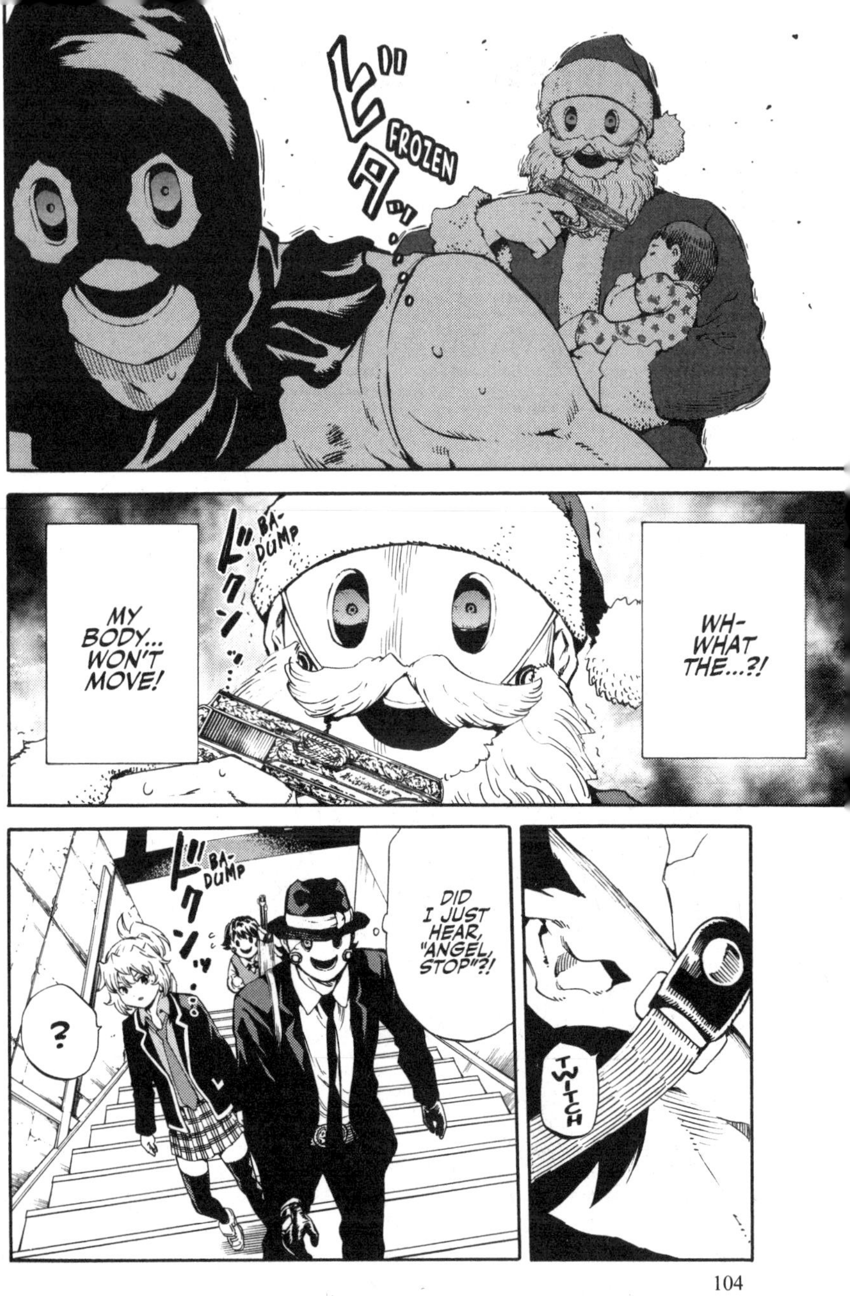
FROZEN
WH- WHAT THE...?!
BA-DUMP
MY BODY... WON'T MOVE!
TWITCH
DID I JUST HEAR, "ANGEL, STOP"?!
BA-DUMP
?

CHAPTER 181: How Should We Handle It?

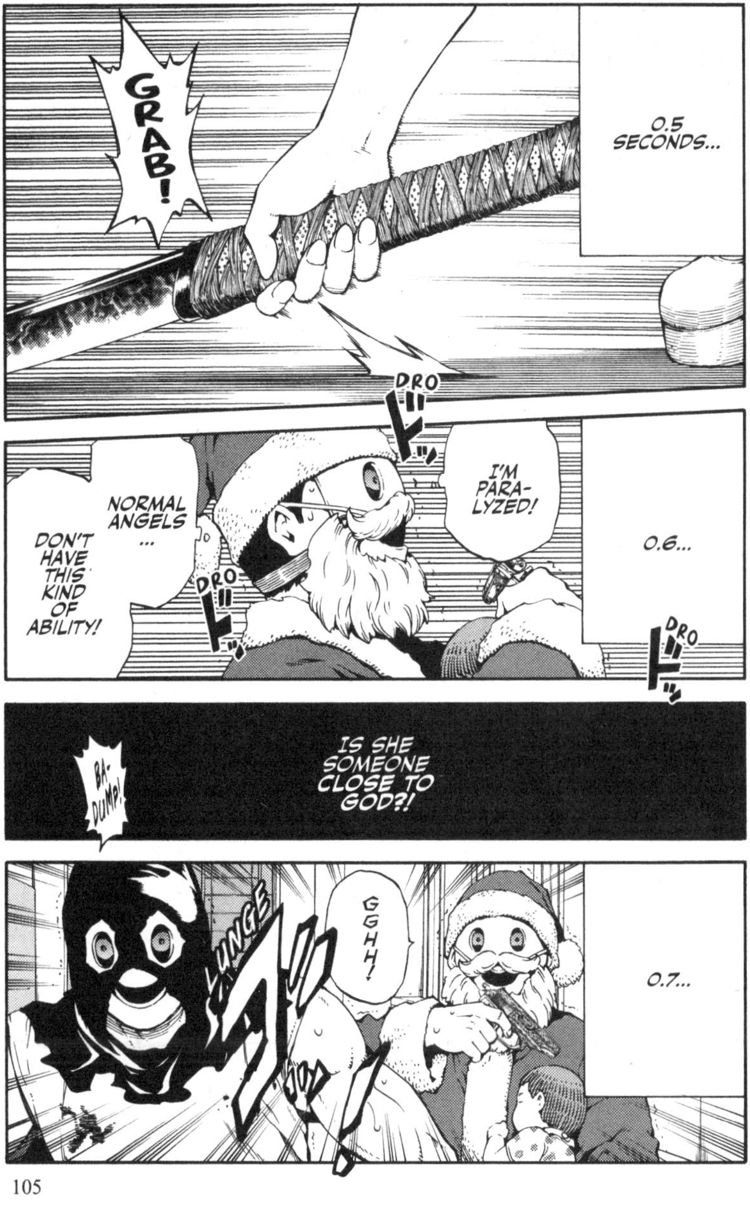
0.5 SECONDS...
GRAB!
DRO
0.6...
DRO
I'M PARA-LYZED!
DRO
NORMAL ANGELS ... DON'T HAVE THIS KIND OF ABILITY!
IS SHE SOMEONE CLOSE TO GOD?!
BA-DUMP!
0.7...
GGHH!
LUNGE

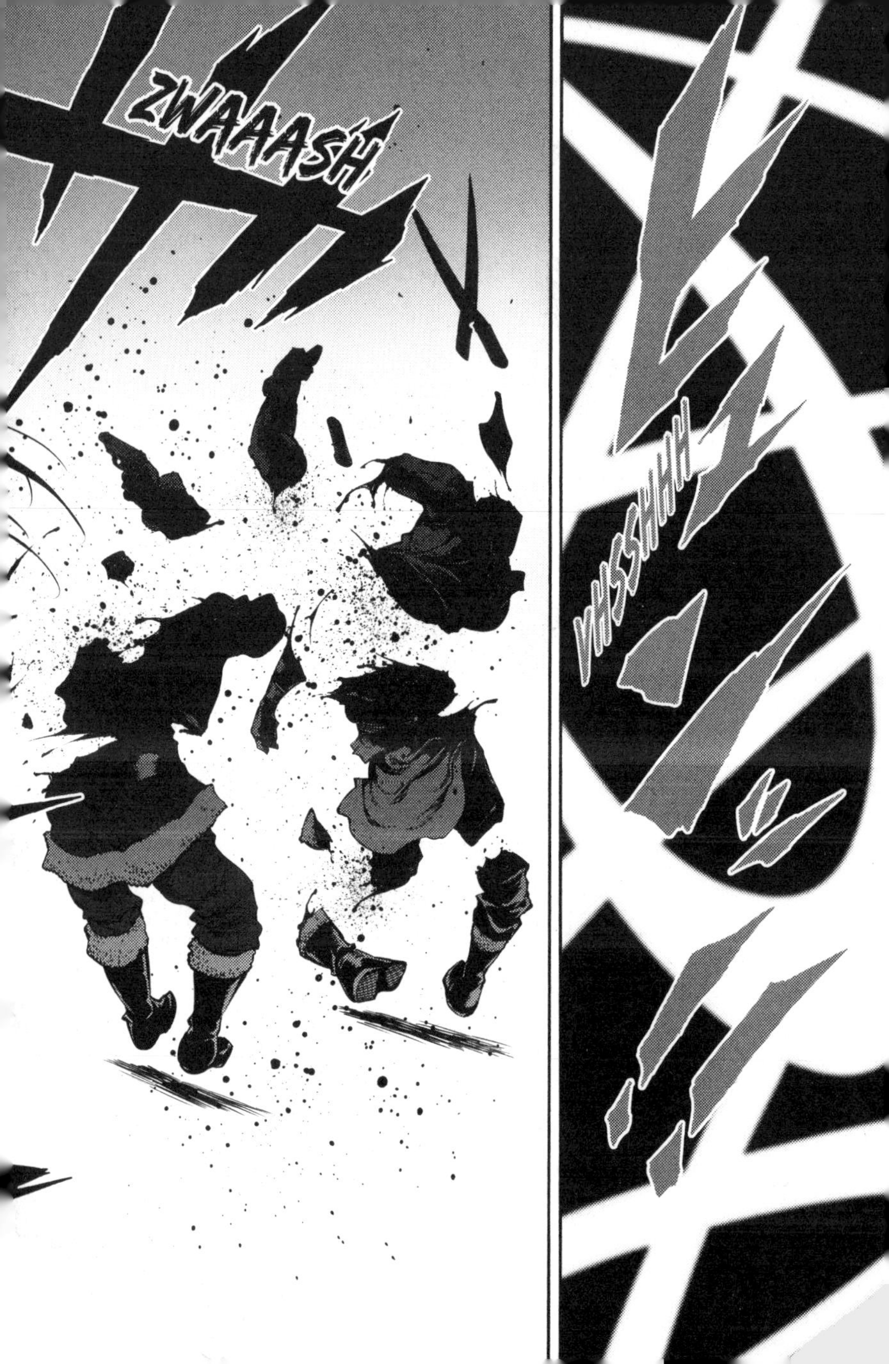
VHSSHHH
ZWAAASH

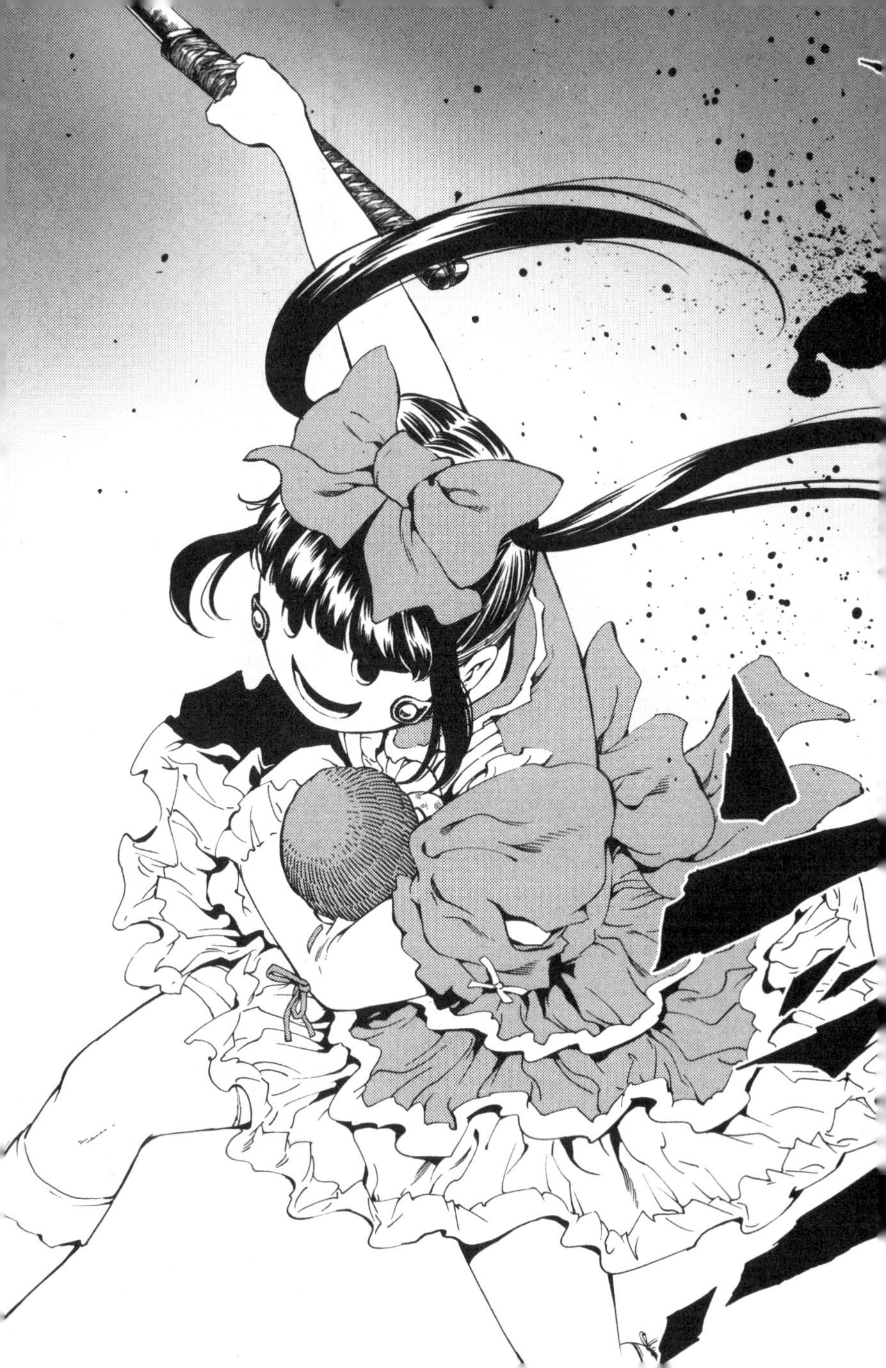

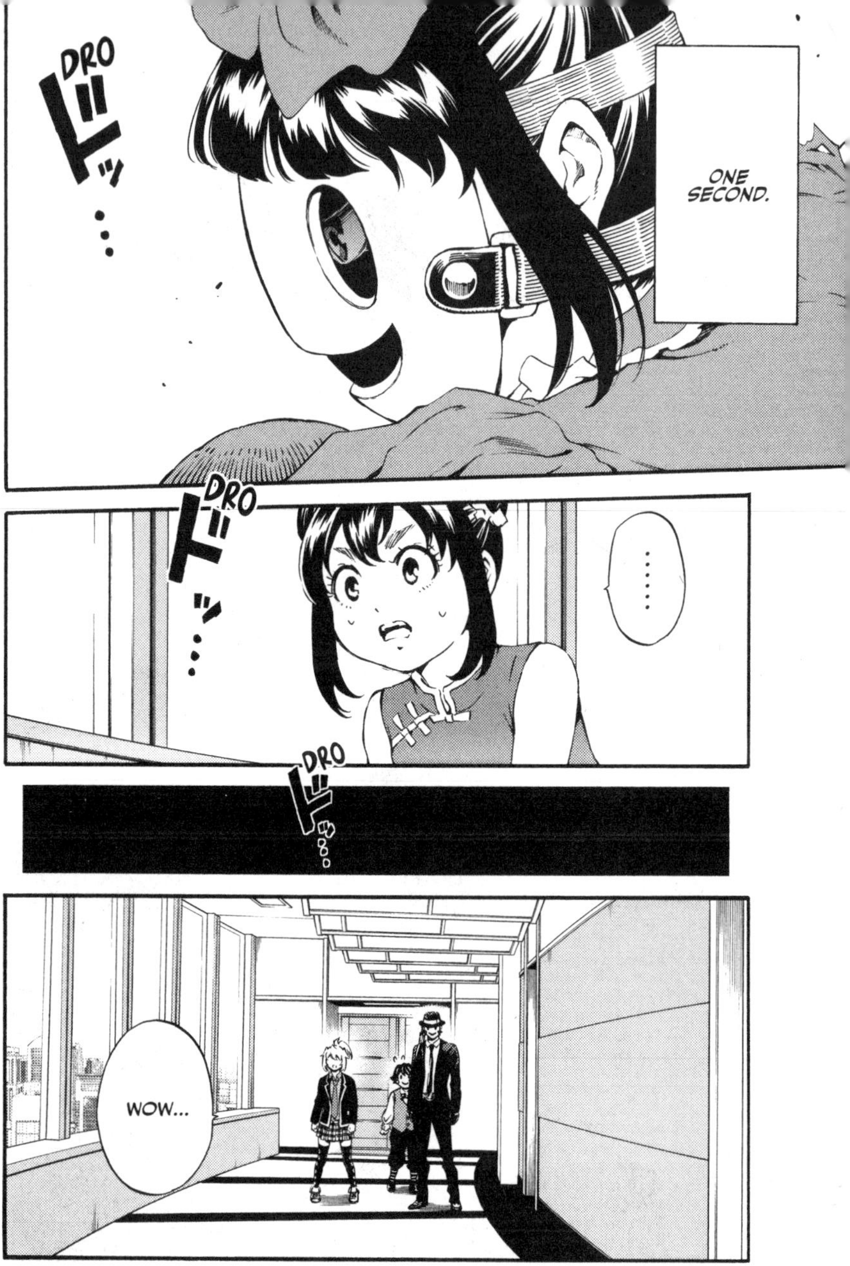
ONE SECOND.
DRO ドッ...
......
DRO ドッ...
DRO
WOW...

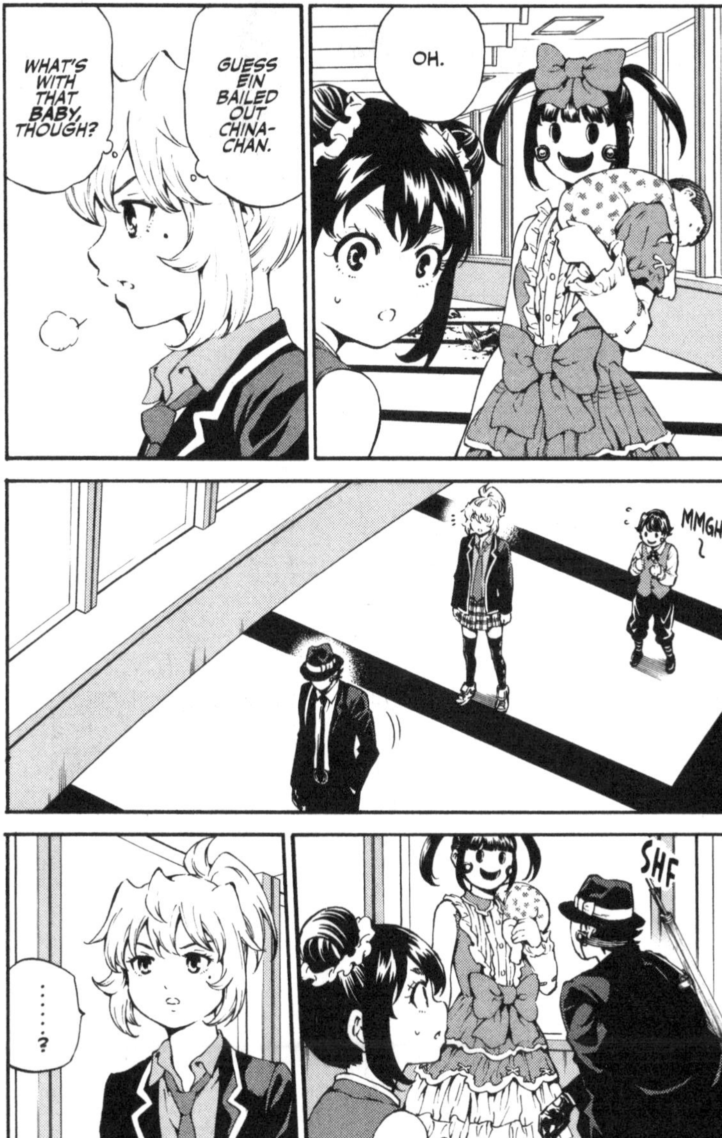
OH.
GUESS EIN BAILED OUT CHINA-CHAN.
WHAT'S WITH THAT BABY, THOUGH?
MMGH!
SHF
......?

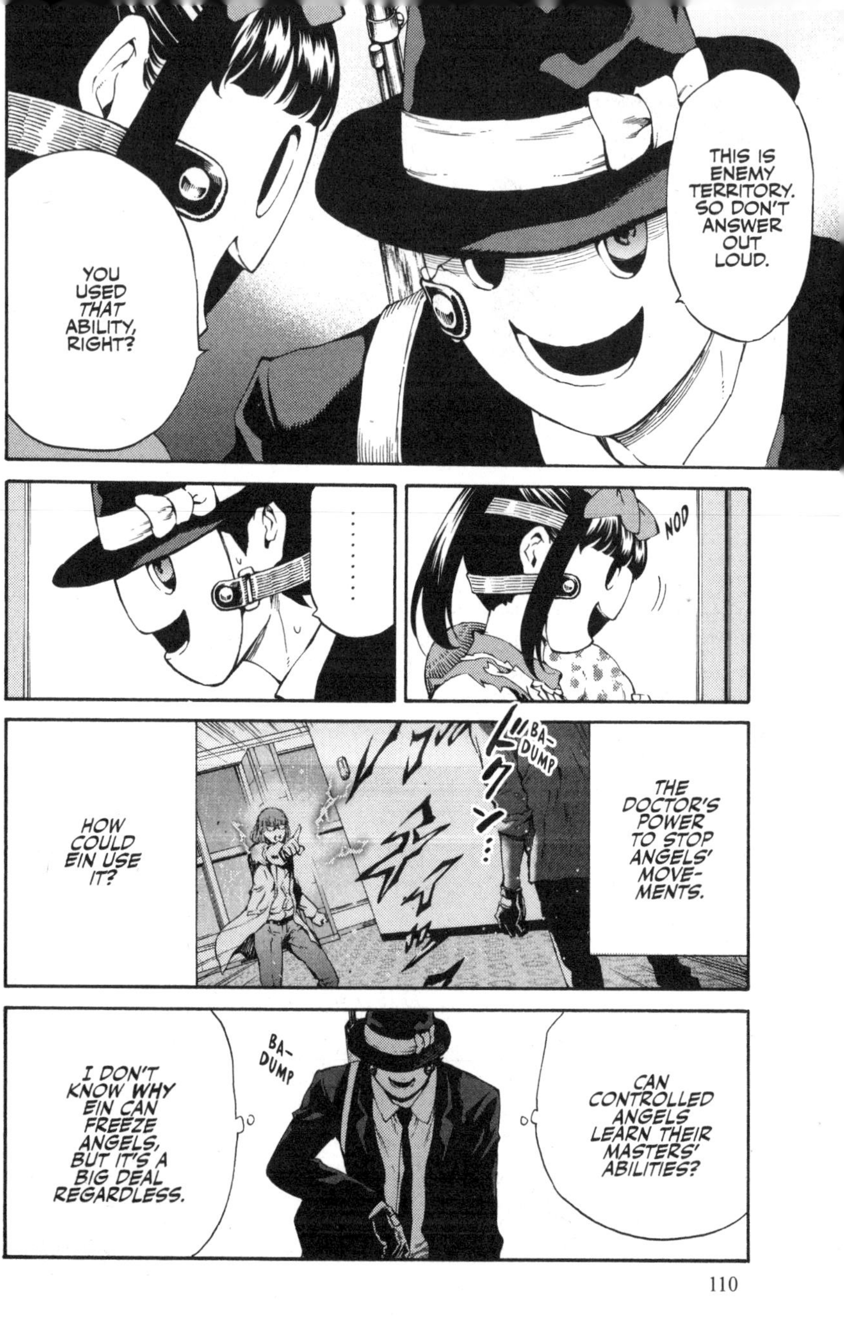
THIS IS ENEMY TERRITORY. SO DON'T ANSWER OUT LOUD.
YOU USED THAT ABILITY, RIGHT?
NOD
......
THE DOCTOR'S POWER TO STOP ANGELS' MOVE-MENTS.
BA-DUMP
HOW COULD EIN USE IT?
CAN CONTROLLED ANGELS LEARN THEIR MASTERS' ABILITIES?
BA-DUMP
I DON'T KNOW WHY EIN CAN FREEZE ANGELS, BUT IT'S A BIG DEAL REGARDLESS.

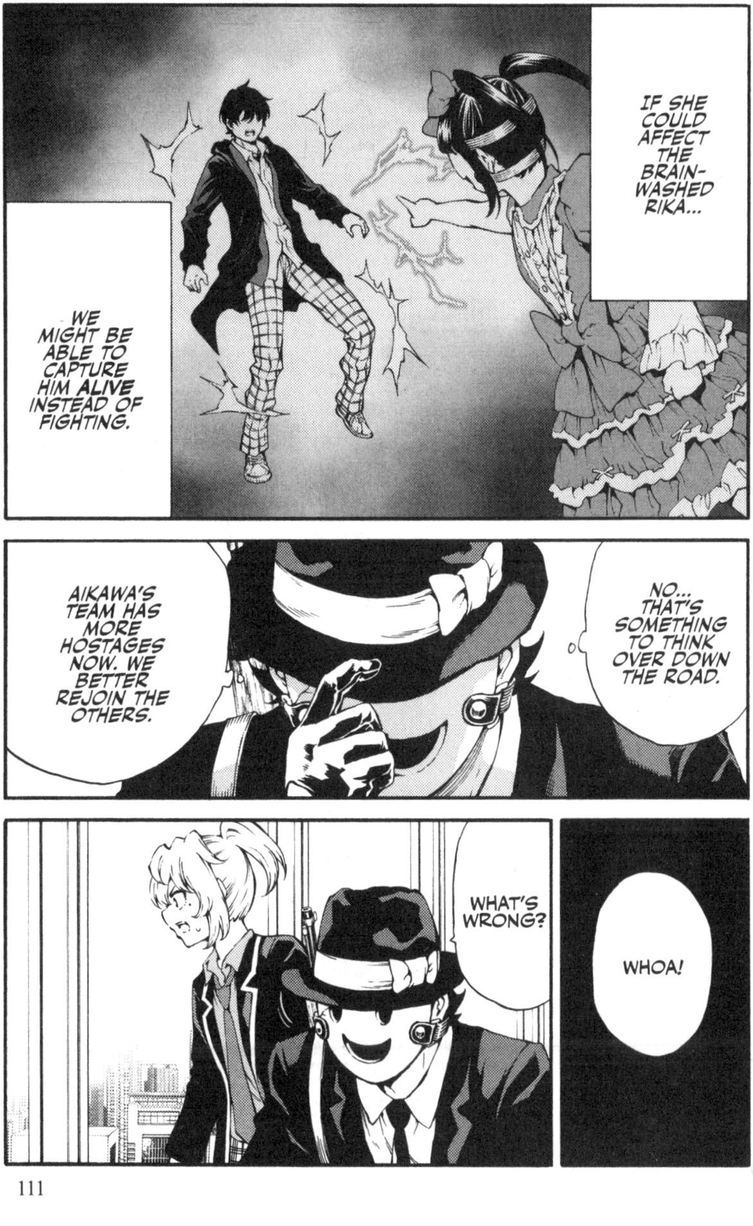
IF SHE COULD AFFECT THE BRAIN-WASHED RIKA...
WE MIGHT BE ABLE TO CAPTURE HIM ALIVE INSTEAD OF FIGHTING.
NO... THAT'S SOMETHING TO THINK OVER DOWN THE ROAD.
AIKAWA'S TEAM HAS MORE HOSTAGES NOW. WE BETTER REJOIN THE OTHERS.
WHOA!
WHAT'S WRONG?

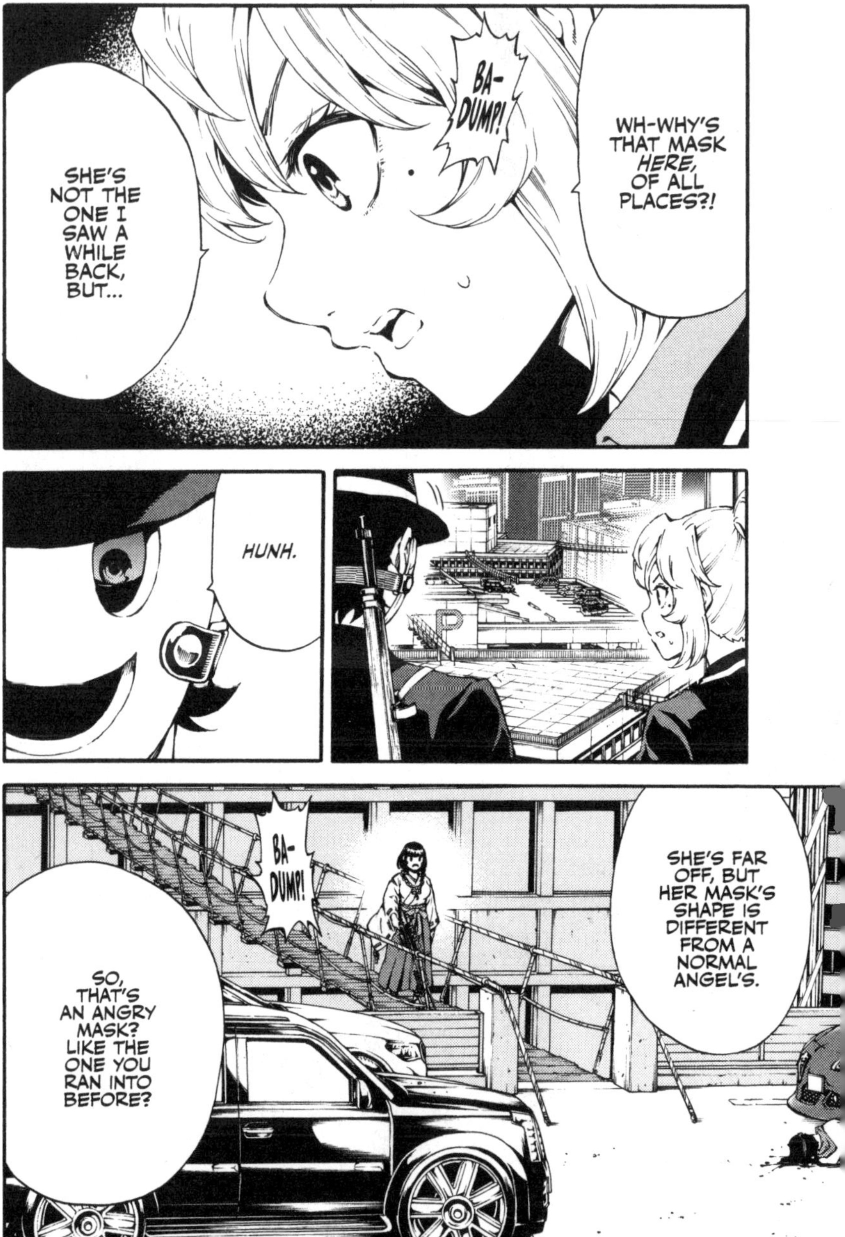
WH-WHY'S THAT MASK *HERE,* OF ALL PLACES?!
BA-DUMP!
SHE'S NOT THE ONE I SAW A WHILE BACK, BUT...
HUNH.
SHE'S FAR OFF, BUT HER MASK'S SHAPE IS DIFFERENT FROM A NORMAL ANGEL'S.
BA-DUMP!
SO, THAT'S AN ANGRY MASK? LIKE THE ONE YOU RAN INTO BEFORE?

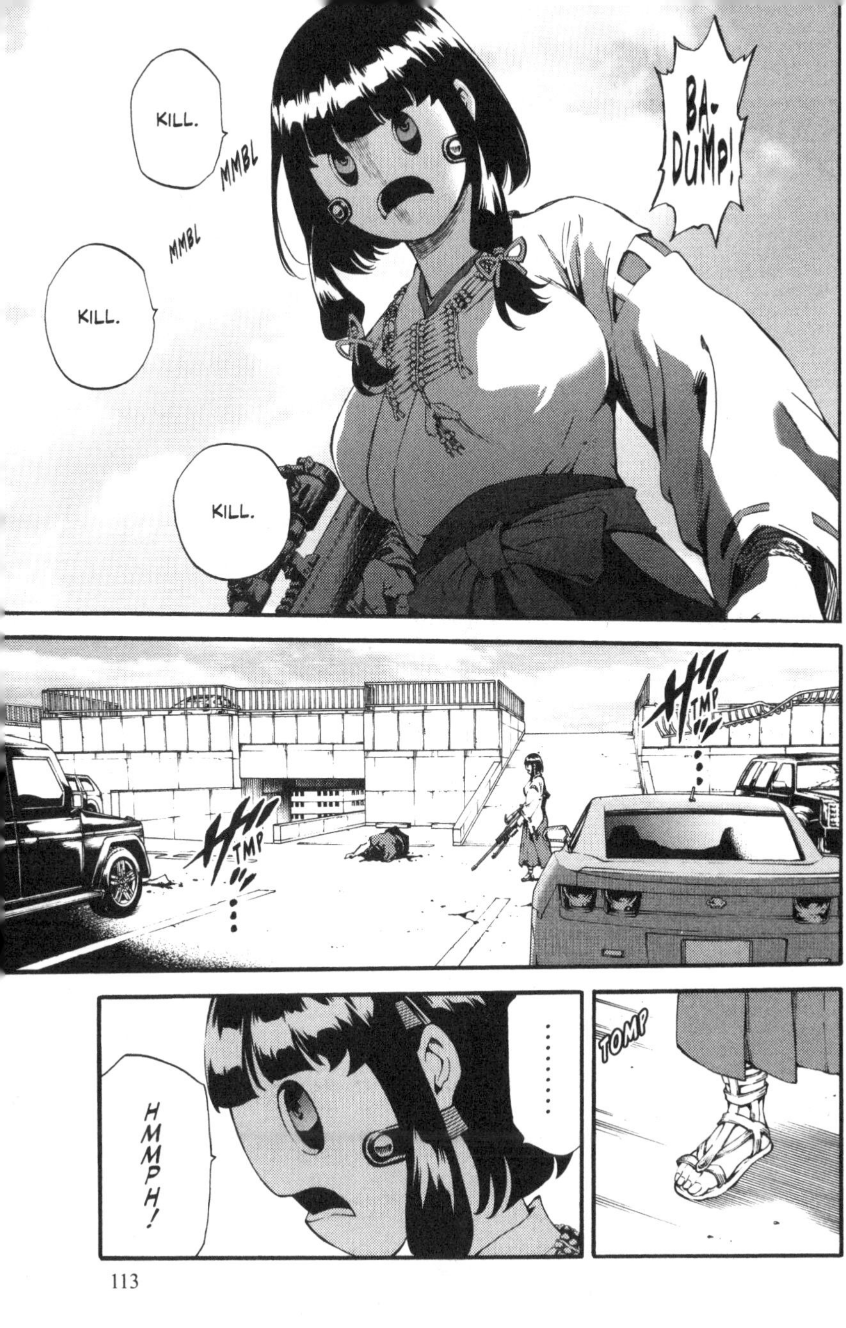
BA-DUMP!
KILL.
MMBL
MMBL
KILL.
KILL.
TMP
...
TMP
...
TOMP
....
HMMPH!

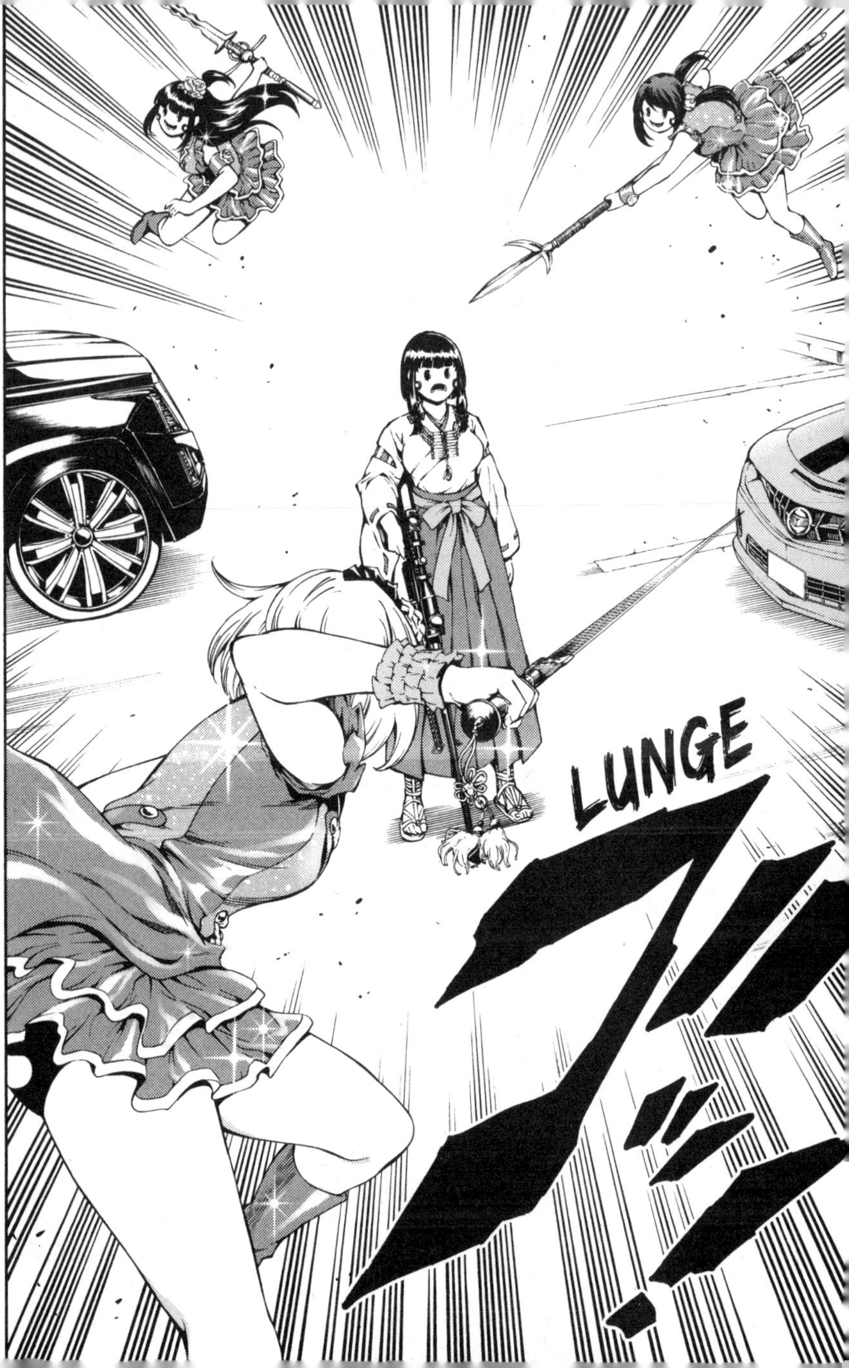
LUNGE

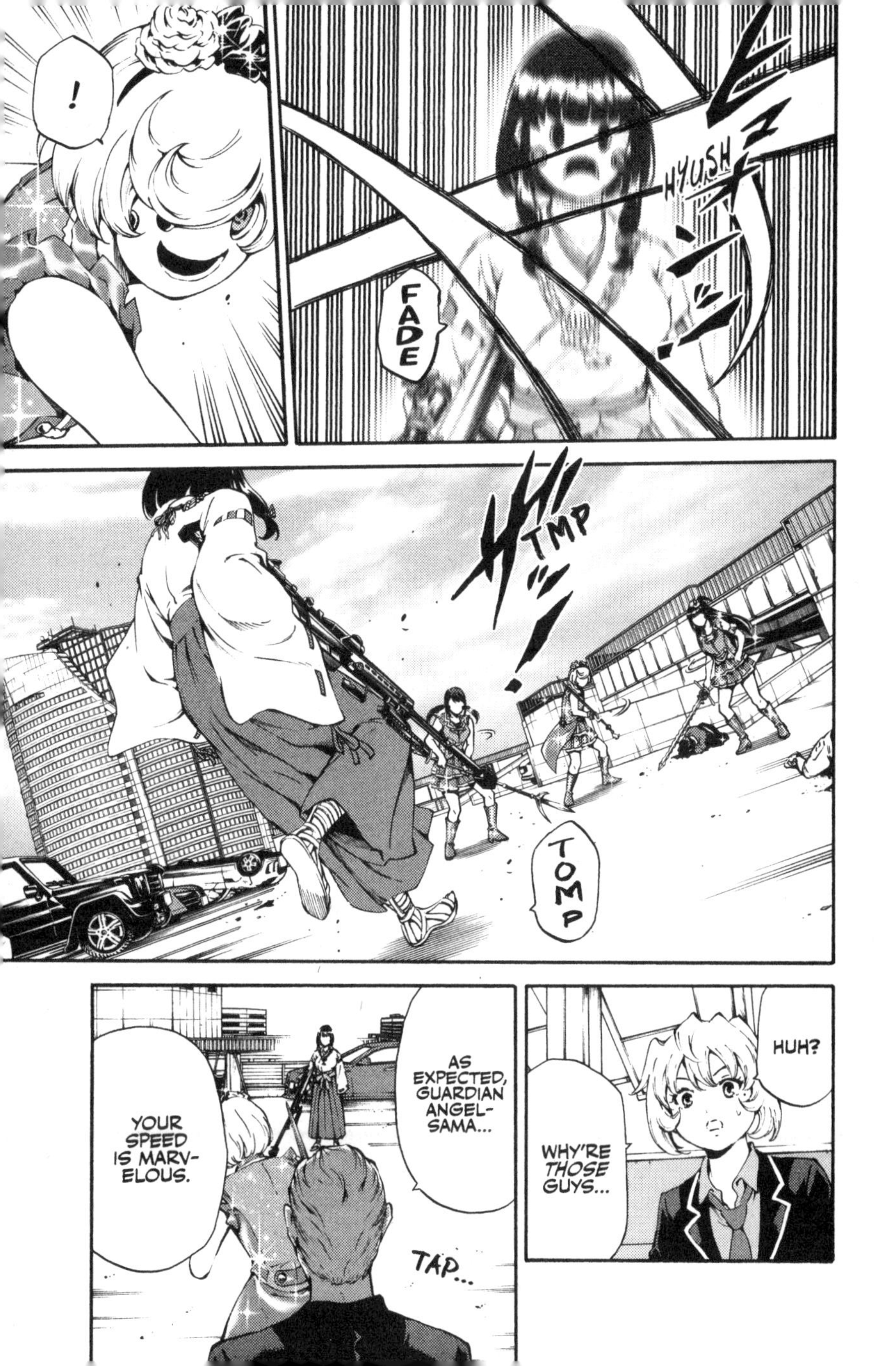
HYUSH
FADE
!
TMP
TOMP
HUH?
WHY'RE *THOSE* GUYS...
AS EXPECTED, GUARDIAN ANGEL-SAMA...
YOUR SPEED IS MARVELOUS.
TAP...

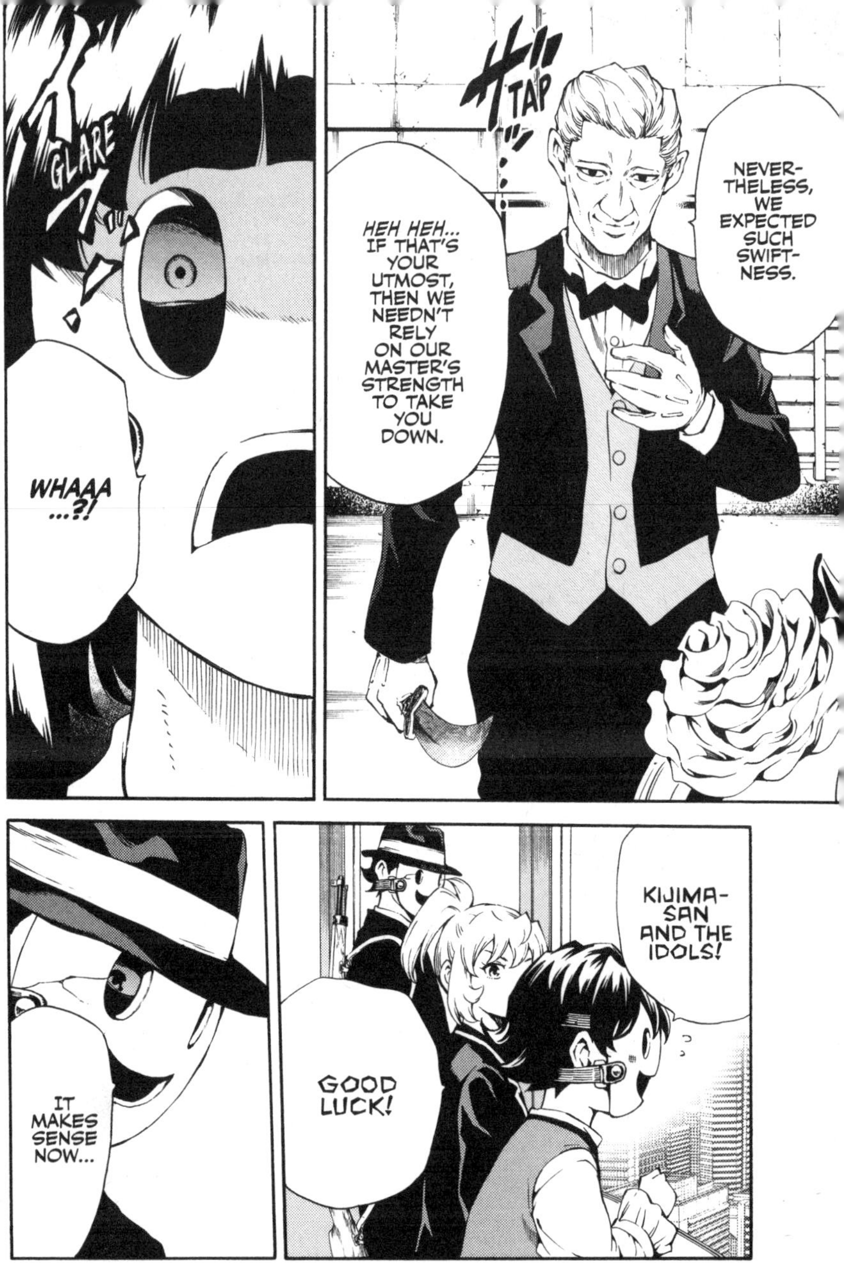
TAP
NEVER-THELESS, WE EXPECTED SUCH SWIFT-NESS.
HEH HEH... IF THAT'S YOUR UTMOST, THEN WE NEEDN'T RELY ON OUR MASTER'S STRENGTH TO TAKE YOU DOWN.
GLARE
WHAAA ...?!
KIJIMA-SAN AND THE IDOLS!
GOOD LUCK!
IT MAKES SENSE NOW...

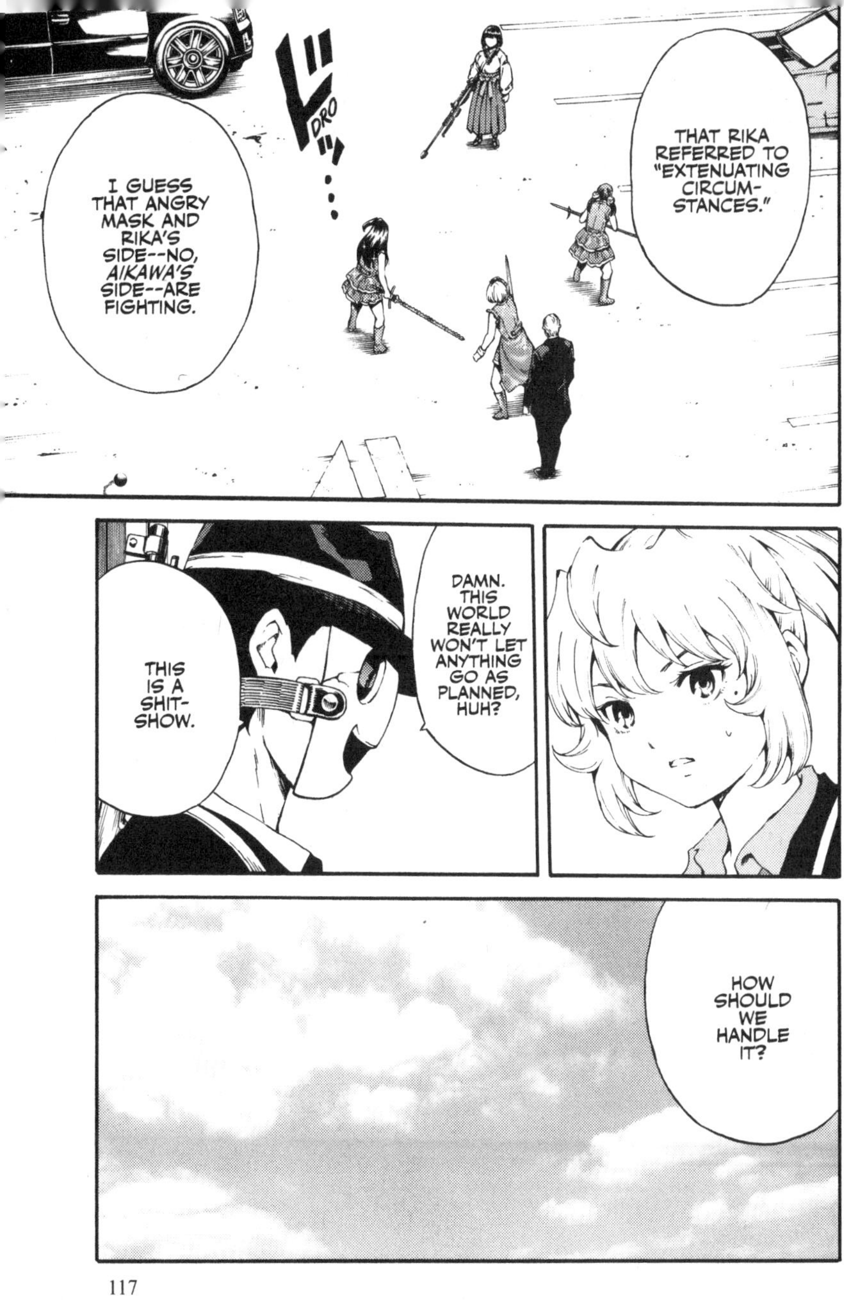
THAT RIKA REFERRED TO "EXTENUATING CIRCUM-STANCES."
DRO
I GUESS THAT ANGRY MASK AND RIKA'S SIDE--NO, *AIKAWA'S* SIDE--ARE FIGHTING.
DAMN. THIS WORLD REALLY WON'T LET ANYTHING GO AS PLANNED, HUH?
THIS IS A SHIT-SHOW.
HOW SHOULD WE HANDLE IT?

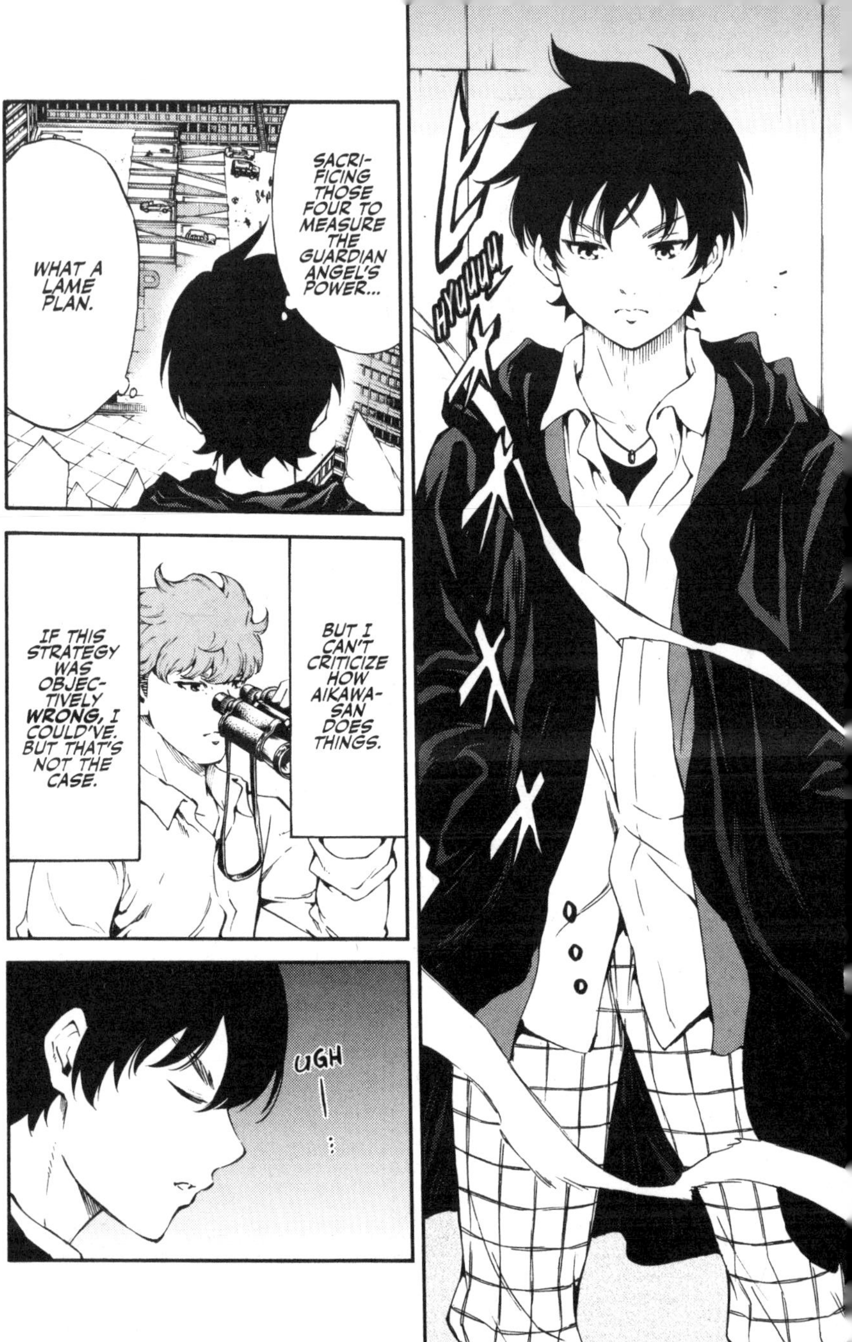
SACRI-FICING THOSE FOUR TO MEASURE THE GUARDIAN ANGEL'S POWER...
WHAT A LAME PLAN.
BUT I CAN'T CRITICIZE HOW AIKAWA-SAN DOES THINGS.
IF THIS STRATEGY WAS OBJEC-TIVELY **WRONG**, I COULD'VE. BUT THAT'S NOT THE CASE.
UGH —...

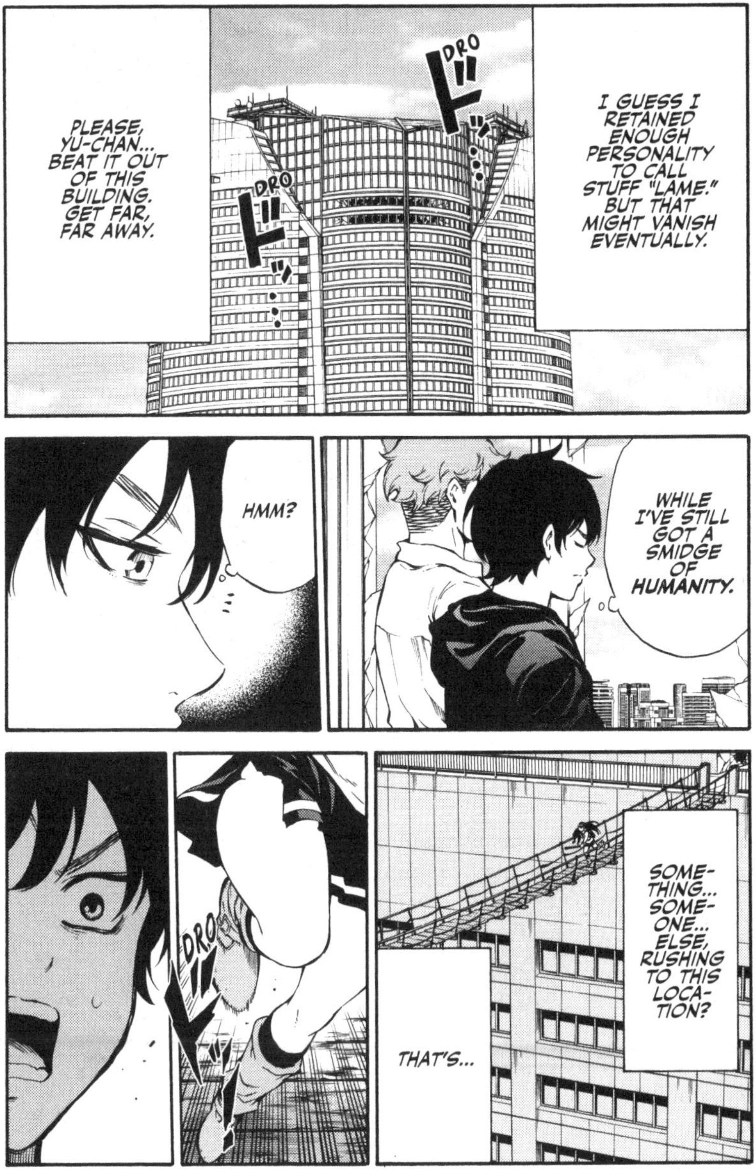

I GUESS I RETAINED ENOUGH PERSONALITY TO CALL STUFF "LAME." BUT THAT MIGHT VANISH EVENTUALLY.
DRO
DRO
PLEASE, YU-CHAN... BEAT IT OUT OF THIS BUILDING. GET FAR, FAR AWAY.
WHILE I'VE STILL GOT A SMIDGE OF **HUMANITY.**
HMM?
SOME-THING... SOME-ONE... ELSE, RUSHING TO THIS LOCA-TION?
THAT'S...
DRO

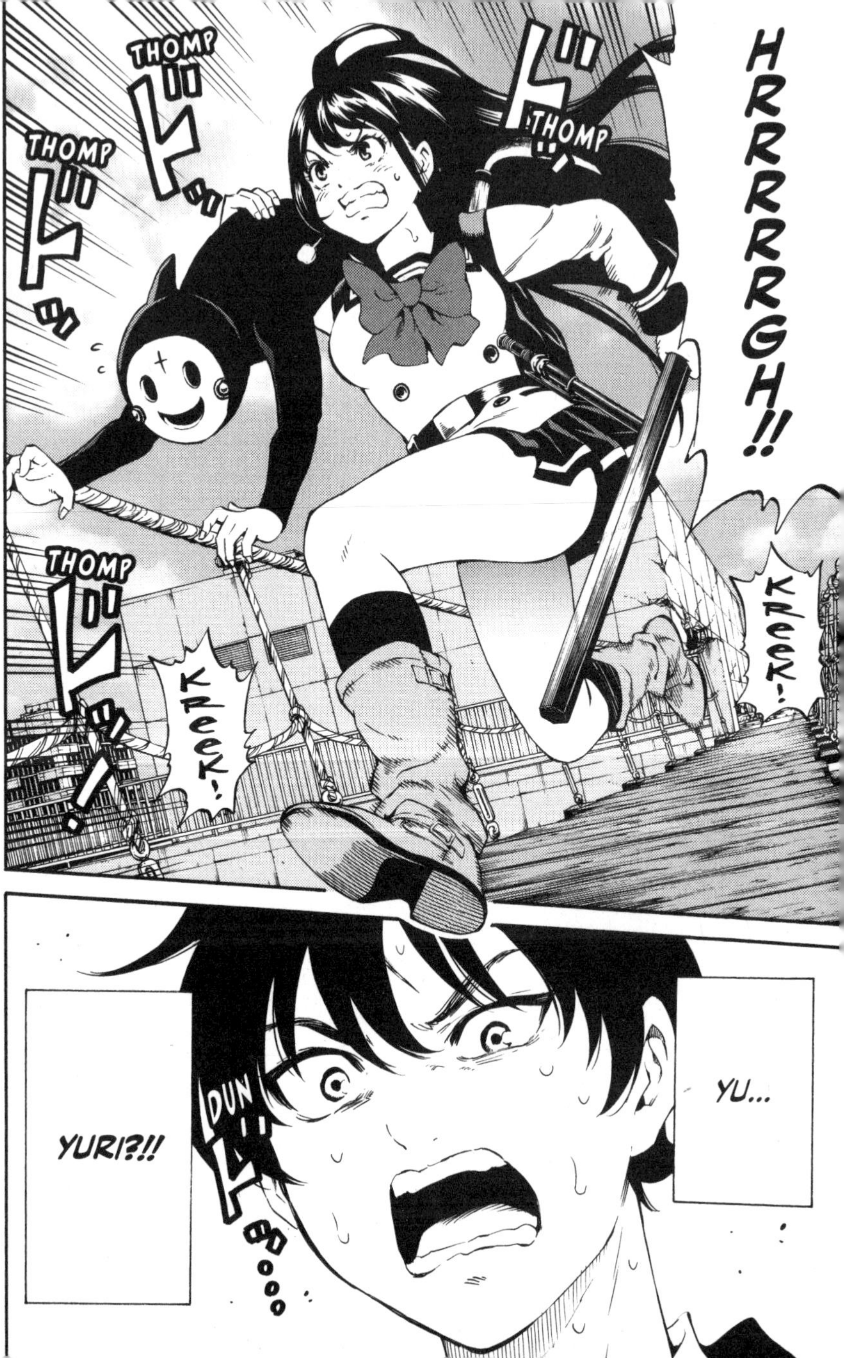
HRRRRRGH!!
THOMP
THOMP
THOMP
KREEK!
THOMP
KREEK!
YU...
DUN
YURI?!!

I love
the curve
babies'
cheeks
have
right
here!

HIGH-RISE
INVASION

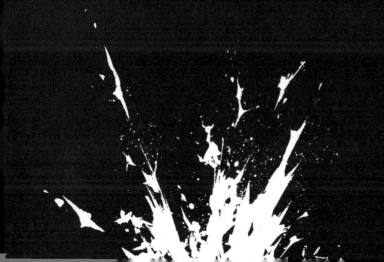

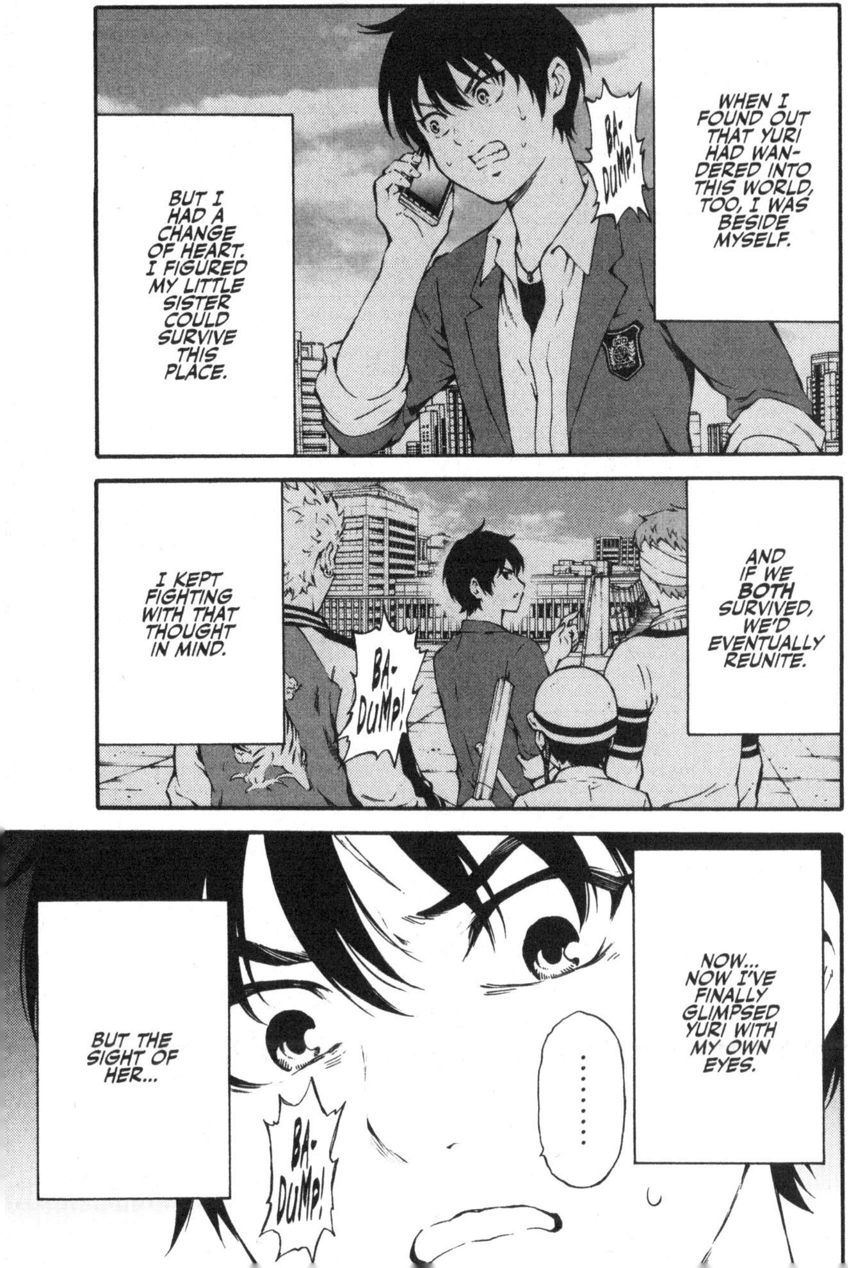
WHEN I FOUND OUT THAT YURI HAD WANDERED INTO THIS WORLD, TOO, I WAS BESIDE MYSELF.
BA-DUMP!
BUT I HAD A CHANGE OF HEART. I FIGURED MY LITTLE SISTER COULD SURVIVE THIS PLACE.
AND IF WE BOTH SURVIVED, WE'D EVENTUALLY REUNITE.
BA-DUMP!
I KEPT FIGHTING WITH THAT THOUGHT IN MIND.
NOW... NOW I'VE FINALLY GLIMPSED YURI WITH MY OWN EYES.
....
BA-DUMP!
BUT THE SIGHT OF HER...

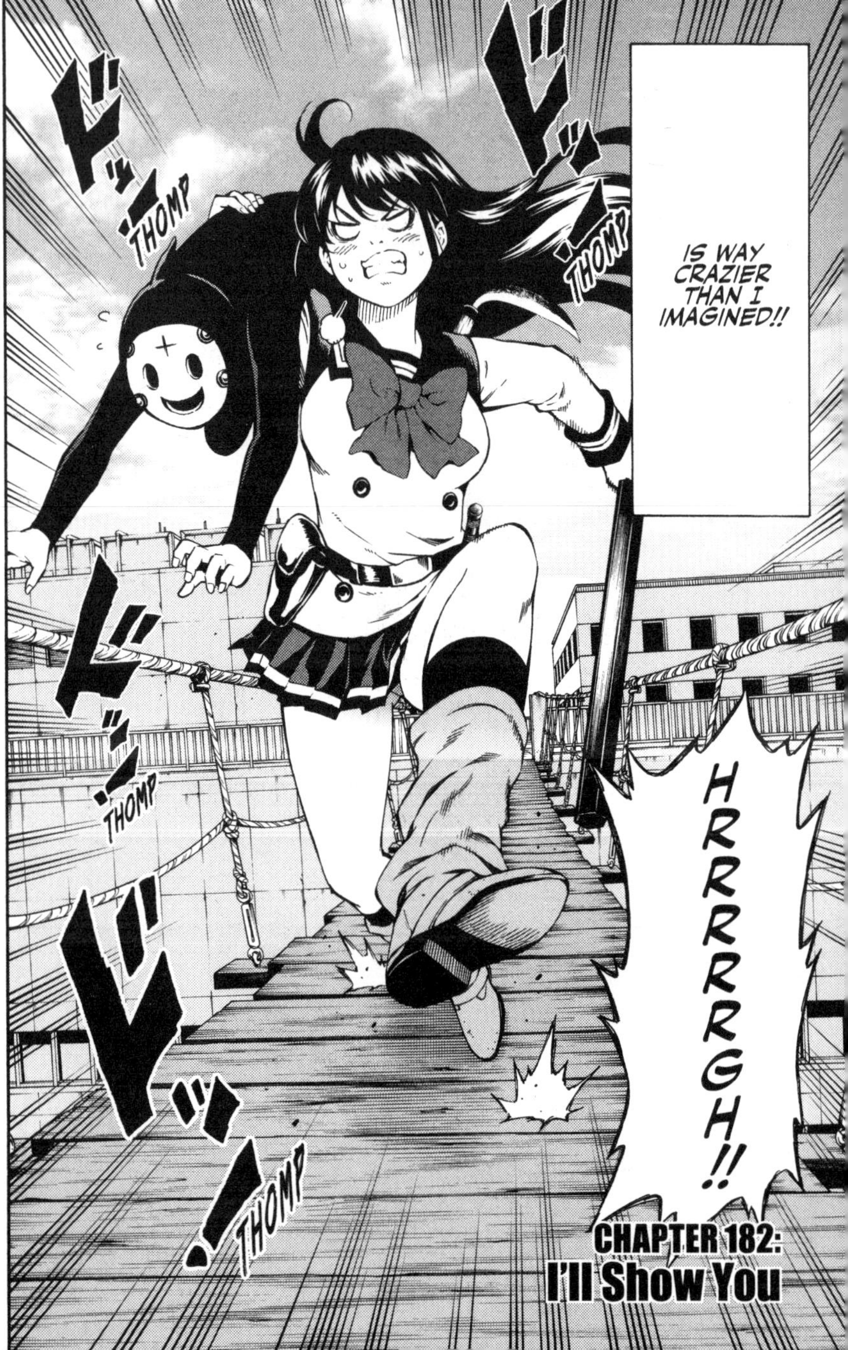
IS WAY CRAZIER THAN I IMAGINED!!
THOMP
THOMP
HRRRRRRGH!!
THOMP
THOMP
CHAPTER 182:
I'll Show You

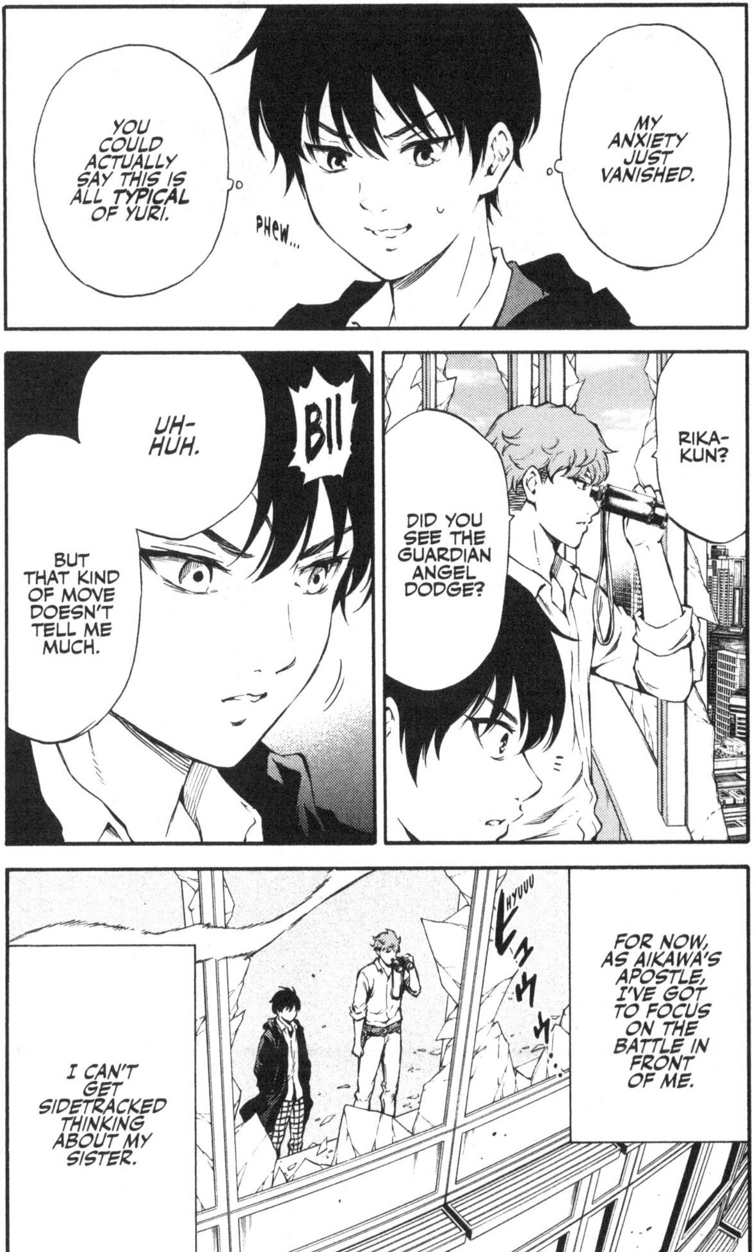
MY ANXIETY JUST VANISHED.
PHEW...
YOU COULD ACTUALLY SAY THIS IS ALL TYPICAL OF YURI.
RIKA-KUN?
DID YOU SEE THE GUARDIAN ANGEL DODGE?
BII
UH-HUH.
BUT THAT KIND OF MOVE DOESN'T TELL ME MUCH.
HYUUU
FOR NOW, AS AIKAWA'S APOSTLE, I'VE GOT TO FOCUS ON THE BATTLE IN FRONT OF ME.
I CAN'T GET SIDETRACKED THINKING ABOUT MY SISTER.

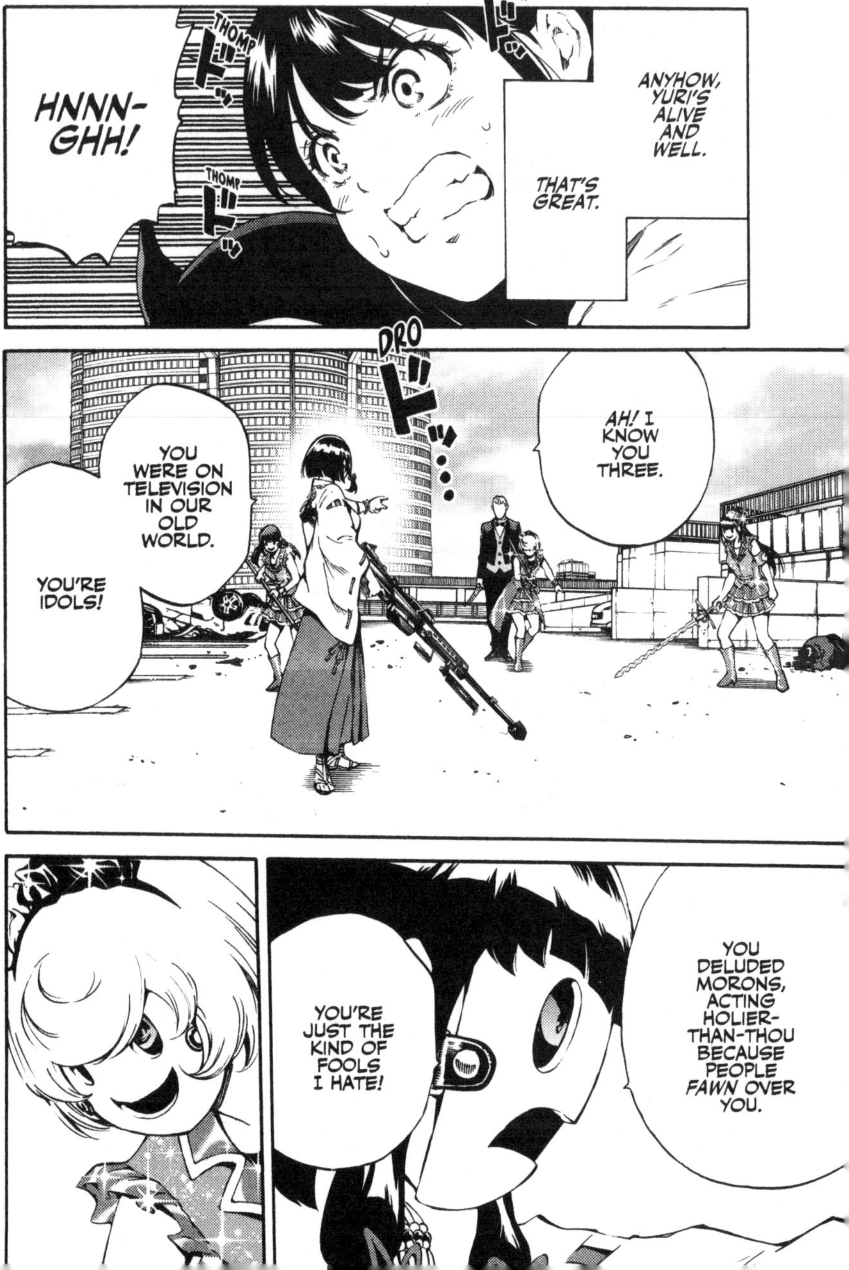
THOMP
ANYHOW, YURI'S ALIVE AND WELL.
THAT'S GREAT.
THOMP
HNNN-GHH!
THOMP
AH! I KNOW YOU THREE.
DRO
YOU WERE ON TELEVISION IN OUR OLD WORLD.
YOU'RE IDOLS!
YOU DELUDED MORONS, ACTING HOLIER-THAN-THOU BECAUSE PEOPLE FAWN OVER YOU.
YOU'RE JUST THE KIND OF FOOLS I HATE!

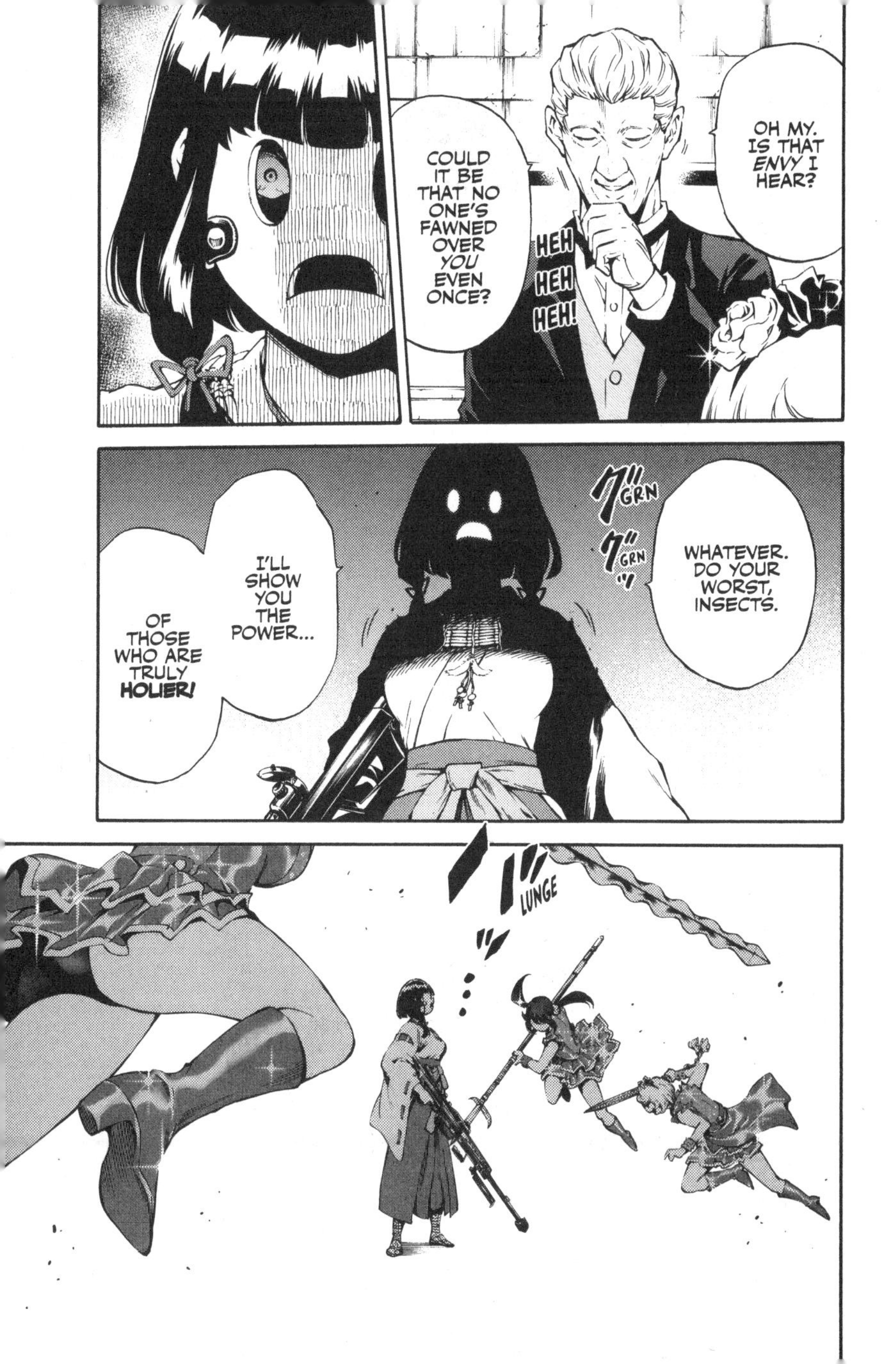
OH MY. IS THAT *ENVY* I HEAR?
HEH HEH HEH!
COULD IT BE THAT NO ONE'S FAWNED OVER *YOU* EVEN ONCE?
GRN
GRN
WHATEVER. DO YOUR WORST, INSECTS.
I'LL SHOW YOU THE POWER...
OF THOSE WHO ARE TRULY **HOLIER!**
LUNGE
...

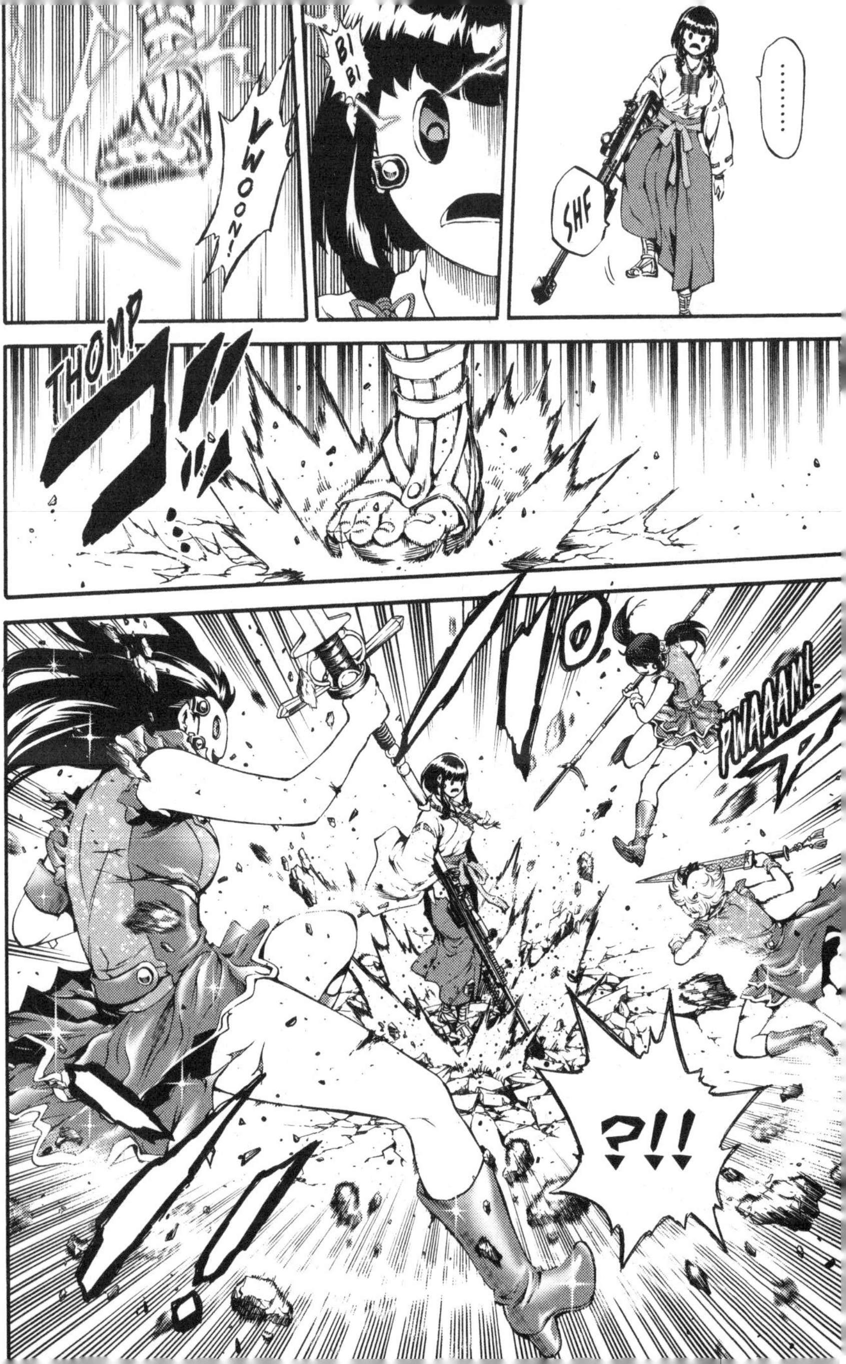
……
SHF
BI BI
VWOOON!
THOMP
PWAAAM!
?!!

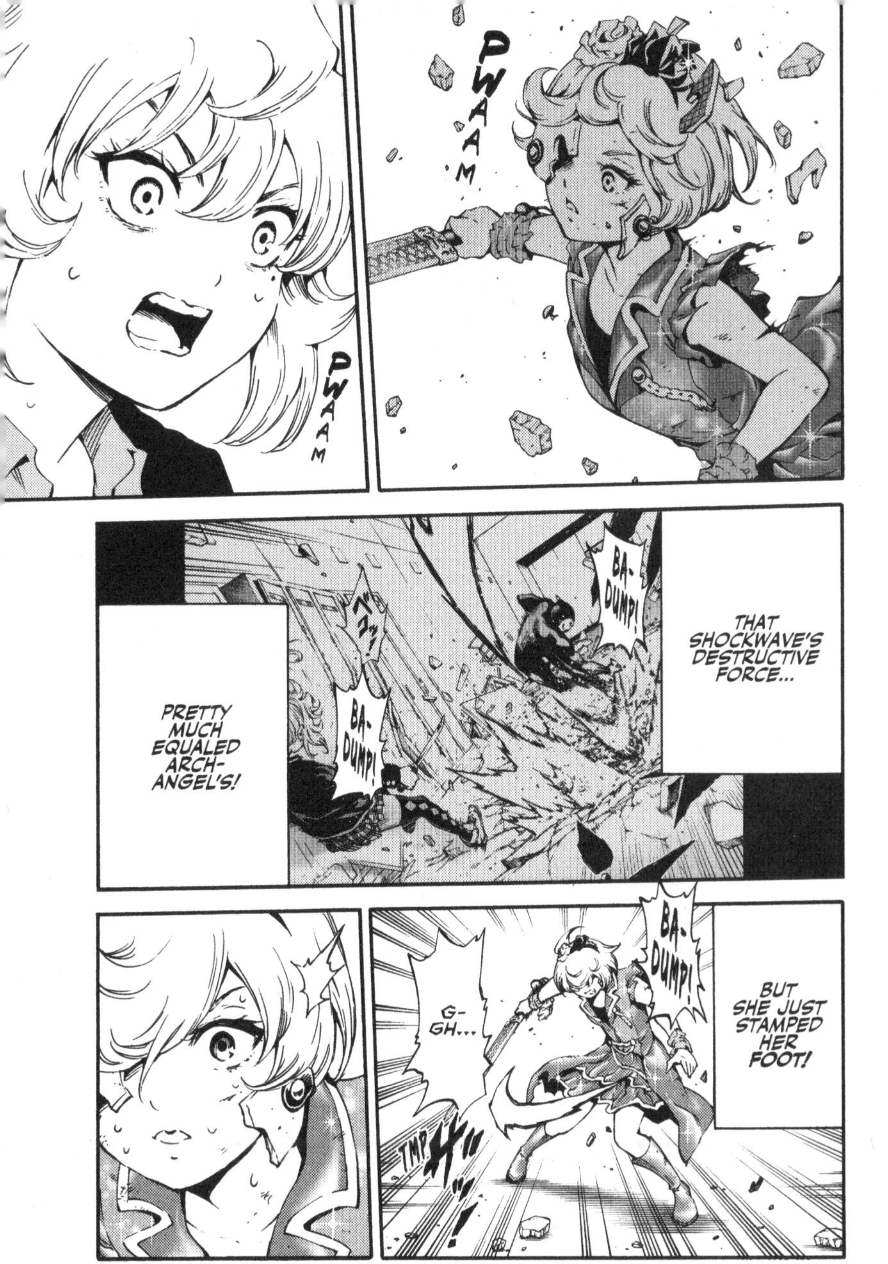
PWAAAM
PWAAAM
THAT SHOCKWAVE'S DESTRUCTIVE FORCE...
BA-DUMP!
BA-DUMP!
PRETTY MUCH EQUALED ARCH-ANGEL'S!
BUT SHE JUST STAMPED HER FOOT!
BA-DUMP!
G-GH...
TMP

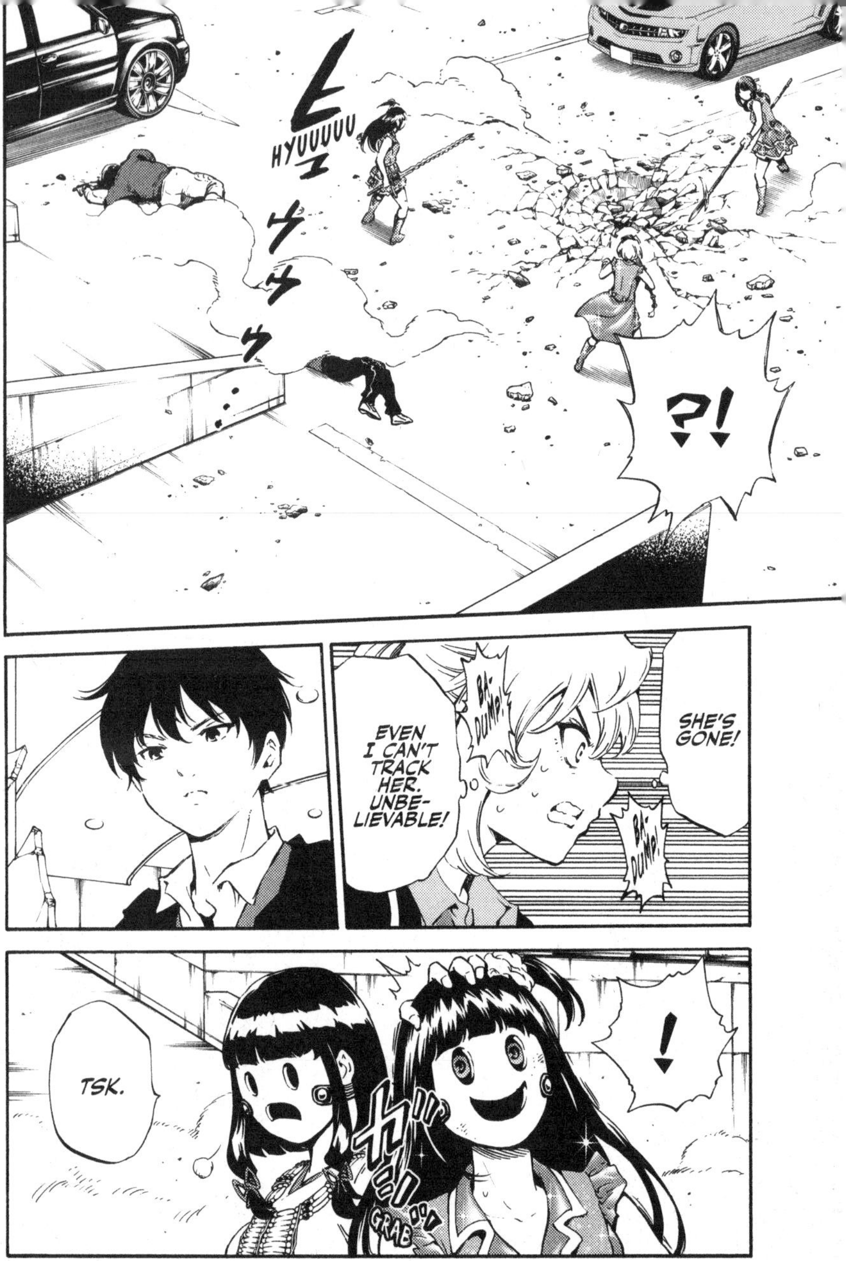
HYUUUUU
?!
SHE'S GONE!
BA-DUMP!
EVEN I CAN'T TRACK HER. UNBE-LIEVABLE!
BA-DUMP!
!
GRAB
TSK.

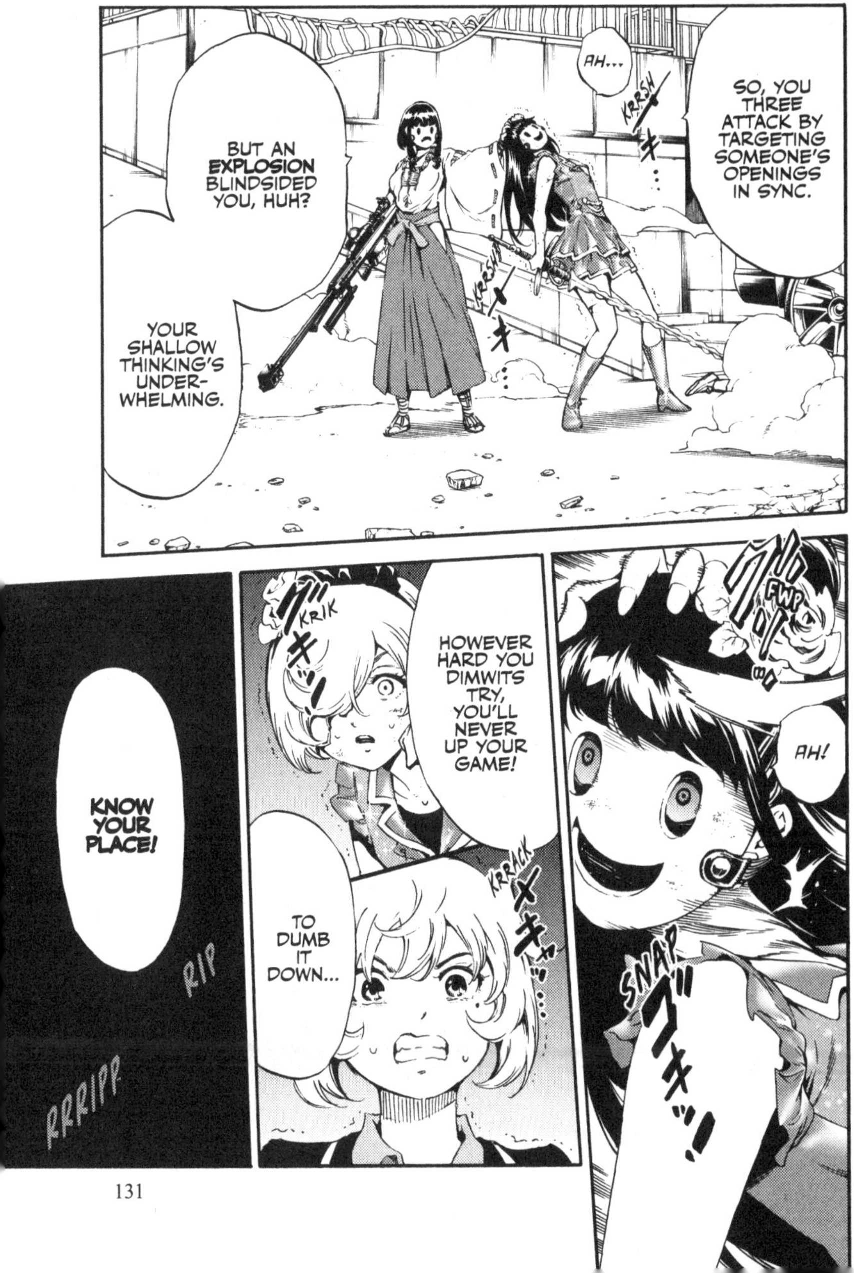
SO, YOU THREE ATTACK BY TARGETING SOMEONE'S OPENINGS IN SYNC.
AH...
KRRSH
KRRSH
BUT AN **EXPLOSION** BLINDSIDED YOU, HUH?
YOUR SHALLOW THINKING'S UNDER-WHELMING.
FWP
AH!
SNAP
KRIK
HOWEVER HARD YOU DIMWITS TRY, YOU'LL NEVER UP YOUR GAME!
TO DUMB IT DOWN...
KRRACK
KNOW YOUR PLACE!
RIP
RRRIPP

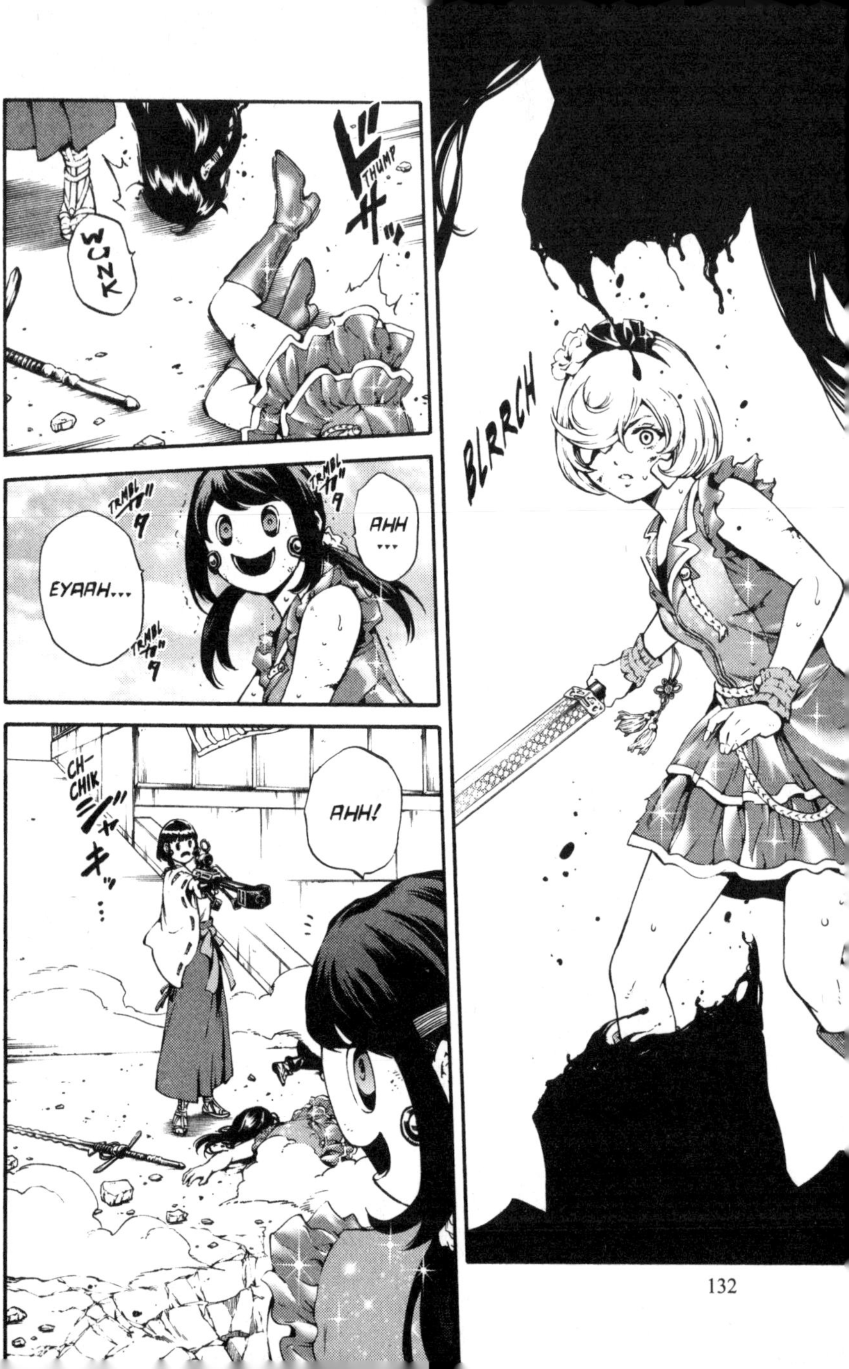
BLRRCH
THUMP
WUNK
TRMBL
AHH...
TRMBL
EYAAH...
TRMBL
CH-CHIK
AHH!

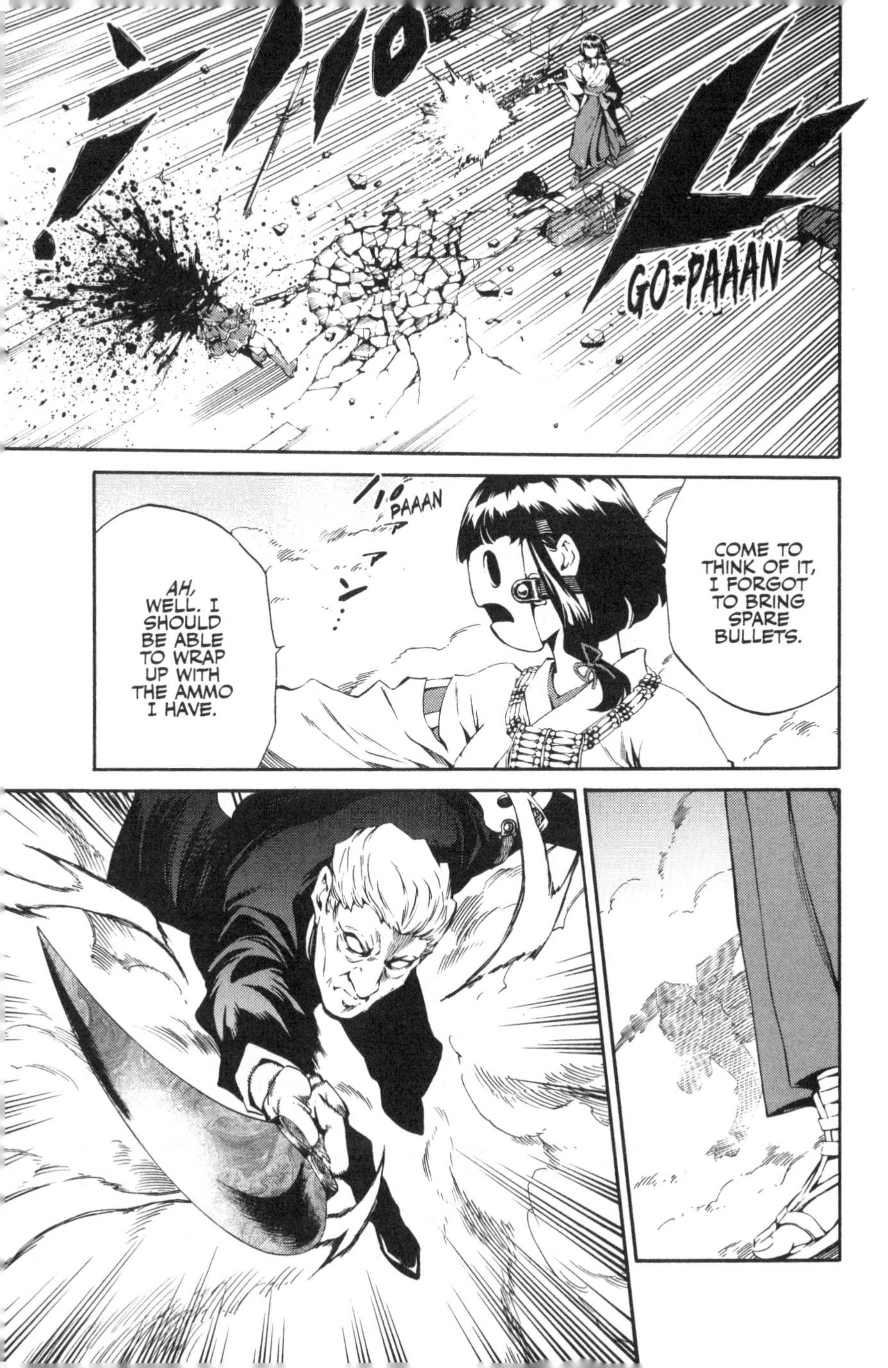
GO-PAAAN
COME TO THINK OF IT, I FORGOT TO BRING SPARE BULLETS.
PAAAN
AH, WELL. I SHOULD BE ABLE TO WRAP UP WITH THE AMMO I HAVE.

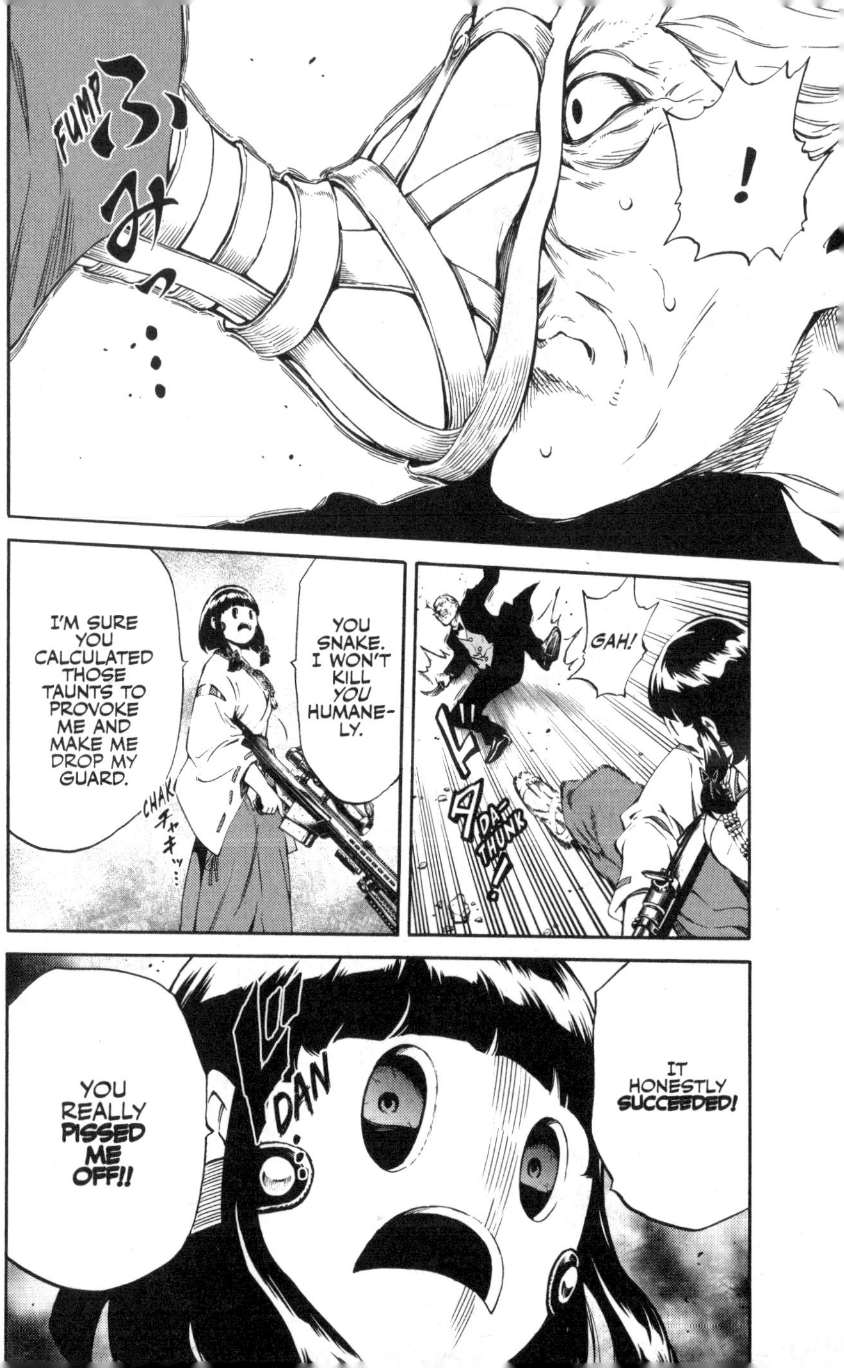
!
FUMP
ふみっ
GAH!
DA-THUNK!
YOU SNAKE. I WON'T KILL YOU HUMANE-LY.
I'M SURE YOU CALCULATED THOSE TAUNTS TO PROVOKE ME AND MAKE ME DROP MY GUARD.
CHAK
チャキッ…
IT HONESTLY SUCCEEDED!
DAN
YOU REALLY PISSED ME OFF!!

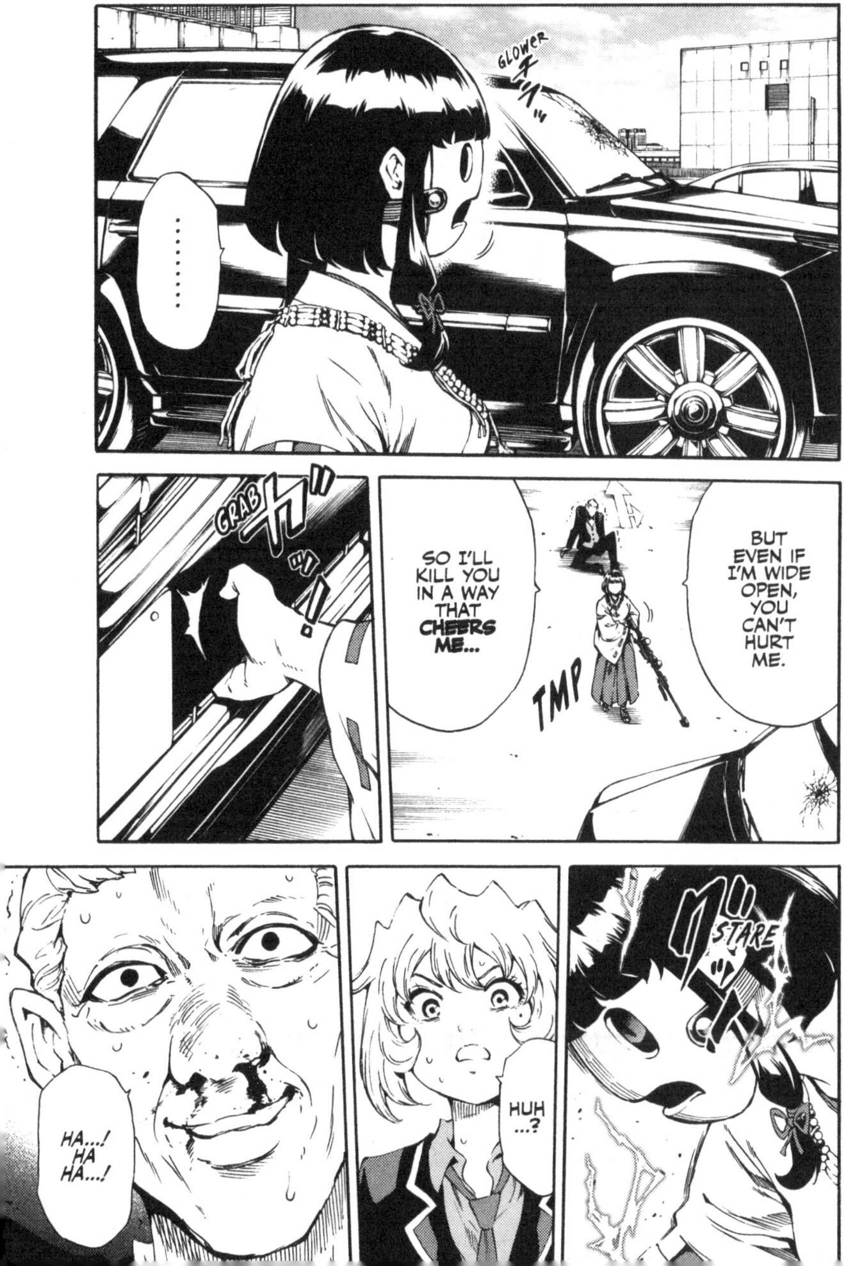
GLOWER
……
BUT EVEN IF I'M WIDE OPEN, YOU CAN'T HURT ME.
SO I'LL KILL YOU IN A WAY THAT **CHEERS ME...**
TMP
GRAB
STARE
HUH ...?
HA...! HA HA...!

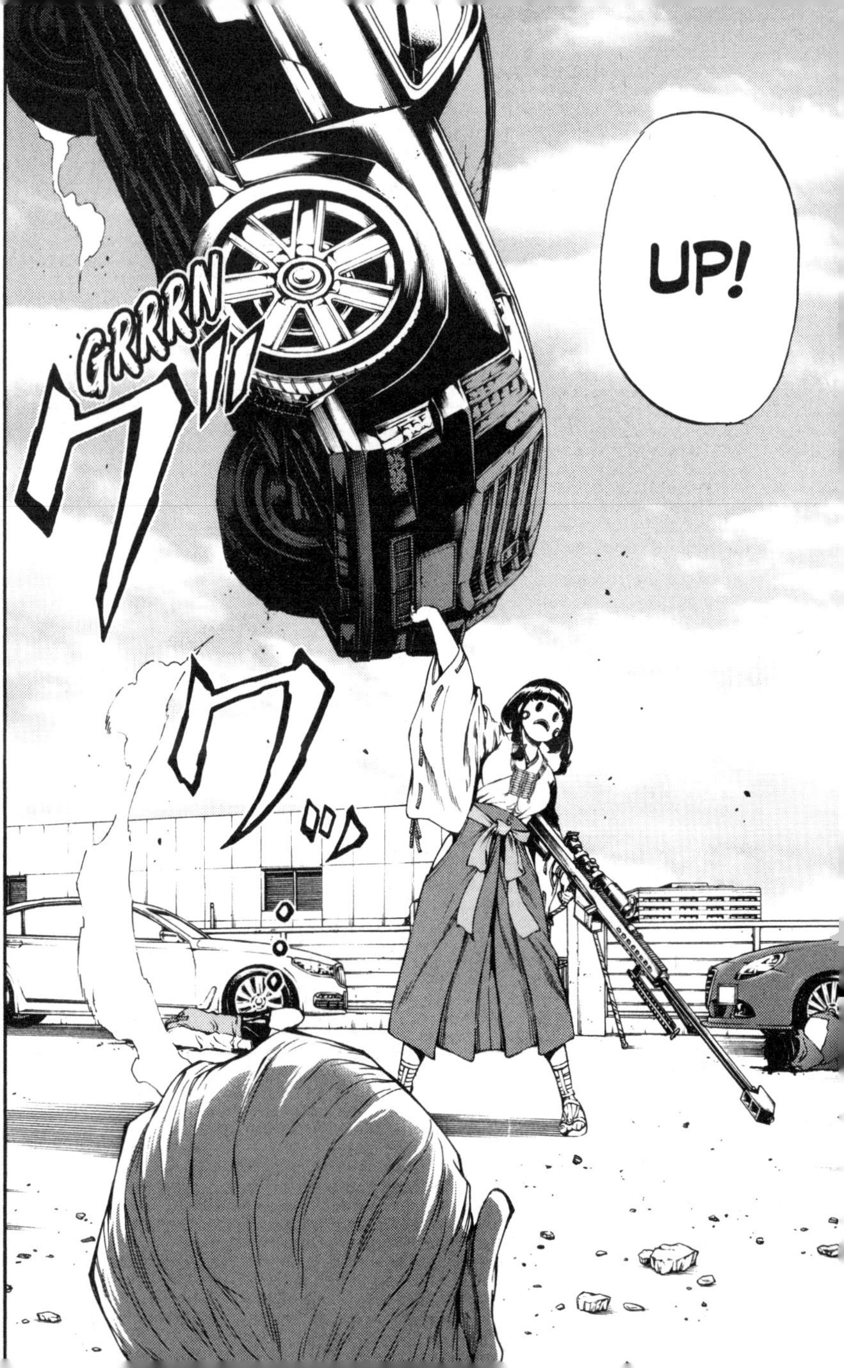
UP!
GRRRN
ググッ

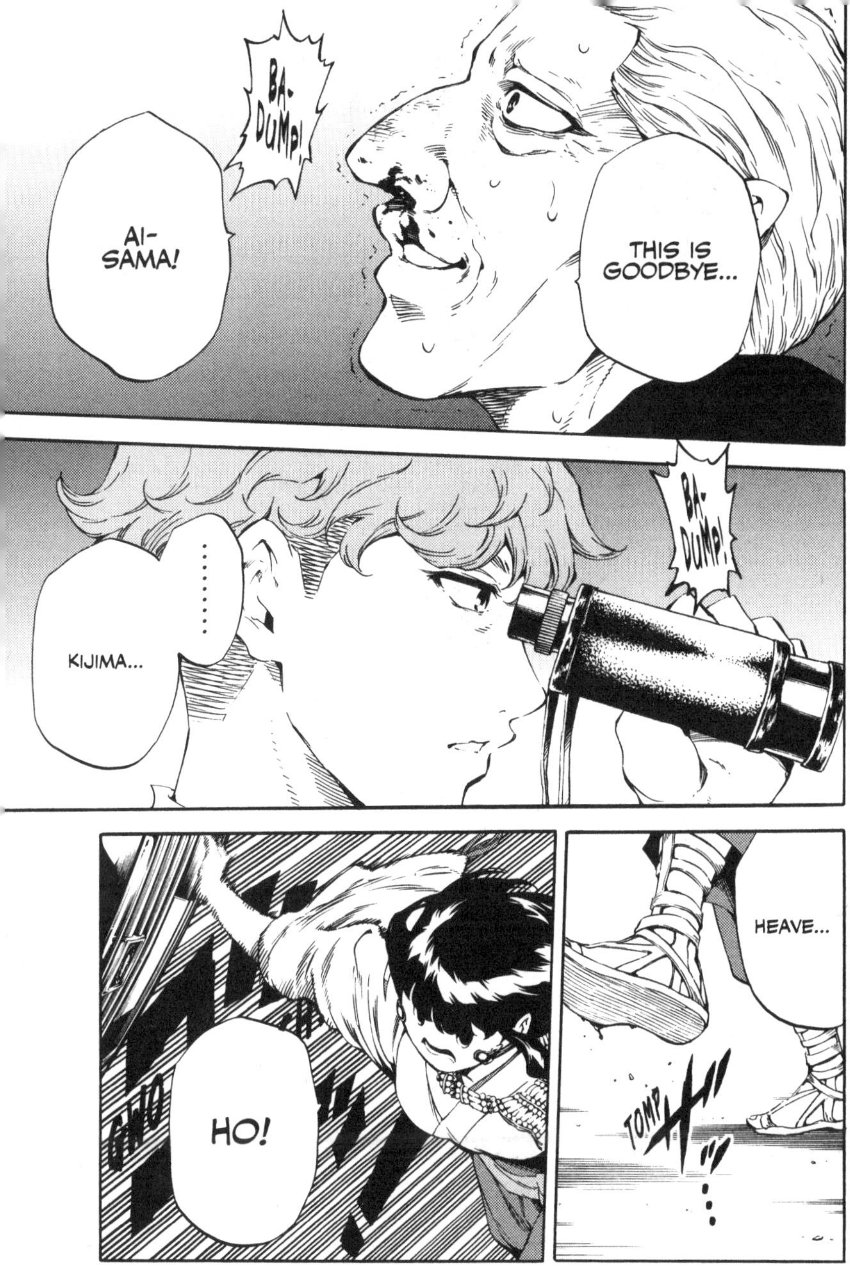
THIS IS GOODBYE...
BA-DUMP!
AI-SAMA!
BA-DUMP!
......
KIJIMA...
HEAVE...
TOMP
GWO
HO!

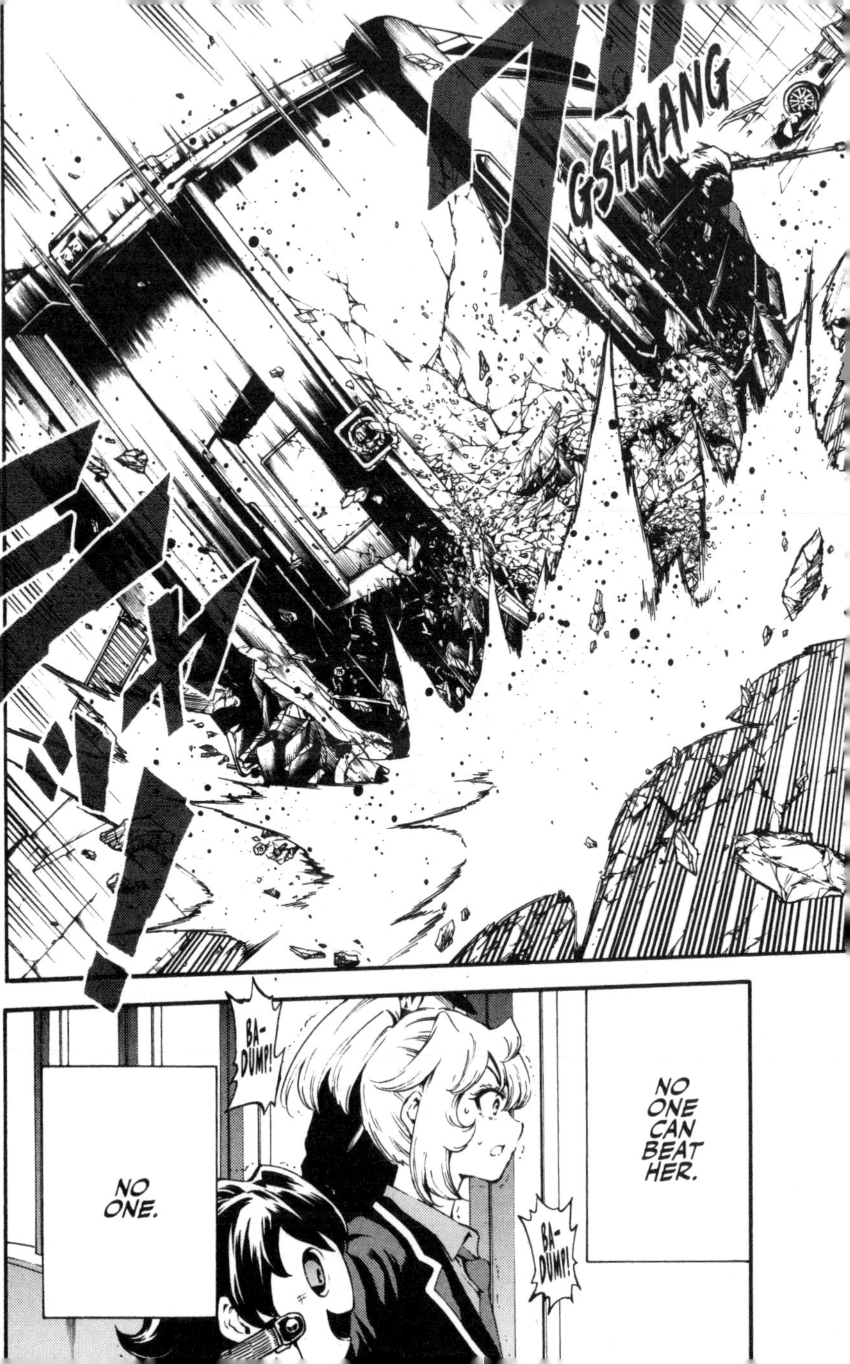
GSHAANG
NO ONE CAN BEAT HER.
BA-DUMP!
BA-DUMP!
NO ONE.

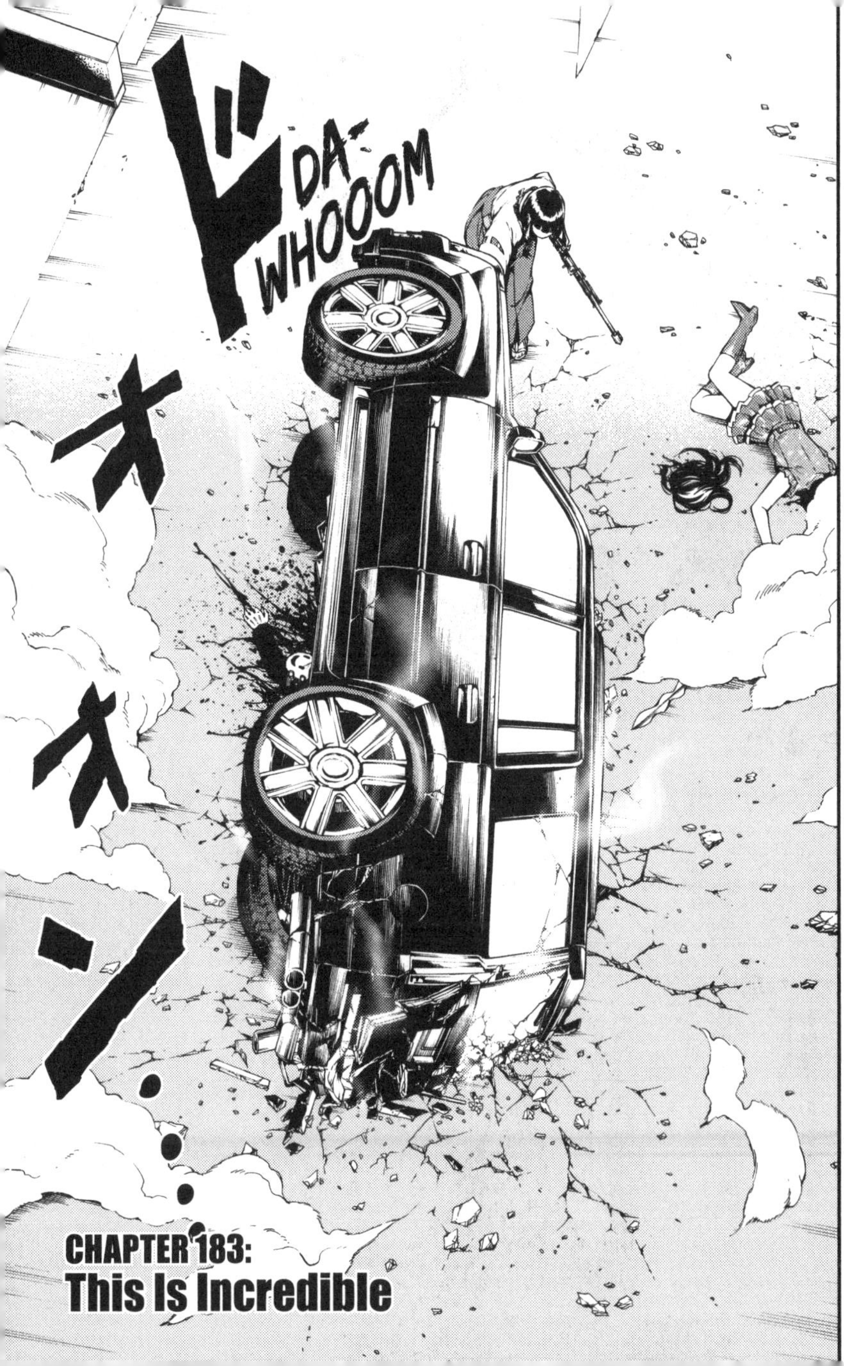
ドオオン…
DA-WHOOOM

CHAPTER 183: This Is Incredible

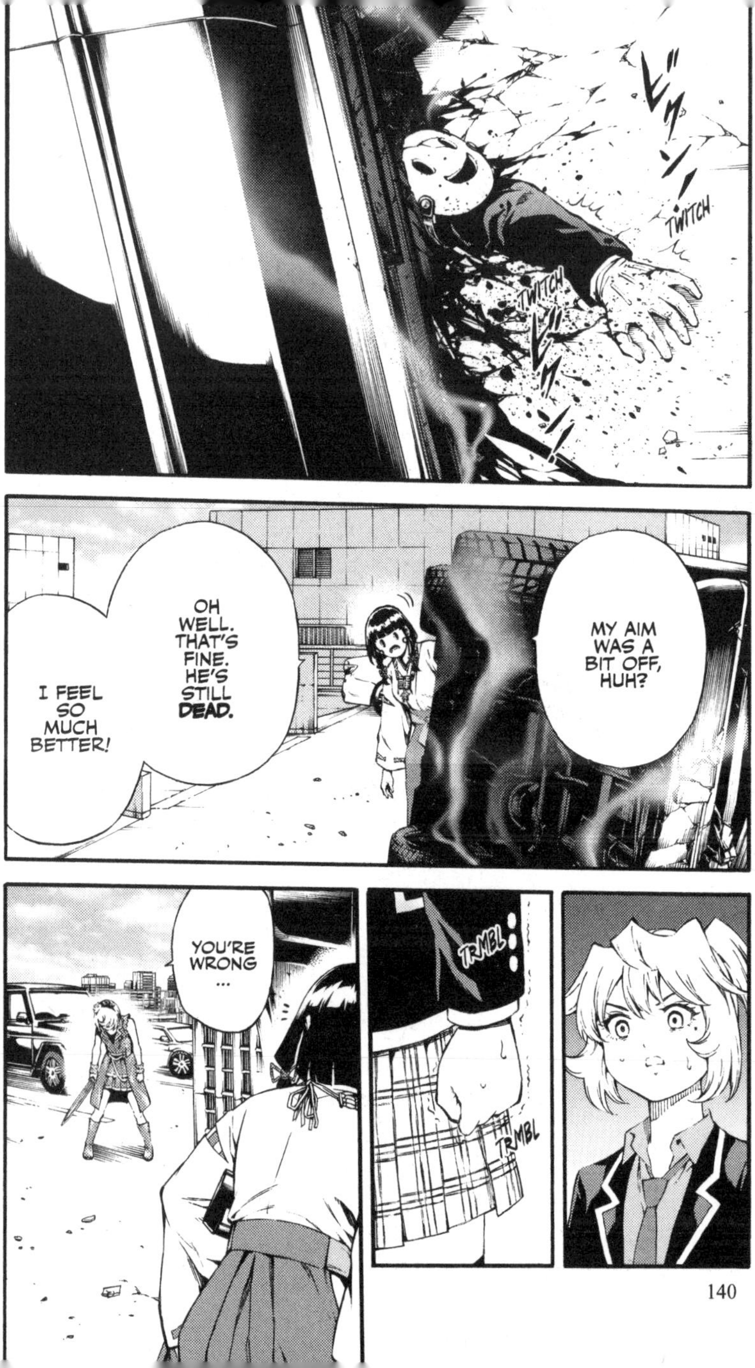
TWITCH
TWITCH
MY AIM WAS A BIT OFF, HUH?
OH WELL. THAT'S FINE. HE'S STILL **DEAD.**
I FEEL SO MUCH BETTER!
TRMBL
TRMBL
YOU'RE WRONG ...

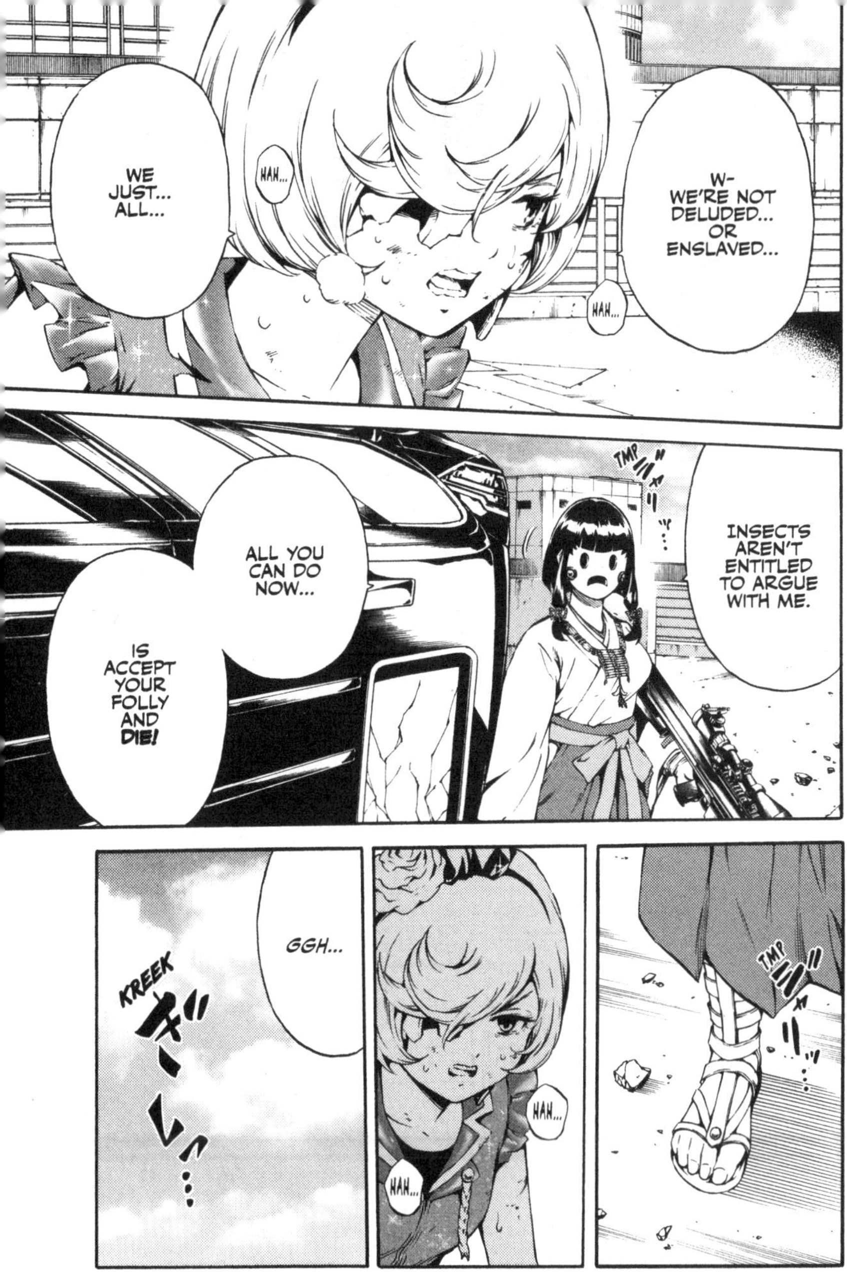
W- WE'RE NOT DELUDED... OR ENSLAVED...
HAH...
HAH...
WE JUST... ALL...
TMP
INSECTS AREN'T ENTITLED TO ARGUE WITH ME.
ALL YOU CAN DO NOW...
IS ACCEPT YOUR FOLLY AND DIE!
TMP
HAH...
HAH...
GGH...
KREEK

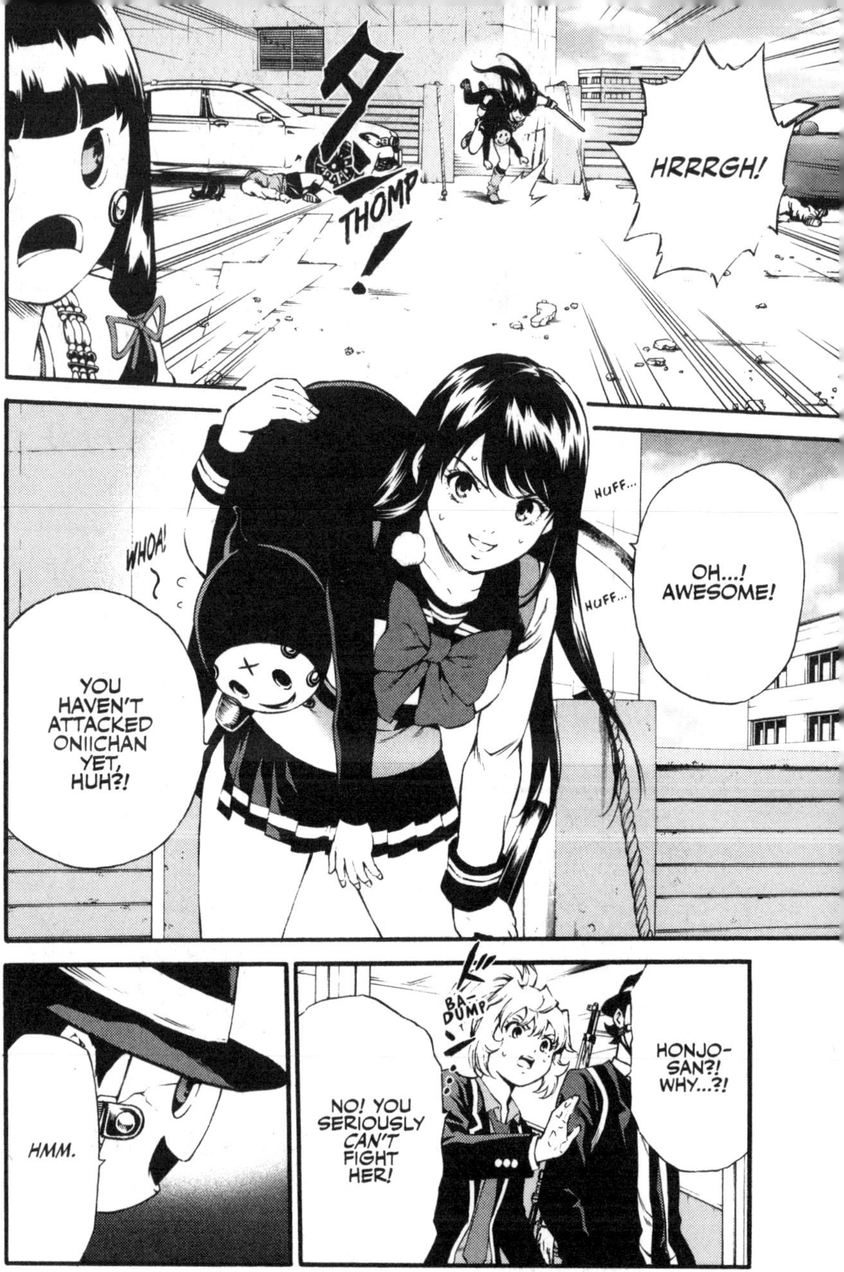
HRRRGH!
タ
THOMP
HUFF...
HUFF...
OH...! AWESOME!
WHOA!
YOU HAVEN'T ATTACKED ONIICHAN YET, HUH?!
HONJO-SAN?! WHY...?!
BA-DUMP
NO! YOU SERIOUSLY CAN'T FIGHT HER!
HMM.

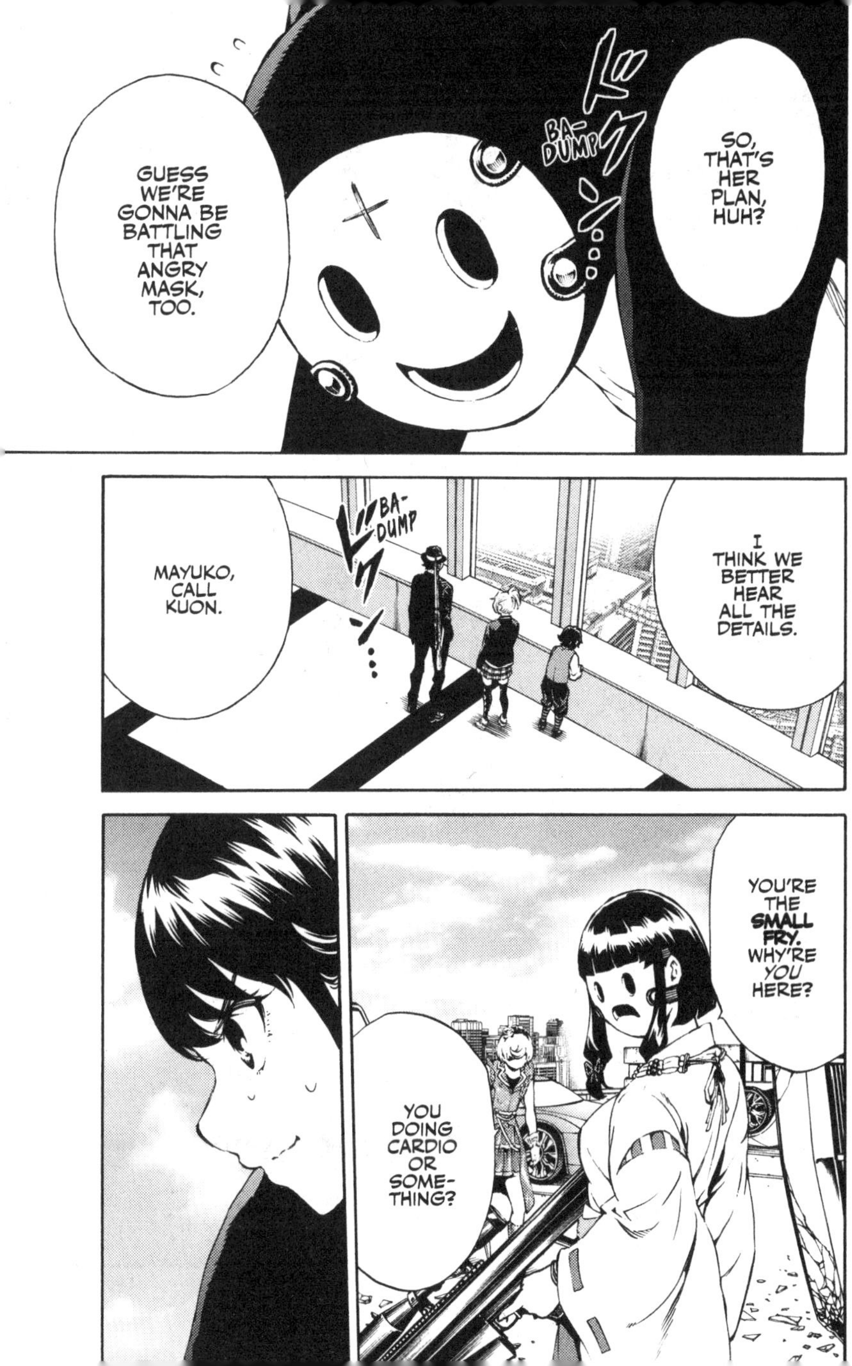
SO, THAT'S HER PLAN, HUH?
BA-DUMP
GUESS WE'RE GONNA BE BATTLING THAT ANGRY MASK, TOO.
I THINK WE BETTER HEAR ALL THE DETAILS.
BA-DUMP
MAYUKO, CALL KUON.
YOU'RE THE **SMALL FRY.** WHY'RE *YOU* HERE?
YOU DOING CARDIO OR SOMETHING?

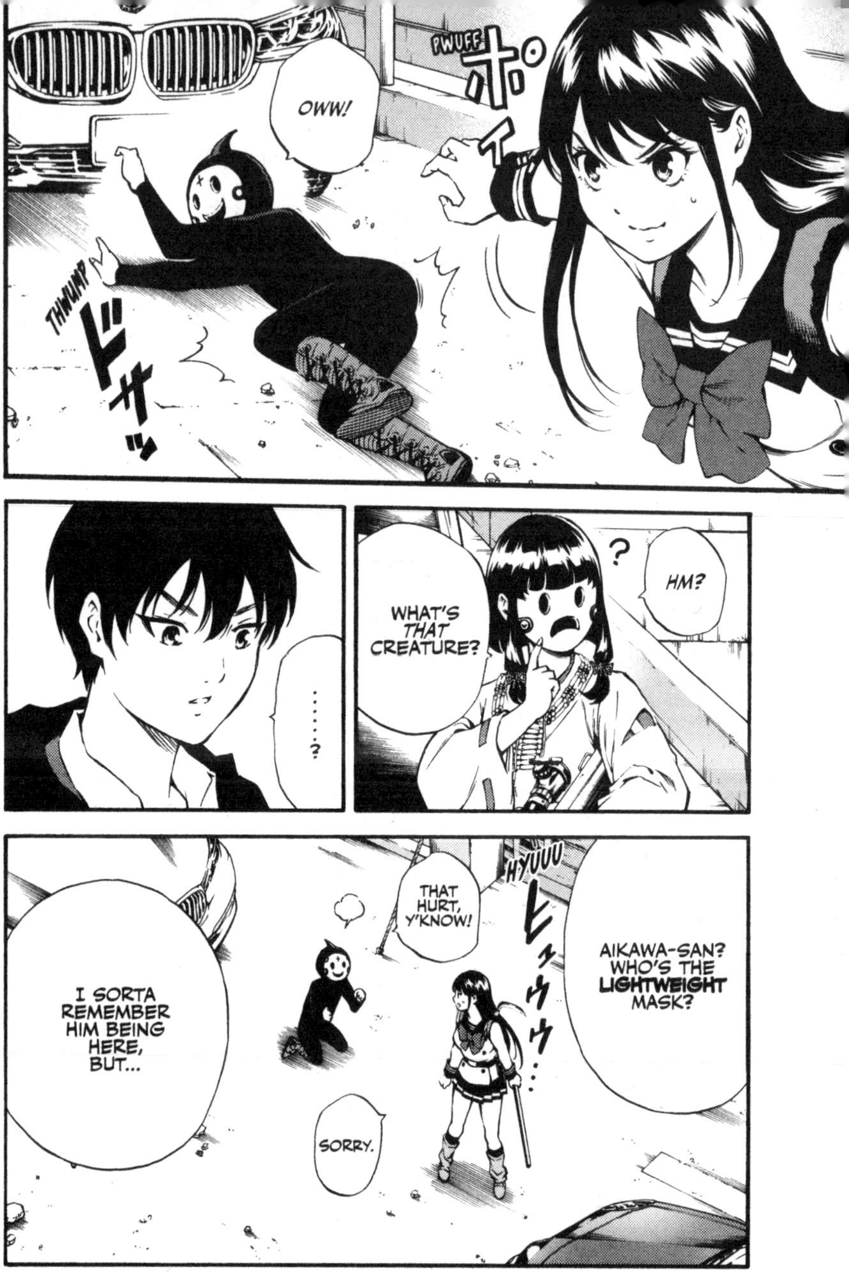

PWUFF
ポイ
OWW!
THWUMP
ドサッ
HM?
?
WHAT'S THAT CREATURE?
......?
HYUUU
ヒュウウ...
AIKAWA-SAN? WHO'S THE LIGHTWEIGHT MASK?
THAT HURT, Y'KNOW!
SORRY.
I SORTA REMEMBER HIM BEING HERE, BUT...

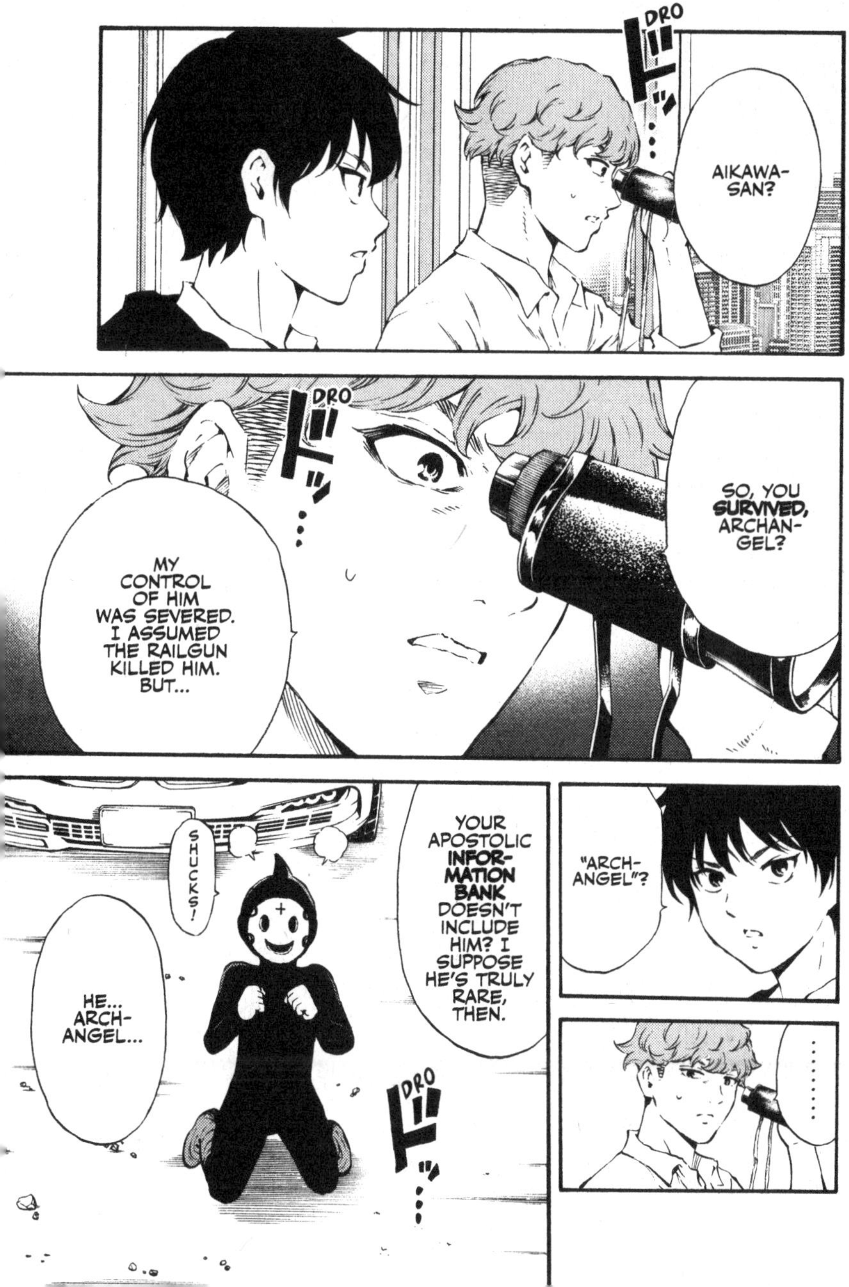
AIKAWA-SAN?
DRO
...
SO, YOU **SURVIVED,** ARCHANGEL?
DRO
...
MY CONTROL OF HIM WAS SEVERED. I ASSUMED THE RAILGUN KILLED HIM. BUT...
"ARCH-ANGEL"?
......
YOUR APOSTOLIC **INFORMATION BANK** DOESN'T INCLUDE HIM? I SUPPOSE HE'S TRULY RARE, THEN.
SHUCKS!
HE... ARCH-ANGEL...
DRO
...

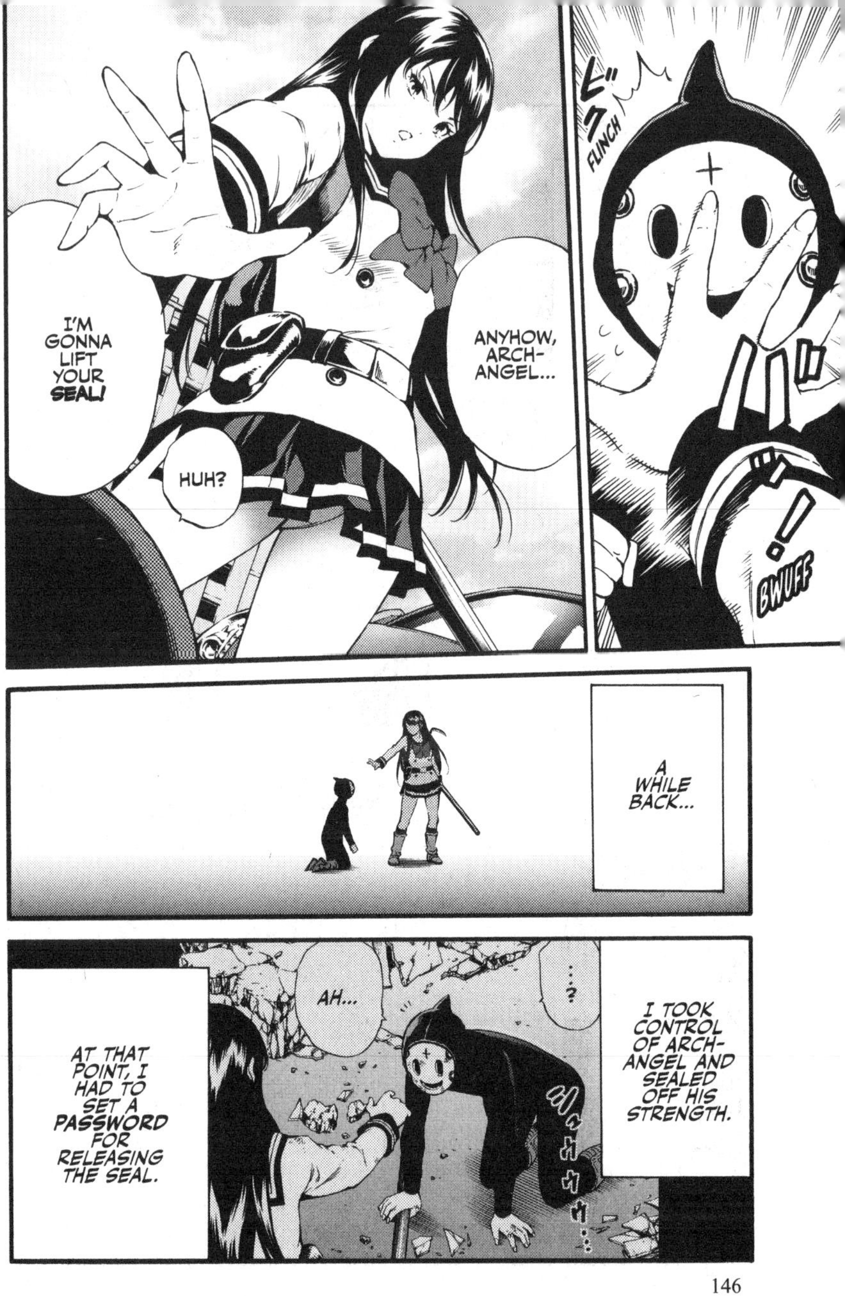
ビク
FLINCH
!
BWUFF
ANYHOW, ARCH-ANGEL...
I'M GONNA LIFT YOUR **SEAL!**
HUH?
A WHILE BACK...
I TOOK CONTROL OF ARCH-ANGEL AND SEALED OFF HIS STRENGTH.
...?
AH...
AT THAT POINT, I HAD TO SET A **PASSWORD** FOR RELEASING THE SEAL.

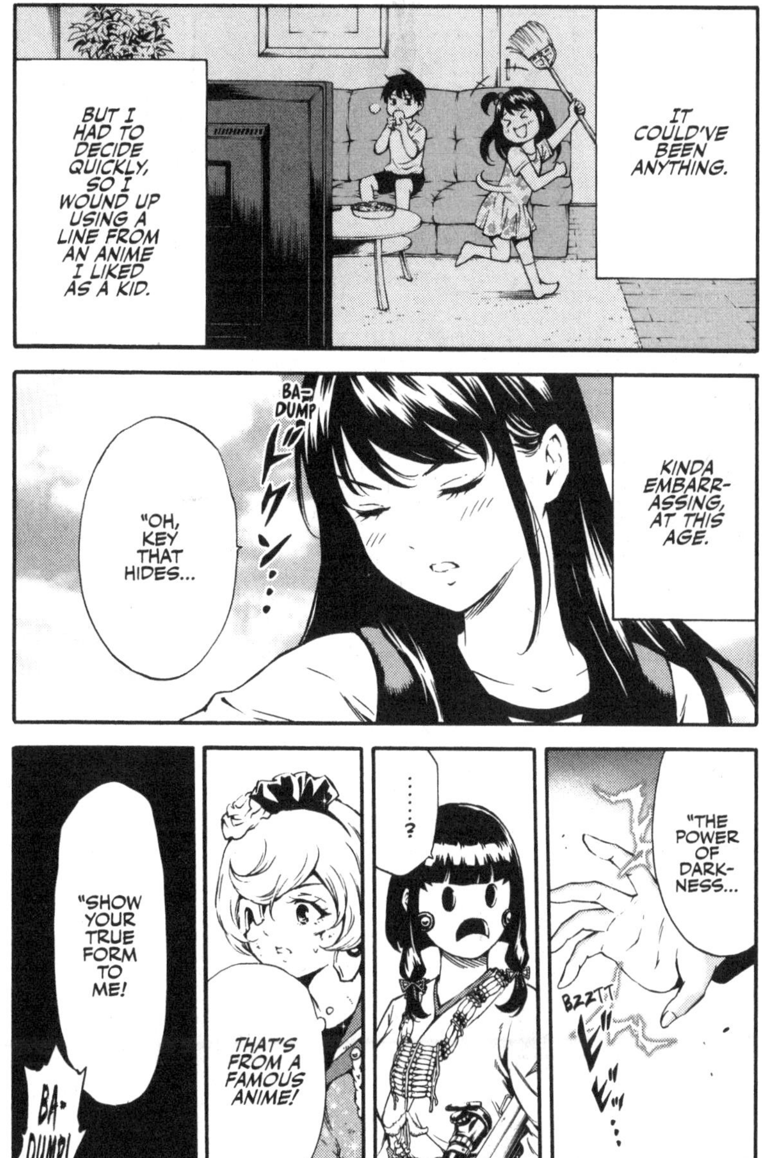
IT COULD'VE BEEN ANYTHING.
BUT I HAD TO DECIDE QUICKLY, SO I WOUND UP USING A LINE FROM AN ANIME I LIKED AS A KID.
KINDA EMBARRASSING, AT THIS AGE.
BA-DUMP
"OH, KEY THAT HIDES...
"THE POWER OF DARKNESS...
BZZTT
......?
THAT'S FROM A FAMOUS ANIME!
"SHOW YOUR TRUE FORM TO ME!
BA-DUMP!

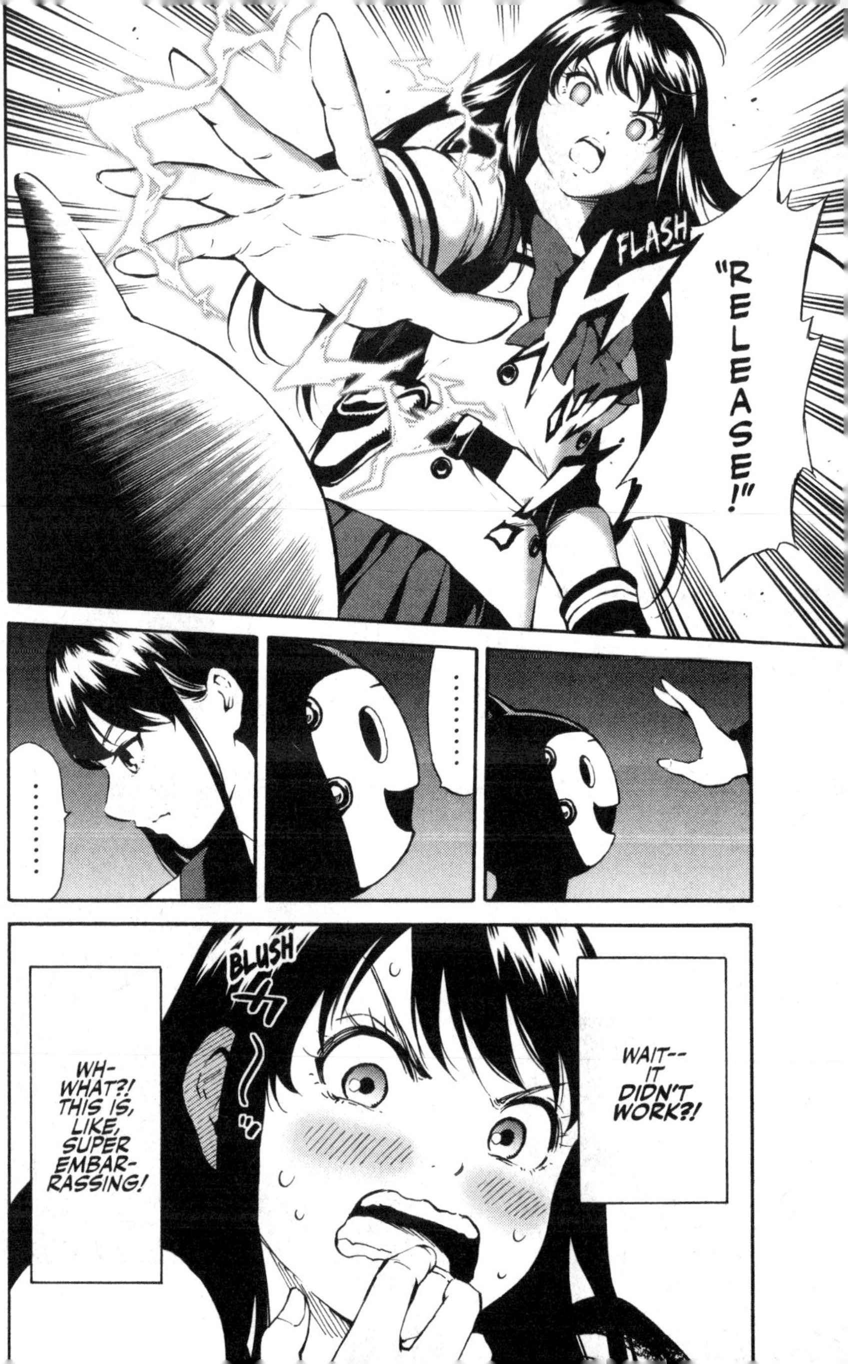
"RELEASE!"
FLASH
......
......
WAIT-- IT DIDN'T WORK?!
BLUSH
WH-WHAT?! THIS IS, LIKE, SUPER EMBAR-RASSING!

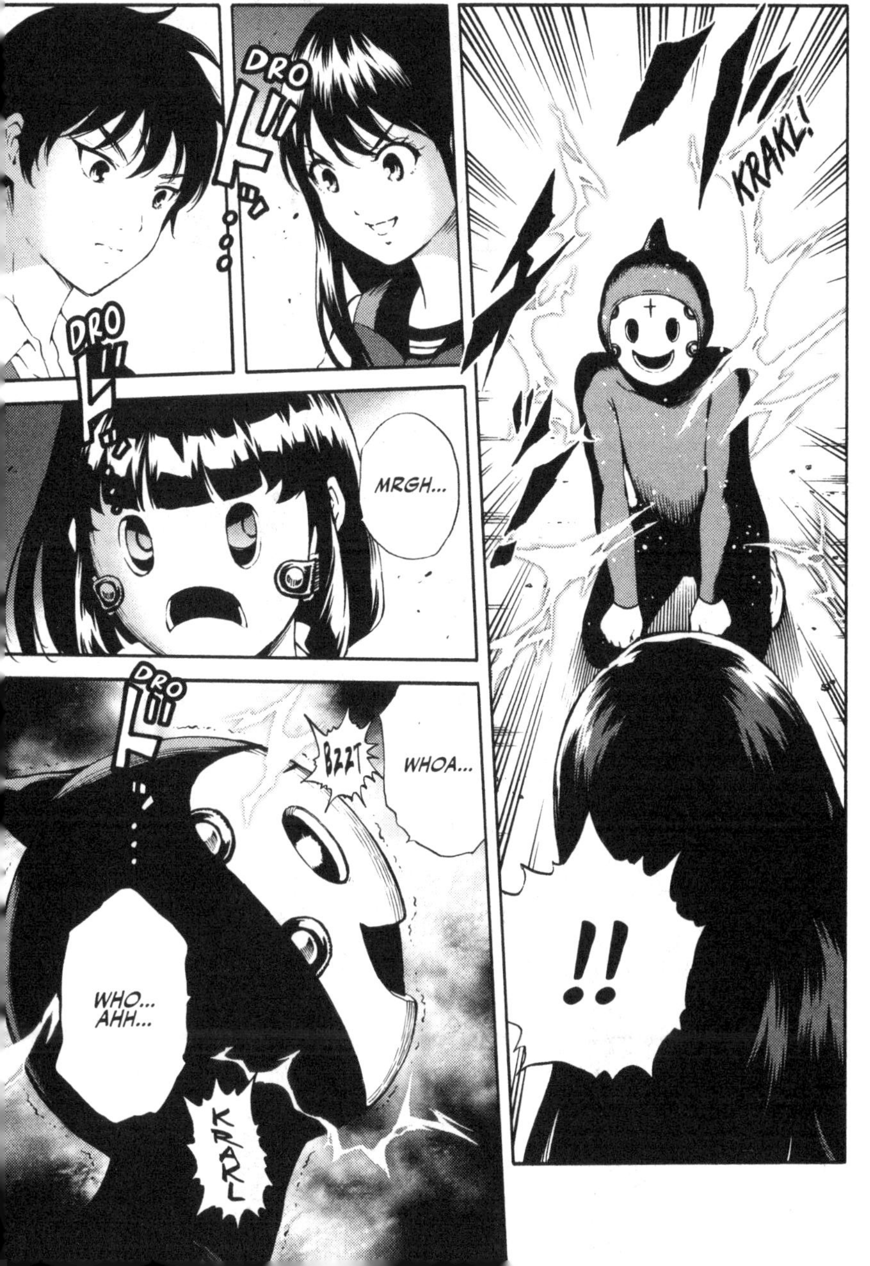
KRAKL!
!!
DRO
DRO
MRGH...
DRO
WHOA...
BZZT
WHO...
AHH...
KRAKL

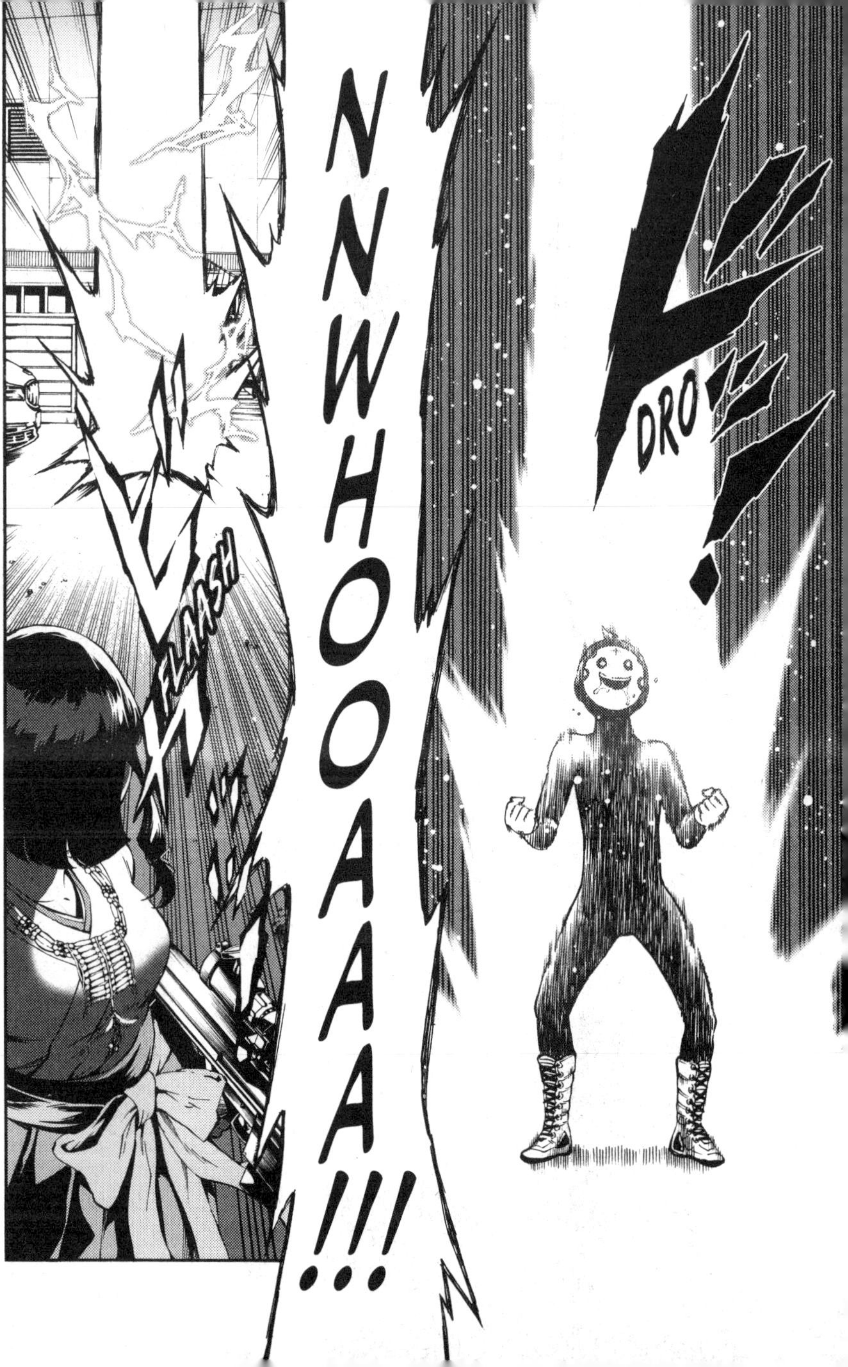
DRO
NNWHOOOAAAA!!!
FLAASH

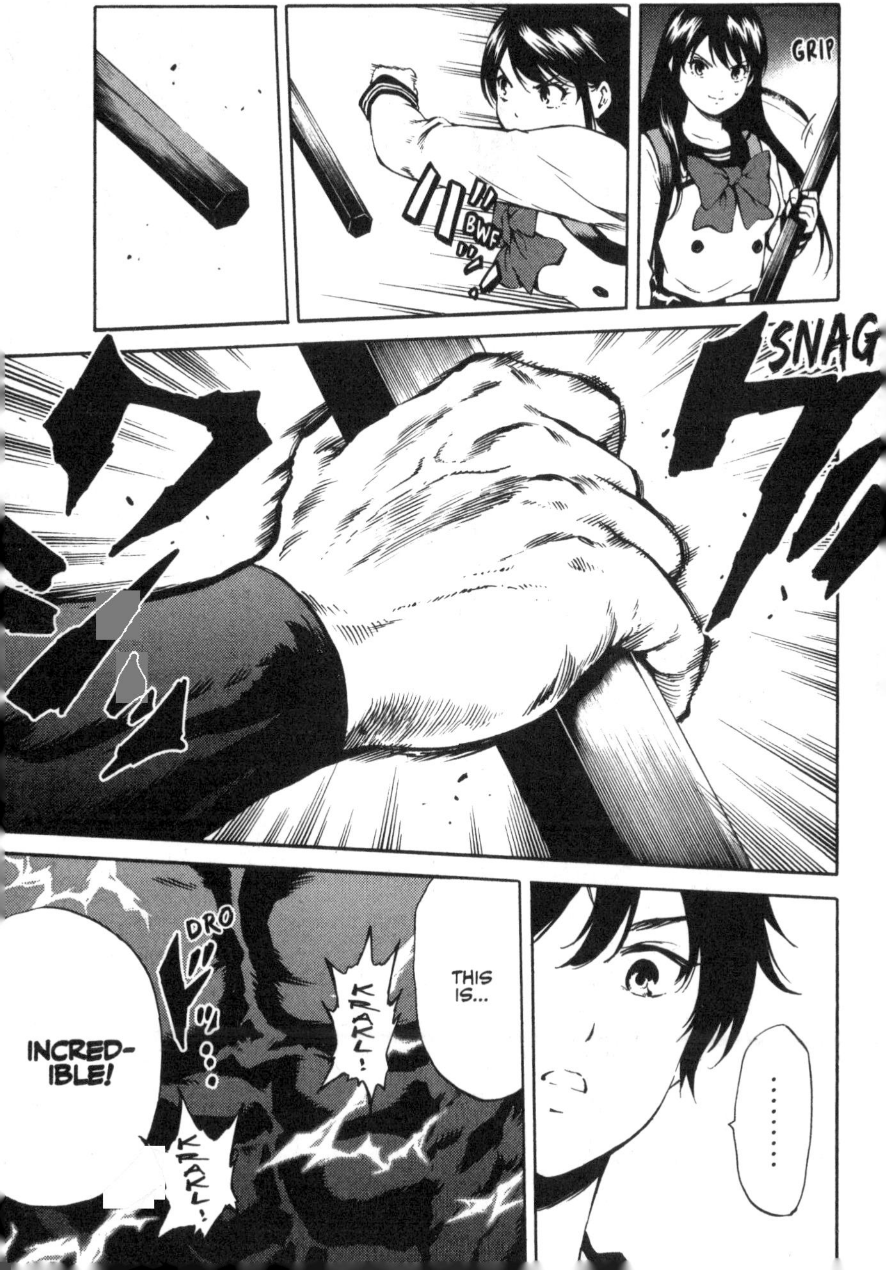
GRIP
BWF
SNAG
....
THIS IS...
KRAKL!
DRO
INCRED-IBLE!
KRAKL!

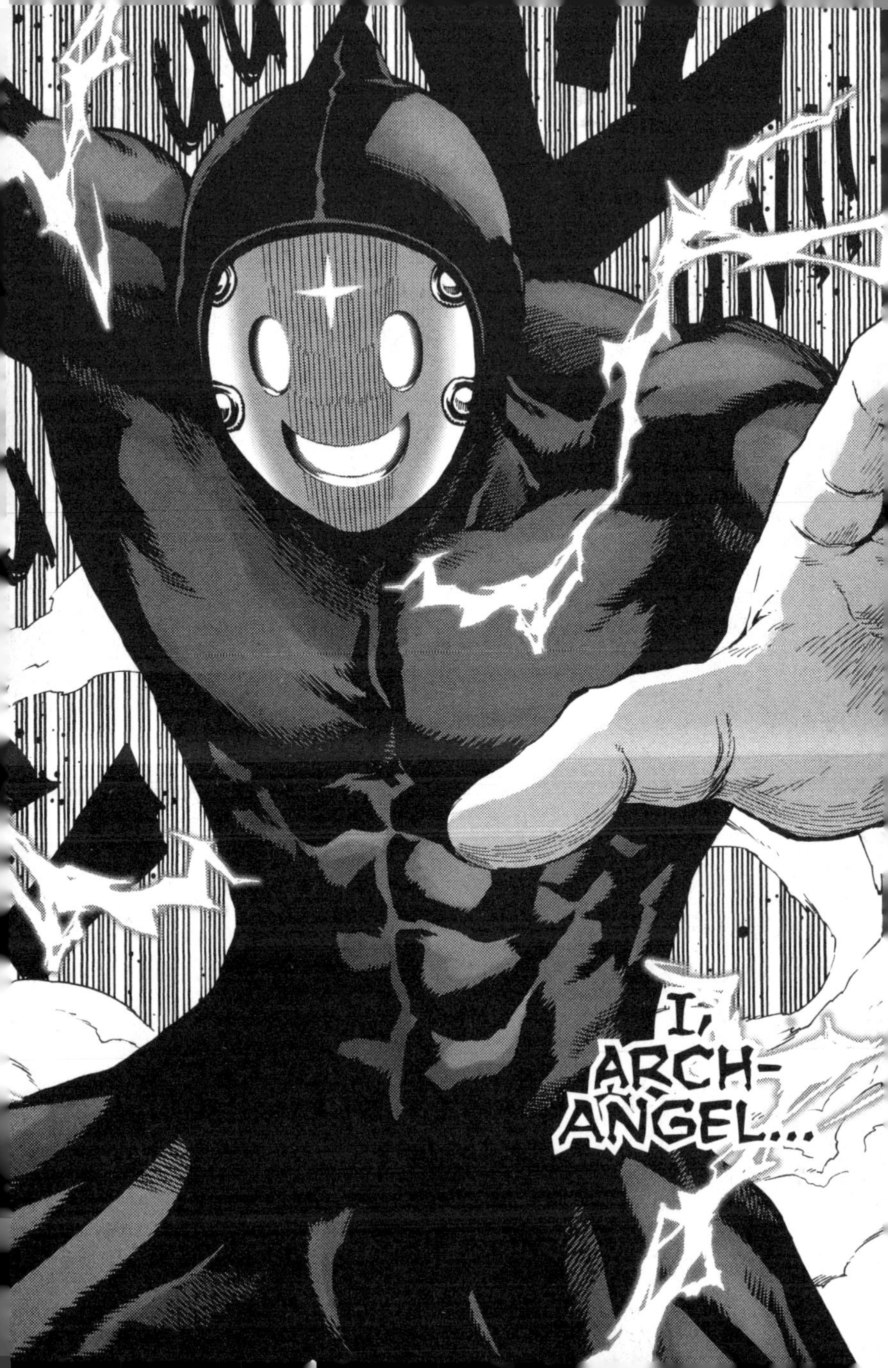
I, ARCH-ANGEL...

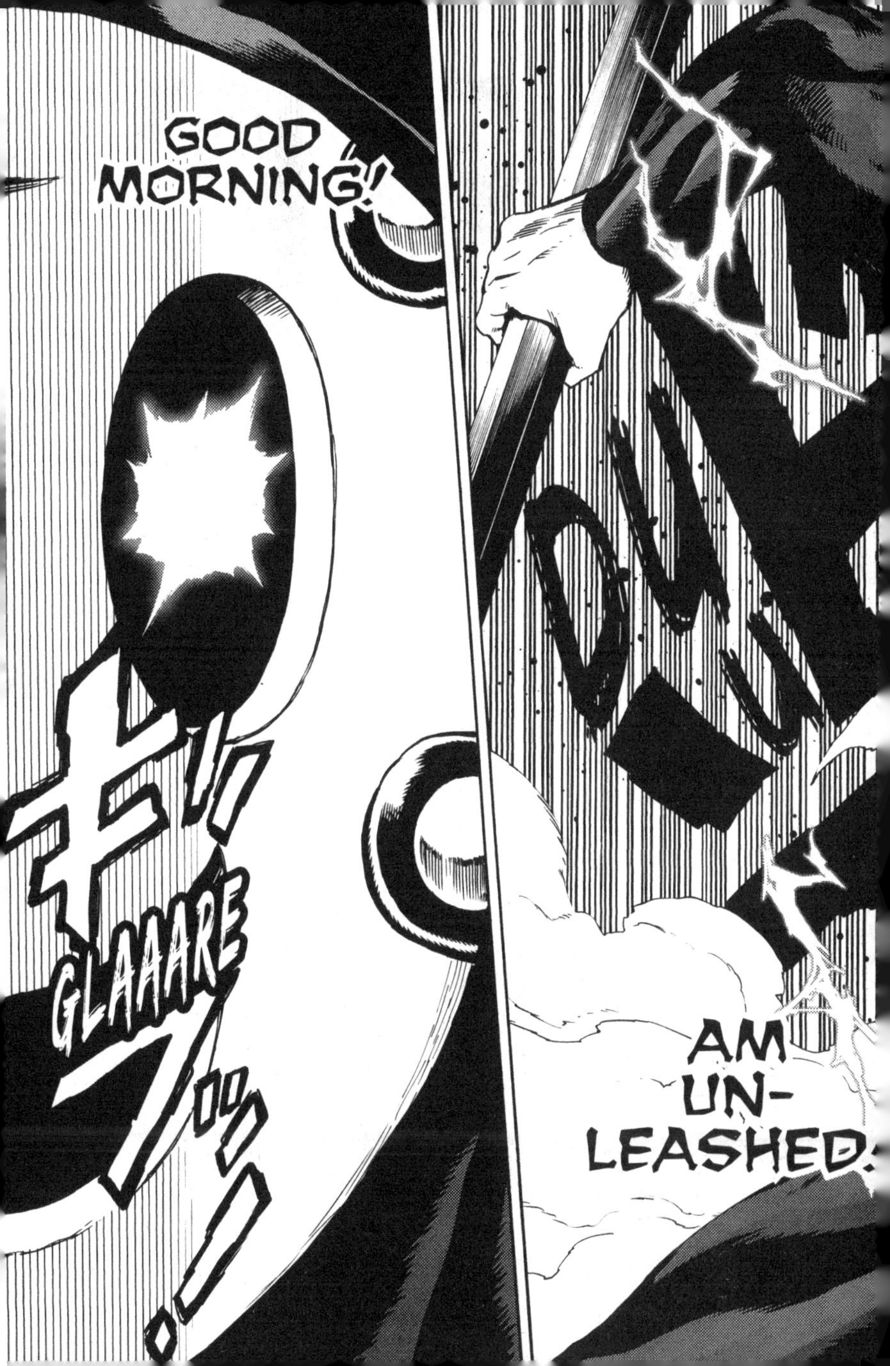
AM UN-LEASHED.
GOOD MORNING!
GLAAARE

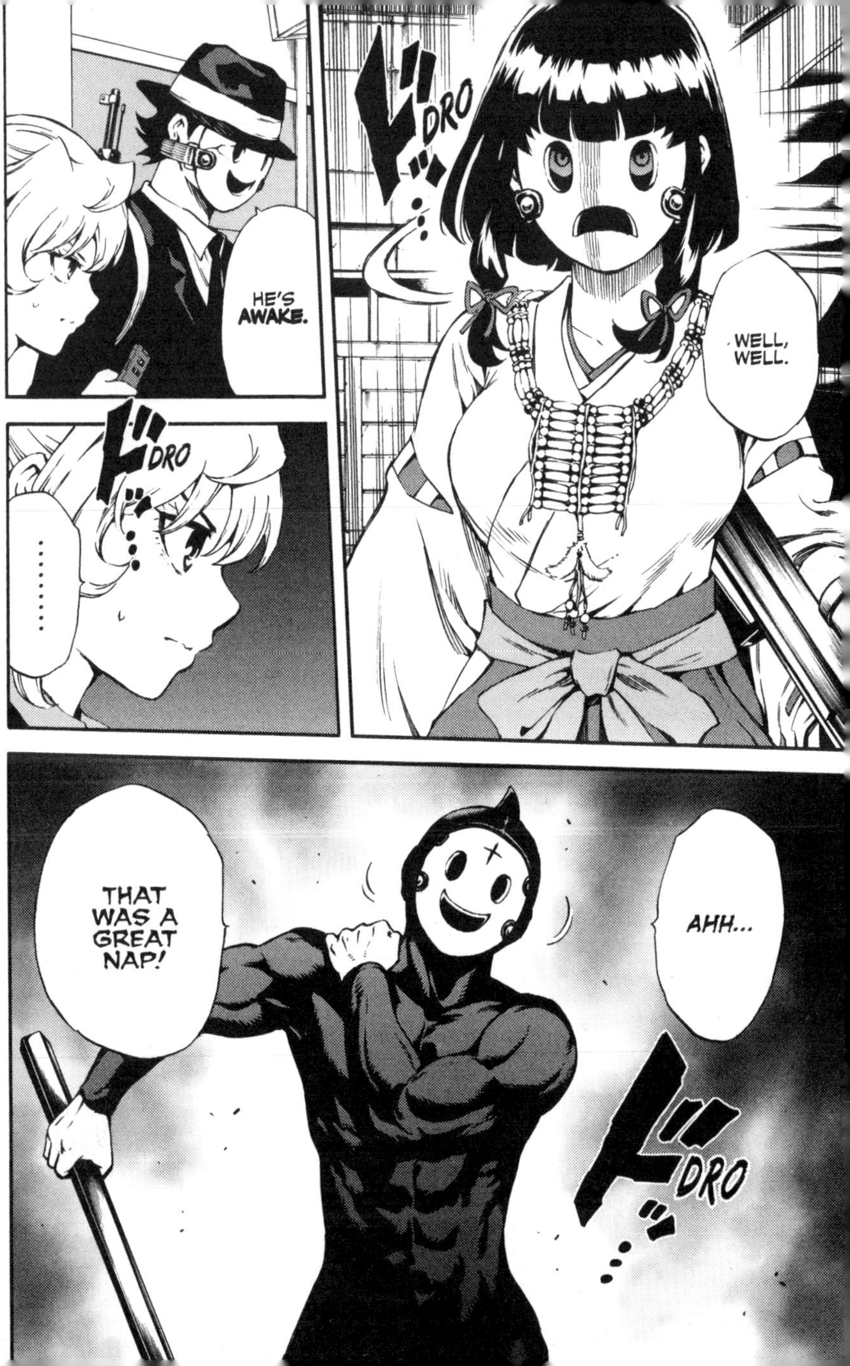
DRO
WELL, WELL.
HE'S AWAKE.
DRO
....
AHH...
THAT WAS A GREAT NAP!
DRO

HIGH-RISE
INVASION

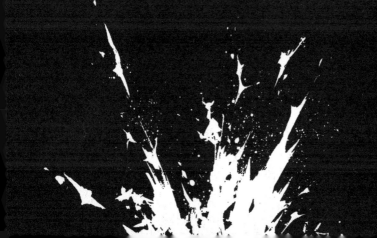

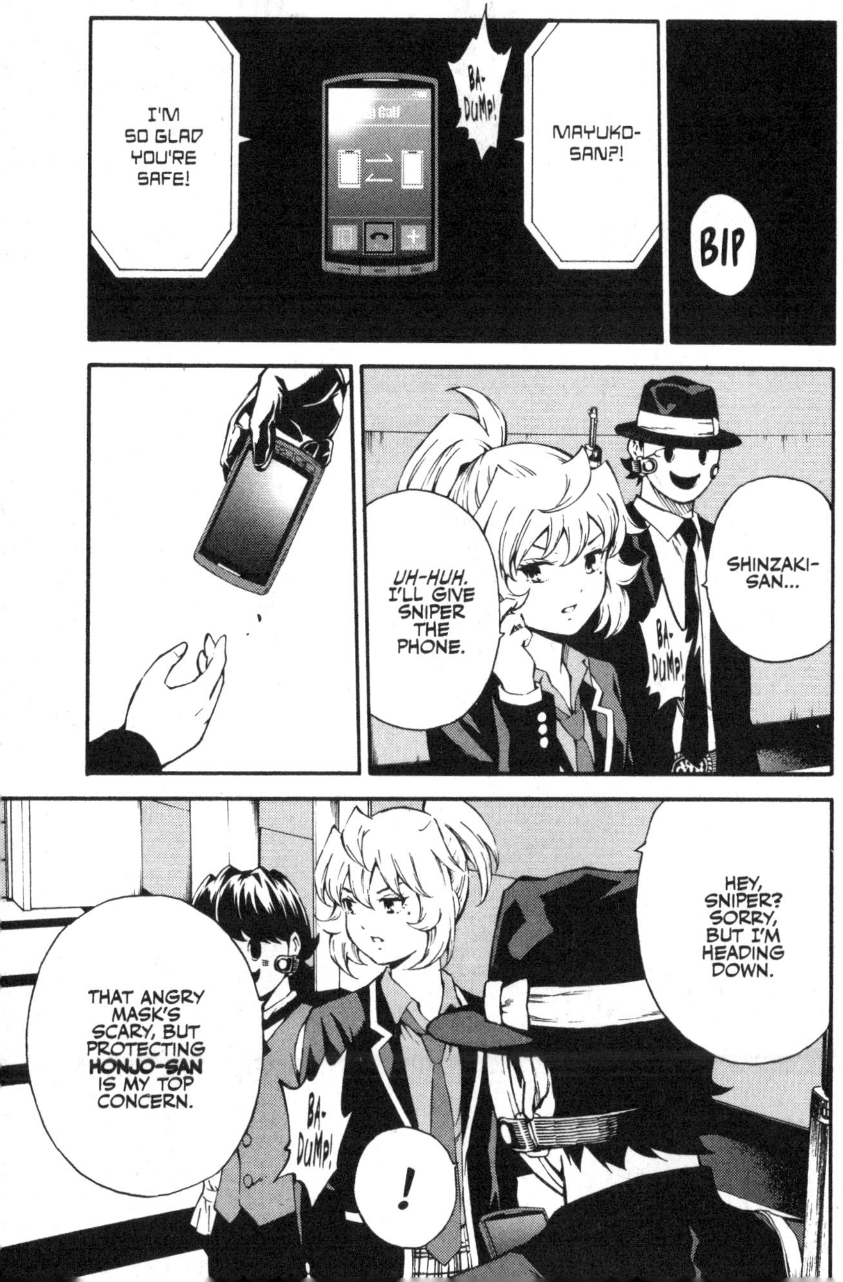
BIP
MAYUKO-SAN?!
BA-DUMP!
I'M SO GLAD YOU'RE SAFE!
SHINZAKI-SAN...
BA-DUMP!
UH-HUH. I'LL GIVE SNIPER THE PHONE.
HEY, SNIPER? SORRY, BUT I'M HEADING DOWN.
THAT ANGRY MASK'S SCARY, BUT PROTECTING **HONJO-SAN** IS MY TOP CONCERN.
BA-DUMP!
!

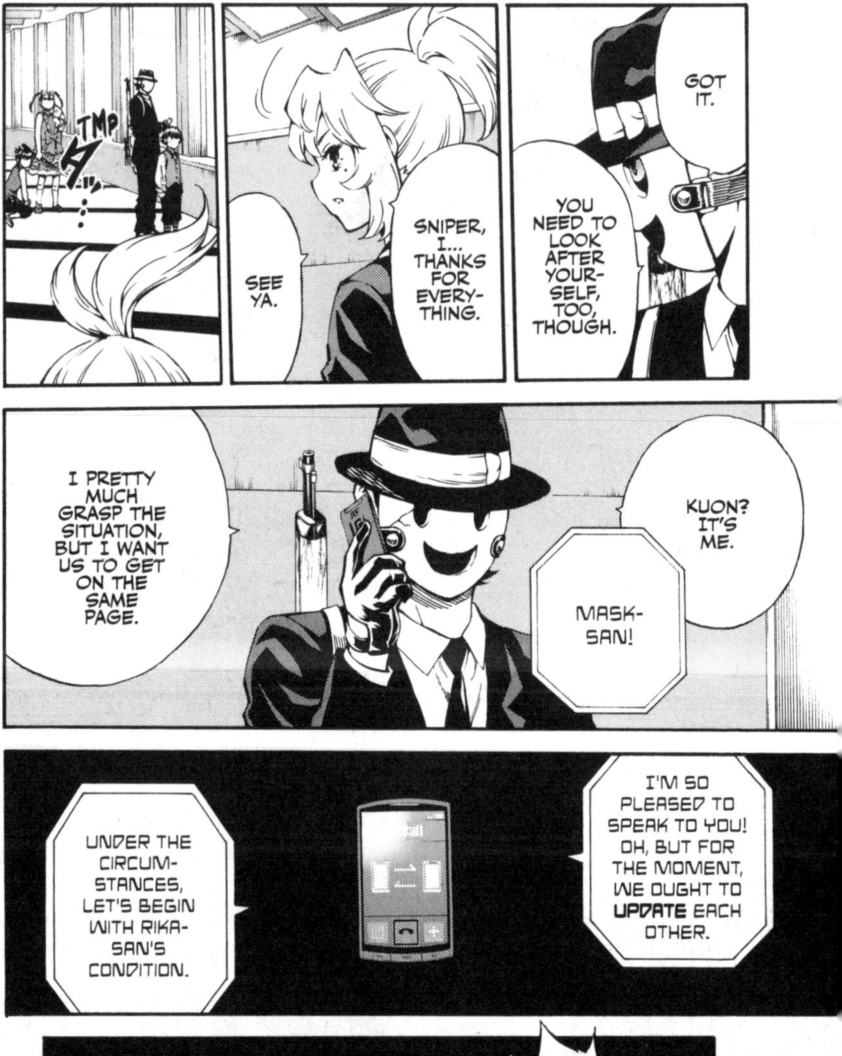
GOT IT.
YOU NEED TO LOOK AFTER YOURSELF, TOO, THOUGH.
SNIPER, I... THANKS FOR EVERYTHING.
SEE YA.
TMP
KUON? IT'S ME.
MASK-SAN!
I PRETTY MUCH GRASP THE SITUATION, BUT I WANT US TO GET ON THE SAME PAGE.
I'M SO PLEASED TO SPEAK TO YOU! OH, BUT FOR THE MOMENT, WE OUGHT TO UPDATE EACH OTHER.
UNDER THE CIRCUMSTANCES, LET'S BEGIN WITH RIKA-SAN'S CONDITION.
BA-DUMP!

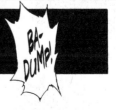

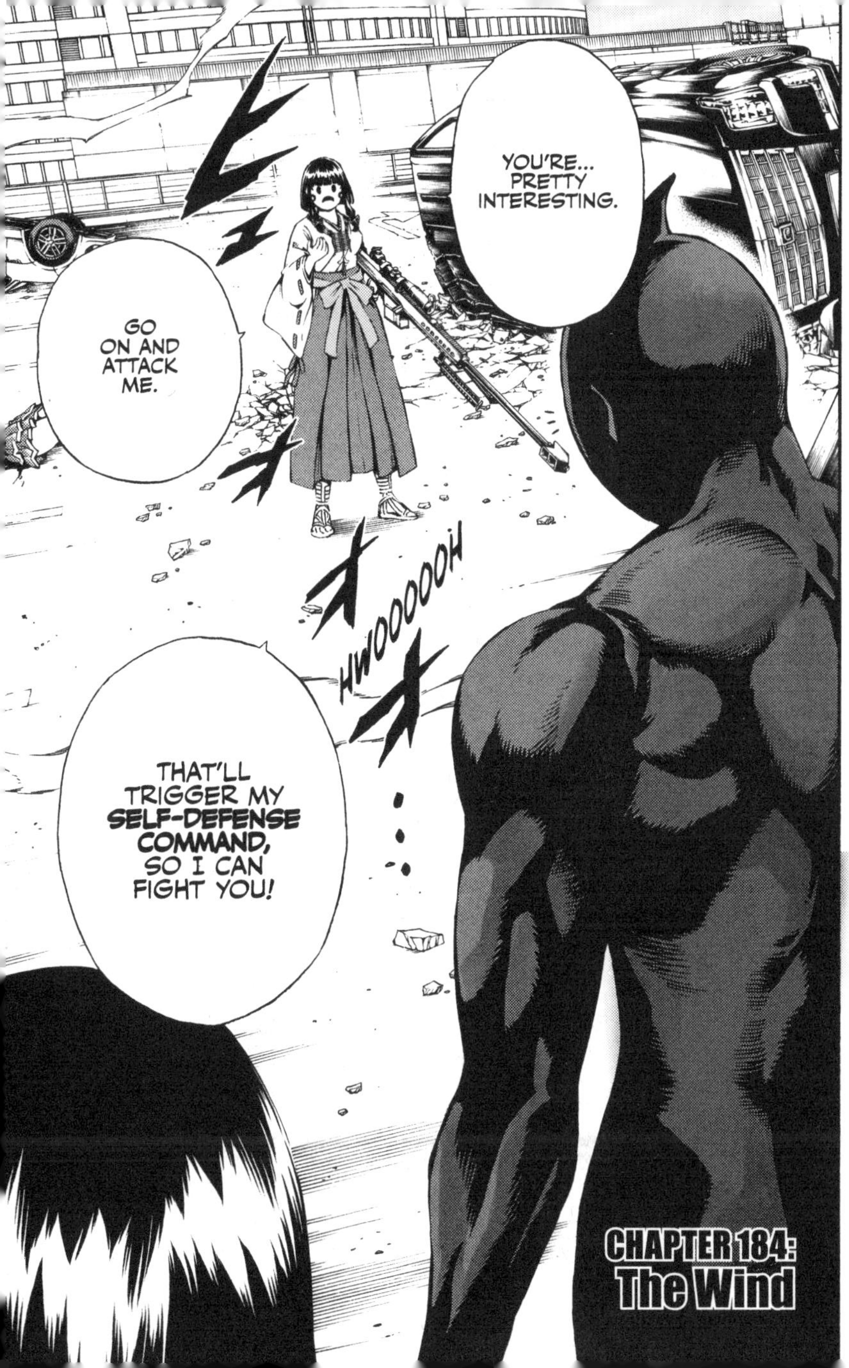
YOU'RE... PRETTY INTERESTING.
GO ON AND ATTACK ME.
HWOOOOOOH
...
THAT'LL TRIGGER MY **SELF-DEFENSE COMMAND,** SO I CAN FIGHT YOU!
CHAPTER 184: The Wind

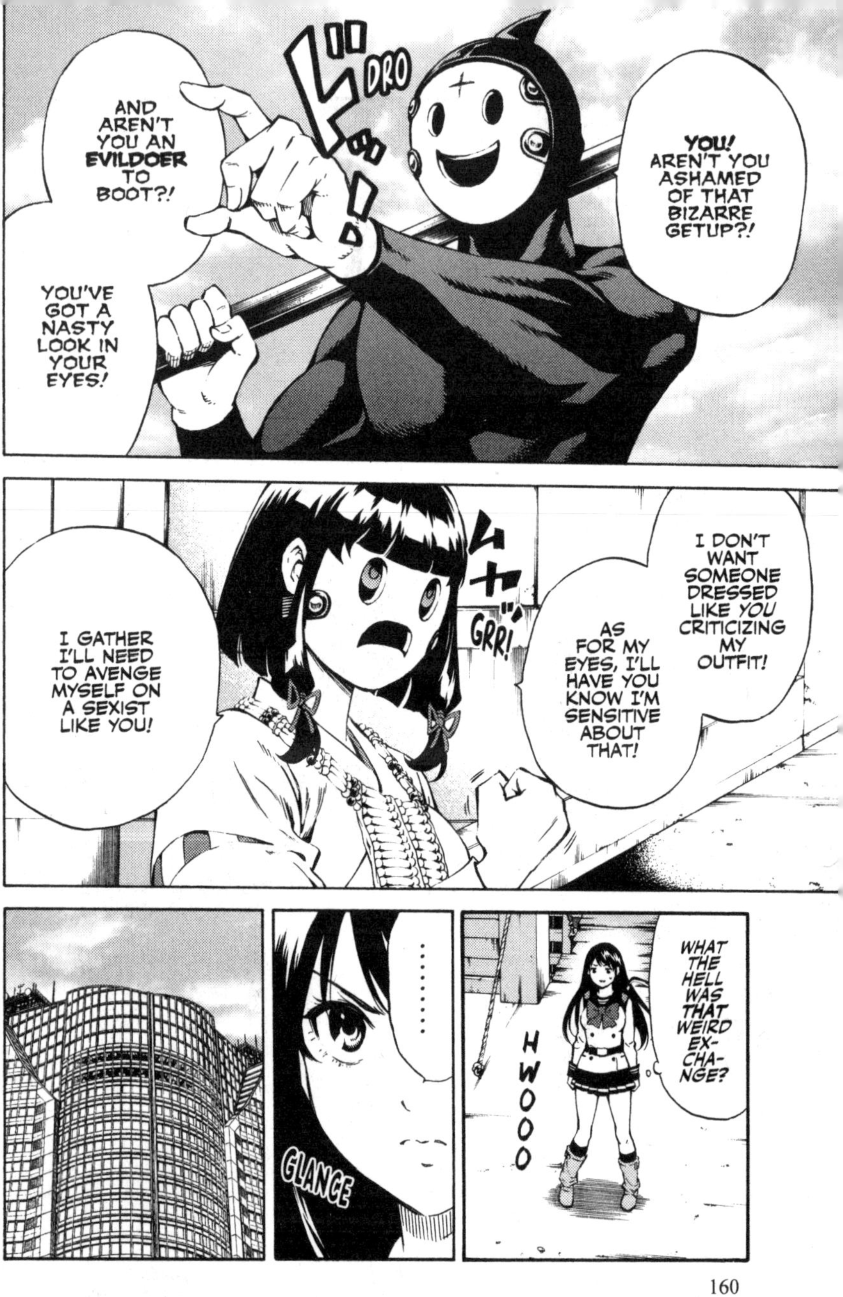

YOU! AREN'T YOU ASHAMED OF THAT BIZARRE GETUP?!
DRO
AND AREN'T YOU AN EVILDOER TO BOOT?!
YOU'VE GOT A NASTY LOOK IN YOUR EYES!
I DON'T WANT SOMEONE DRESSED LIKE YOU CRITICIZING MY OUTFIT!
AS FOR MY EYES, I'LL HAVE YOU KNOW I'M SENSITIVE ABOUT THAT!
GRR!
I GATHER I'LL NEED TO AVENGE MYSELF ON A SEXIST LIKE YOU!
WHAT THE HELL WAS THAT WEIRD EX-CHA-NGE?
HWOOO
....
GLANCE

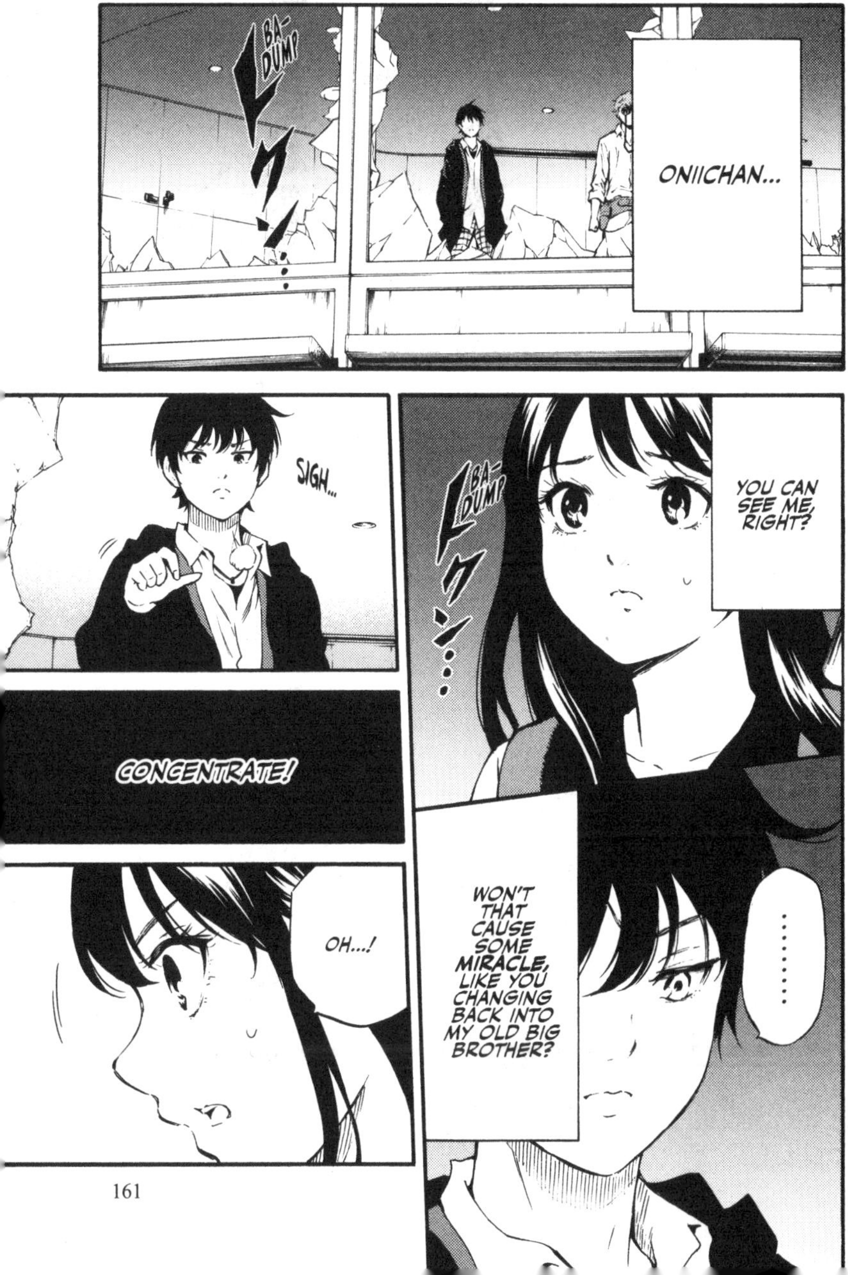
ONIICHAN...
BA-DUMP
YOU CAN SEE ME, RIGHT?
BA-DUMP
WON'T THAT CAUSE SOME MIRACLE, LIKE YOU CHANGING BACK INTO MY OLD BIG BROTHER?
....
SIGH...
CONCENTRATE!
OH...!

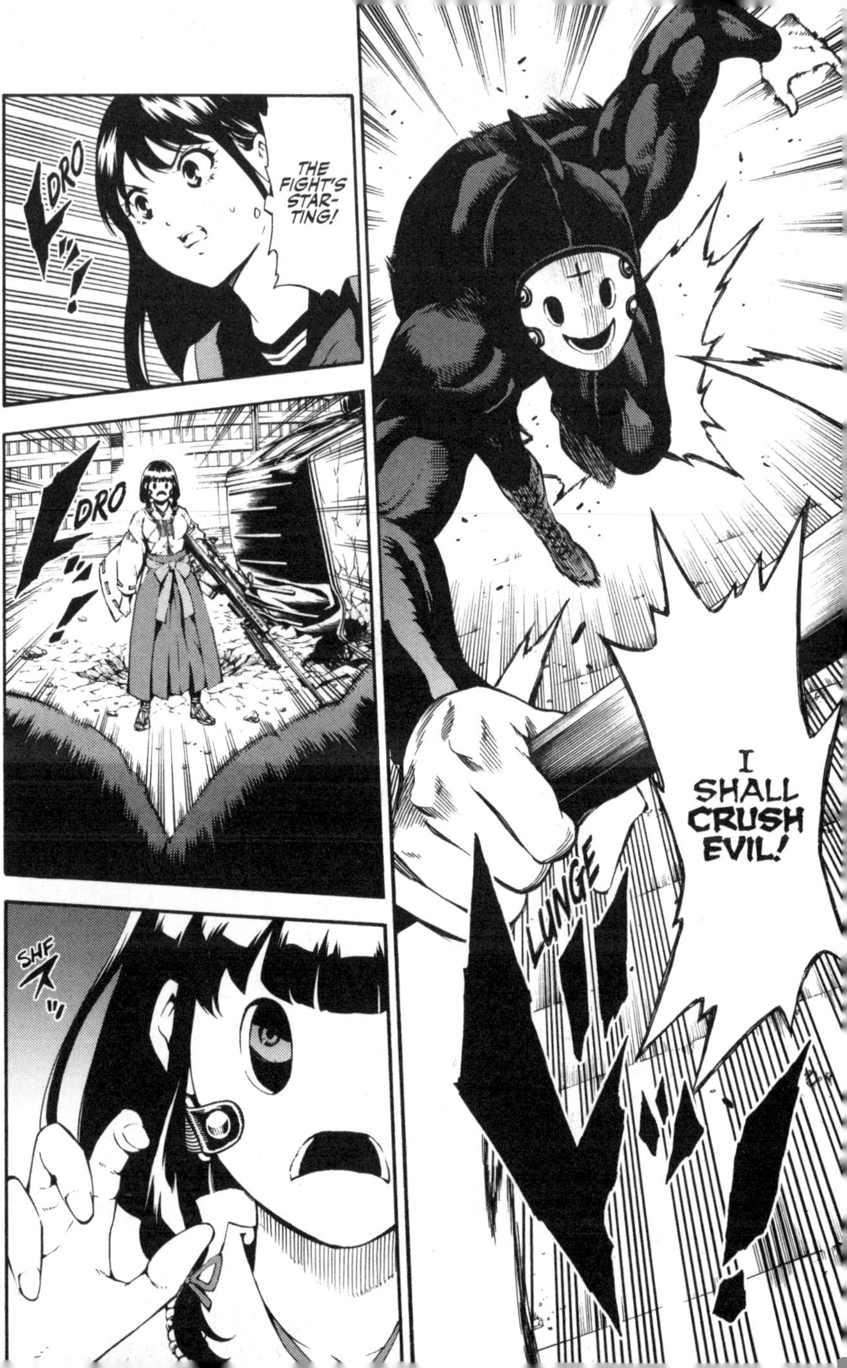
I SHALL CRUSH EVIL!
LUNGE
DRO
THE FIGHT'S STAR-TING!
DRO
SHF

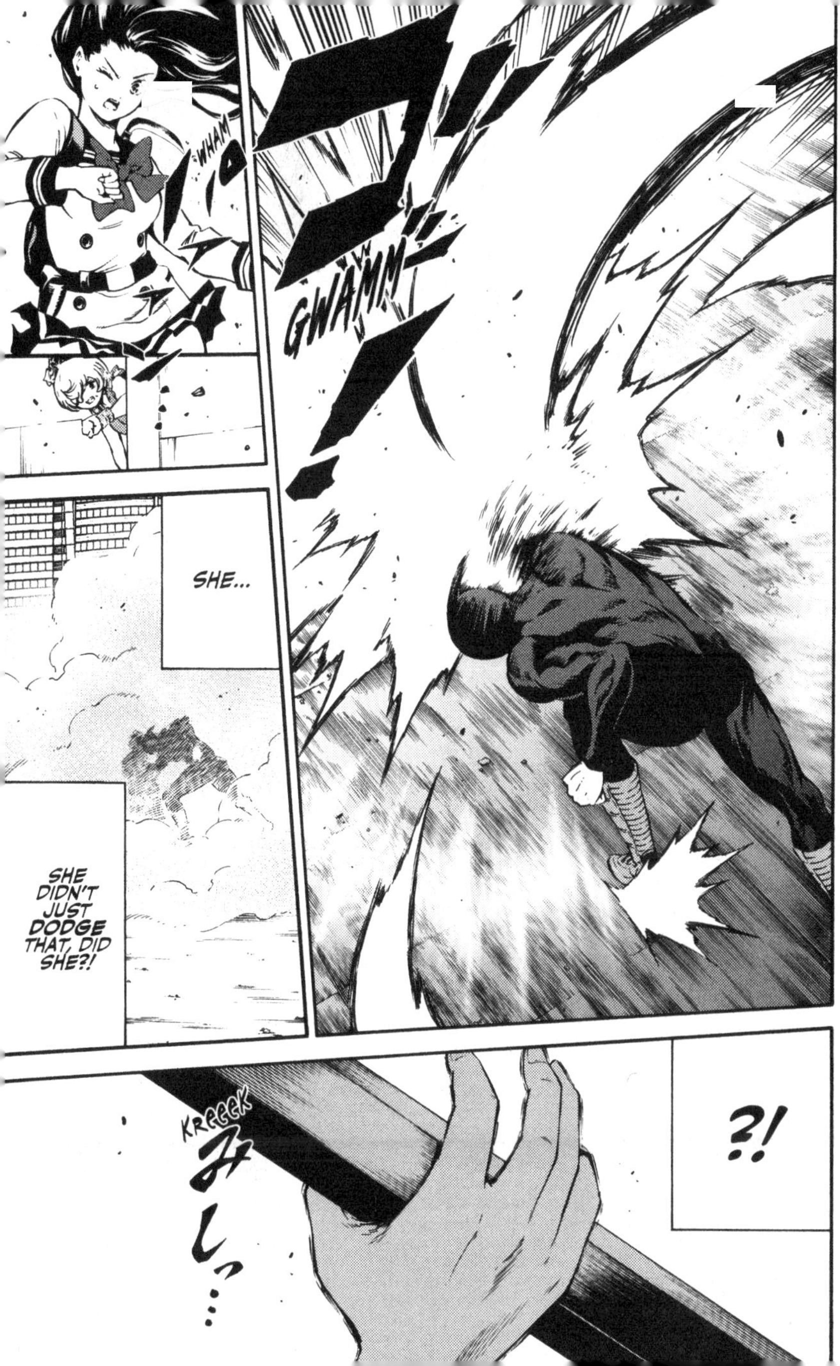
GWAMM
WHAM
SHE...
SHE DIDN'T JUST DODGE THAT, DID SHE?!
?!
KREEEK
みしっ…

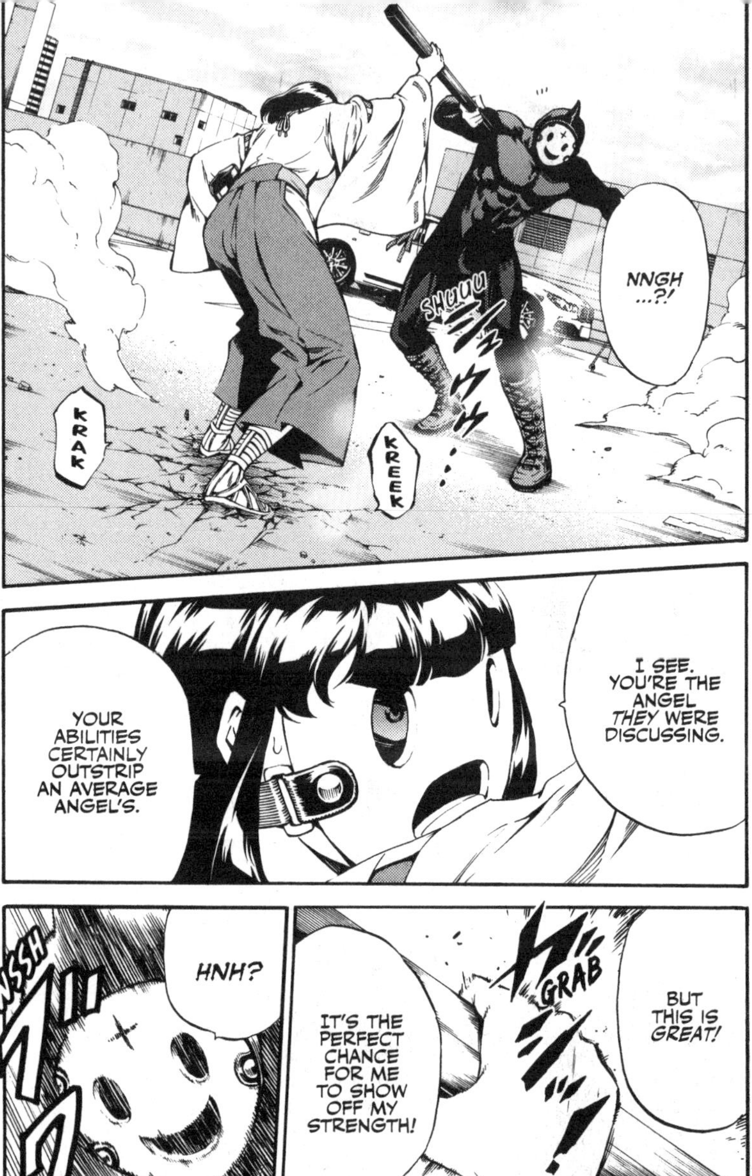
NNGH ...?!
SHUUU
KREEK
KRAK
I SEE. YOU'RE THE ANGEL *THEY* WERE DISCUSSING.
YOUR ABILITIES CERTAINLY OUTSTRIP AN AVERAGE ANGEL'S.
BUT THIS IS *GREAT!*
GRAB
IT'S THE PERFECT CHANCE FOR ME TO SHOW OFF MY STRENGTH!
HNH?
GWSSH

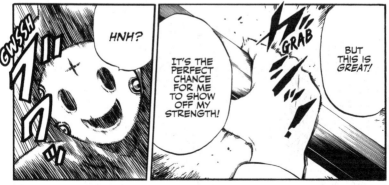

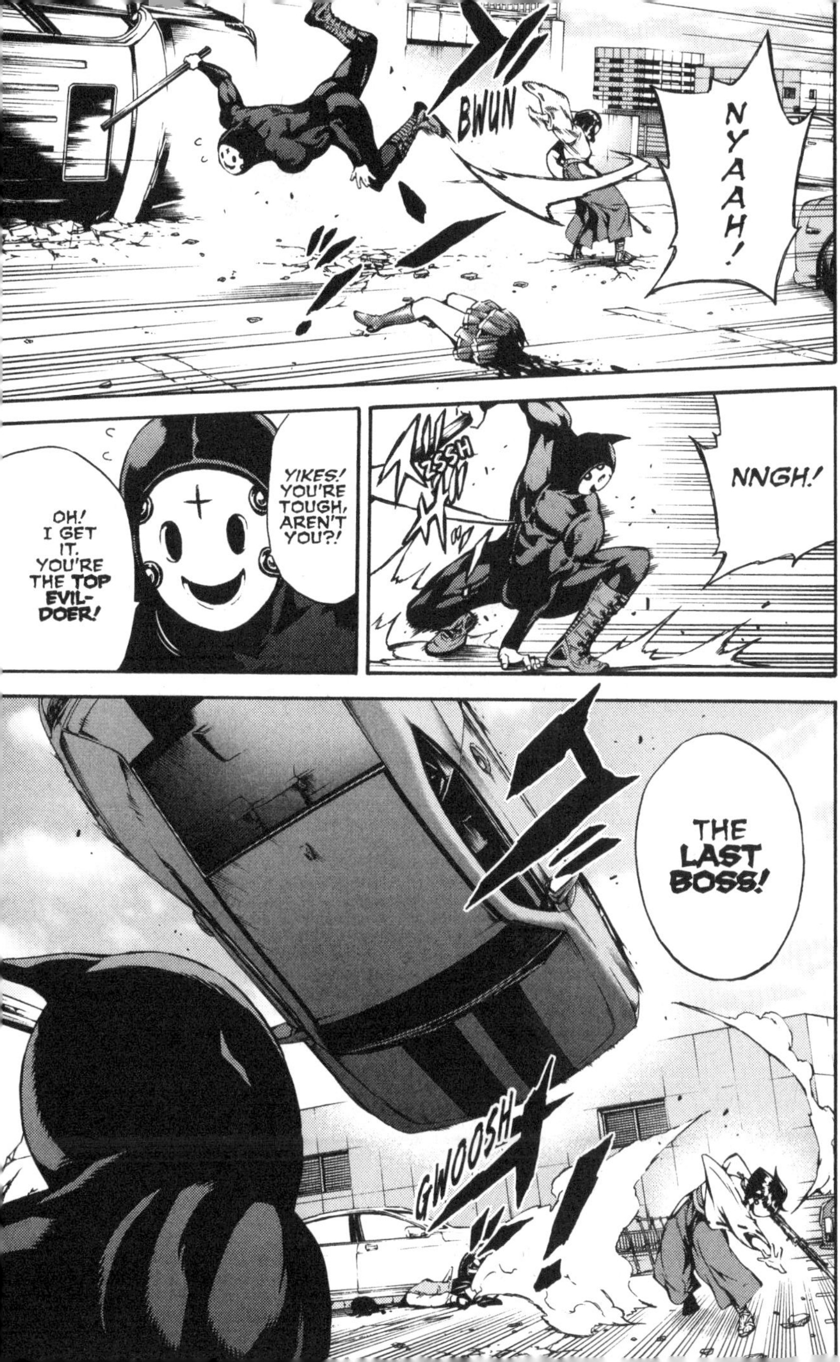
NYAAH!
BWUN
NNGH!
ZSSH
YIKES! YOU'RE TOUGH, AREN'T YOU?!
OH! I GET IT. YOU'RE THE **TOP EVIL-DOER**!
THE **LAST BOSS**!
GWOOSH

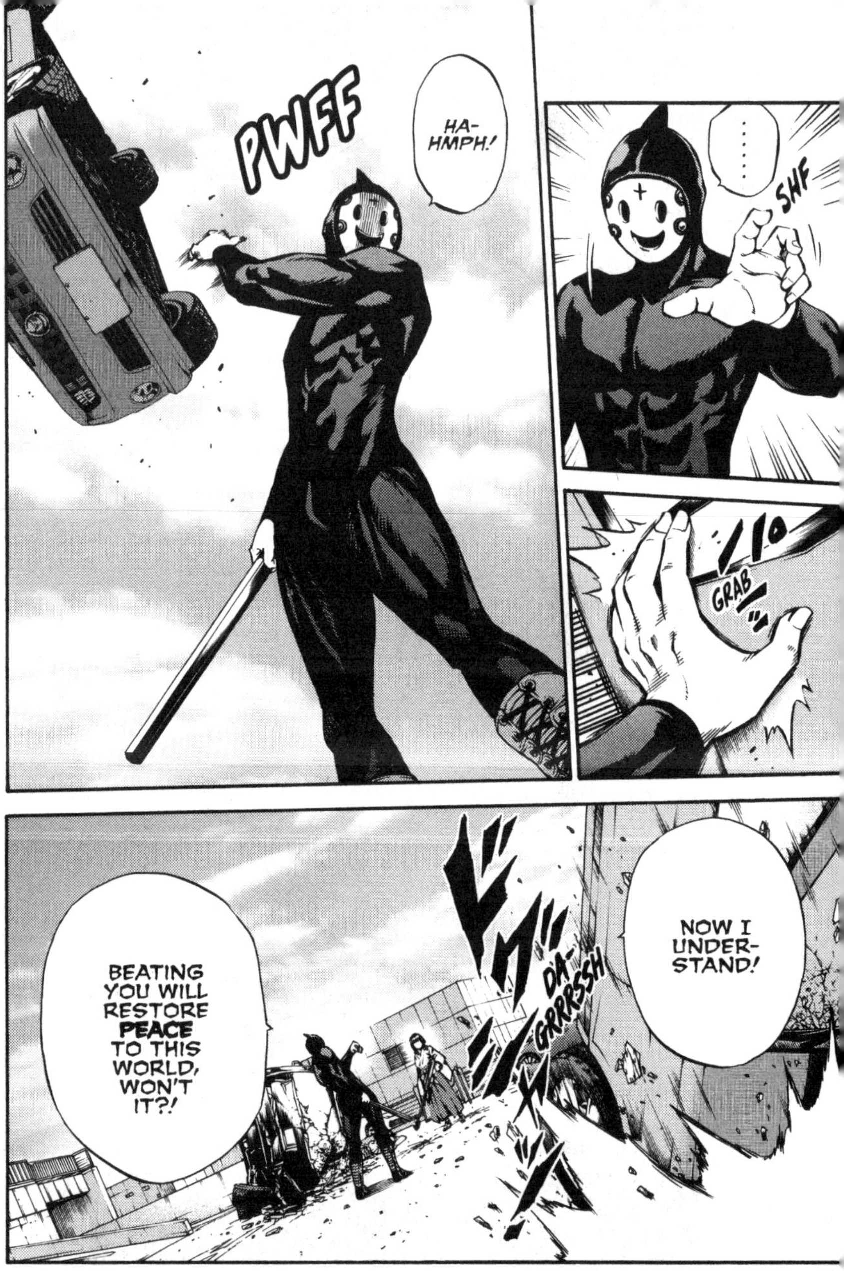
......
SHF
GRAB
PWFF
HA-HMPH!
NOW I UNDER-STAND!
DA-GRRRSSH
BEATING YOU WILL RESTORE **PEACE** TO THIS WORLD, WON'T IT?!

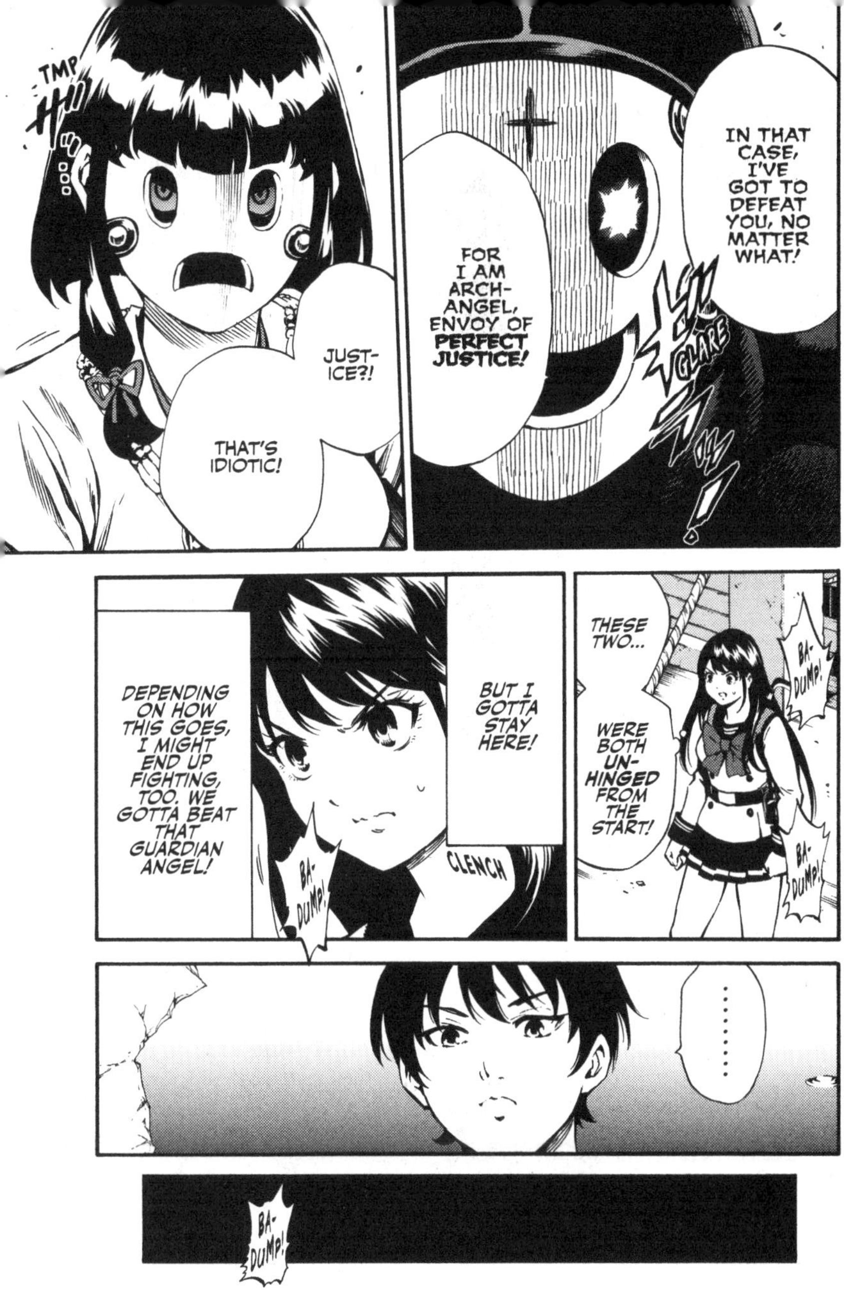
IN THAT CASE, I'VE GOT TO DEFEAT YOU, NO MATTER WHAT!
FOR I AM ARCH-ANGEL, ENVOY OF **PERFECT JUSTICE!**
GLARE
TMP
JUST-ICE?!
THAT'S IDIOTIC!
THESE TWO...
WERE BOTH UN-HINGED FROM THE START!
BA-DUMP!
BA-DUMP!
BUT I GOTTA STAY HERE!
DEPENDING ON HOW THIS GOES, I MIGHT END UP FIGHTING, TOO. WE GOTTA BEAT THAT GUARDIAN ANGEL!
CLENCH
BA-DUMP!
....
BA-DUMP!

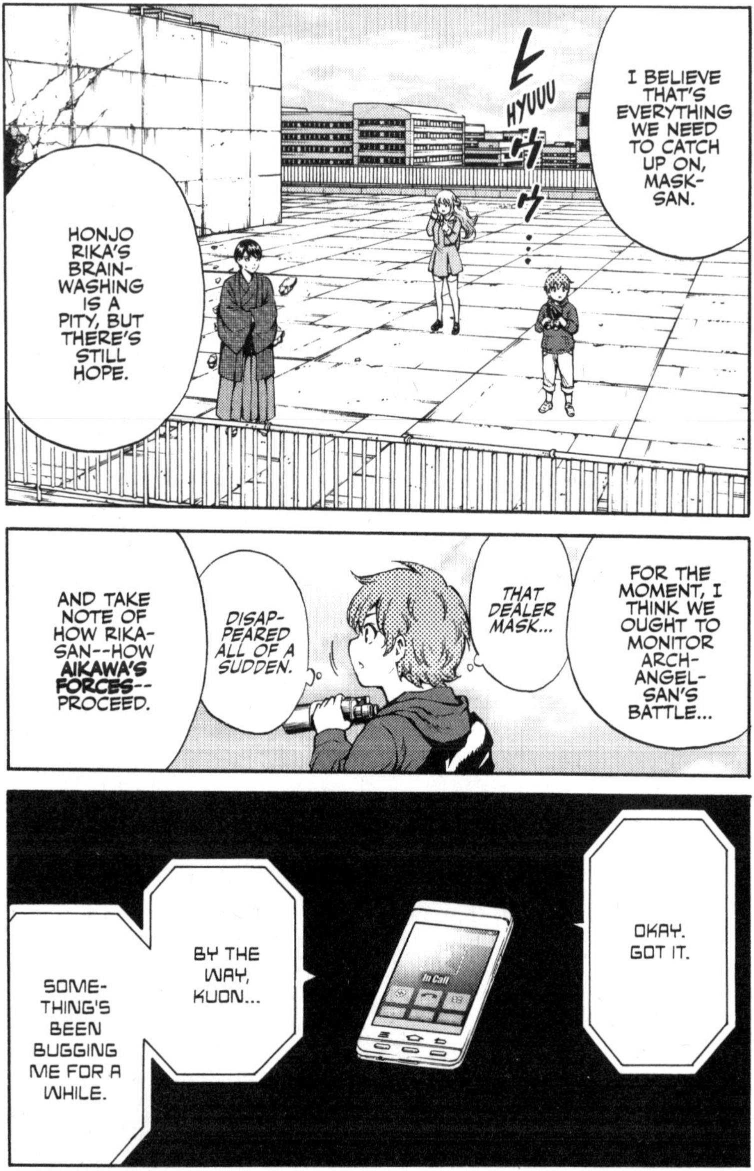
I BELIEVE THAT'S EVERYTHING WE NEED TO CATCH UP ON, MASK-SAN.
HYUUU
HONJO RIKA'S BRAINWASHING IS A PITY, BUT THERE'S STILL HOPE.
FOR THE MOMENT, I THINK WE OUGHT TO MONITOR ARCHANGEL-SAN'S BATTLE...
THAT DEALER MASK...
DISAPPEARED ALL OF A SUDDEN.
AND TAKE NOTE OF HOW RIKA-SAN--HOW **AIKAWA'S FORCES**--PROCEED.
OKAY. GOT IT.
In Call
BY THE WAY, KUON...
SOMETHING'S BEEN BUGGING ME FOR A WHILE.

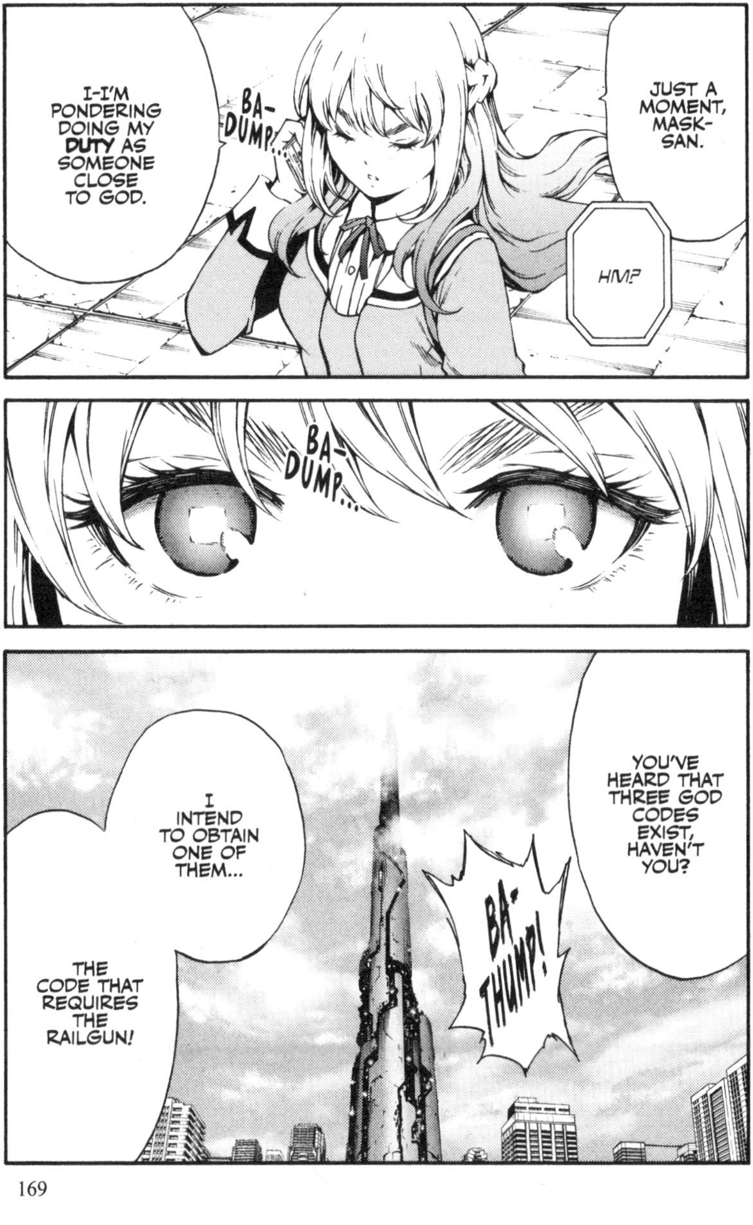
JUST A MOMENT, MASK-SAN.
HM?
BA-DUMP...
I-I'M PONDERING DOING MY **DUTY** AS SOMEONE CLOSE TO GOD.
BA-DUMP...
YOU'VE HEARD THAT THREE GOD CODES EXIST, HAVEN'T YOU?
BA-THUMP!
I INTEND TO OBTAIN ONE OF THEM...
THE CODE THAT REQUIRES THE RAILGUN!

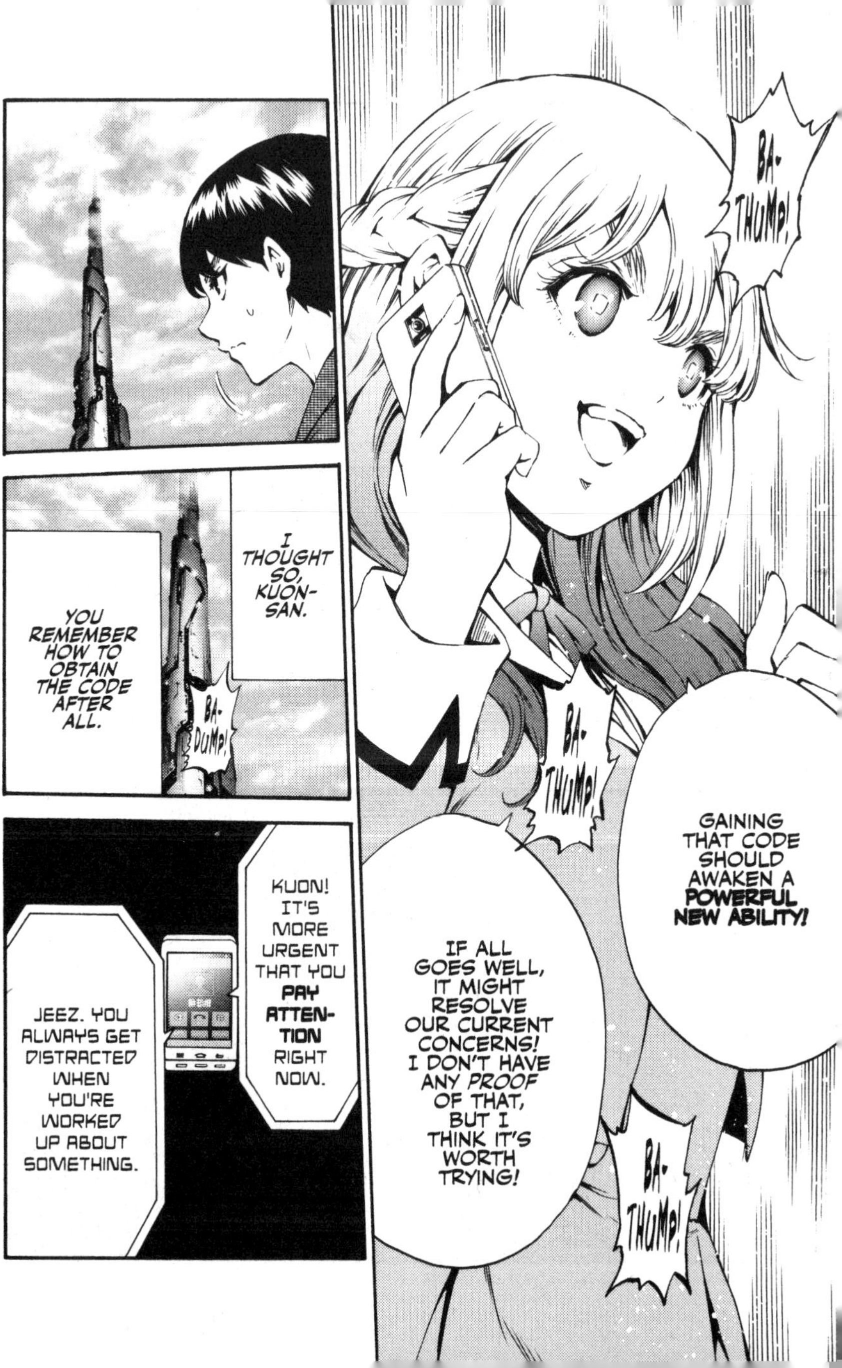
BA-THUMP!
GAINING THAT CODE SHOULD AWAKEN A **POWERFUL NEW ABILITY!**
BA-THUMP!
IF ALL GOES WELL, IT MIGHT RESOLVE OUR CURRENT CONCERNS! I DON'T HAVE ANY *PROOF* OF THAT, BUT I THINK IT'S WORTH TRYING!
BA-THUMP!
I THOUGHT SO, KUON-SAN.
YOU REMEMBER HOW TO OBTAIN THE CODE AFTER ALL.
BA-DUMP!
KUON! IT'S MORE URGENT THAT YOU **PAY ATTEN-TION** RIGHT NOW.
JEEZ. YOU ALWAYS GET DISTRACTED WHEN YOU'RE WORKED UP ABOUT SOMETHING.

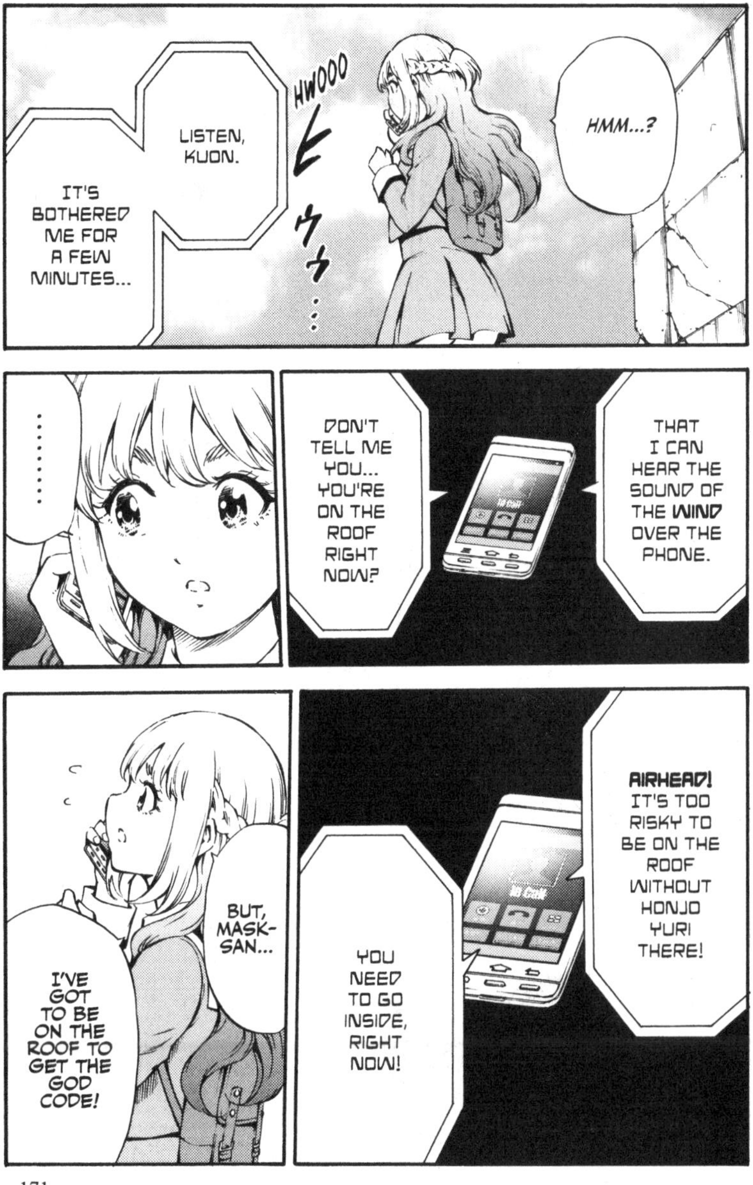
HMM...?
HWOOO
LISTEN, KUON.
IT'S BOTHERED ME FOR A FEW MINUTES...
THAT I CAN HEAR THE SOUND OF THE **WIND** OVER THE PHONE.
DON'T TELL ME YOU... YOU'RE ON THE ROOF RIGHT NOW?
....
AIRHEAD! IT'S TOO RISKY TO BE ON THE ROOF WITHOUT HONJO YURI THERE!
YOU NEED TO GO INSIDE, RIGHT NOW!
BUT, MASK-SAN...
I'VE GOT TO BE ON THE ROOF TO GET THE GOD CODE!

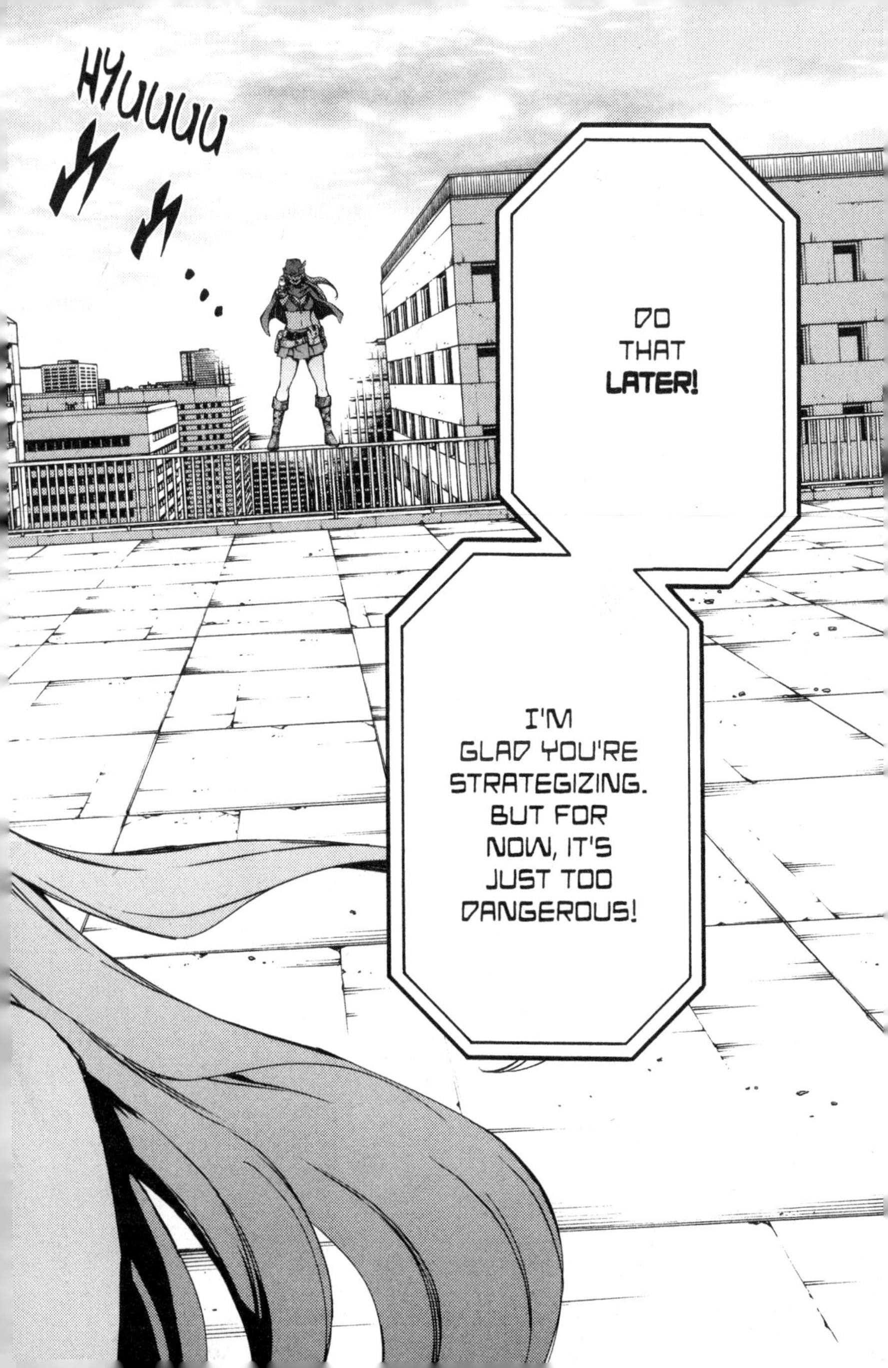
HYUUUU
DO THAT LATER!
I'M GLAD YOU'RE STRATEGIZING. BUT FOR NOW, IT'S JUST TOO DANGEROUS!

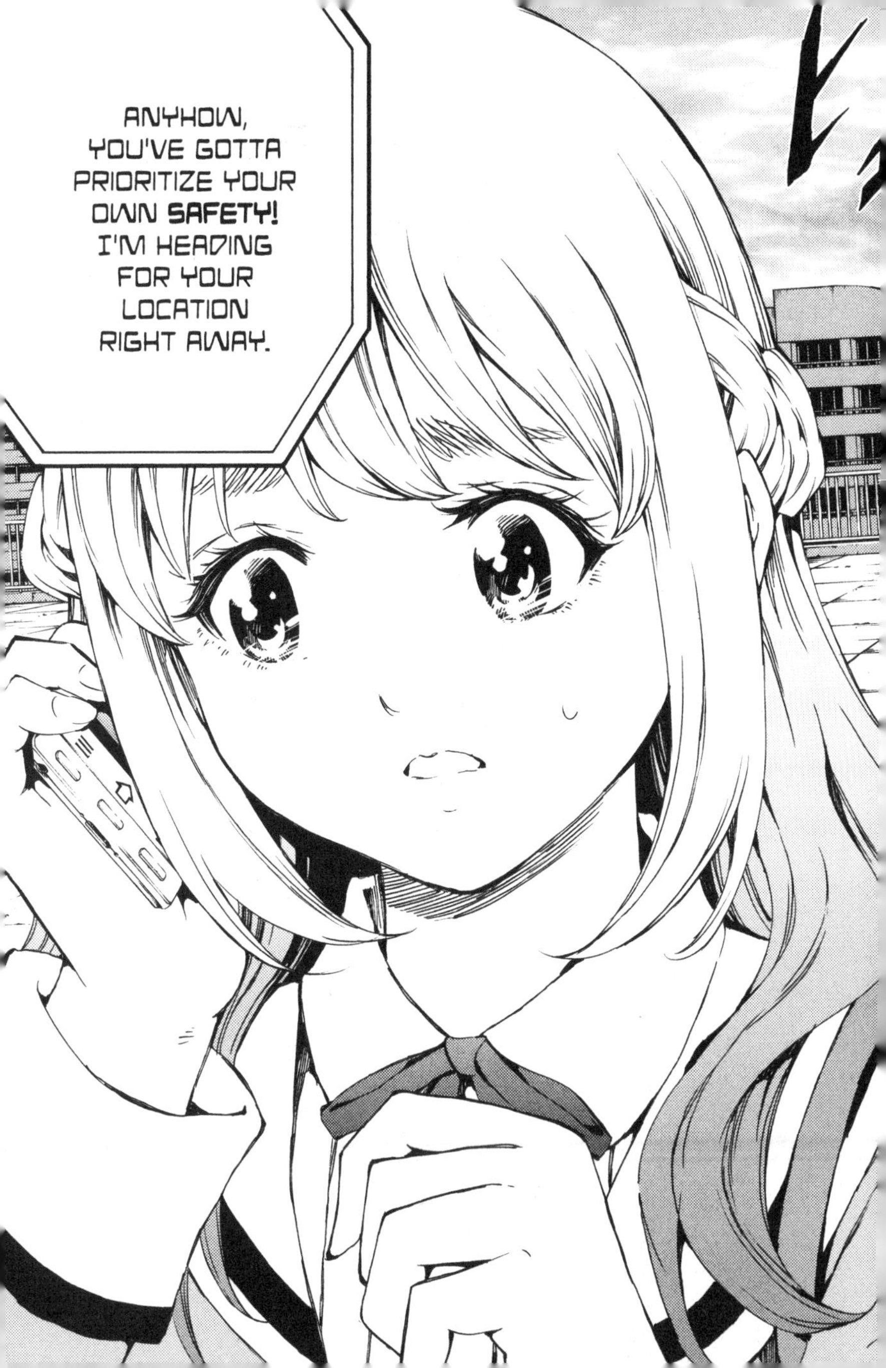
ANYHOW, YOU'VE GOTTA PRIORITIZE YOUR OWN **SAFETY!** I'M HEADING FOR YOUR LOCATION RIGHT AWAY.

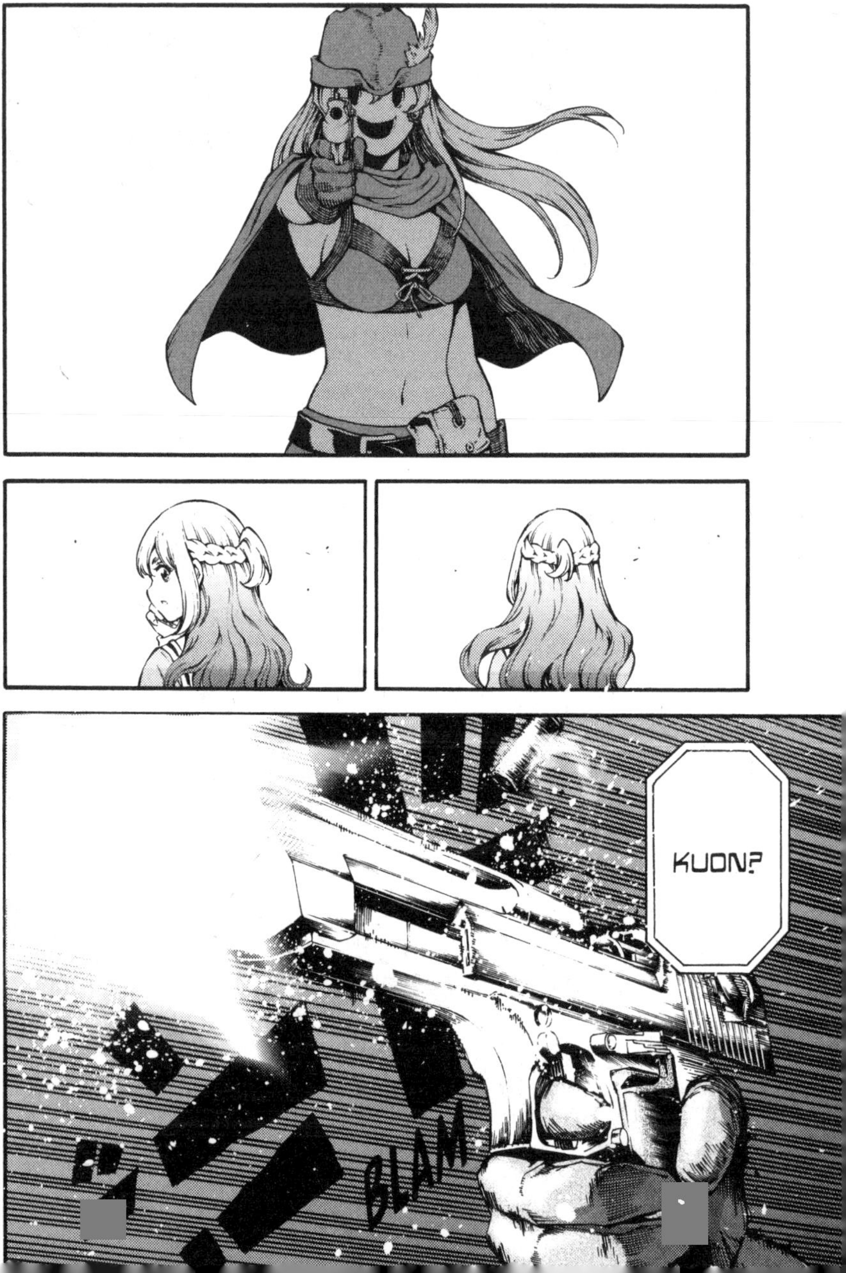
KUON?
BLAM

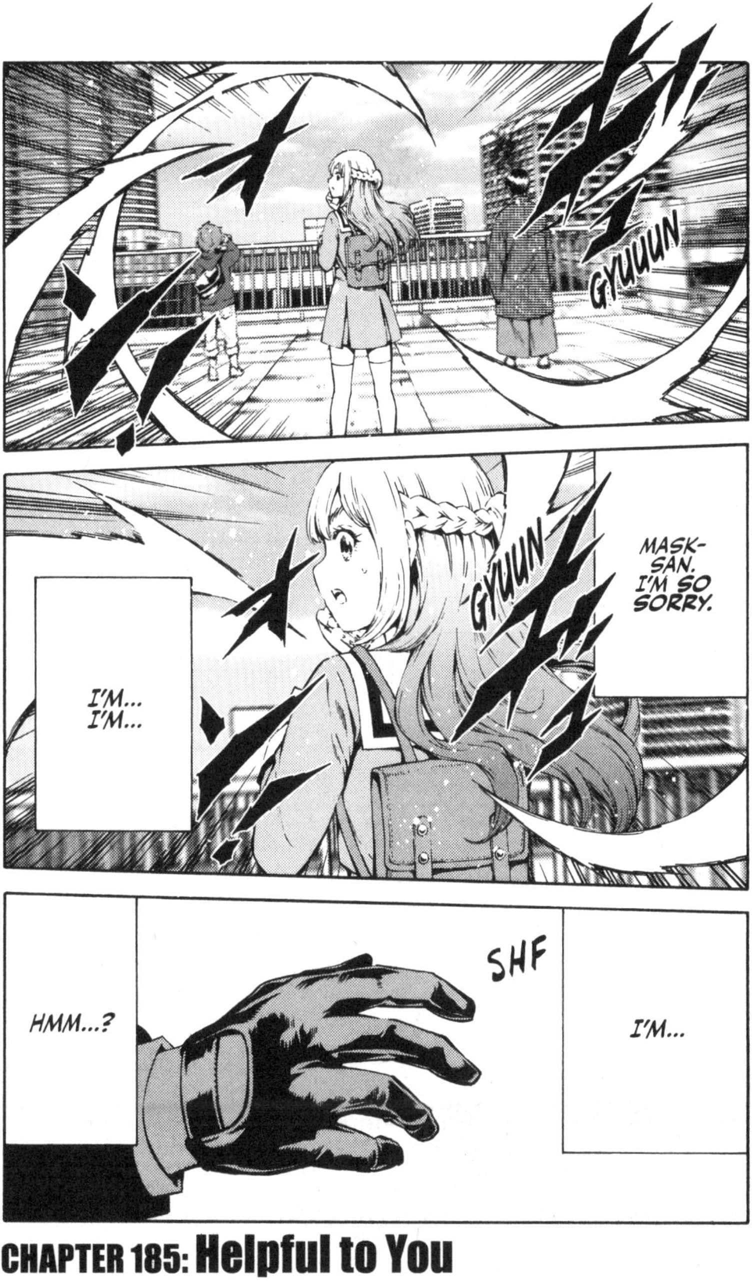
GYUUUN
MASK-SAN. I'M SO SORRY.
GYUUN
I'M... I'M...
I'M...
SHF
HMM...?

CHAPTER 185: Helpful to You

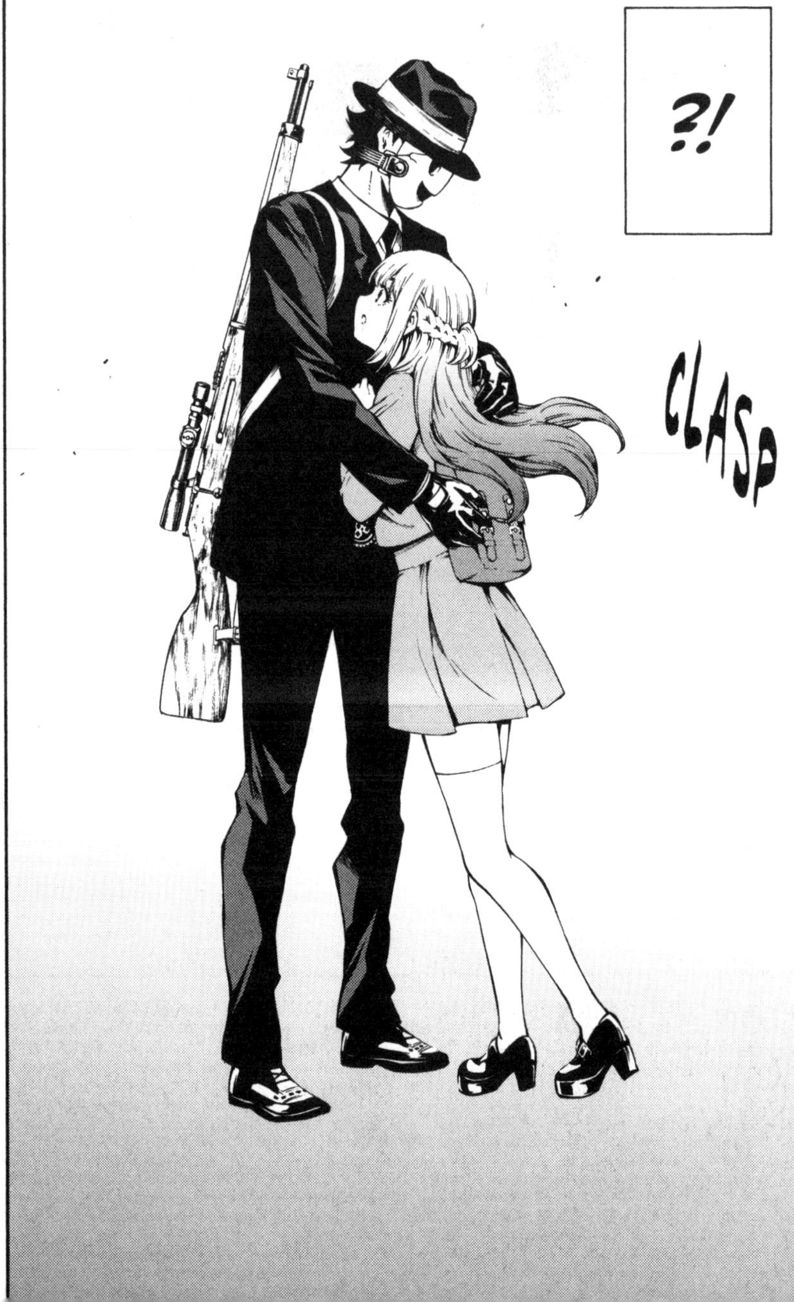
?!
CLASP

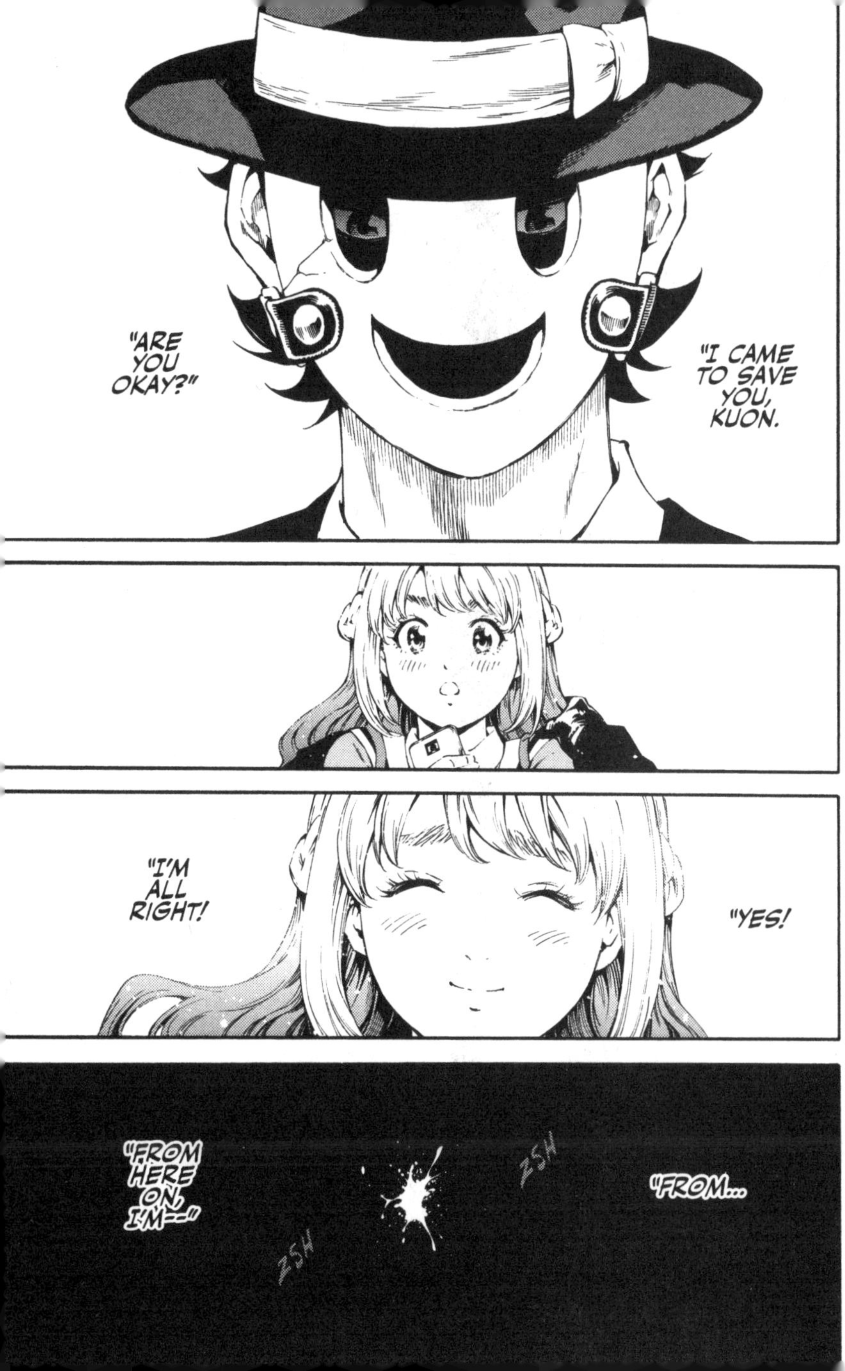
"I CAME TO SAVE YOU, KUON.
"ARE YOU OKAY?"
"YES!
"I'M ALL RIGHT!
"FROM...
ZSH
ZSH
"FROM HERE ON, I'M--"

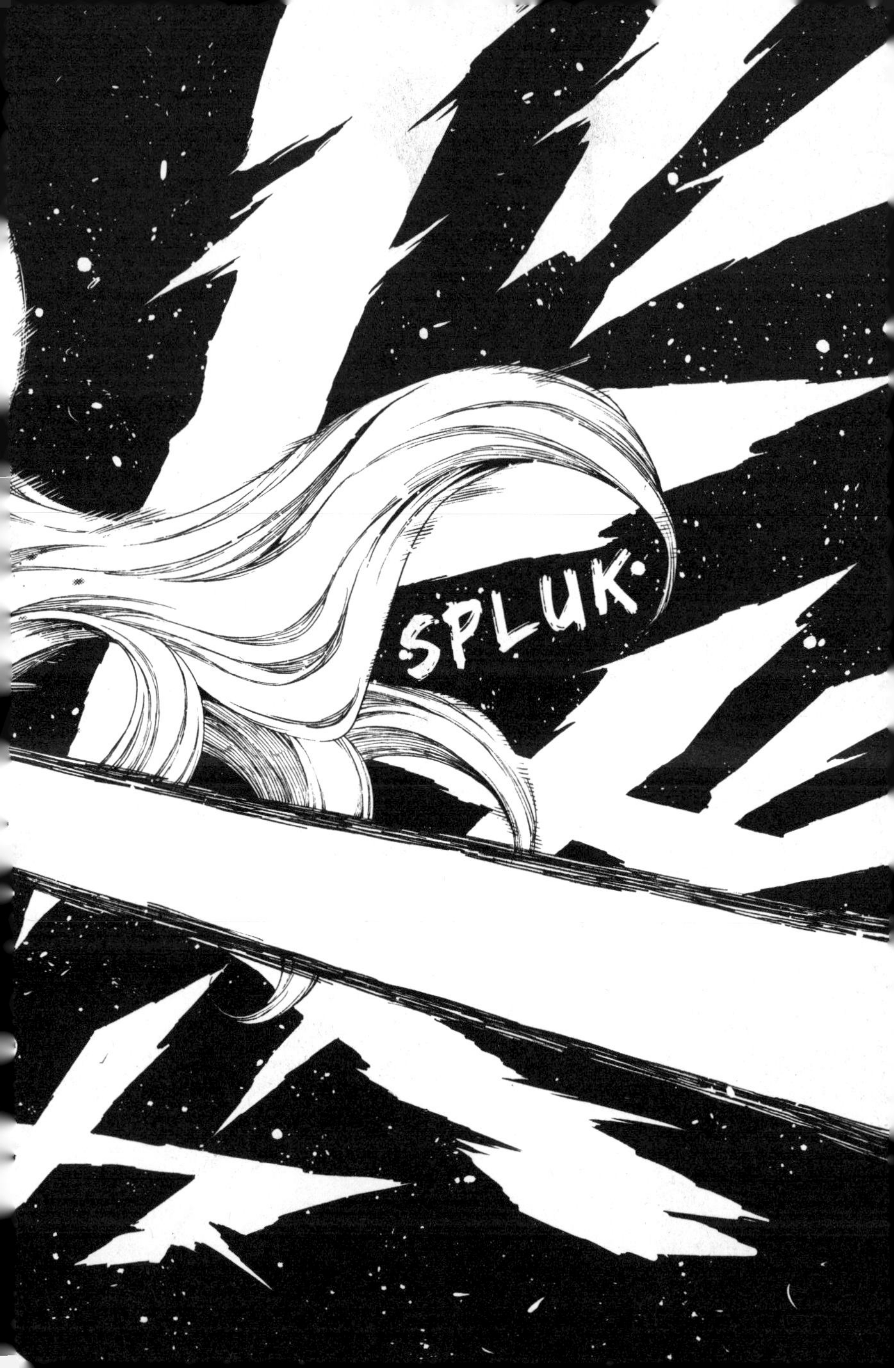
SPLUK

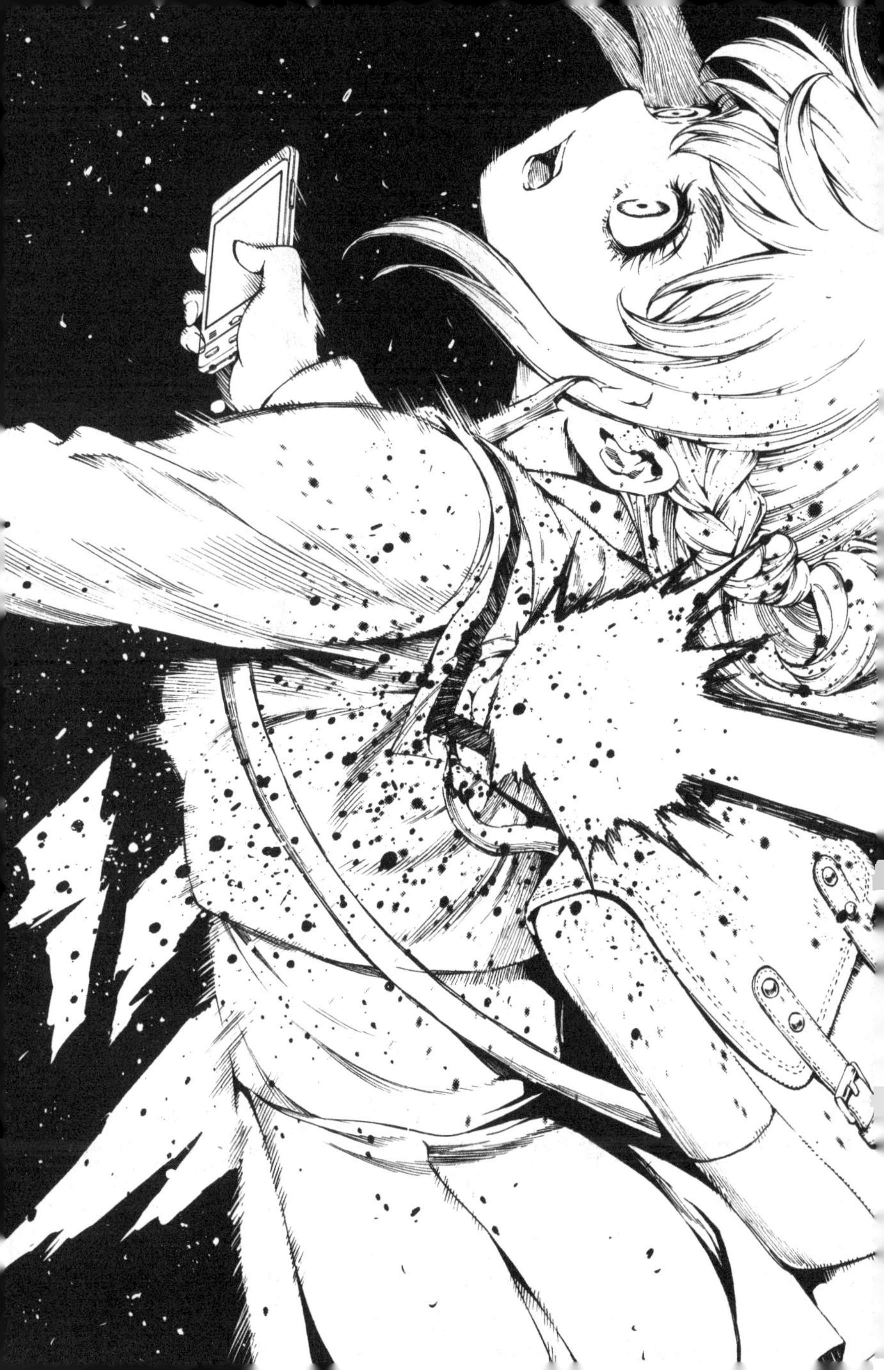

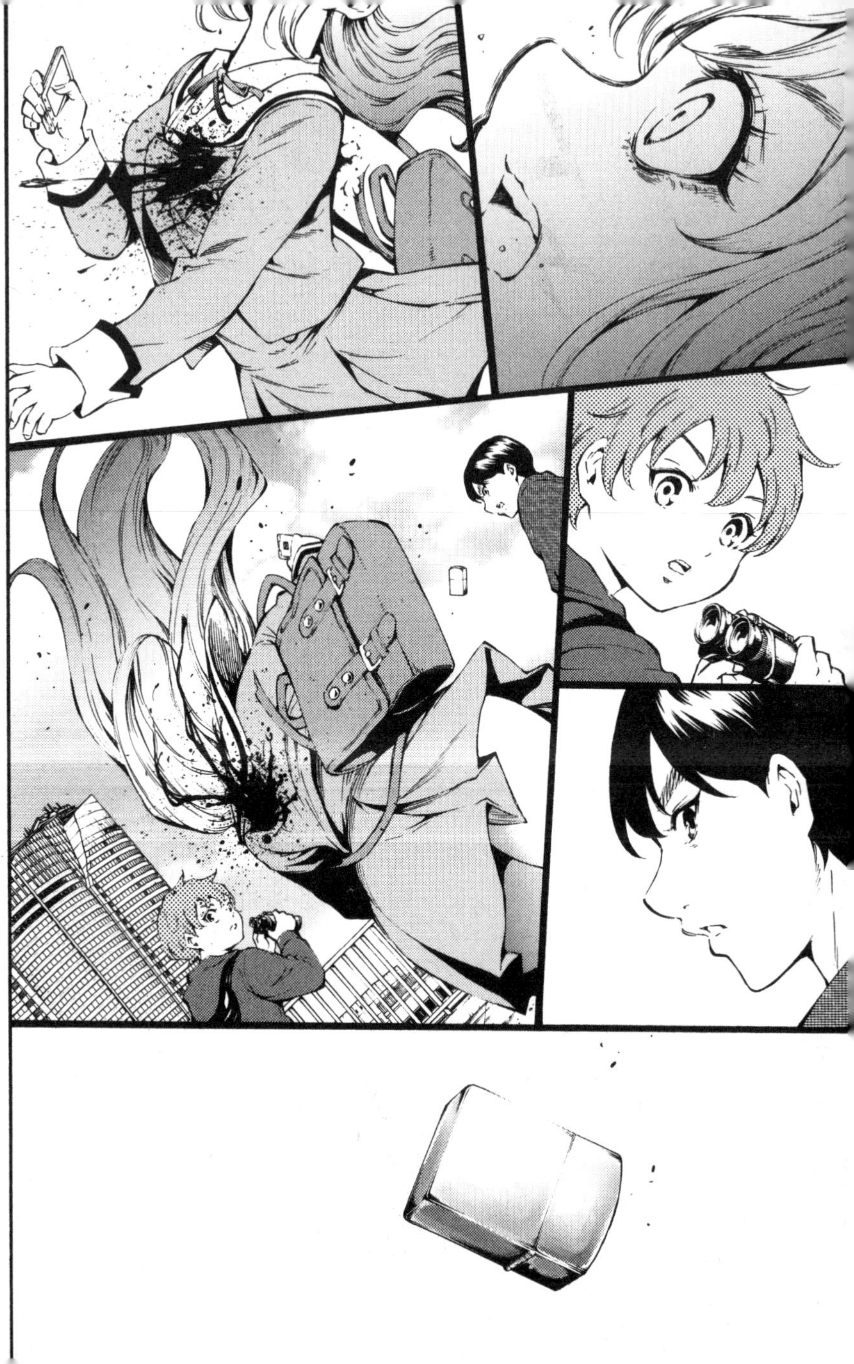

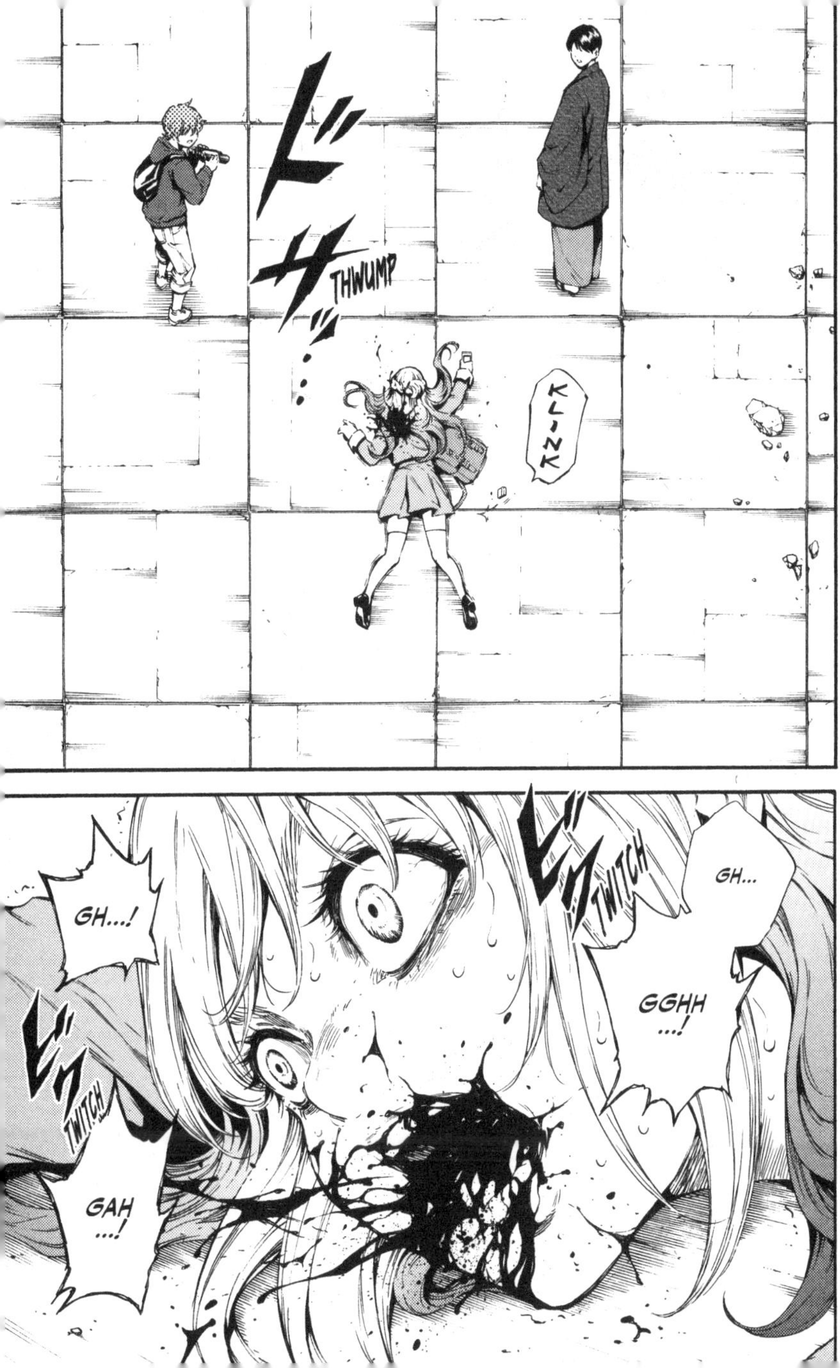
THWUMP
KLINK
GH... GGHH ...!
TWITCH
GH...!
TWITCH
GAH ...!

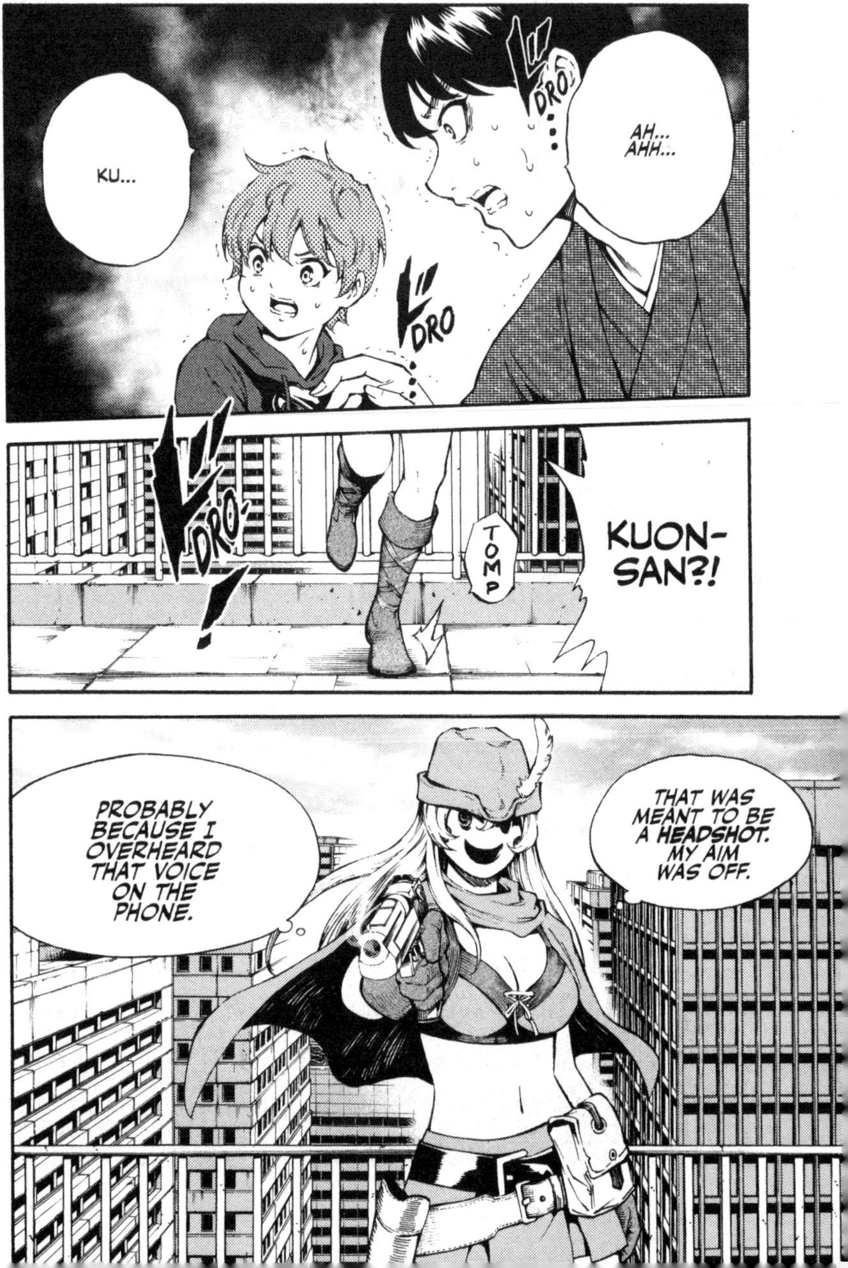
AH... AHH...
DRO
KU...
DRO
KUON-SAN?!
TOMP
DRO
THAT WAS MEANT TO BE A **HEADSHOT**. MY AIM WAS OFF.
PROBABLY BECAUSE I OVERHEARD THAT VOICE ON THE PHONE.

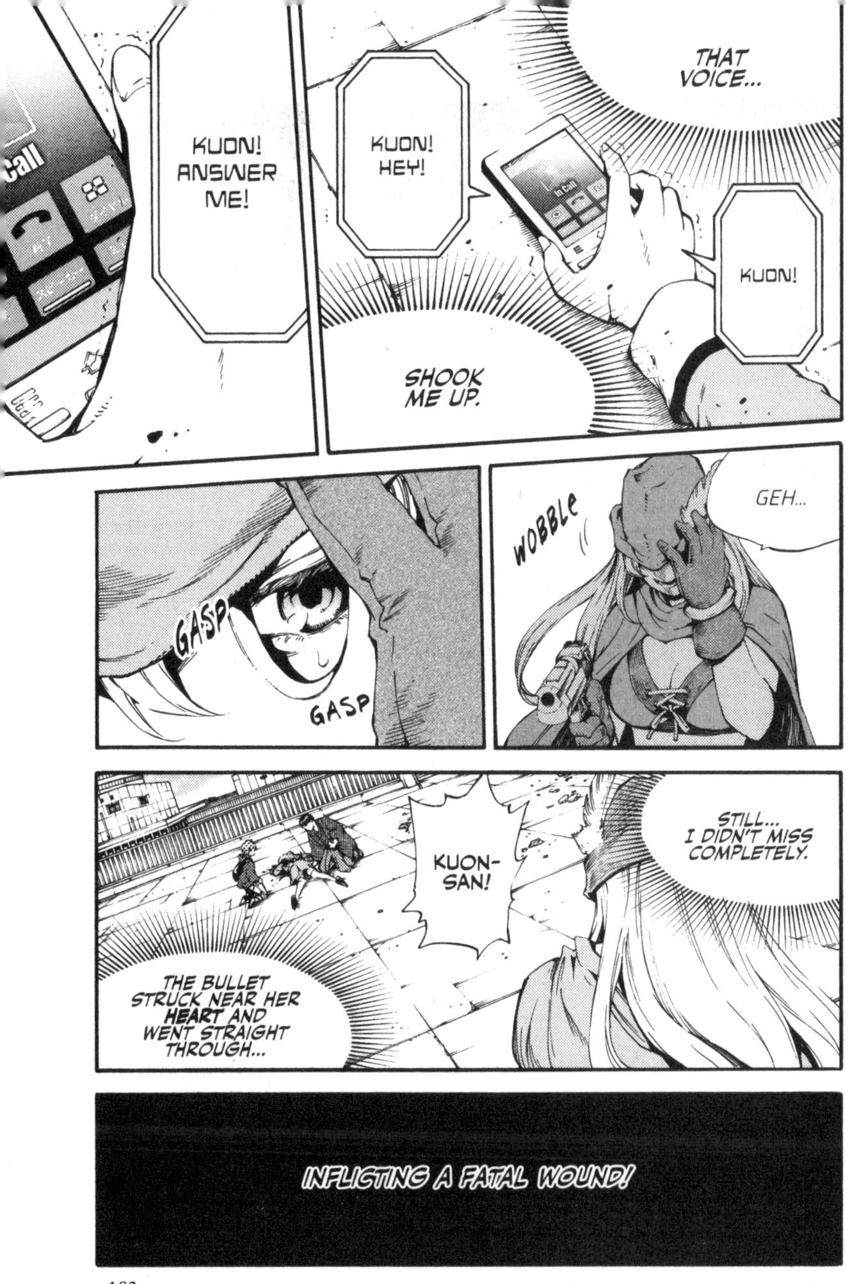
THAT VOICE...
KUON!
KUON! HEY!
SHOOK ME UP.
KUON! ANSWER ME!
GEH...
WOBBLE
GASP
GASP
STILL... I DIDN'T MISS COMPLETELY.
KUON-SAN!
THE BULLET STRUCK NEAR HER HEART AND WENT STRAIGHT THROUGH...
INFLICTING A FATAL WOUND!

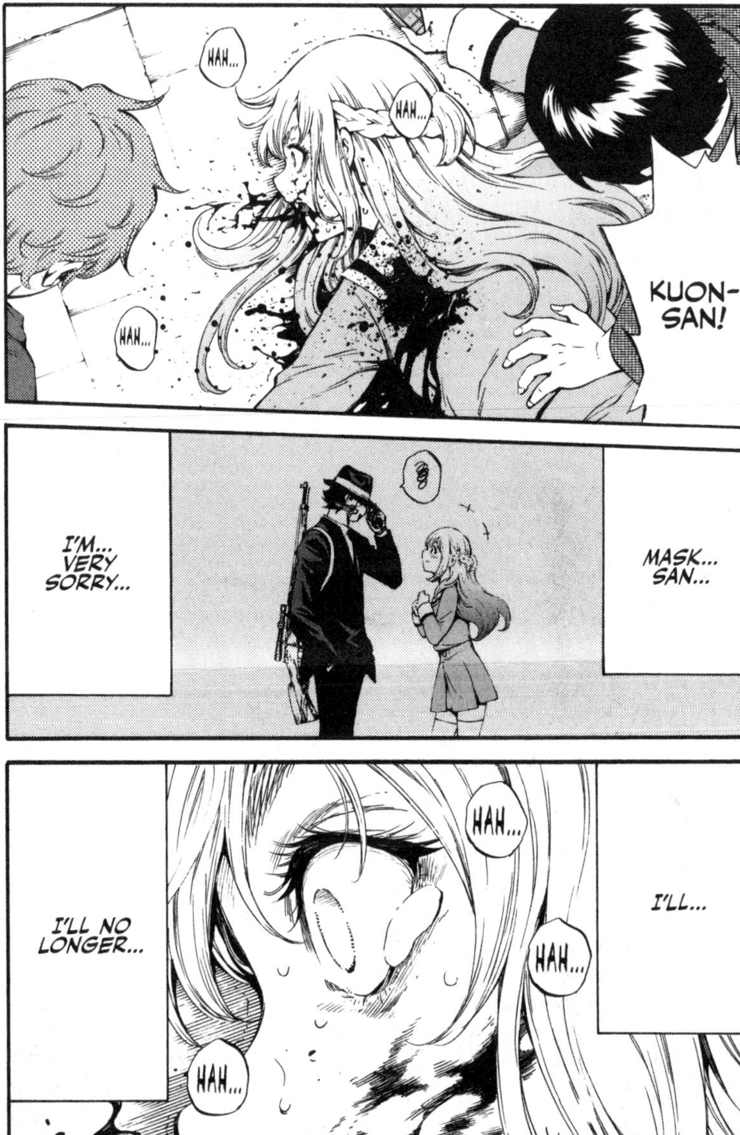
KUON-SAN!
HAH...
HAH...
HAH...
MASK... SAN...
I'M... VERY SORRY...
I'LL...
HAH...
HAH...
I'LL NO LONGER...
HAH...

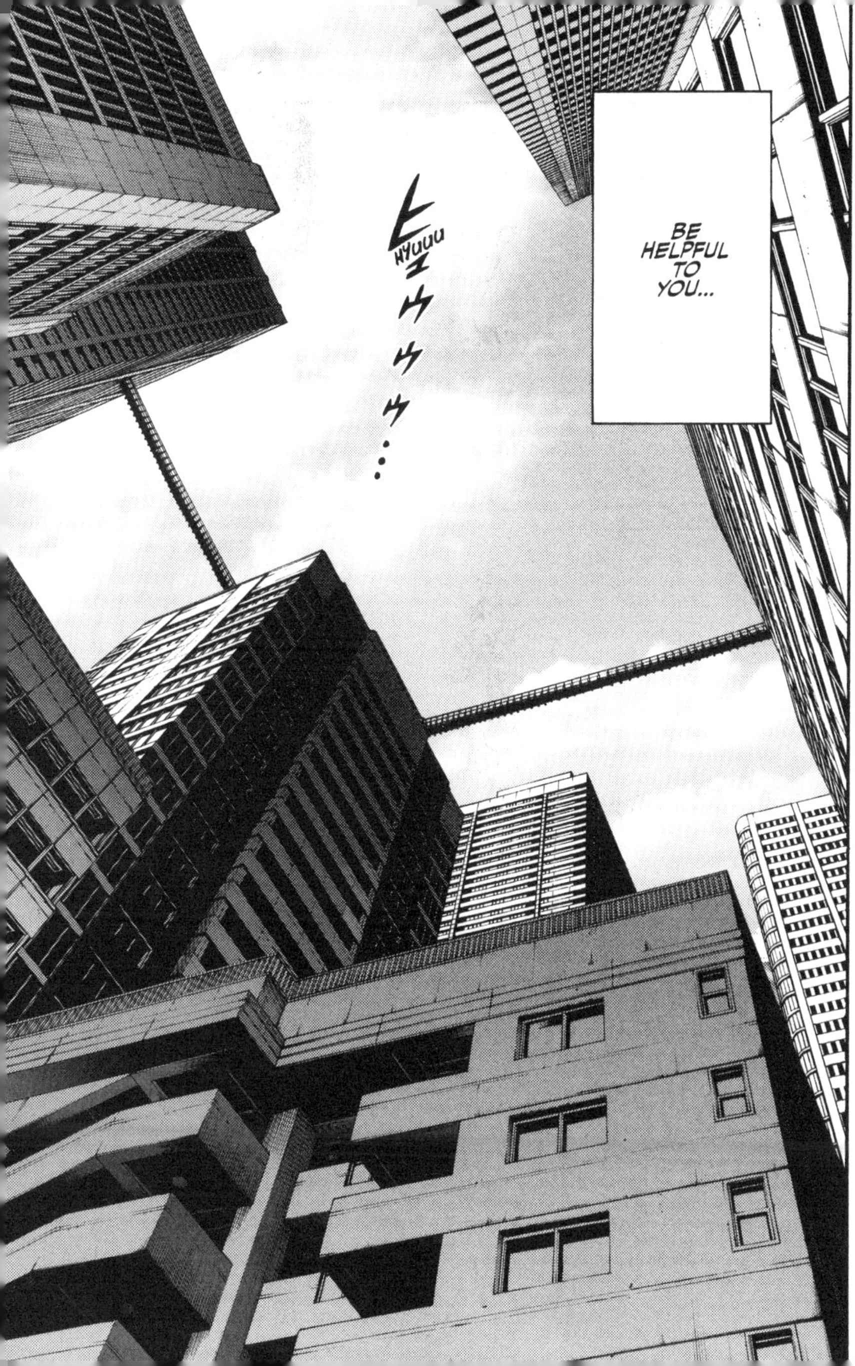
BE HELPFUL TO YOU...
HYUUU
ヒュウウウ…

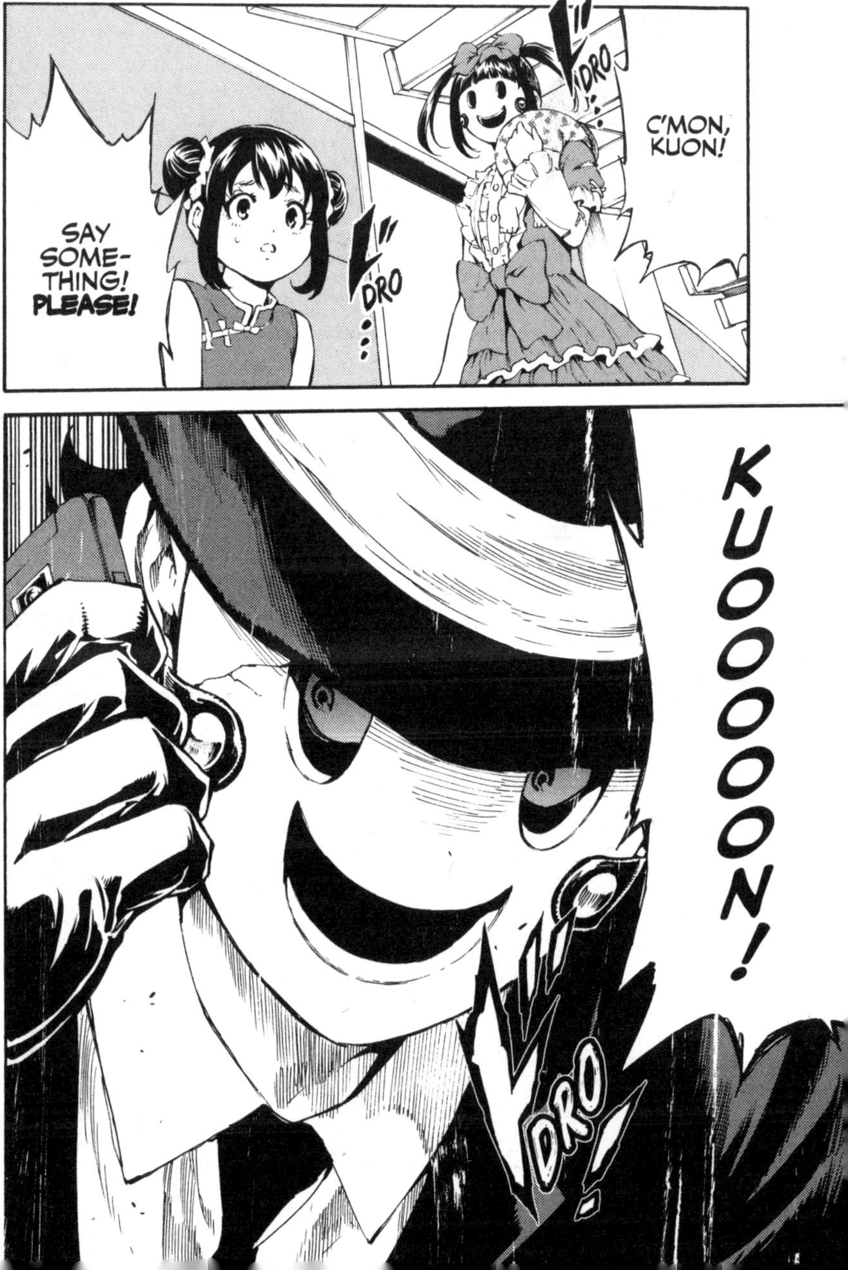
DRO
C'MON, KUON!
DRO
SAY SOME-THING! **PLEASE!**
KUOOOOOON!
DRO!

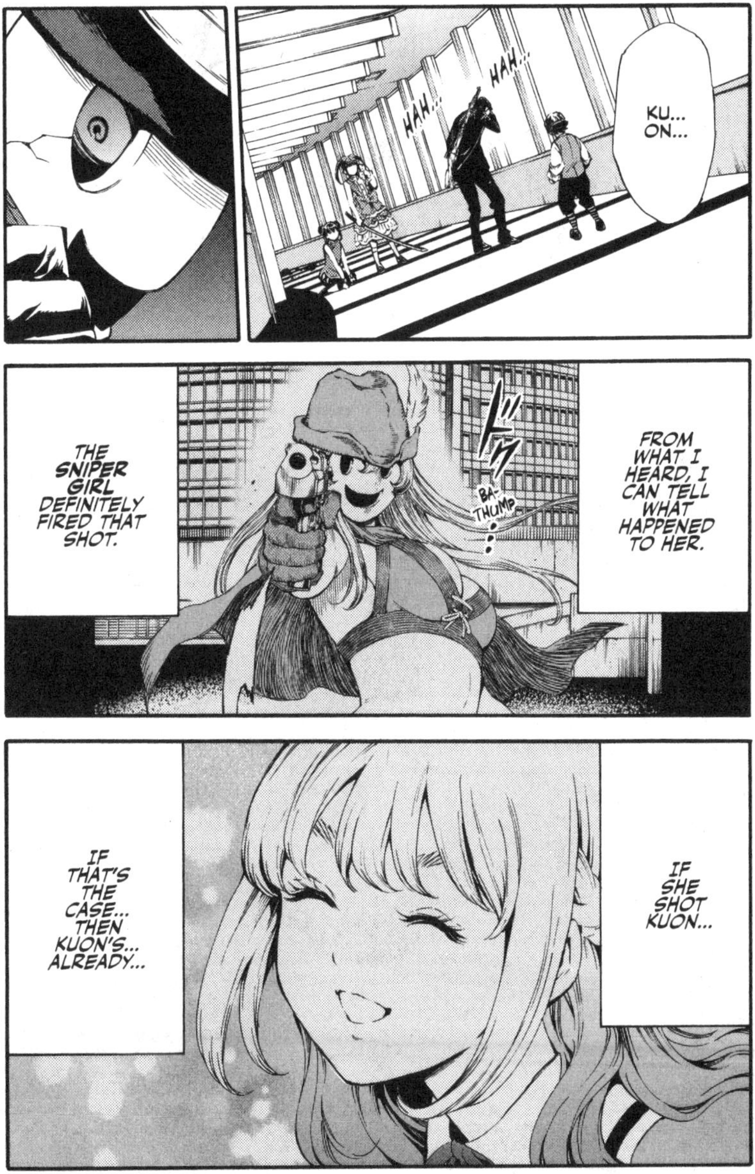
KU... ON...
HAH... HAH...
FROM WHAT I HEARD, I CAN TELL WHAT HAPPENED TO HER.
BA-THUMP
THE SNIPER GIRL DEFINITELY FIRED THAT SHOT.
IF SHE SHOT KUON...
IF THAT'S THE CASE... THEN KUON'S... ALREADY...

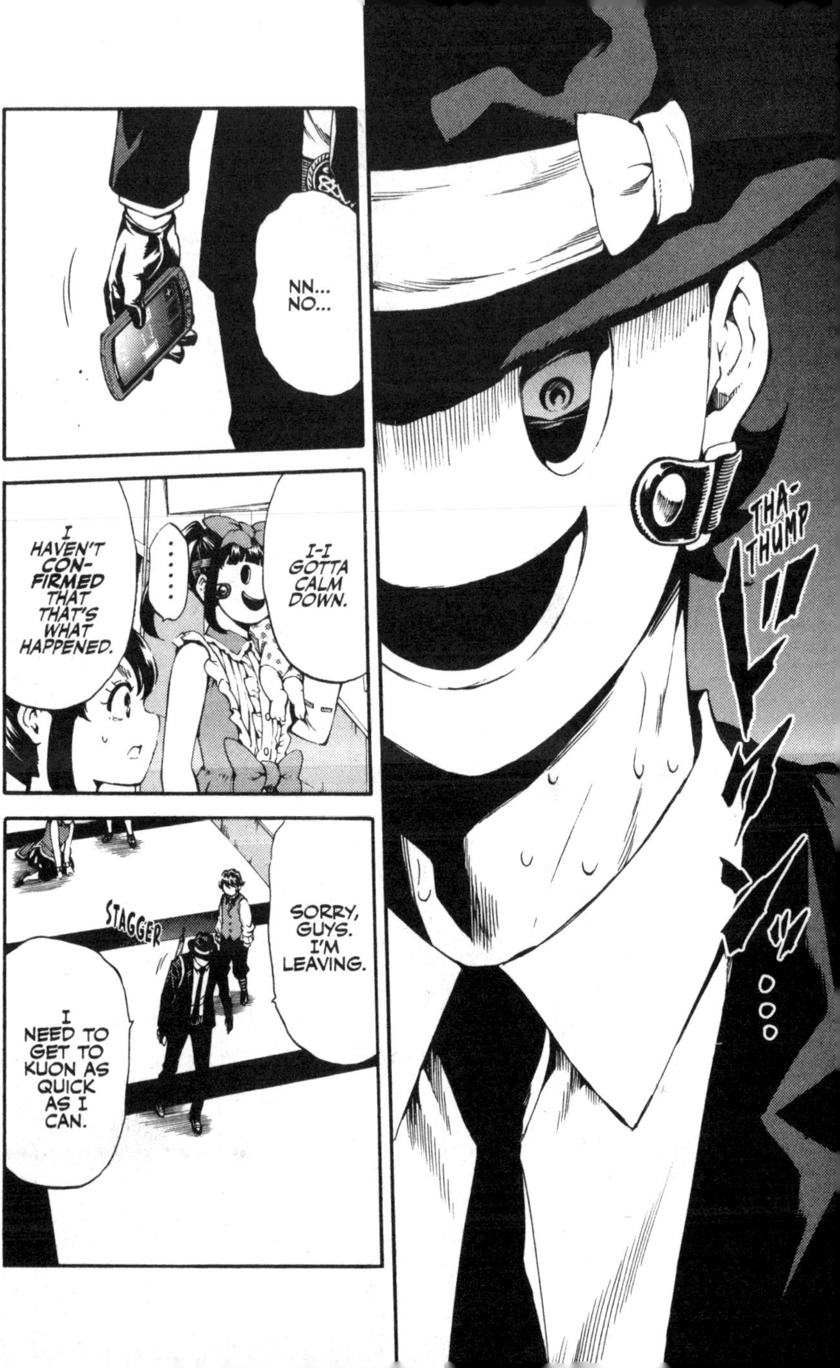
THA-THUMP
NN... NO...
I-I GOTTA CALM DOWN.
......
I HAVEN'T CONFIRMED THAT THAT'S WHAT HAPPENED.
SORRY, GUYS. I'M LEAVING.
STAGGER
I NEED TO GET TO KUON AS QUICK AS I CAN.

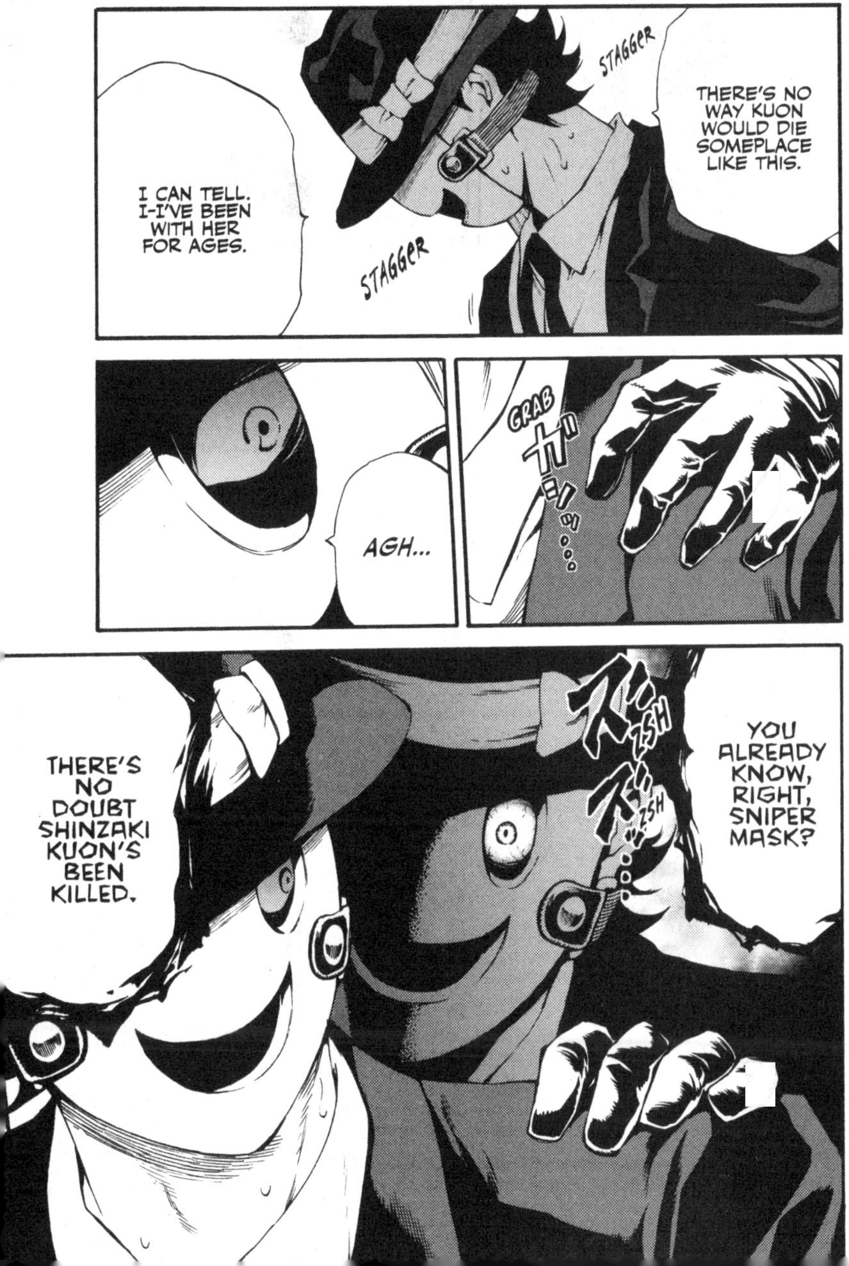
STAGGER
THERE'S NO WAY KUON WOULD DIE SOMEPLACE LIKE THIS.
I CAN TELL. I-I'VE BEEN WITH HER FOR AGES.
STAGGER
GRAB
AGH...
YOU ALREADY KNOW, RIGHT, SNIPER MASK?
ZSH
ZSH
THERE'S NO DOUBT SHINZAKI KUON'S BEEN KILLED.

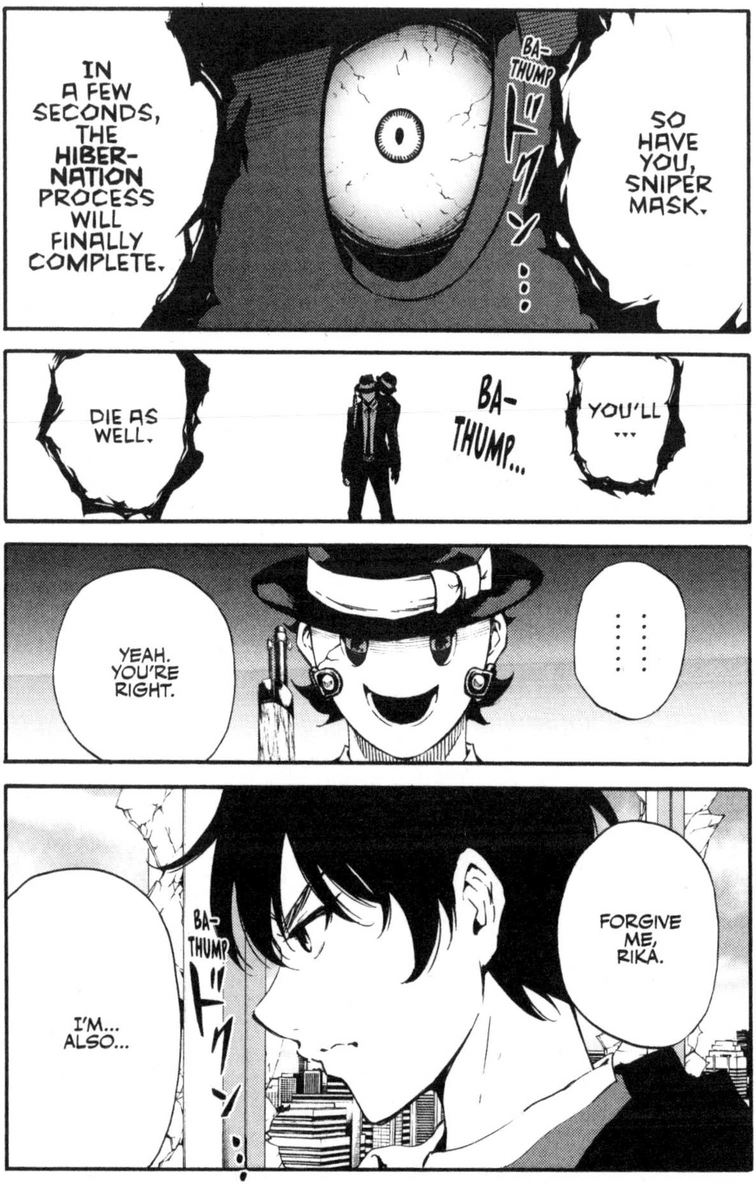
SO HAVE YOU, SNIPER MASK.
BA-THUMP
IN A FEW SECONDS, THE HIBERNATION PROCESS WILL FINALLY COMPLETE.
YOU'LL ...
BA-THUMP...
DIE AS WELL.
......
YEAH. YOU'RE RIGHT.
FORGIVE ME, RIKA.
BA-THUMP
I'M... ALSO...

HIGH-RISE INVASION

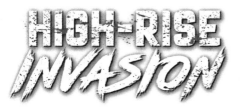

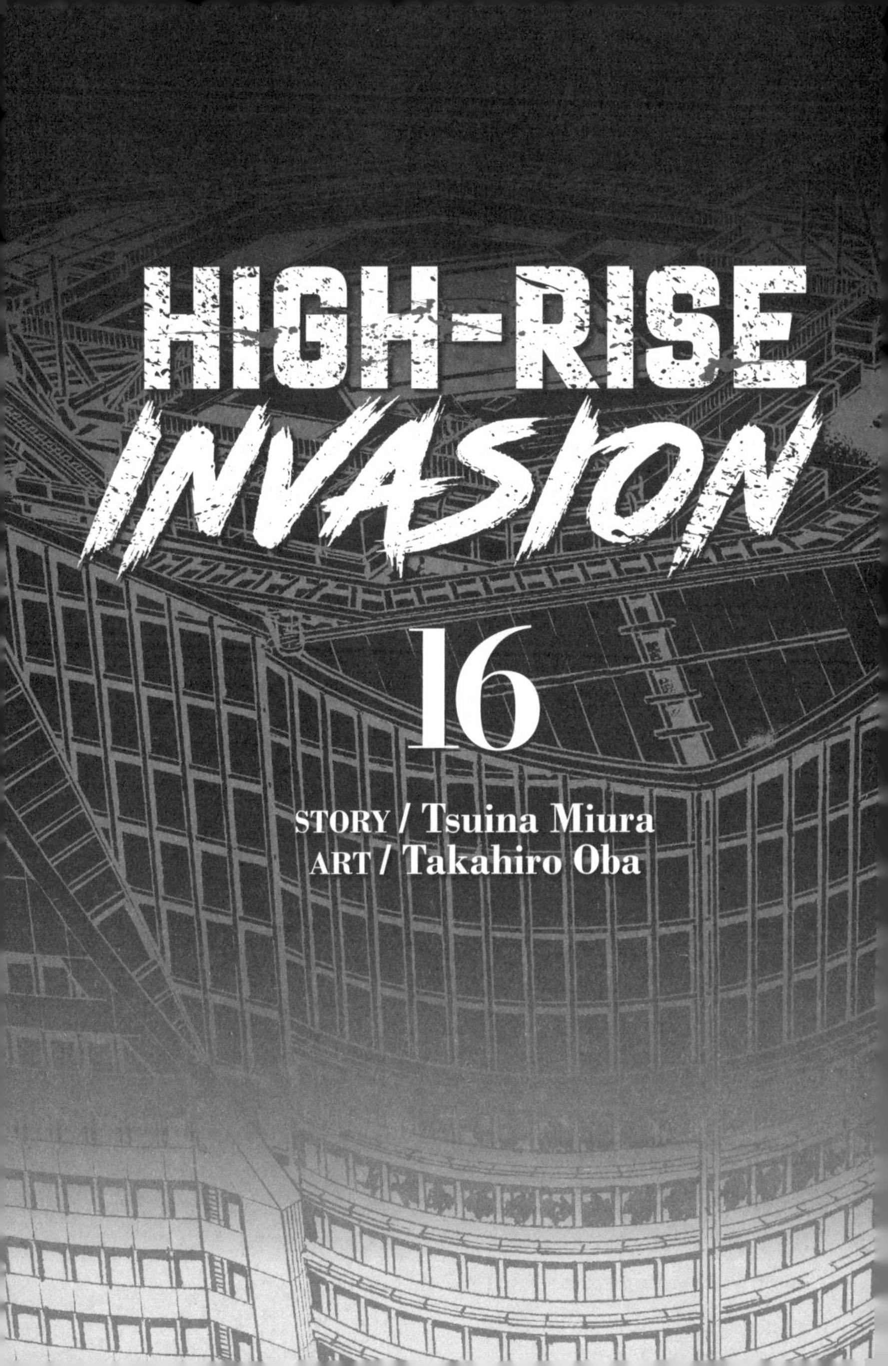

HIGH-RISE INVASION

16

STORY / Tsuina Miura
ART / Takahiro Oba

HIGH-RISE INVASION 16

CONTENTS

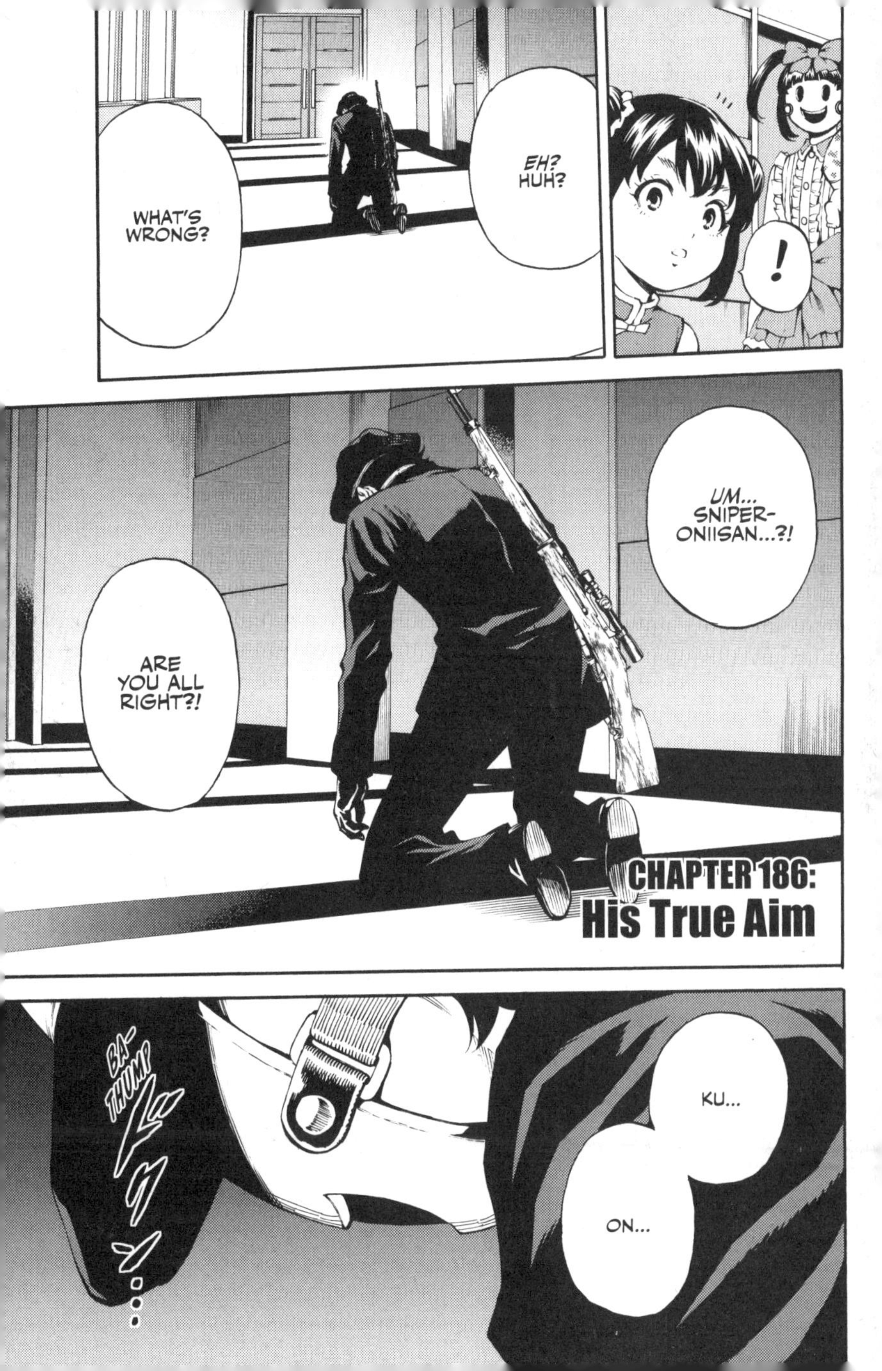
!
EH? HUH?
WHAT'S WRONG?
UM... SNIPER-ONIISAN...?!
ARE YOU ALL RIGHT?!
CHAPTER 186: His True Aim
KU...
ON...
BA-THUMP

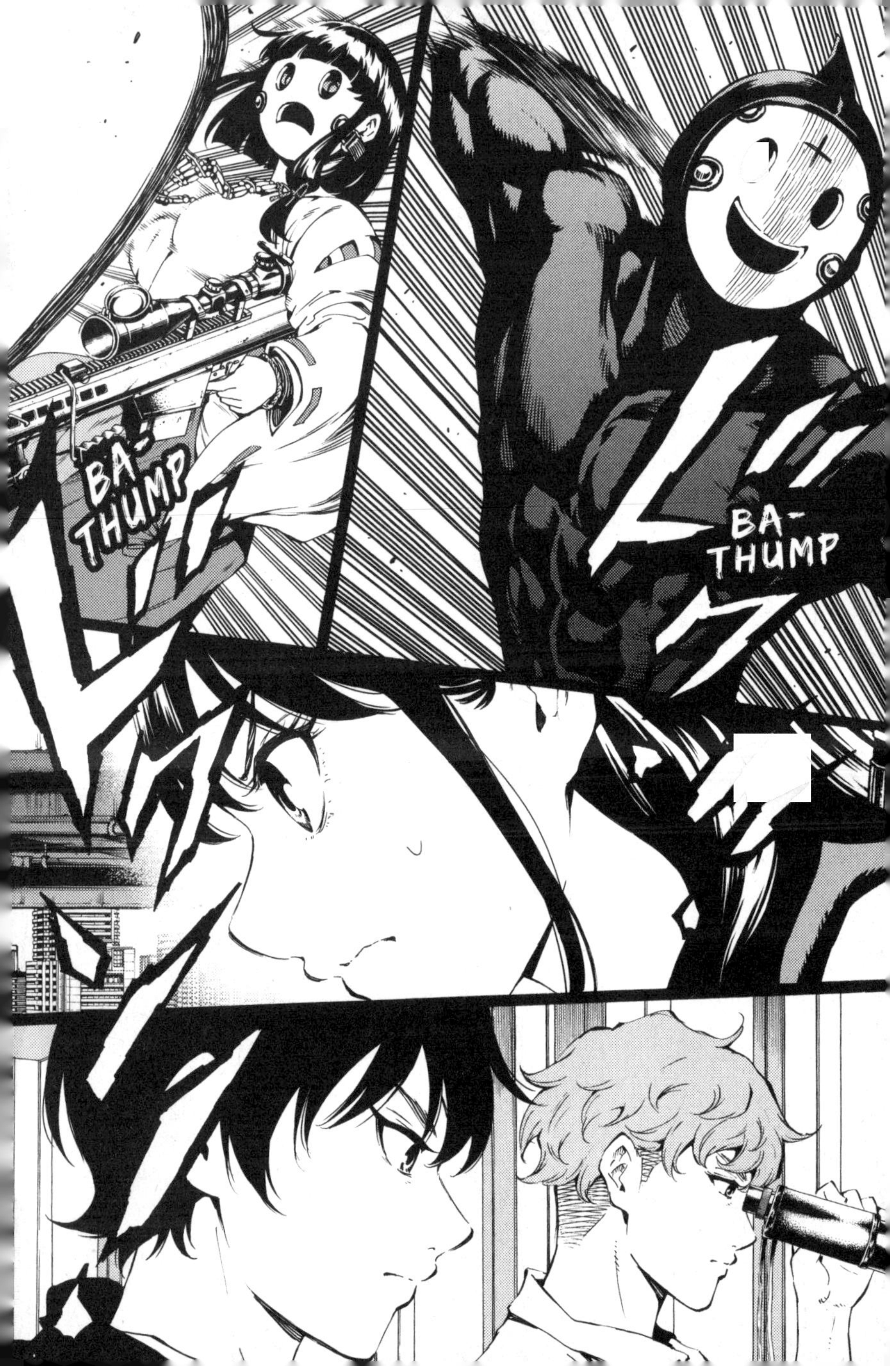
BA-
THUMP
BA-
THUMP

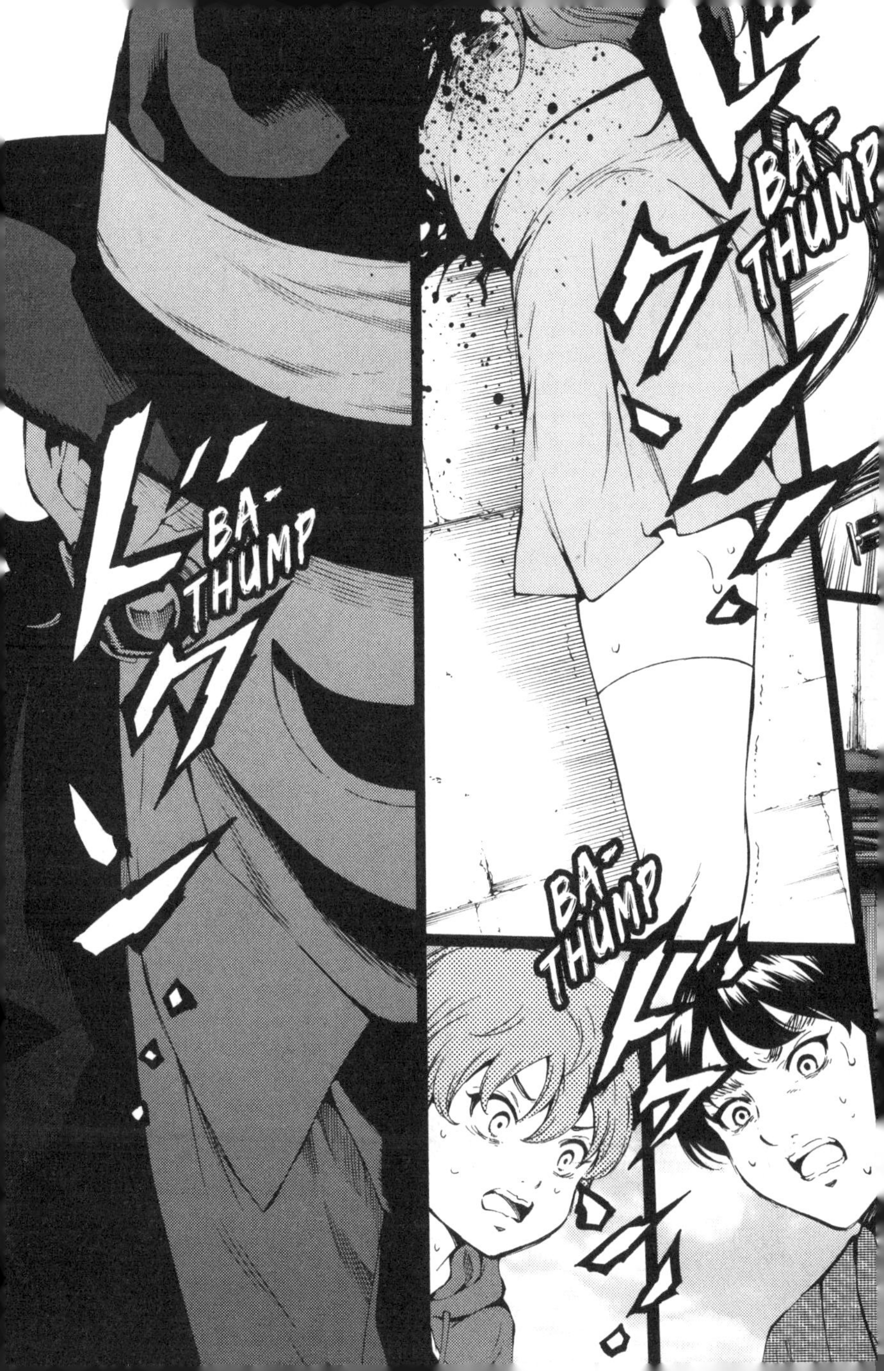
BA-THUMP
BA-THUMP
BA-THUMP

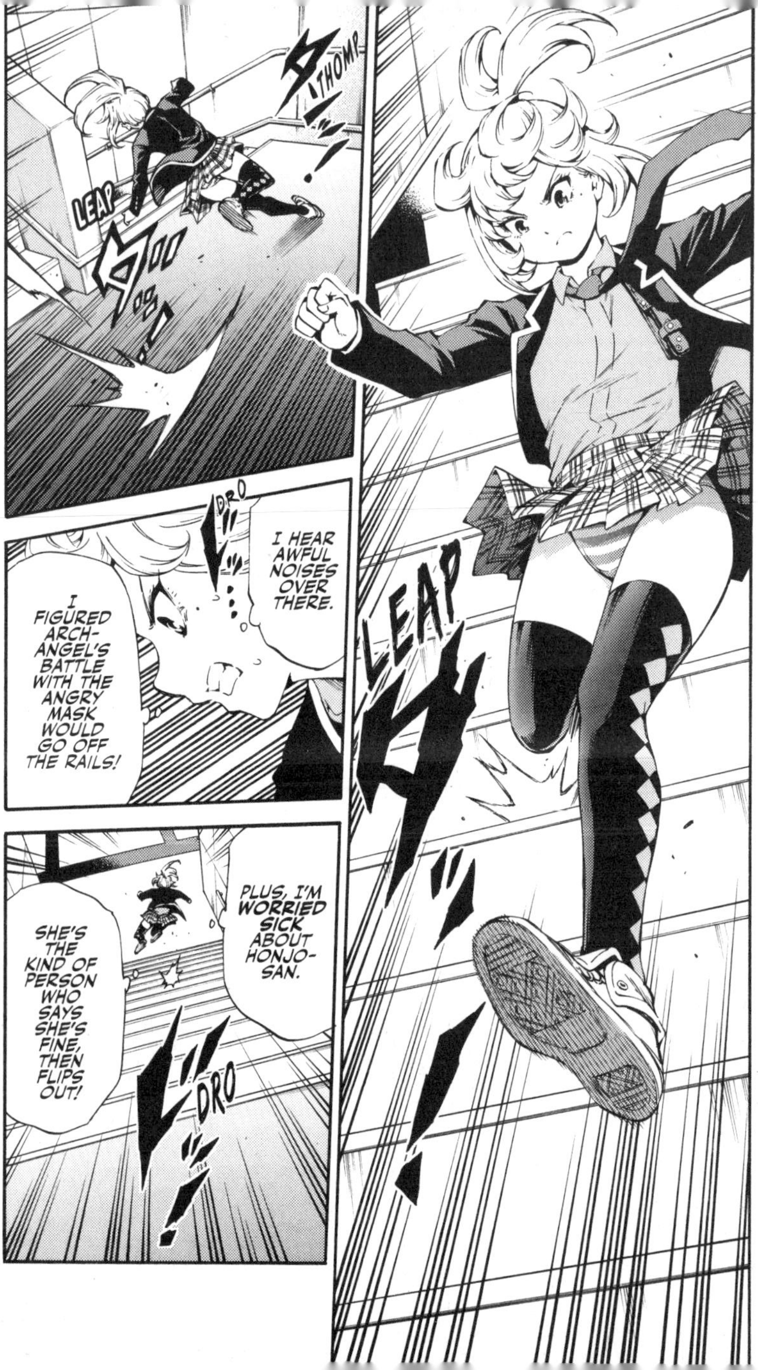
LEAP
THOMP
LEAP
DRO
I HEAR AWFUL NOISES OVER THERE.
I FIGURED ARCH-ANGEL'S BATTLE WITH THE ANGRY MASK WOULD GO OFF THE RAILS!
PLUS, I'M WORRIED SICK ABOUT HONJO-SAN.
SHE'S THE KIND OF PERSON WHO SAYS SHE'S FINE, THEN FLIPS OUT!
DRO

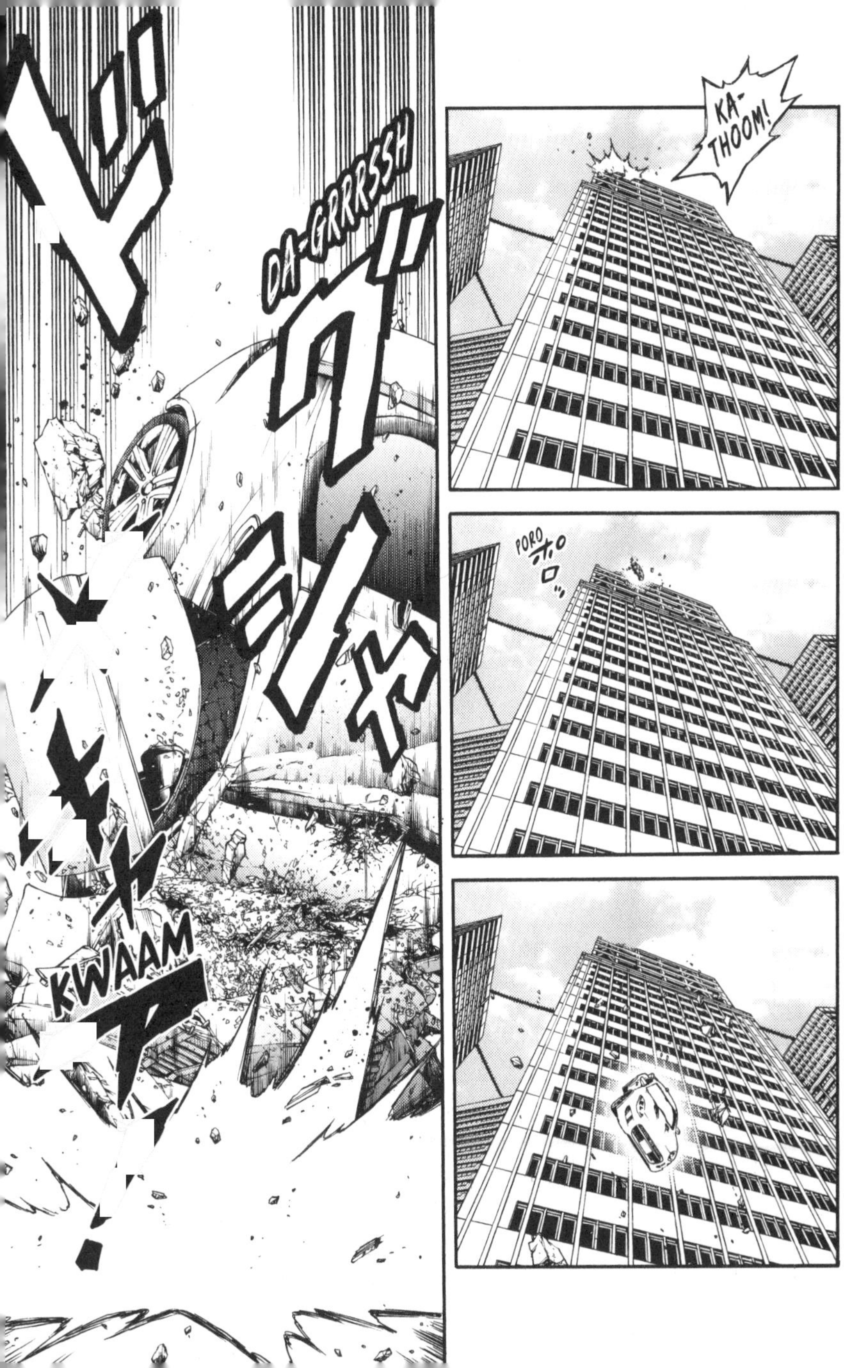
KA-
THOOM!
PORO
DA-GRRRSSH
KWAAM

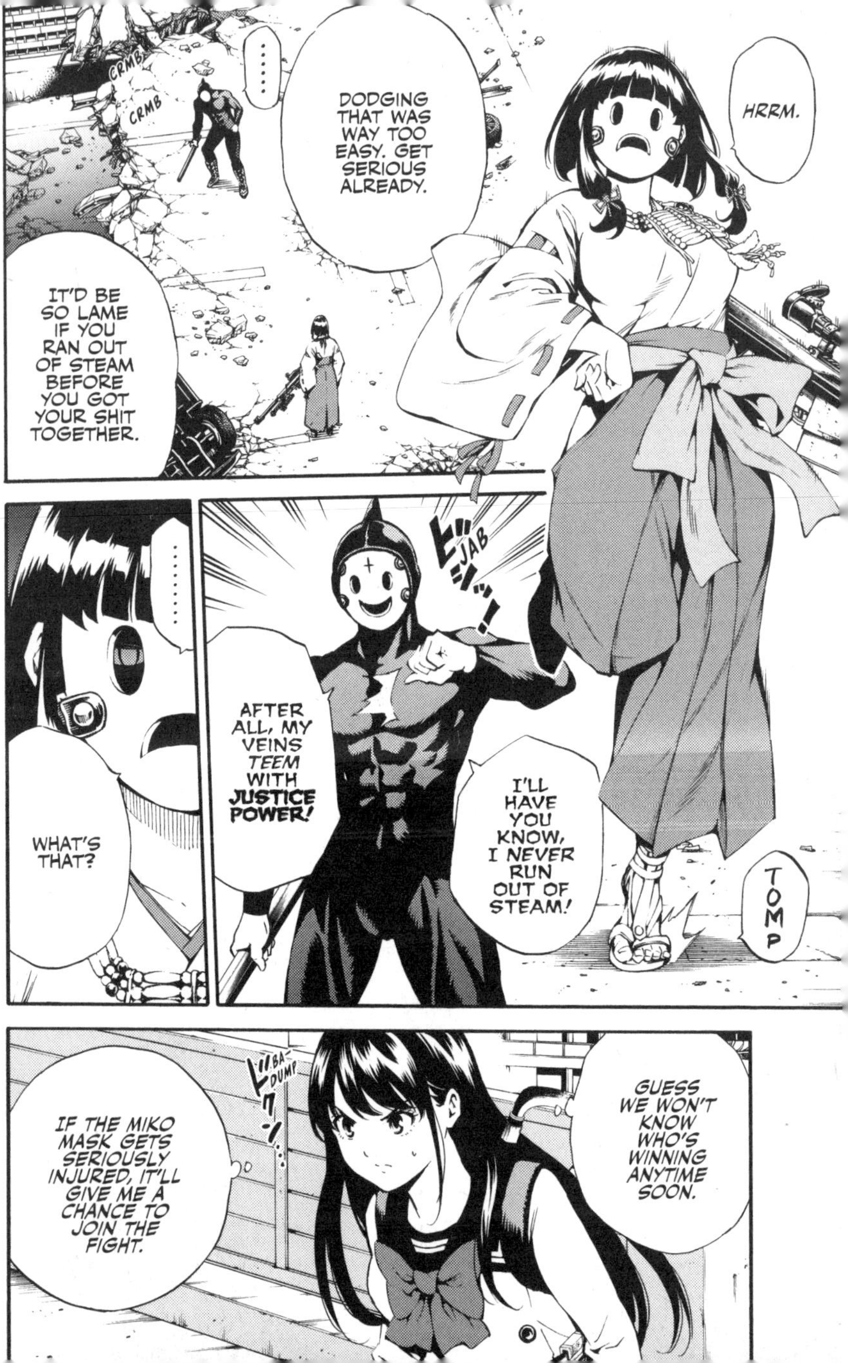
HRRM.
DODGING THAT WAS WAY TOO EASY. GET SERIOUS ALREADY.
......
CRMB
CRMB
IT'D BE SO LAME IF YOU RAN OUT OF STEAM BEFORE YOU GOT YOUR SHIT TOGETHER.
TOMP
JAB
I'LL HAVE YOU KNOW, I NEVER RUN OUT OF STEAM!
AFTER ALL, MY VEINS *TEEM* WITH **JUSTICE POWER!**
......
WHAT'S THAT?
GUESS WE WON'T KNOW WHO'S WINNING ANYTIME SOON.
BA-DUMP
IF THE MIKO MASK GETS SERIOUSLY INJURED, IT'LL GIVE ME A CHANCE TO JOIN THE FIGHT.

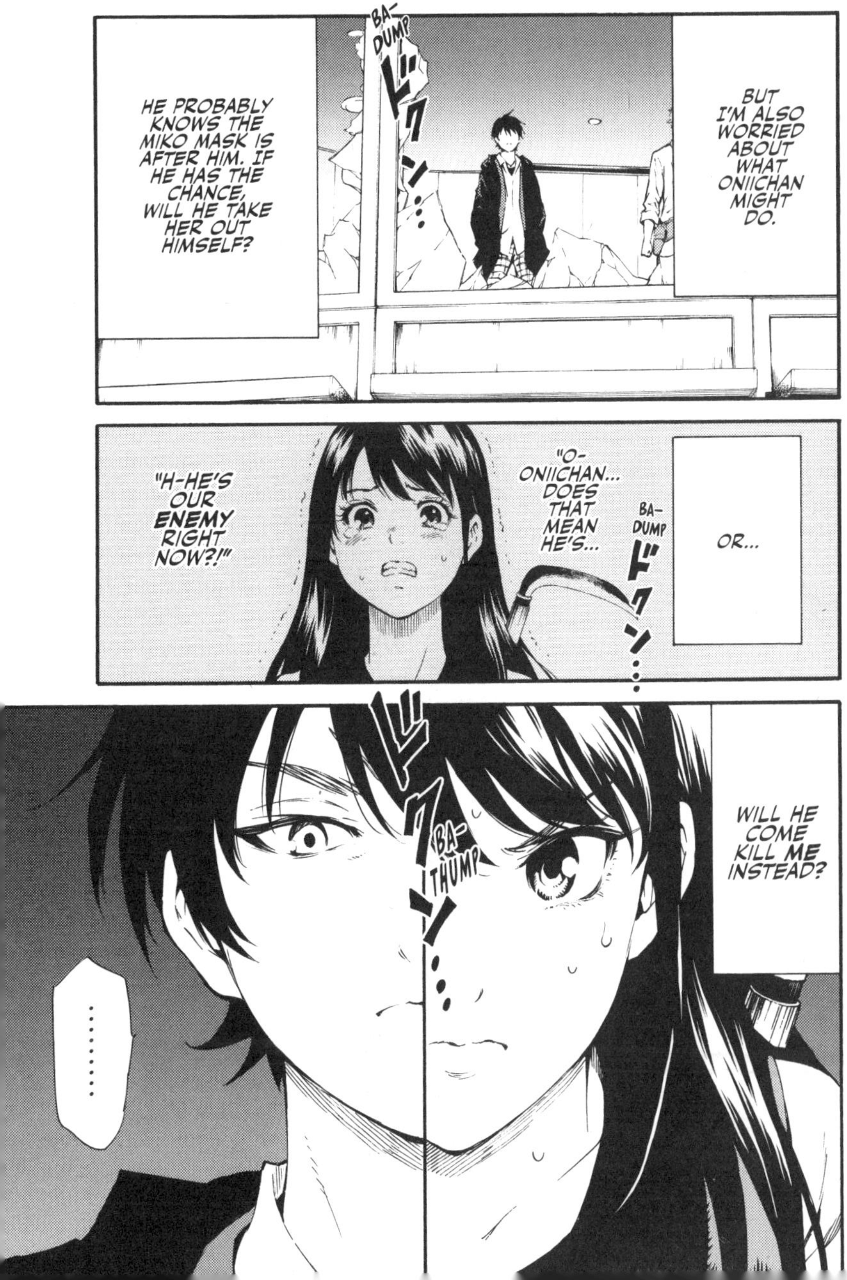
BUT I'M ALSO WORRIED ABOUT WHAT ONIICHAN MIGHT DO.
BA-DUMP
ドクン…
HE PROBABLY KNOWS THE MIKO MASK IS AFTER HIM. IF HE HAS THE CHANCE, WILL HE TAKE HER OUT HIMSELF?
OR...
BA-DUMP
ドクン…
"O-ONIICHAN... DOES THAT MEAN HE'S...
"H-HE'S OUR ENEMY RIGHT NOW?!"
WILL HE COME KILL ME INSTEAD?
ドクン…
BA-THUMP
....

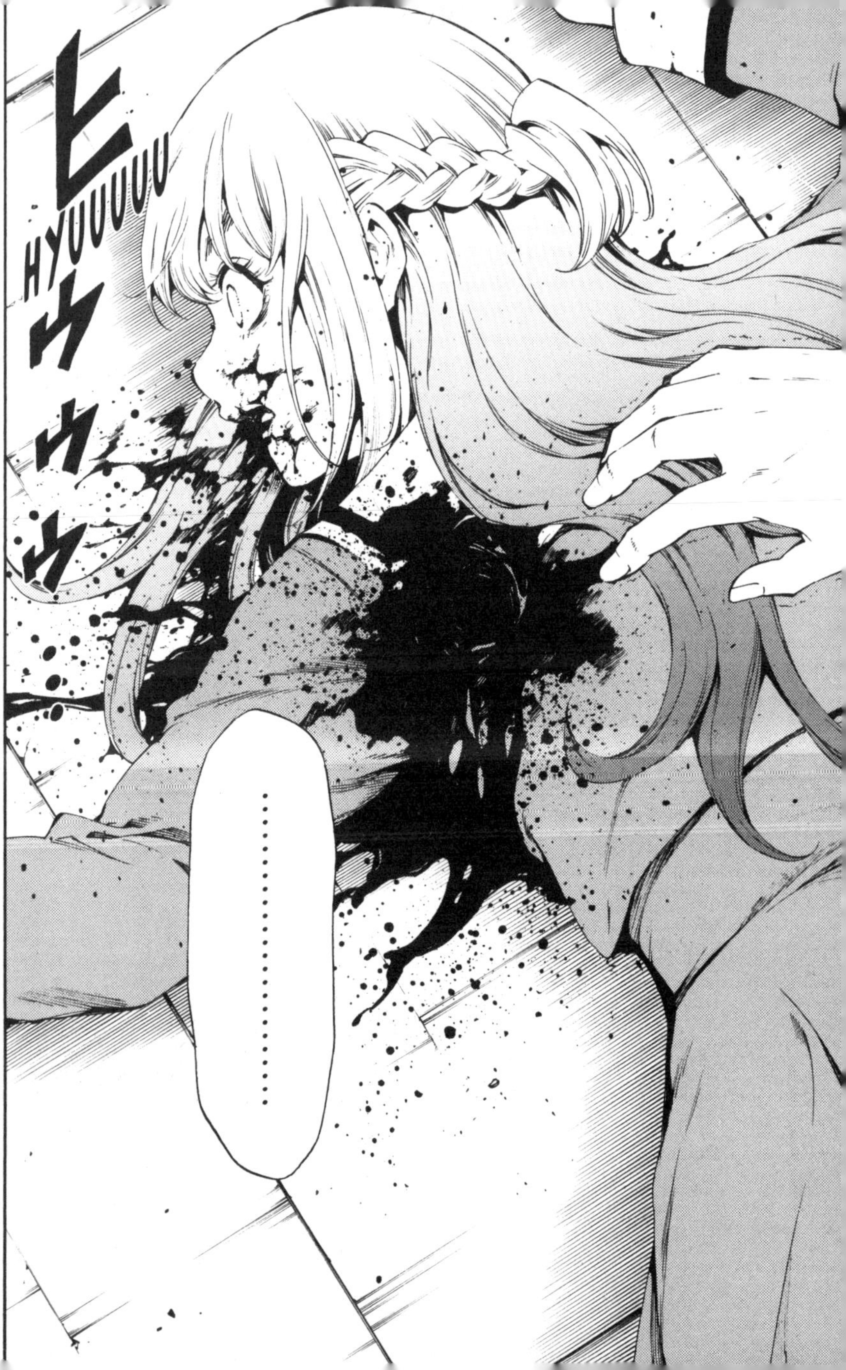
HYUUUUU
....

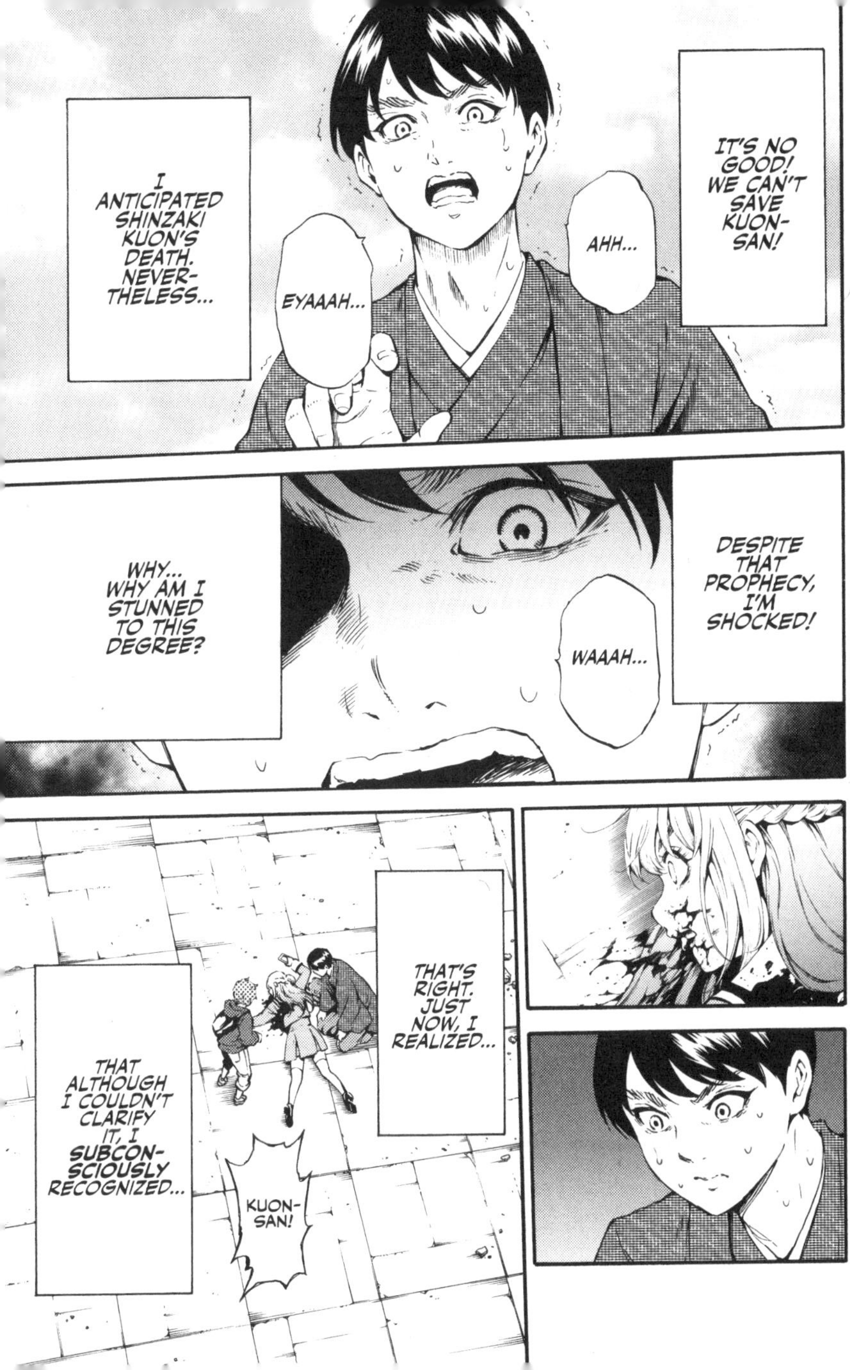
IT'S NO GOOD! WE CAN'T SAVE KUON-SAN!
AHH...
EYAAAH...
I ANTICIPATED SHINZAKI KUON'S DEATH. NEVERTHELESS...
DESPITE THAT PROPHECY, I'M SHOCKED!
WAAAH...
WHY... WHY AM I STUNNED TO THIS DEGREE?
THAT'S RIGHT. JUST NOW, I REALIZED...
KUON-SAN!
THAT ALTHOUGH I COULDN'T CLARIFY IT, I **SUBCONSCIOUSLY** RECOGNIZED...

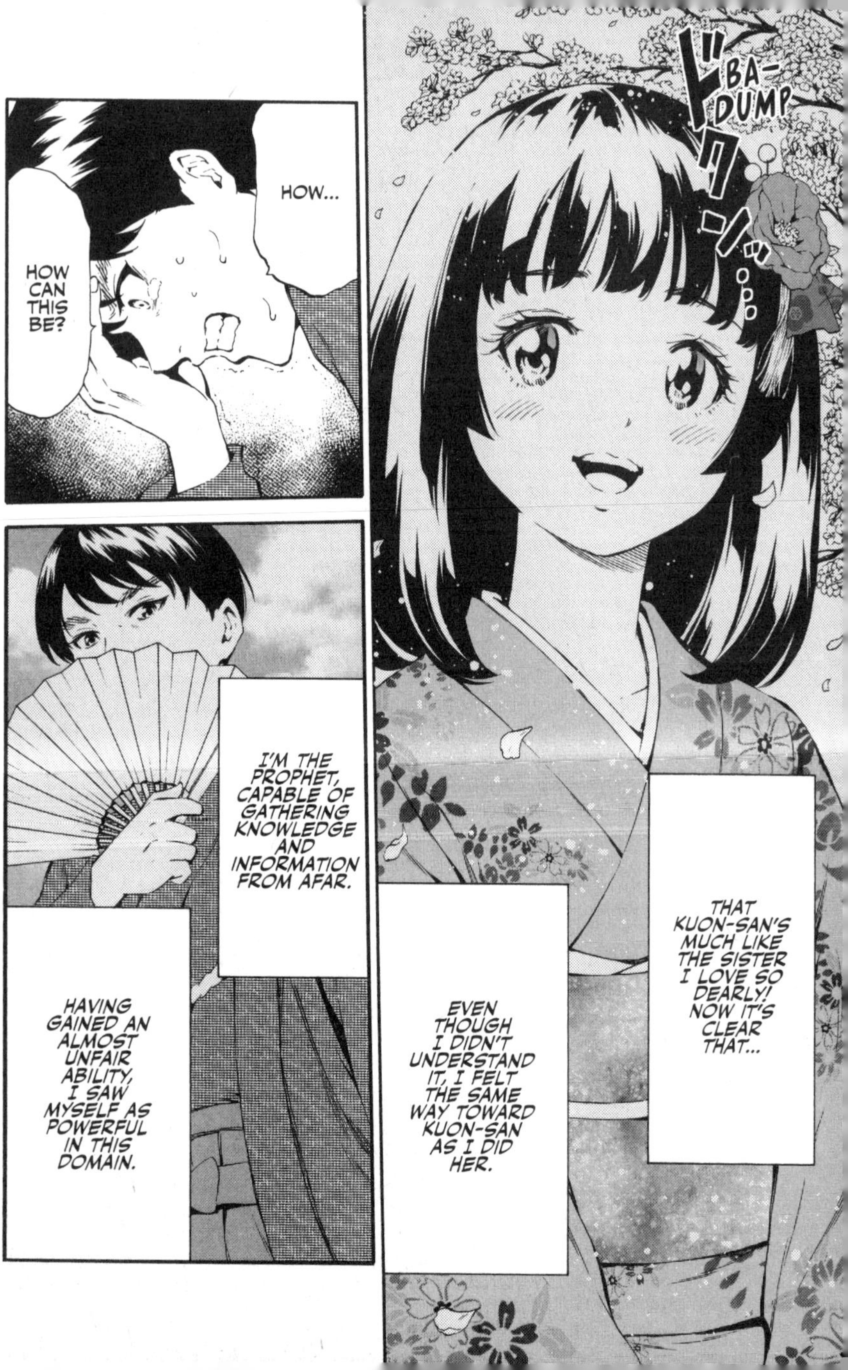
BA-DUMP
THAT KUON-SAN'S MUCH LIKE THE SISTER I LOVE SO DEARLY! NOW IT'S CLEAR THAT...
EVEN THOUGH I DIDN'T UNDERSTAND IT, I FELT THE SAME WAY TOWARD KUON-SAN AS I DID HER.
HOW...
HOW CAN THIS BE?
I'M THE PROPHET, CAPABLE OF GATHERING KNOWLEDGE AND INFORMATION FROM AFAR.
HAVING GAINED AN ALMOST UNFAIR ABILITY, I SAW MYSELF AS POWERFUL IN THIS DOMAIN.

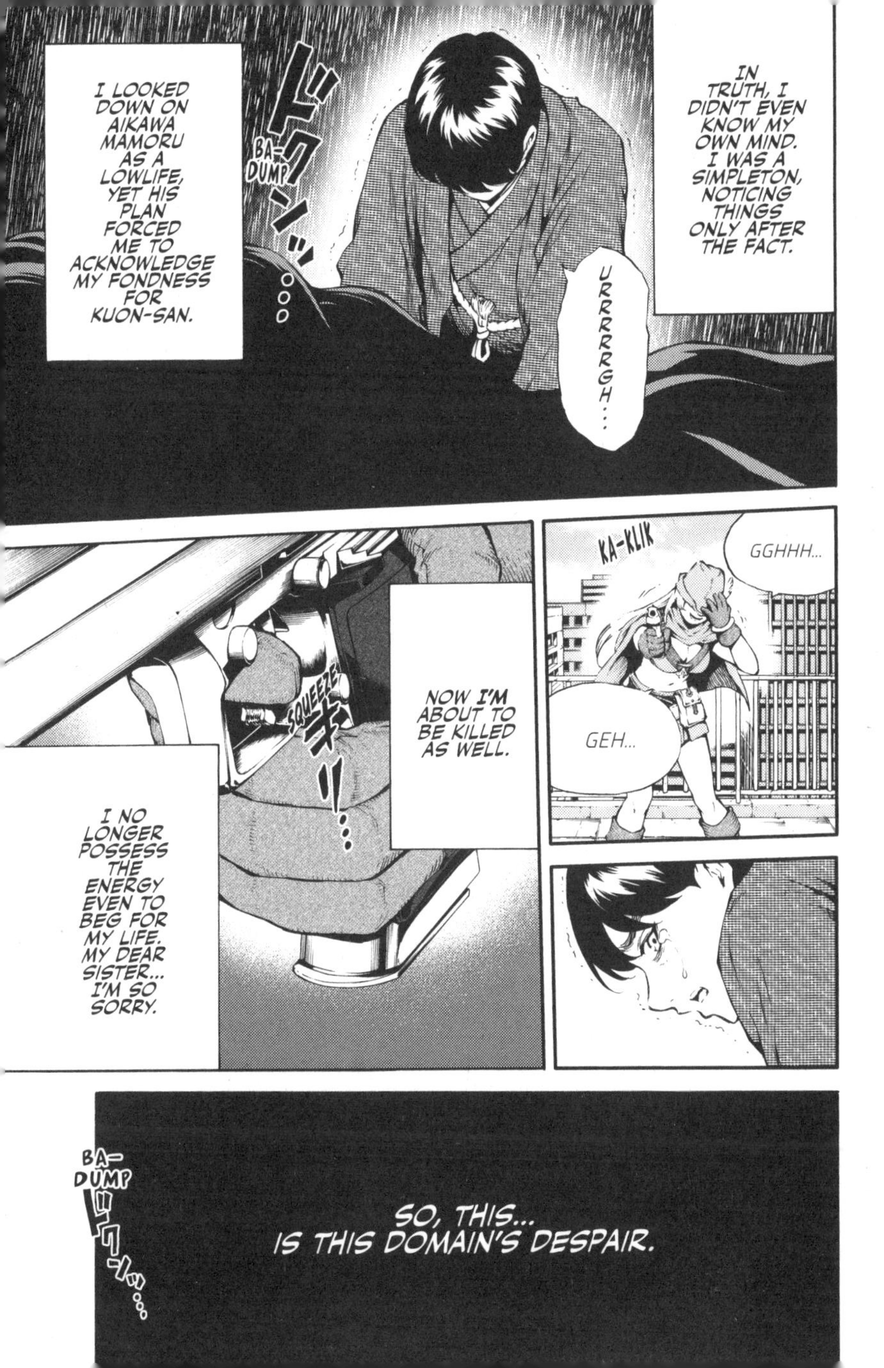
IN TRUTH, I DIDN'T EVEN KNOW MY OWN MIND. I WAS A SIMPLETON, NOTICING THINGS ONLY AFTER THE FACT.
URRRRGH...
BA-DUMP
I LOOKED DOWN ON AIKAWA MAMORU AS A LOWLIFE, YET HIS PLAN FORCED ME TO ACKNOWLEDGE MY FONDNESS FOR KUON-SAN.
KA-KLIK
GGHHH...
GEH...
NOW I'M ABOUT TO BE KILLED AS WELL.
SQUEEZE
I NO LONGER POSSESS THE ENERGY EVEN TO BEG FOR MY LIFE. MY DEAR SISTER... I'M SO SORRY.
BA-DUMP
SO, THIS... IS THIS DOMAIN'S DESPAIR.

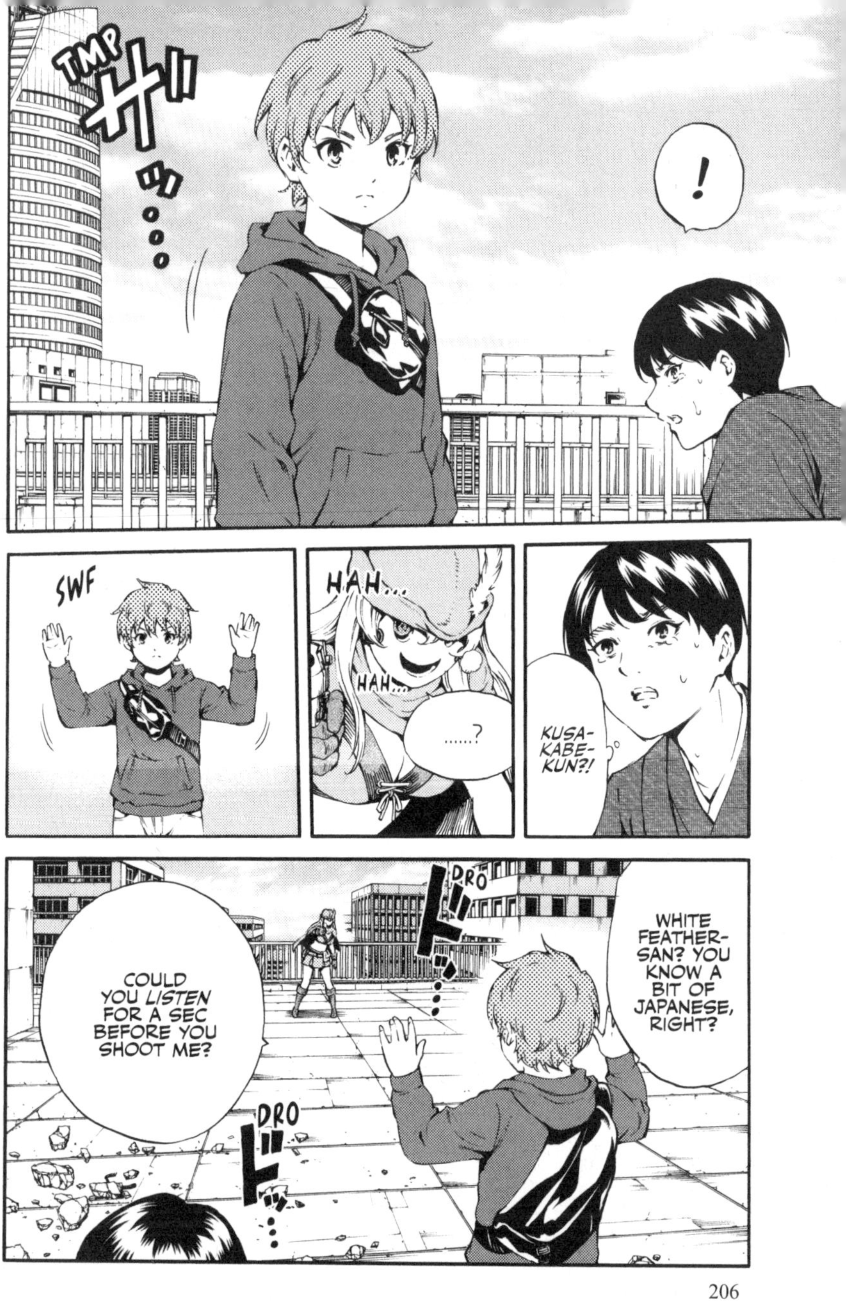
!
TMP
KUSA-KABE-KUN?!
HAH...
HAH...
......?
SWF
WHITE FEATHER-SAN? YOU KNOW A BIT OF JAPANESE, RIGHT?
DRO
COULD YOU *LISTEN* FOR A SEC BEFORE YOU SHOOT ME?
DRO

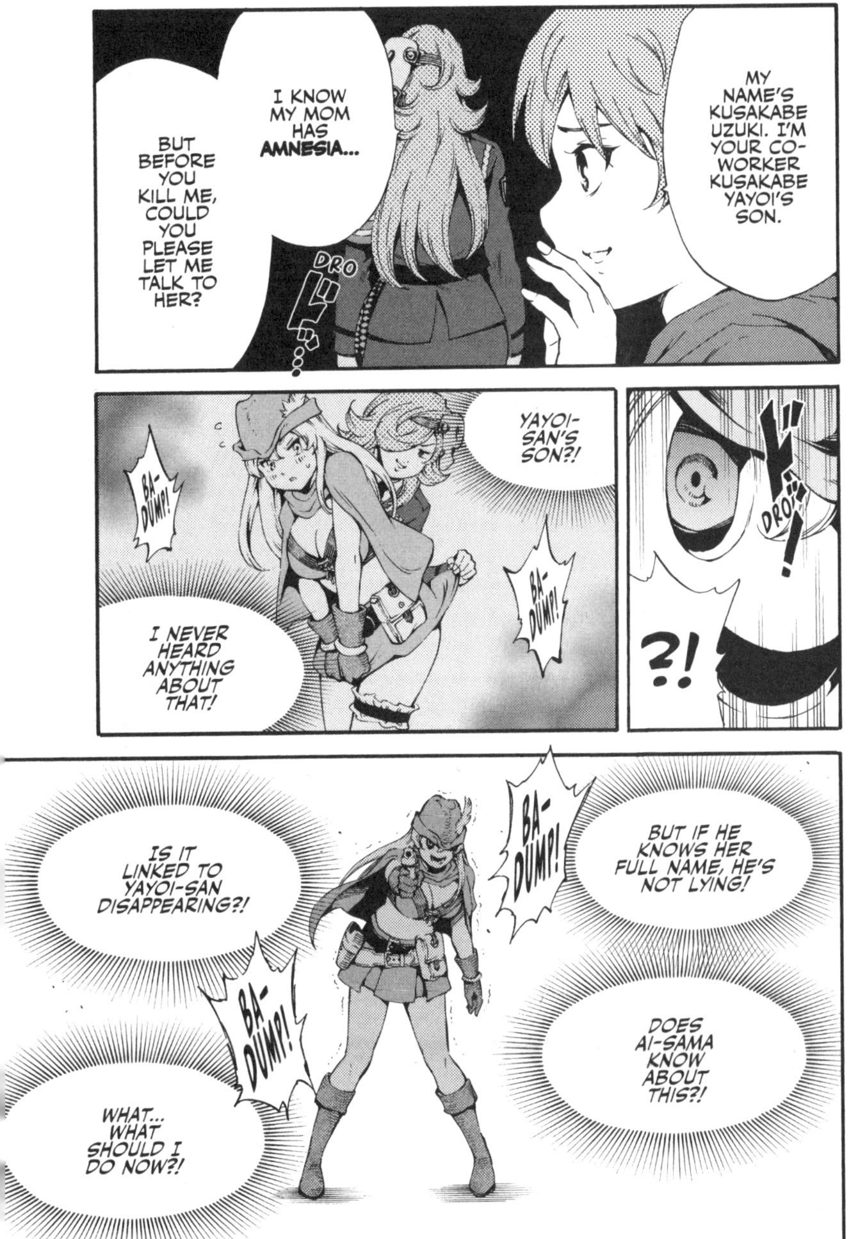
MY NAME'S KUSAKABE UZUKI. I'M YOUR CO-WORKER KUSAKABE YAYOI'S SON.
I KNOW MY MOM HAS **AMNESIA...**
BUT BEFORE YOU KILL ME, COULD YOU PLEASE LET ME TALK TO HER?
DRO
DRO
?!
YAYOI-SAN'S SON?!
BA-DUMP!
BA-DUMP!
I NEVER HEARD ANYTHING ABOUT THAT!
BUT IF HE KNOWS HER FULL NAME, HE'S NOT LYING!
BA-DUMP!
IS IT LINKED TO YAYOI-SAN DISAPPEARING?!
DOES AI-SAMA KNOW ABOUT THIS?!
BA-DUMP!
WHAT... WHAT SHOULD I DO NOW?!

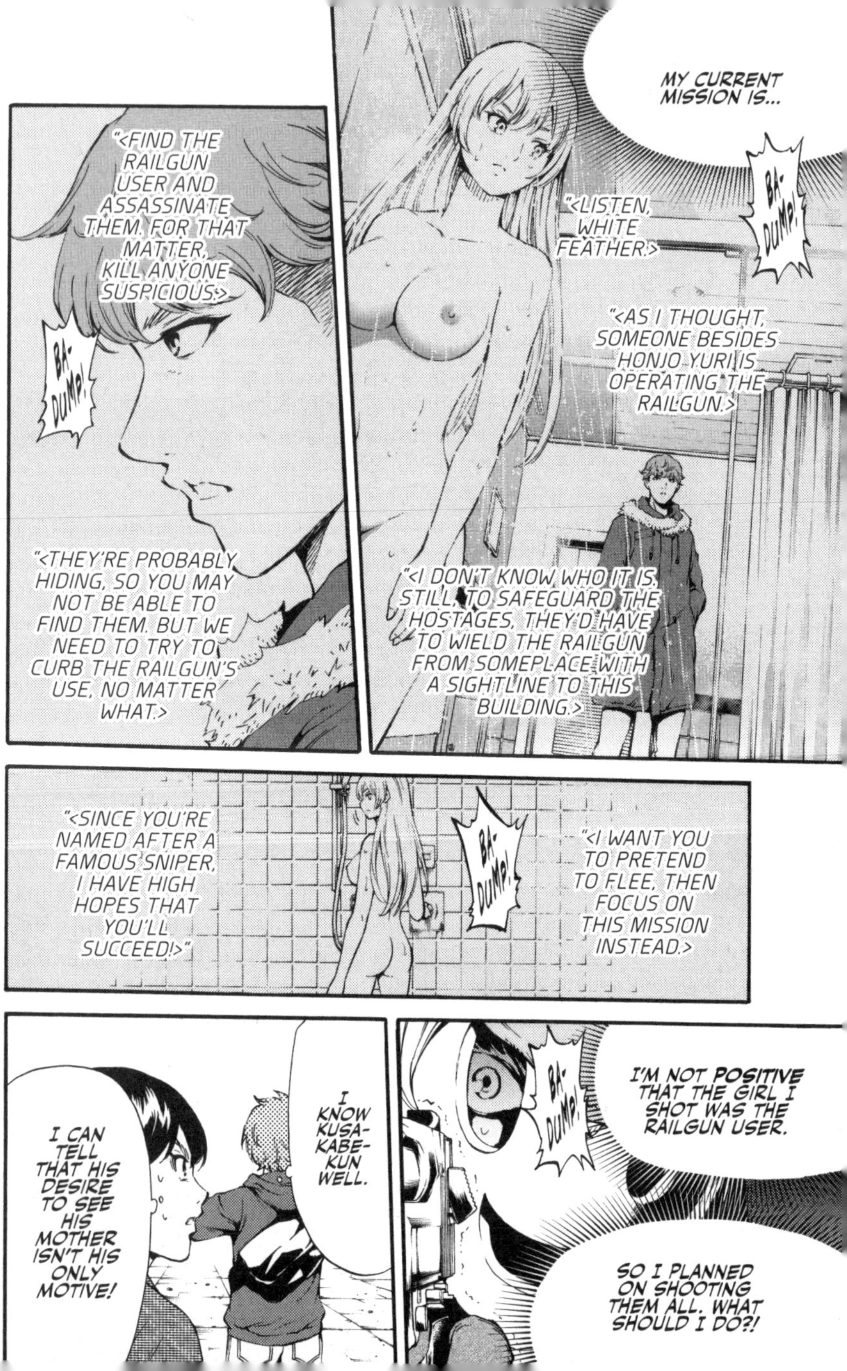

MY CURRENT MISSION IS...
BA-DUMP!
“<LISTEN, WHITE FEATHER.>
“<AS I THOUGHT, SOMEONE BESIDES HONJO YURI IS OPERATING THE RAILGUN.>
“<I DON'T KNOW WHO IT IS. STILL, TO SAFEGUARD THE HOSTAGES, THEY'D HAVE TO WIELD THE RAILGUN FROM SOMEPLACE WITH A SIGHTLINE TO THIS BUILDING.>
“<FIND THE RAILGUN USER AND ASSASSINATE THEM. FOR THAT MATTER, KILL ANYONE SUSPICIOUS.>
BA-DUMP!
“<THEY'RE PROBABLY HIDING, SO YOU MAY NOT BE ABLE TO FIND THEM. BUT WE NEED TO TRY TO CURB THE RAILGUN'S USE, NO MATTER WHAT.>
“<I WANT YOU TO PRETEND TO FLEE, THEN FOCUS ON THIS MISSION INSTEAD.>
BA-DUMP!
“<SINCE YOU'RE NAMED AFTER A FAMOUS SNIPER, I HAVE HIGH HOPES THAT YOU'LL SUCCEED!>”
I'M NOT POSITIVE THAT THE GIRL I SHOT WAS THE RAILGUN USER.
BA-DUMP!
SO I PLANNED ON SHOOTING THEM ALL. WHAT SHOULD I DO?!
I KNOW KUSAKABE-KUN WELL.
I CAN TELL THAT HIS DESIRE TO SEE HIS MOTHER ISN'T HIS ONLY MOTIVE!

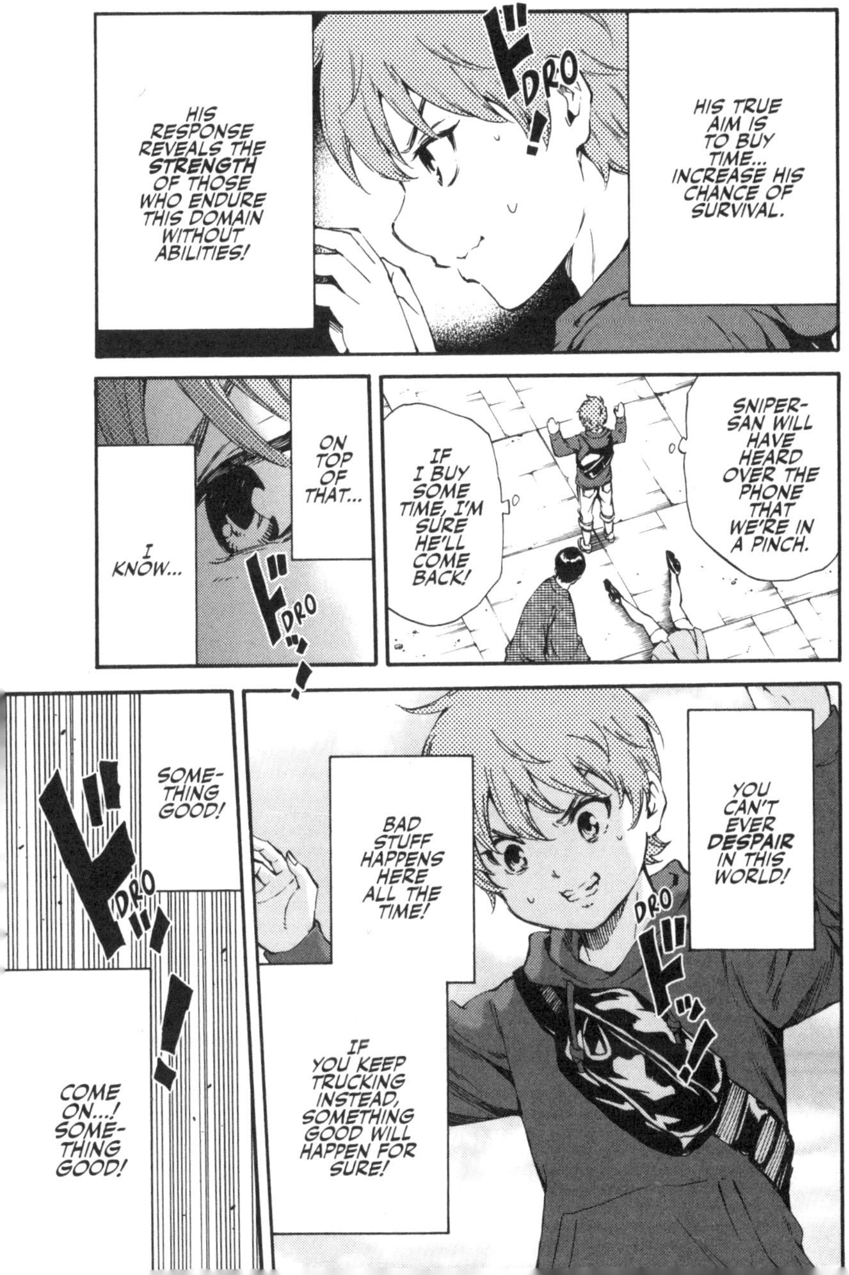
HIS TRUE AIM IS TO BUY TIME... INCREASE HIS CHANCE OF SURVIVAL.
ドDRO!
HIS RESPONSE REVEALS THE STRENGTH OF THOSE WHO ENDURE THIS DOMAIN WITHOUT ABILITIES!
SNIPER-SAN WILL HAVE HEARD OVER THE PHONE THAT WE'RE IN A PINCH.
IF I BUY SOME TIME, I'M SURE HE'LL COME BACK!
ON TOP OF THAT...
I KNOW...
ドDRO!
YOU CAN'T EVER DESPAIR IN THIS WORLD!
BAD STUFF HAPPENS HERE ALL THE TIME!
DRO ド!
IF YOU KEEP TRUCKING INSTEAD, SOMETHING GOOD WILL HAPPEN FOR SURE!
SOME-THING GOOD!
ドDRO!
COME ON...! SOME-THING GOOD!

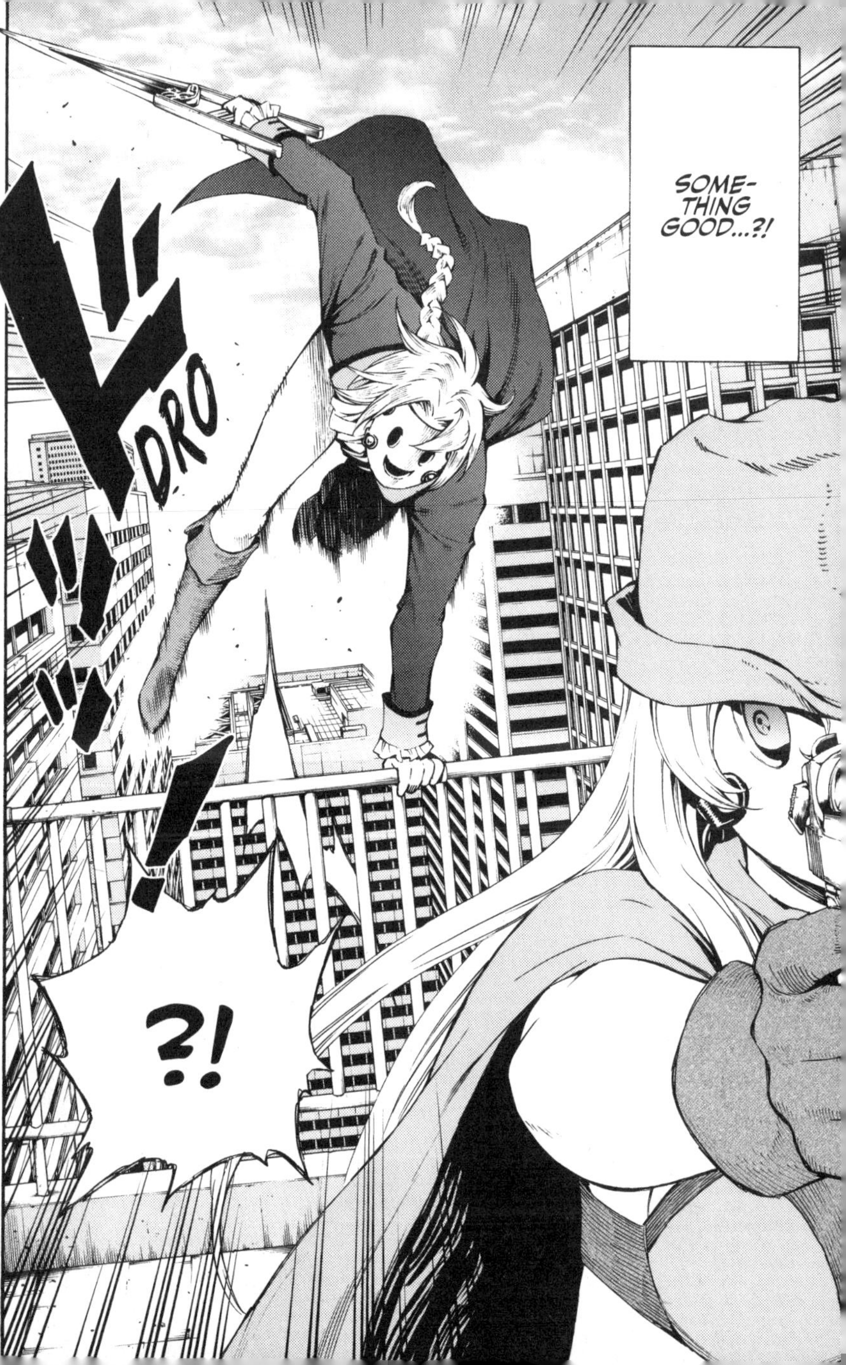
SOME-
THING
GOOD...?!
DRO
?!

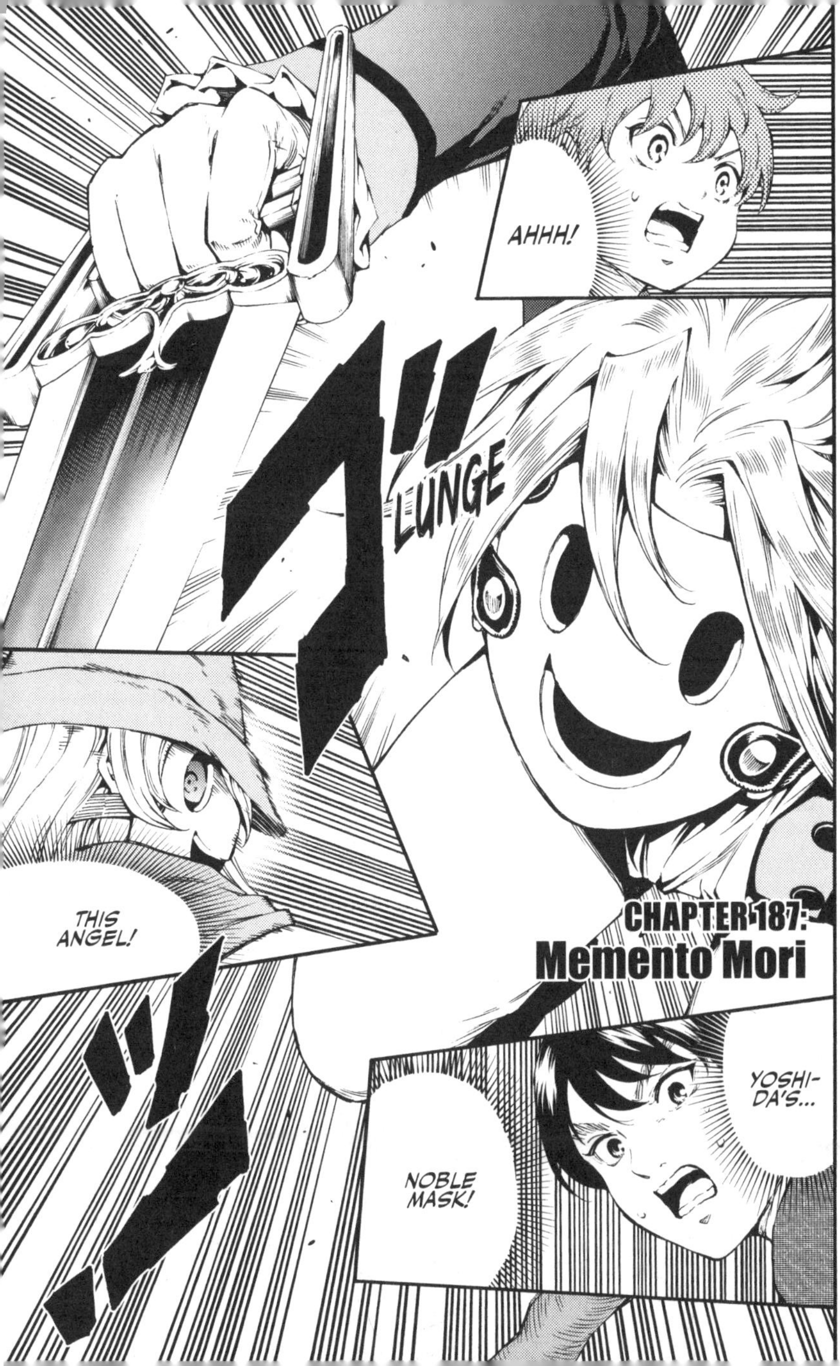
AHHH!
LUNGE
CHAPTER 187:
Memento Mori
THIS ANGEL!
YOSHI-DA'S...
NOBLE MASK!

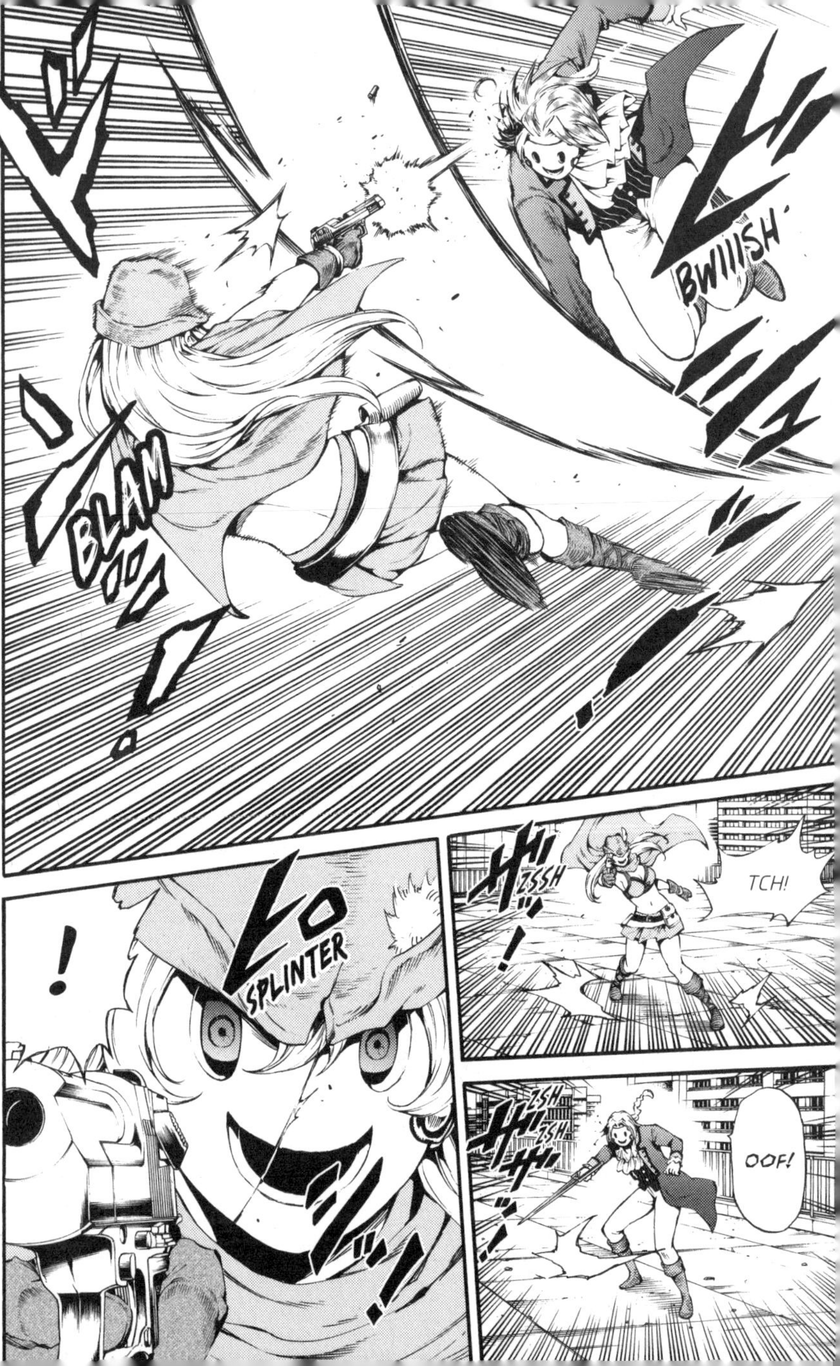
BWIIISH
BLAM
ZSSH
TCH!
ZSH
ZSH
OOF!
SPLINTER

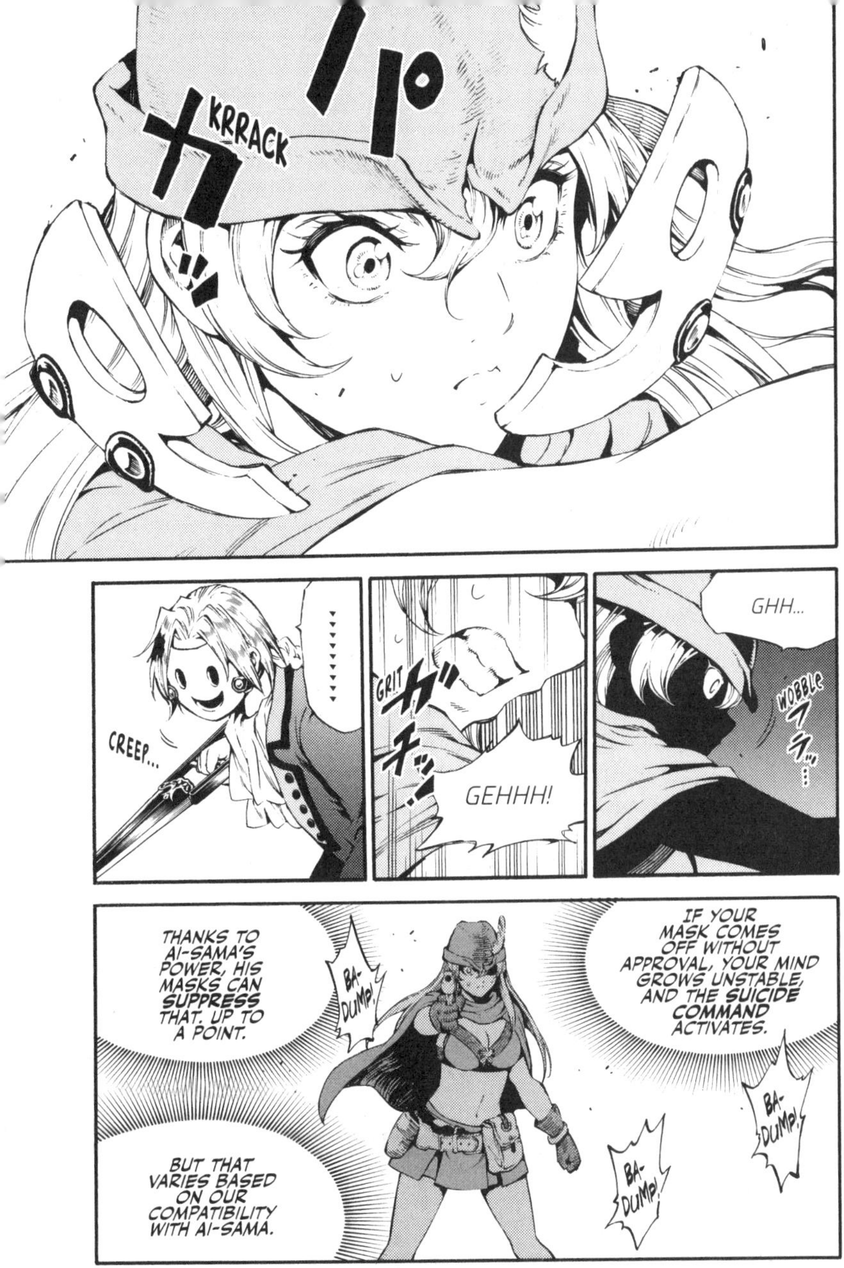

パカッ!
KRRACK
GHH...
フラ...
WOBBLE
ガチッ!
GRIT
GEHHH!
......
CREEP...
IF YOUR MASK COMES OFF WITHOUT APPROVAL, YOUR MIND GROWS UNSTABLE, AND THE **SUICIDE COMMAND** ACTIVATES.
THANKS TO AI-SAMA'S POWER, HIS MASKS CAN **SUPPRESS** THAT. UP TO A POINT.
BA-DUMP!
BA-DUMP!
BA-DUMP!
BUT THAT VARIES BASED ON OUR COMPATIBILITY WITH AI-SAMA.

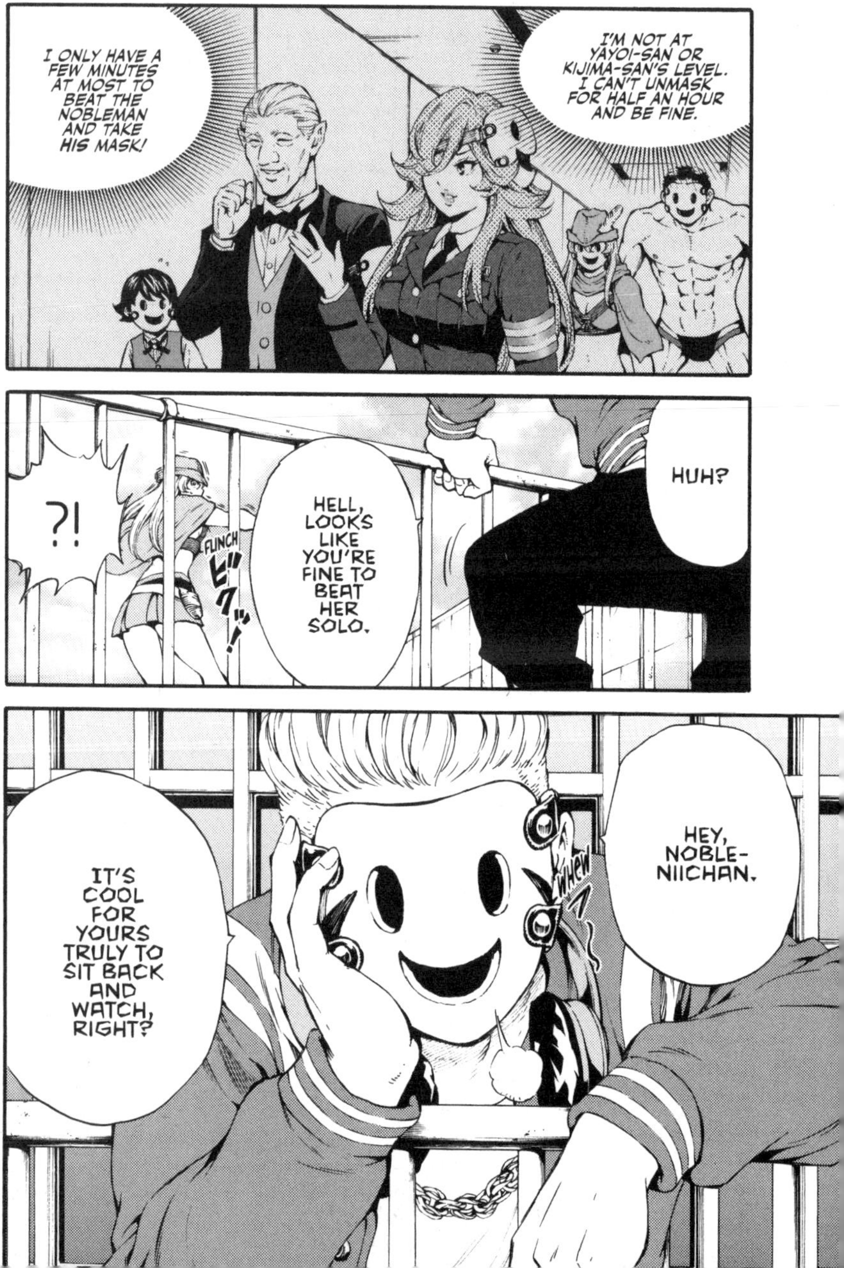
I'M NOT AT YAYOI-SAN OR KIJIMA-SAN'S LEVEL. I CAN'T UNMASK FOR HALF AN HOUR AND BE FINE.
I ONLY HAVE A FEW MINUTES AT MOST TO BEAT THE NOBLEMAN AND TAKE HIS MASK!
HUH?
HELL, LOOKS LIKE YOU'RE FINE TO BEAT HER SOLO.
FLINCH
?!
HEY, NOBLE-NIICHAN.
WHEW
IT'S COOL FOR YOURS TRULY TO SIT BACK AND WATCH, RIGHT?

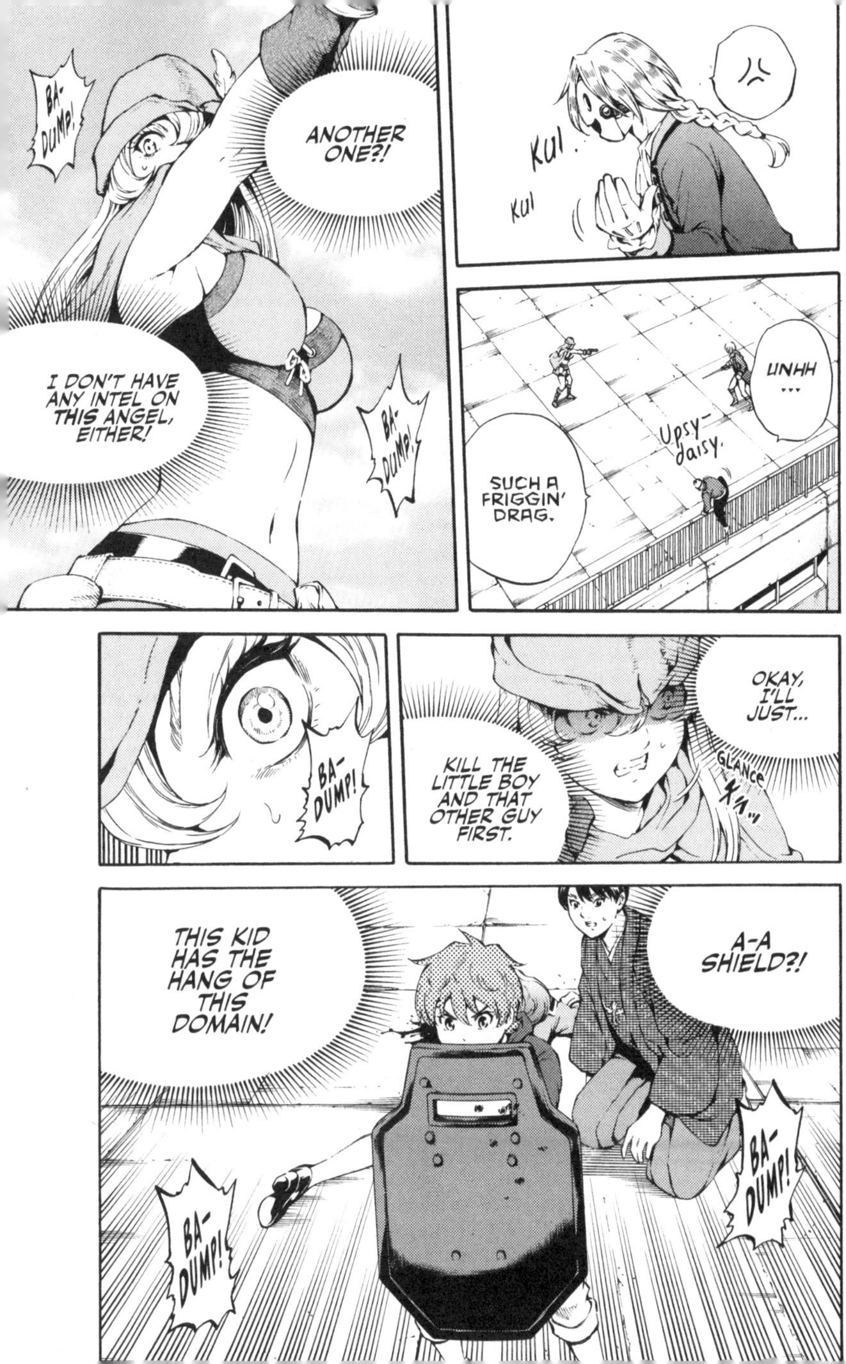

Kul
Kul
UNHH...
Upsy-daisy.
SUCH A FRIGGIN' DRAG.
ANOTHER ONE?!
BA-DUMP!
I DON'T HAVE ANY INTEL ON THIS ANGEL, EITHER!
BA-DUMP!
OKAY, I'LL JUST...
GLANCE
KILL THE LITTLE BOY AND THAT OTHER GUY FIRST.
BA-DUMP!
A-A SHIELD?!
THIS KID HAS THE HANG OF THIS DOMAIN!
BA-DUMP!
BA-DUMP!

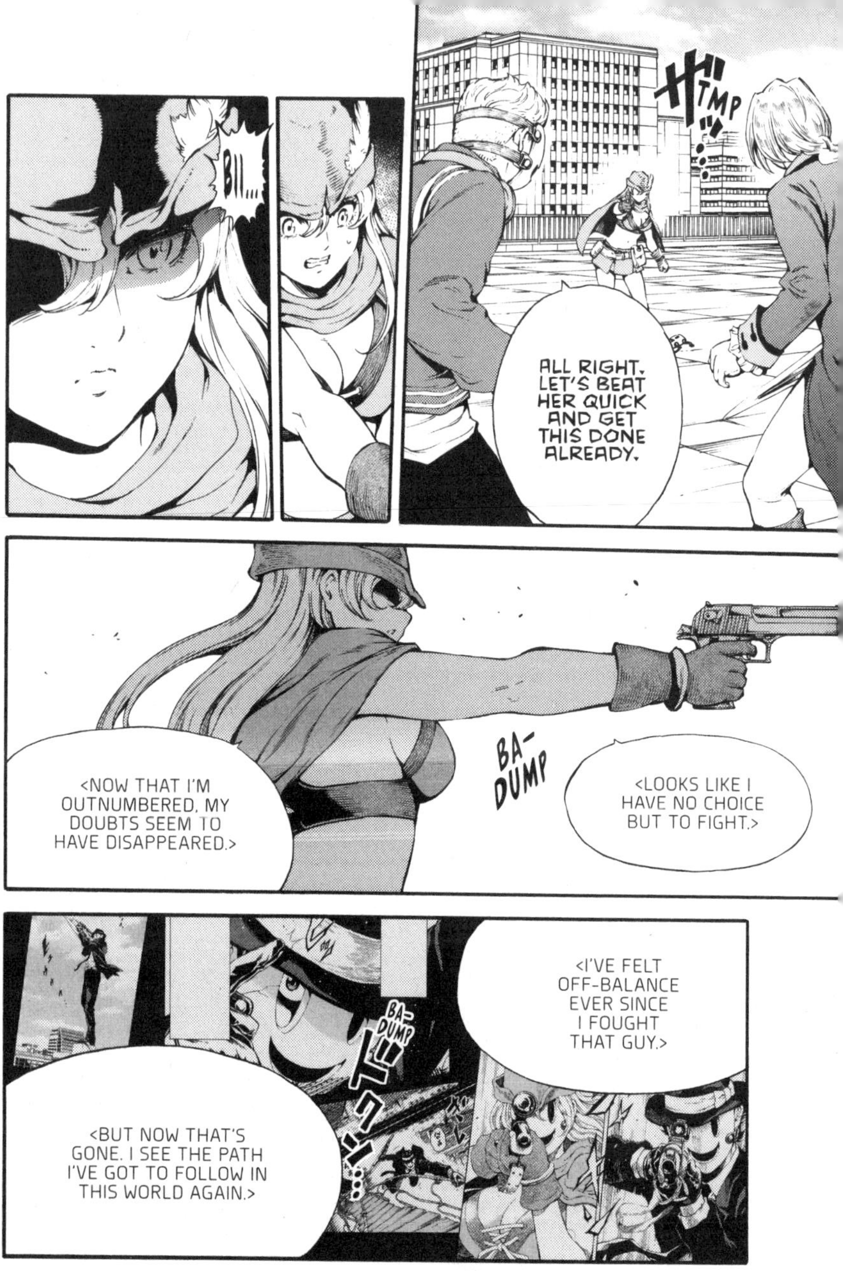
TMP
ALL RIGHT. LET'S BEAT HER QUICK AND GET THIS DONE ALREADY.
BII...!
<LOOKS LIKE I HAVE NO CHOICE BUT TO FIGHT.>
BA-DUMP
<NOW THAT I'M OUTNUMBERED, MY DOUBTS SEEM TO HAVE DISAPPEARED.>
<I'VE FELT OFF-BALANCE EVER SINCE I FOUGHT THAT GUY.>
BA-DUMP
<BUT NOW THAT'S GONE. I SEE THE PATH I'VE GOT TO FOLLOW IN THIS WORLD AGAIN.>

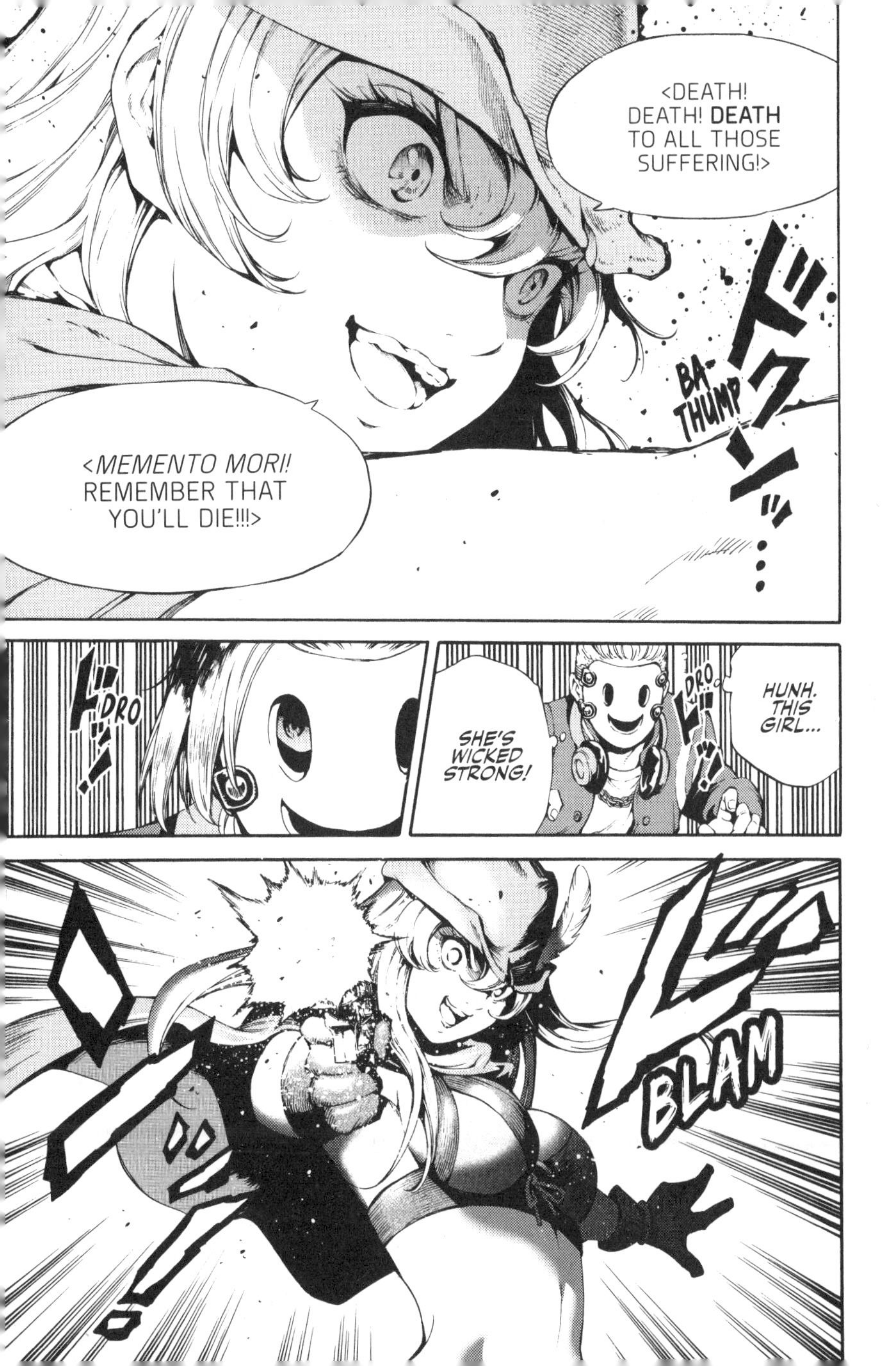

<DEATH! DEATH! **DEATH** TO ALL THOSE SUFFERING!>
BA-THUMP
<*MEMENTO MORI!* REMEMBER THAT YOU'LL DIE!!!>
HUNH. THIS GIRL...
DRO
SHE'S WICKED STRONG!
DRO
BLAM

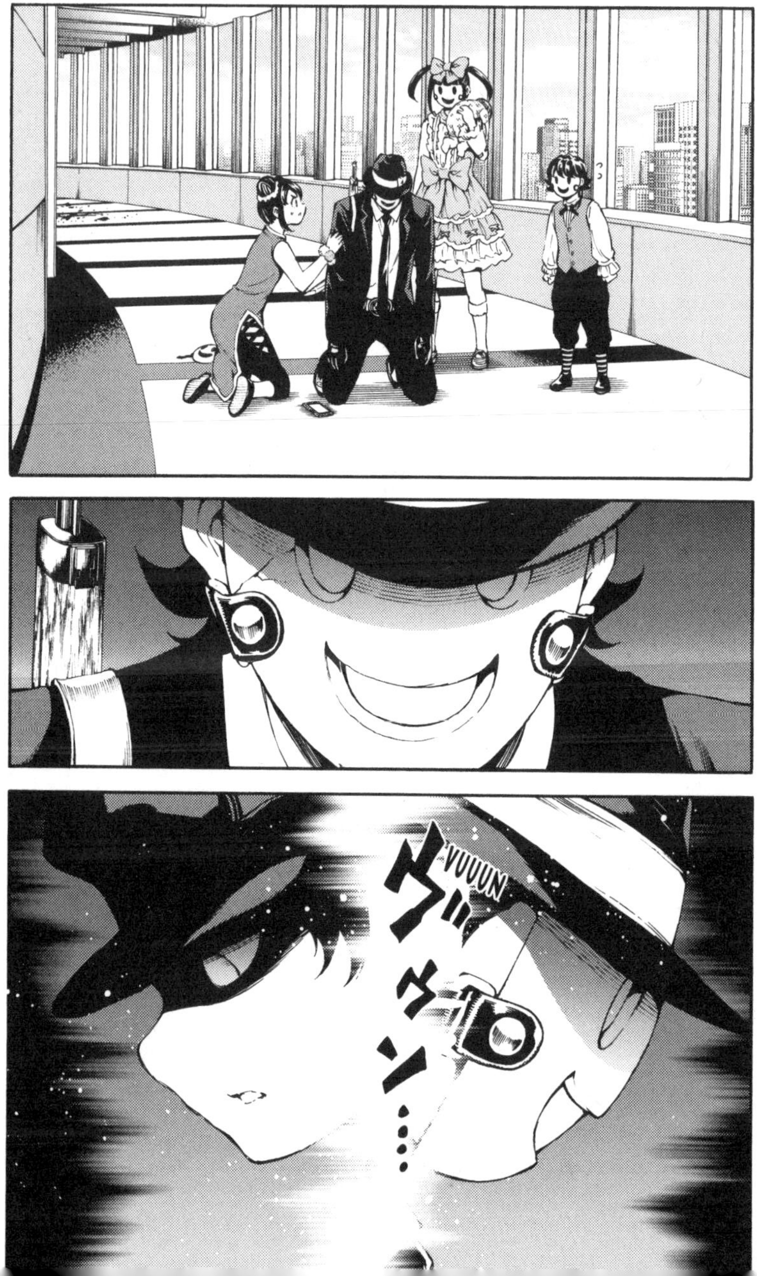
VUUUN
ヴゥン…

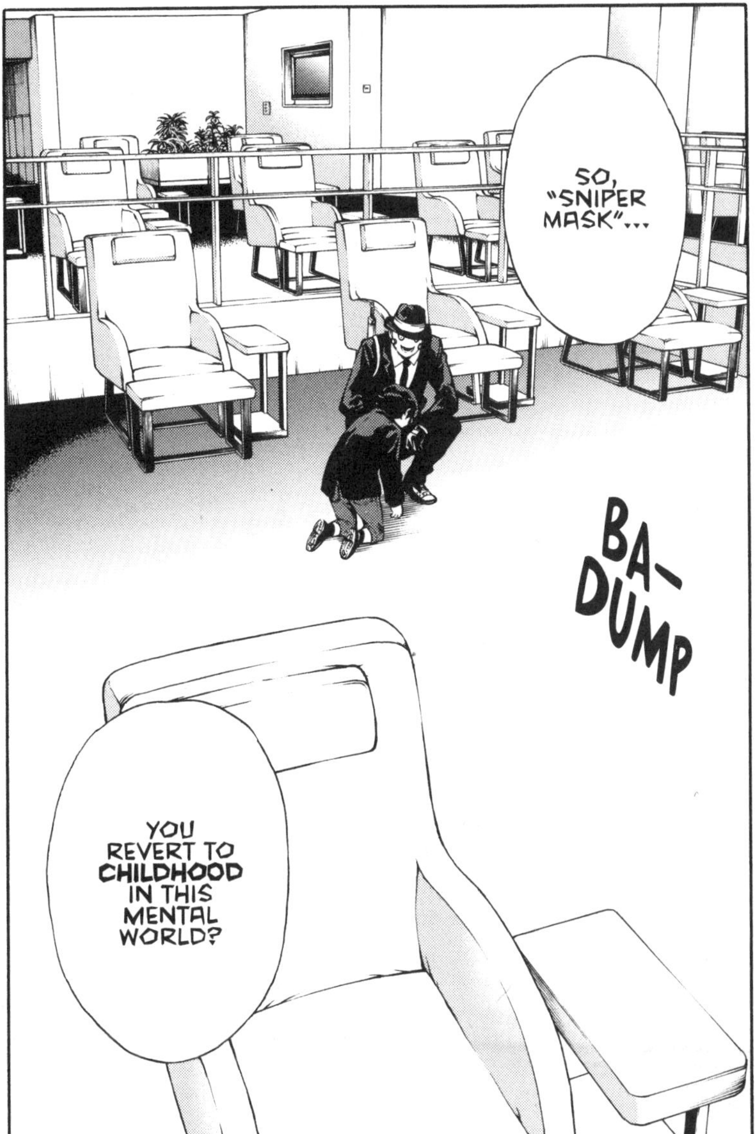
SO, "SNIPER MASK"...
BA-DUMP
YOU REVERT TO CHILDHOOD IN THIS MENTAL WORLD?

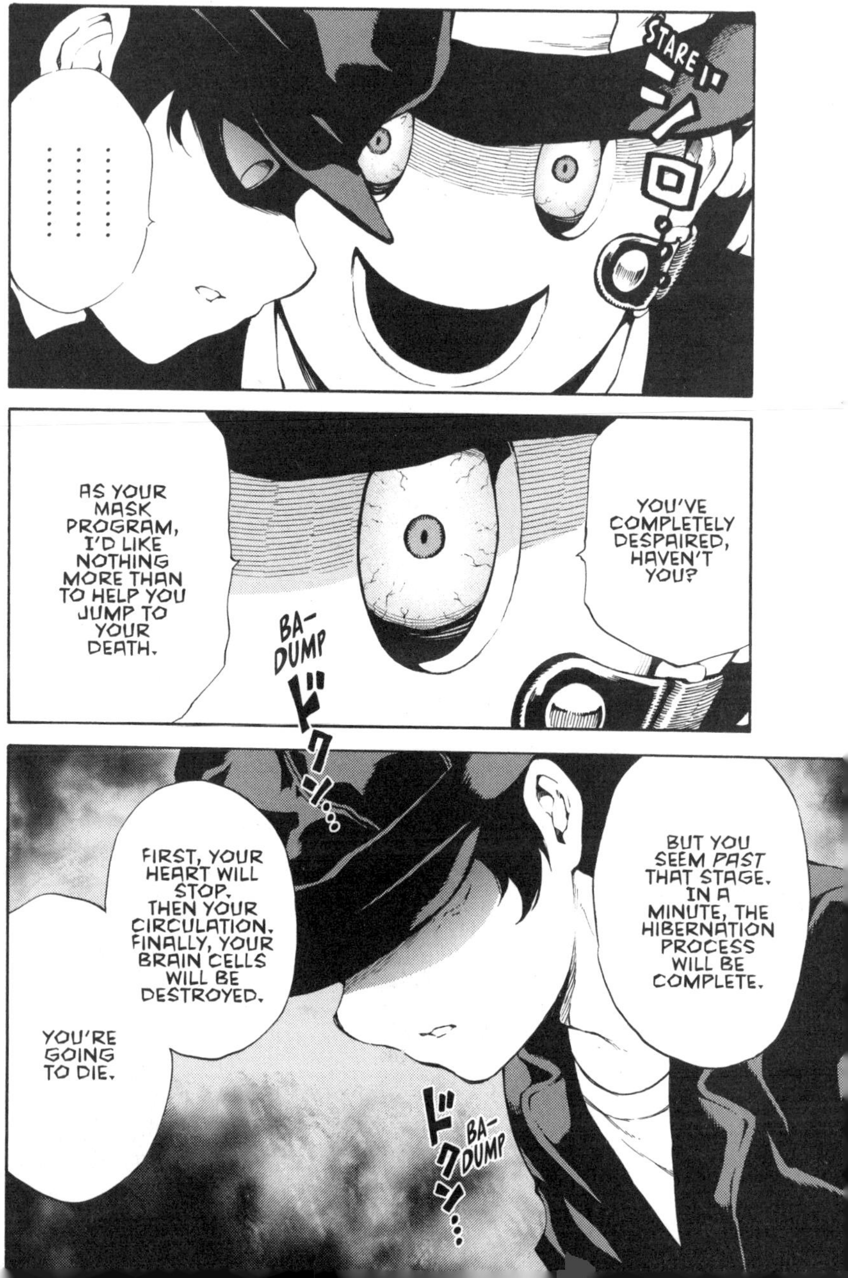
STARE
......
YOU'VE COMPLETELY DESPAIRED, HAVEN'T YOU?
AS YOUR MASK PROGRAM, I'D LIKE NOTHING MORE THAN TO HELP YOU JUMP TO YOUR DEATH.
BA-DUMP
BUT YOU SEEM *PAST* THAT STAGE. IN A MINUTE, THE HIBERNATION PROCESS WILL BE COMPLETE.
FIRST, YOUR HEART WILL STOP. THEN YOUR CIRCULATION. FINALLY, YOUR BRAIN CELLS WILL BE DESTROYED.
YOU'RE GOING TO DIE.
BA-DUMP

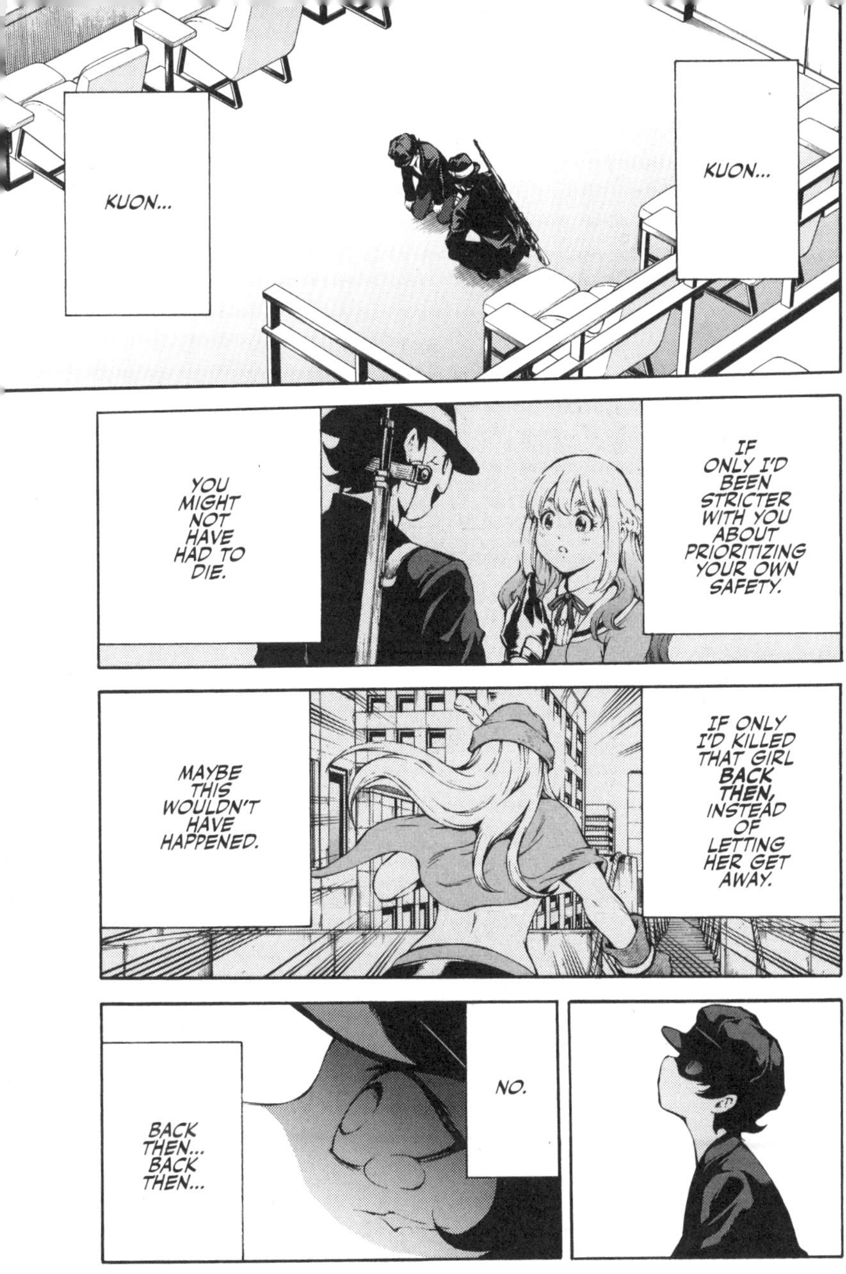
KUON...
KUON...
IF ONLY I'D BEEN STRICTER WITH YOU ABOUT PRIORITIZING YOUR OWN SAFETY.
YOU MIGHT NOT HAVE HAD TO DIE.
IF ONLY I'D KILLED THAT GIRL BACK THEN, INSTEAD OF LETTING HER GET AWAY.
MAYBE THIS WOULDN'T HAVE HAPPENED.
NO.
BACK THEN... BACK THEN...

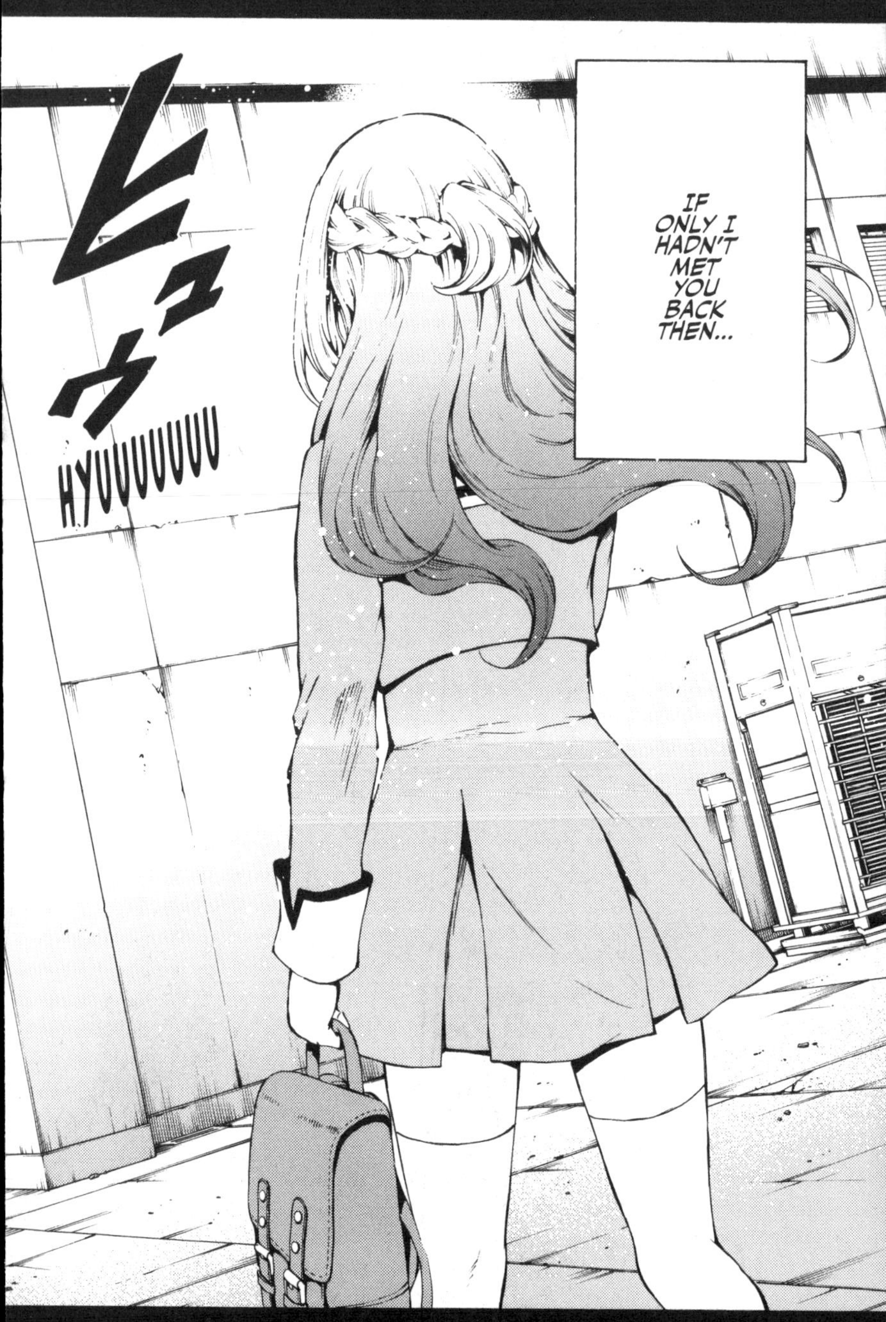
IF ONLY I HADN'T MET YOU BACK THEN...
ヒュウ
HYUUUUUUU

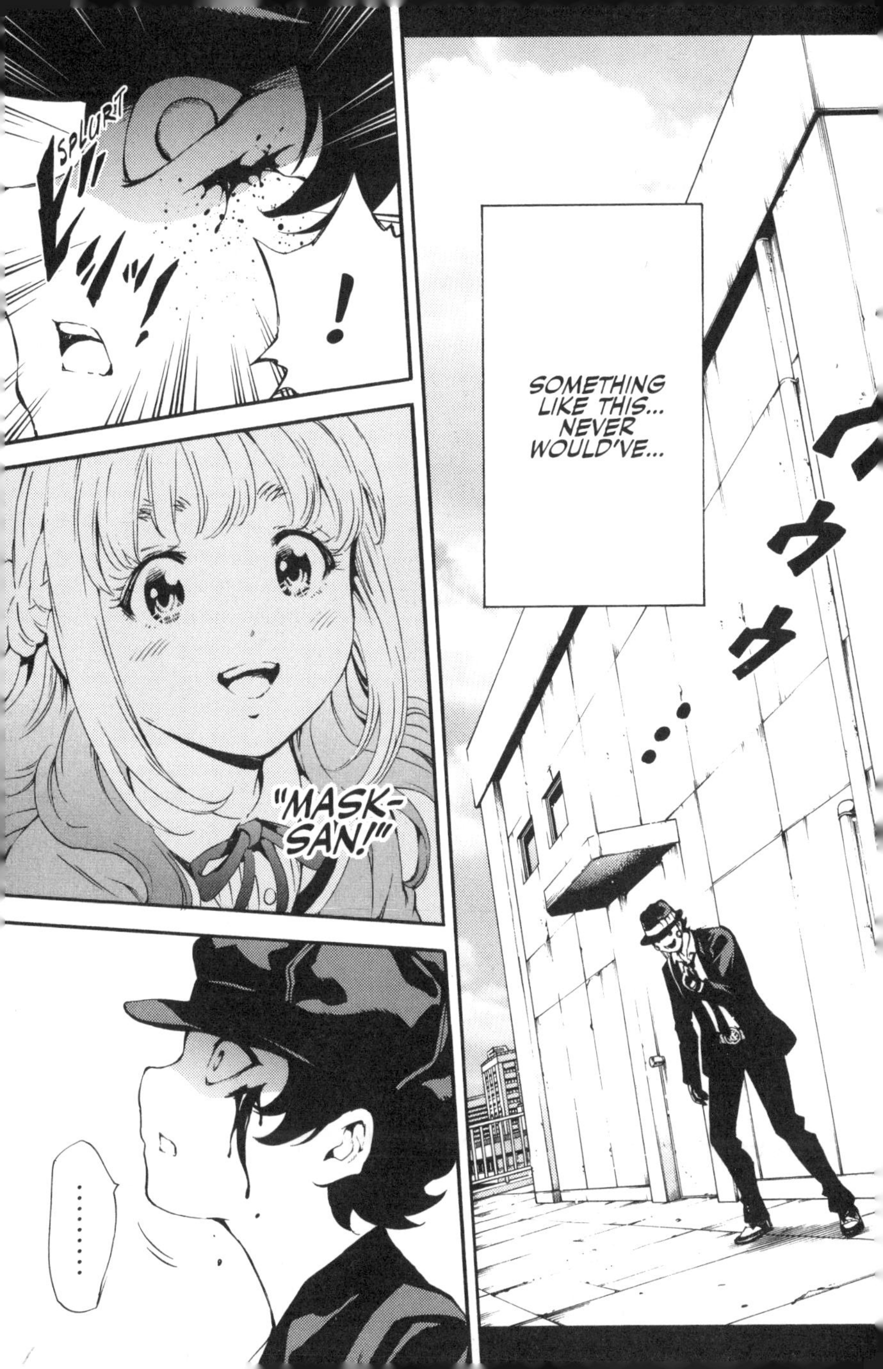
SOMETHING LIKE THIS... NEVER WOULD'VE...
SPLURT
!
"MASK-SAN!"
......

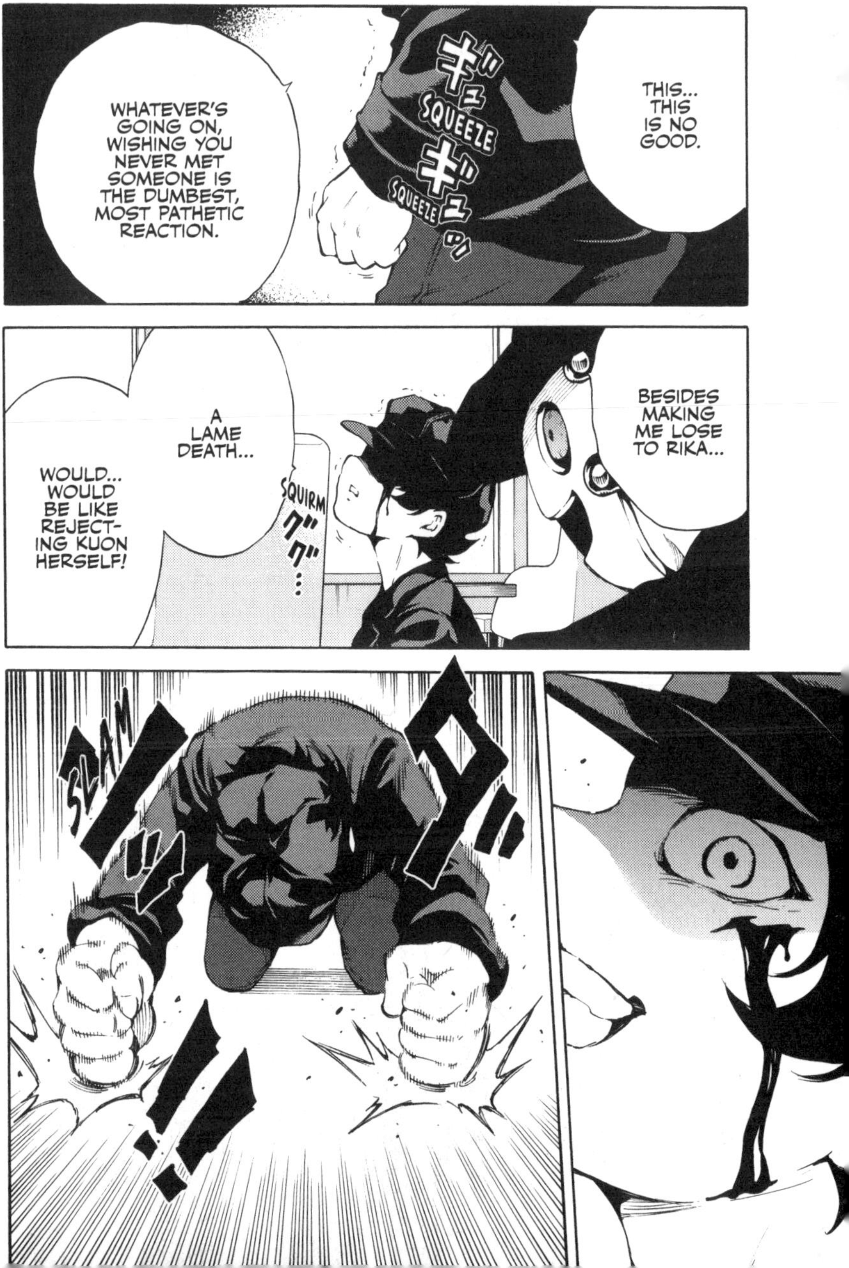
THIS... THIS IS NO GOOD.
SQUEEZE
SQUEEZE
WHATEVER'S GOING ON, WISHING YOU NEVER MET SOMEONE IS THE DUMBEST, MOST PATHETIC REACTION.
BESIDES MAKING ME LOSE TO RIKA...
A LAME DEATH...
WOULD... WOULD BE LIKE REJECTING KUON HERSELF!
SQUIRM
SLAM

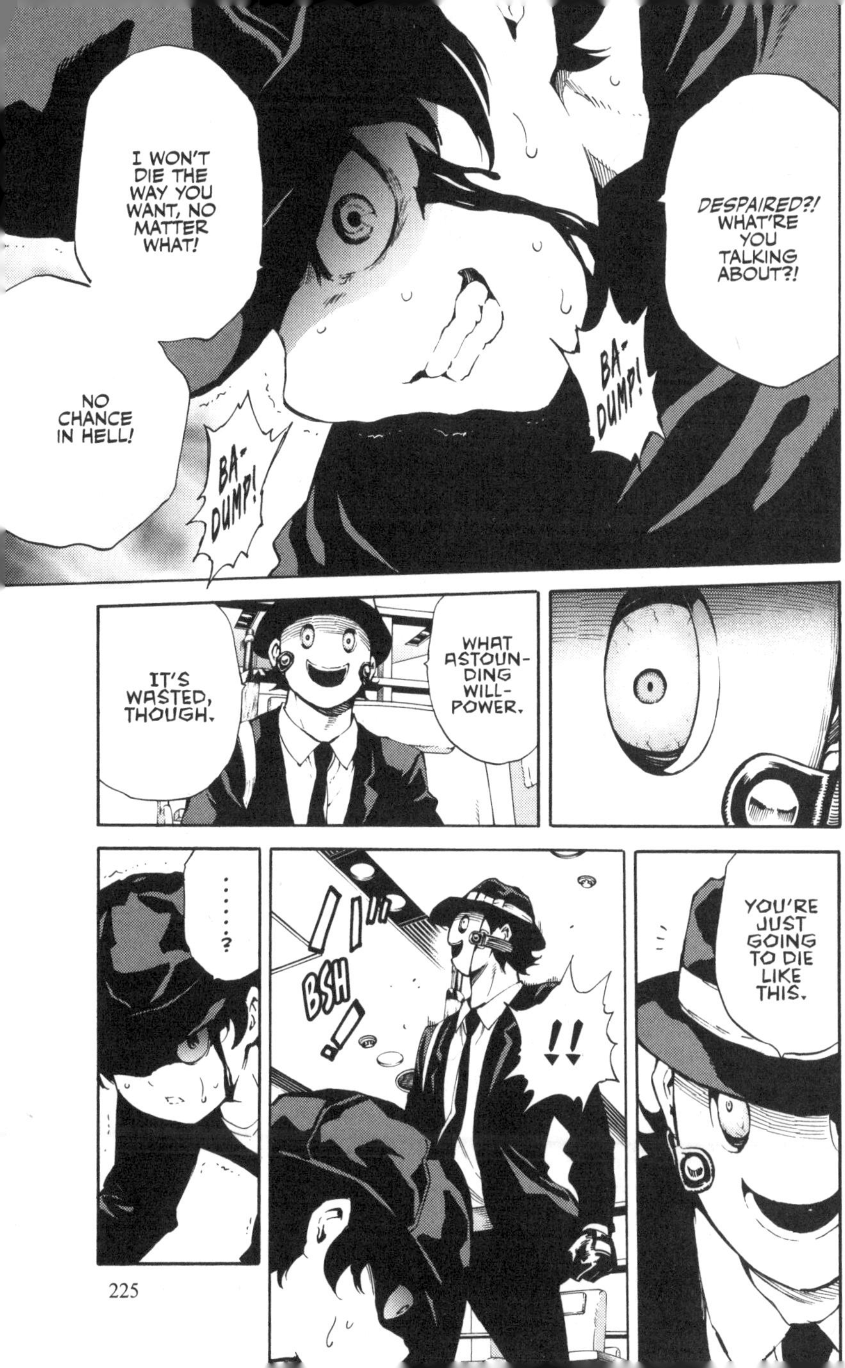
DESPAIRED?! WHAT'RE YOU TALKING ABOUT?!
BA-DUMP!
I WON'T DIE THE WAY YOU WANT, NO MATTER WHAT!
NO CHANCE IN HELL!
BA-DUMP!
WHAT ASTOUNDING WILLPOWER.
IT'S WASTED, THOUGH.
YOU'RE JUST GOING TO DIE LIKE THIS.
!!
BSH!
......?

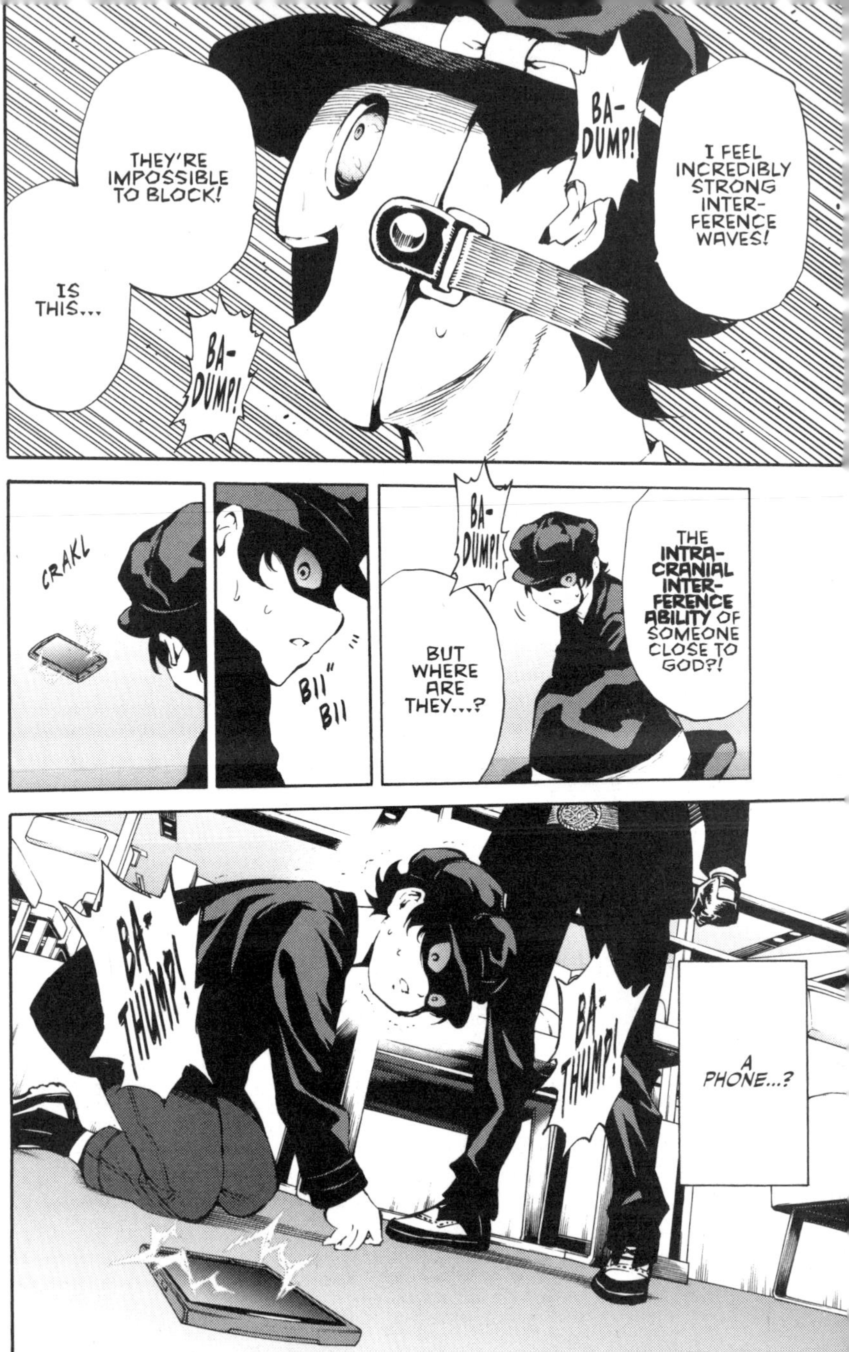
BA-DUMP!
I FEEL INCREDIBLY STRONG INTER-FERENCE WAVES!
THEY'RE IMPOSSIBLE TO BLOCK!
IS THIS...
BA-DUMP!
BA-DUMP!
THE **INTRA-CRANIAL INTER-FERENCE ABILITY** OF SOMEONE CLOSE TO GOD?!
BUT WHERE ARE THEY...?
BII" BII
CRAKL
A PHONE...?
BA-THUMP!
BA-THUMP!

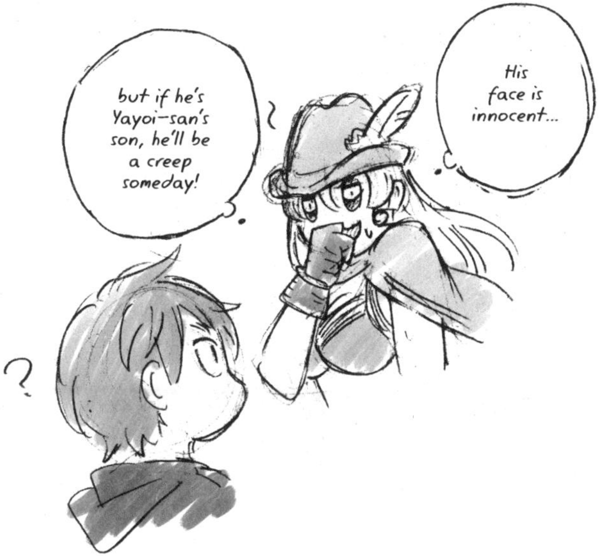
His face is innocent...
but if he's Yayoi-san's son, he'll be a creep someday!
?

HIGH-RISE INVASION

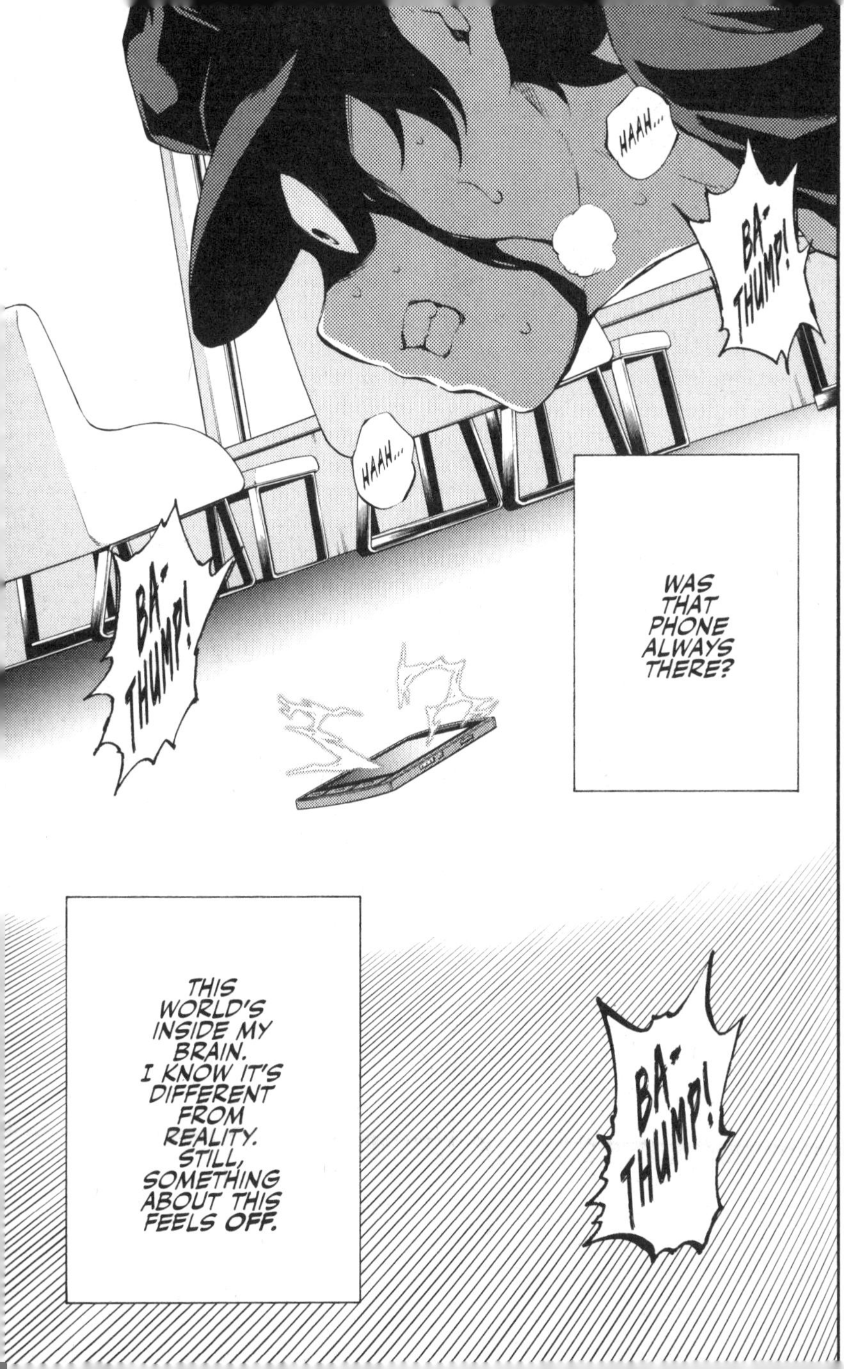
HAAH...
BA-THUMP!
HAAH...
BA-THUMP!
WAS THAT PHONE ALWAYS THERE?
BA-THUMP!
THIS WORLD'S INSIDE MY BRAIN. I KNOW IT'S DIFFERENT FROM REALITY. STILL, SOMETHING ABOUT THIS FEELS OFF.

CHAPTER 188: If I Boil It Down

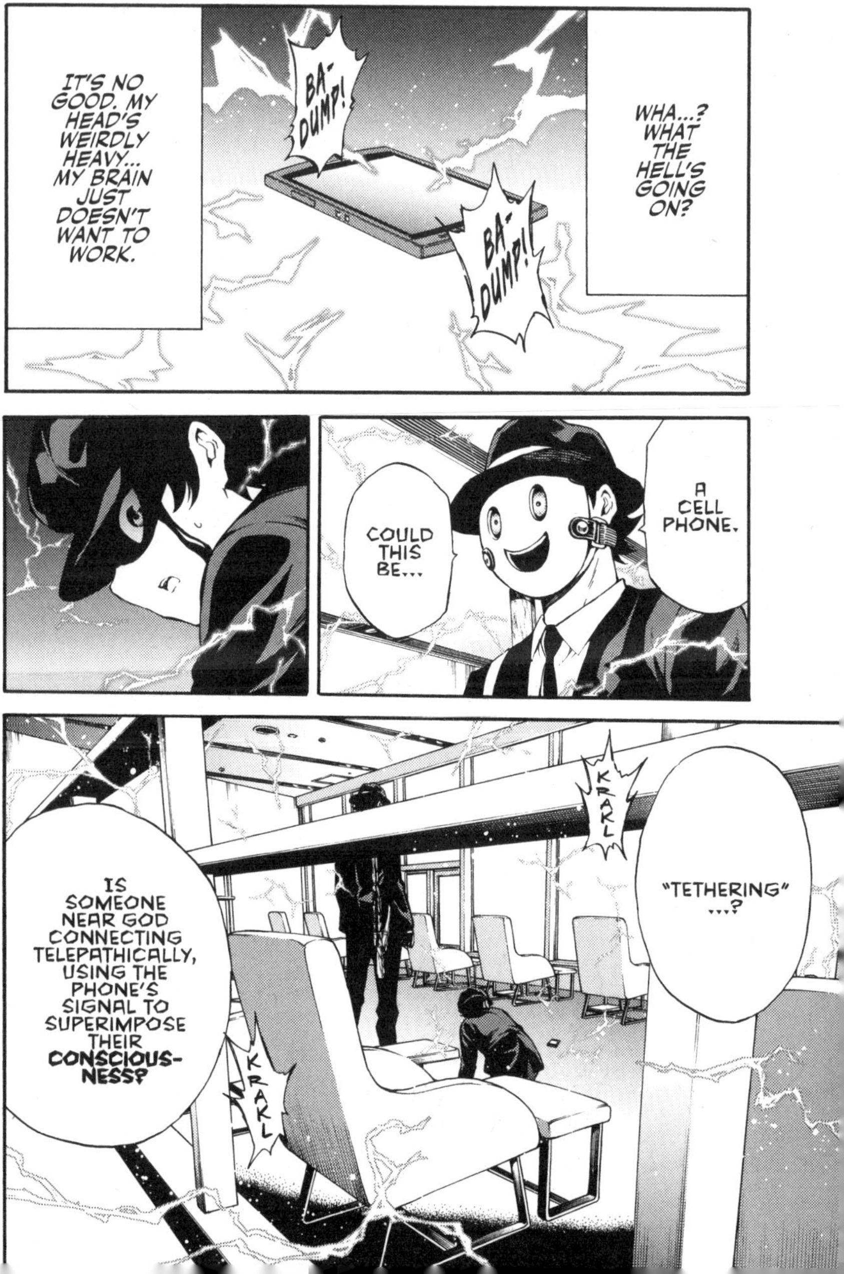
WHA...? WHAT THE HELL'S GOING ON?
BA-DUMP!
BA-DUMP!
IT'S NO GOOD. MY HEAD'S WEIRDLY HEAVY... MY BRAIN JUST DOESN'T WANT TO WORK.
A CELL PHONE.
COULD THIS BE...
KRAKL
"TETHERING"...?
IS SOMEONE NEAR GOD CONNECTING TELEPATHICALLY, USING THE PHONE'S SIGNAL TO SUPERIMPOSE THEIR **CONSCIOUSNESS?**
KRAKL

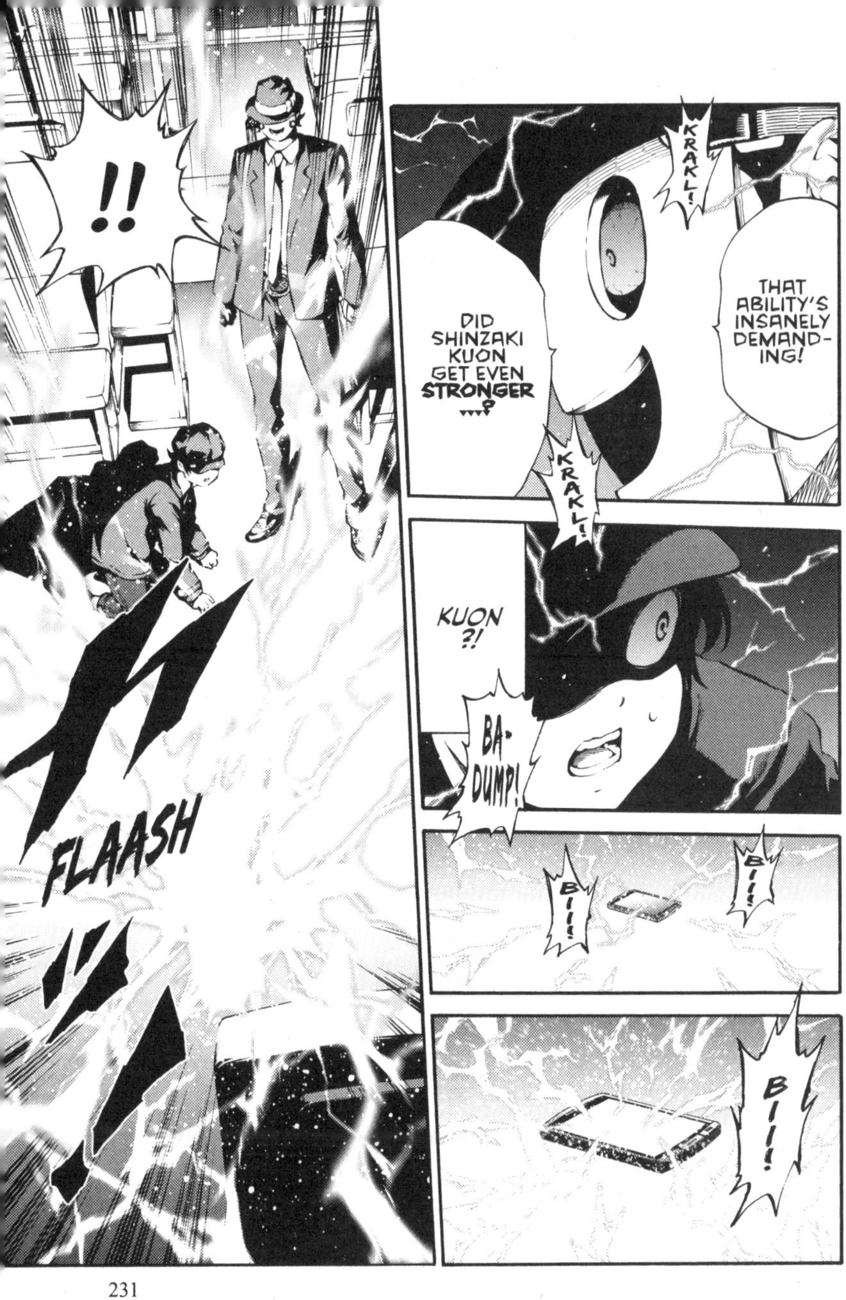
KRAKL!
THAT ABILITY'S INSANELY DEMANDING!
DID SHINZAKI KUON GET EVEN STRONGER...?
KRAKL!
KUON ?!
BA-DUMP!
BI!!!
BI!!!
BI!!!
!!
FLAASH
!!

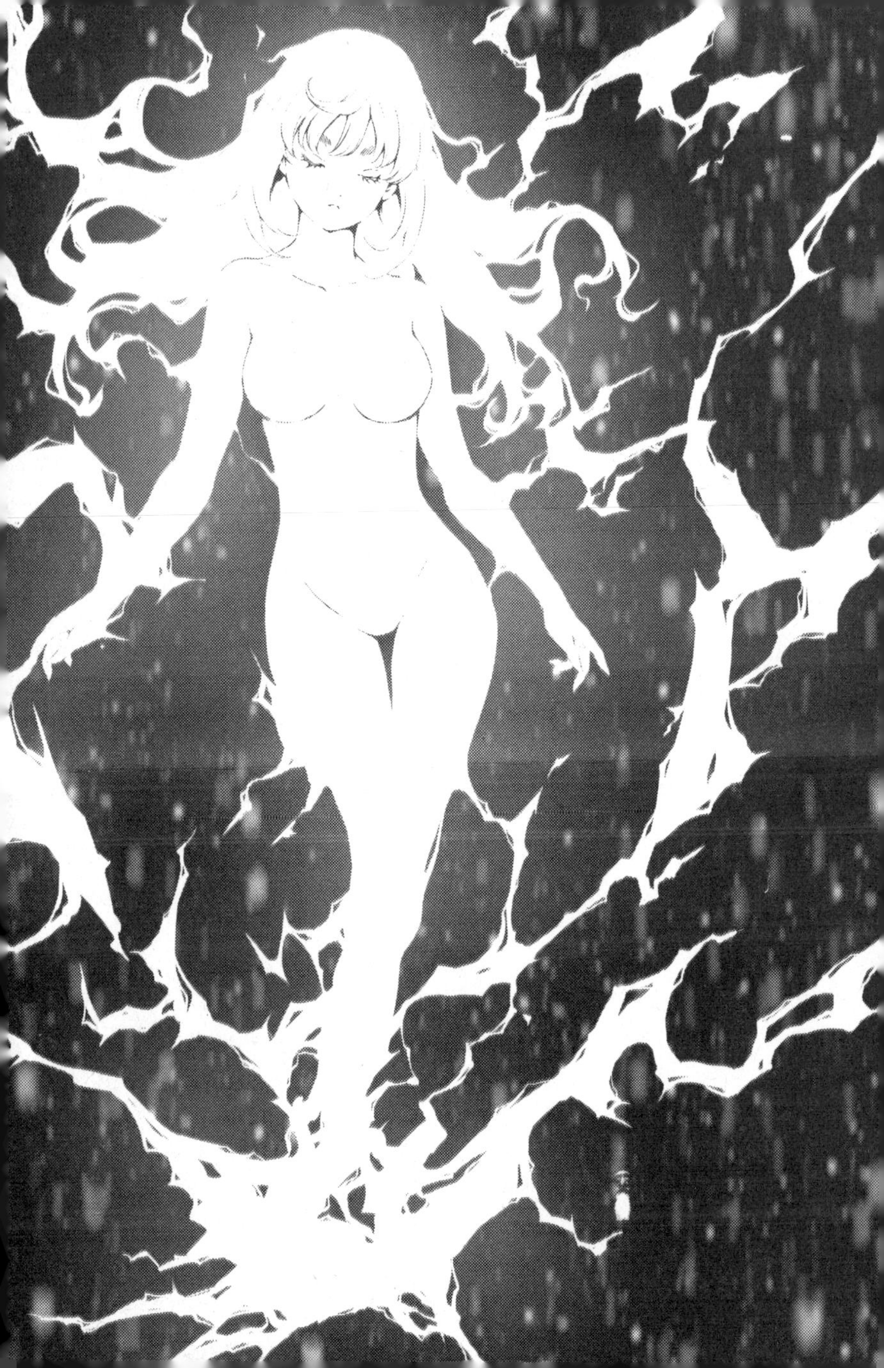

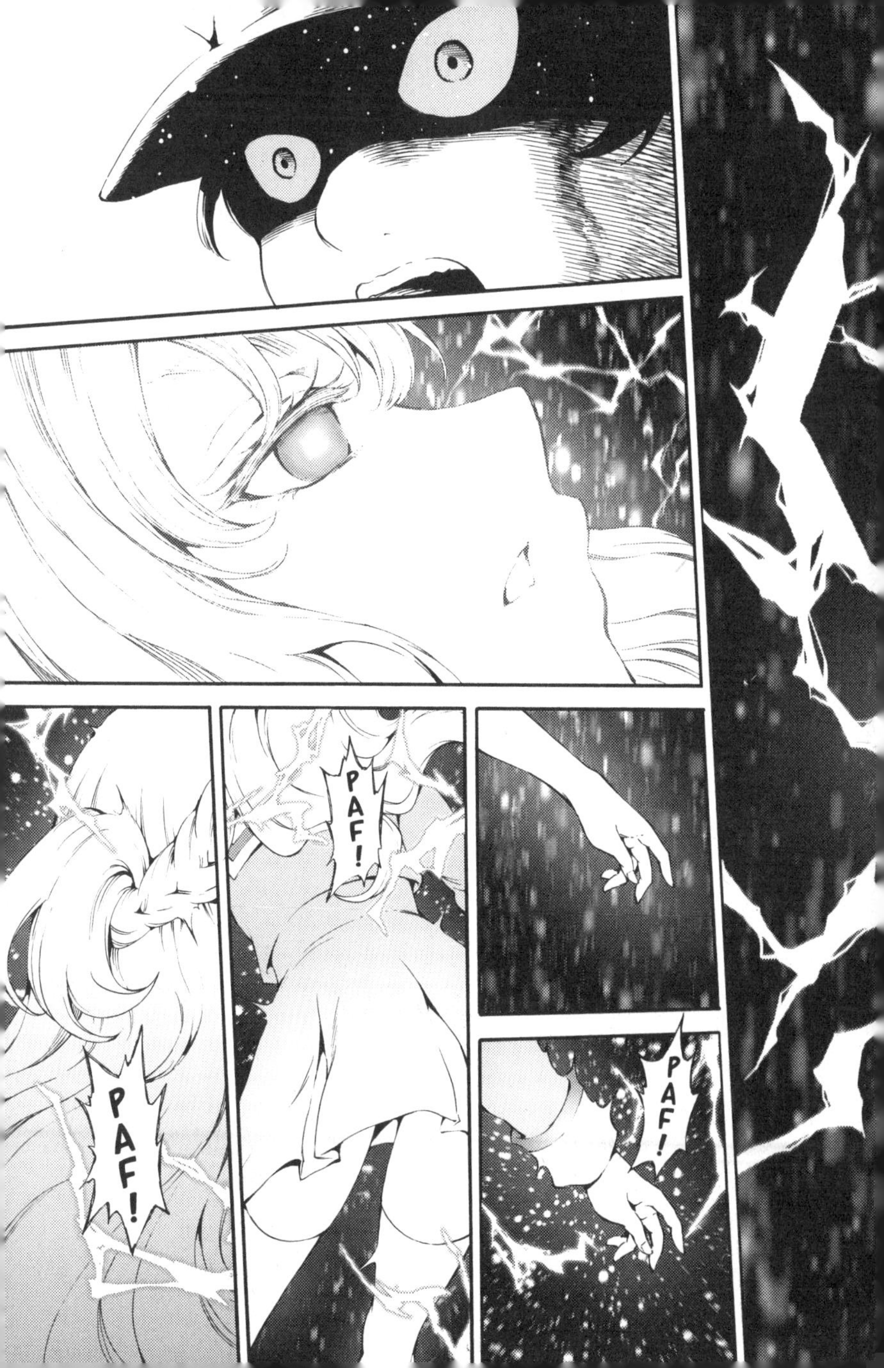
PAF!
PAF!
PAF!

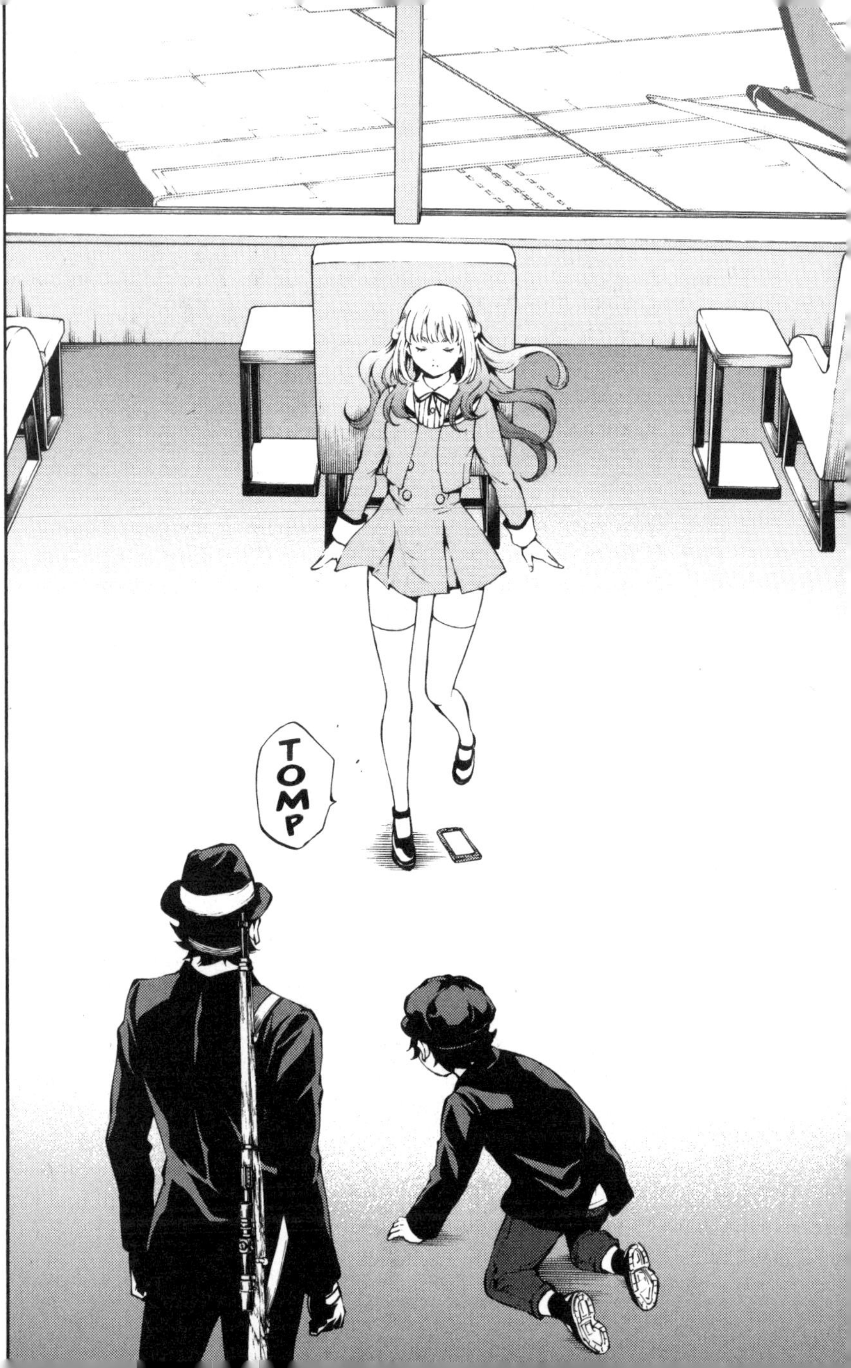
TOMP

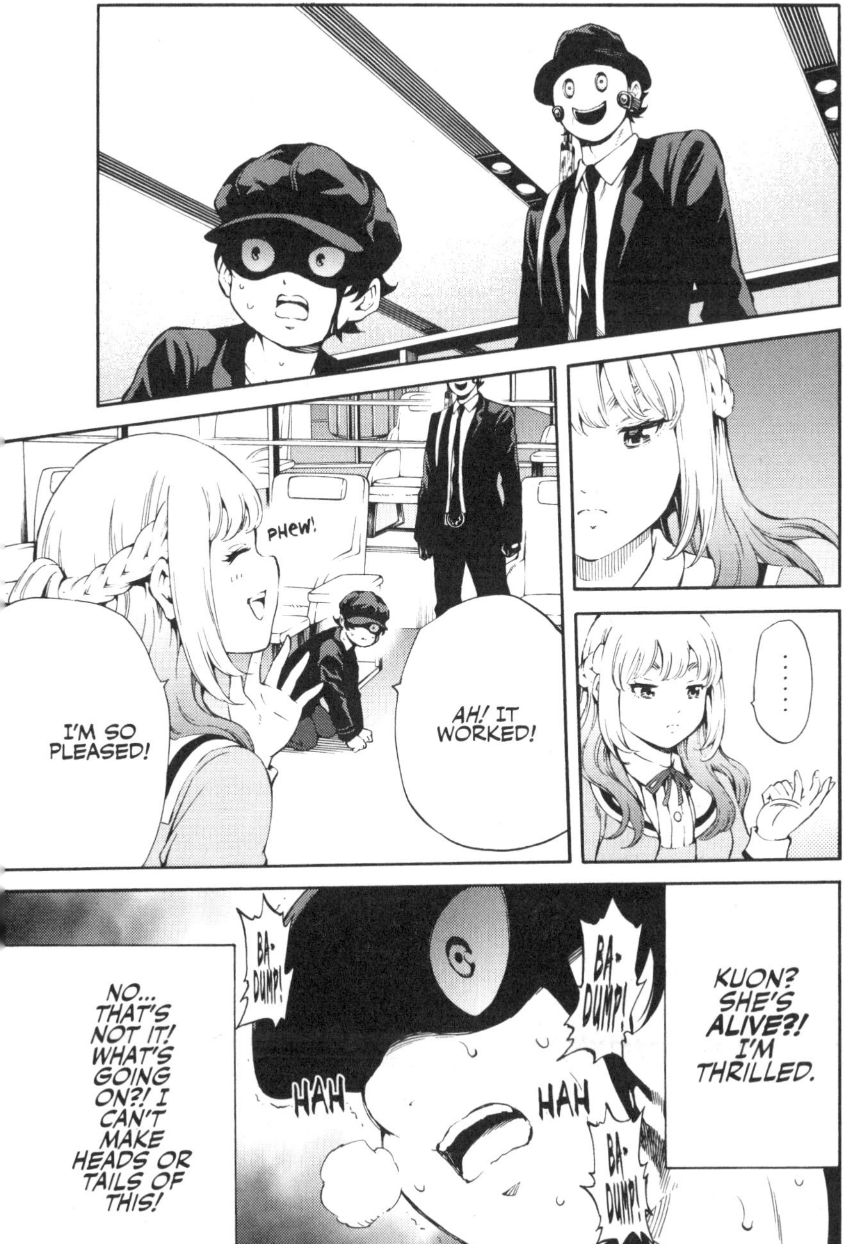
......
PHEW!
AH! IT WORKED!
I'M SO PLEASED!
KUON? SHE'S ALIVE?! I'M THRILLED.
BA-DUMP!
HAH
HAH
BA-DUMP!
BA-DUMP!
NO... THAT'S NOT IT! WHAT'S GOING ON?! I CAN'T MAKE HEADS OR TAILS OF THIS!

KRAKL

!!

SHF

NOW TO END THE HIBER-NATION PROCESS!

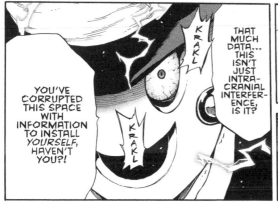

KRAKL

THAT MUCH DATA... THIS ISN'T JUST INTRA-CRANIAL INTERFER-ENCE, IS IT?

YOU'VE CORRUPTED THIS SPACE WITH INFORMATION TO INSTALL *YOURSELF*, HAVEN'T YOU?!

KRAKL

MY BREATH...

STAGGER

GG-HHH...

YOU DID A **LIFE TRANSFER!**

KRAKL

WHEN IT COMES TO PROCESSING DATA, YOU'RE ALREADY WELL BEYOND ME!

KRAKL

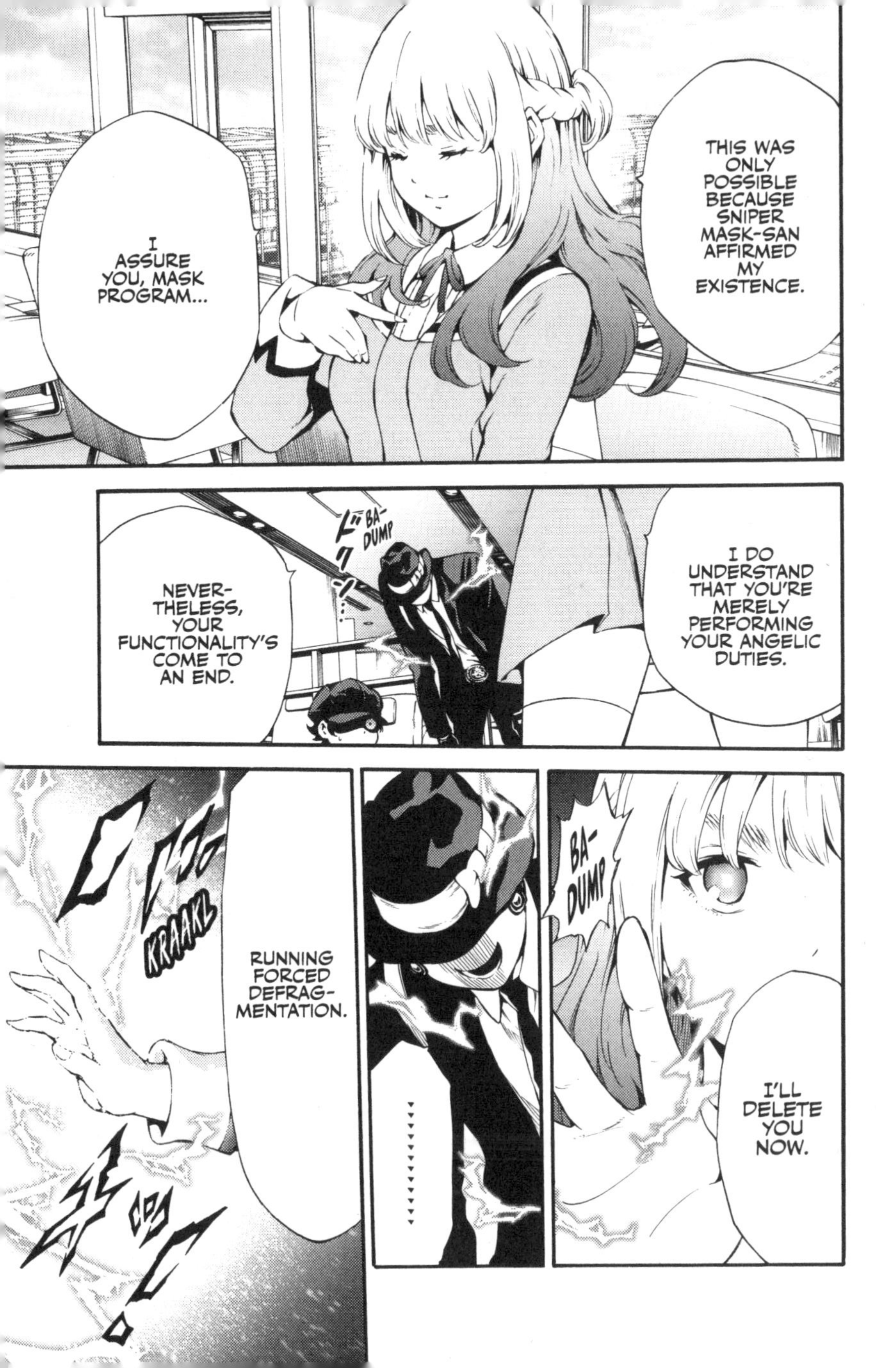
THIS WAS ONLY POSSIBLE BECAUSE SNIPER MASK-SAN AFFIRMED MY EXISTENCE.
I ASSURE YOU, MASK PROGRAM...
I DO UNDERSTAND THAT YOU'RE MERELY PERFORMING YOUR ANGELIC DUTIES.
BA-DUMP
NEVER-THELESS, YOUR FUNCTIONALITY'S COME TO AN END.
BA-DUMP
I'LL DELETE YOU NOW.
....
RUNNING FORCED DEFRAG-MENTATION.
KRAAKL

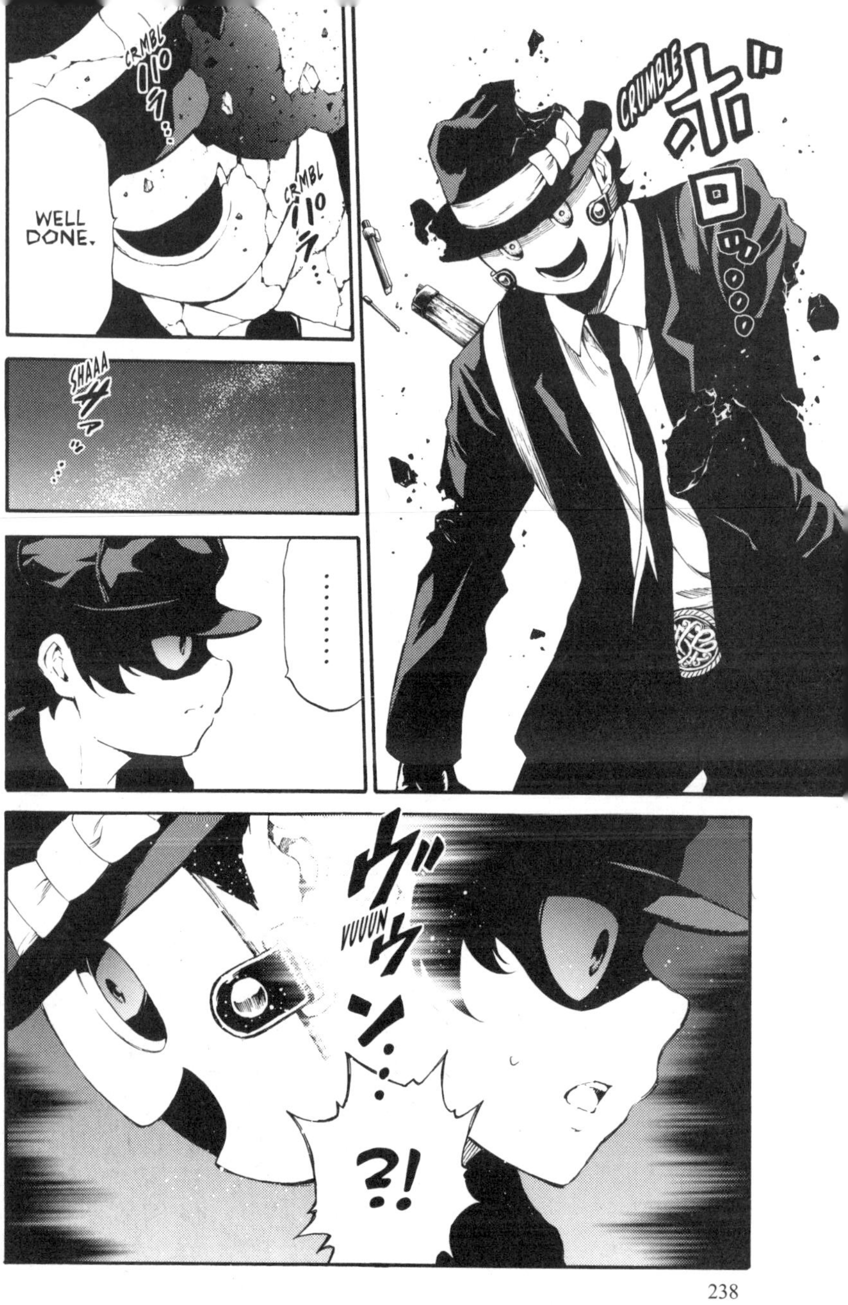
CRUMBLE
CRMBL
CRMBL
WELL DONE.
SHAAA
......
VUUUN
?!

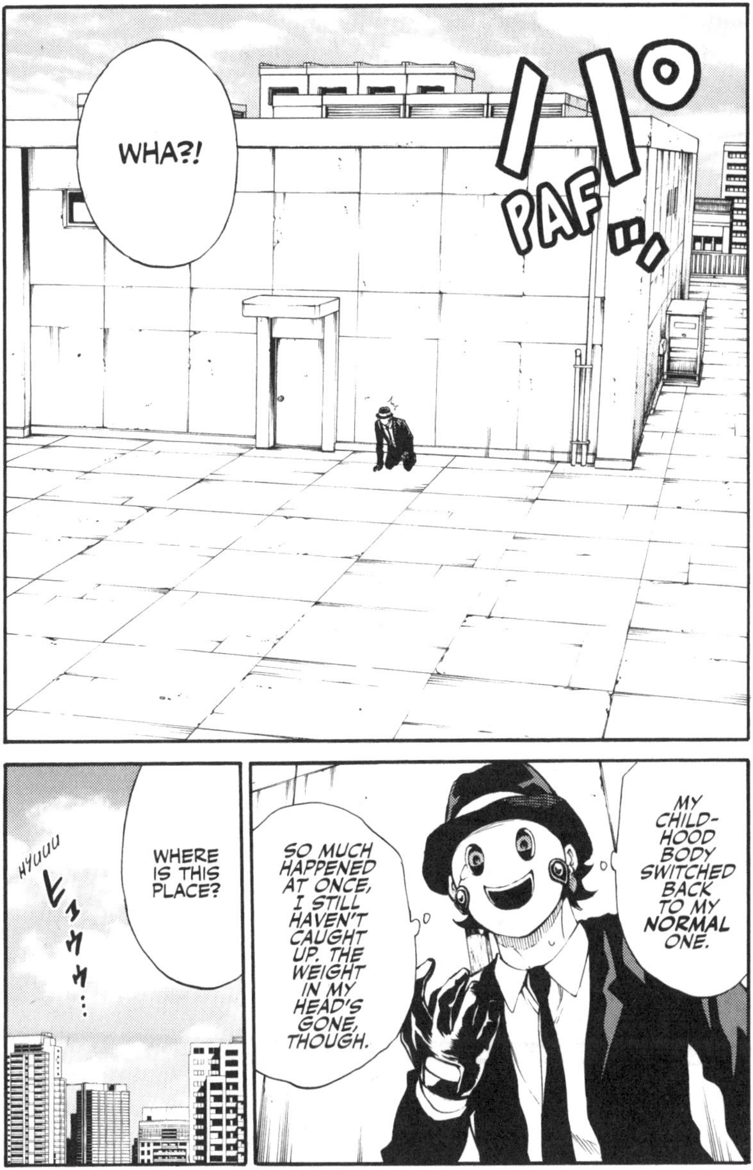
PAF
WHA?!
MY CHILDHOOD BODY SWITCHED BACK TO MY NORMAL ONE.
SO MUCH HAPPENED AT ONCE, I STILL HAVEN'T CAUGHT UP. THE WEIGHT IN MY HEAD'S GONE, THOUGH.
HYUUU
WHERE IS THIS PLACE?

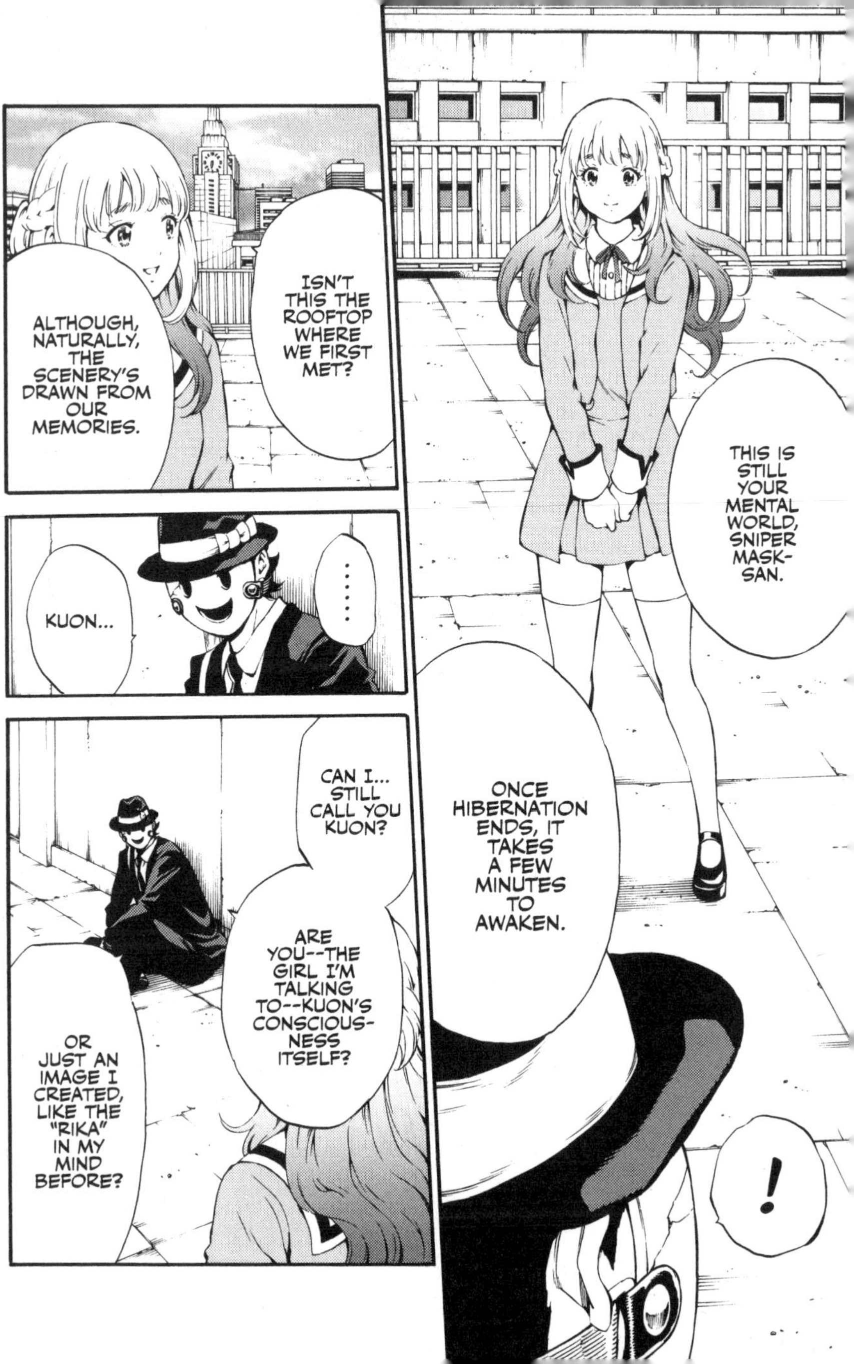
THIS IS STILL YOUR MENTAL WORLD, SNIPER MASK-SAN.
ONCE HIBERNATION ENDS, IT TAKES A FEW MINUTES TO AWAKEN.
!
ISN'T THIS THE ROOFTOP WHERE WE FIRST MET?
ALTHOUGH, NATURALLY, THE SCENERY'S DRAWN FROM OUR MEMORIES.
......
KUON...
CAN I... STILL CALL YOU KUON?
ARE YOU--THE GIRL I'M TALKING TO--KUON'S CONSCIOUSNESS ITSELF?
OR JUST AN IMAGE I CREATED, LIKE THE "RIKA" IN MY MIND BEFORE?

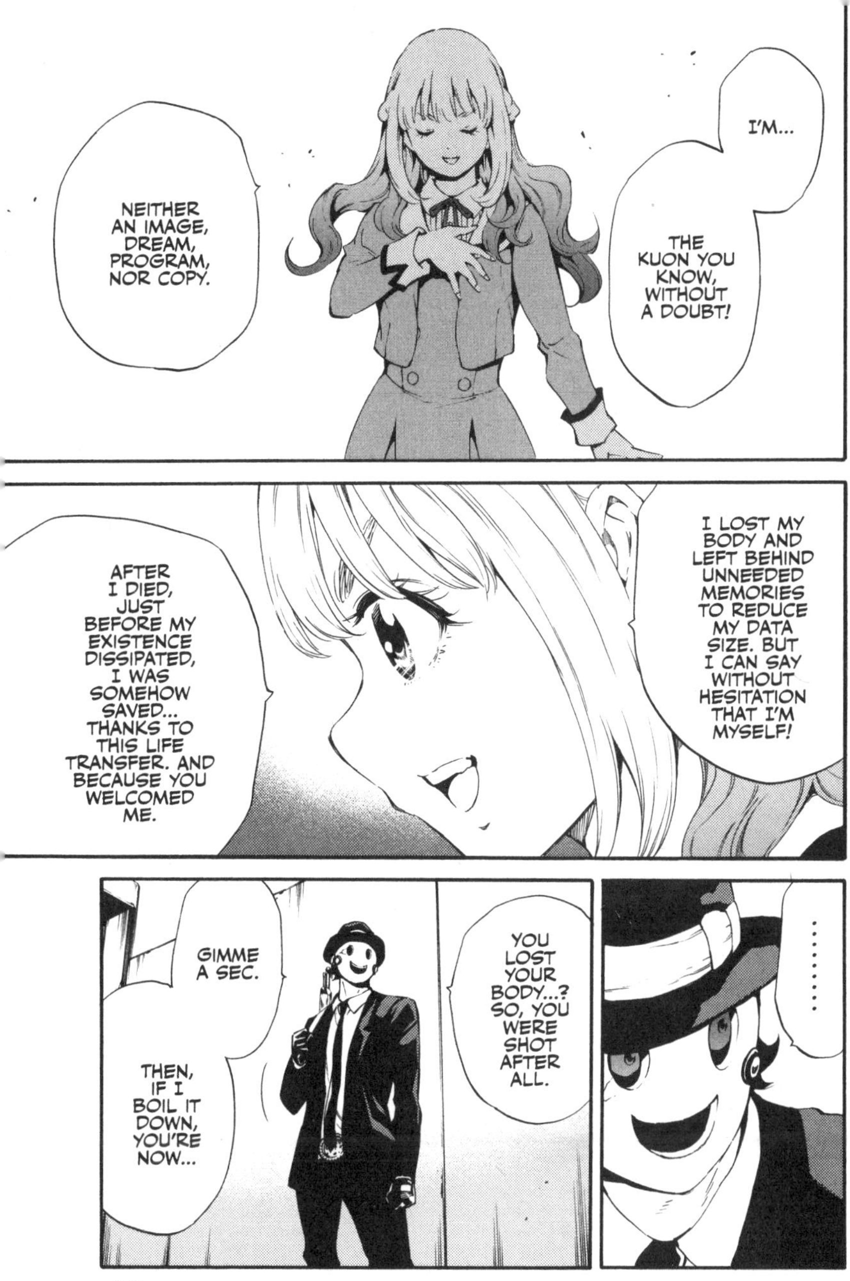
I'M...
THE KUON YOU KNOW, WITHOUT A DOUBT!
NEITHER AN IMAGE, DREAM, PROGRAM, NOR COPY.
I LOST MY BODY AND LEFT BEHIND UNNEEDED MEMORIES TO REDUCE MY DATA SIZE. BUT I CAN SAY WITHOUT HESITATION THAT I'M MYSELF!
AFTER I DIED, JUST BEFORE MY EXISTENCE DISSIPATED, I WAS SOMEHOW SAVED... THANKS TO THIS LIFE TRANSFER. AND BECAUSE YOU WELCOMED ME.
....
YOU LOST YOUR BODY...? SO, YOU WERE SHOT AFTER ALL.
GIMME A SEC.
THEN, IF I BOIL IT DOWN, YOU'RE NOW...

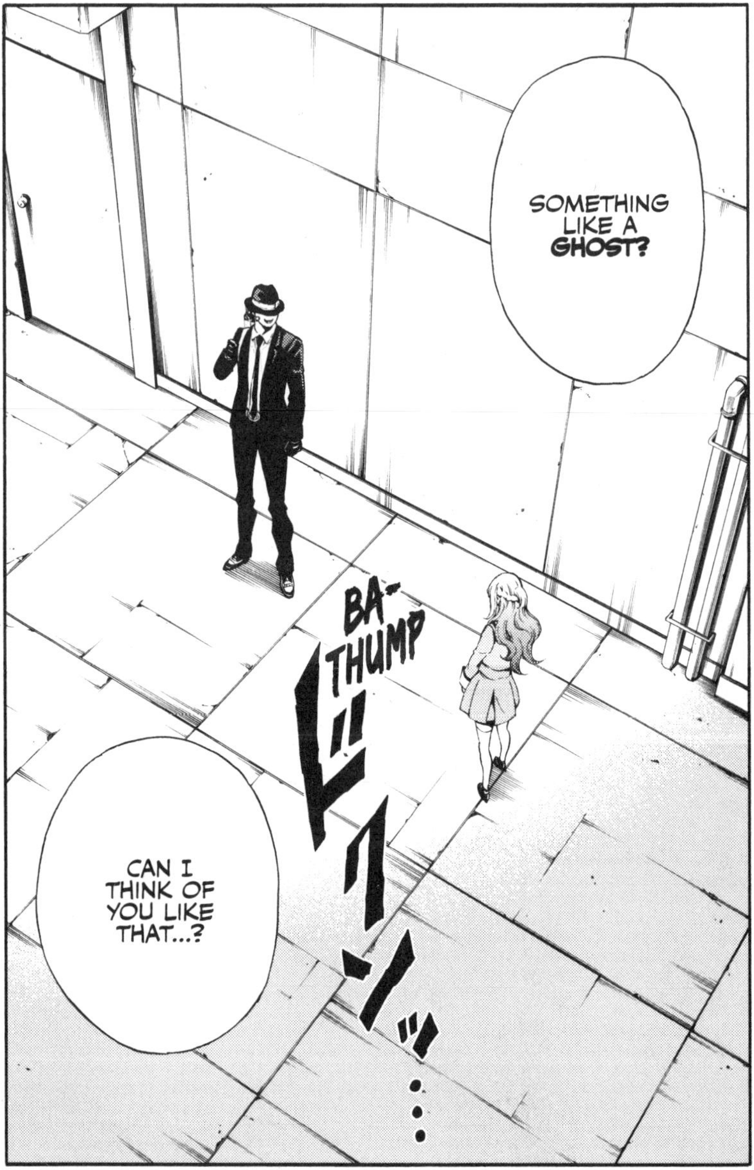
SOMETHING LIKE A **GHOST?**
BA-THUMP
CAN I THINK OF YOU LIKE THAT...?

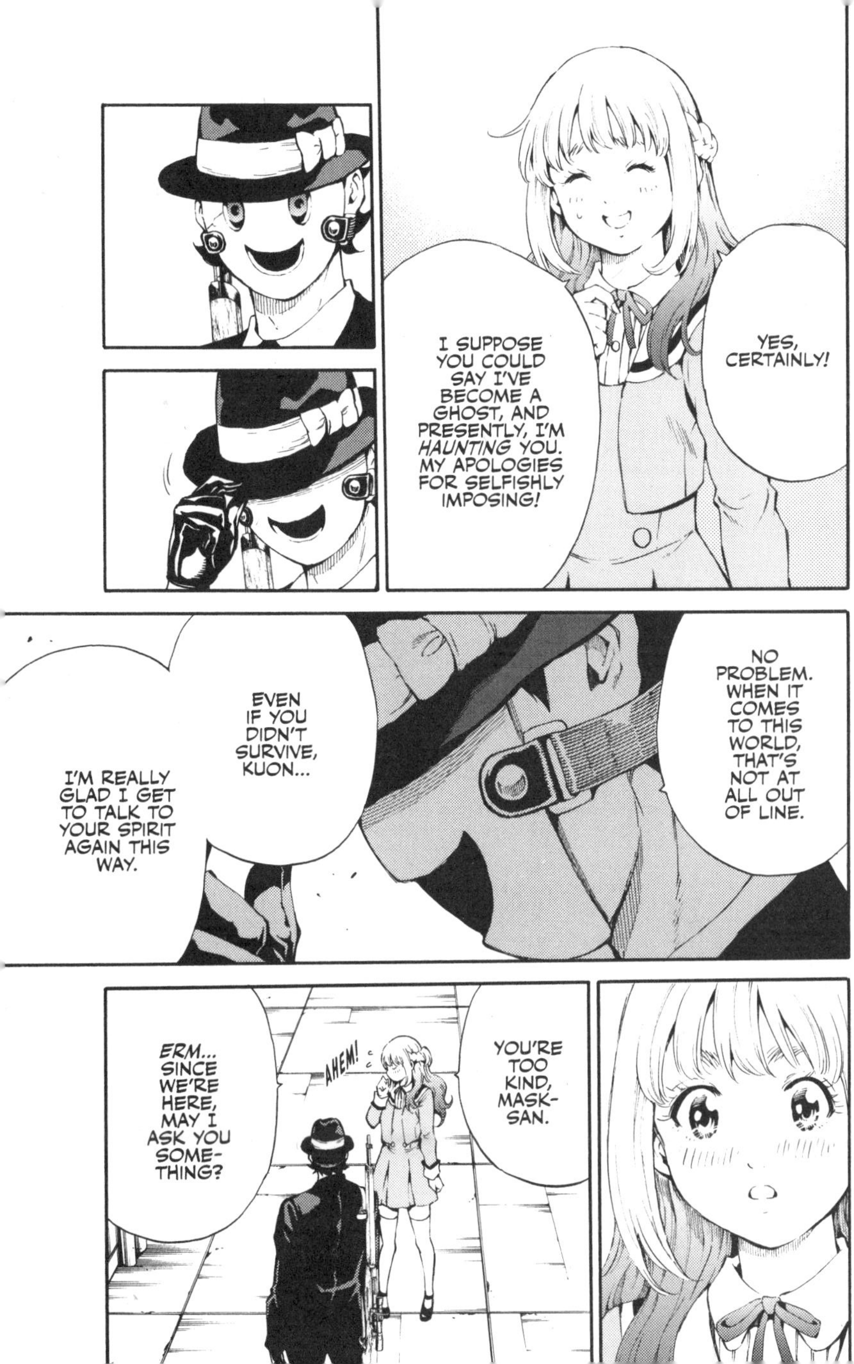
YES, CERTAINLY!
I SUPPOSE YOU COULD SAY I'VE BECOME A GHOST, AND PRESENTLY, I'M *HAUNTING* YOU. MY APOLOGIES FOR SELFISHLY IMPOSING!
NO PROBLEM. WHEN IT COMES TO THIS WORLD, THAT'S NOT AT ALL OUT OF LINE.
EVEN IF YOU DIDN'T SURVIVE, KUON...
I'M REALLY GLAD I GET TO TALK TO YOUR SPIRIT AGAIN THIS WAY.
YOU'RE TOO KIND, MASK-SAN.
AHEM!
ERM... SINCE WE'RE HERE, MAY I ASK YOU SOME-THING?

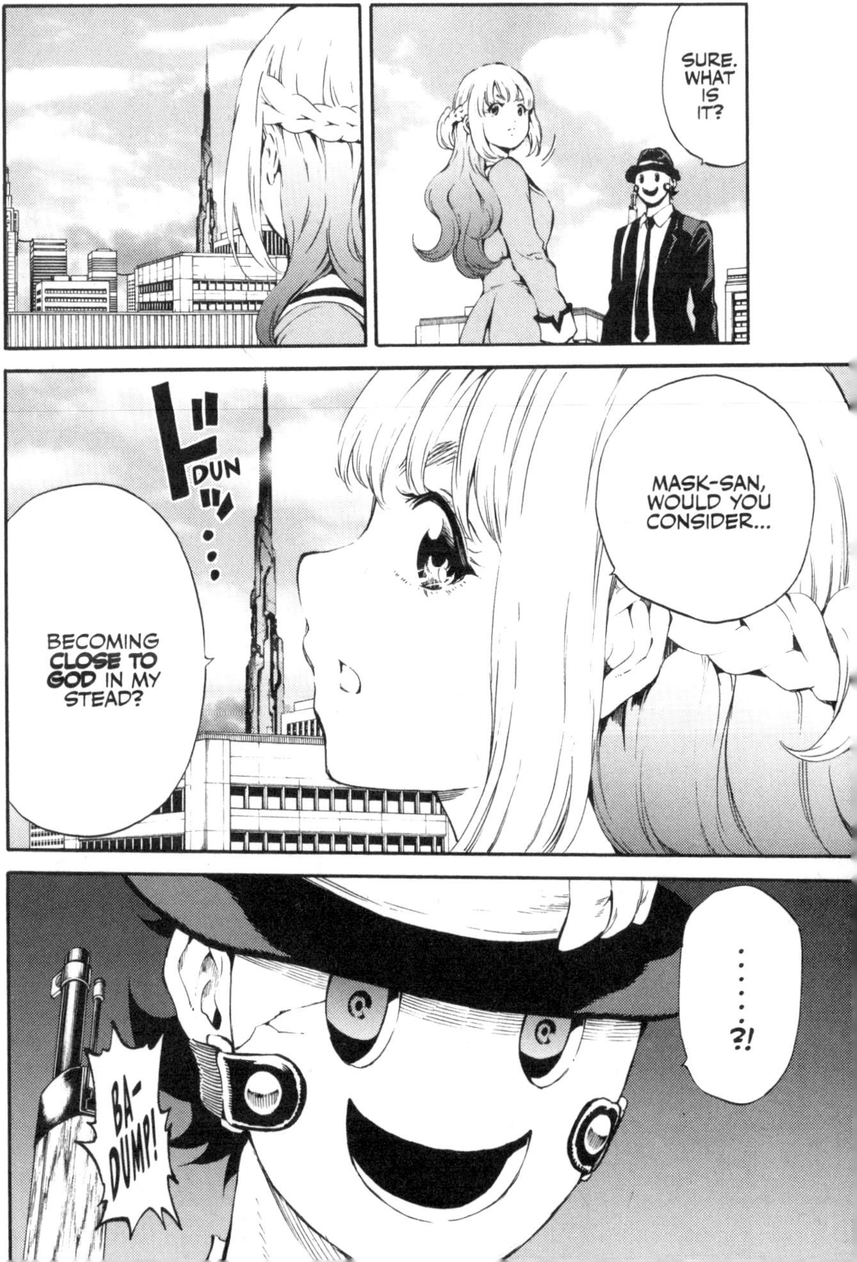
SURE. WHAT IS IT?
MASK-SAN, WOULD YOU CONSIDER...
ド DUN
...
BECOMING **CLOSE TO GOD** IN MY STEAD?
......?!
BA-DUMP!

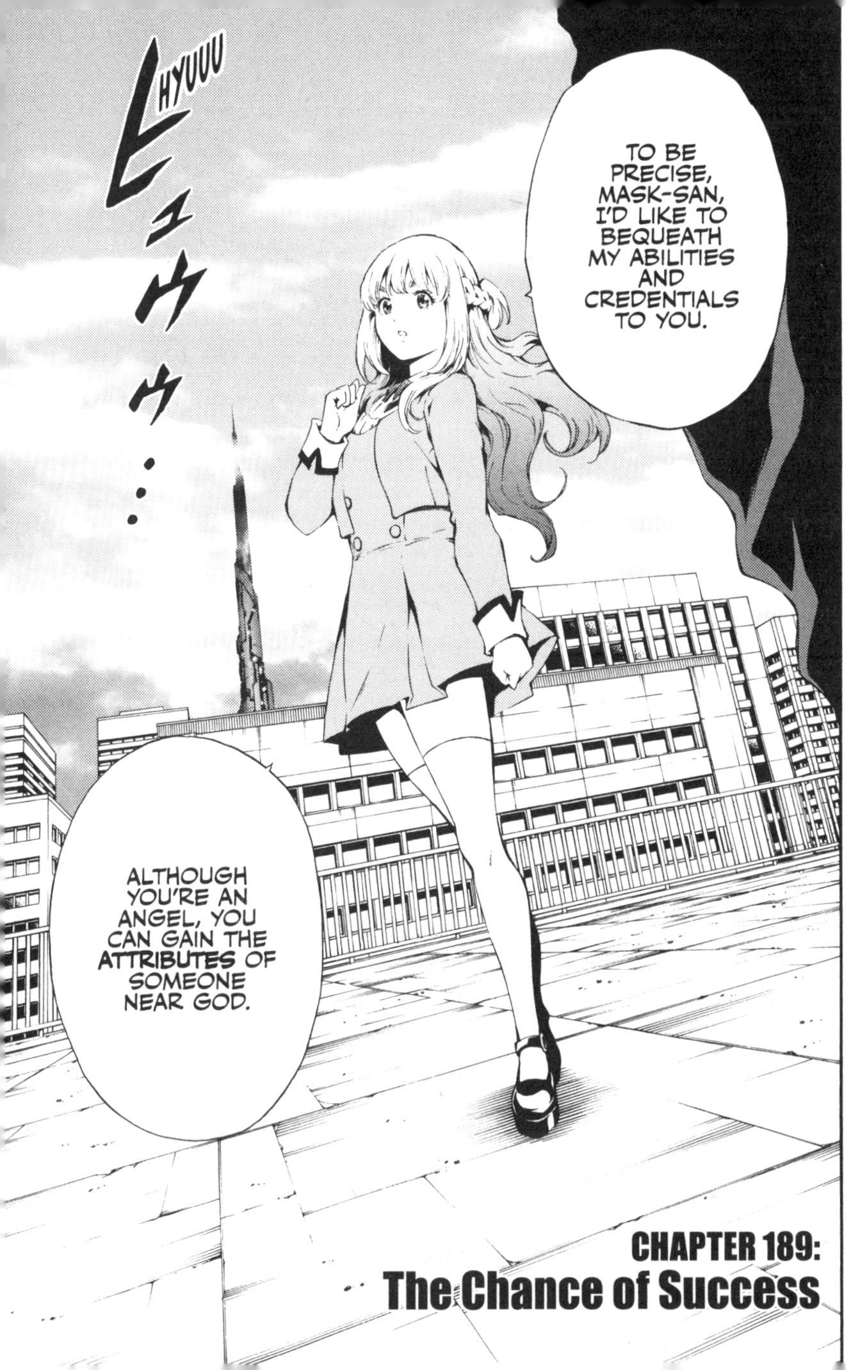
TO BE PRECISE, MASK-SAN, I'D LIKE TO BEQUEATH MY ABILITIES AND CREDENTIALS TO YOU.
HYUUU
ヒュウウ…
ALTHOUGH YOU'RE AN ANGEL, YOU CAN GAIN THE **ATTRIBUTES** OF SOMEONE NEAR GOD.

CHAPTER 189: The Chance of Success

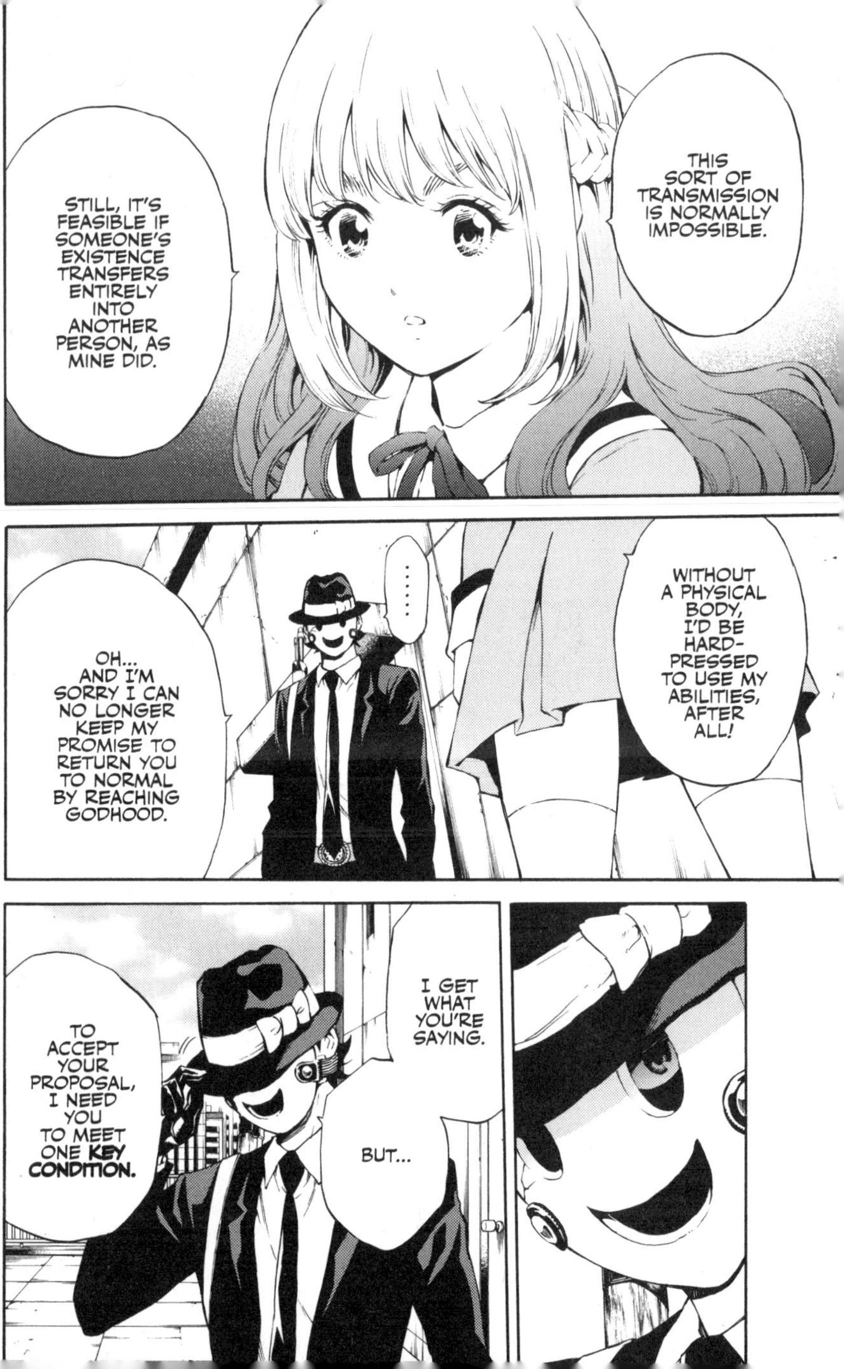
THIS SORT OF TRANSMISSION IS NORMALLY IMPOSSIBLE.
STILL, IT'S FEASIBLE IF SOMEONE'S EXISTENCE TRANSFERS ENTIRELY INTO ANOTHER PERSON, AS MINE DID.
WITHOUT A PHYSICAL BODY, I'D BE HARD-PRESSED TO USE MY ABILITIES, AFTER ALL!
......
OH... AND I'M SORRY I CAN NO LONGER KEEP MY PROMISE TO RETURN YOU TO NORMAL BY REACHING GODHOOD.
I GET WHAT YOU'RE SAYING.
BUT...
TO ACCEPT YOUR PROPOSAL, I NEED YOU TO MEET ONE **KEY CONDITION.**

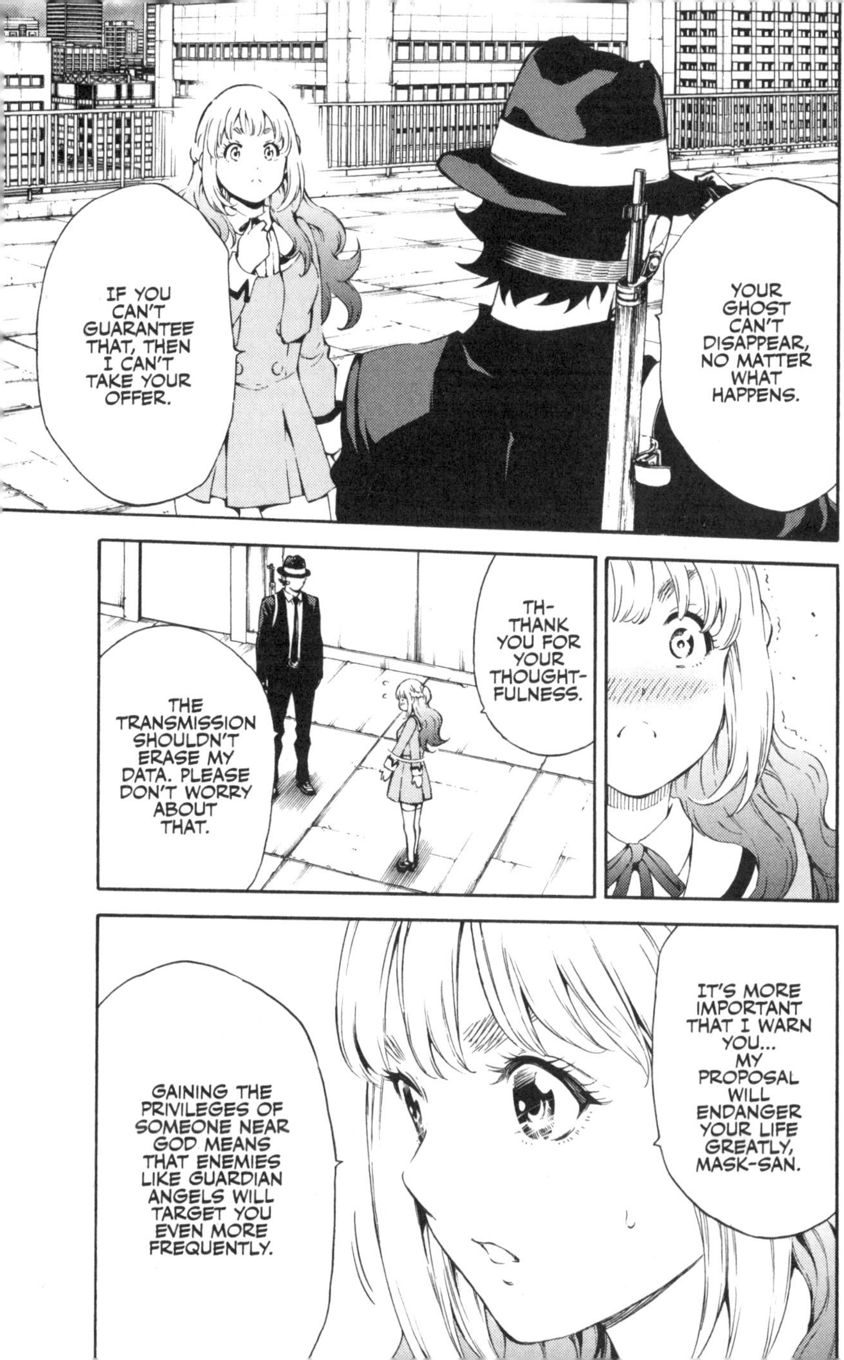
YOUR GHOST CAN'T DISAPPEAR, NO MATTER WHAT HAPPENS.
IF YOU CAN'T GUARANTEE THAT, THEN I CAN'T TAKE YOUR OFFER.
TH-THANK YOU FOR YOUR THOUGHTFULNESS.
THE TRANSMISSION SHOULDN'T ERASE MY DATA. PLEASE DON'T WORRY ABOUT THAT.
IT'S MORE IMPORTANT THAT I WARN YOU... MY PROPOSAL WILL ENDANGER YOUR LIFE GREATLY, MASK-SAN.
GAINING THE PRIVILEGES OF SOMEONE NEAR GOD MEANS THAT ENEMIES LIKE GUARDIAN ANGELS WILL TARGET YOU EVEN MORE FREQUENTLY.

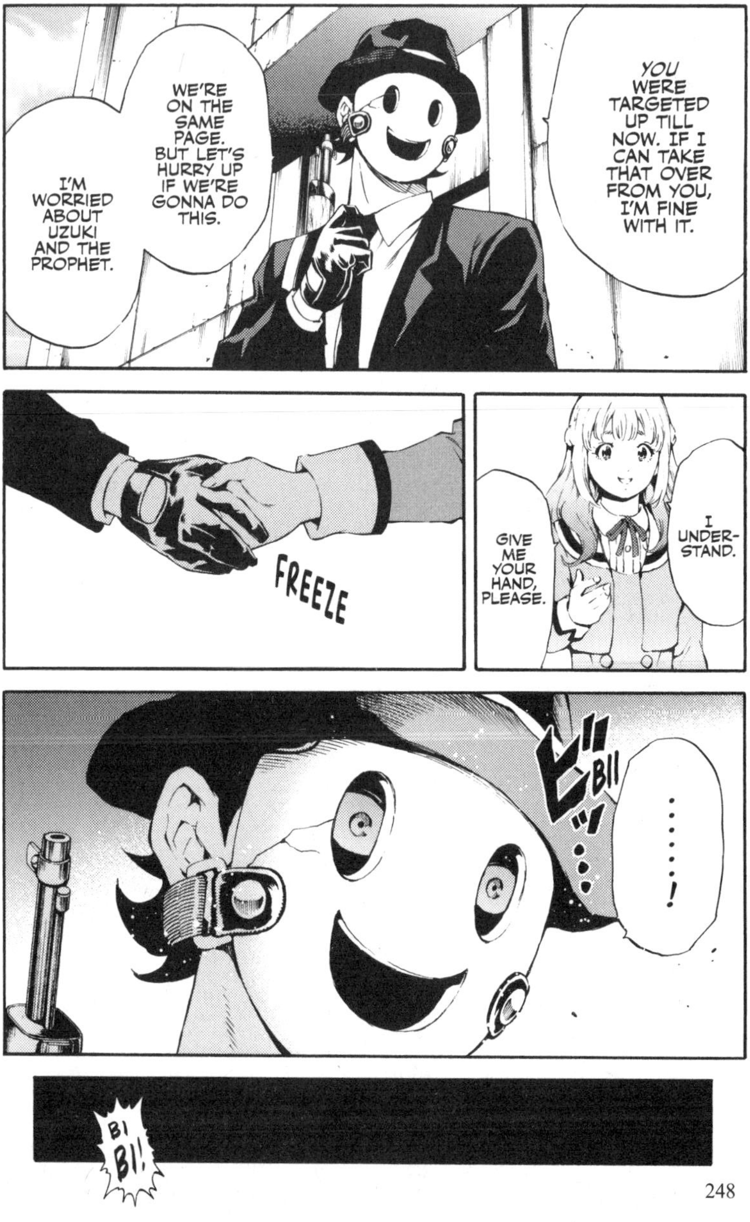
YOU WERE TARGETED UP TILL NOW. IF I CAN TAKE THAT OVER FROM YOU, I'M FINE WITH IT.
WE'RE ON THE SAME PAGE. BUT LET'S HURRY UP IF WE'RE GONNA DO THIS.
I'M WORRIED ABOUT UZUKI AND THE PROPHET.
I UNDER-STAND.
GIVE ME YOUR HAND, PLEASE.
FREEZE
BII
........!
BI BI!

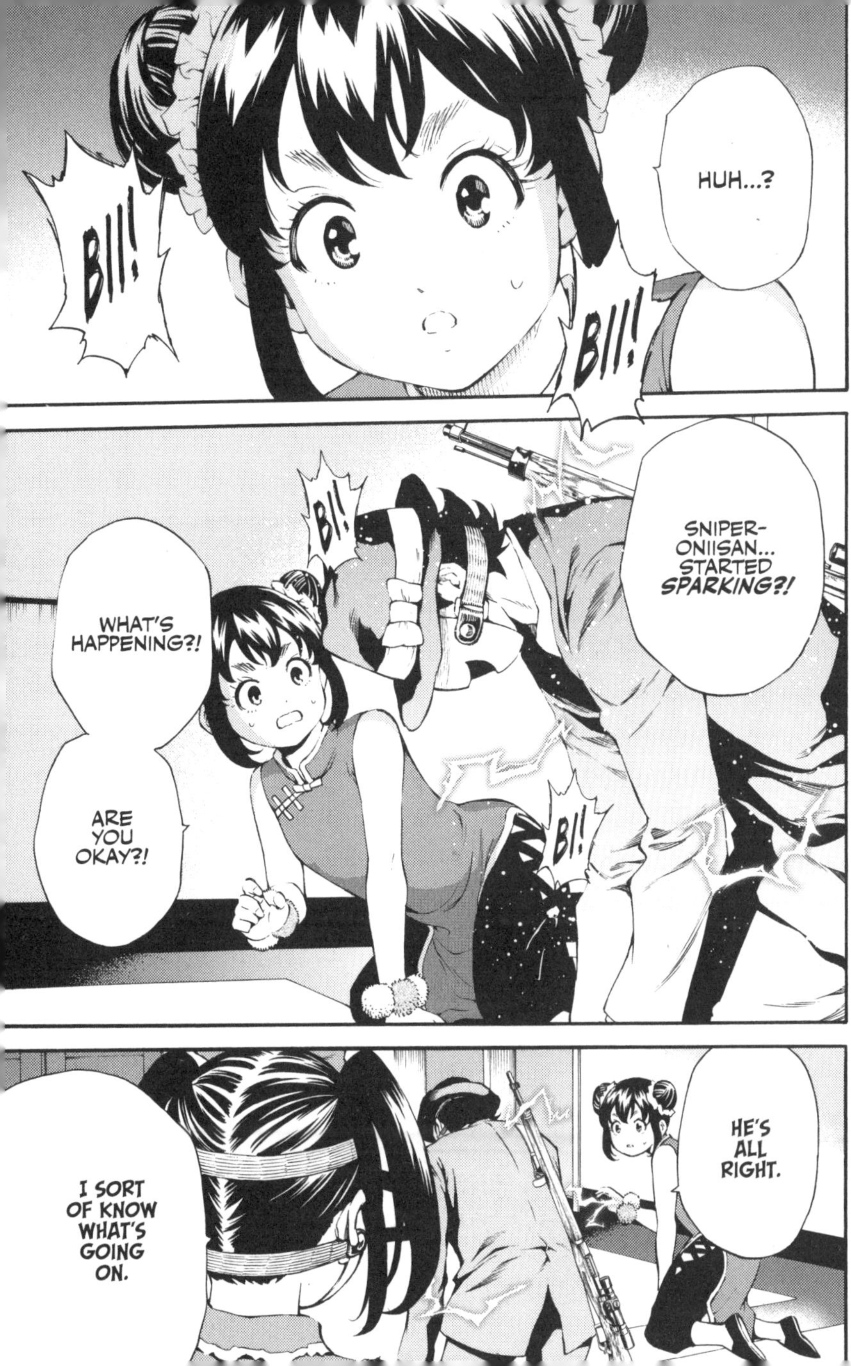
HUH...?
BII!
BII!
SNIPER-ONIISAN... STARTED SPARKING?!
BI!
WHAT'S HAPPENING?!
ARE YOU OKAY?!
BI!
HE'S ALL RIGHT.
I SORT OF KNOW WHAT'S GOING ON.

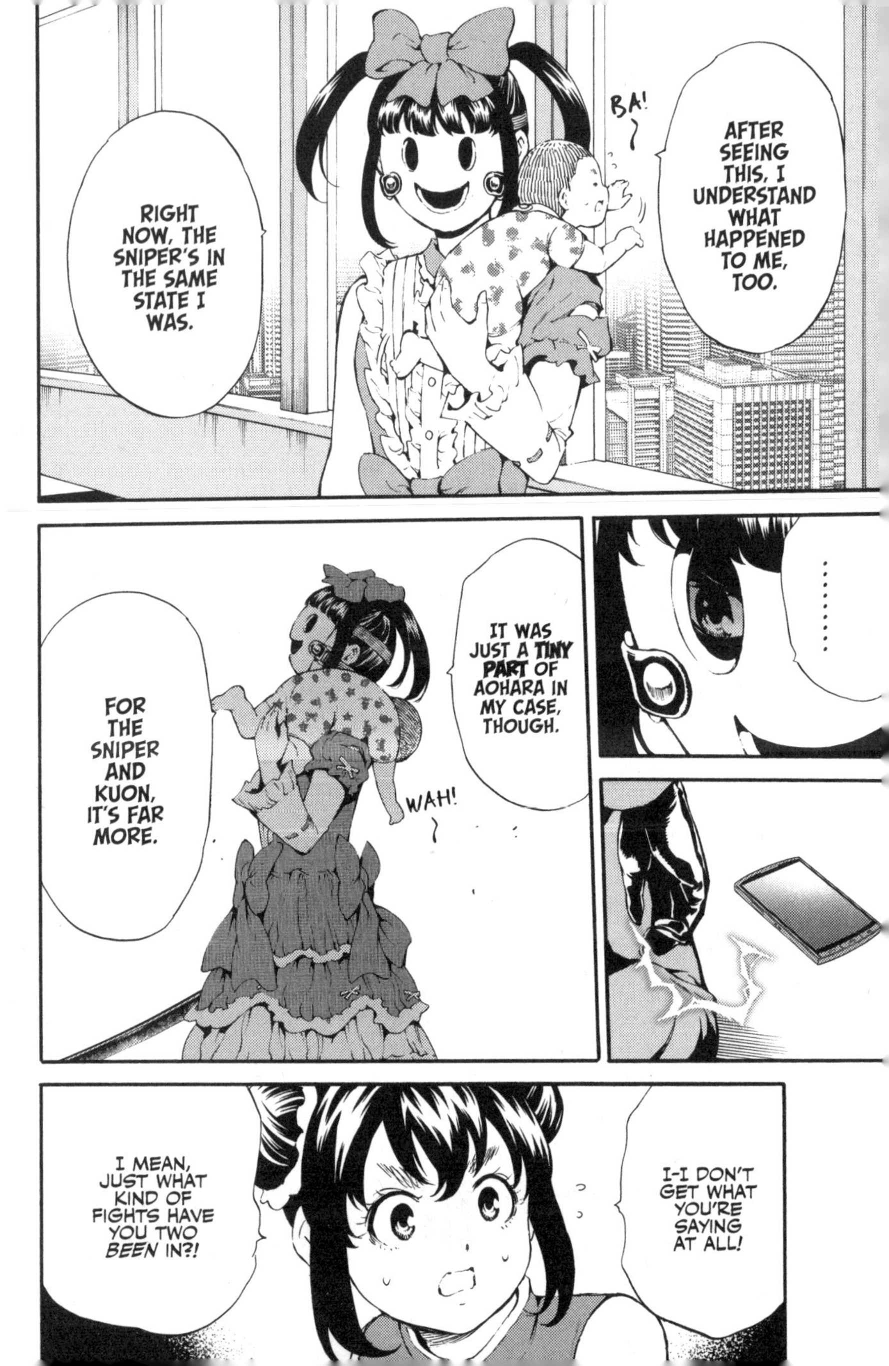
AFTER SEEING THIS, I UNDERSTAND WHAT HAPPENED TO ME, TOO.
BA!
RIGHT NOW, THE SNIPER'S IN THE SAME STATE I WAS.
......
IT WAS JUST A TINY PART OF AOHARA IN MY CASE, THOUGH.
WAH!
FOR THE SNIPER AND KUON, IT'S FAR MORE.
I-I DON'T GET WHAT YOU'RE SAYING AT ALL!
I MEAN, JUST WHAT KIND OF FIGHTS HAVE YOU TWO BEEN IN?!

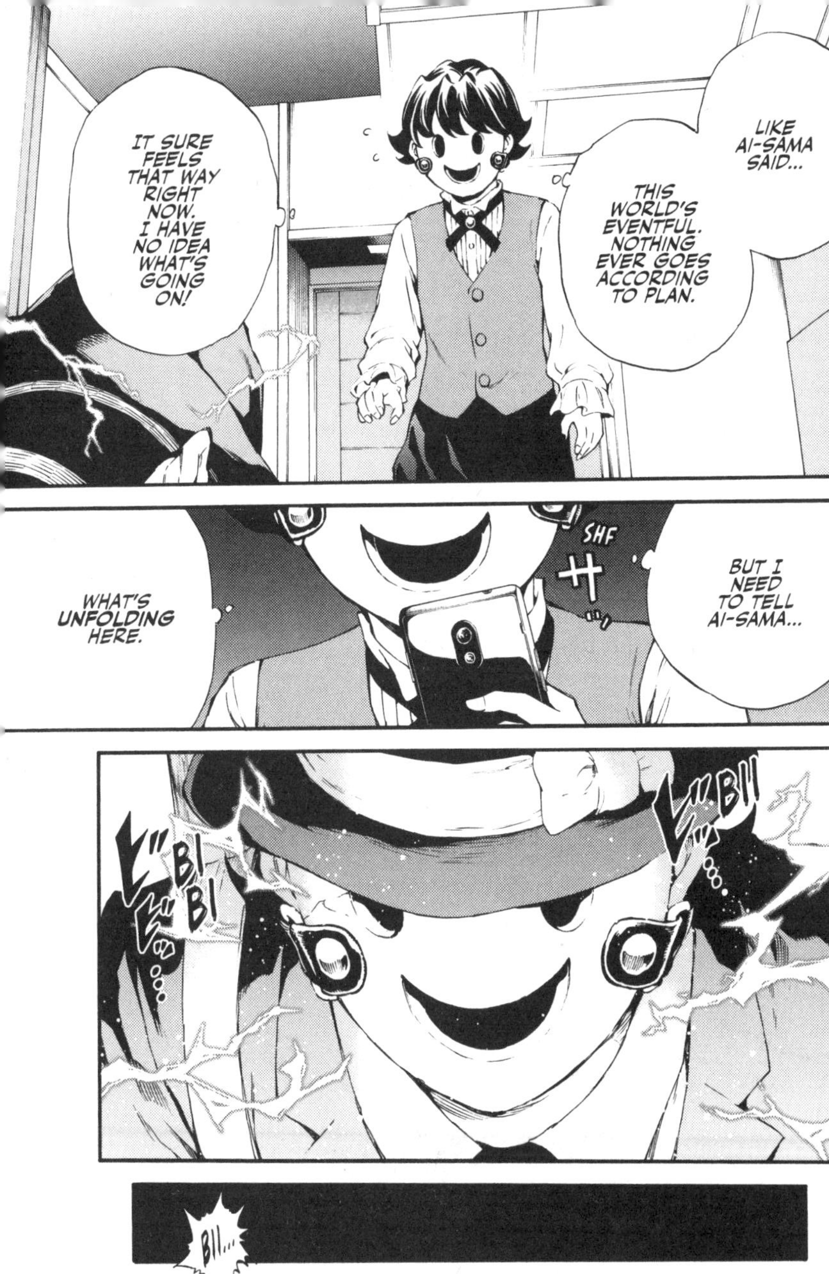
LIKE AI-SAMA SAID...
THIS WORLD'S EVENTFUL. NOTHING EVER GOES ACCORDING TO PLAN.
IT SURE FEELS THAT WAY RIGHT NOW. I HAVE NO IDEA WHAT'S GOING ON!
SHF
BUT I NEED TO TELL AI-SAMA...
WHAT'S UNFOLDING HERE.
BII
BI
BI
BII...

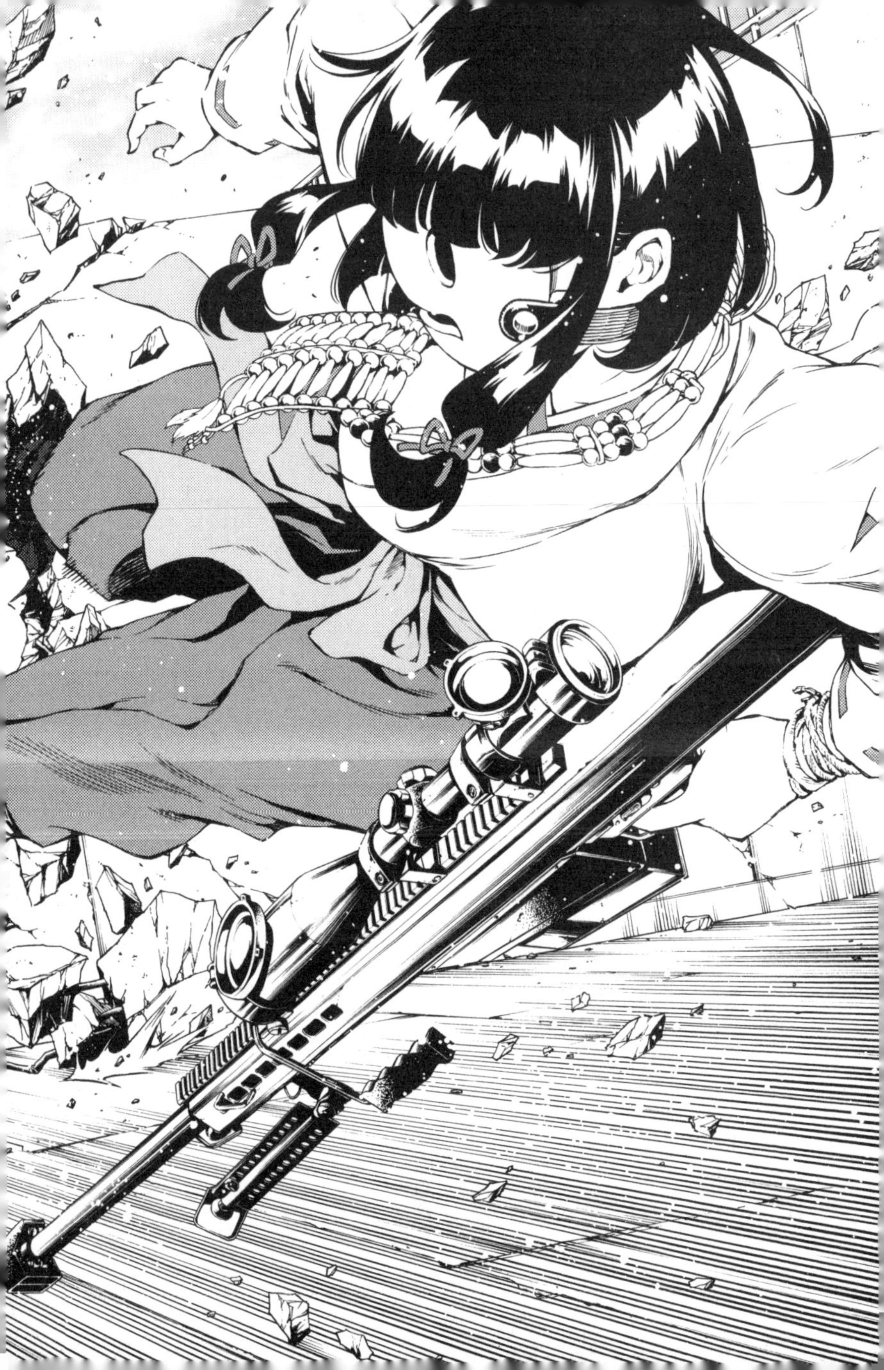

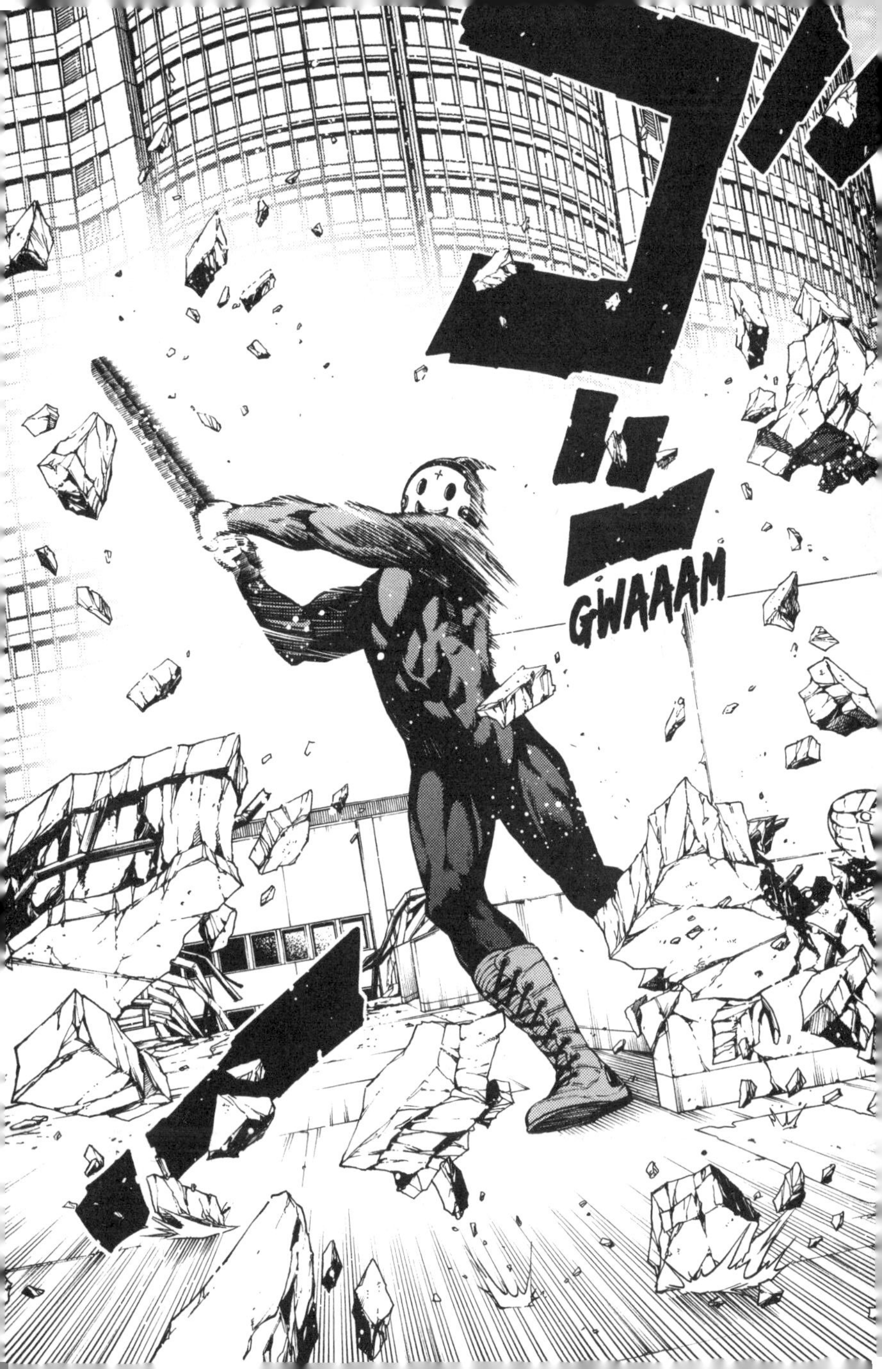
GWAAAM

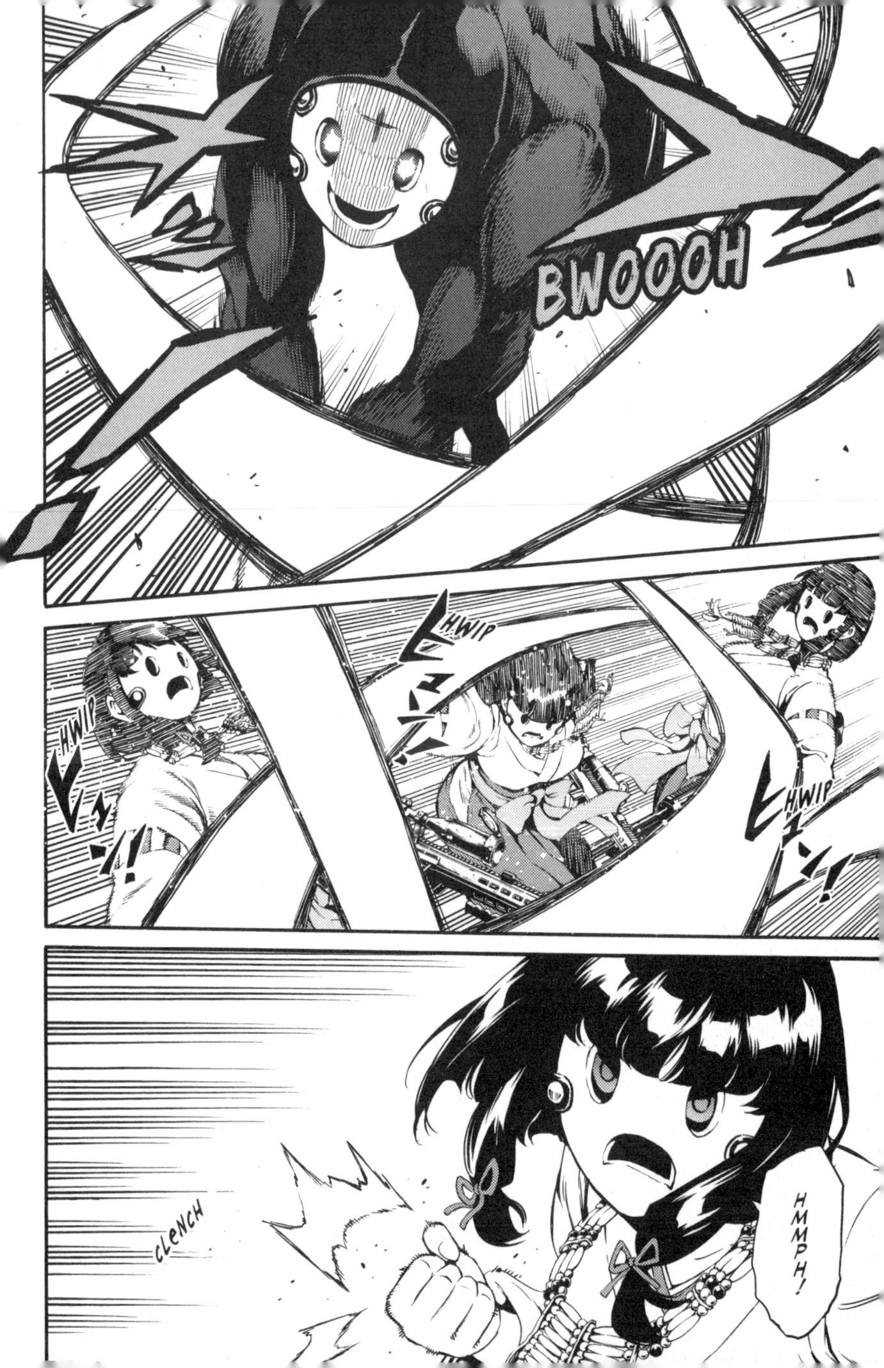
BWOOOH
HWIP
HWIP
HWIP
HMMPH!
CLENCH

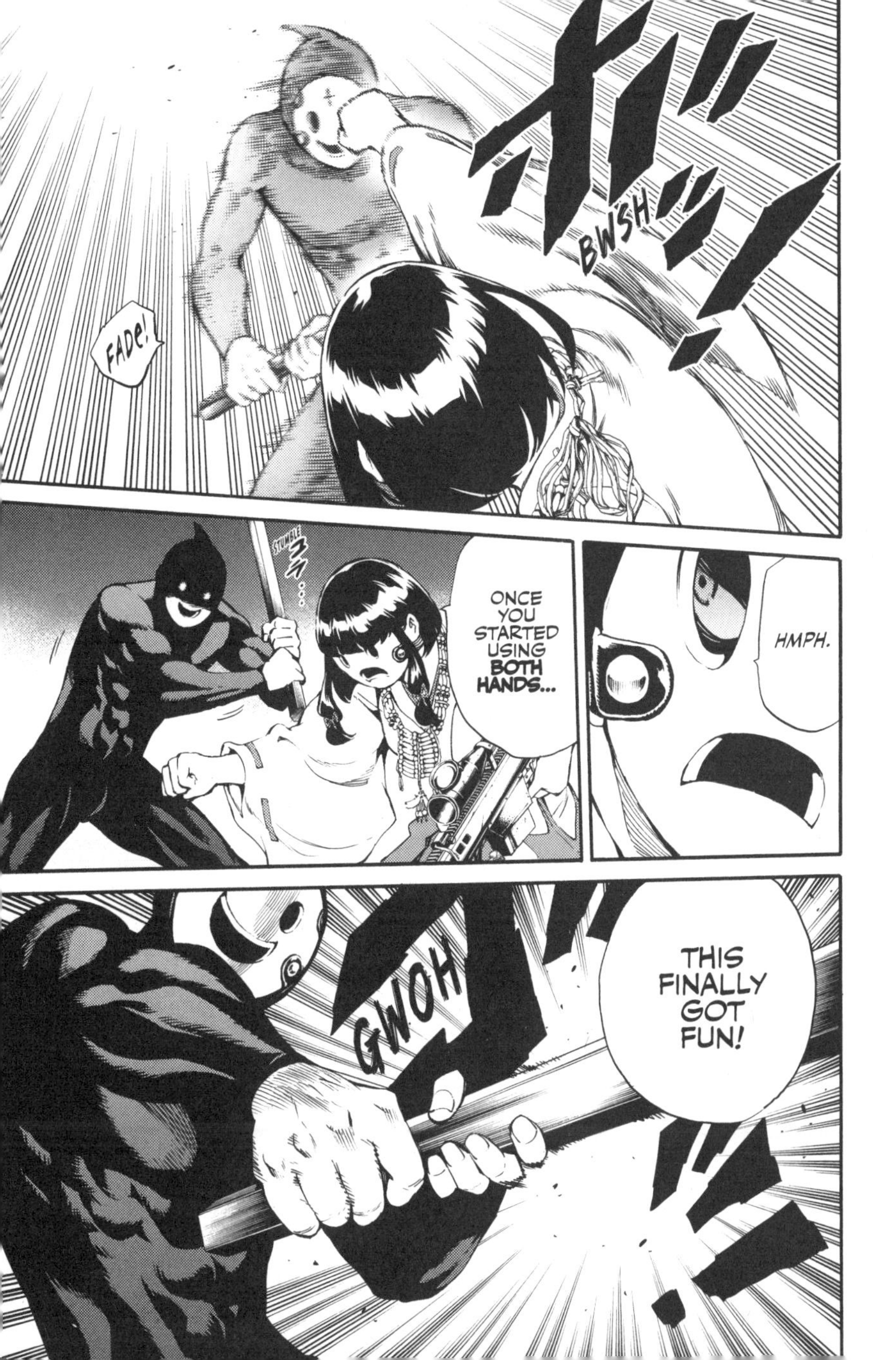
BWSH
FADE!
HMPH.
ONCE YOU STARTED USING **BOTH HANDS...**
STUMBLE
THIS FINALLY GOT FUN!
GWOH

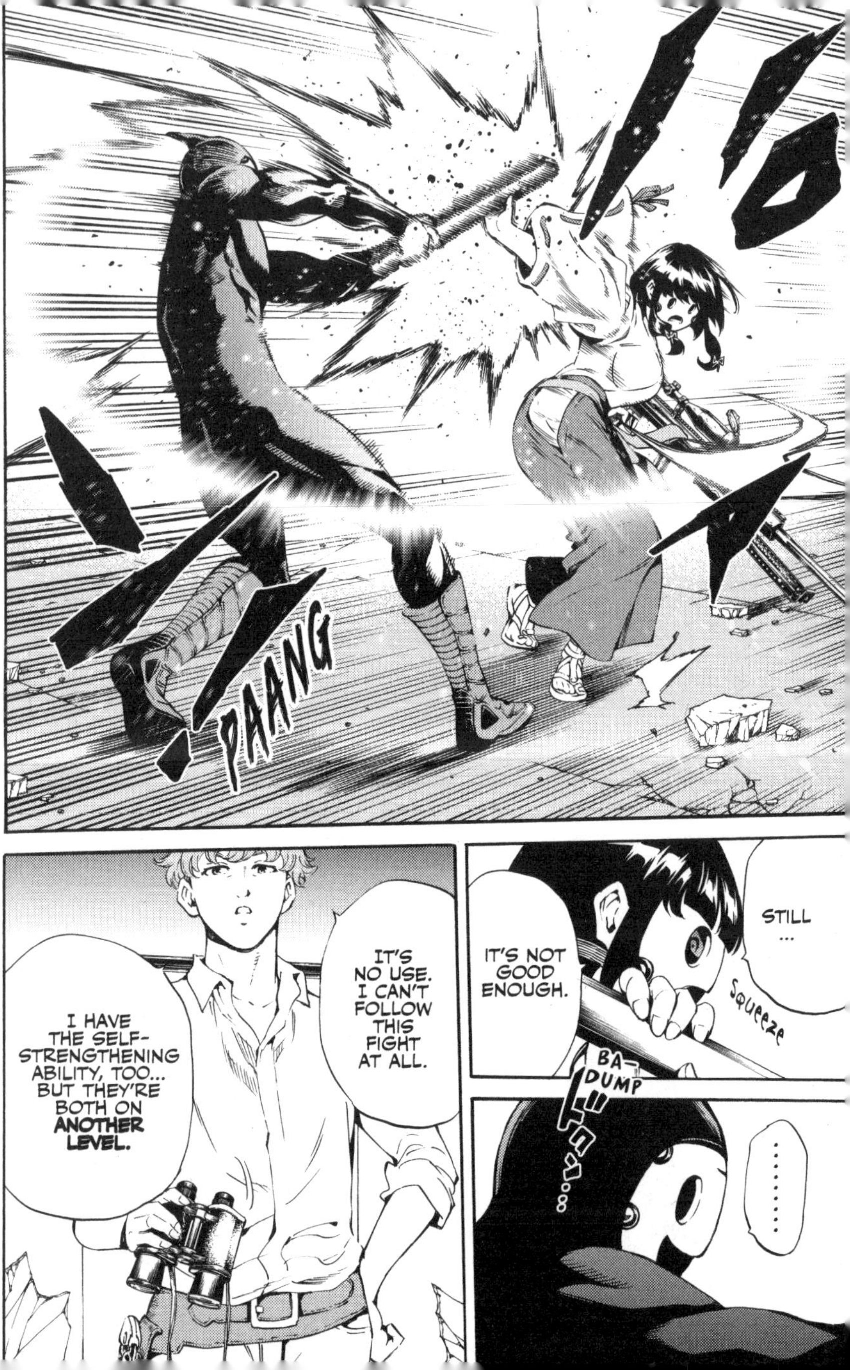
PAANG
STILL ...
IT'S NOT GOOD ENOUGH.
Squeeze
BA-DUMP
....
IT'S NO USE. I CAN'T FOLLOW THIS FIGHT AT ALL.
I HAVE THE SELF-STRENGTHENING ABILITY, TOO... BUT THEY'RE BOTH ON **ANOTHER LEVEL.**

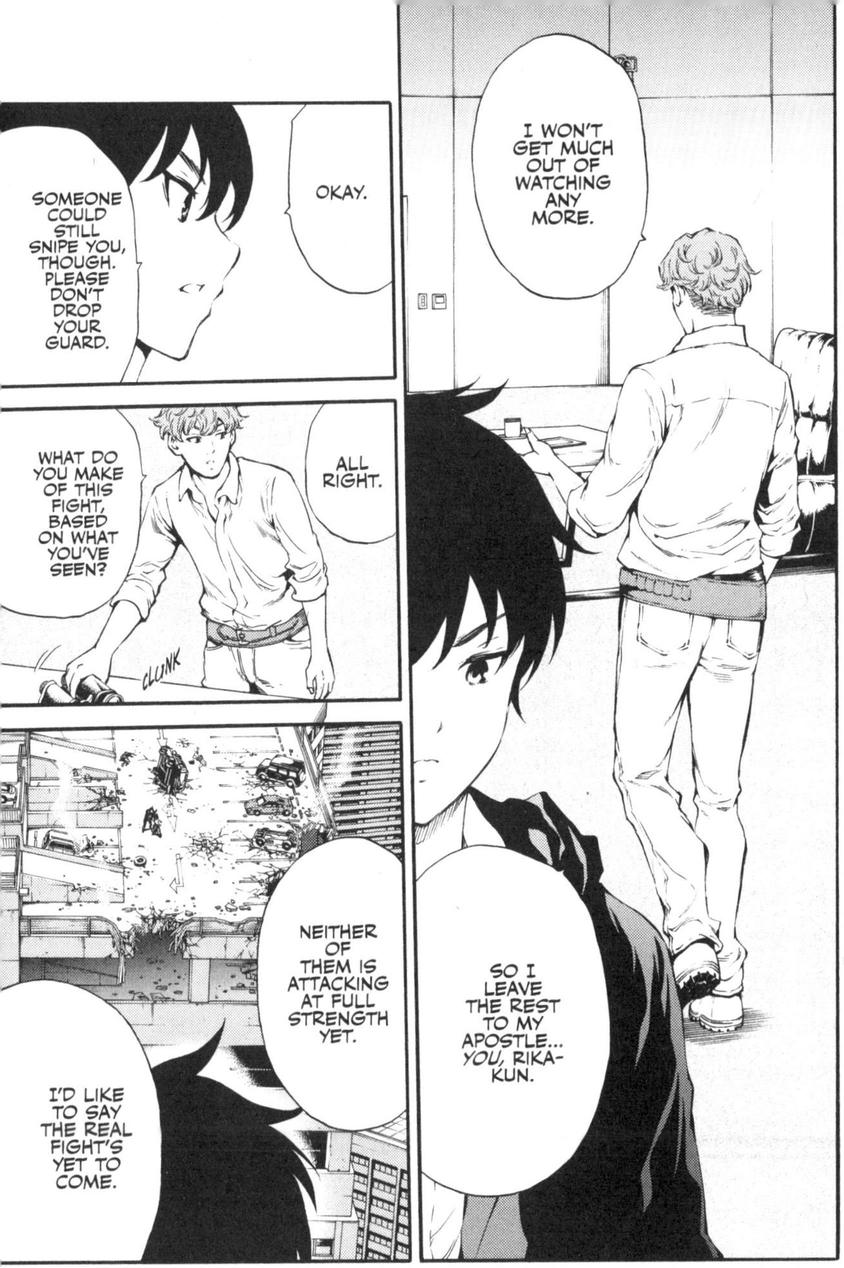
I WON'T GET MUCH OUT OF WATCHING ANY MORE.
SO I LEAVE THE REST TO MY APOSTLE... *YOU,* RIKA-KUN.
OKAY.
SOMEONE COULD STILL SNIPE YOU, THOUGH. PLEASE DON'T DROP YOUR GUARD.
ALL RIGHT.
WHAT DO YOU MAKE OF THIS FIGHT, BASED ON WHAT YOU'VE SEEN?
CLUNK
NEITHER OF THEM IS ATTACKING AT FULL STRENGTH YET.
I'D LIKE TO SAY THE REAL FIGHT'S YET TO COME.

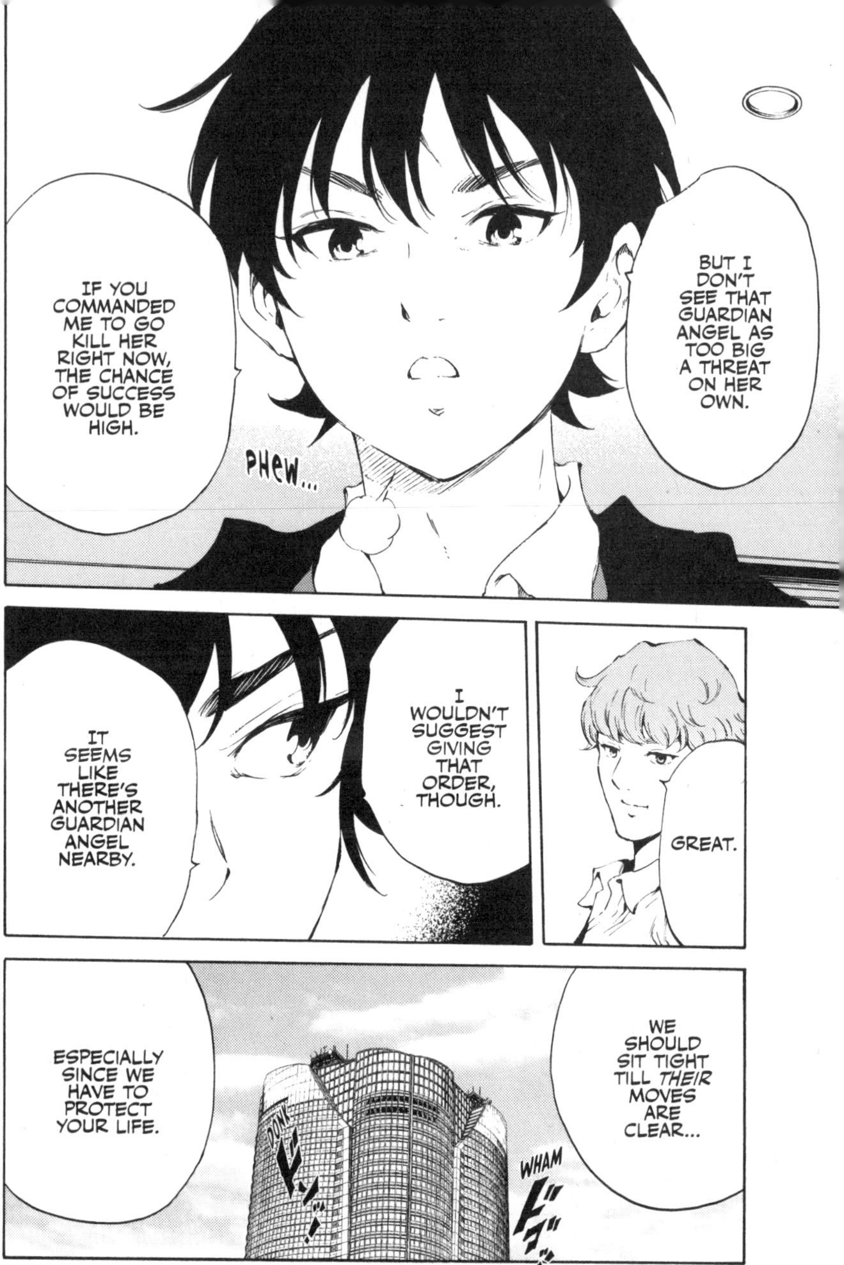
BUT I DON'T SEE THAT GUARDIAN ANGEL AS TOO BIG A THREAT ON HER OWN.
PHEW...
IF YOU COMMANDED ME TO GO KILL HER RIGHT NOW, THE CHANCE OF SUCCESS WOULD BE HIGH.
GREAT.
I WOULDN'T SUGGEST GIVING THAT ORDER, THOUGH.
IT SEEMS LIKE THERE'S ANOTHER GUARDIAN ANGEL NEARBY.
WE SHOULD SIT TIGHT TILL *THEIR* MOVES ARE CLEAR...
WHAM
DONK
ESPECIALLY SINCE WE HAVE TO PROTECT YOUR LIFE.

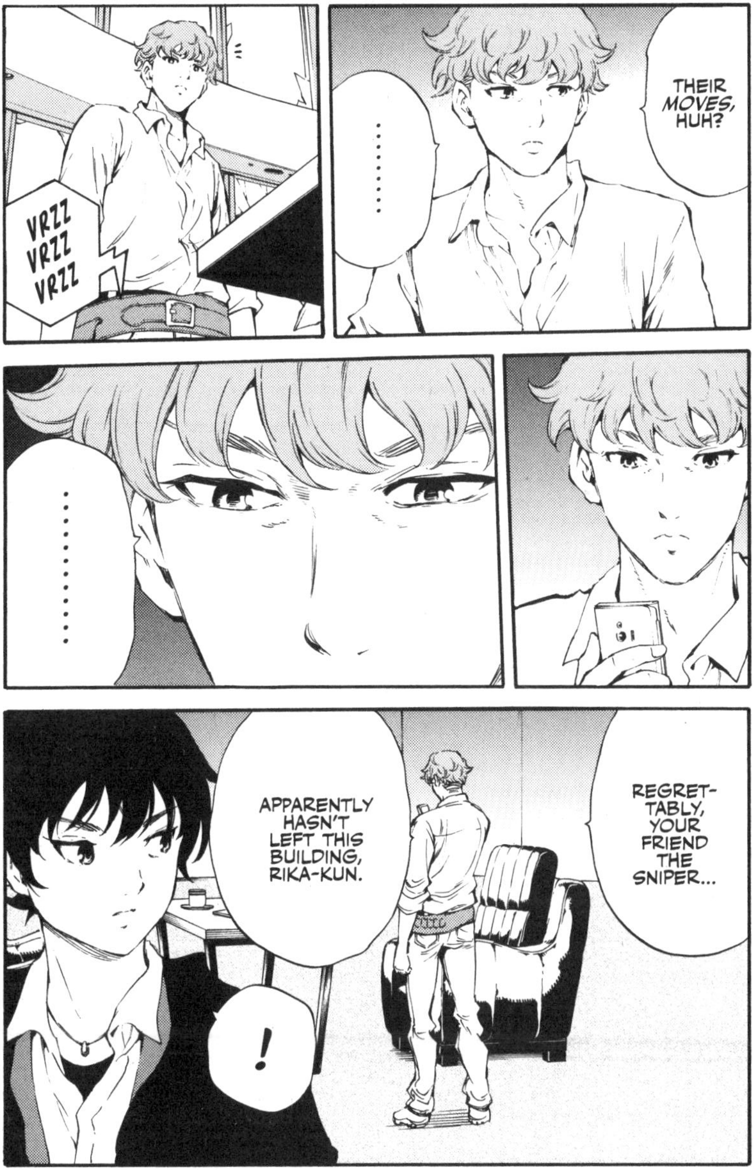
THEIR MOVES, HUH?
....
VRZZ VRZZ VRZZ
....
REGRET-TABLY, YOUR FRIEND THE SNIPER...
APPARENTLY HASN'T LEFT THIS BUILDING, RIKA-KUN.
!

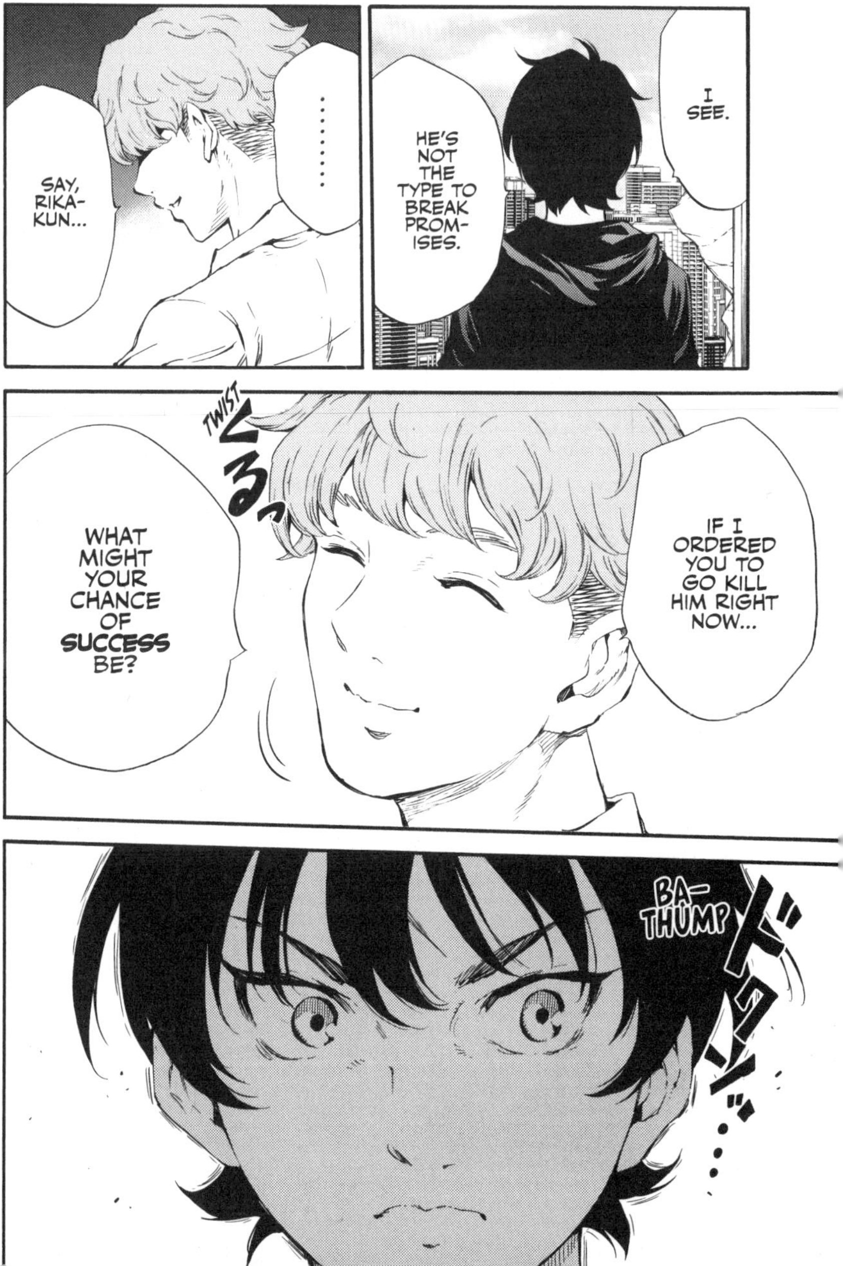

I SEE.
HE'S NOT THE TYPE TO BREAK PROMISES.
....
SAY, RIKA-KUN...
IF I ORDERED YOU TO GO KILL HIM RIGHT NOW...
TWIST
WHAT MIGHT YOUR CHANCE OF **SUCCESS** BE?
BA-THUMP

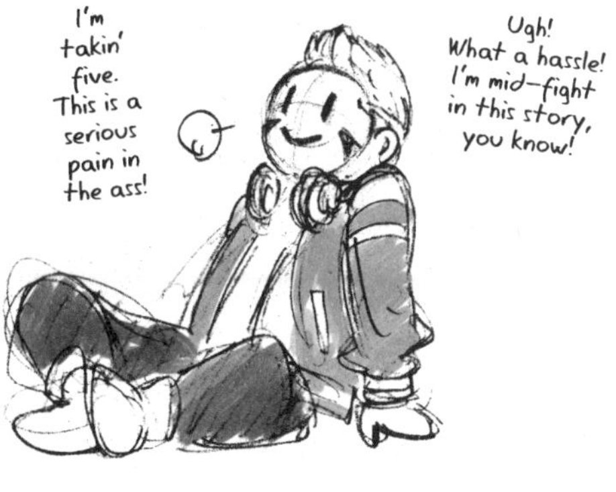
Ugh! What a hassle! I'm mid-fight in this story, you know!
I'm takin' five. This is a serious pain in the ass!

HIGH-RISE
INVASION

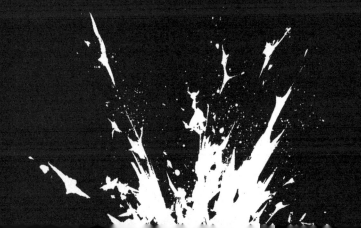

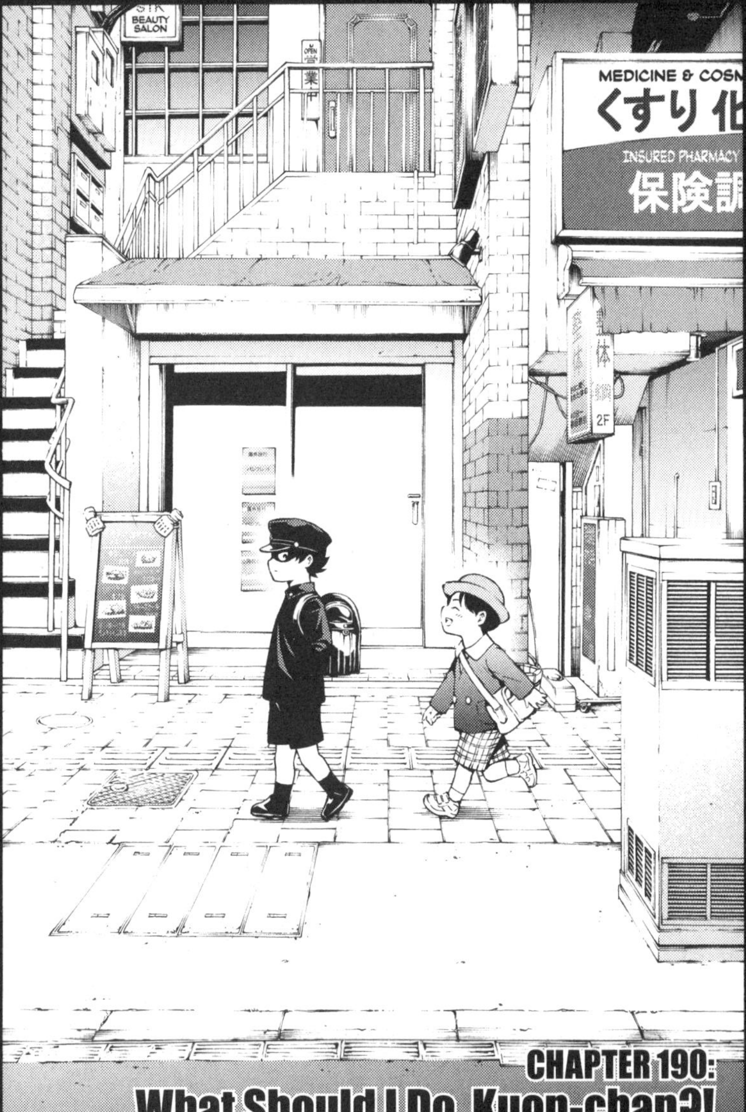
BEAUTY SALON
OPEN
MEDICINE & COSM
くすり 化
INSURED PHARMACY
2F

CHAPTER 190:
What Should I Do, Kuon-chan?!

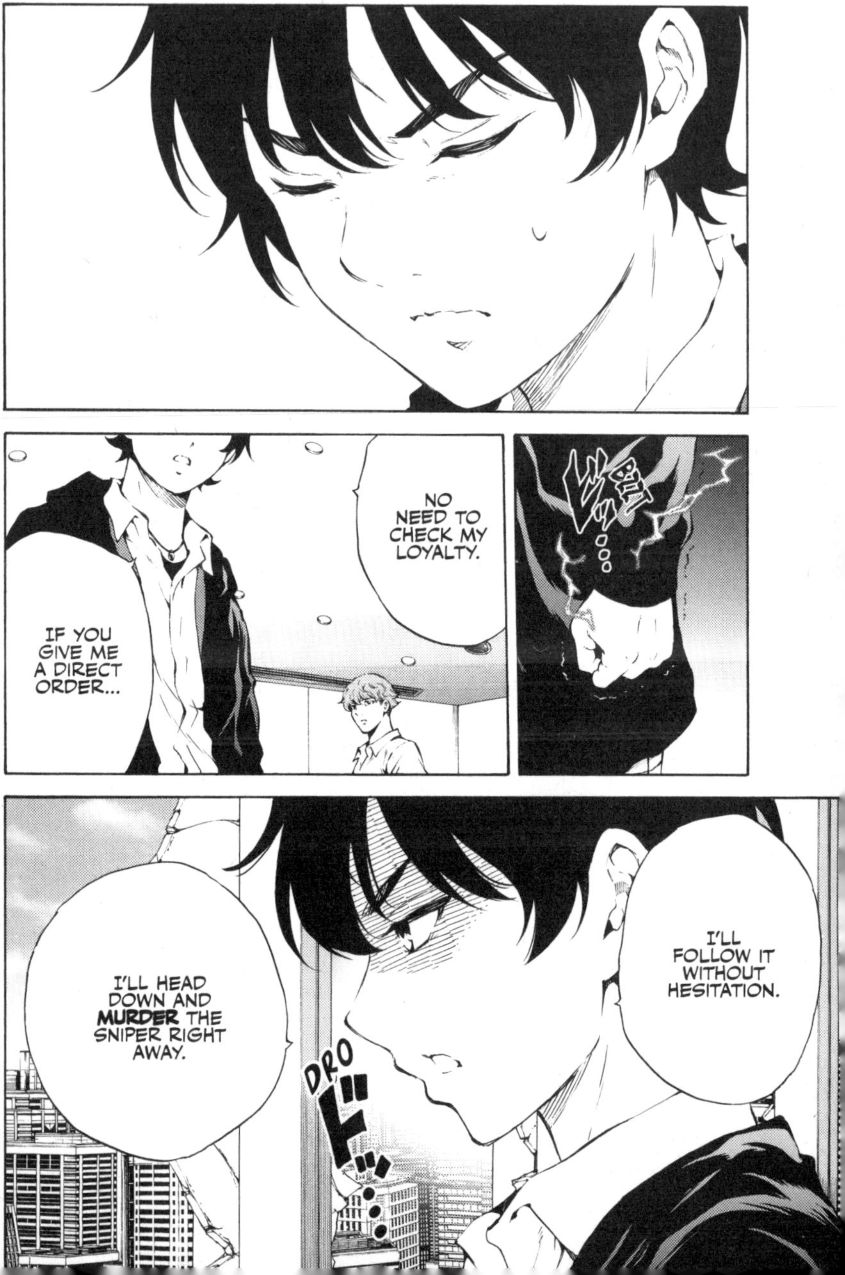
NO NEED TO CHECK MY LOYALTY.
IF YOU GIVE ME A DIRECT ORDER...
I'LL FOLLOW IT WITHOUT HESITATION.
I'LL HEAD DOWN AND **MURDER** THE SNIPER RIGHT AWAY.
DRO

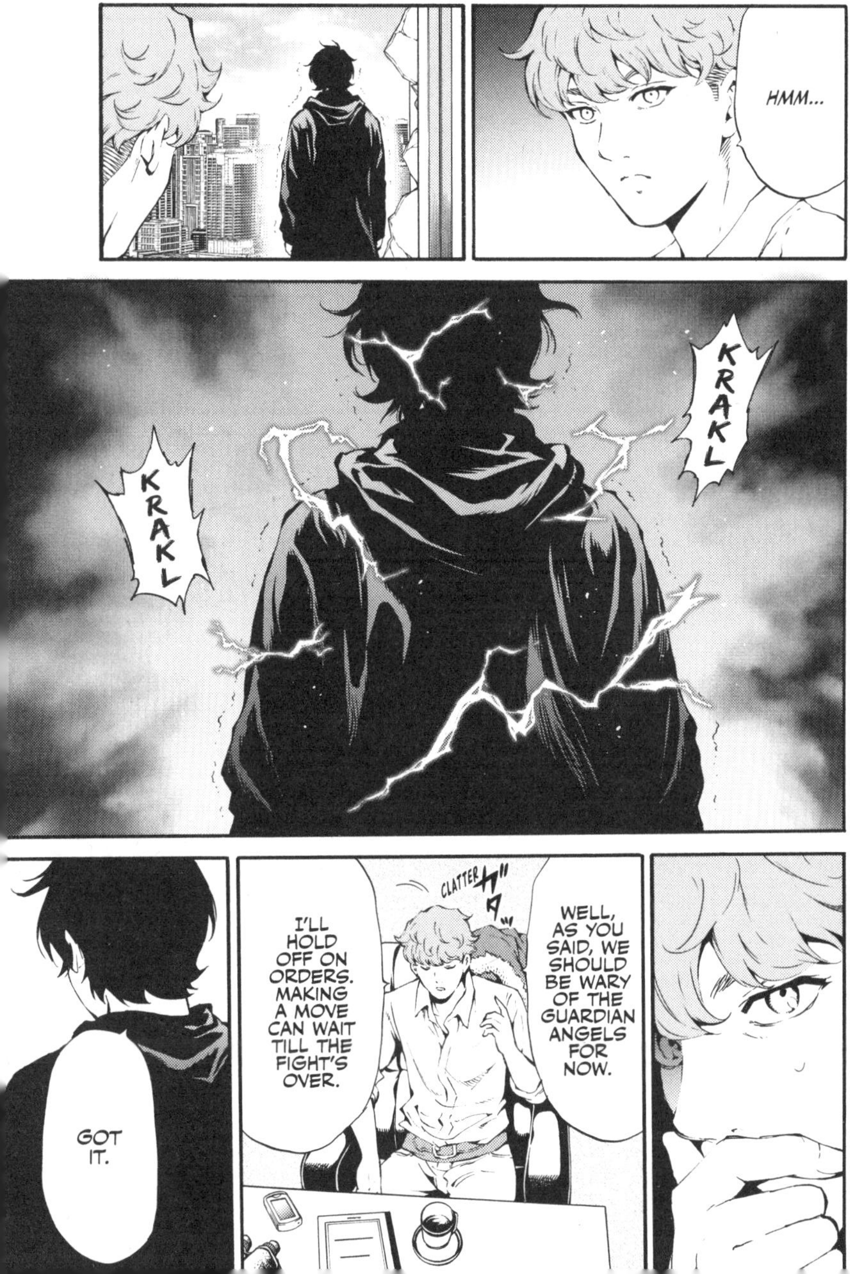
HMM...
KRAKL
KRAKL
WELL, AS YOU SAID, WE SHOULD BE WARY OF THE GUARDIAN ANGELS FOR NOW.
CLATTER
I'LL HOLD OFF ON ORDERS. MAKING A MOVE CAN WAIT TILL THE FIGHT'S OVER.
GOT IT.

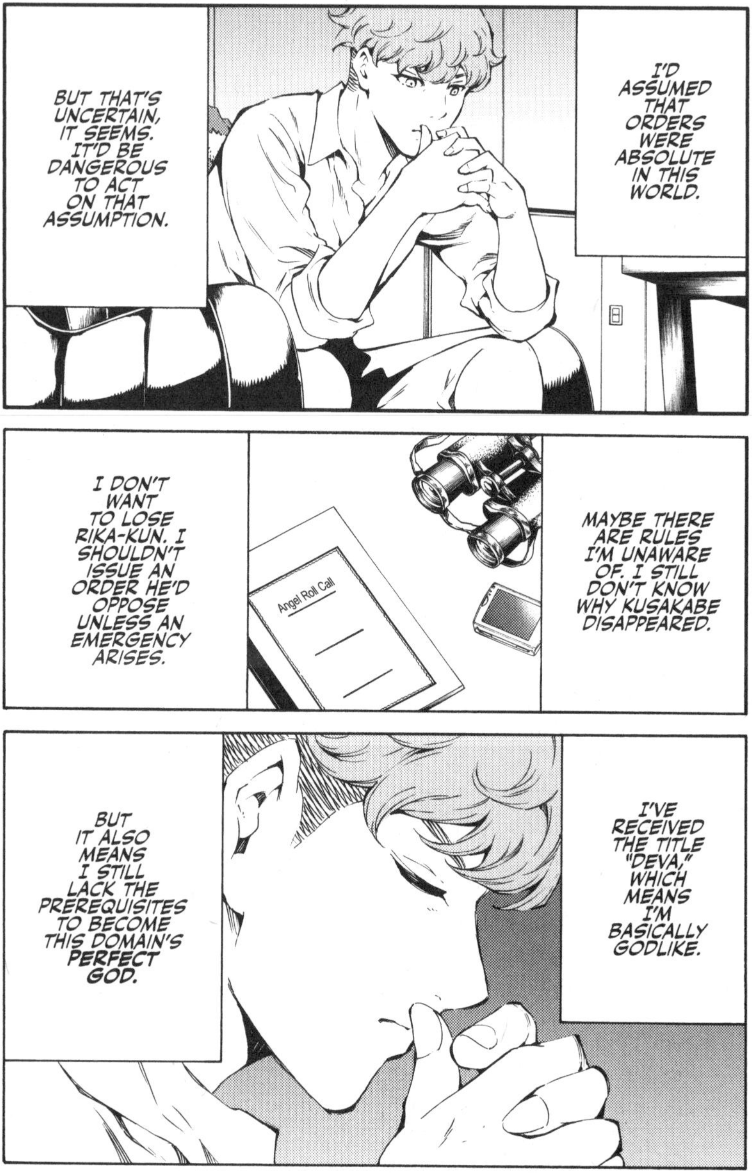
I'D ASSUMED THAT ORDERS WERE ABSOLUTE IN THIS WORLD.
BUT THAT'S UNCERTAIN, IT SEEMS. IT'D BE DANGEROUS TO ACT ON THAT ASSUMPTION.
MAYBE THERE ARE RULES I'M UNAWARE OF. I STILL DON'T KNOW WHY KUSAKABE DISAPPEARED.
Angel Roll Call
I DON'T WANT TO LOSE RIKA-KUN. I SHOULDN'T ISSUE AN ORDER HE'D OPPOSE UNLESS AN EMERGENCY ARISES.
I'VE RECEIVED THE TITLE "DEVA," WHICH MEANS I'M BASICALLY GODLIKE.
BUT IT ALSO MEANS I STILL LACK THE PREREQUISITES TO BECOME THIS DOMAIN'S **PERFECT** GOD.

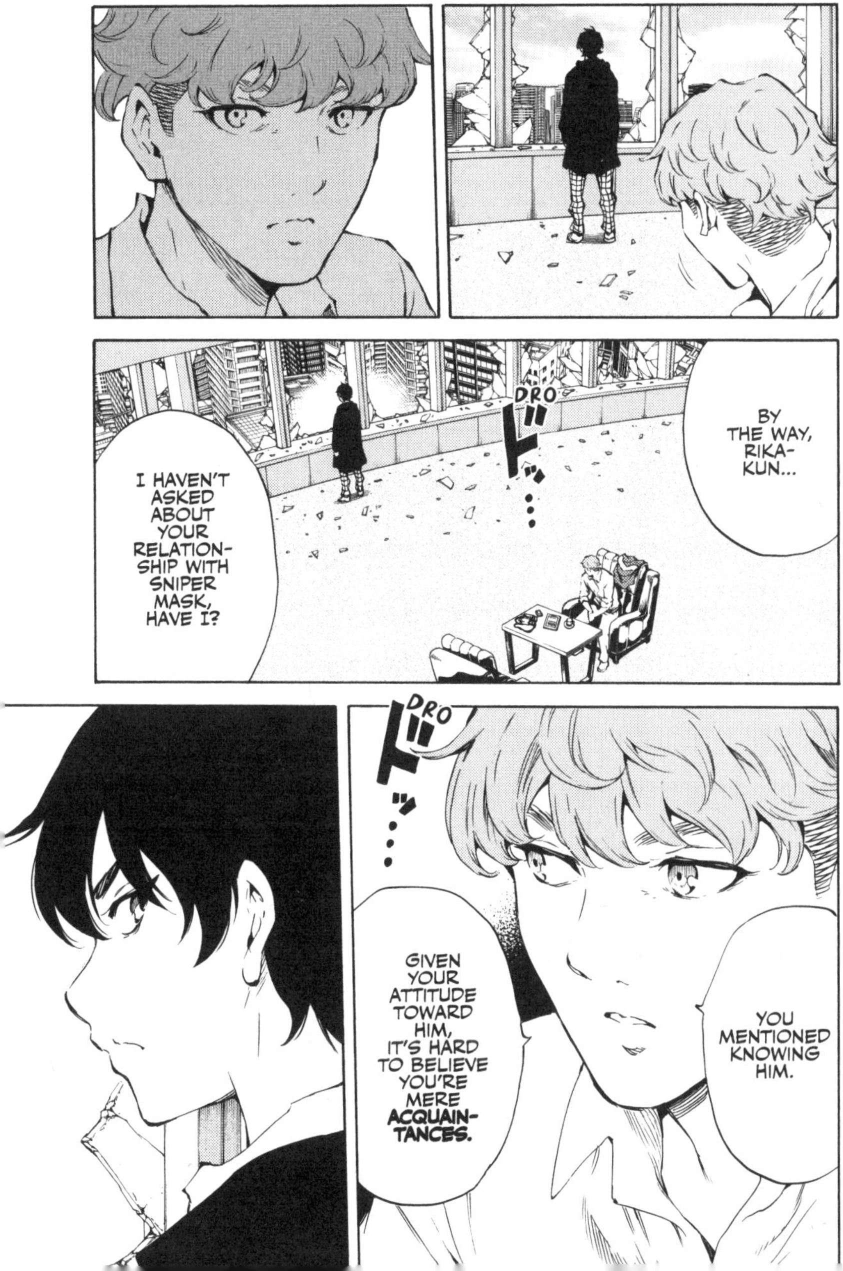
BY THE WAY, RIKA-KUN...
DRO
I HAVEN'T ASKED ABOUT YOUR RELATION-SHIP WITH SNIPER MASK, HAVE I?
DRO
YOU MENTIONED KNOWING HIM.
GIVEN YOUR ATTITUDE TOWARD HIM, IT'S HARD TO BELIEVE YOU'RE MERE **ACQUAIN-TANCES.**

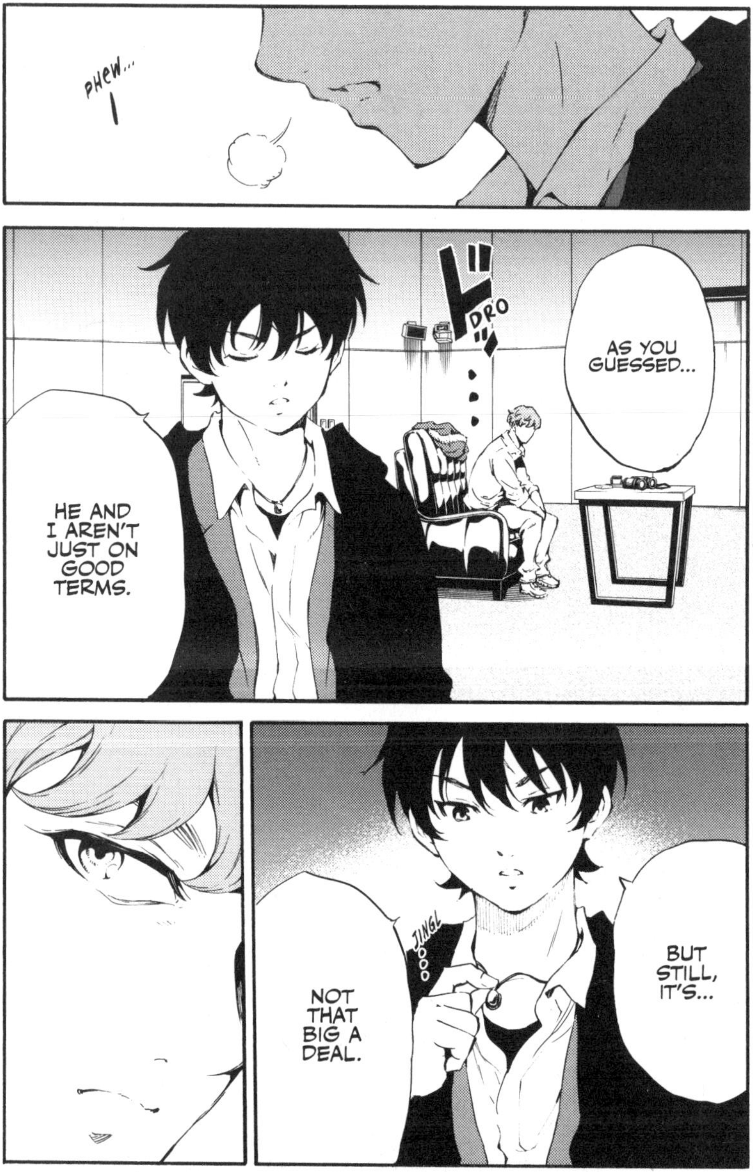
PHEW...
AS YOU GUESSED...
DRO
HE AND I AREN'T JUST ON GOOD TERMS.
BUT STILL, IT'S...
JINGL
NOT THAT BIG A DEAL.

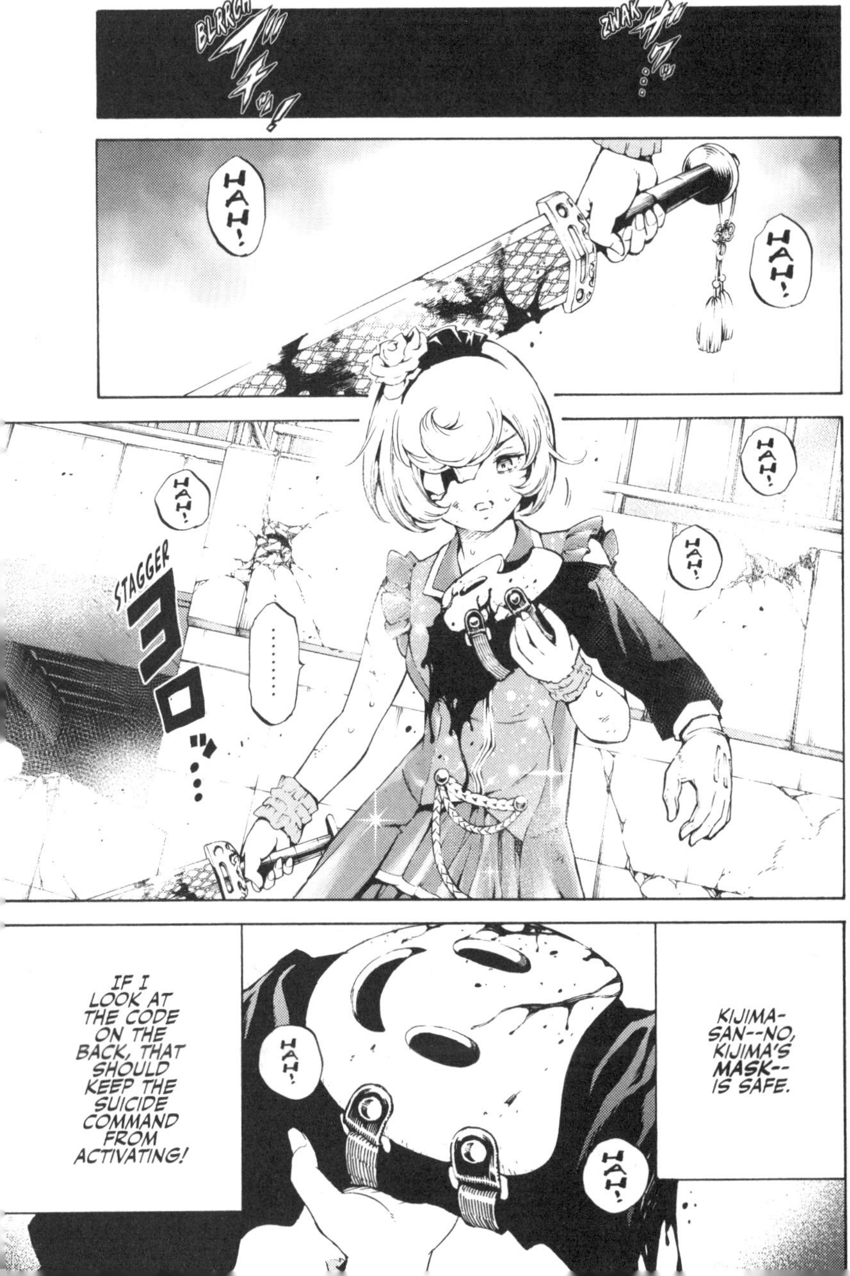
ZWAK
BLRRCH
HAH!
HAH!
HAH!
HAH!
HAH!
STAGGER
......
KIJIMA-SAN--NO, KIJIMA'S MASK--IS SAFE.
HAH!
HAH!
IF I LOOK AT THE CODE ON THE BACK, THAT SHOULD KEEP THE SUICIDE COMMAND FROM ACTIVATING!

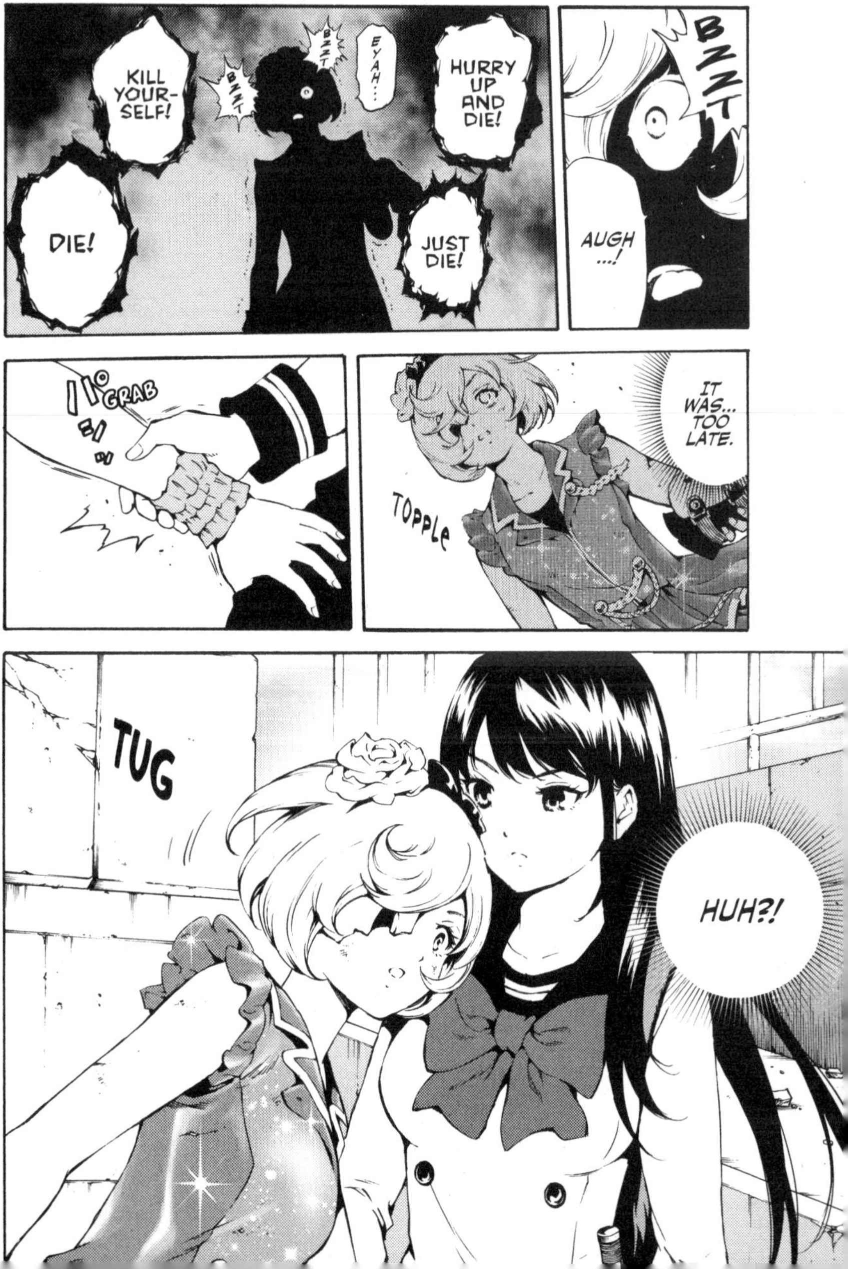
BZZZT
AUGH ...!
HURRY UP AND DIE!
EYAH...
BZZT
BZZT
KILL YOUR-SELF!
JUST DIE!
DIE!
IT WAS... TOO LATE.
TOPPLE
GRAB
HUH?!
TUG

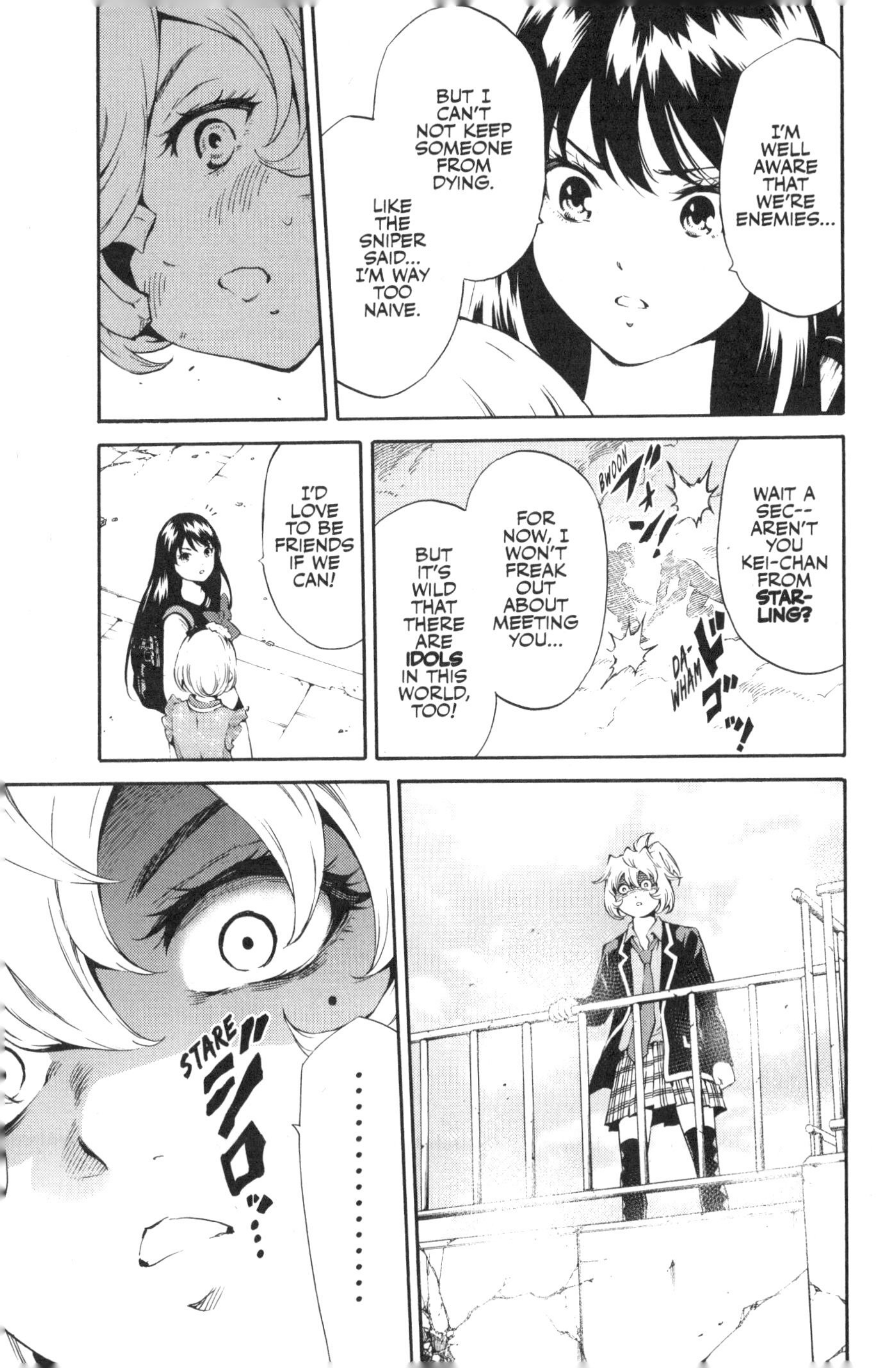
I'M WELL AWARE THAT WE'RE ENEMIES...
BUT I CAN'T NOT KEEP SOMEONE FROM DYING.
LIKE THE SNIPER SAID... I'M WAY TOO NAIVE.
WAIT A SEC-- AREN'T YOU KEI-CHAN FROM **STAR-LING?**
BWOON
FOR NOW, I WON'T FREAK OUT ABOUT MEETING YOU...
DA-WHAM
BUT IT'S WILD THAT THERE ARE **IDOLS** IN THIS WORLD, TOO!
I'D LOVE TO BE FRIENDS IF WE CAN!
STARE
......

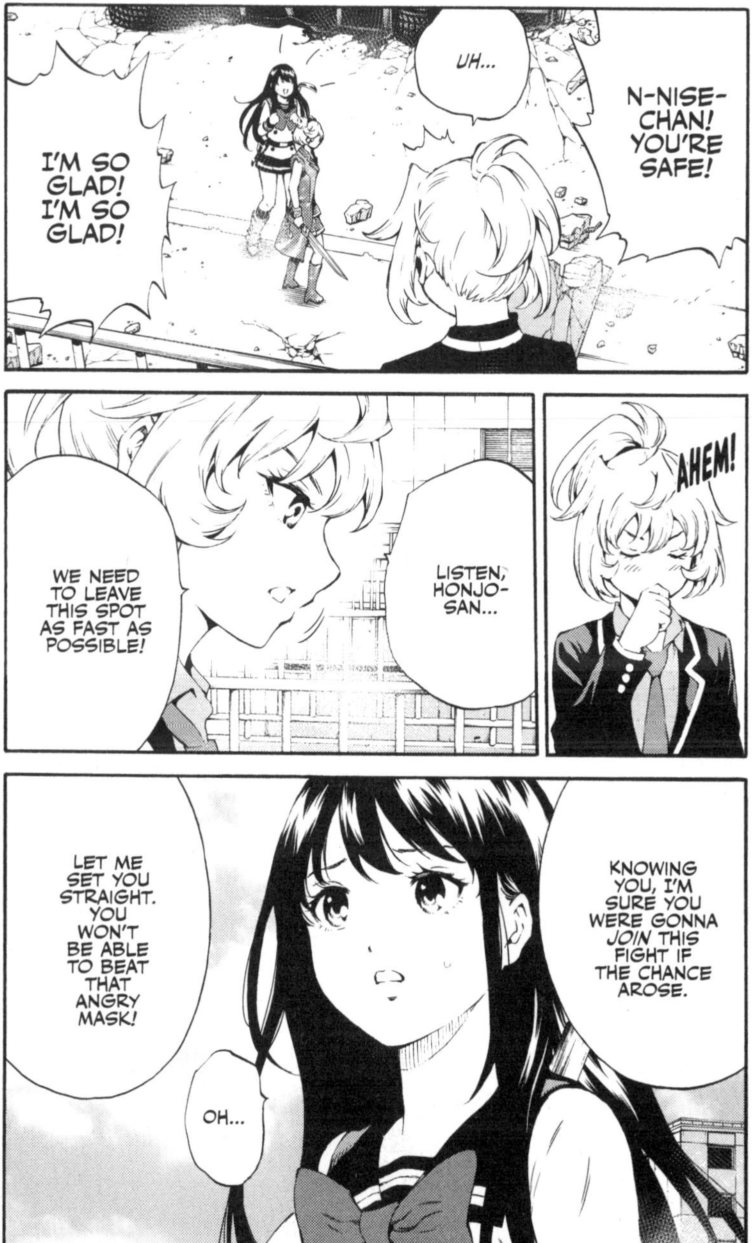
N-NISE-CHAN! YOU'RE SAFE!
UH...
I'M SO GLAD! I'M SO GLAD!
AHEM!
LISTEN, HONJO-SAN...
WE NEED TO LEAVE THIS SPOT AS FAST AS POSSIBLE!
KNOWING YOU, I'M SURE YOU WERE GONNA *JOIN* THIS FIGHT IF THE CHANCE AROSE.
LET ME SET YOU STRAIGHT. YOU WON'T BE ABLE TO BEAT THAT ANGRY MASK!
OH...

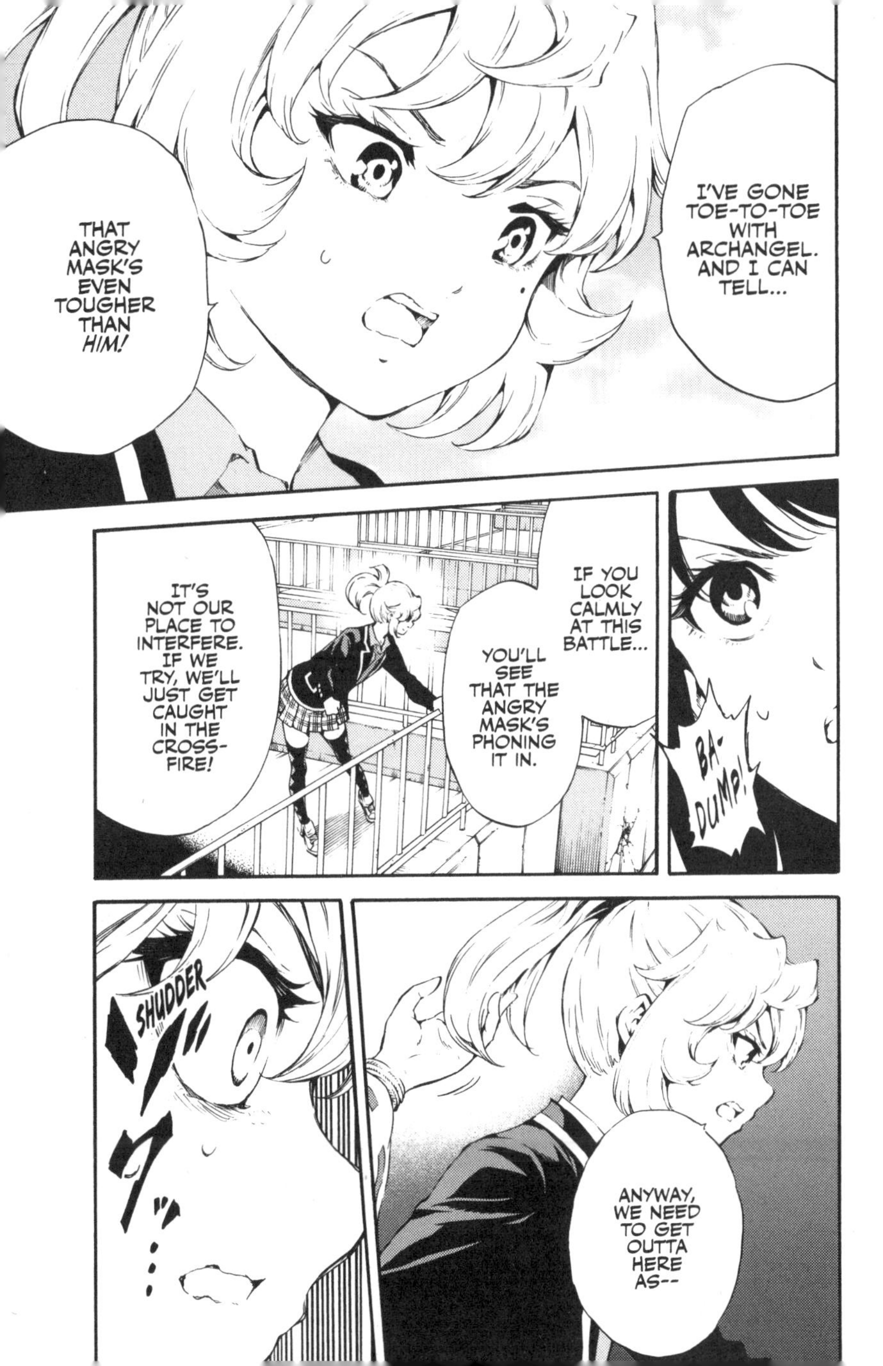
I'VE GONE TOE-TO-TOE WITH ARCHANGEL. AND I CAN TELL...
THAT ANGRY MASK'S EVEN TOUGHER THAN *HIM!*
BA-DUMP!
IF YOU LOOK CALMLY AT THIS BATTLE...
YOU'LL SEE THAT THE ANGRY MASK'S PHONING IT IN.
IT'S NOT OUR PLACE TO INTERFERE. IF WE TRY, WE'LL JUST GET CAUGHT IN THE CROSS-FIRE!
ANYWAY, WE NEED TO GET OUTTA HERE AS--
SHUDDER

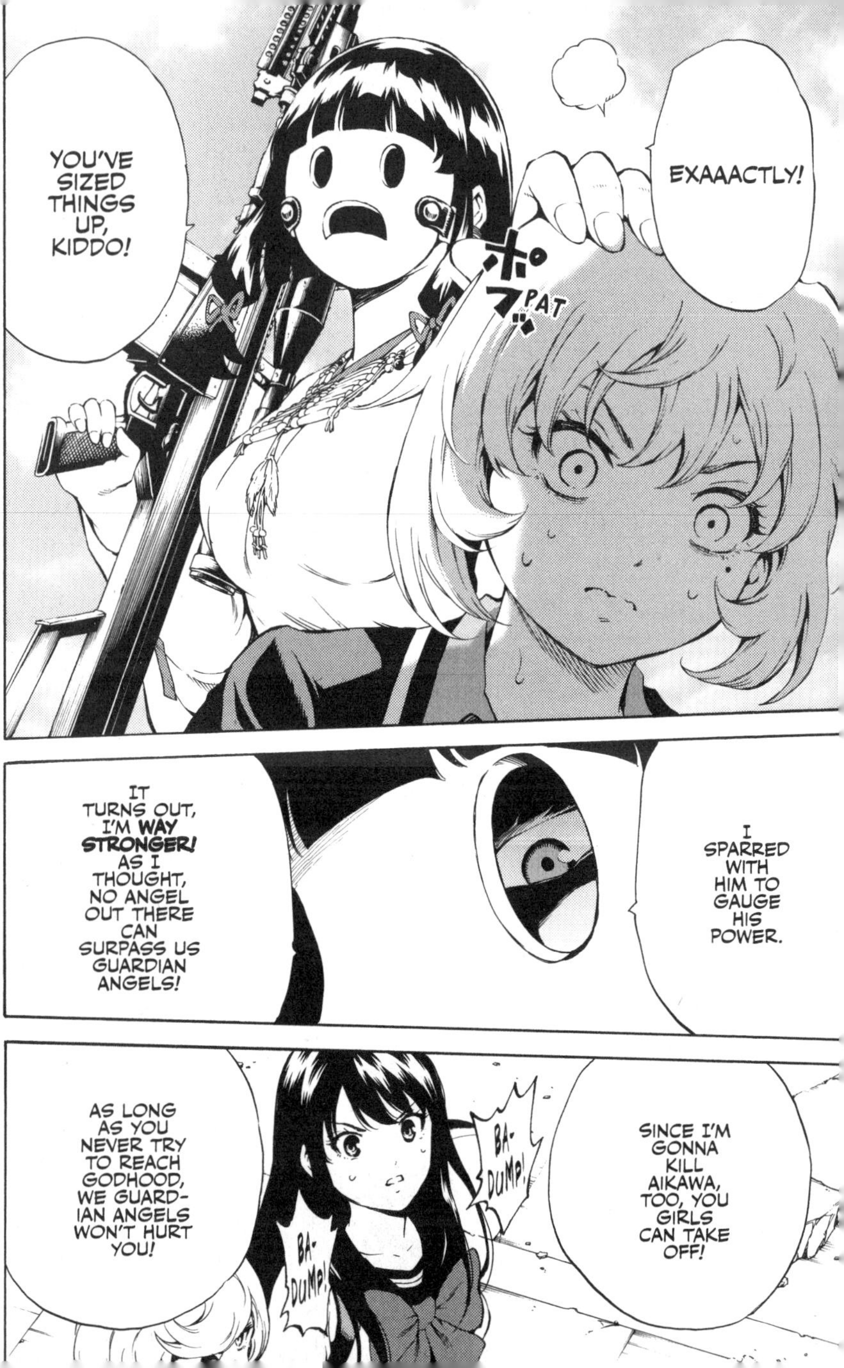
EXAAACTLY!
PAT
YOU'VE SIZED THINGS UP, KIDDO!
I SPARRED WITH HIM TO GAUGE HIS POWER.
IT TURNS OUT, I'M **WAY STRONGER!** AS I THOUGHT, NO ANGEL OUT THERE CAN SURPASS US GUARDIAN ANGELS!
SINCE I'M GONNA KILL AIKAWA, TOO, YOU GIRLS CAN TAKE OFF!
BA-DUMP!
AS LONG AS YOU NEVER TRY TO REACH GODHOOD, WE GUARD-IAN ANGELS WON'T HURT YOU!
BA-DUMP!

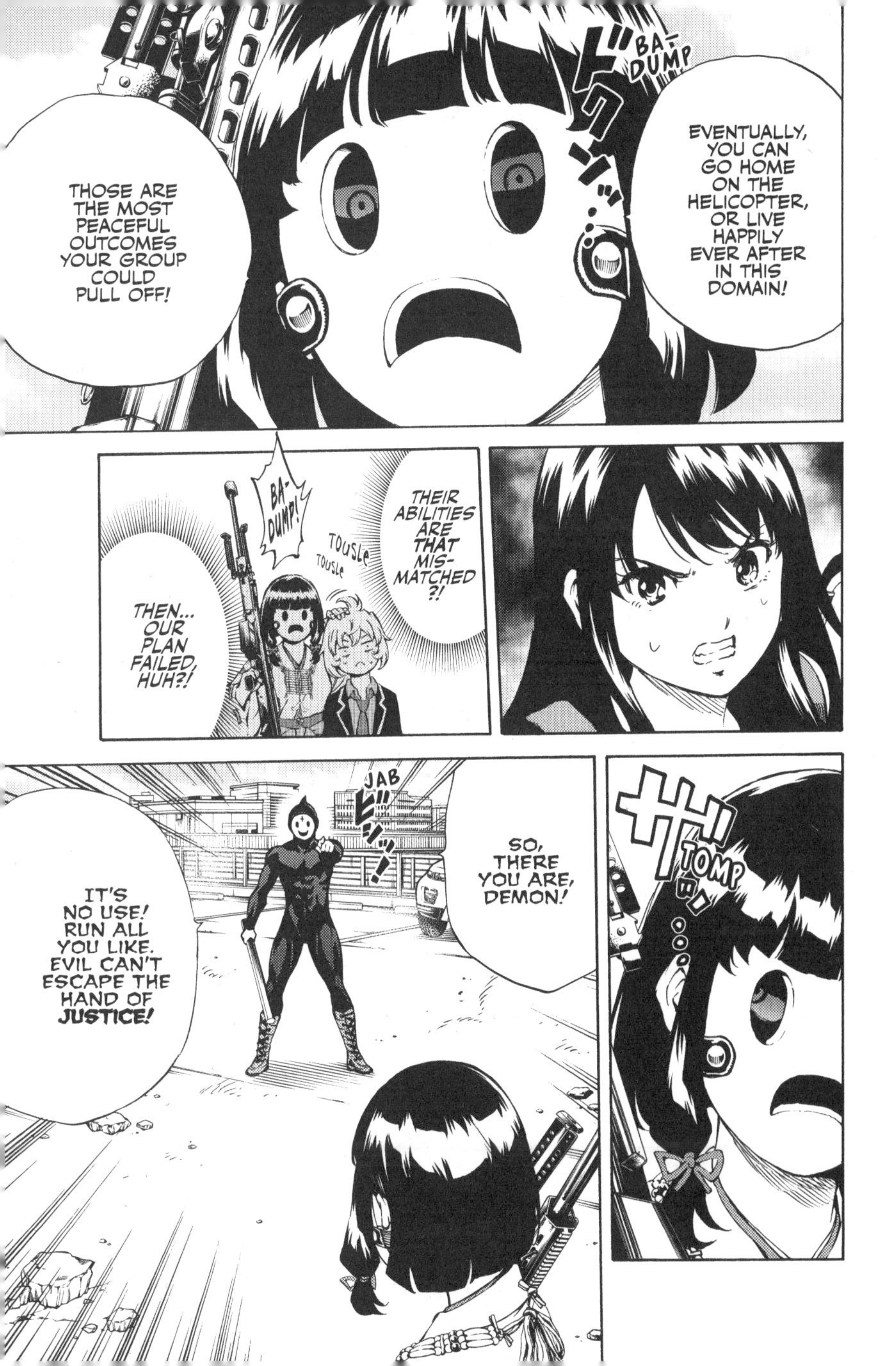
BA-DUMP
EVENTUALLY, YOU CAN GO HOME ON THE HELICOPTER, OR LIVE HAPPILY EVER AFTER IN THIS DOMAIN!
THOSE ARE THE MOST PEACEFUL OUTCOMES YOUR GROUP COULD PULL OFF!
THEIR ABILITIES ARE THAT MIS-MATCHED?!
BA-DUMP!
TOUSLE TOUSLE
THEN... OUR PLAN FAILED, HUH?!
TOMP
JAB
SO, THERE YOU ARE, DEMON!
IT'S NO USE! RUN ALL YOU LIKE. EVIL CAN'T ESCAPE THE HAND OF JUSTICE!

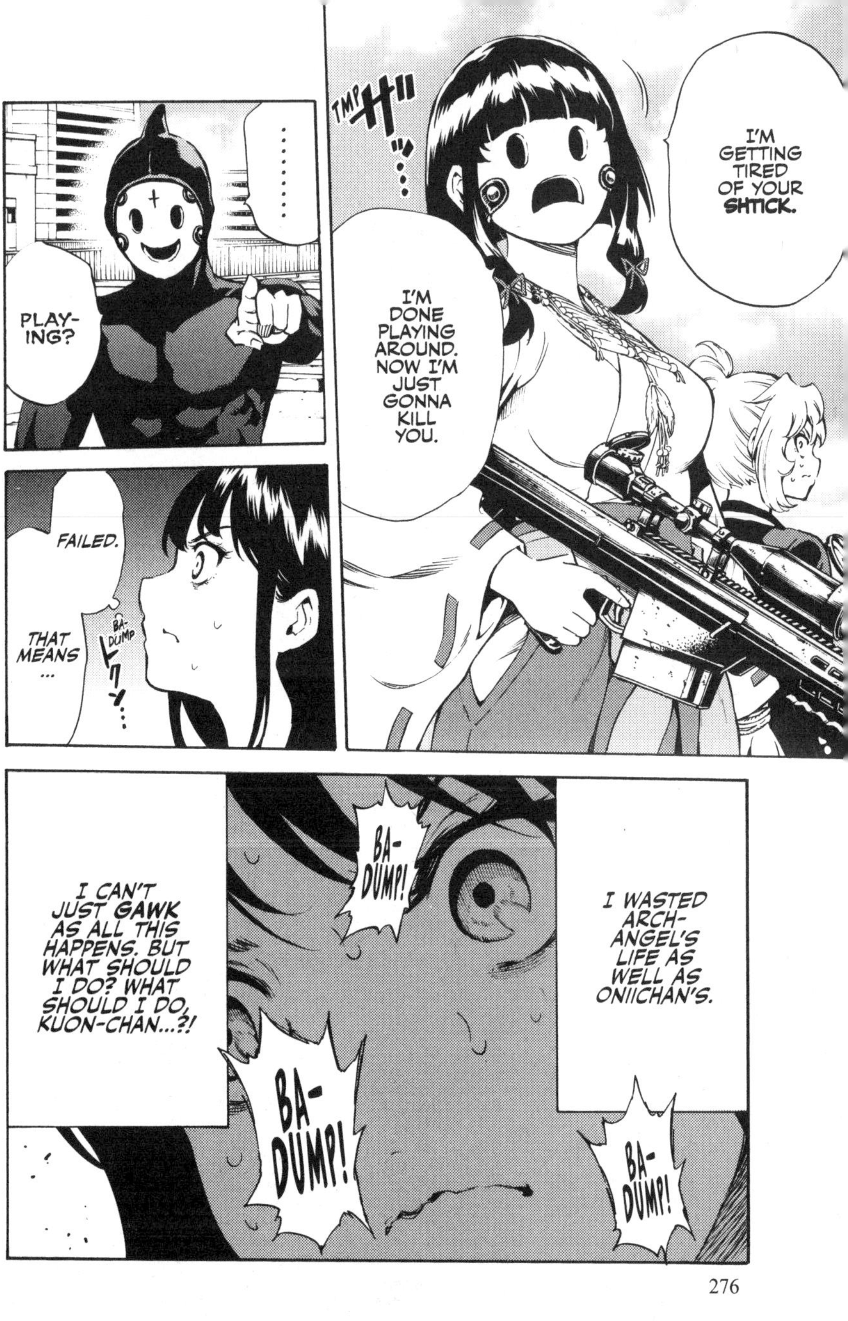
TMP
I'M GETTING TIRED OF YOUR **SHTICK.**
I'M DONE PLAYING AROUND. NOW I'M JUST GONNA KILL YOU.
....
PLAYING?
FAILED.
THAT MEANS ...
BA-DUMP
I WASTED ARCH-ANGEL'S LIFE AS WELL AS ONIICHAN'S.
BA-DUMP!
BA-DUMP!
*I CAN'T JUST **GAWK** AS ALL THIS HAPPENS. BUT WHAT SHOULD I DO? WHAT SHOULD I DO, KUON-CHAN...?!*
BA-DUMP!

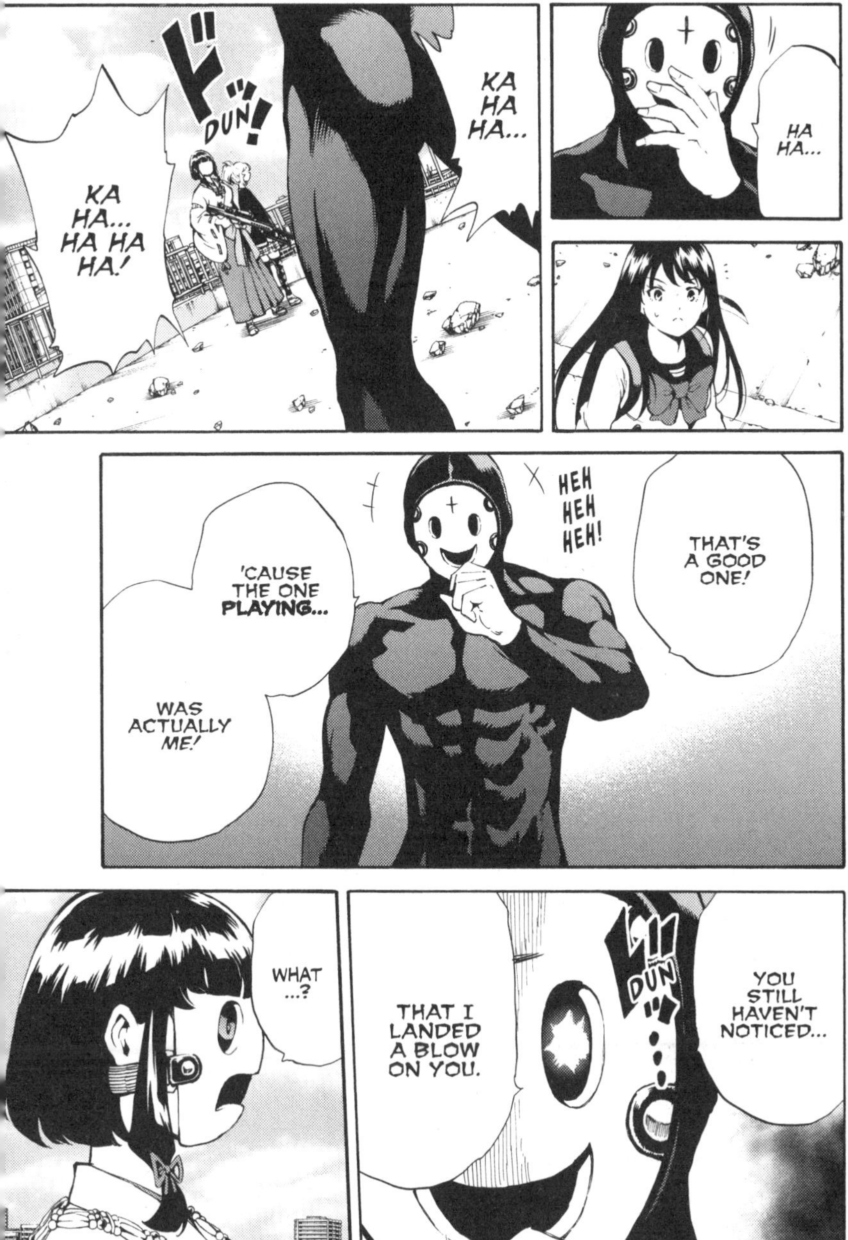
HA HA...
KA HA HA...
ド DUN!
KA HA... HA HA HA!
THAT'S A GOOD ONE!
HEH HEH HEH!
'CAUSE THE ONE PLAYING...
WAS ACTUALLY ME!
YOU STILL HAVEN'T NOTICED...
DUN
THAT I LANDED A BLOW ON YOU.
WHAT ...?

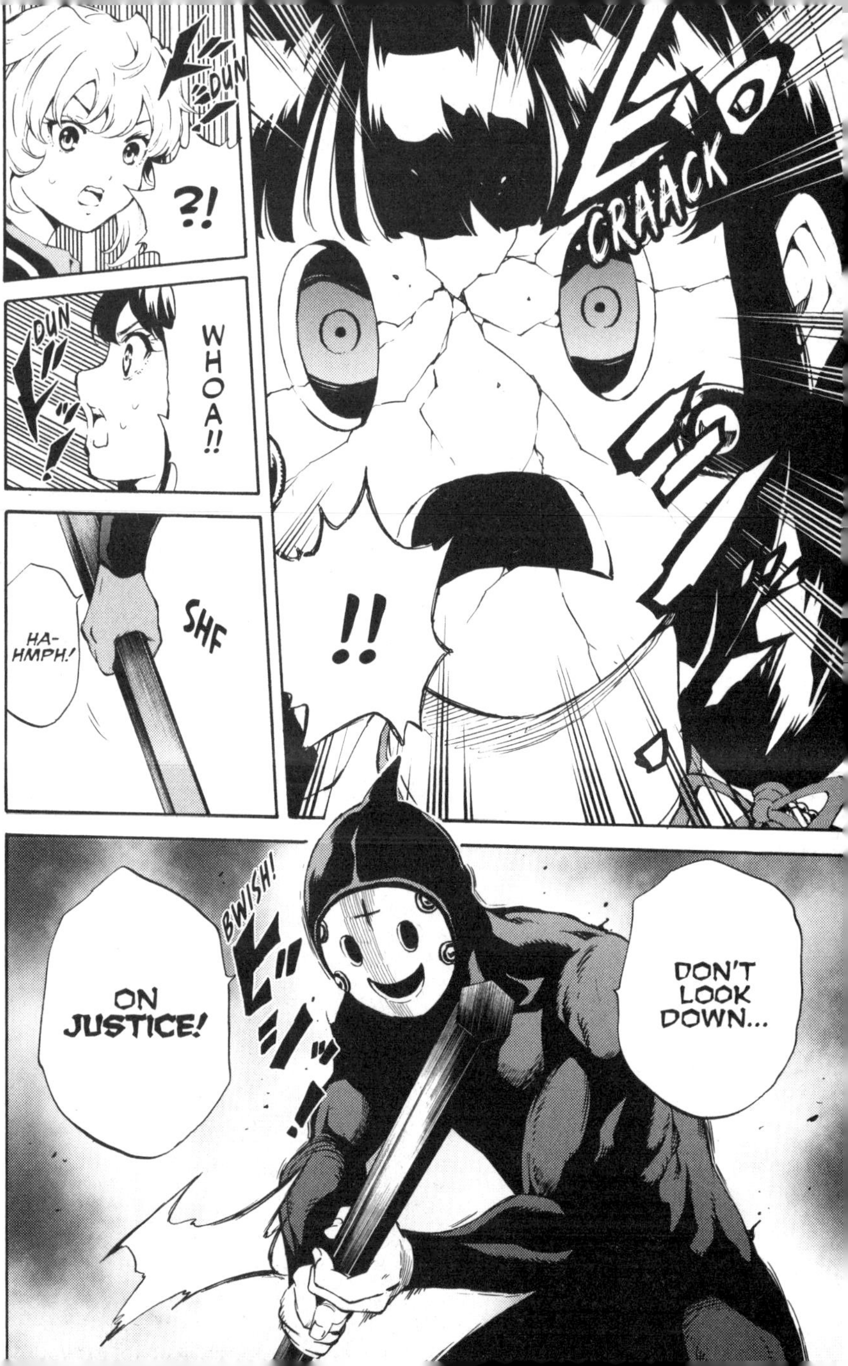

CRAACK
!!
DUN
?!
DUN
WHOA!!
SHF
HA-HMPH!
DON'T LOOK DOWN...
BWISH!
ON JUSTICE!

CHAPTER 191: Honjo-san's Weaknesses

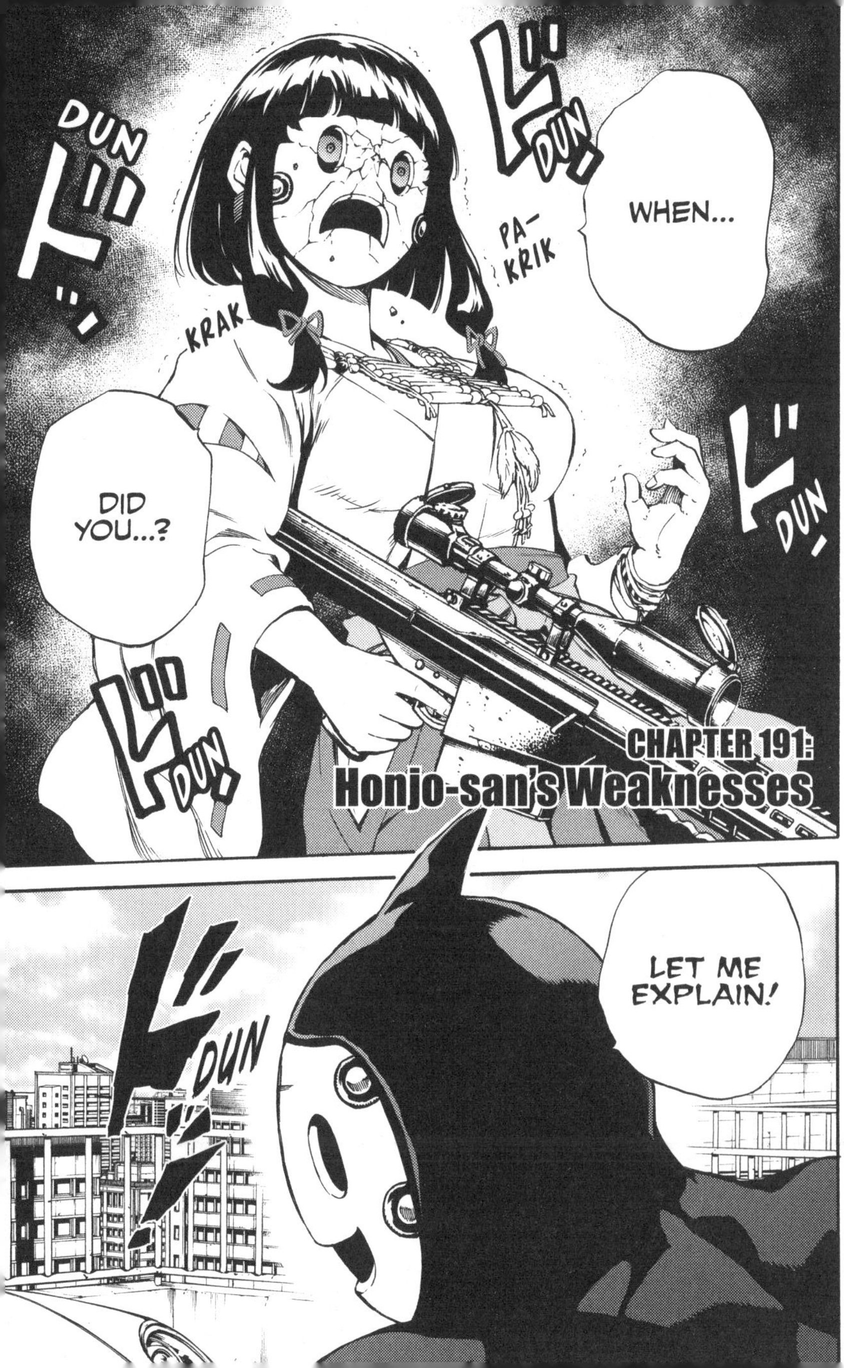
DUN
WHEN...
PA-KRIK
DUN
KRAK
DUN
DID YOU...?
DUN
LET ME EXPLAIN!
DUN

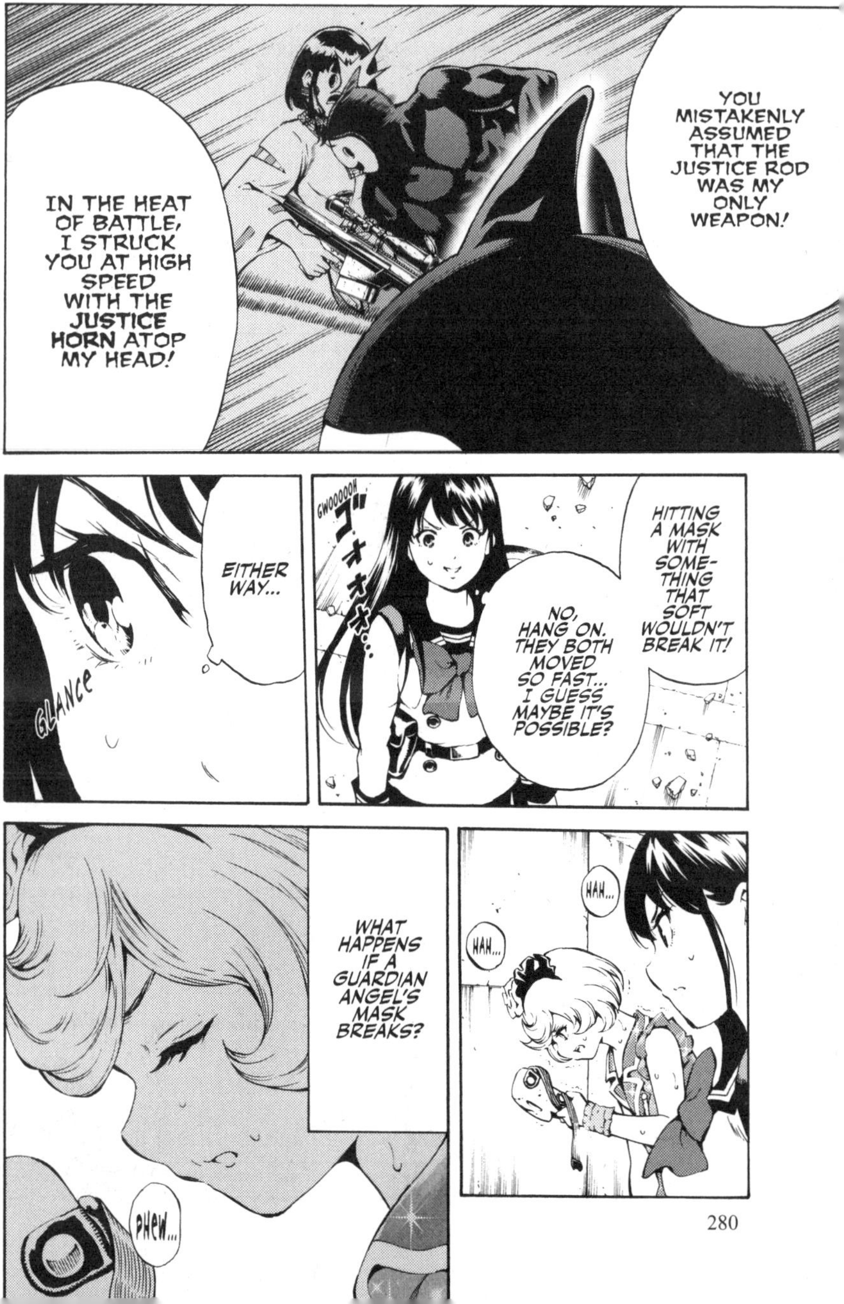
YOU MISTAKENLY ASSUMED THAT THE JUSTICE ROD WAS MY ONLY WEAPON!
IN THE HEAT OF BATTLE, I STRUCK YOU AT HIGH SPEED WITH THE **JUSTICE HORN** ATOP MY HEAD!
HITTING A MASK WITH SOME-THING THAT SOFT WOULDN'T BREAK IT!
GWOOOOOH
ゴオオオ…
NO, HANG ON. THEY BOTH MOVED SO FAST... I GUESS MAYBE IT'S POSSIBLE?
EITHER WAY...
GLANCE
HAH...
HAH...
WHAT HAPPENS IF A GUARDIAN ANGEL'S MASK BREAKS?
PHEW...

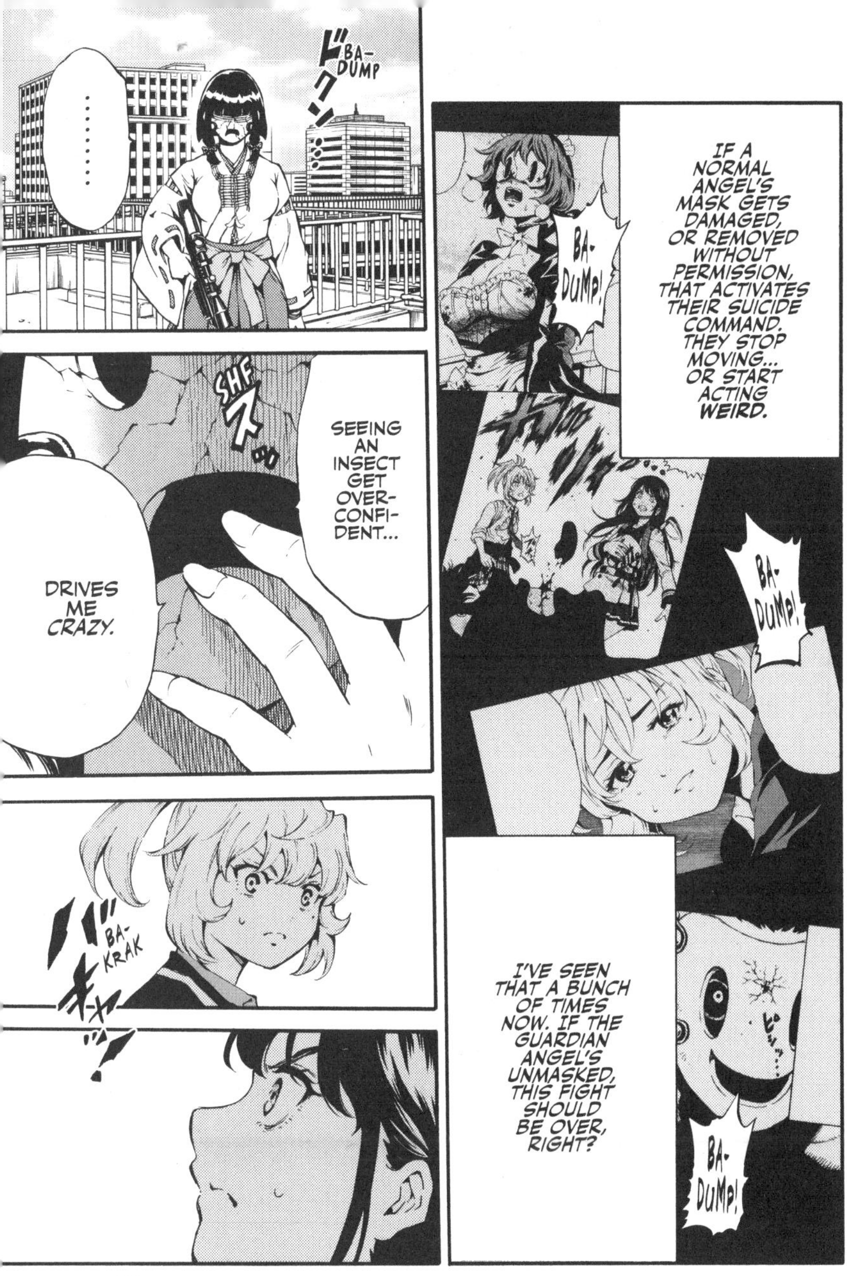

IF A NORMAL ANGEL'S MASK GETS DAMAGED, OR REMOVED WITHOUT PERMISSION, THAT ACTIVATES THEIR SUICIDE COMMAND. THEY STOP MOVING... OR START ACTING **WEIRD.**
BA-DUMP!
BA-DUMP!
I'VE SEEN THAT A BUNCH OF TIMES NOW. IF THE GUARDIAN ANGEL'S UNMASKED, THIS FIGHT SHOULD BE OVER, RIGHT?
BA-DUMP!
BA-DUMP
......
SHF
SEEING AN INSECT GET OVER-CONFI-DENT...
DRIVES ME *CRAZY.*
BA-KRAK

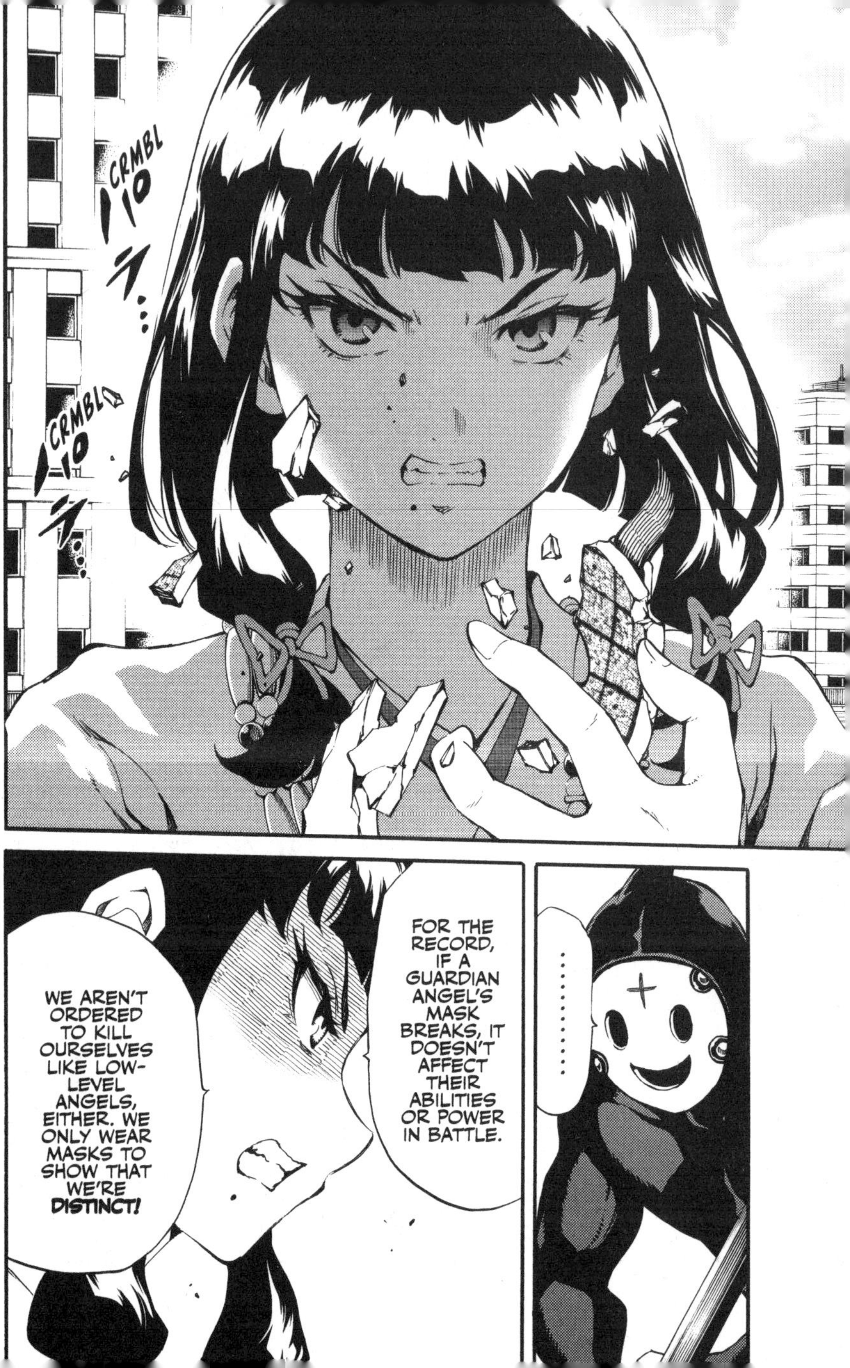
CRMBL
CRMBL
....
FOR THE RECORD, IF A GUARDIAN ANGEL'S MASK BREAKS, IT DOESN'T AFFECT THEIR ABILITIES OR POWER IN BATTLE.
WE AREN'T ORDERED TO KILL OURSELVES LIKE LOW-LEVEL ANGELS, EITHER. WE ONLY WEAR MASKS TO SHOW THAT WE'RE **DISTINCT!**

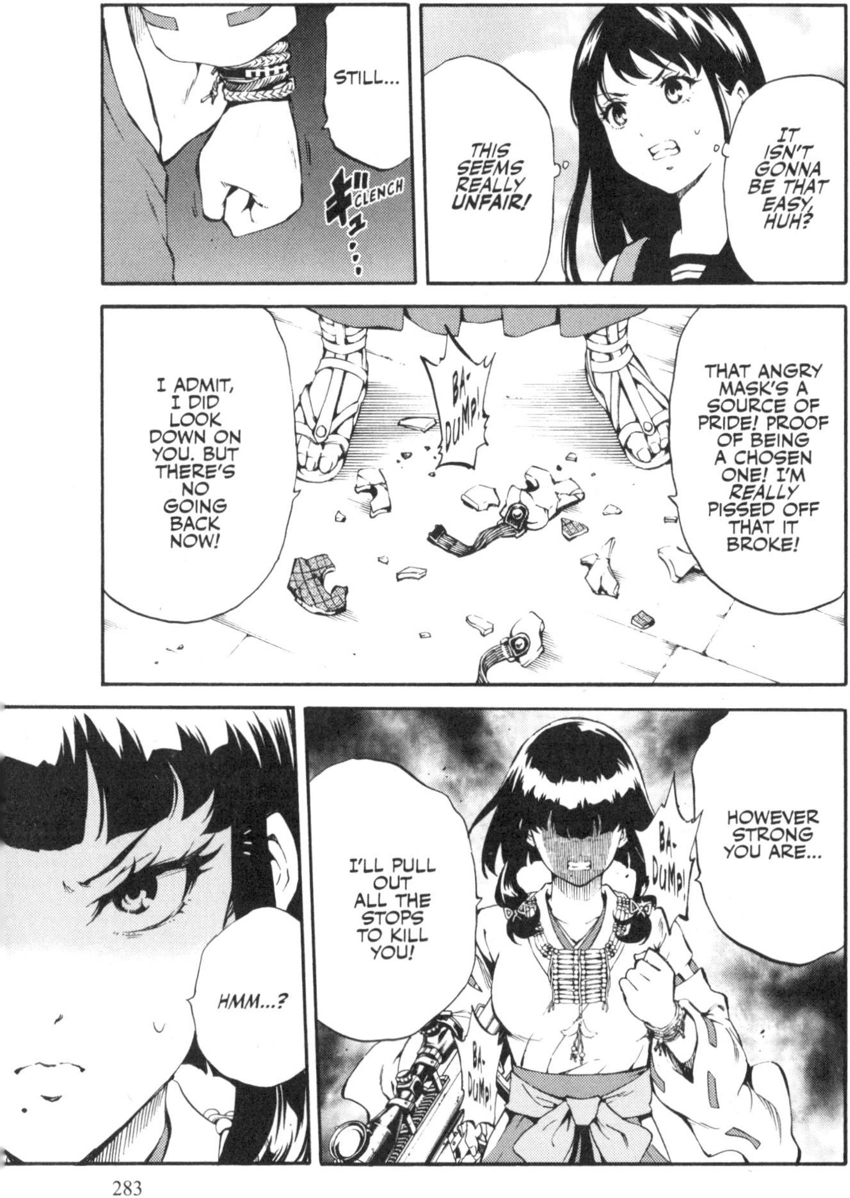
IT ISN'T GONNA BE THAT EASY, HUH?
THIS SEEMS REALLY UNFAIR!
STILL...
CLENCH
THAT ANGRY MASK'S A SOURCE OF PRIDE! PROOF OF BEING A CHOSEN ONE! I'M *REALLY* PISSED OFF THAT IT BROKE!
BA-DUMP!
I ADMIT, I DID LOOK DOWN ON YOU. BUT THERE'S NO GOING BACK NOW!
HOWEVER STRONG YOU ARE...
BA-DUMP!
I'LL PULL OUT ALL THE STOPS TO KILL YOU!
BA-DUMP!
HMM...?

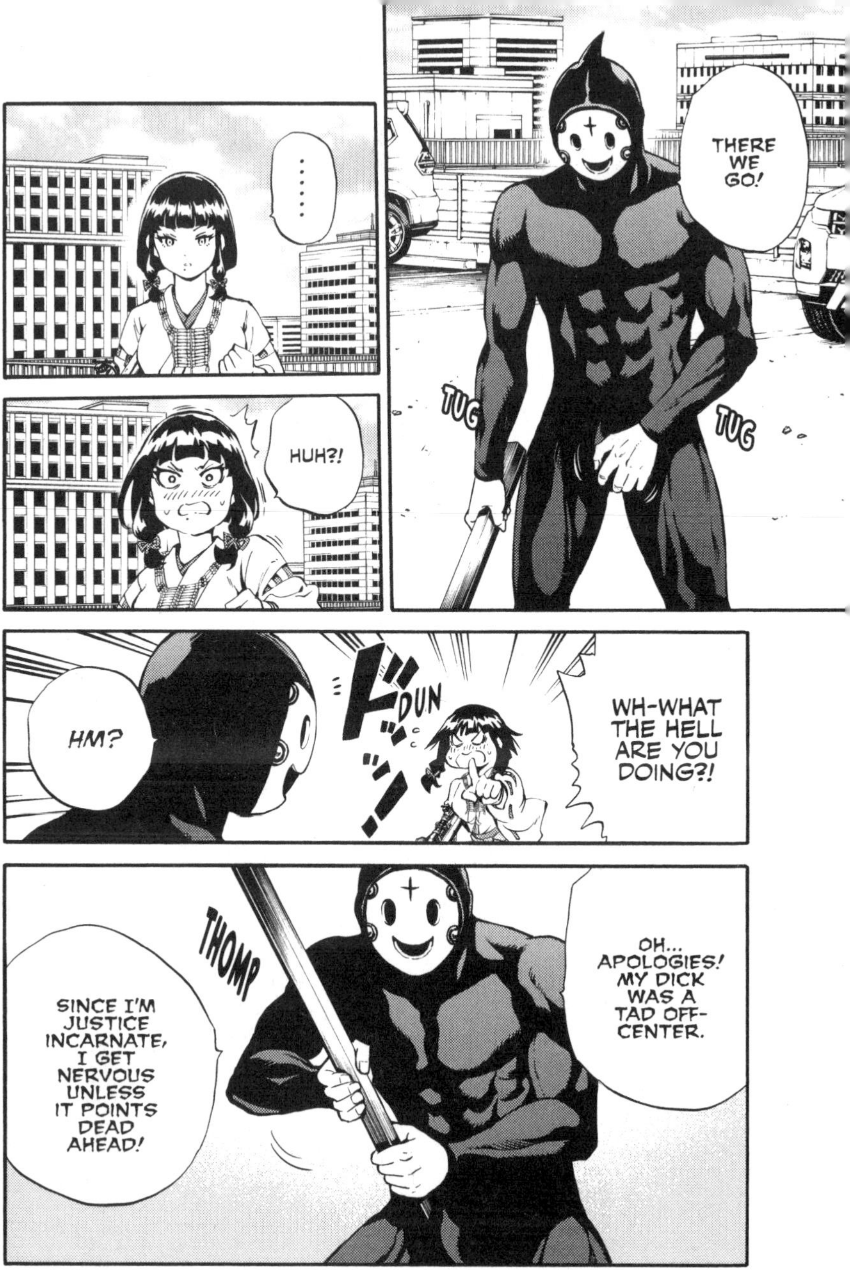
THERE WE GO!
TUG
TUG
......
HUH?!
WH-WHAT THE HELL ARE YOU DOING?!
DUN
HM?
OH... APOLOGIES! MY DICK WAS A TAD OFF-CENTER.
THOMP
SINCE I'M JUSTICE INCARNATE, I GET NERVOUS UNLESS IT POINTS DEAD AHEAD!

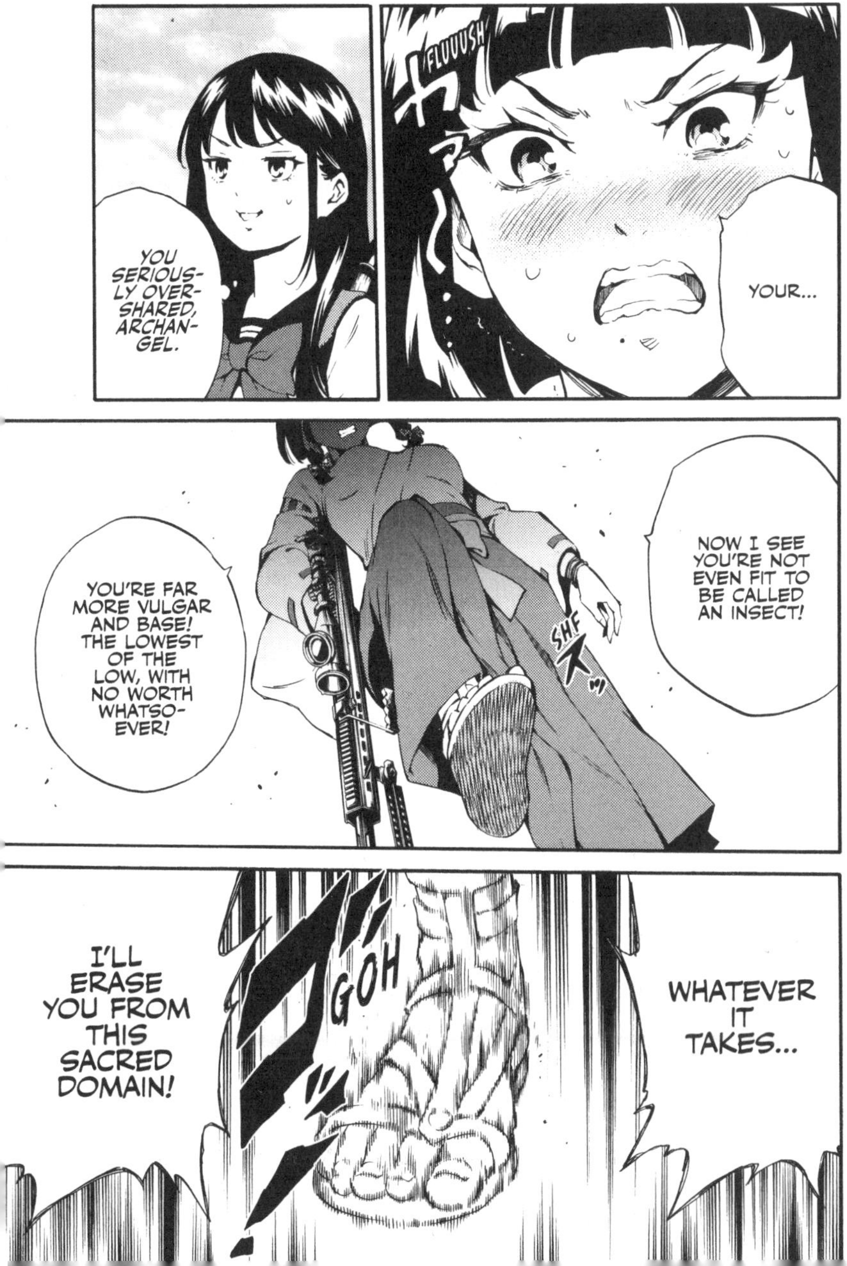
FLUUUSH
YOUR...
YOU SERIOUSLY OVERSHARED, ARCHANGEL.
NOW I SEE YOU'RE NOT EVEN FIT TO BE CALLED AN INSECT!
SHF
YOU'RE FAR MORE VULGAR AND BASE! THE LOWEST OF THE LOW, WITH NO WORTH WHATSOEVER!
WHATEVER IT TAKES...
GOH
I'LL ERASE YOU FROM THIS SACRED DOMAIN!

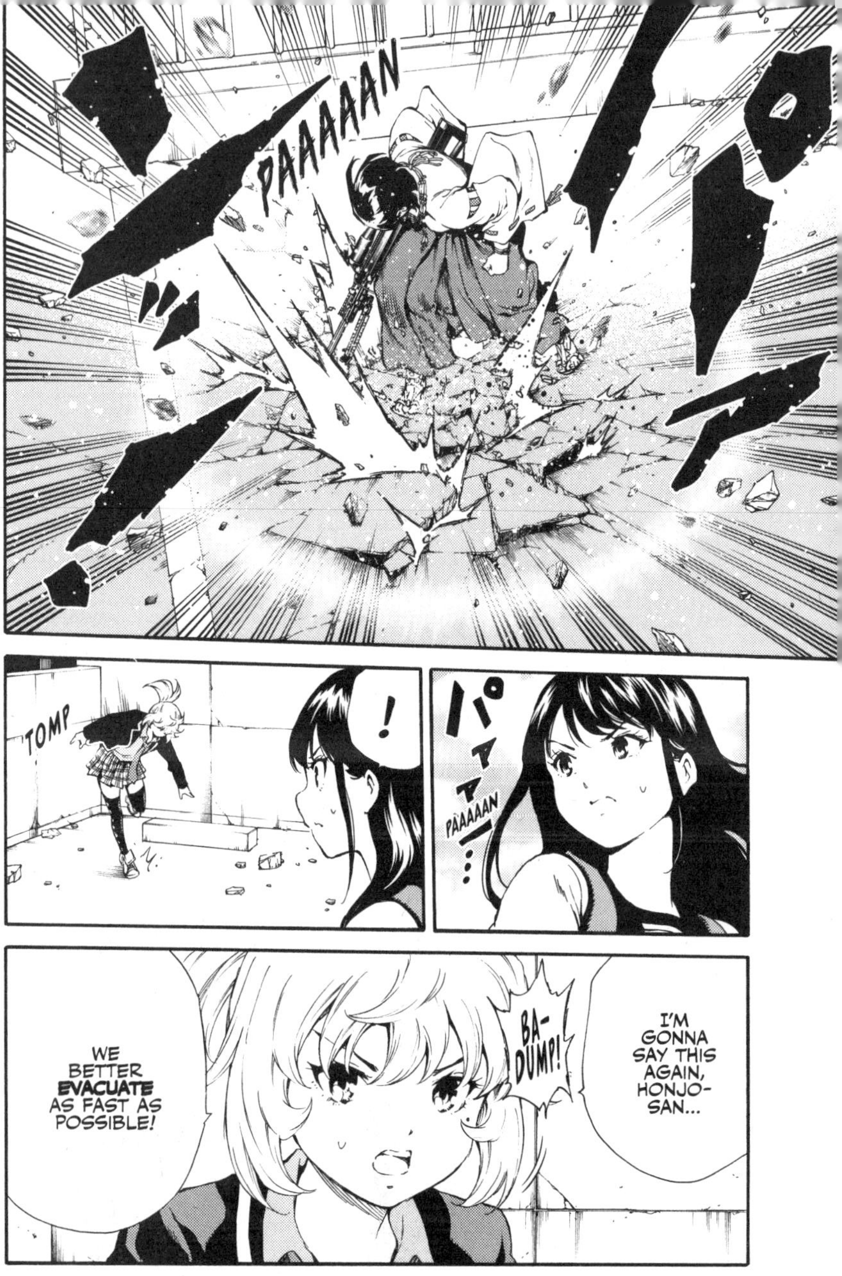
PAAAAAN
PAAAAAN...
!
TOMP
I'M GONNA SAY THIS AGAIN, HONJO-SAN...
BA-DUMP!
WE BETTER **EVACUATE** AS FAST AS POSSIBLE!

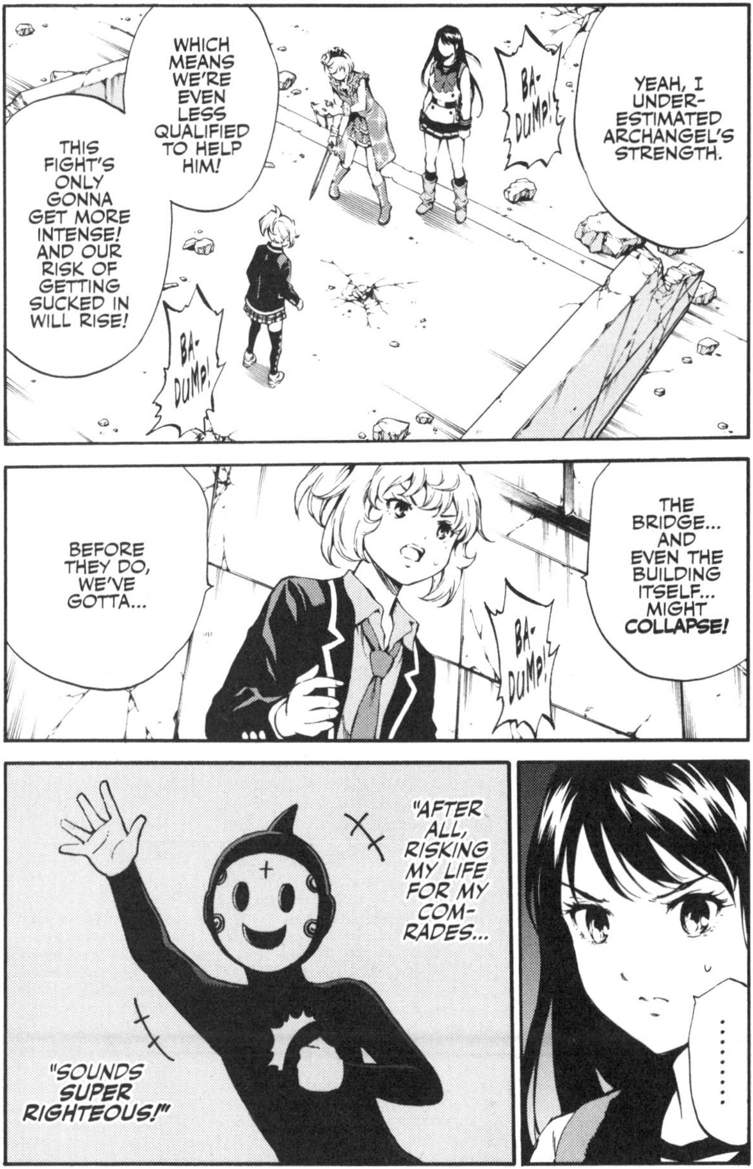
YEAH, I UNDER-ESTIMATED ARCHANGEL'S STRENGTH.
BA-DUMP!
WHICH MEANS WE'RE EVEN LESS QUALIFIED TO HELP HIM!
THIS FIGHT'S ONLY GONNA GET MORE INTENSE! AND OUR RISK OF GETTING SUCKED IN WILL RISE!
BA-DUMP!
THE BRIDGE... AND EVEN THE BUILDING ITSELF... MIGHT **COLLAPSE!**
BA-DUMP!
BEFORE THEY DO, WE'VE GOTTA...
....
"AFTER ALL, RISKING MY LIFE FOR MY COM-RADES...
"SOUNDS SUPER RIGHTEOUS!"

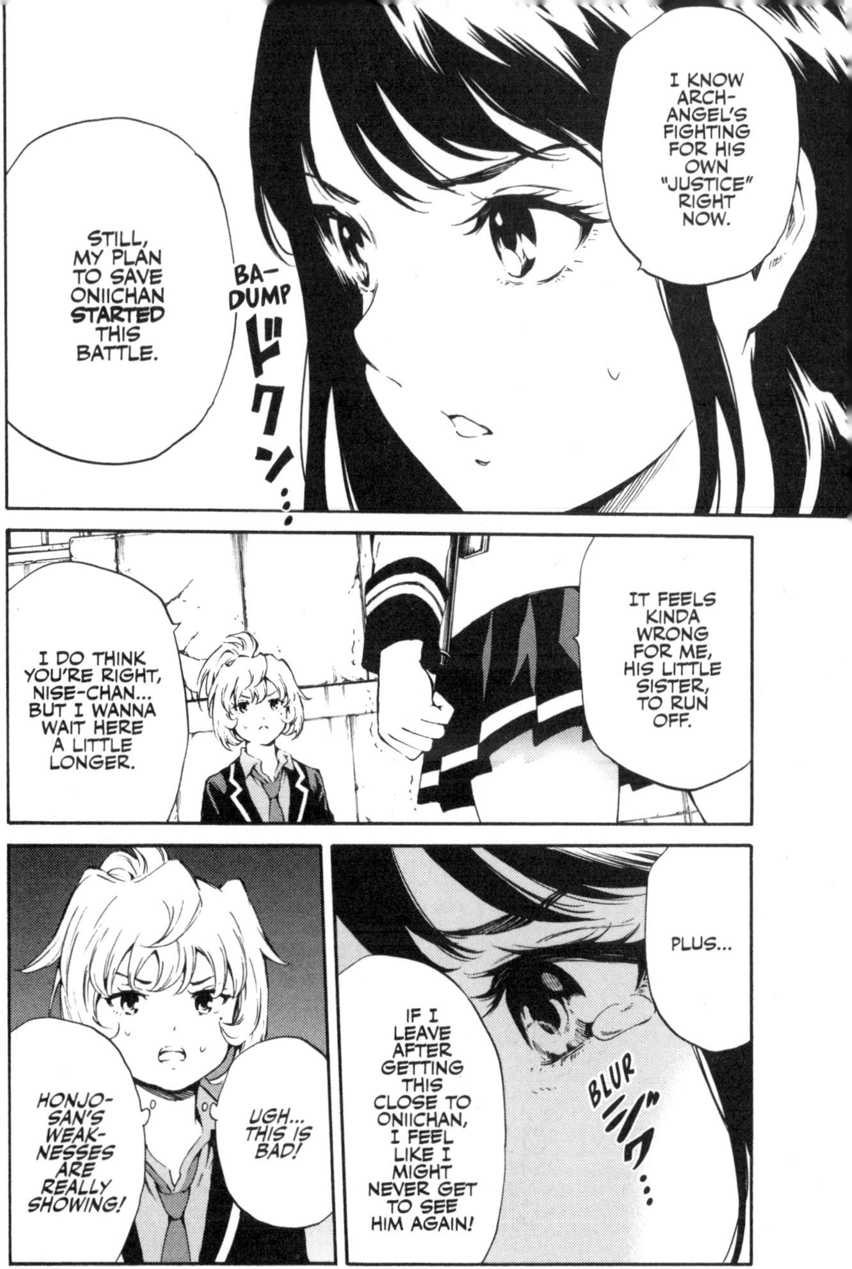
I KNOW ARCH-ANGEL'S FIGHTING FOR HIS OWN "JUSTICE" RIGHT NOW.
BA-DUMP
ドクン…
STILL, MY PLAN TO SAVE ONIICHAN **STARTED** THIS BATTLE.
IT FEELS KINDA WRONG FOR ME, HIS LITTLE SISTER, TO RUN OFF.
I DO THINK YOU'RE RIGHT, NISE-CHAN... BUT I WANNA WAIT HERE A LITTLE LONGER.
PLUS...
IF I LEAVE AFTER GETTING THIS CLOSE TO ONIICHAN, I FEEL LIKE I MIGHT NEVER GET TO SEE HIM AGAIN!
BLUR
UGH... THIS IS BAD!
HONJO-SAN'S WEAK-NESSES ARE REALLY SHOWING!

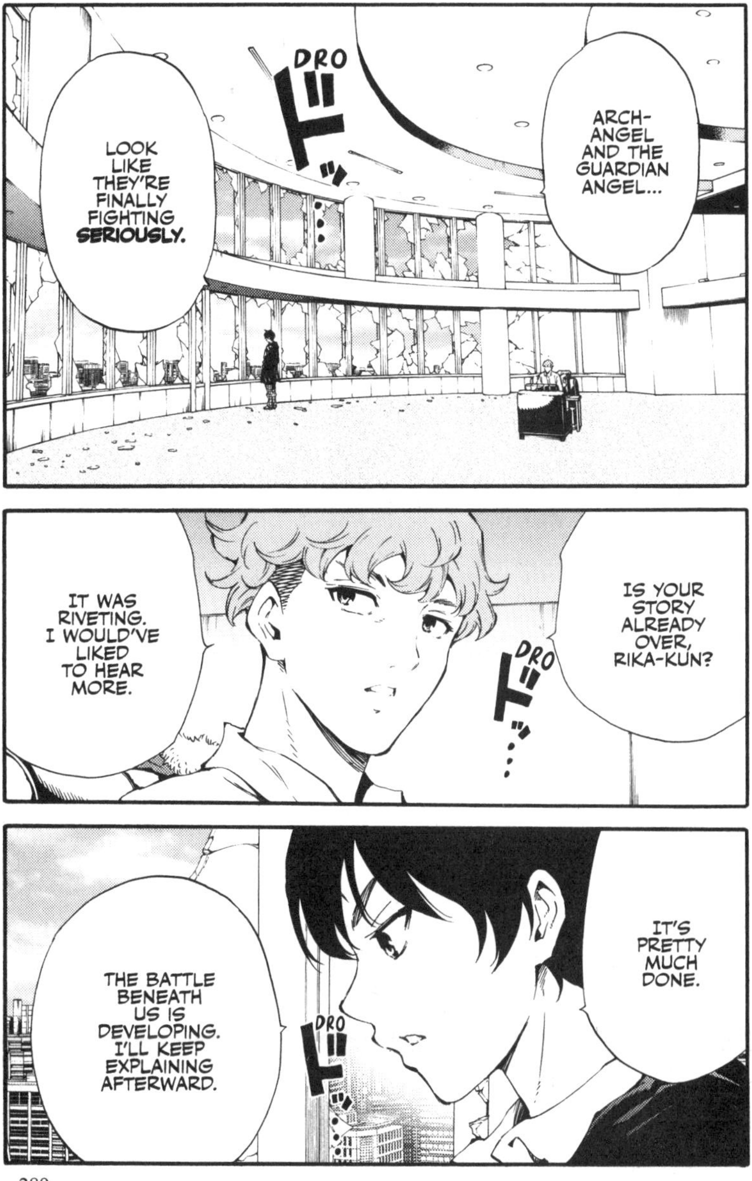
ARCH-ANGEL AND THE GUARDIAN ANGEL...
DRO
LOOK LIKE THEY'RE FINALLY FIGHTING SERIOUSLY.
IS YOUR STORY ALREADY OVER, RIKA-KUN?
DRO
IT WAS RIVETING. I WOULD'VE LIKED TO HEAR MORE.
IT'S PRETTY MUCH DONE.
DRO
THE BATTLE BENEATH US IS DEVELOPING. I'LL KEEP EXPLAINING AFTERWARD.

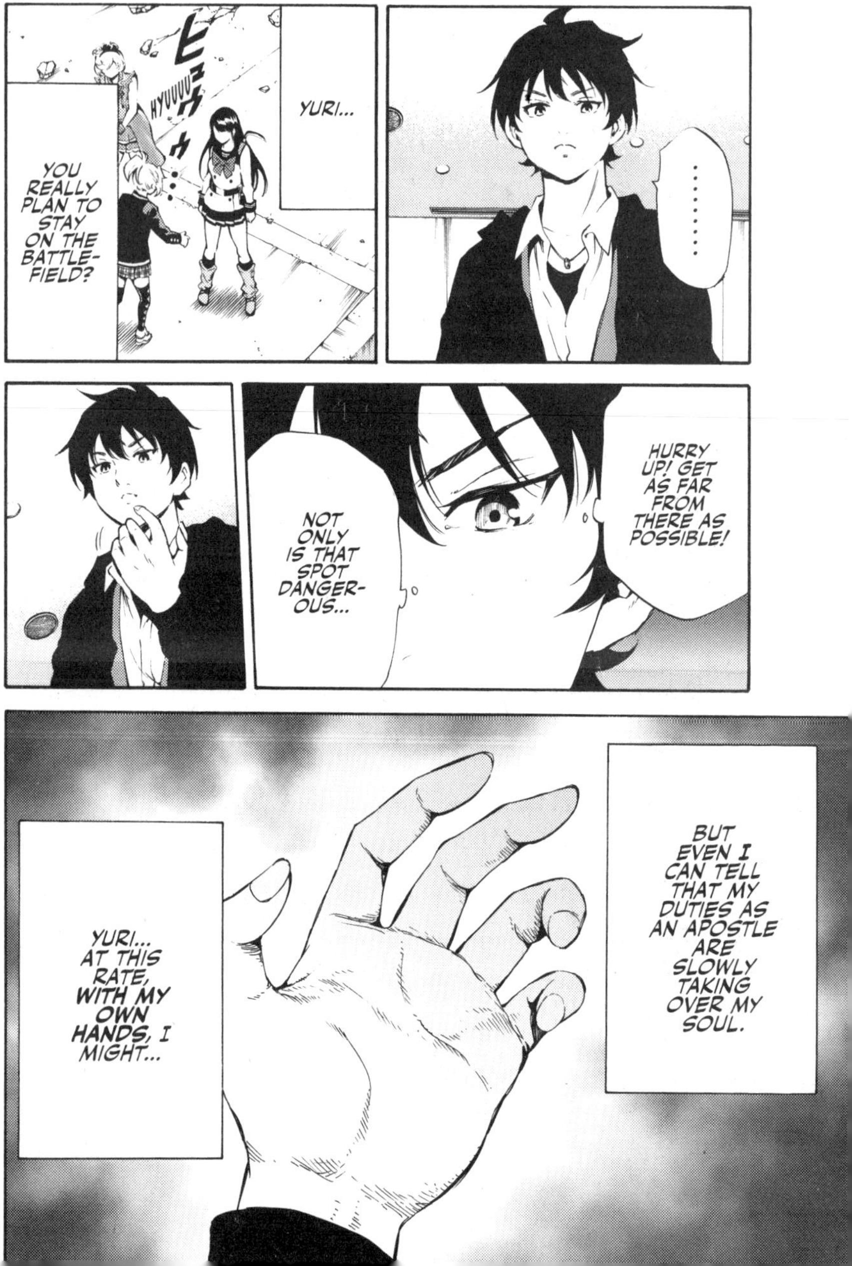

....
YURI...
HYUUUU
YOU REALLY PLAN TO STAY ON THE BATTLE-FIELD?
HURRY UP! GET AS FAR FROM THERE AS POSSIBLE!
NOT ONLY IS THAT SPOT DANGER-OUS...
BUT EVEN I CAN TELL THAT MY DUTIES AS AN APOSTLE ARE SLOWLY TAKING OVER MY SOUL.
YURI... AT THIS RATE, **WITH MY OWN HANDS,** I MIGHT...

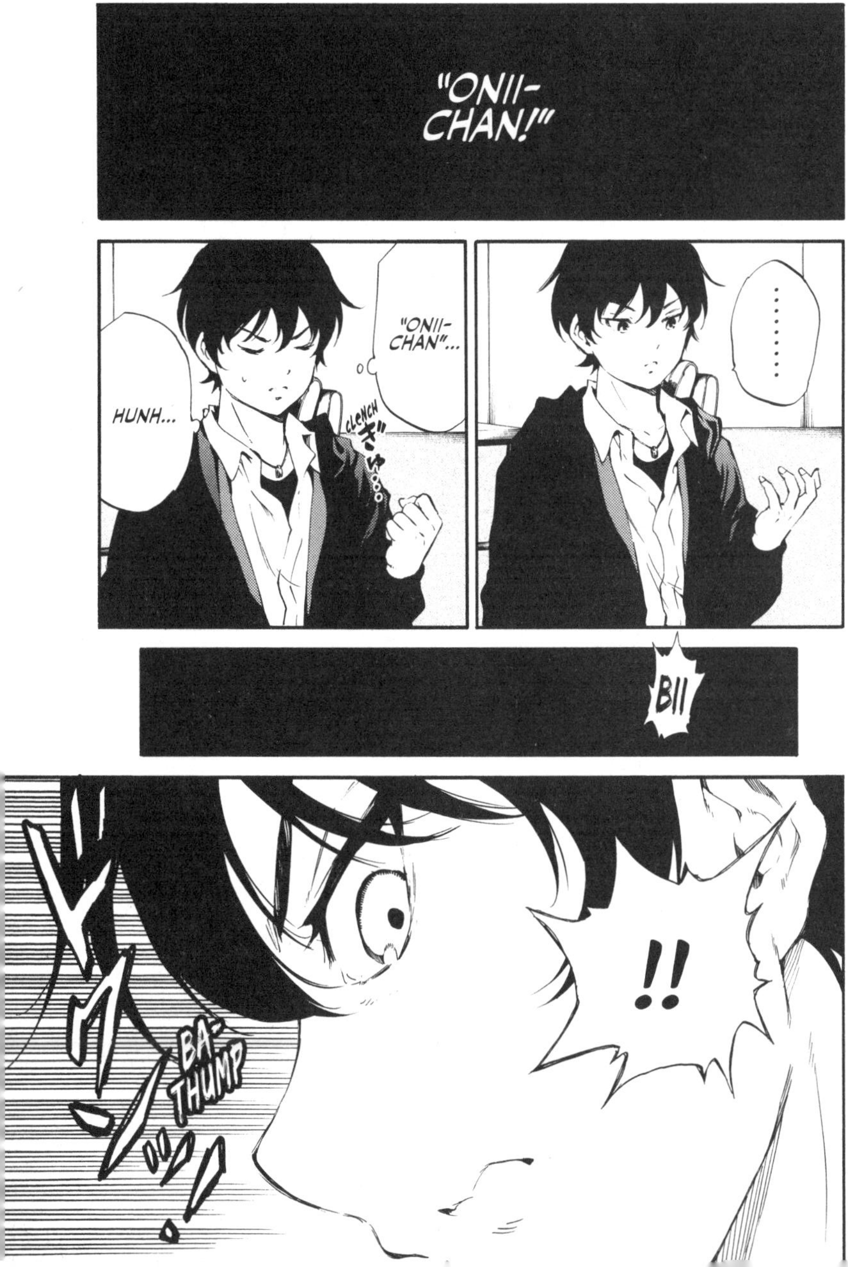
"ONII-CHAN!"
....
"ONII-CHAN"...
CLENCH
HUNH...
BII
!!
BA-THUMP

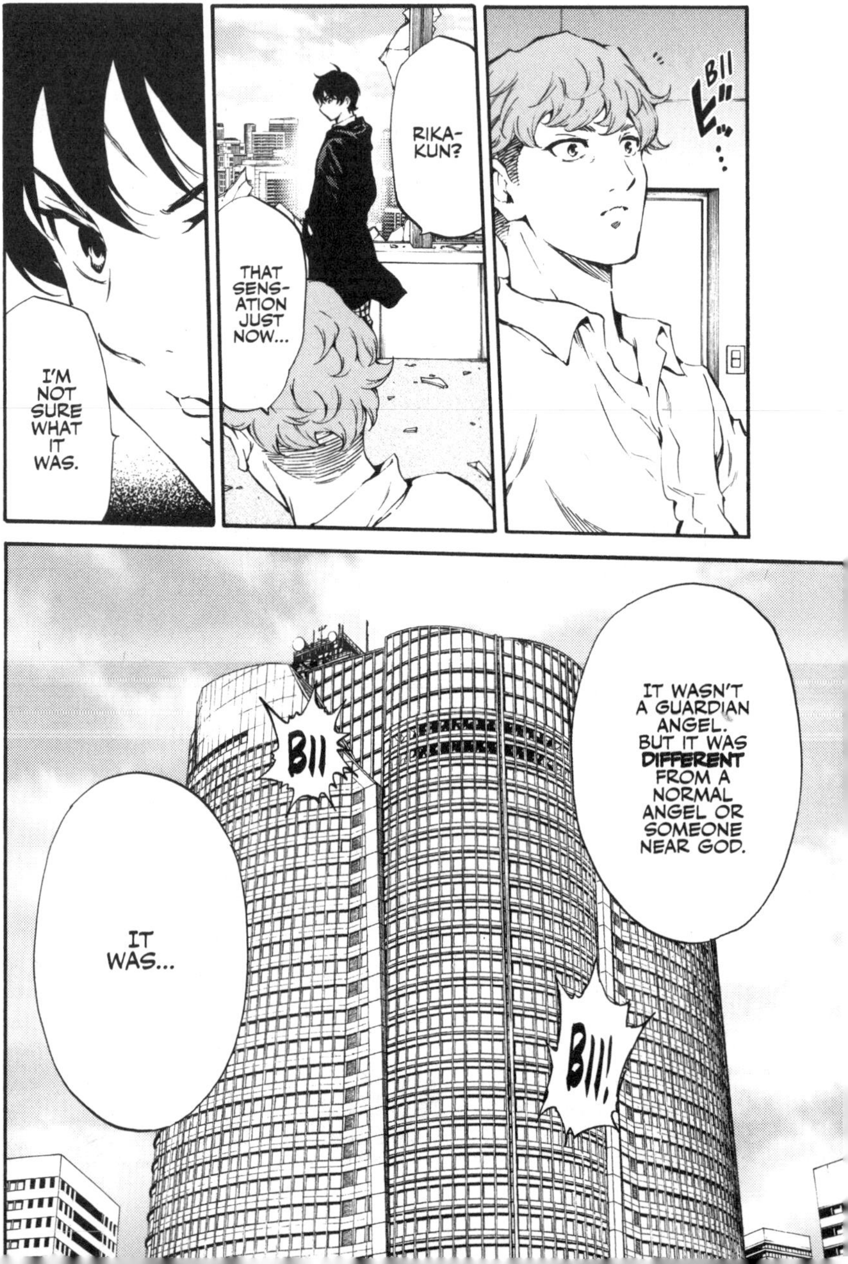
BII
RIKA-KUN?
THAT SENSATION JUST NOW...
I'M NOT SURE WHAT IT WAS.
IT WASN'T A GUARDIAN ANGEL. BUT IT WAS **DIFFERENT** FROM A NORMAL ANGEL OR SOMEONE NEAR GOD.
BII
IT WAS...
BII!

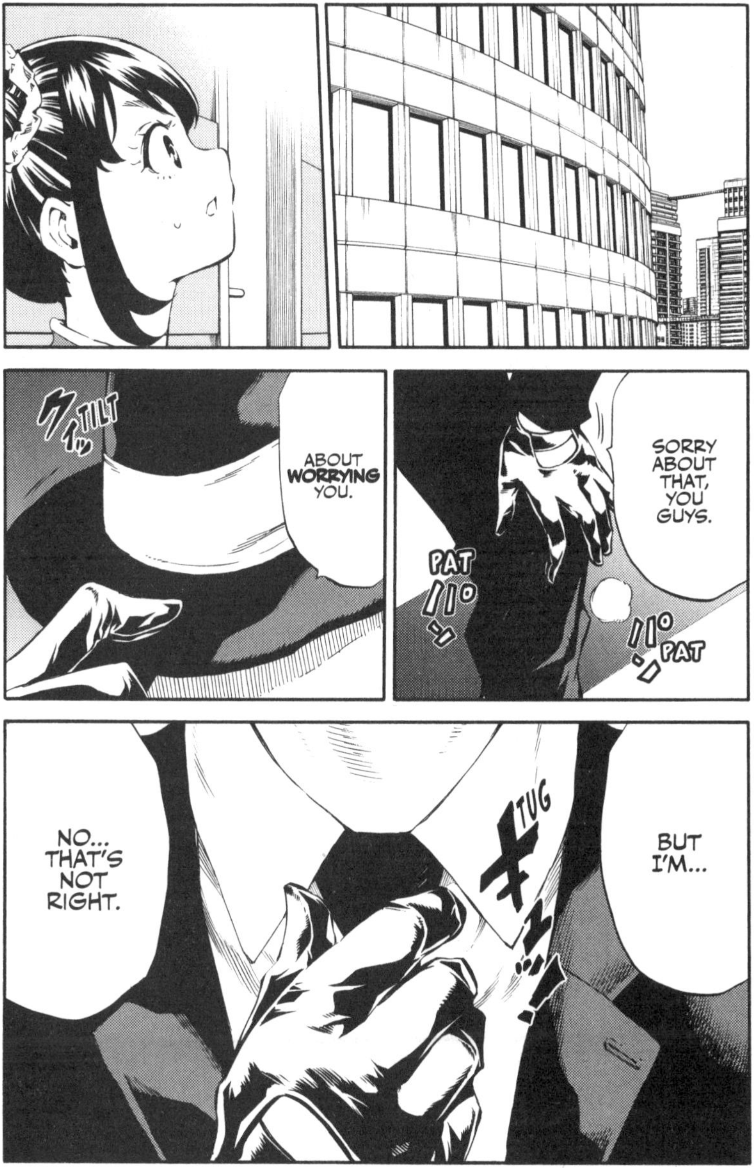
SORRY ABOUT THAT, YOU GUYS.
PAT
PAT
ABOUT WORRYING YOU.
クイッ TILT
BUT I'M...
TUG
NO... THAT'S NOT RIGHT.

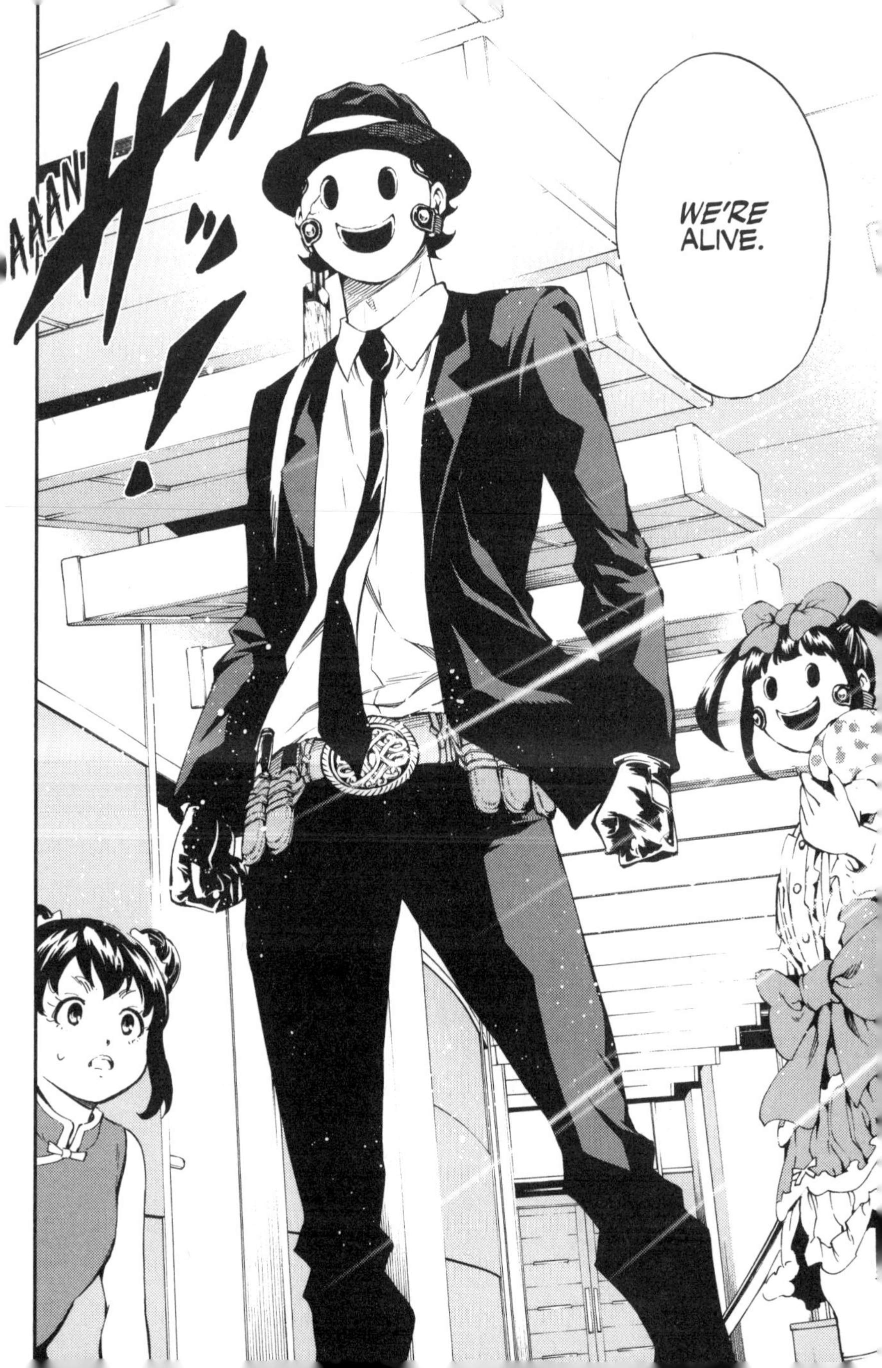
WE'RE ALIVE.
AAAN'

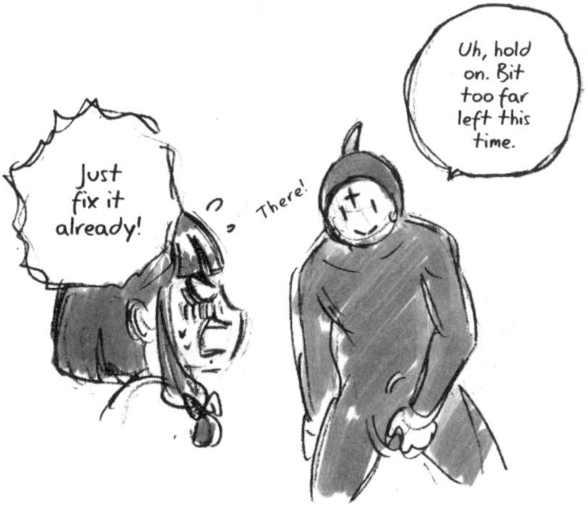
Uh, hold on. Bit too far left this time.
There!
Just fix it already!

HIGH-RISE INVASION

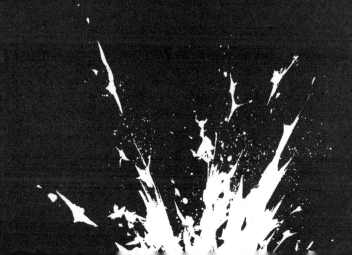

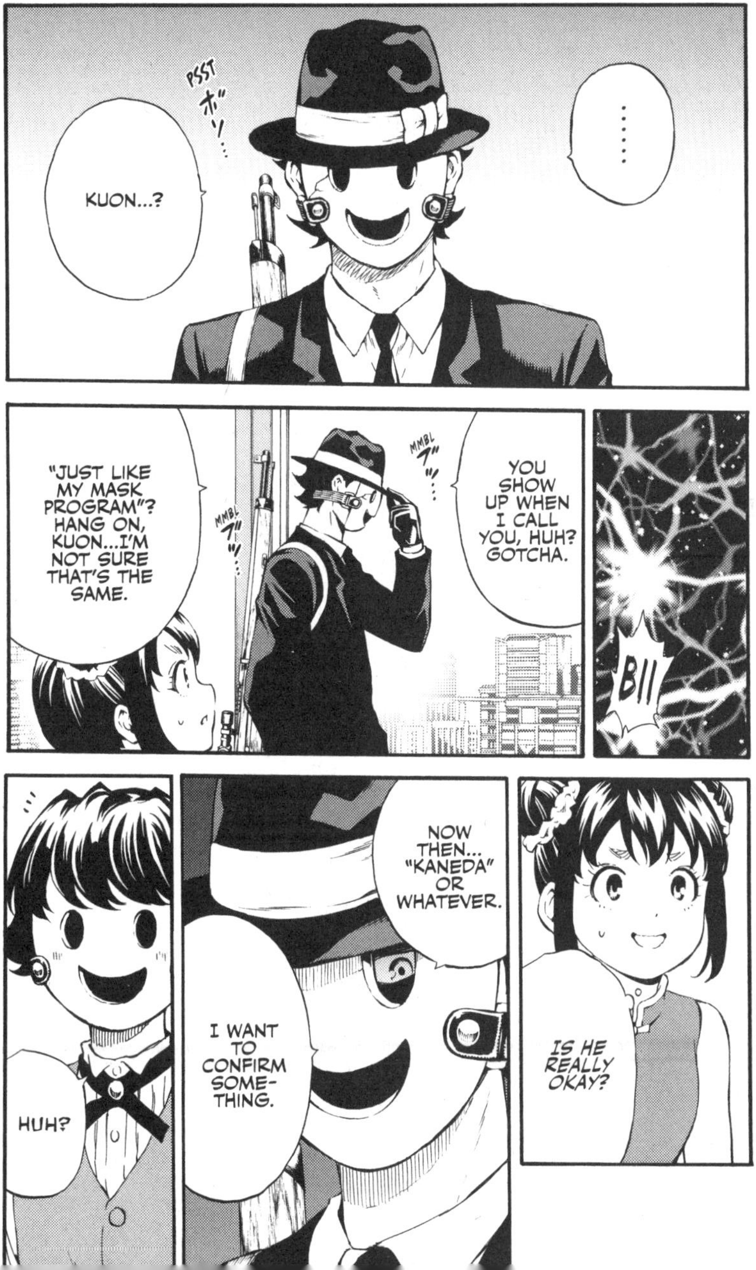
......
PSST
ボソ…
KUON...?
BII
MMBL
ブツ…
YOU SHOW UP WHEN I CALL YOU, HUH? GOTCHA.
MMBL
ブツ…
"JUST LIKE MY MASK PROGRAM"? HANG ON, KUON...I'M NOT SURE THAT'S THE SAME.
IS HE REALLY OKAY?
NOW THEN... "KANEDA" OR WHATEVER.
I WANT TO CONFIRM SOME-THING.
HUH?

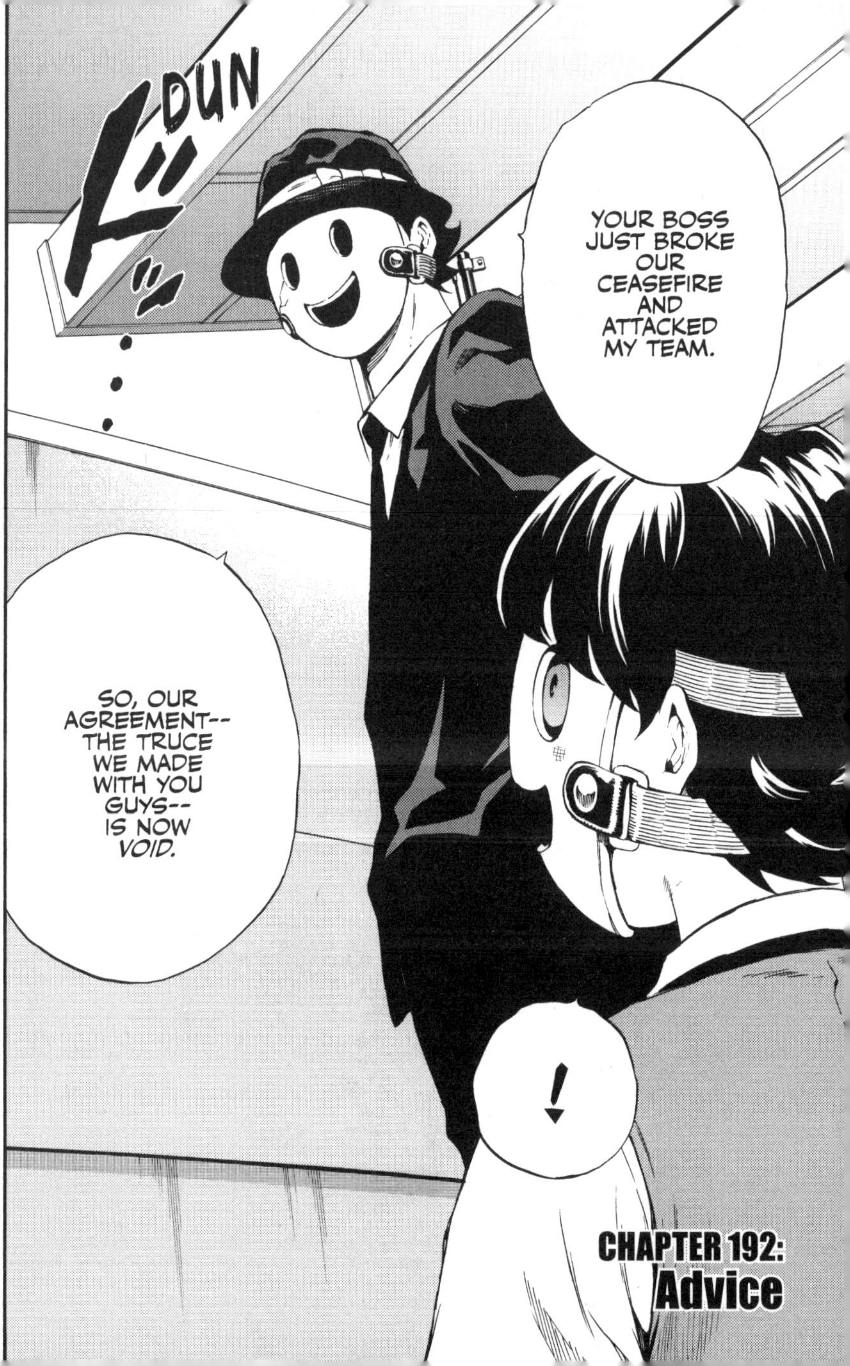
YOUR BOSS JUST BROKE OUR CEASEFIRE AND ATTACKED MY TEAM.
DUN
SO, OUR AGREEMENT-- THE TRUCE WE MADE WITH YOU GUYS-- IS NOW *VOID.*
!
CHAPTER 192: Advice

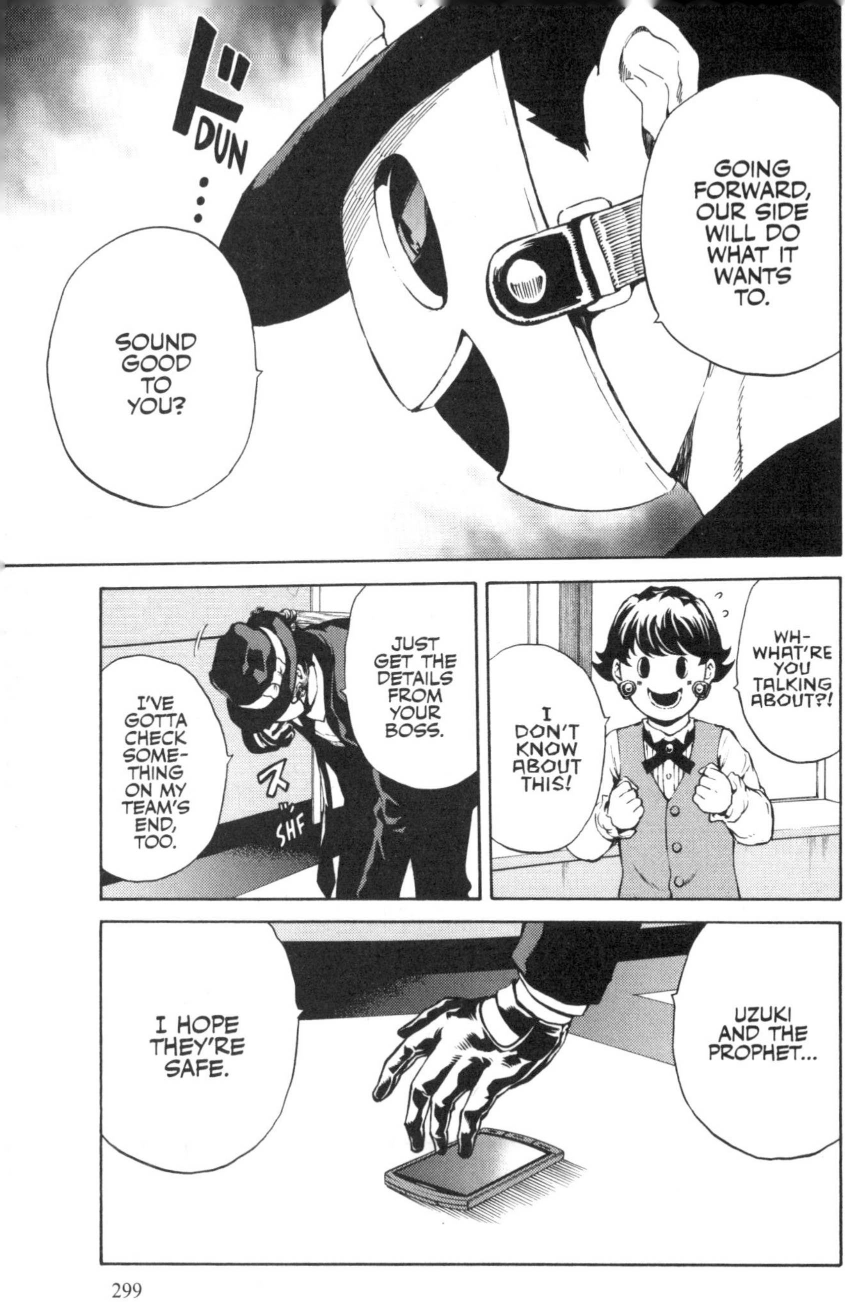
GOING FORWARD, OUR SIDE WILL DO WHAT IT WANTS TO.
ド
DUN
...
SOUND GOOD TO YOU?
WH-WHAT'RE YOU TALKING ABOUT?!
I DON'T KNOW ABOUT THIS!
JUST GET THE DETAILS FROM YOUR BOSS.
I'VE GOTTA CHECK SOME-THING ON MY TEAM'S END, TOO.
ス
SHF
UZUKI AND THE PROPHET...
I HOPE THEY'RE SAFE.

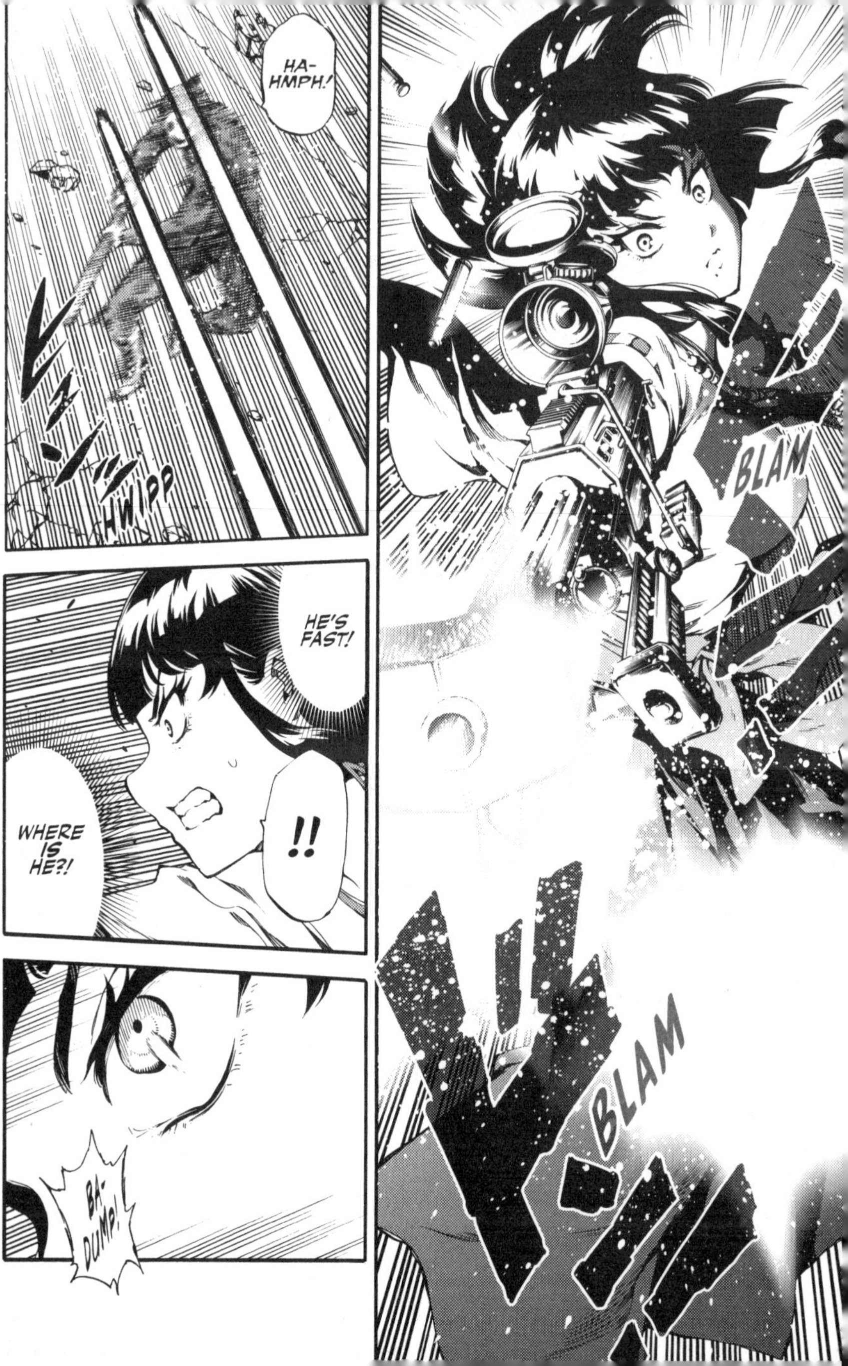
BLAM
BLAM
HA-HMPH!
HWIPP
HE'S FAST!
!!
WHERE IS HE?!
BA-DUMP!

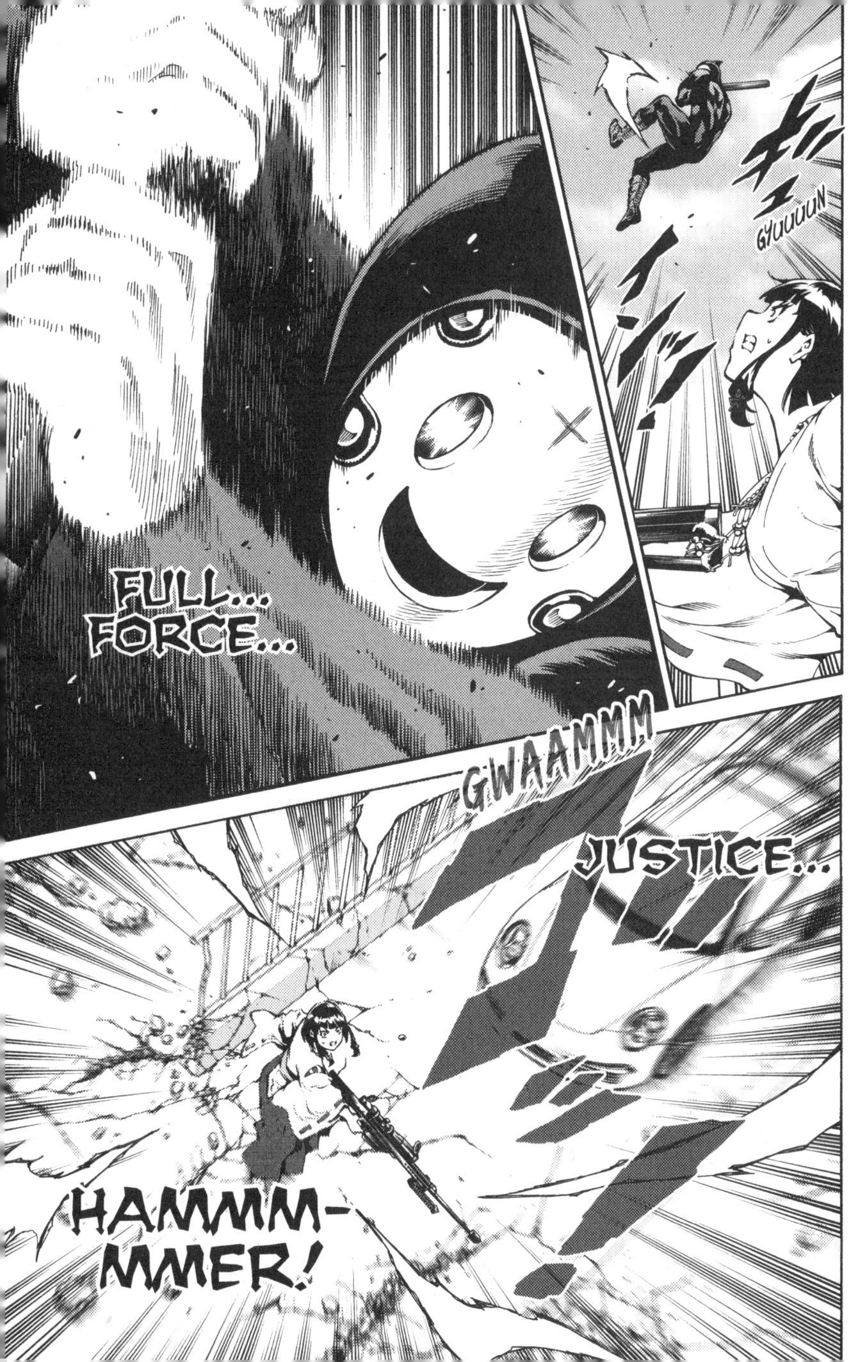
GYUUUUN
FULL... FORCE...
GWAAMMM
JUSTICE...
HAMMMM-MMER!

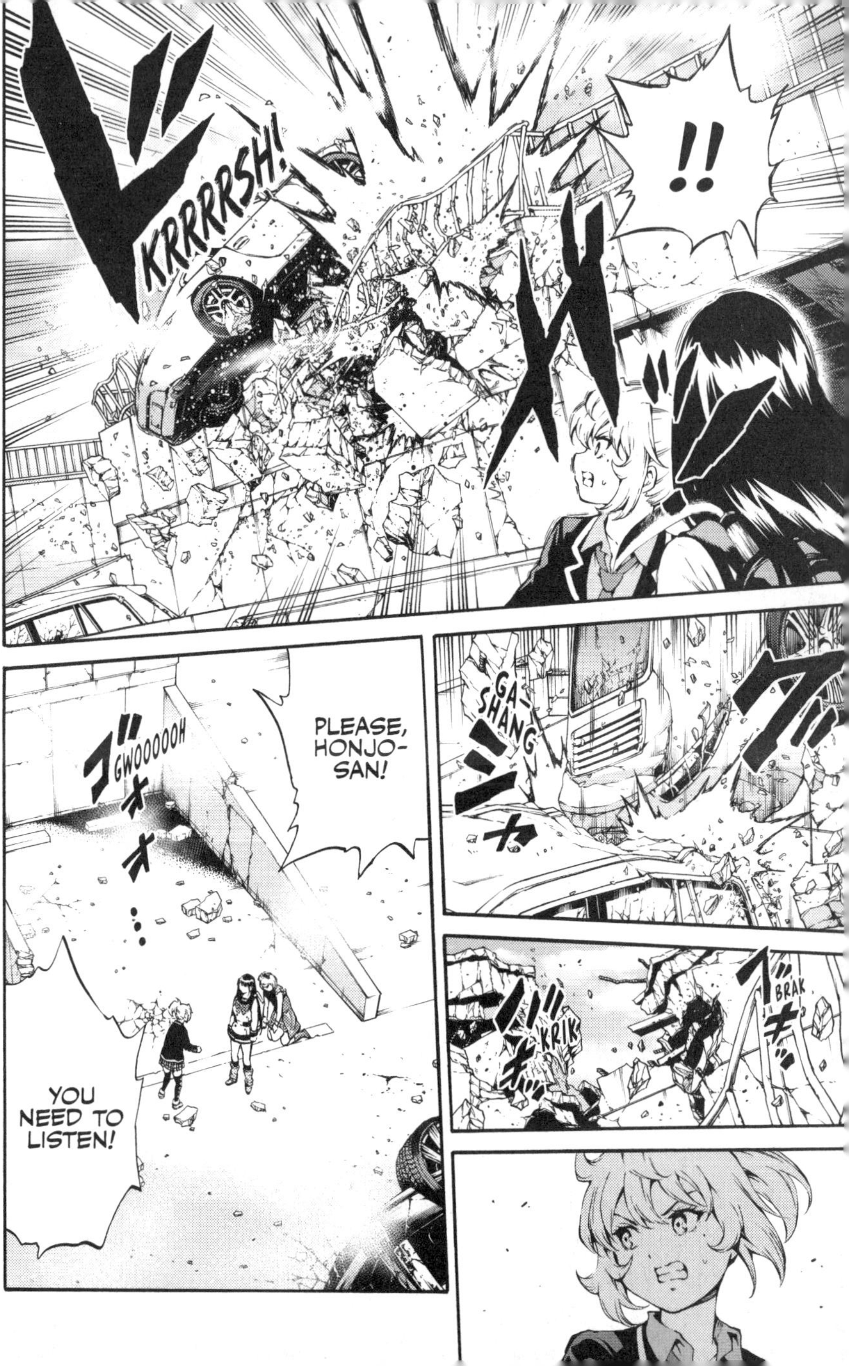
!!
KRRRRSH!
GA-SHANG
BRAK
KRIK
PLEASE, HONJO-SAN!
GWOOOOOH
YOU NEED TO LISTEN!

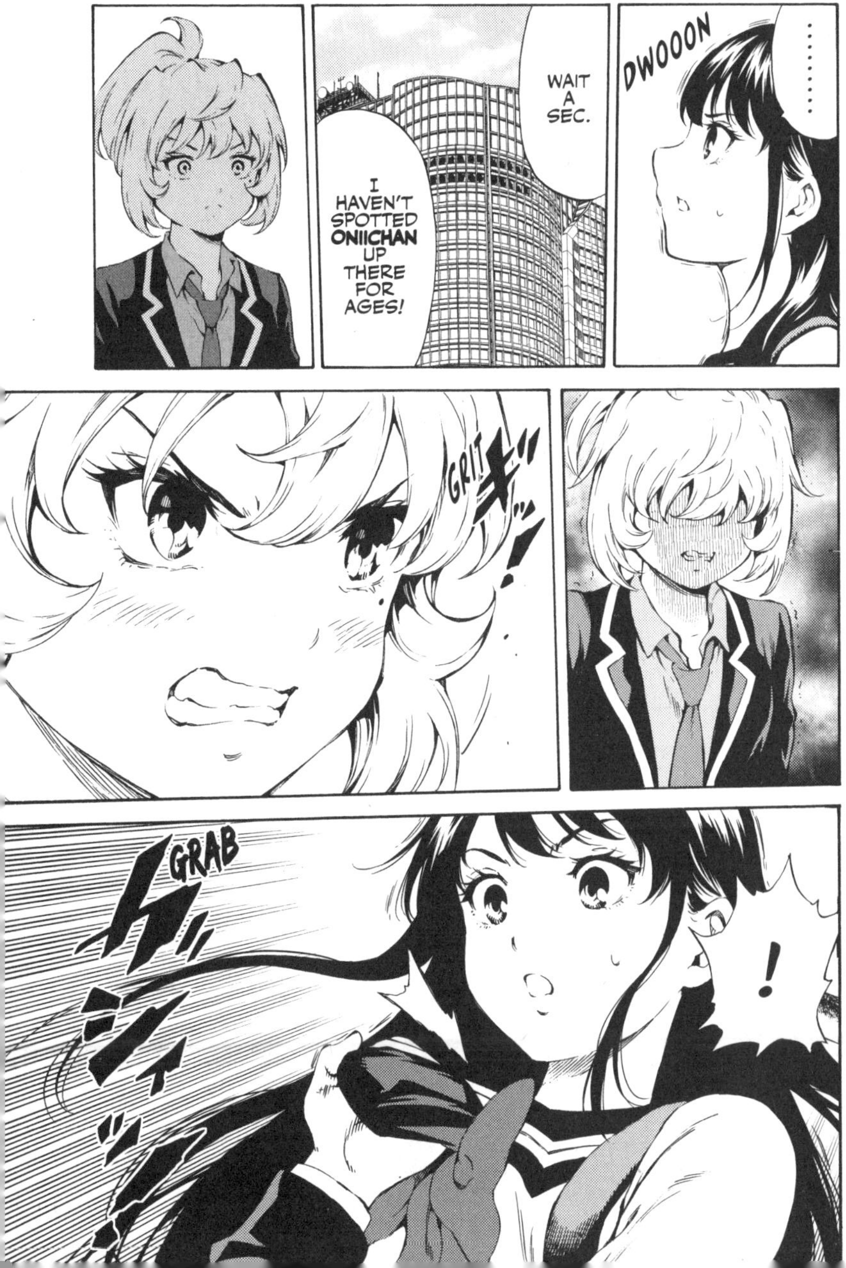
....
DWOOON
WAIT A SEC.
I HAVEN'T SPOTTED ONIICHAN UP THERE FOR AGES!
GRIT
!
GRAB

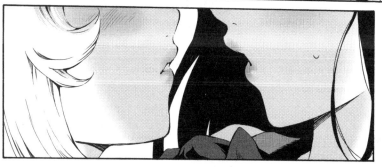

BA-DUMP!

IT'S NOT WHAT YOU... I GOT KINDA **MAD** AND JUST...

BA-DUMP!

I-- WHAT AM I...?!

BA BA

UH...

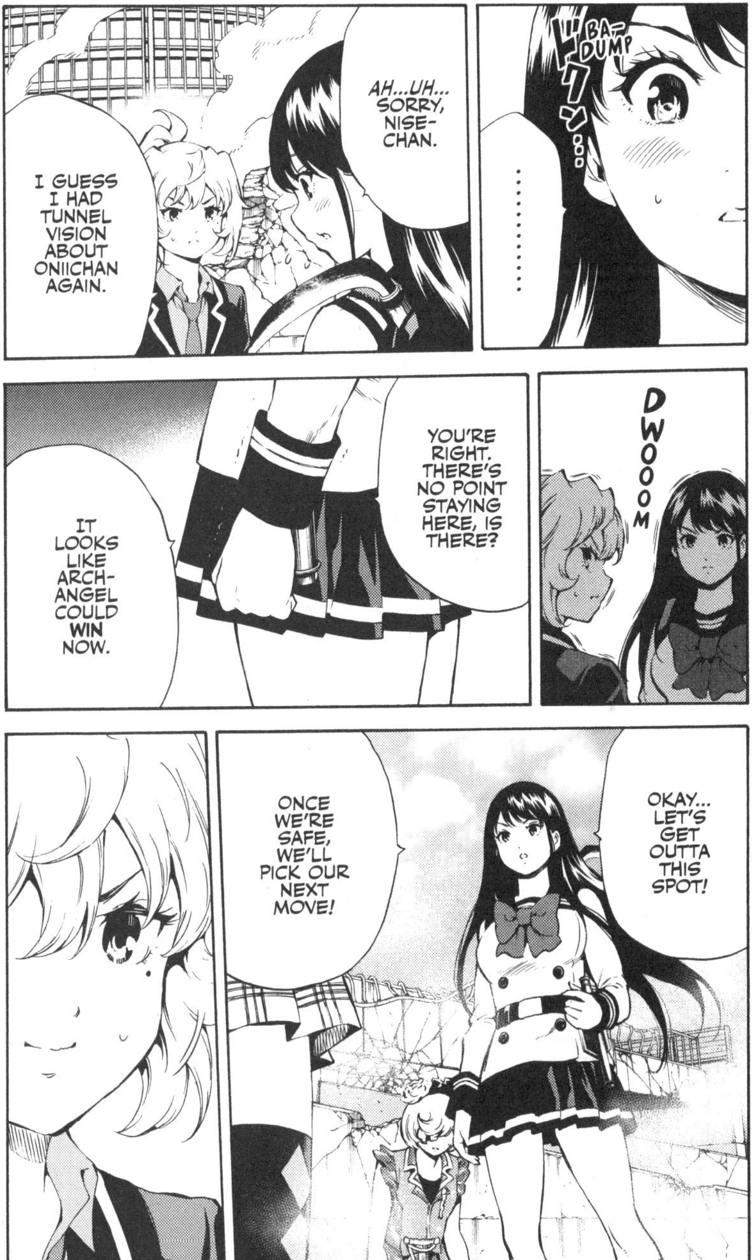
ドクン...
BA-DUMP
......
AH...UH... SORRY, NISE-CHAN.
I GUESS I HAD TUNNEL VISION ABOUT ONIICHAN AGAIN.
DWOOOOM
YOU'RE RIGHT. THERE'S NO POINT STAYING HERE, IS THERE?
IT LOOKS LIKE ARCH-ANGEL COULD **WIN** NOW.
OKAY... LET'S GET OUTTA THIS SPOT!
ONCE WE'RE SAFE, WE'LL PICK OUR NEXT MOVE!

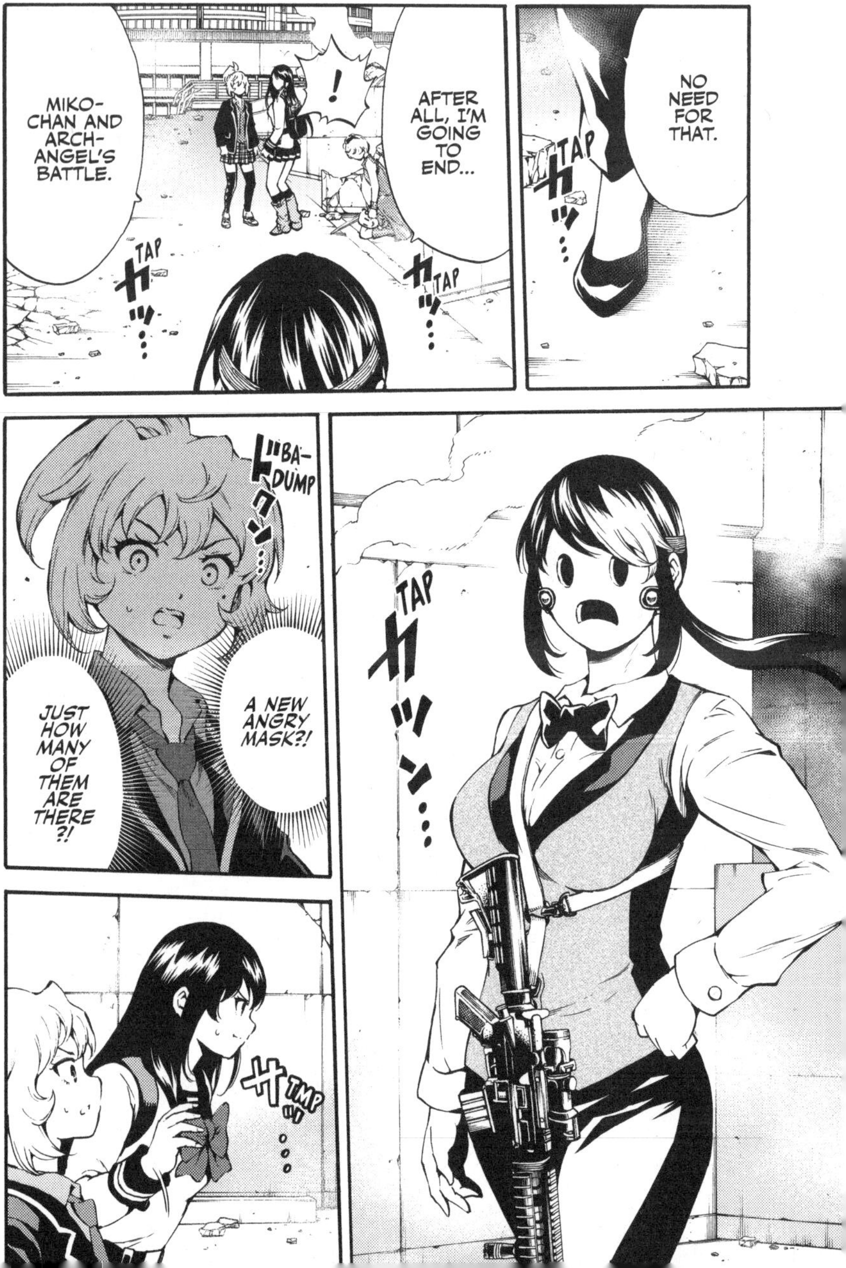
NO NEED FOR THAT.
TAP
カッ…
AFTER ALL, I'M GOING TO END...
!
MIKO-CHAN AND ARCH-ANGEL'S BATTLE.
TAP
カッ…
TAP
カッ…
TAP
カッン…
BA-DUMP
ドクン…
A NEW ANGRY MASK?!
JUST HOW MANY OF THEM ARE THERE?!
TMP
ザッ…

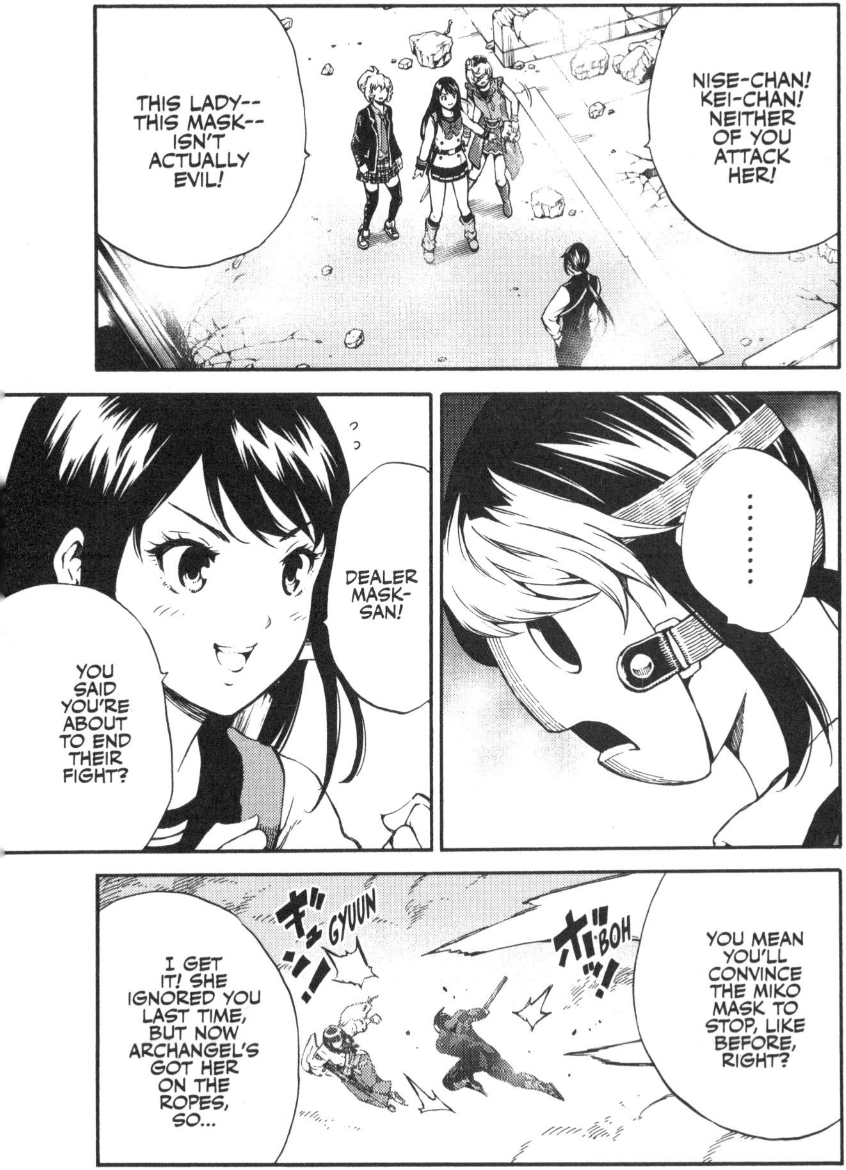
NISE-CHAN! KEI-CHAN! NEITHER OF YOU ATTACK HER!
THIS LADY-- THIS MASK-- ISN'T ACTUALLY EVIL!
....
DEALER MASK-SAN!
YOU SAID YOU'RE ABOUT TO END THEIR FIGHT?
YOU MEAN YOU'LL CONVINCE THE MIKO MASK TO STOP, LIKE BEFORE, RIGHT?
BOH
GYUUN
I GET IT! SHE IGNORED YOU LAST TIME, BUT NOW ARCHANGEL'S GOT HER ON THE ROPES, SO...

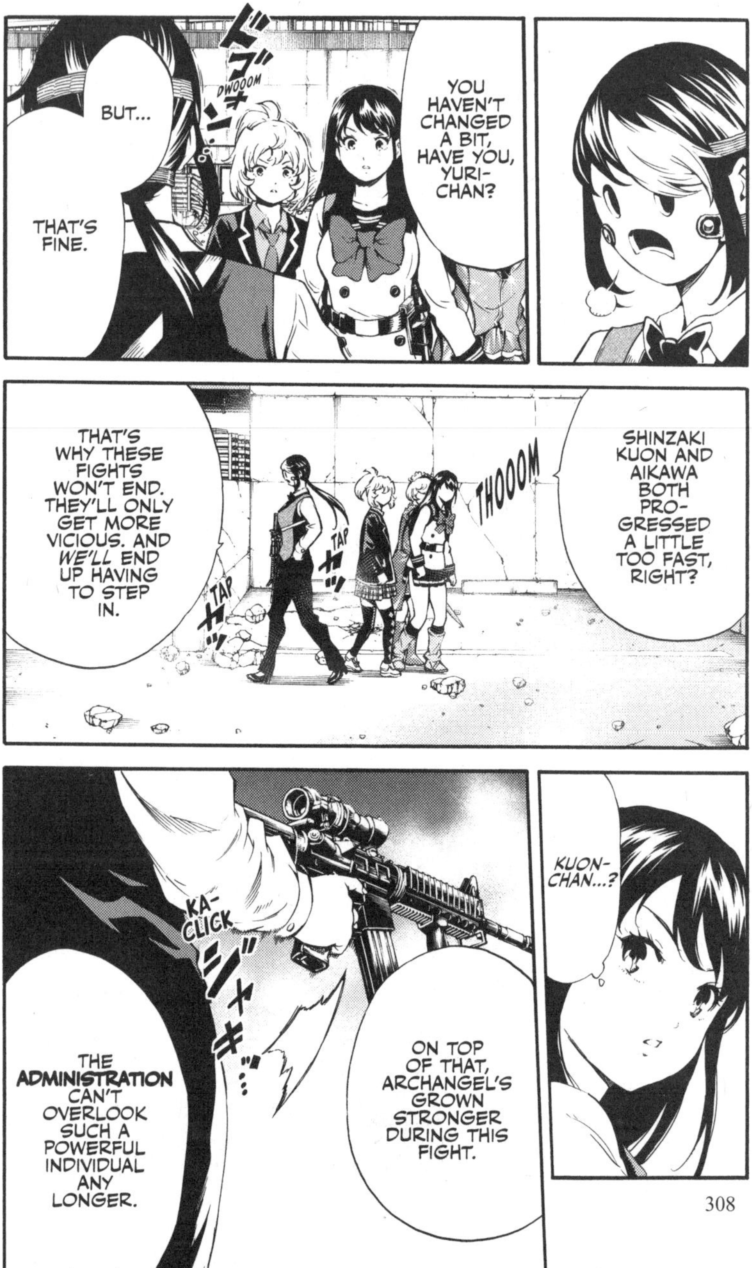
YOU HAVEN'T CHANGED A BIT, HAVE YOU, YURI-CHAN?
DWOOOM
BUT...
THAT'S FINE.
SHINZAKI KUON AND AIKAWA BOTH PRO-GRESSED A LITTLE TOO FAST, RIGHT?
THOOOM
TAP
TAP
THAT'S WHY THESE FIGHTS WON'T END. THEY'LL ONLY GET MORE VICIOUS. AND *WE'LL* END UP HAVING TO STEP IN.
KUON-CHAN...?
ON TOP OF THAT, ARCHANGEL'S GROWN STRONGER DURING THIS FIGHT.
KA-CLICK
THE **ADMINISTRATION** CAN'T OVERLOOK SUCH A POWERFUL INDIVIDUAL ANY LONGER.

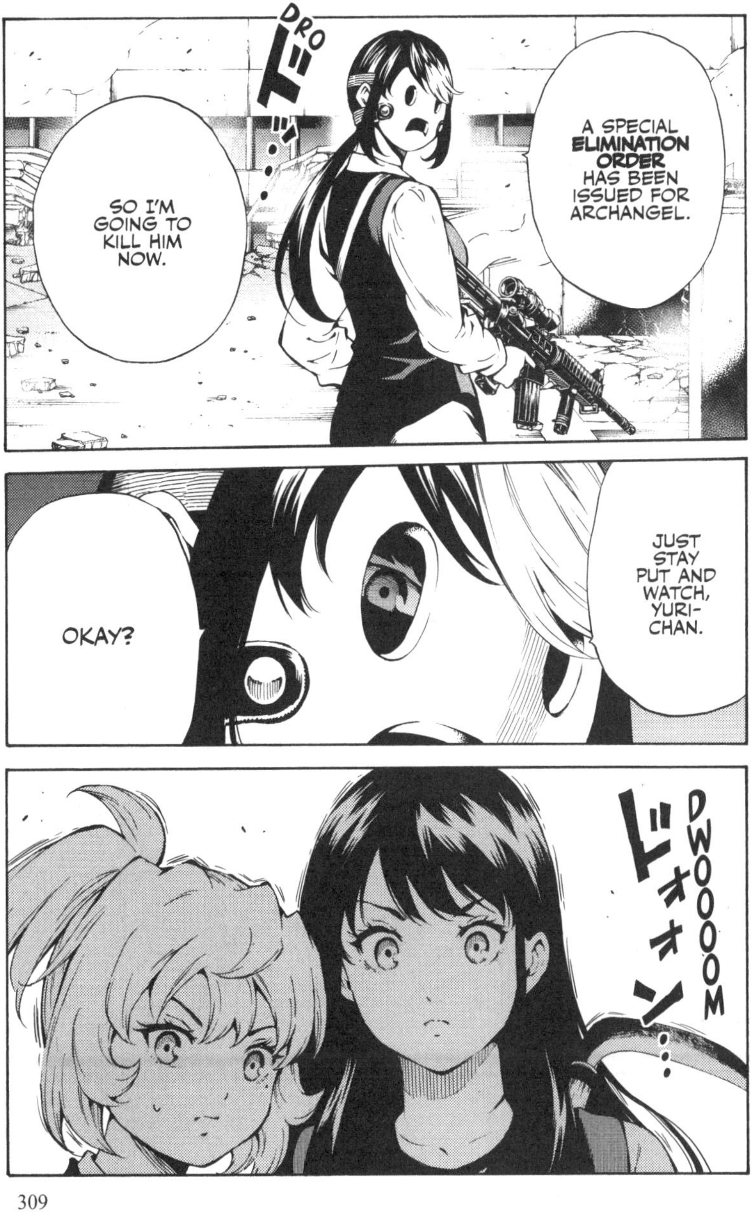
A SPECIAL ELIMINATION ORDER HAS BEEN ISSUED FOR ARCHANGEL.
DRO
SO I'M GOING TO KILL HIM NOW.
JUST STAY PUT AND WATCH, YURI-CHAN.
OKAY?
DWOOOOM

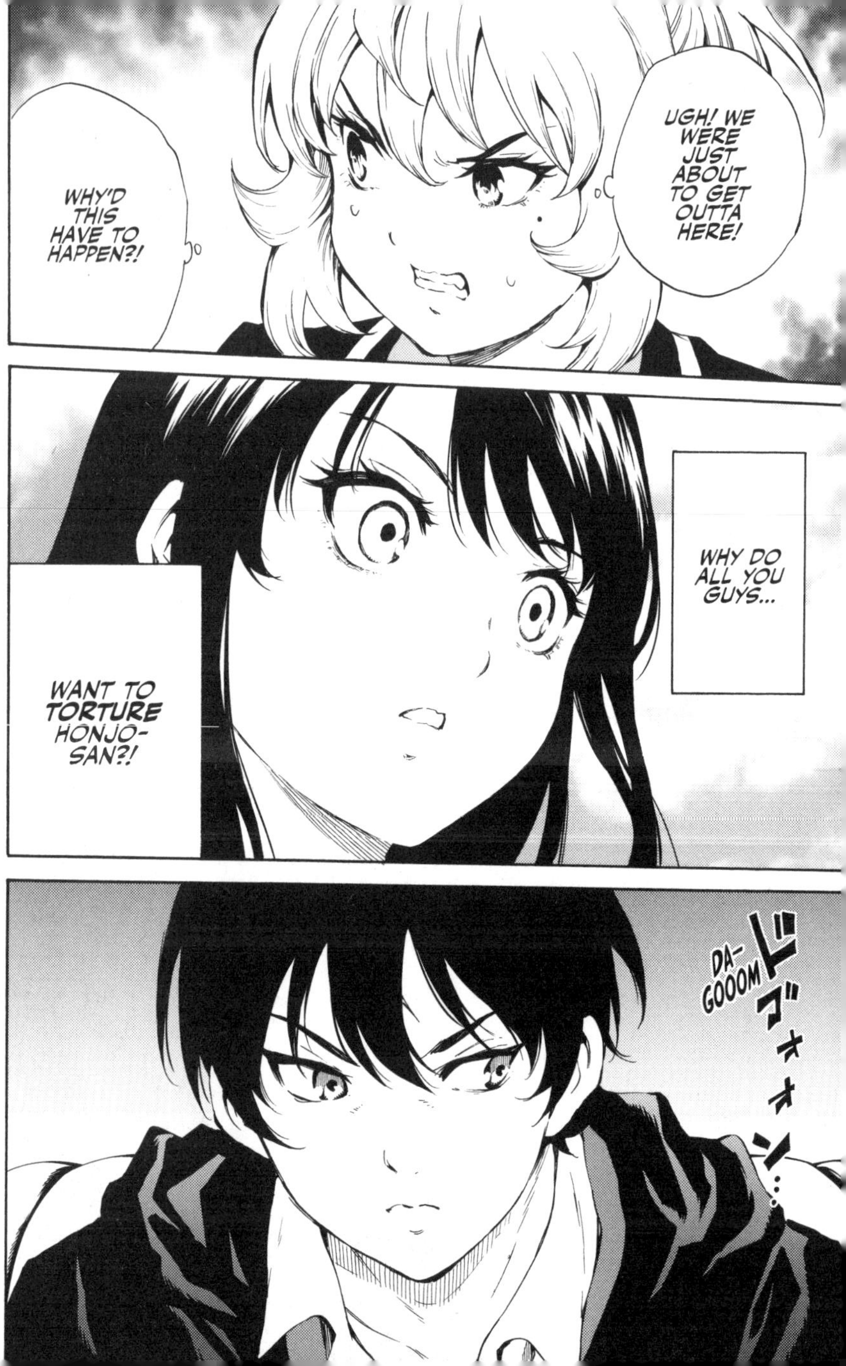
UGH! WE WERE JUST ABOUT TO GET OUTTA HERE!
WHY'D THIS HAVE TO HAPPEN?!
WHY DO ALL YOU GUYS...
WANT TO TORTURE HONJO-SAN?!
DA-GOOOM
ドゴォォン…

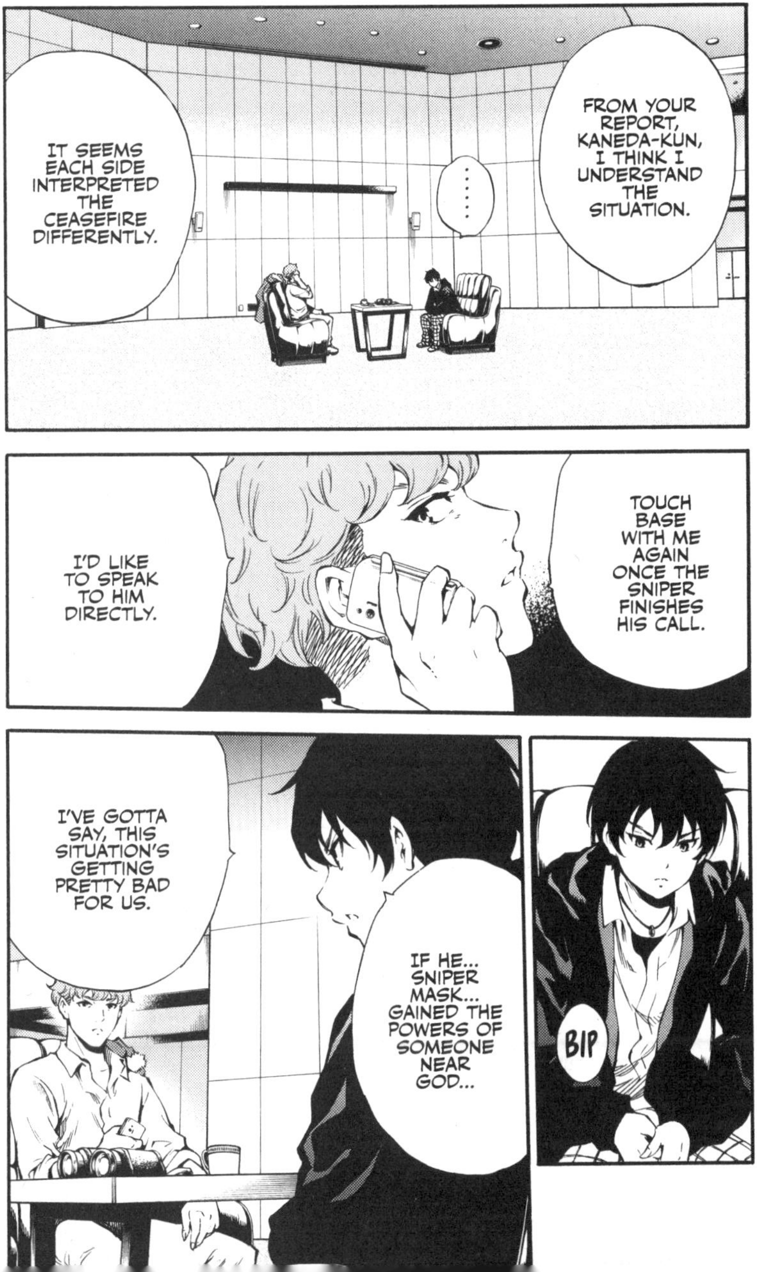
FROM YOUR REPORT, KANEDA-KUN, I THINK I UNDERSTAND THE SITUATION.
......
IT SEEMS EACH SIDE INTERPRETED THE CEASEFIRE DIFFERENTLY.
TOUCH BASE WITH ME AGAIN ONCE THE SNIPER FINISHES HIS CALL.
I'D LIKE TO SPEAK TO HIM DIRECTLY.
BIP
I'VE GOTTA SAY, THIS SITUATION'S GETTING PRETTY BAD FOR US.
IF HE... SNIPER MASK... GAINED THE POWERS OF SOMEONE NEAR GOD...

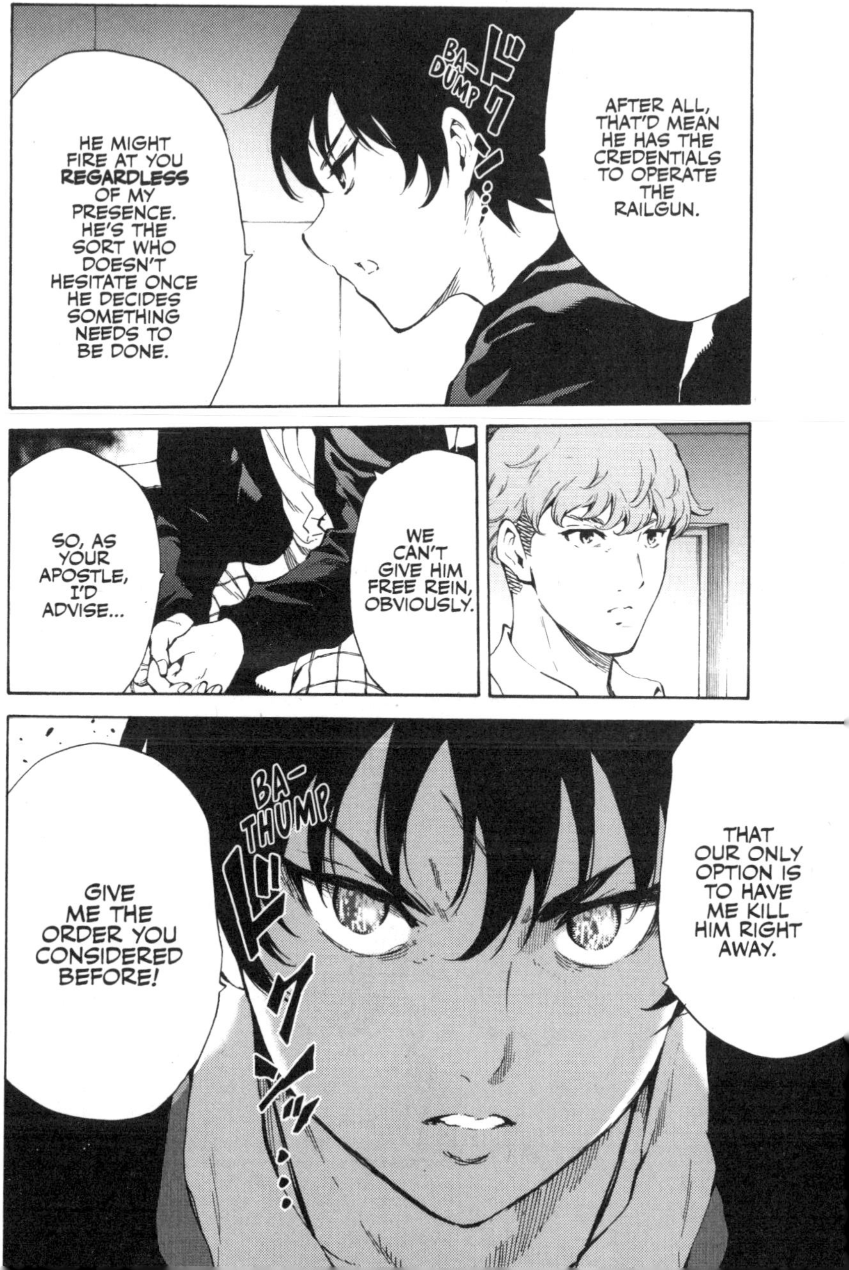
AFTER ALL, THAT'D MEAN HE HAS THE CREDENTIALS TO OPERATE THE RAILGUN.
BA-DUMP
HE MIGHT FIRE AT YOU **REGARDLESS** OF MY PRESENCE. HE'S THE SORT WHO DOESN'T HESITATE ONCE HE DECIDES SOMETHING NEEDS TO BE DONE.
WE CAN'T GIVE HIM FREE REIN, OBVIOUSLY.
SO, AS YOUR APOSTLE, I'D ADVISE...
THAT OUR ONLY OPTION IS TO HAVE ME KILL HIM RIGHT AWAY.
BA-THUMP
GIVE ME THE ORDER YOU CONSIDERED BEFORE!

CHAPTER 193: What You Must Do

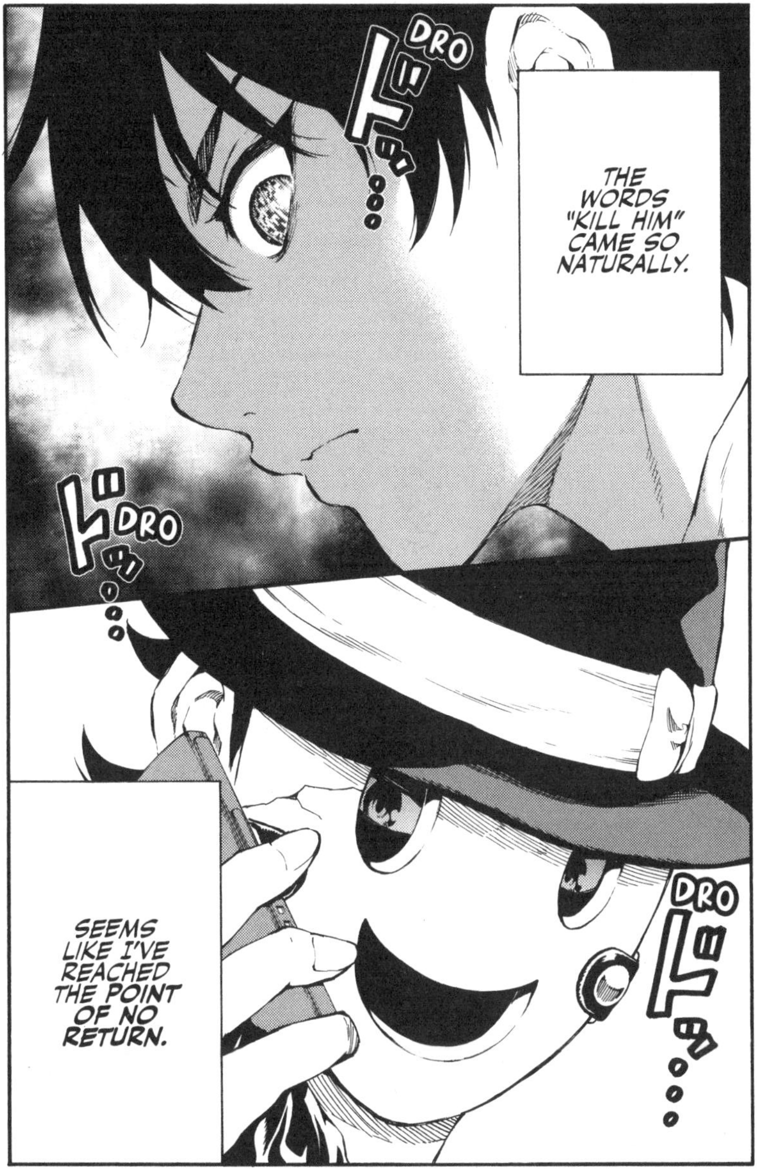
THE WORDS "KILL HIM" CAME SO NATURALLY.
DRO...
DRO...
DRO...
SEEMS LIKE I'VE REACHED THE POINT OF NO RETURN.

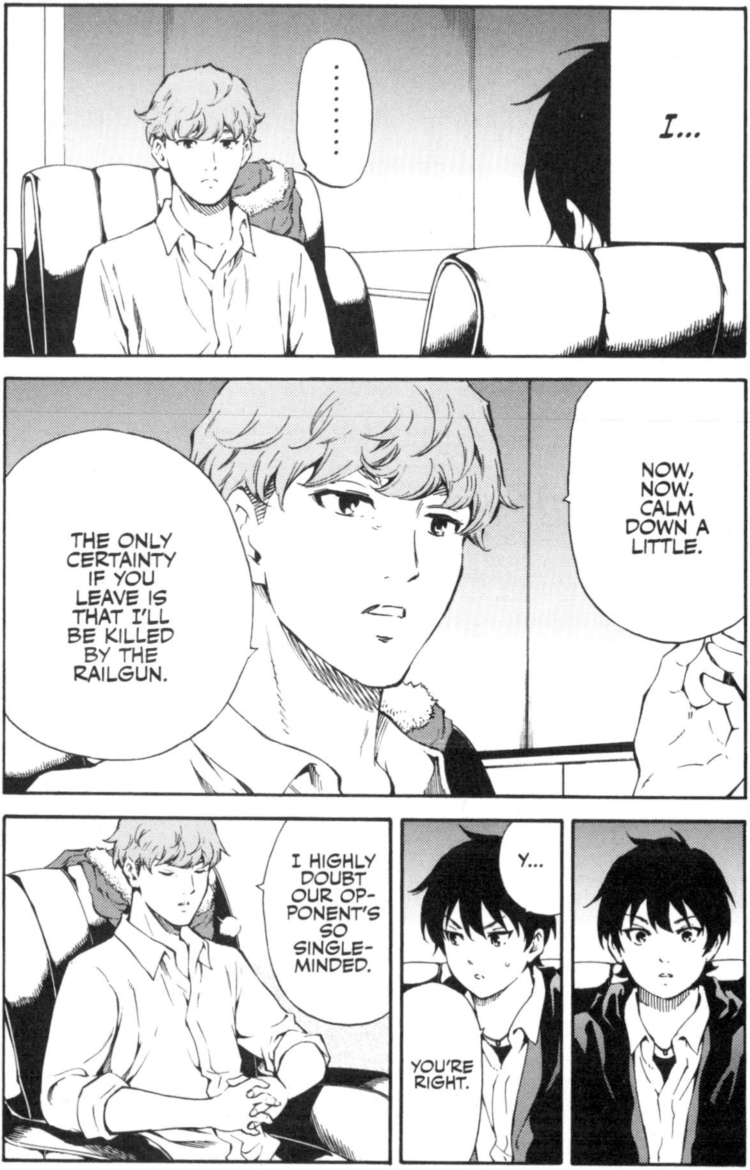
I...
......
NOW, NOW. CALM DOWN A LITTLE.
THE ONLY CERTAINTY IF YOU LEAVE IS THAT I'LL BE KILLED BY THE RAILGUN.
Y...
YOU'RE RIGHT.
I HIGHLY DOUBT OUR OPPONENT'S SO SINGLE-MINDED.

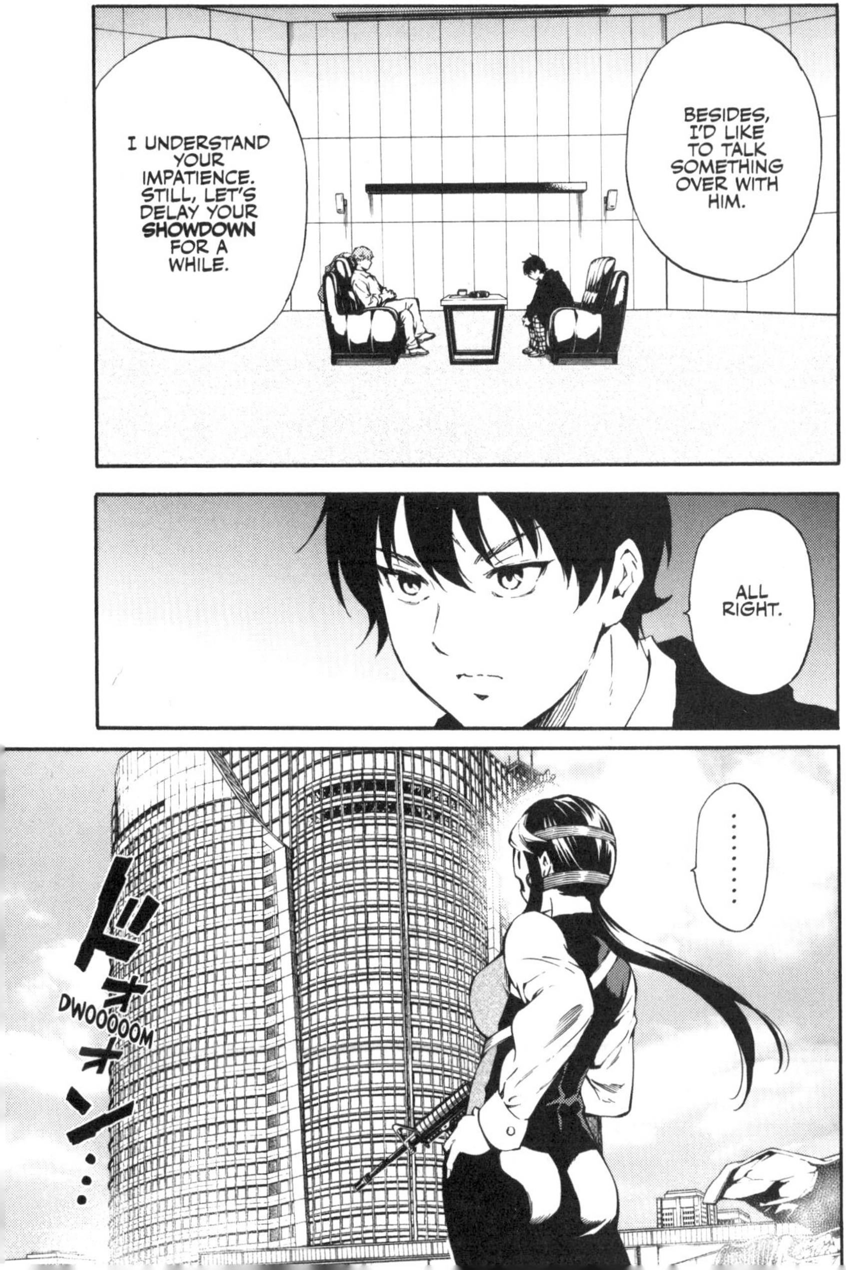

BESIDES, I'D LIKE TO TALK SOMETHING OVER WITH HIM.
I UNDERSTAND YOUR IMPATIENCE. STILL, LET'S DELAY YOUR **SHOWDOWN** FOR A WHILE.
ALL RIGHT.
....
DWOOOOOM

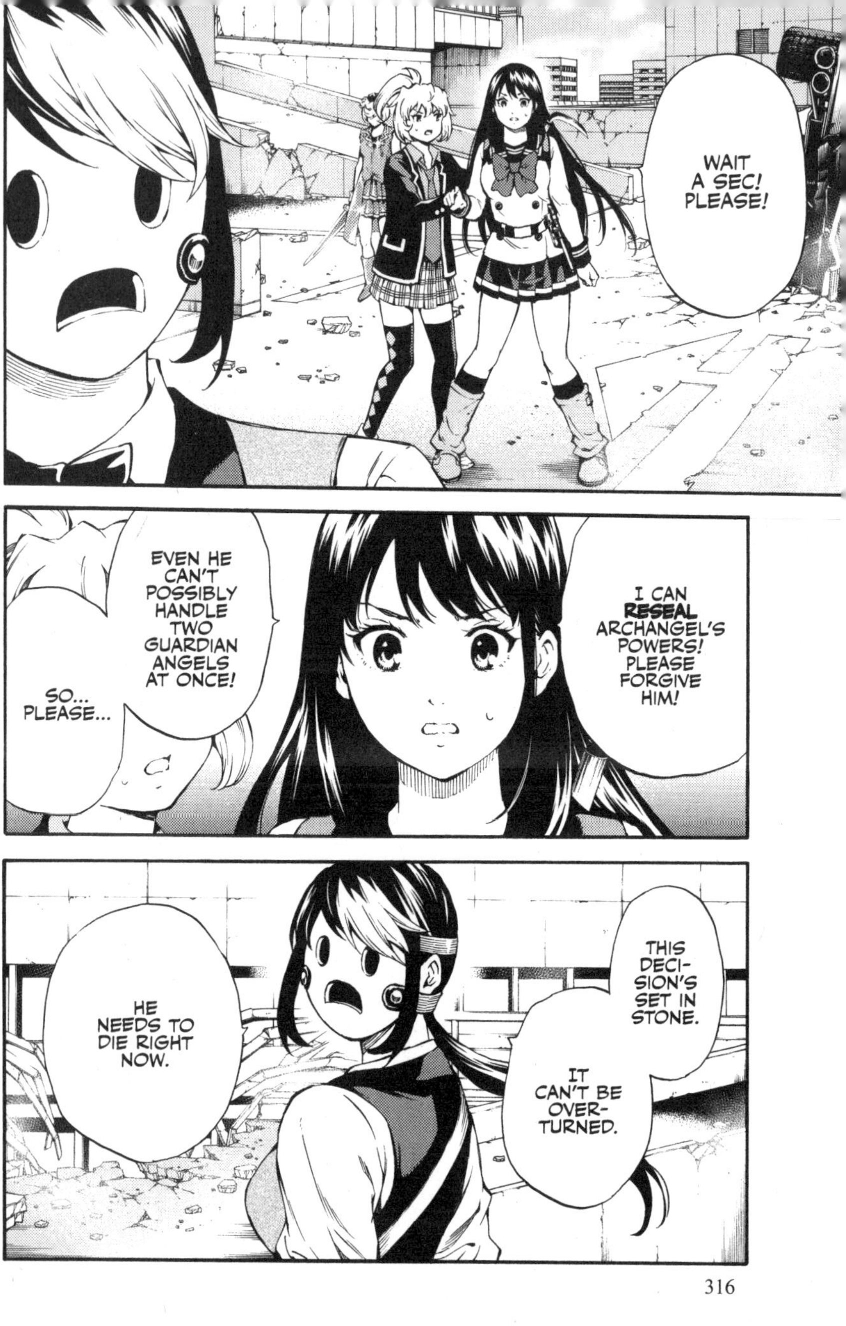
WAIT A SEC! PLEASE!
I CAN **RESEAL** ARCHANGEL'S POWERS! PLEASE FORGIVE HIM!
EVEN HE CAN'T POSSIBLY HANDLE TWO GUARDIAN ANGELS AT ONCE!
SO... PLEASE...
THIS DECISION'S SET IN STONE.
IT CAN'T BE OVERTURNED.
HE NEEDS TO DIE RIGHT NOW.

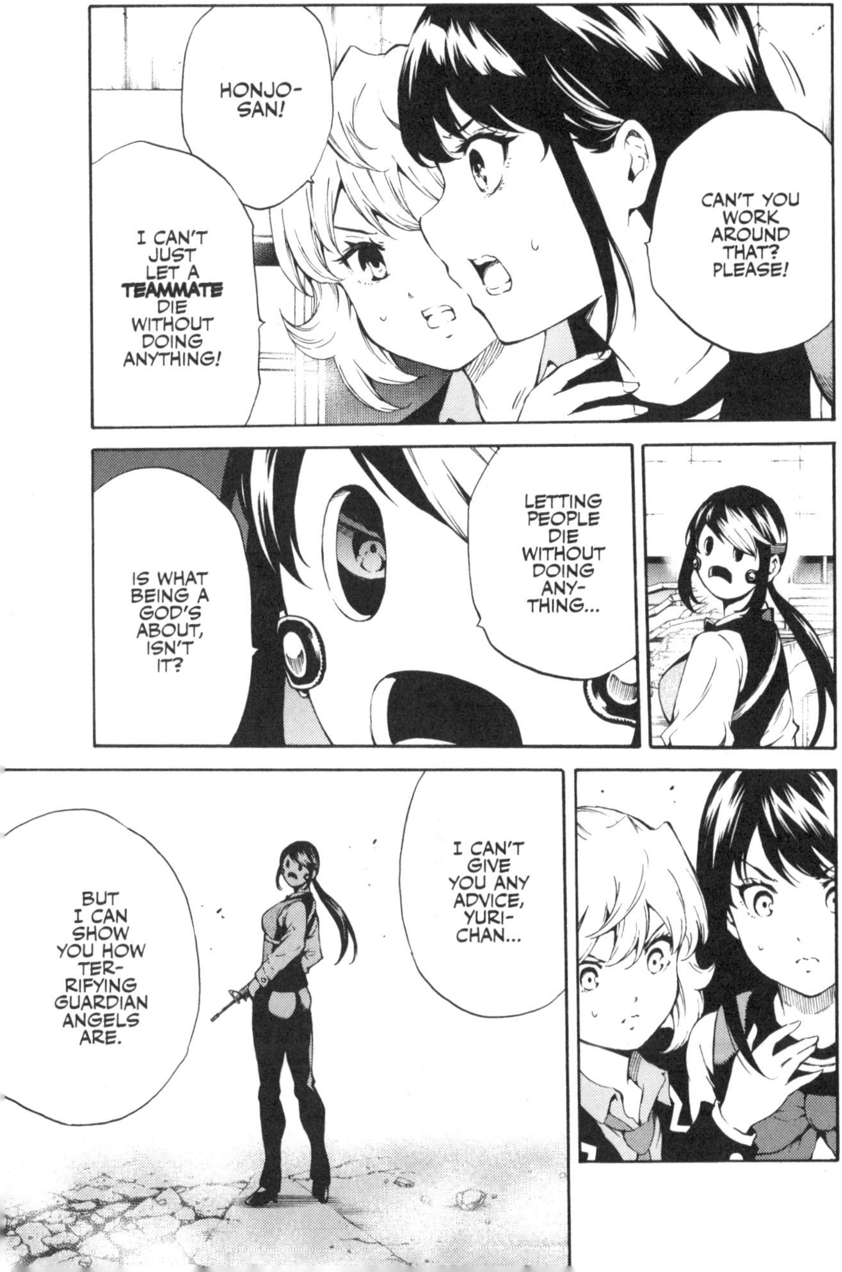
CAN'T YOU WORK AROUND THAT? PLEASE!
HONJO-SAN!
I CAN'T JUST LET A **TEAMMATE** DIE WITHOUT DOING ANYTHING!
LETTING PEOPLE DIE WITHOUT DOING ANY-THING...
IS WHAT BEING A GOD'S ABOUT, ISN'T IT?
I CAN'T GIVE YOU ANY ADVICE, YURI-CHAN...
BUT I CAN SHOW YOU HOW TER-RIFYING GUARDIAN ANGELS ARE.

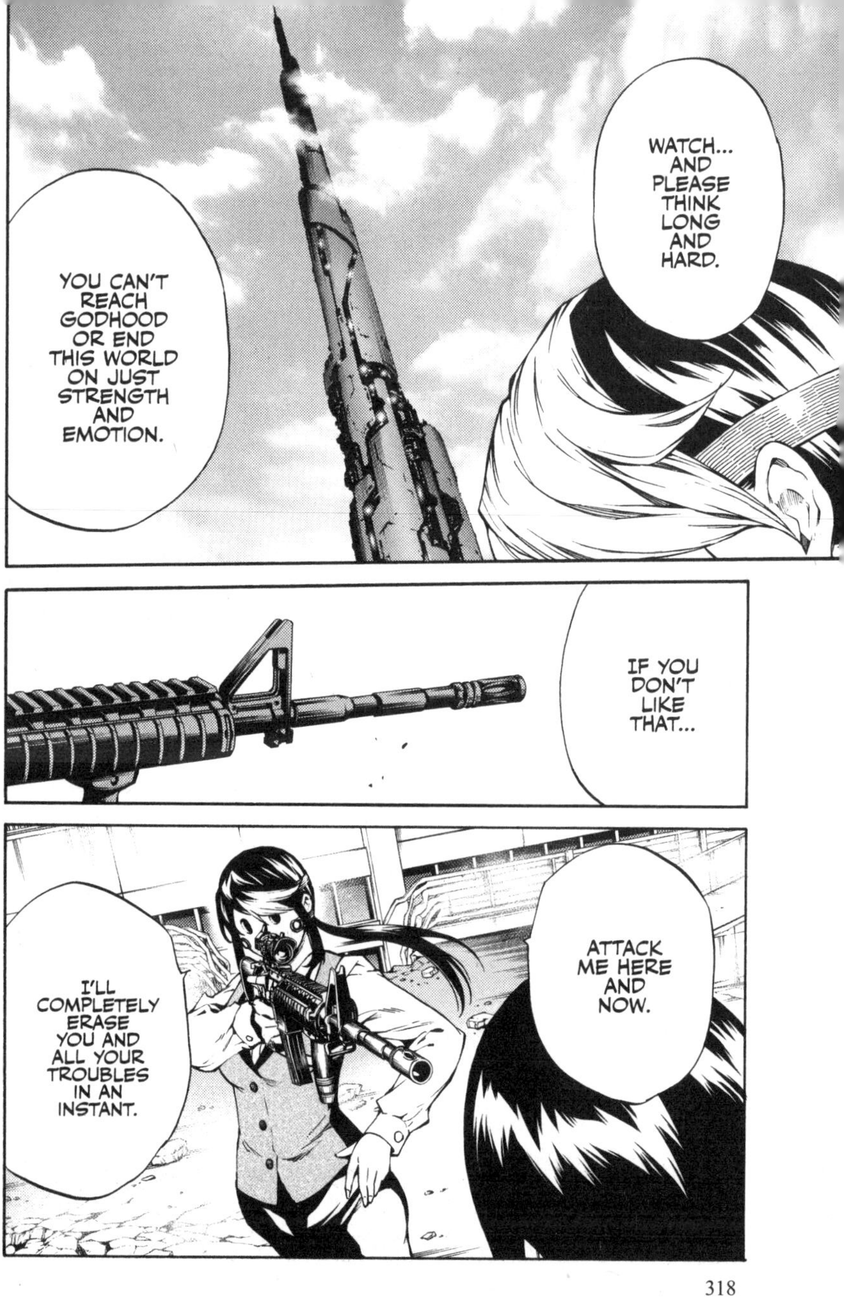
WATCH... AND PLEASE THINK LONG AND HARD.
YOU CAN'T REACH GODHOOD OR END THIS WORLD ON JUST STRENGTH AND EMOTION.
IF YOU DON'T LIKE THAT...
ATTACK ME HERE AND NOW.
I'LL COMPLETELY ERASE YOU AND ALL YOUR TROUBLES IN AN INSTANT.

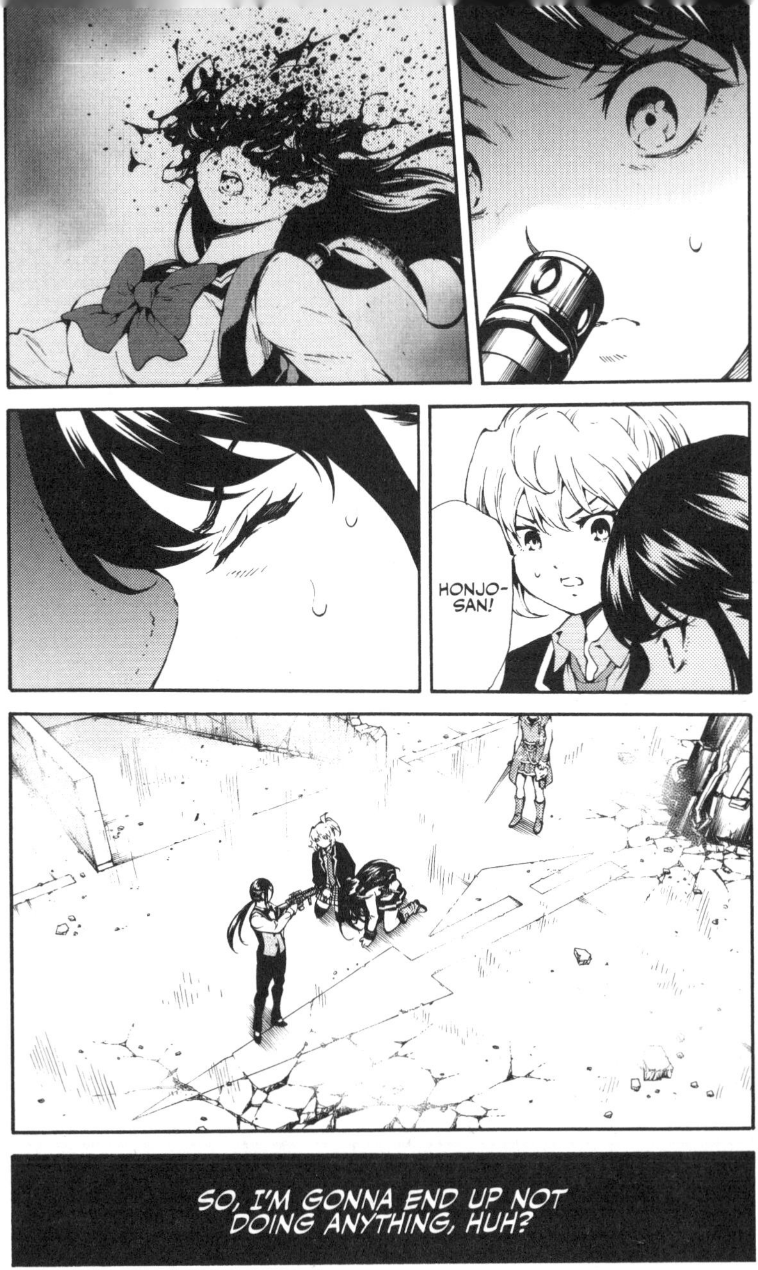
HONJO-SAN!
SO, I'M GONNA END UP NOT DOING ANYTHING, HUH?

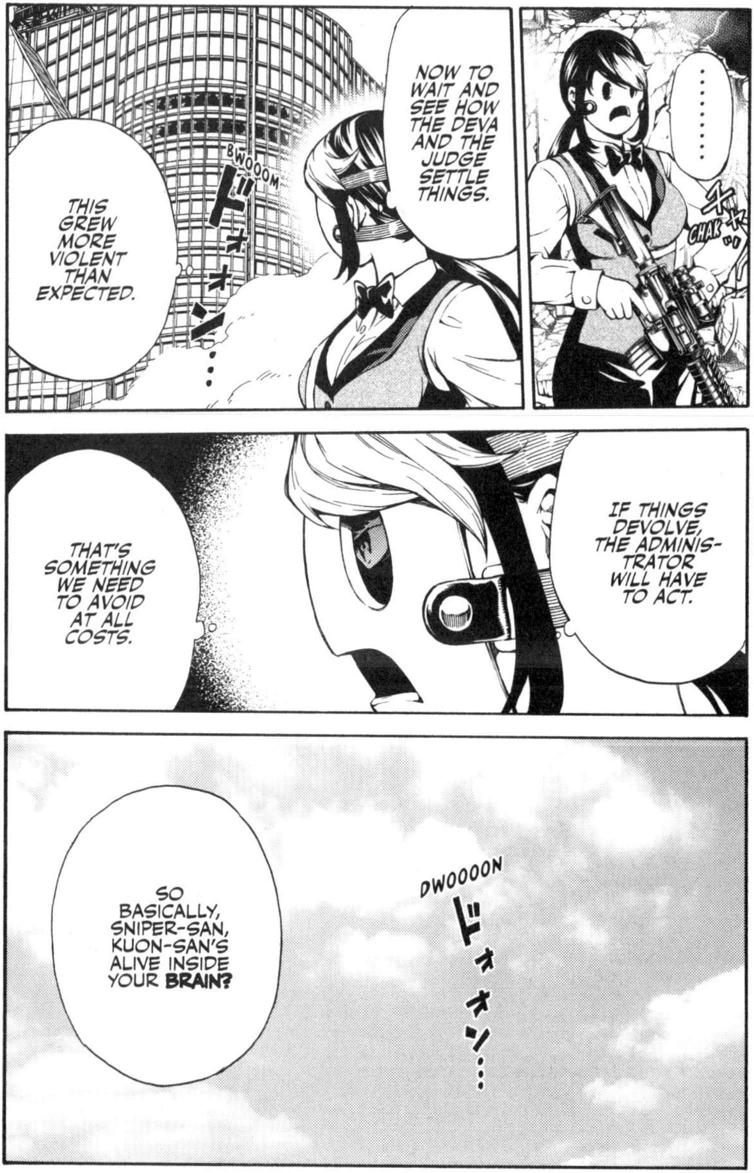
……
CHAK
NOW TO WAIT AND SEE HOW THE DEVA AND THE JUDGE SETTLE THINGS.
BWOOOM
THIS GREW MORE VIOLENT THAN EXPECTED.
IF THINGS DEVOLVE, THE ADMINIS-TRATOR WILL HAVE TO ACT.
THAT'S SOMETHING WE NEED TO AVOID AT ALL COSTS.
DWOOOON
SO BASICALLY, SNIPER-SAN, KUON-SAN'S ALIVE INSIDE YOUR **BRAIN?**

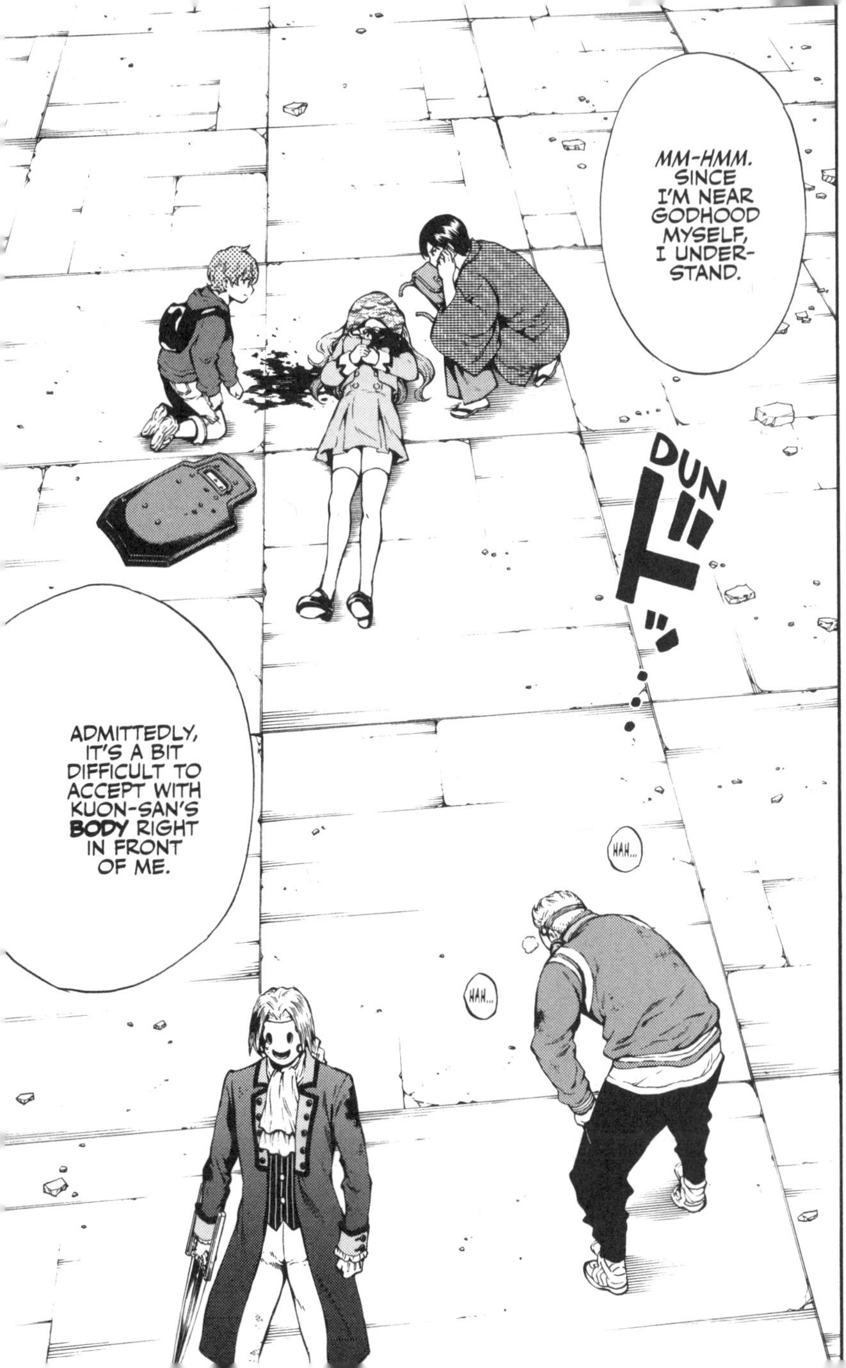
MM-HMM. SINCE I'M NEAR GODHOOD MYSELF, I UNDERSTAND.
DUN
ADMITTEDLY, IT'S A BIT DIFFICULT TO ACCEPT WITH KUON-SAN'S **BODY** RIGHT IN FRONT OF ME.
HAH...
HAH...

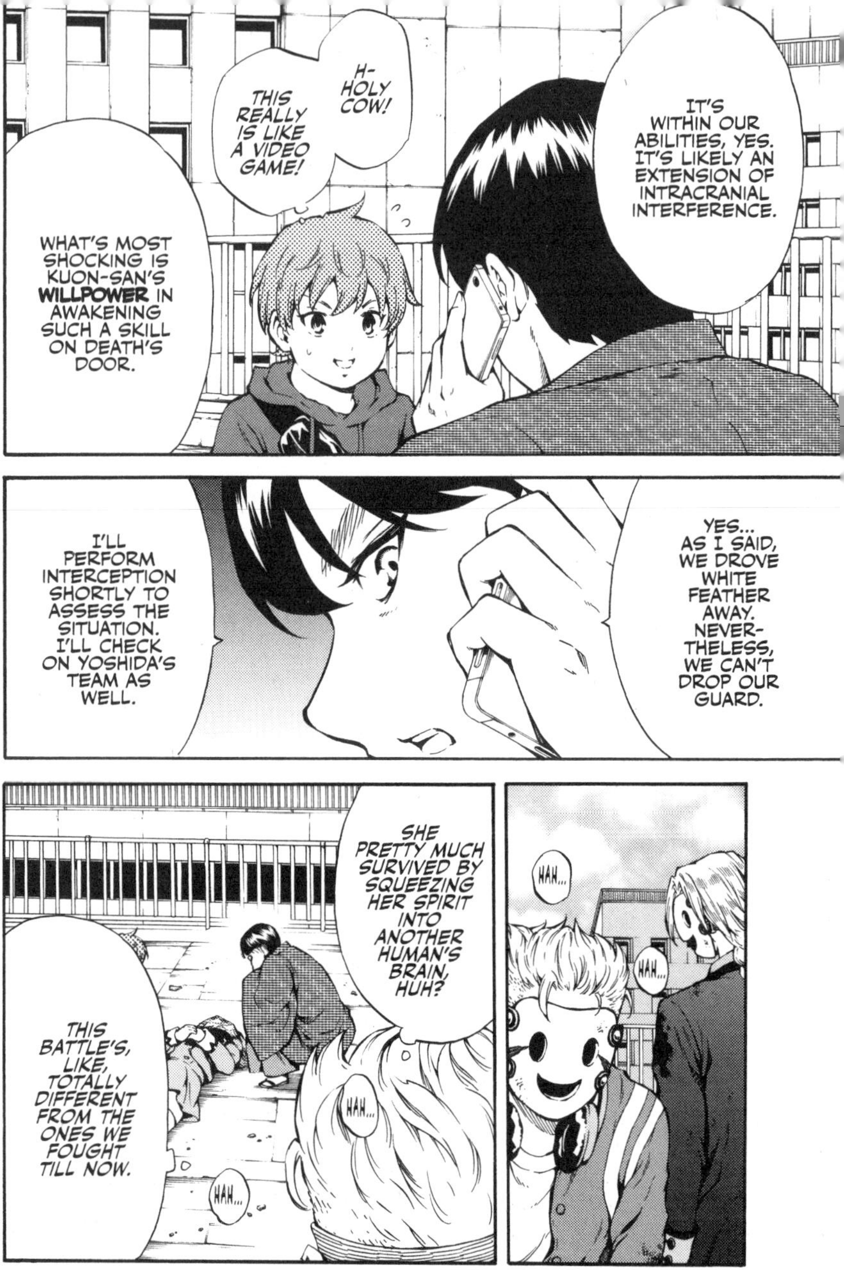
IT'S WITHIN OUR ABILITIES, YES. IT'S LIKELY AN EXTENSION OF INTRACRANIAL INTERFERENCE.
H-HOLY COW!
THIS REALLY IS LIKE A VIDEO GAME!
WHAT'S MOST SHOCKING IS KUON-SAN'S **WILLPOWER** IN AWAKENING SUCH A SKILL ON DEATH'S DOOR.
YES... AS I SAID, WE DROVE WHITE FEATHER AWAY. NEVER-THELESS, WE CAN'T DROP OUR GUARD.
I'LL PERFORM INTERCEPTION SHORTLY TO ASSESS THE SITUATION. I'LL CHECK ON YOSHIDA'S TEAM AS WELL.
HAH...
HAH...
SHE PRETTY MUCH SURVIVED BY SQUEEZING HER SPIRIT INTO ANOTHER HUMAN'S BRAIN, HUH?
HAH...
THIS BATTLE'S, LIKE, TOTALLY DIFFERENT FROM THE ONES WE FOUGHT TILL NOW.
HAH...

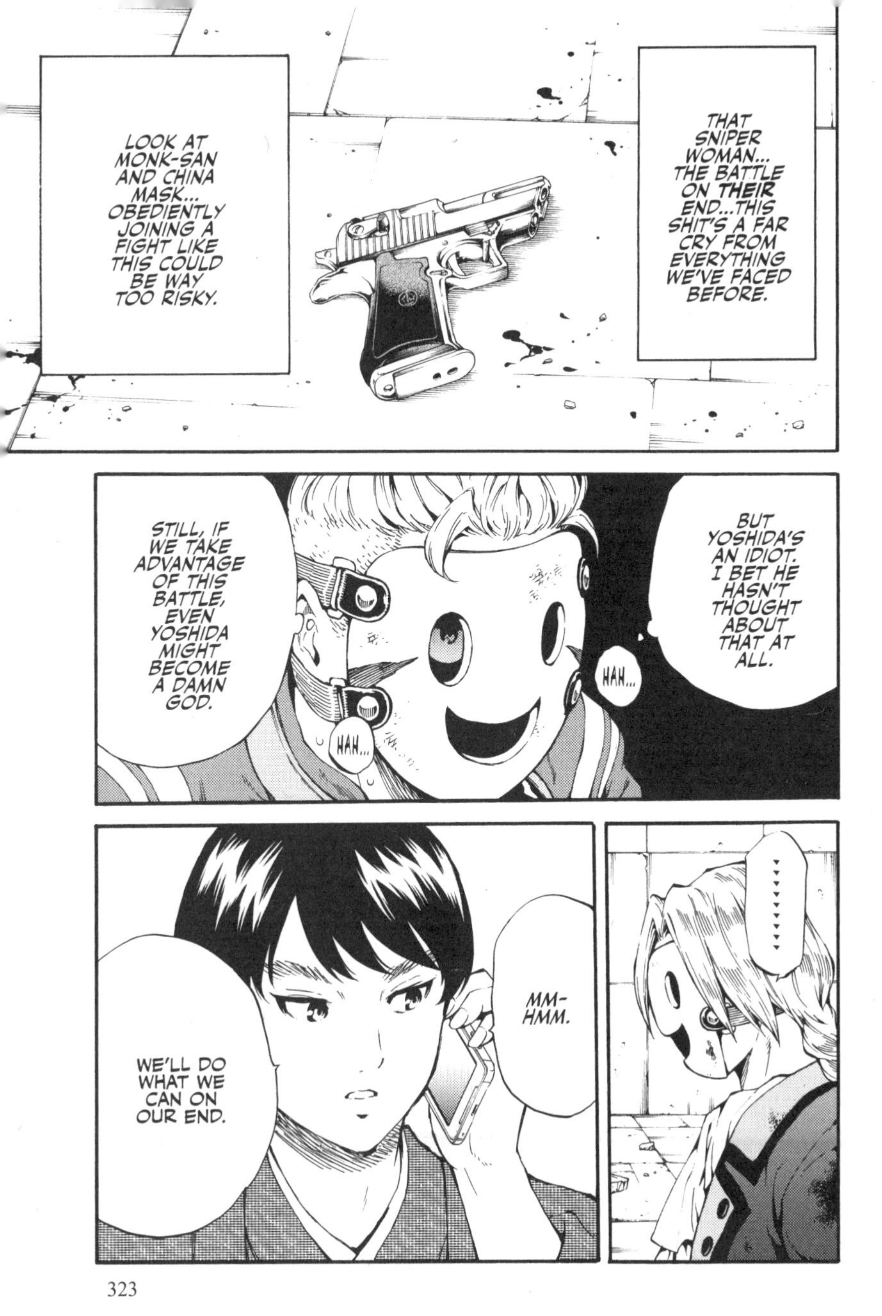
THAT SNIPER WOMAN... THE BATTLE ON **THEIR** END...THIS SHIT'S A FAR CRY FROM EVERYTHING WE'VE FACED BEFORE.
LOOK AT MONK-SAN AND CHINA MASK... OBEDIENTLY JOINING A FIGHT LIKE THIS COULD BE WAY TOO RISKY.
BUT YOSHIDA'S AN IDIOT. I BET HE HASN'T THOUGHT ABOUT THAT AT ALL.
STILL, IF WE TAKE ADVANTAGE OF THIS BATTLE, EVEN YOSHIDA MIGHT BECOME A DAMN GOD.
HAH...
HAH...
....
MM-HMM.
WE'LL DO WHAT WE CAN ON OUR END.

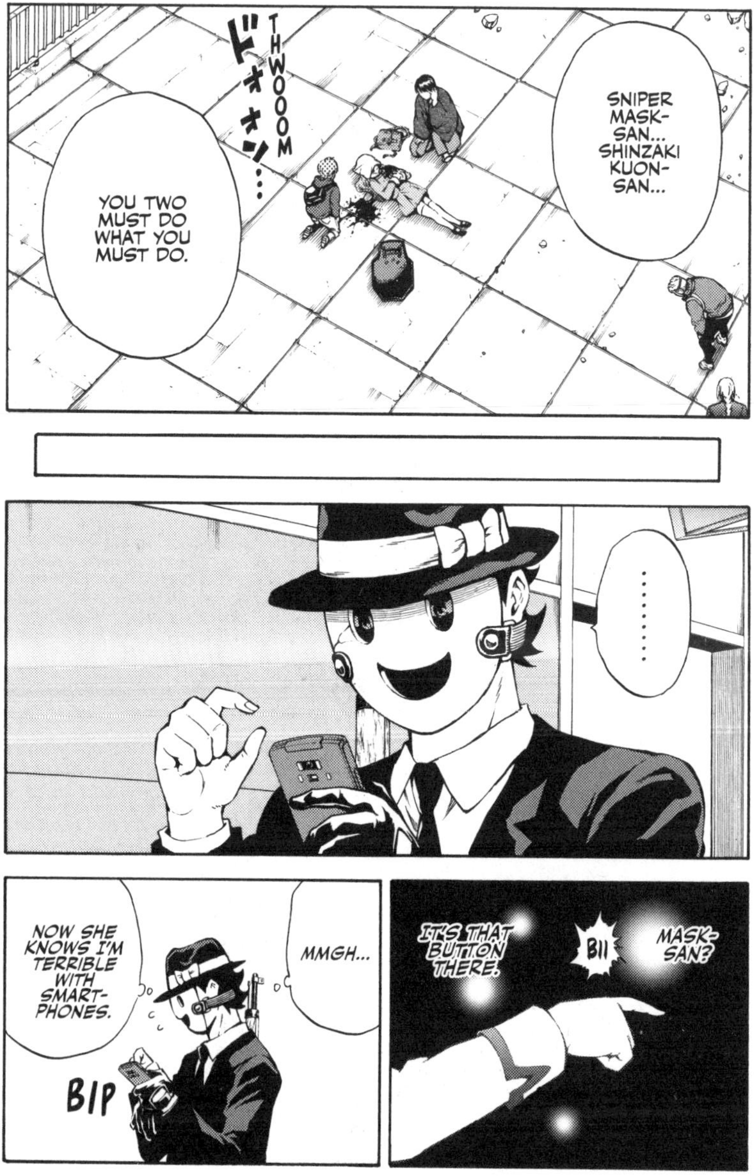
SNIPER MASK-SAN... SHINZAKI KUON-SAN...
ドォォン…
THWOOOM
YOU TWO MUST DO WHAT YOU MUST DO.
......
MASK-SAN?
BII
IT'S THAT BUTTON THERE.
MMGH...
NOW SHE KNOWS I'M TERRIBLE WITH SMARTPHONES.
BIP

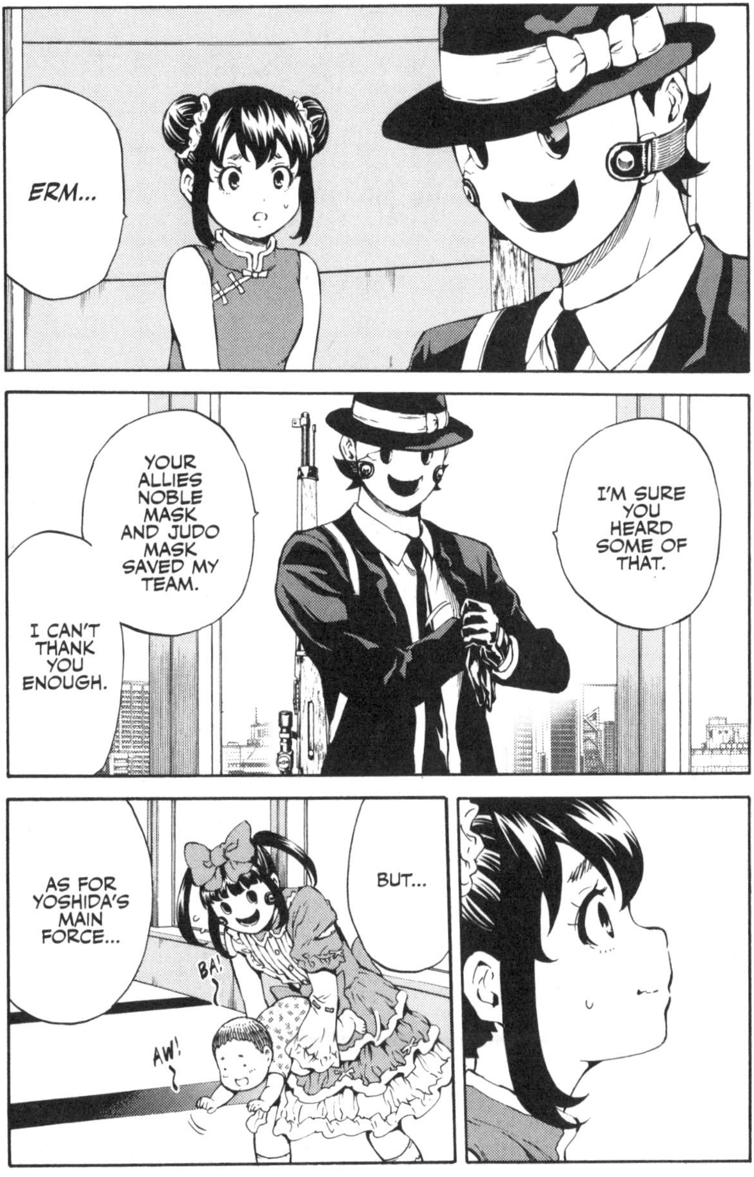
ERM...
I'M SURE YOU HEARD SOME OF THAT.
YOUR ALLIES NOBLE MASK AND JUDO MASK SAVED MY TEAM.
I CAN'T THANK YOU ENOUGH.
BUT...
AS FOR YOSHIDA'S MAIN FORCE...
BA!
AW!

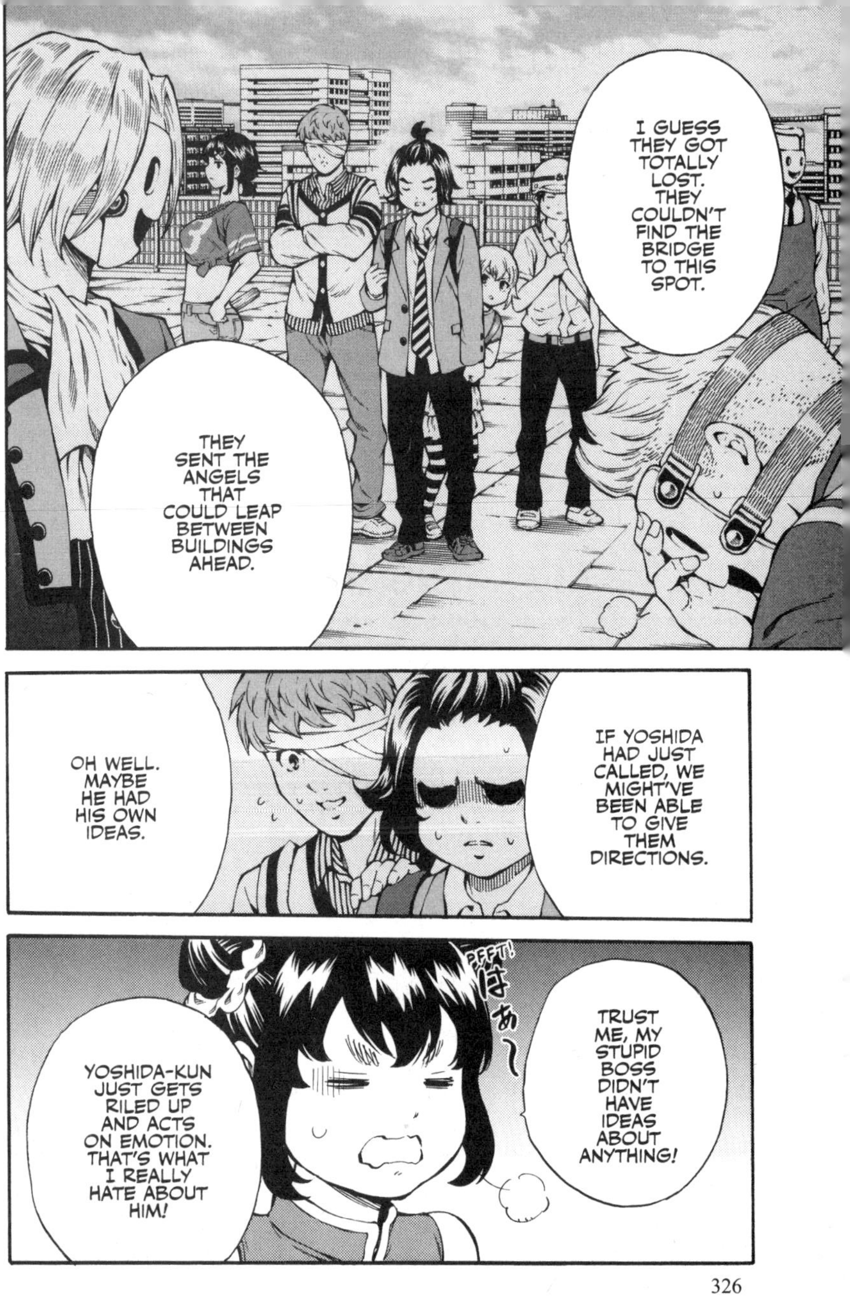
I GUESS THEY GOT TOTALLY LOST. THEY COULDN'T FIND THE BRIDGE TO THIS SPOT.
THEY SENT THE ANGELS THAT COULD LEAP BETWEEN BUILDINGS AHEAD.
IF YOSHIDA HAD JUST CALLED, WE MIGHT'VE BEEN ABLE TO GIVE THEM DIRECTIONS.
OH WELL. MAYBE HE HAD HIS OWN IDEAS.
TRUST ME, MY STUPID BOSS DIDN'T HAVE IDEAS ABOUT ANYTHING!
PFFT! はぁ〜
YOSHIDA-KUN JUST GETS RILED UP AND ACTS ON EMOTION. THAT'S WHAT I REALLY HATE ABOUT HIM!

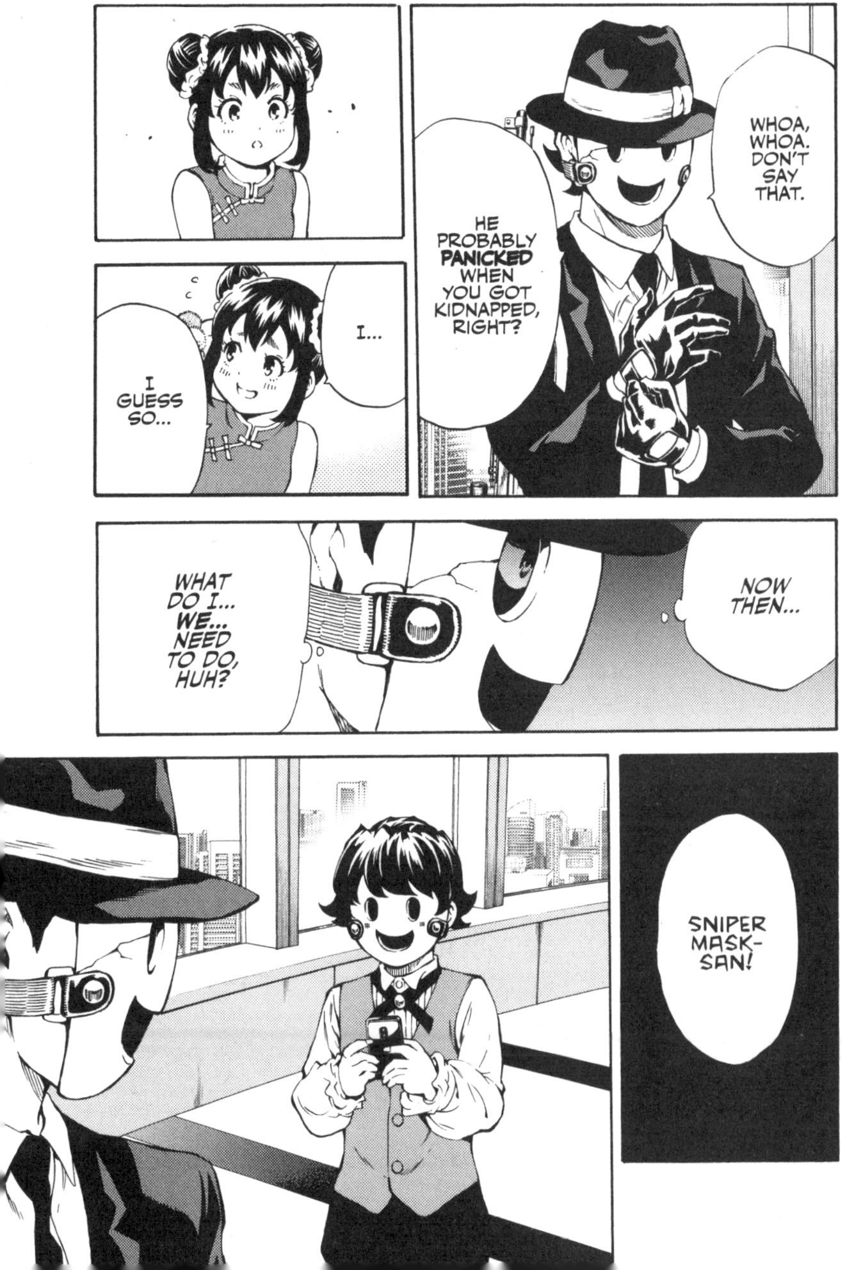
WHOA, WHOA. DON'T SAY THAT.
HE PROBABLY **PANICKED** WHEN YOU GOT KIDNAPPED, RIGHT?
I...
I GUESS SO...
NOW THEN...
WHAT DO I... **WE...** NEED TO DO, HUH?
SNIPER MASK-SAN!

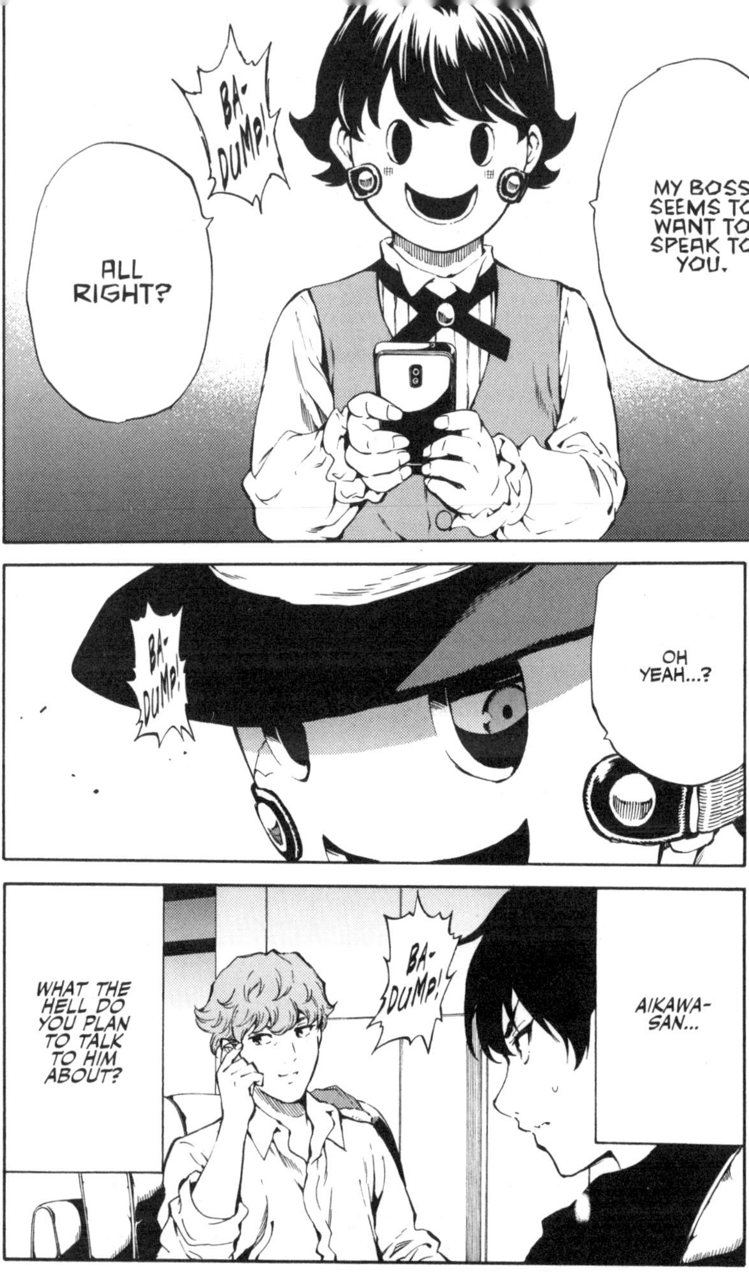
MY BOSS SEEMS TO WANT TO SPEAK TO YOU.
BA-DUMP!
ALL RIGHT?
OH YEAH...?
BA-DUMP!
AIKAWA-SAN...
BA-DUMP!
WHAT THE HELL DO YOU PLAN TO TALK TO HIM ABOUT?

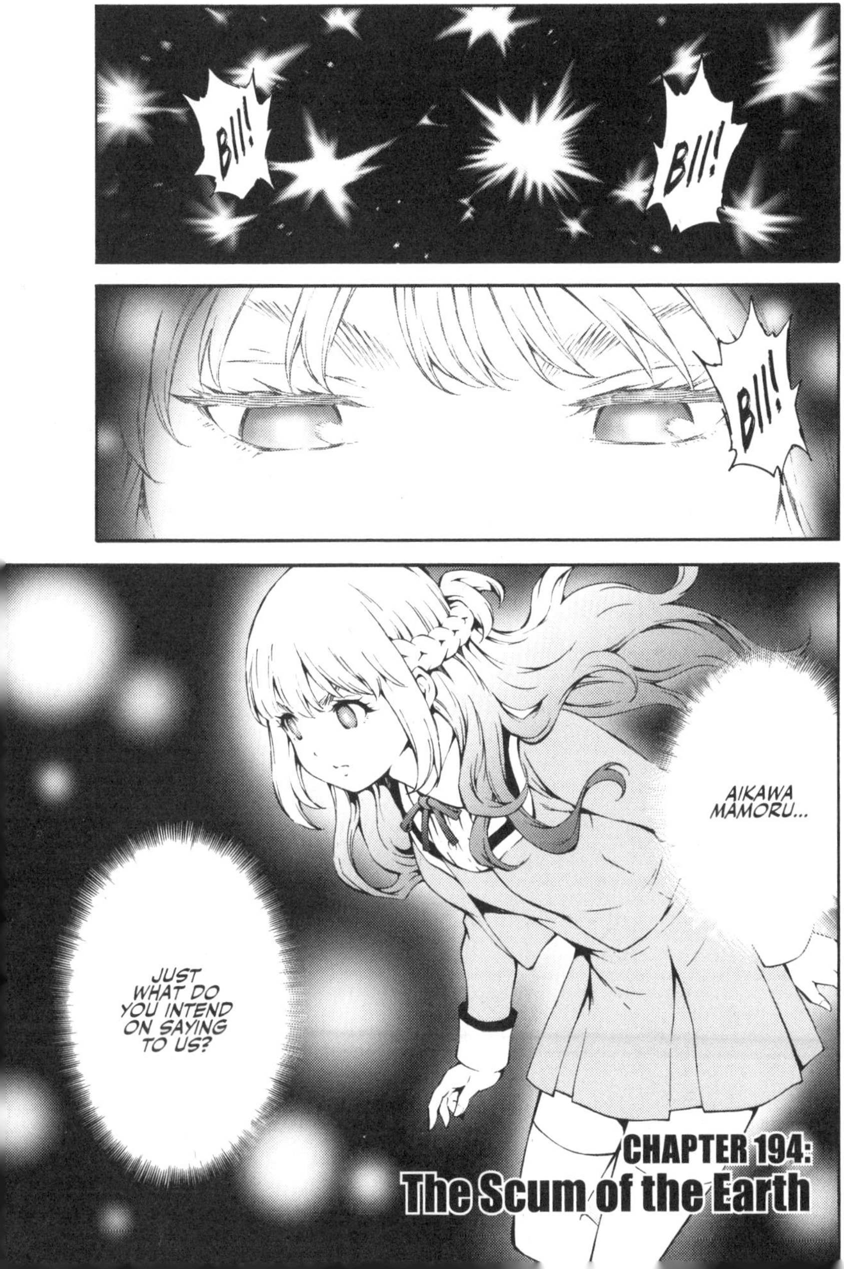
BII!
BII!
BII!
AIKAWA MAMORU...
JUST WHAT DO YOU INTEND ON SAYING TO US?

CHAPTER 194: The Scum of the Earth

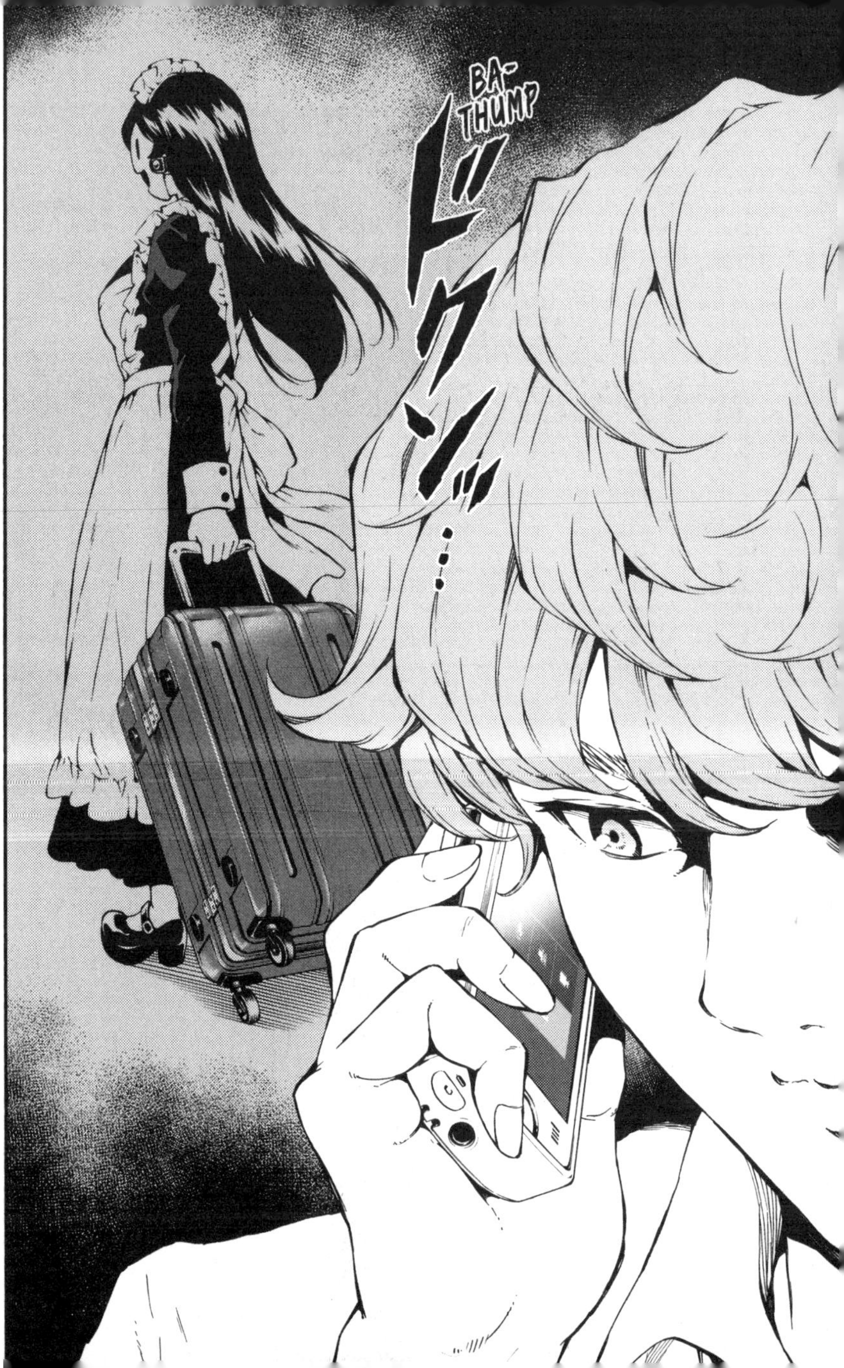
BA-
THUMP
ドクン…

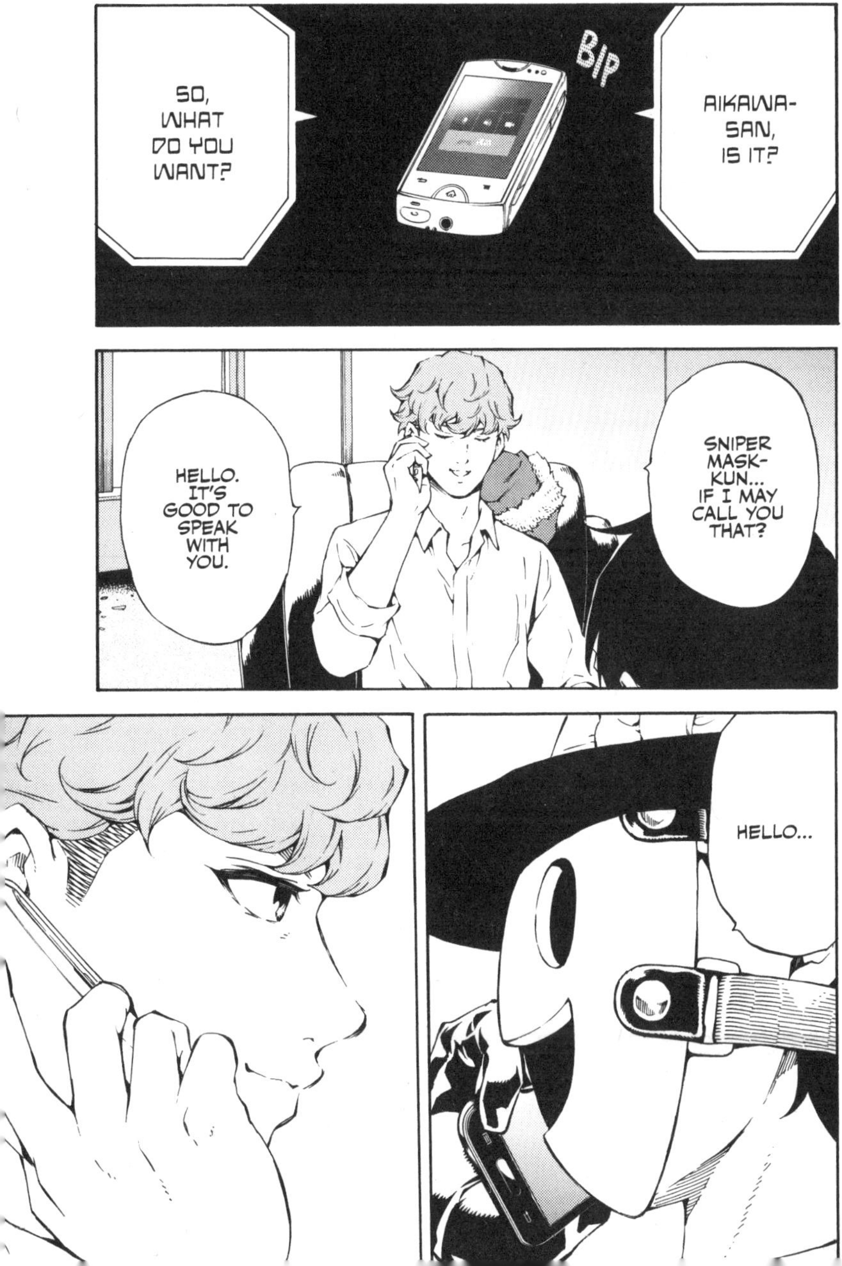
AIKAWA-SAN, IS IT?
BIP
SO, WHAT DO YOU WANT?
SNIPER MASK-KUN... IF I MAY CALL YOU THAT?
HELLO. IT'S GOOD TO SPEAK WITH YOU.
HELLO...

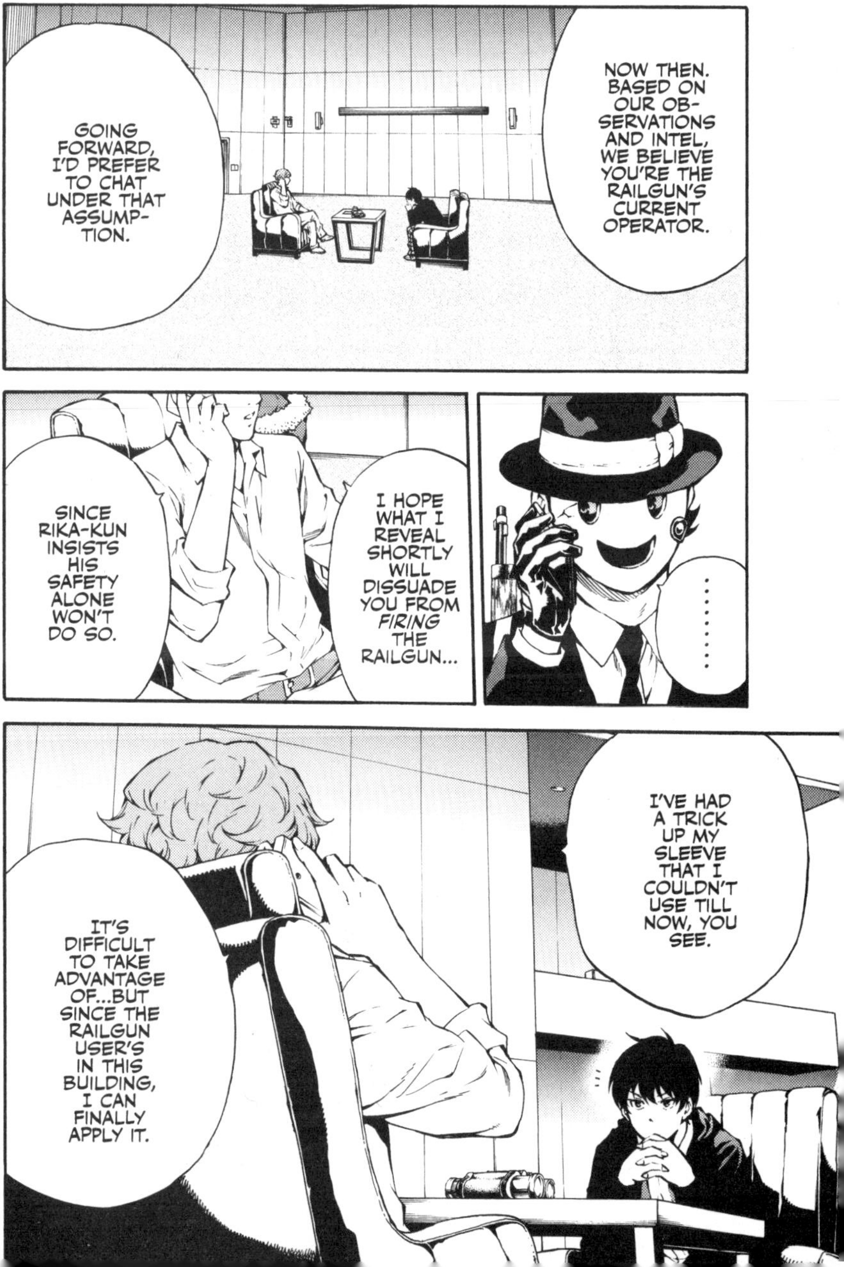
NOW THEN. BASED ON OUR OB-SERVATIONS AND INTEL, WE BELIEVE YOU'RE THE RAILGUN'S CURRENT OPERATOR.
GOING FORWARD, I'D PREFER TO CHAT UNDER THAT ASSUMP-TION.
....
I HOPE WHAT I REVEAL SHORTLY WILL DISSUADE YOU FROM *FIRING* THE RAILGUN...
SINCE RIKA-KUN INSISTS HIS SAFETY ALONE WON'T DO SO.
I'VE HAD A TRICK UP MY SLEEVE THAT I COULDN'T USE TILL NOW, YOU SEE.
IT'S DIFFICULT TO TAKE ADVANTAGE OF...BUT SINCE THE RAILGUN USER'S IN THIS BUILDING, I CAN FINALLY APPLY IT.

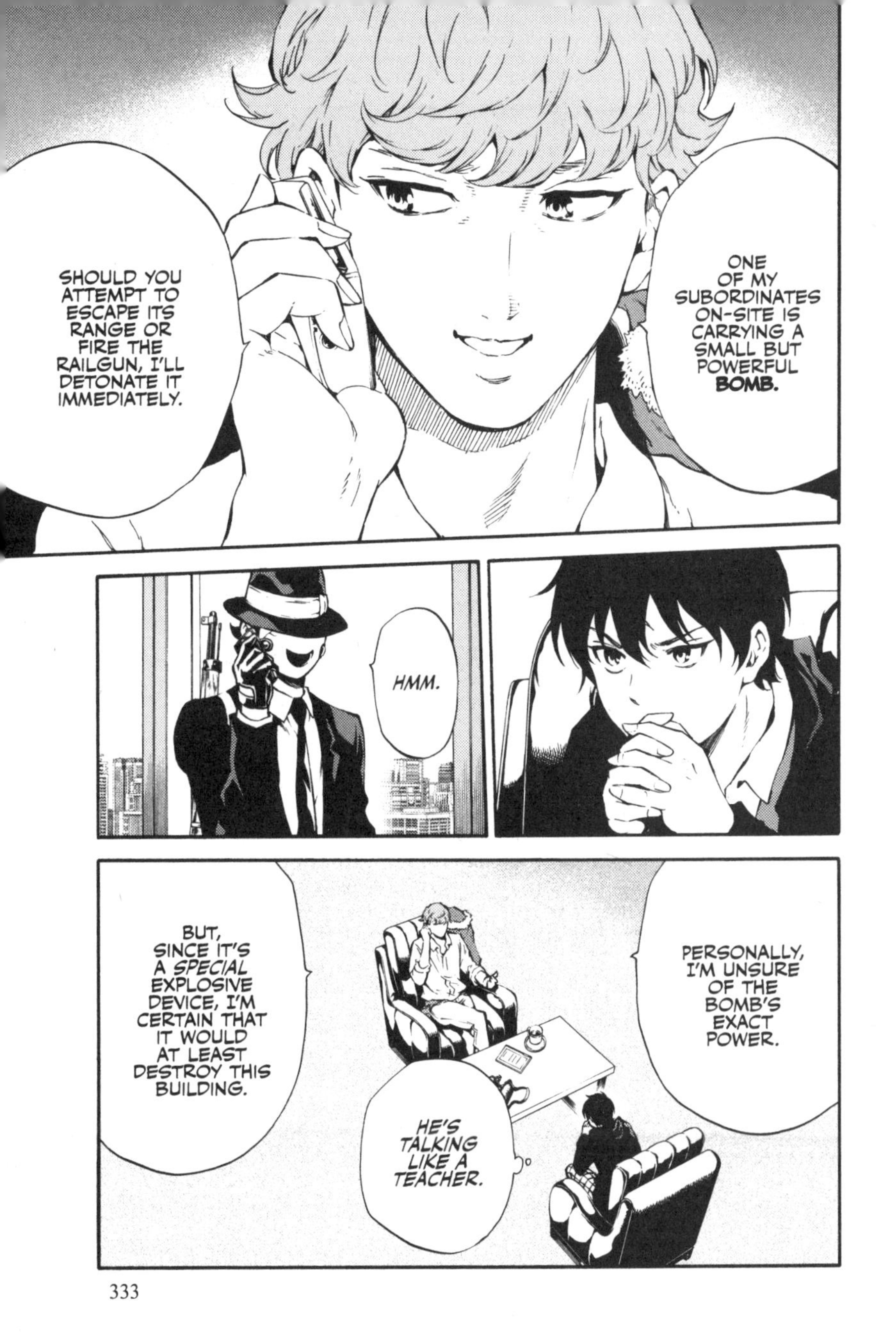
ONE OF MY SUBORDINATES ON-SITE IS CARRYING A SMALL BUT POWERFUL **BOMB.**
SHOULD YOU ATTEMPT TO ESCAPE ITS RANGE OR FIRE THE RAILGUN, I'LL DETONATE IT IMMEDIATELY.
HMM.
PERSONALLY, I'M UNSURE OF THE BOMB'S EXACT POWER.
BUT, SINCE IT'S A *SPECIAL* EXPLOSIVE DEVICE, I'M CERTAIN THAT IT WOULD AT LEAST DESTROY THIS BUILDING.
HE'S TALKING LIKE A TEACHER.

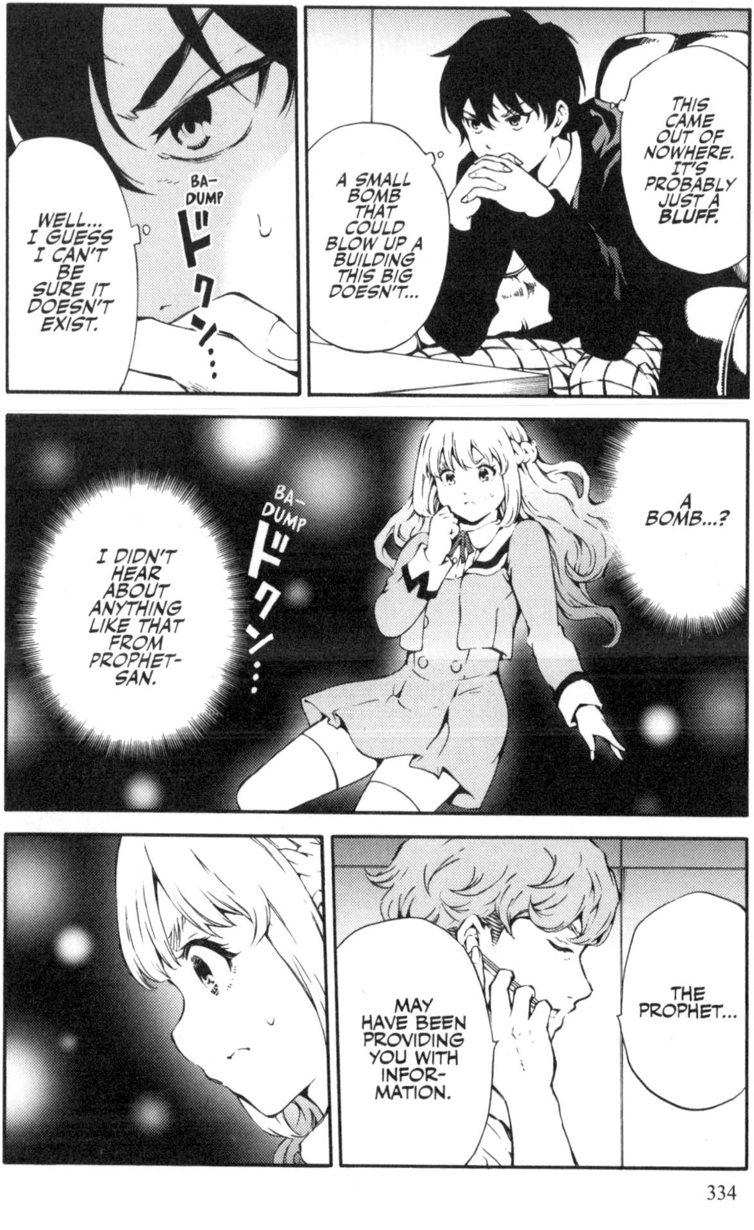
THIS CAME OUT OF NOWHERE. IT'S PROBABLY JUST A BLUFF.
A SMALL BOMB THAT COULD BLOW UP A BUILDING THIS BIG DOESN'T...
BA-DUMP
WELL... I GUESS I CAN'T BE SURE IT DOESN'T EXIST.
A BOMB...?
BA-DUMP
I DIDN'T HEAR ABOUT ANYTHING LIKE THAT FROM PROPHET-SAN.
THE PROPHET...
MAY HAVE BEEN PROVIDING YOU WITH INFORMATION.

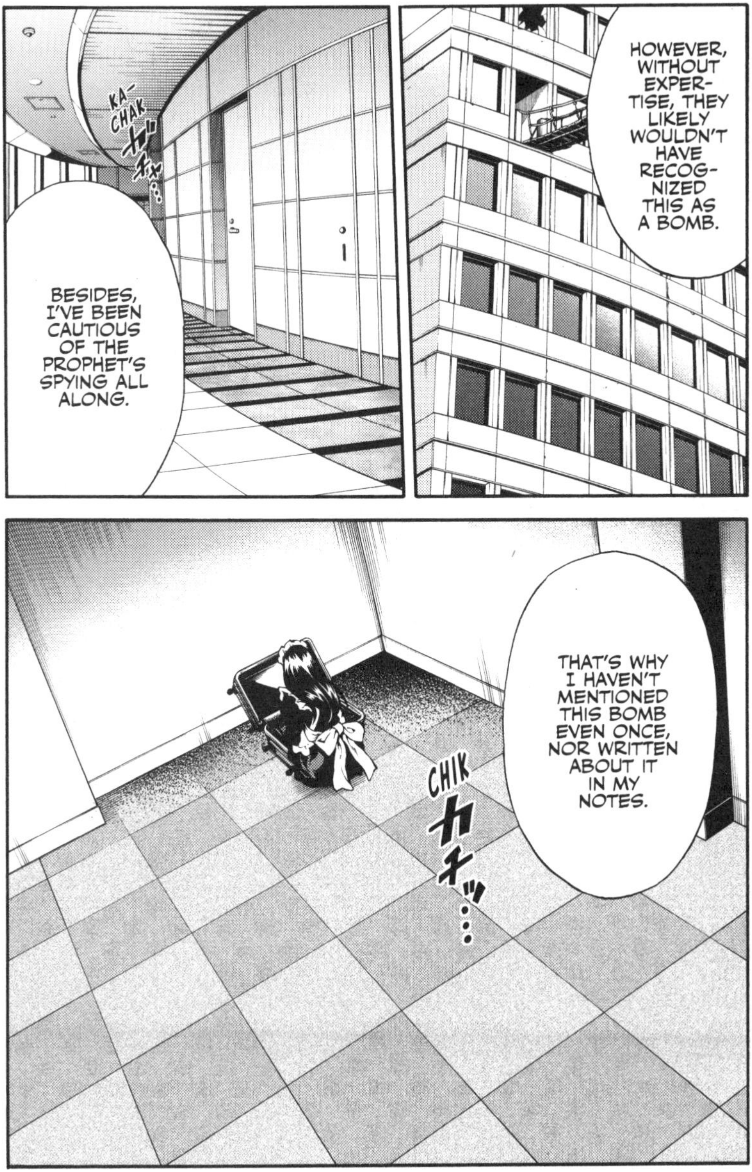
HOWEVER, WITHOUT EXPER- TISE, THEY LIKELY WOULDN'T HAVE RECOG- NIZED THIS AS A BOMB.
KA- CHAK
ガチャ…
BESIDES, I'VE BEEN CAUTIOUS OF THE PROPHET'S SPYING ALL ALONG.
THAT'S WHY I HAVEN'T MENTIONED THIS BOMB EVEN ONCE, NOR WRITTEN ABOUT IT IN MY NOTES.
CHIK
カチッ…

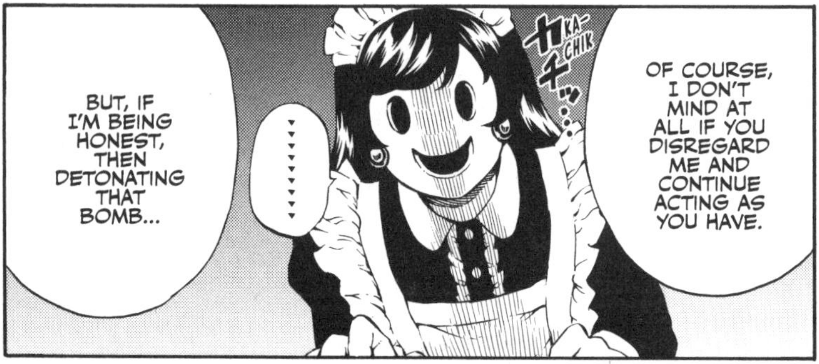
OF COURSE, I DON'T MIND AT ALL IF YOU DISREGARD ME AND CONTINUE ACTING AS YOU HAVE.
KA-CHIK
......
BUT, IF I'M BEING HONEST, THEN DETONATING THAT BOMB...

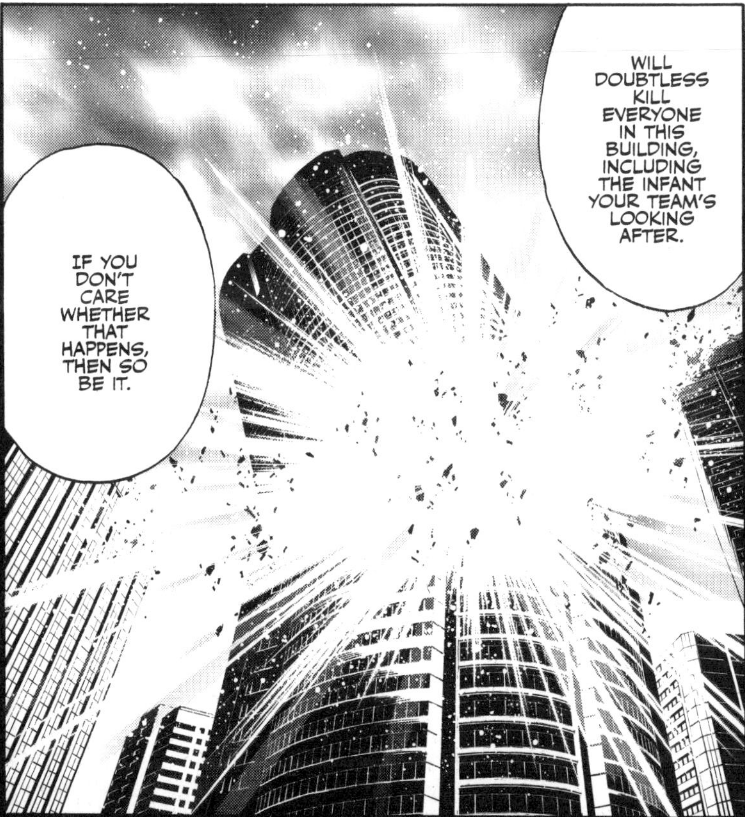
WILL DOUBTLESS KILL EVERYONE IN THIS BUILDING, INCLUDING THE INFANT YOUR TEAM'S LOOKING AFTER.
IF YOU DON'T CARE WHETHER THAT HAPPENS, THEN SO BE IT.

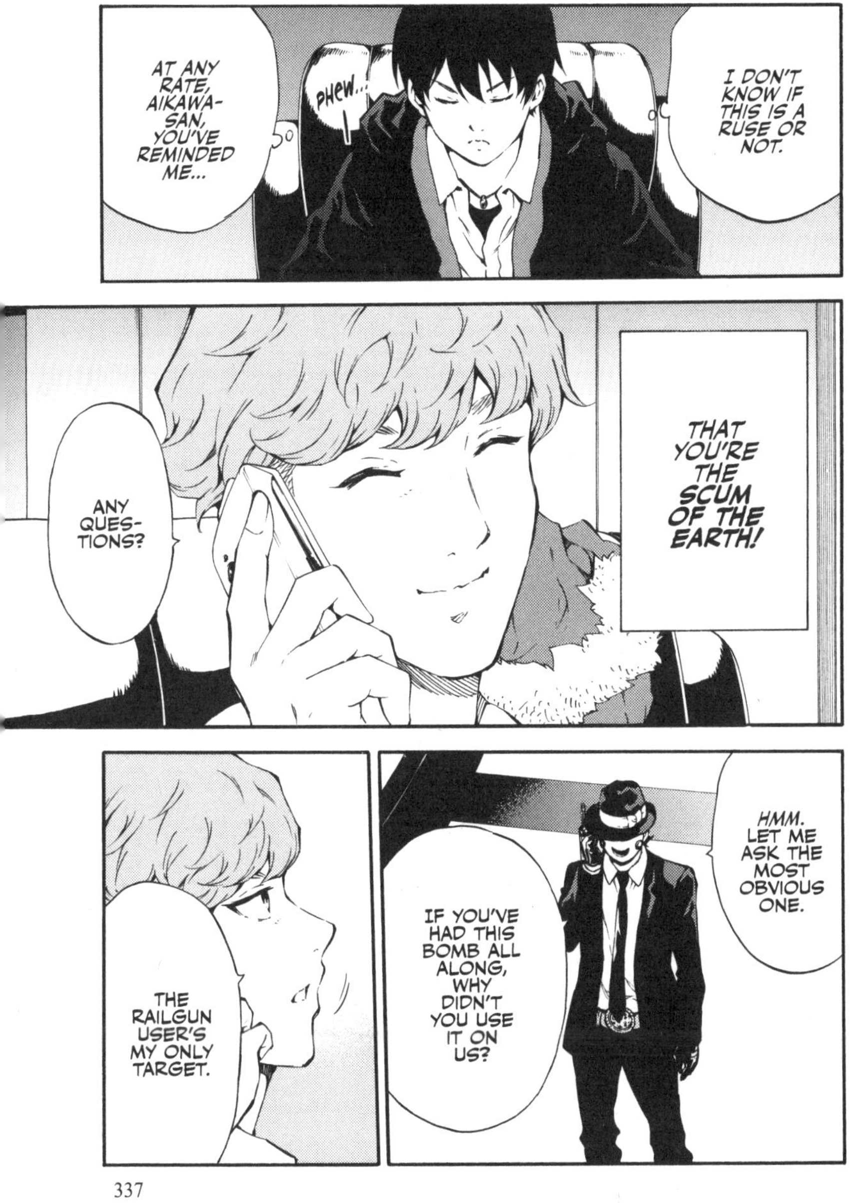
I DON'T KNOW IF THIS IS A RUSE OR NOT.
PHEW...
AT ANY RATE, AIKAWA-SAN, YOU'VE REMINDED ME...
THAT YOU'RE THE SCUM OF THE EARTH!
ANY QUES-TIONS?
HMM. LET ME ASK THE MOST OBVIOUS ONE.
IF YOU'VE HAD THIS BOMB ALL ALONG, WHY DIDN'T YOU USE IT ON US?
THE RAILGUN USER'S MY ONLY TARGET.

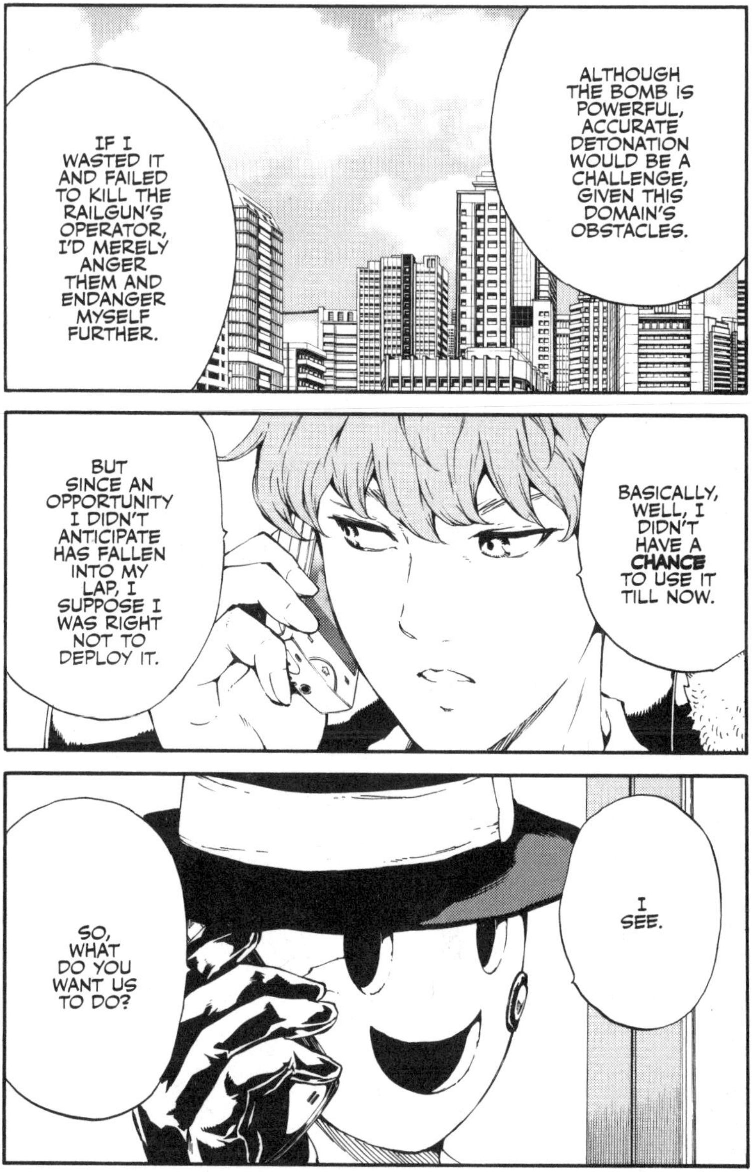
ALTHOUGH THE BOMB IS POWERFUL, ACCURATE DETONATION WOULD BE A CHALLENGE, GIVEN THIS DOMAIN'S OBSTACLES.
IF I WASTED IT AND FAILED TO KILL THE RAILGUN'S OPERATOR, I'D MERELY ANGER THEM AND ENDANGER MYSELF FURTHER.
BASICALLY, WELL, I DIDN'T HAVE A **CHANCE** TO USE IT TILL NOW.
BUT SINCE AN OPPORTUNITY I DIDN'T ANTICIPATE HAS FALLEN INTO MY LAP, I SUPPOSE I WAS RIGHT NOT TO DEPLOY IT.
I SEE.
SO, WHAT DO YOU WANT US TO DO?

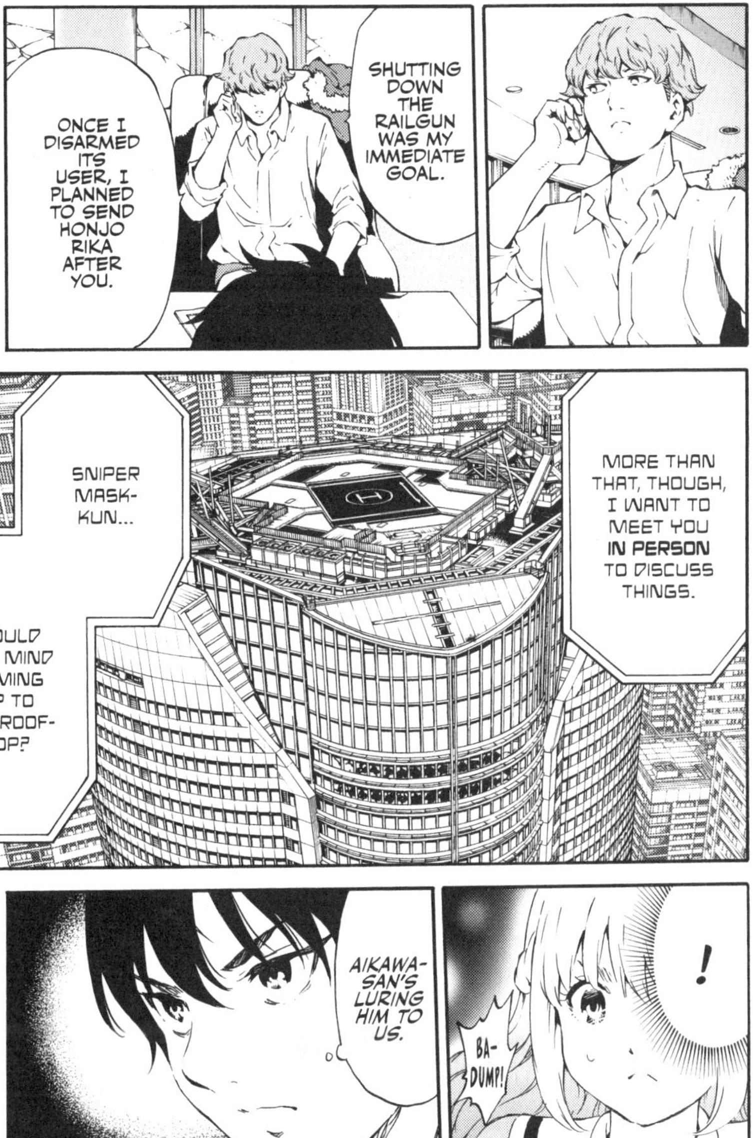
SHUTTING DOWN THE RAILGUN WAS MY IMMEDIATE GOAL.
ONCE I DISARMED ITS USER, I PLANNED TO SEND HONJO RIKA AFTER YOU.
MORE THAN THAT, THOUGH, I WANT TO MEET YOU **IN PERSON** TO DISCUSS THINGS.
SNIPER MASK-KUN...
WOULD YOU MIND COMING UP TO THE ROOF-TOP?
!
BA-DUMP!
AIKAWA-SAN'S LURING HIM TO US.

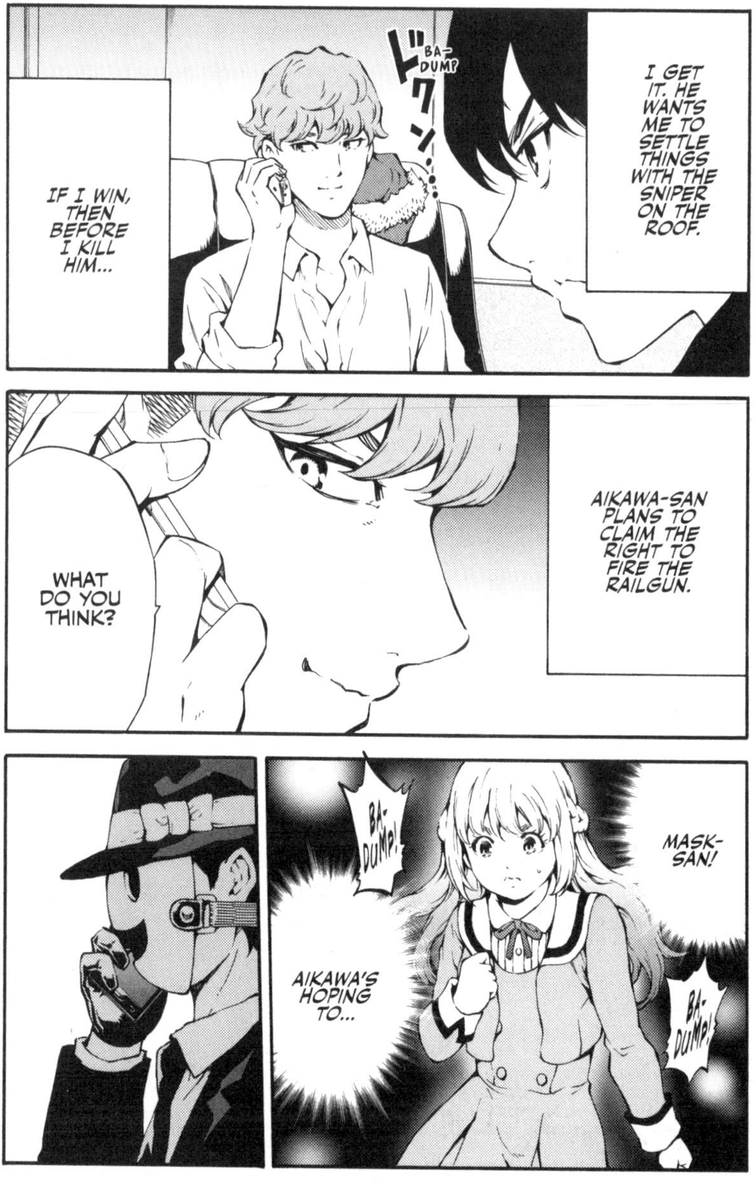
I GET IT. HE WANTS ME TO SETTLE THINGS WITH THE SNIPER ON THE ROOF.
BA-DUMP
ドクン
IF I WIN, THEN BEFORE I KILL HIM...
AIKAWA-SAN PLANS TO CLAIM THE RIGHT TO FIRE THE RAILGUN.
WHAT DO YOU THINK?
MASK-SAN!
BA-DUMP!
AIKAWA'S HOPING TO...
BA-DUMP!

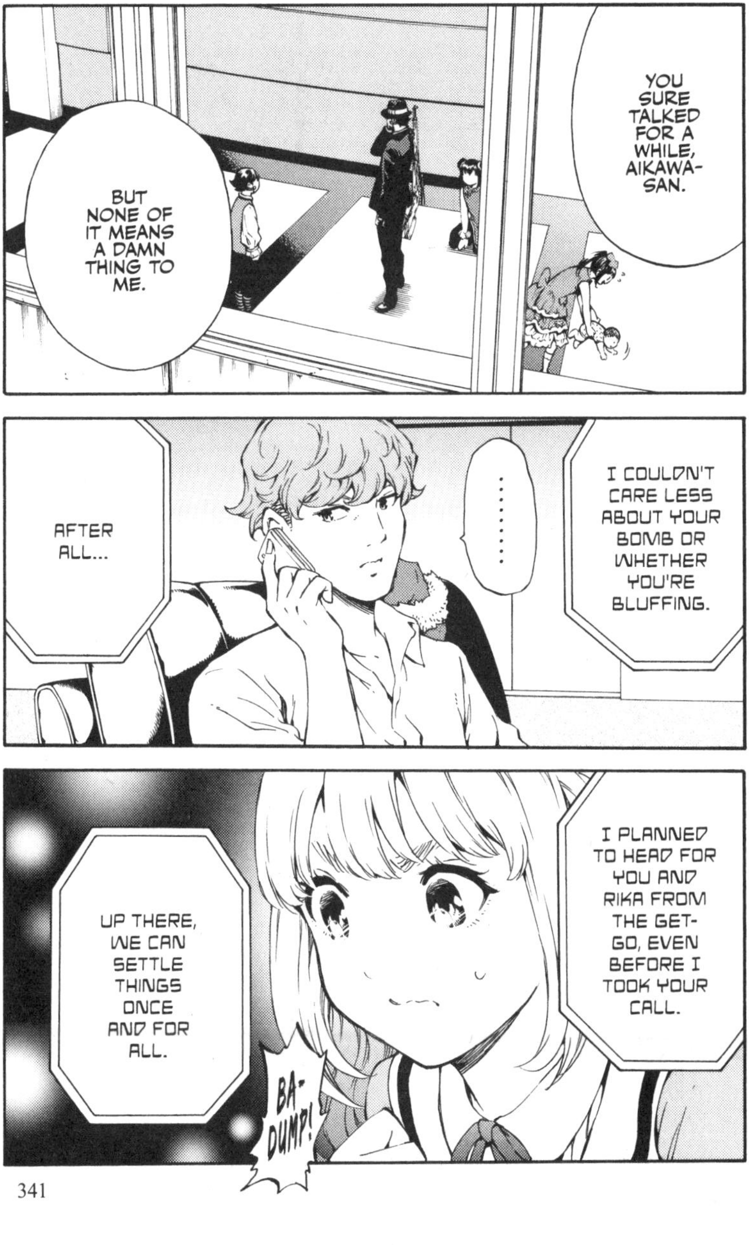
YOU SURE TALKED FOR A WHILE, AIKAWA-SAN.
BUT NONE OF IT MEANS A DAMN THING TO ME.
I COULDN'T CARE LESS ABOUT YOUR BOMB OR WHETHER YOU'RE BLUFFING.
....
AFTER ALL...
I PLANNED TO HEAD FOR YOU AND RIKA FROM THE GET-GO, EVEN BEFORE I TOOK YOUR CALL.
UP THERE, WE CAN SETTLE THINGS ONCE AND FOR ALL.
BA-DUMP!

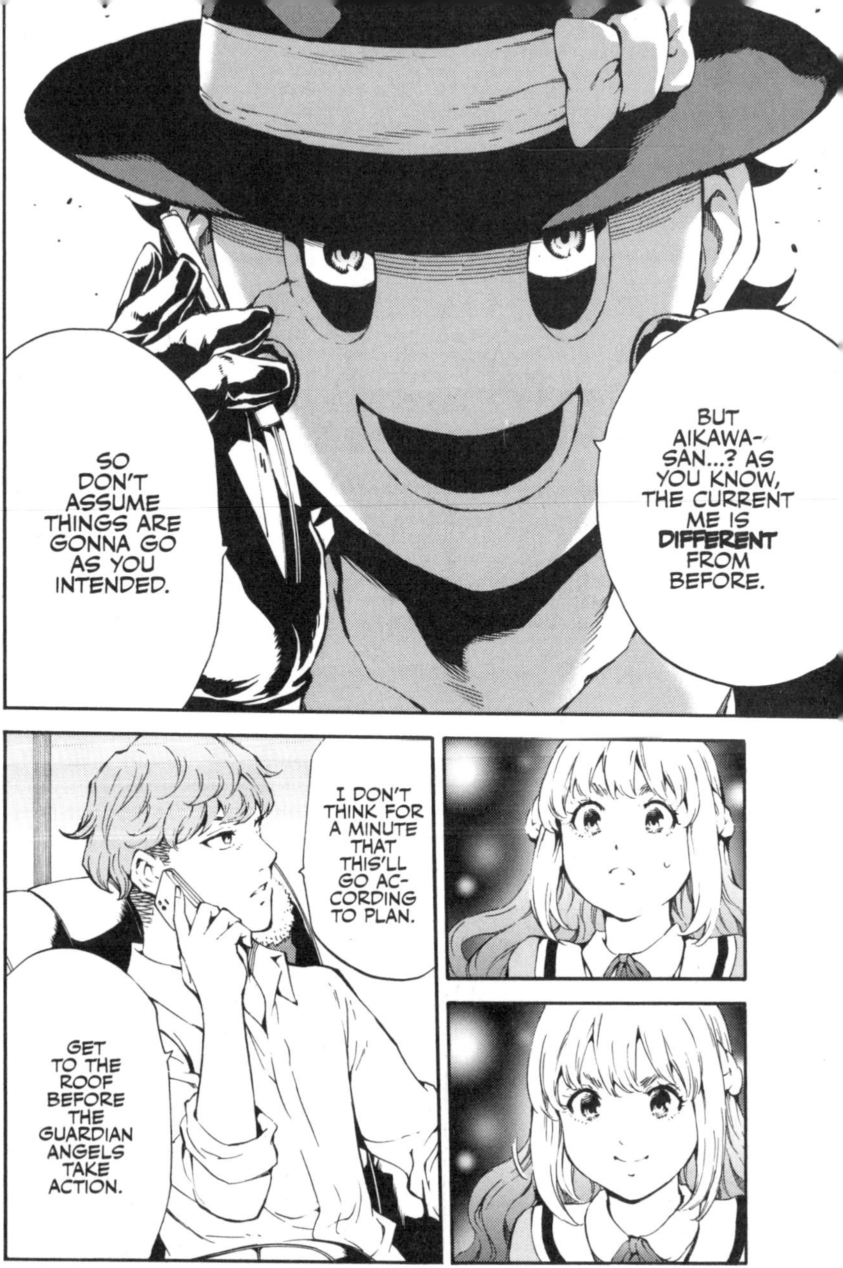
BUT AIKAWA-SAN...? AS YOU KNOW, THE CURRENT ME IS **DIFFERENT** FROM BEFORE.
SO DON'T ASSUME THINGS ARE GONNA GO AS YOU INTENDED.
I DON'T THINK FOR A MINUTE THAT THIS'LL GO AC-CORDING TO PLAN.
GET TO THE ROOF BEFORE THE GUARDIAN ANGELS TAKE ACTION.

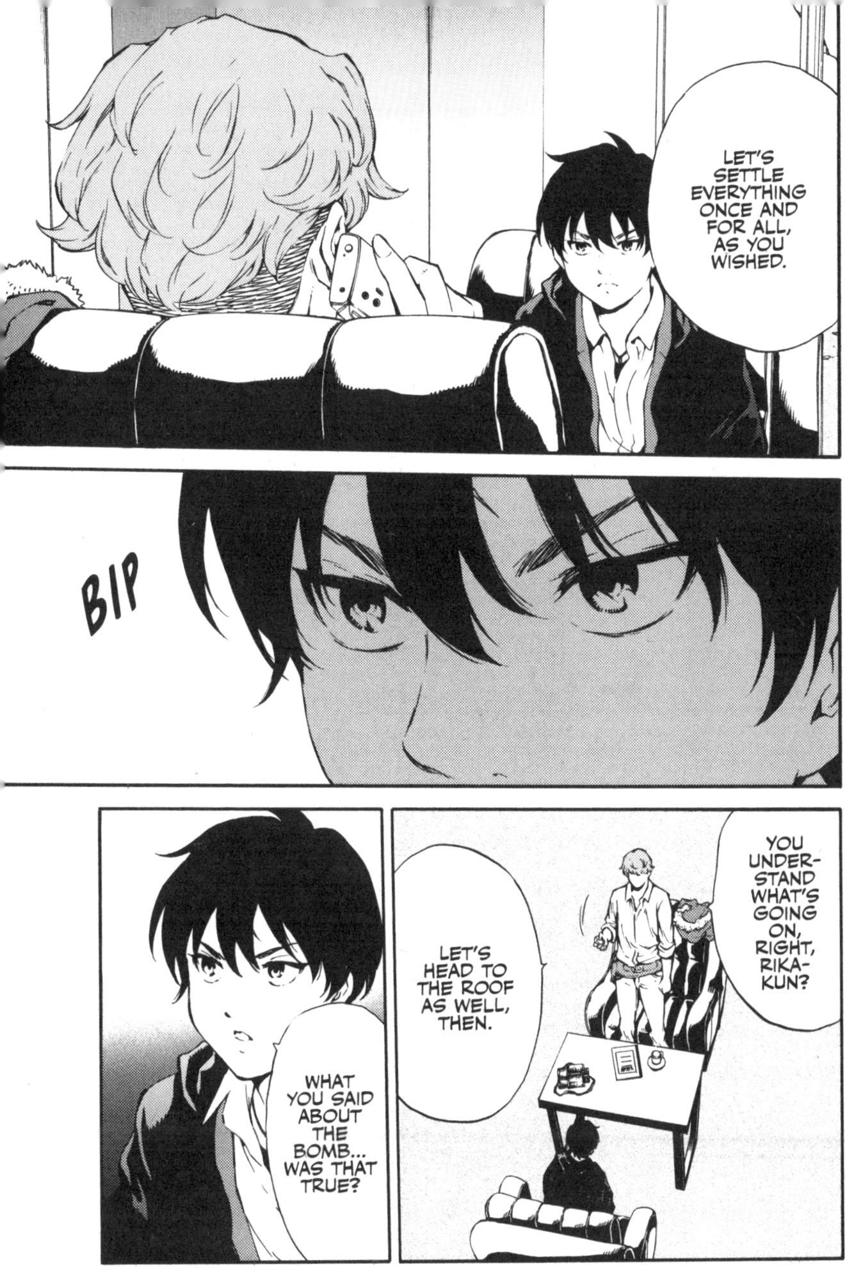
LET'S SETTLE EVERYTHING ONCE AND FOR ALL, AS YOU WISHED.
BIP
YOU UNDER-STAND WHAT'S GOING ON, RIGHT, RIKA-KUN?
LET'S HEAD TO THE ROOF AS WELL, THEN.
WHAT YOU SAID ABOUT THE BOMB... WAS THAT TRUE?

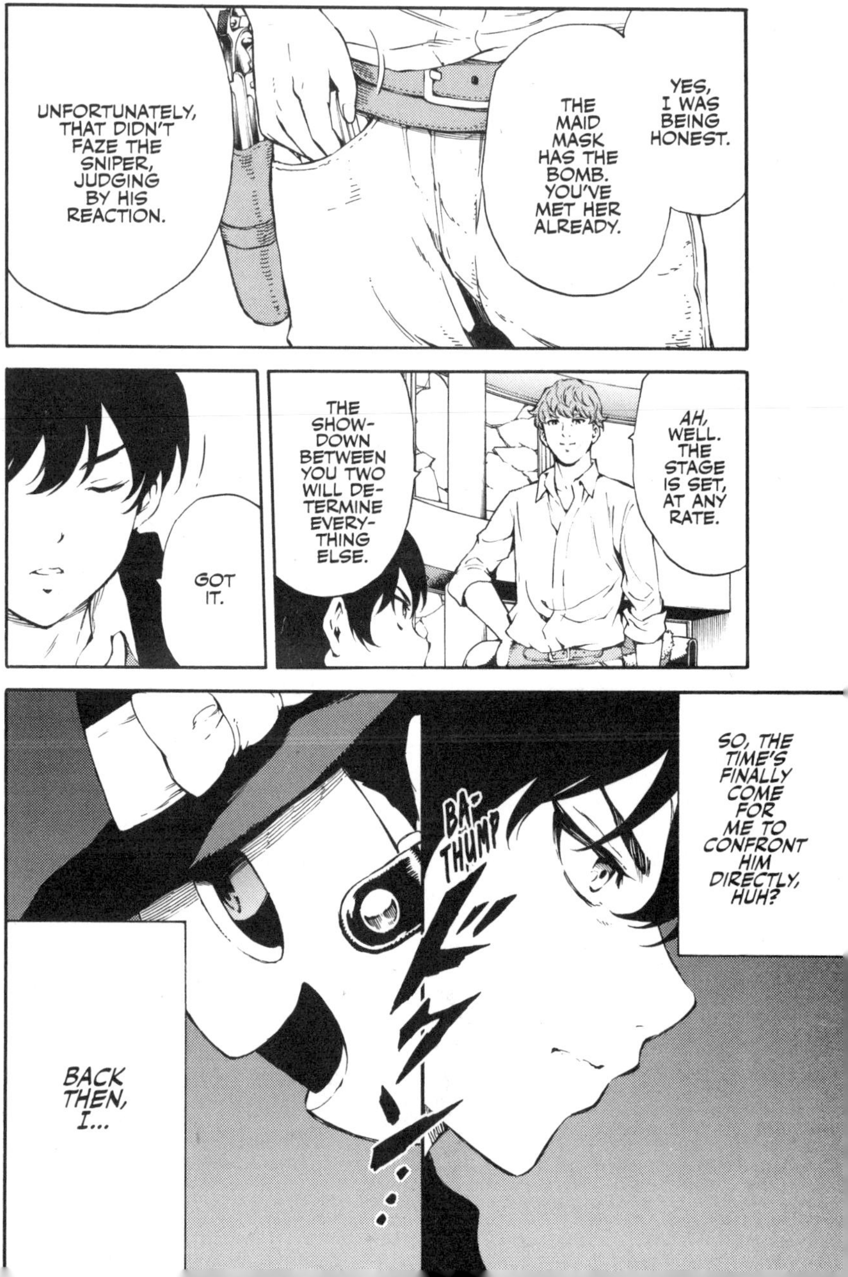
YES, I WAS BEING HONEST.
THE MAID MASK HAS THE BOMB. YOU'VE MET HER ALREADY.
UNFORTUNATELY, THAT DIDN'T FAZE THE SNIPER, JUDGING BY HIS REACTION.
AH, WELL. THE STAGE IS SET, AT ANY RATE.
THE SHOW-DOWN BETWEEN YOU TWO WILL DE-TERMINE EVERY-THING ELSE.
GOT IT.
SO, THE TIME'S FINALLY COME FOR ME TO CONFRONT HIM DIRECTLY, HUH?
BA-THUMP
BACK THEN, I...

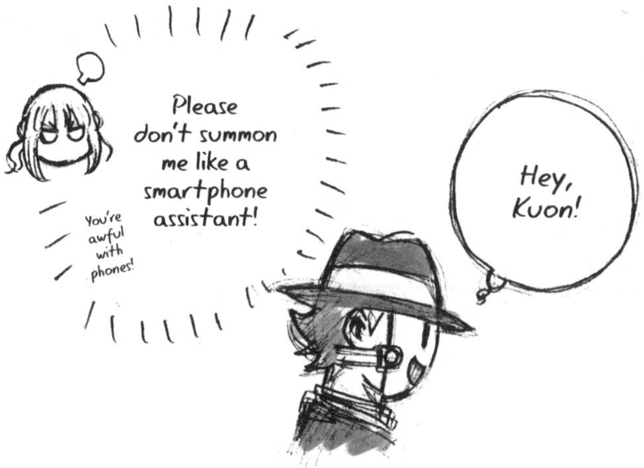
Hey, Kuon!
Please don't summon me like a smartphone assistant!
You're awful with phones!

HIGH-RISE INVASION

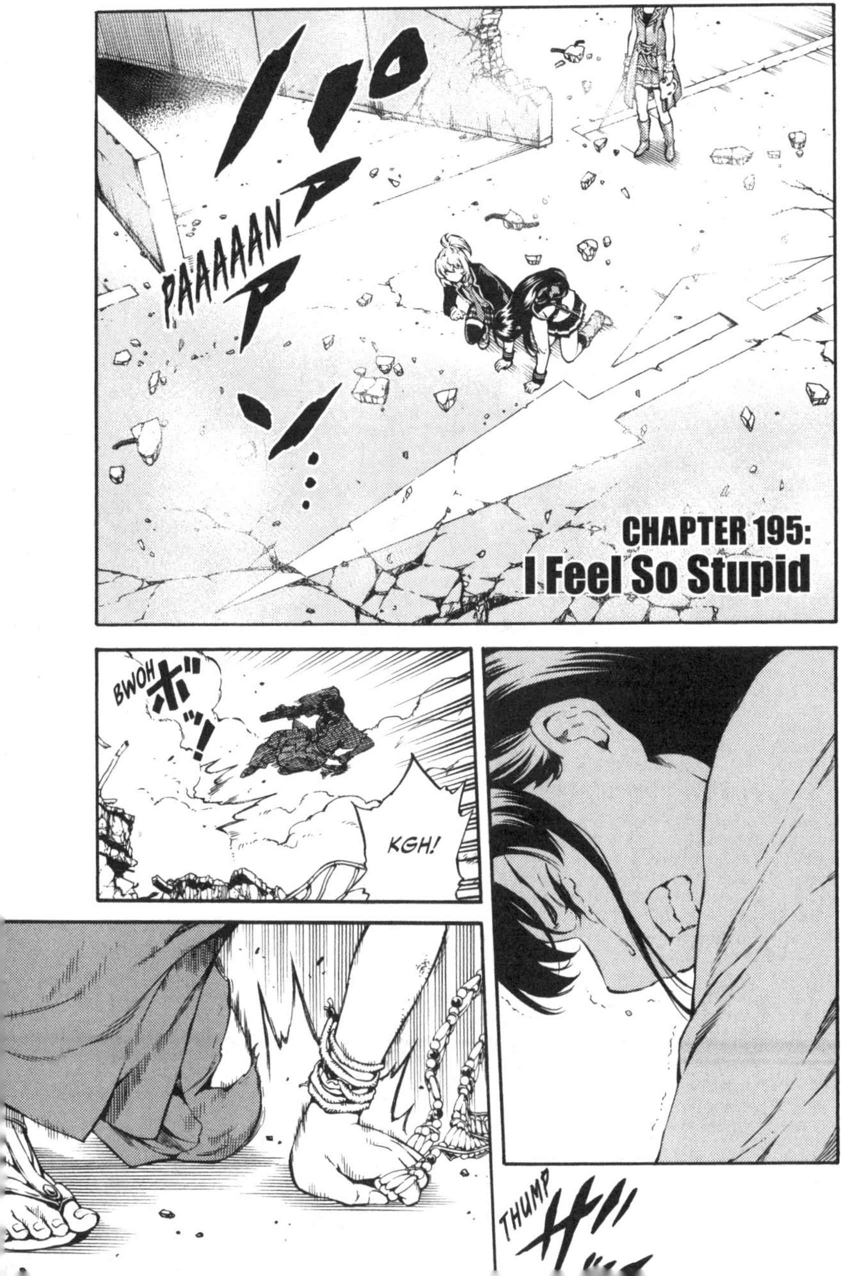
PAAAAAN
CHAPTER 195:
I Feel So Stupid
BWOH
KGH!
THUMP

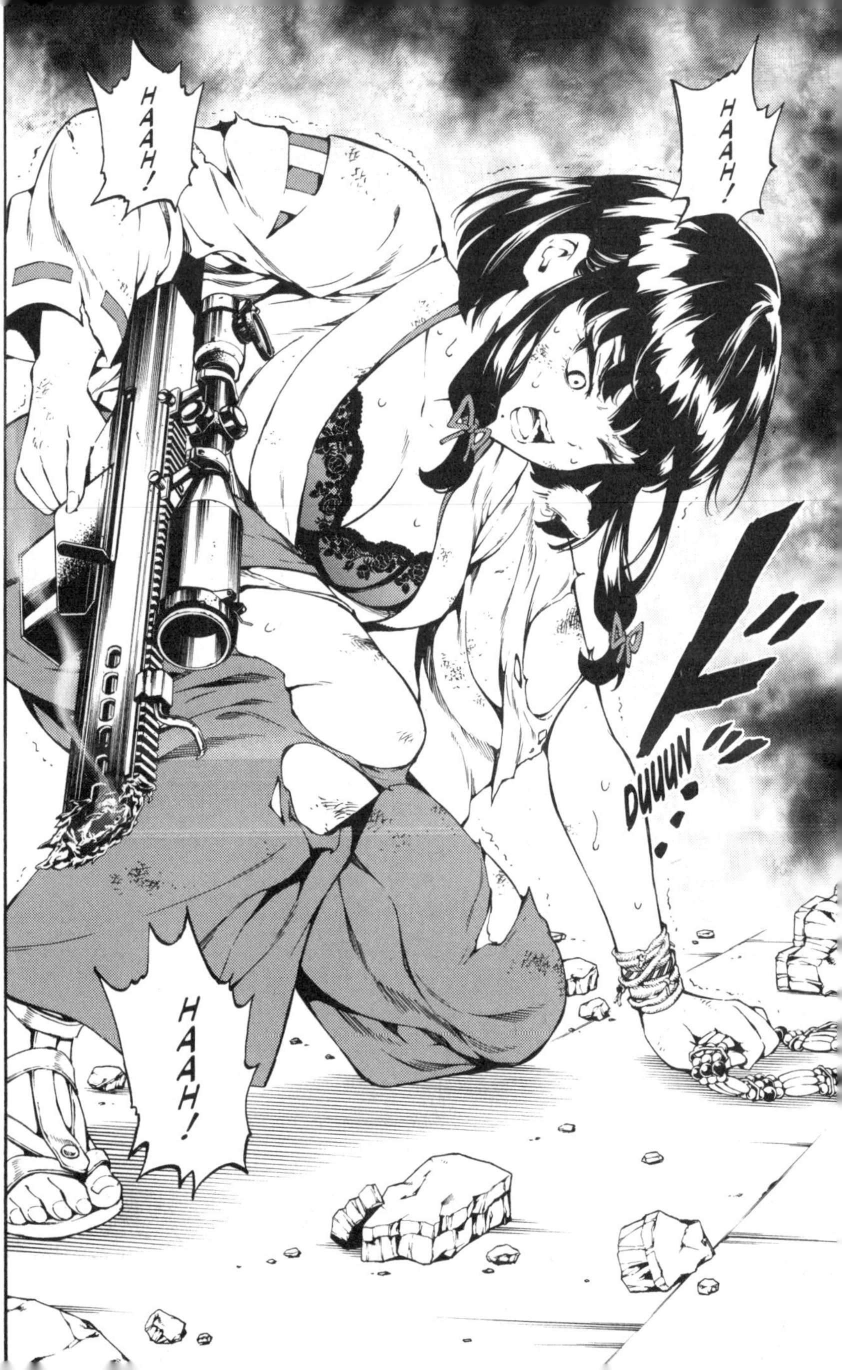
HAAAH!
DUUUN!
HAAAH!
HAAAH!

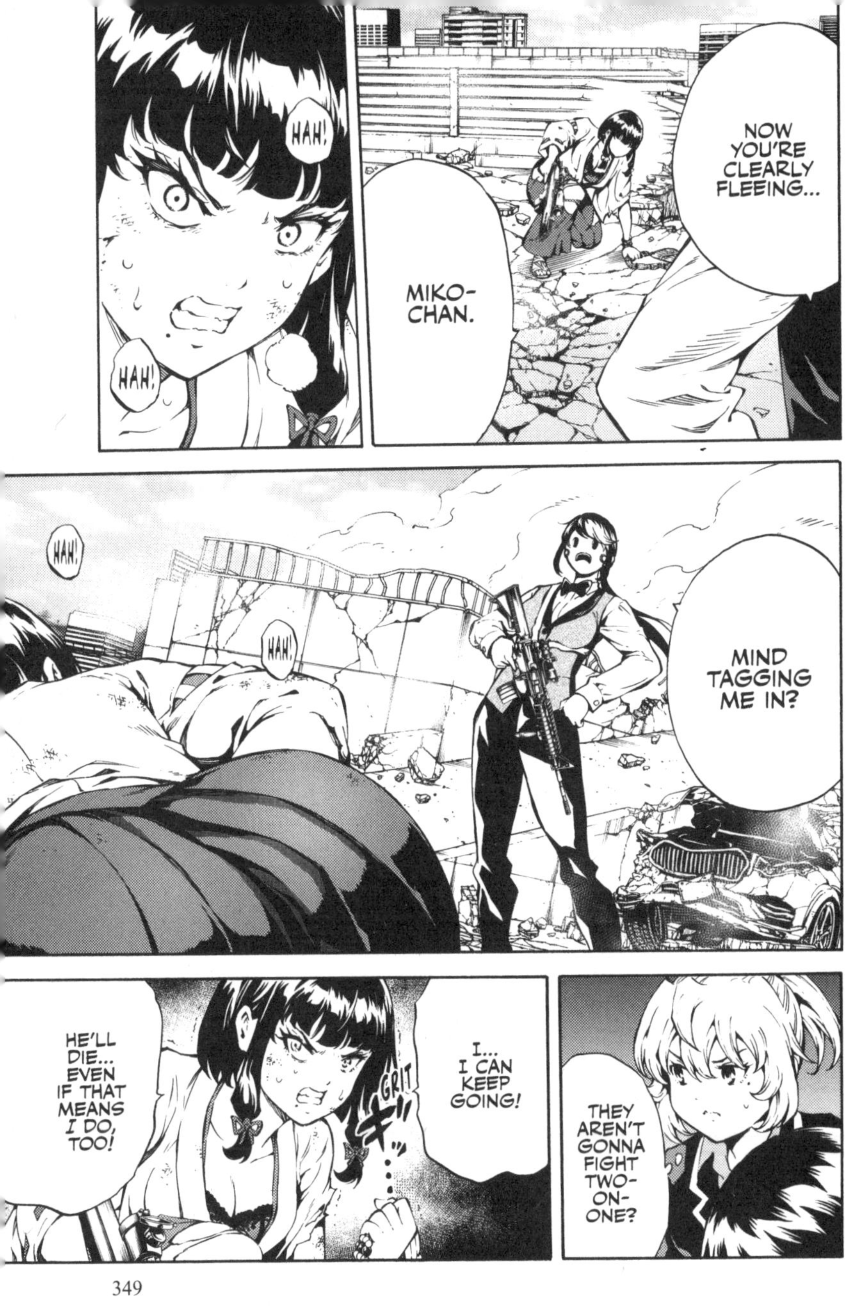
NOW YOU'RE CLEARLY FLEEING...
MIKO-CHAN.
HAH!
HAH!
MIND TAGGING ME IN?
HAH!
HAH!
THEY AREN'T GONNA FIGHT TWO-ON-ONE?
I... I CAN KEEP GOING!
GRIT
HE'LL DIE... EVEN IF THAT MEANS I DO, TOO!

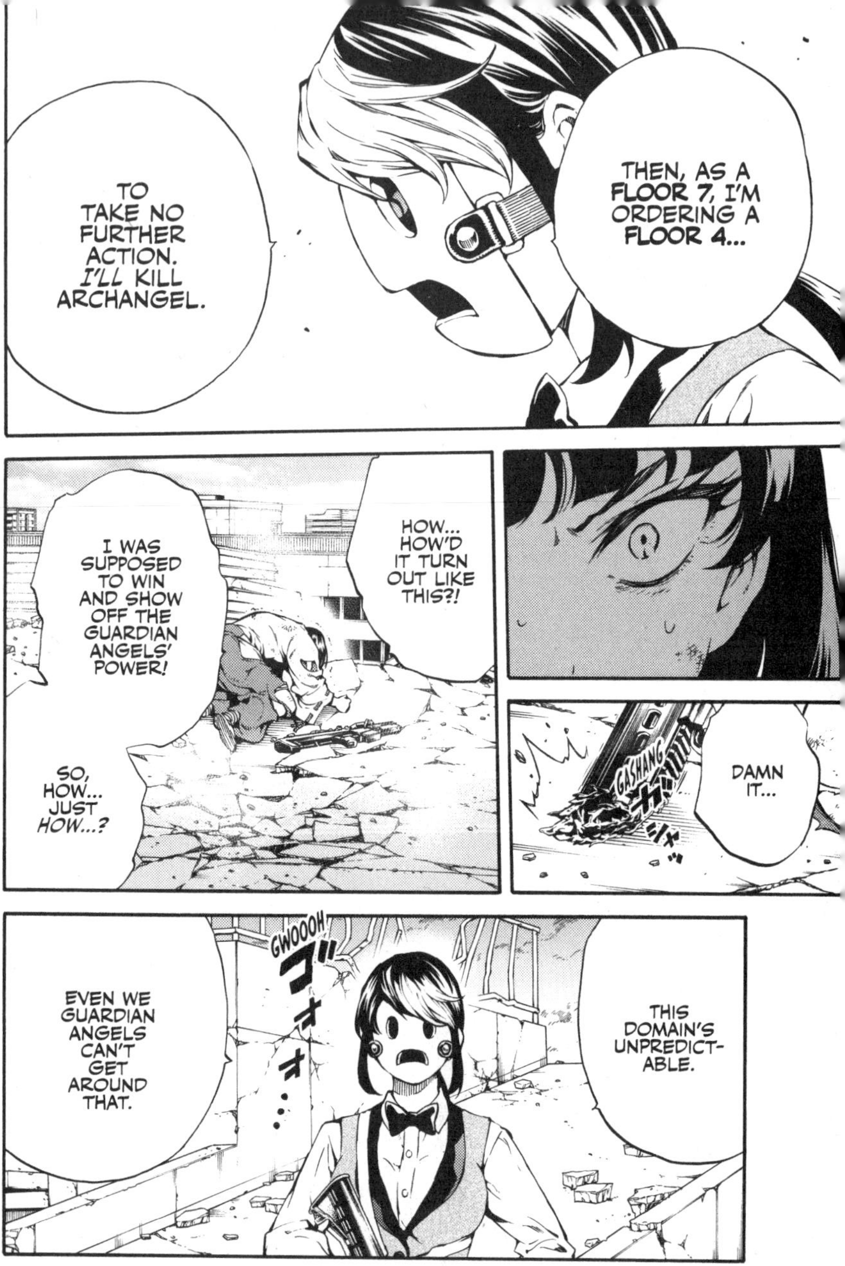
THEN, AS A FLOOR 7, I'M ORDERING A FLOOR 4...
TO TAKE NO FURTHER ACTION. *I'LL* KILL ARCHANGEL.
GASHANG
DAMN IT...
HOW... HOW'D IT TURN OUT LIKE THIS?!
I WAS SUPPOSED TO WIN AND SHOW OFF THE GUARDIAN ANGELS' POWER!
SO, HOW... JUST *HOW...?*
GWOOOH
THIS DOMAIN'S UNPREDICT-ABLE.
EVEN WE GUARDIAN ANGELS CAN'T GET AROUND THAT.

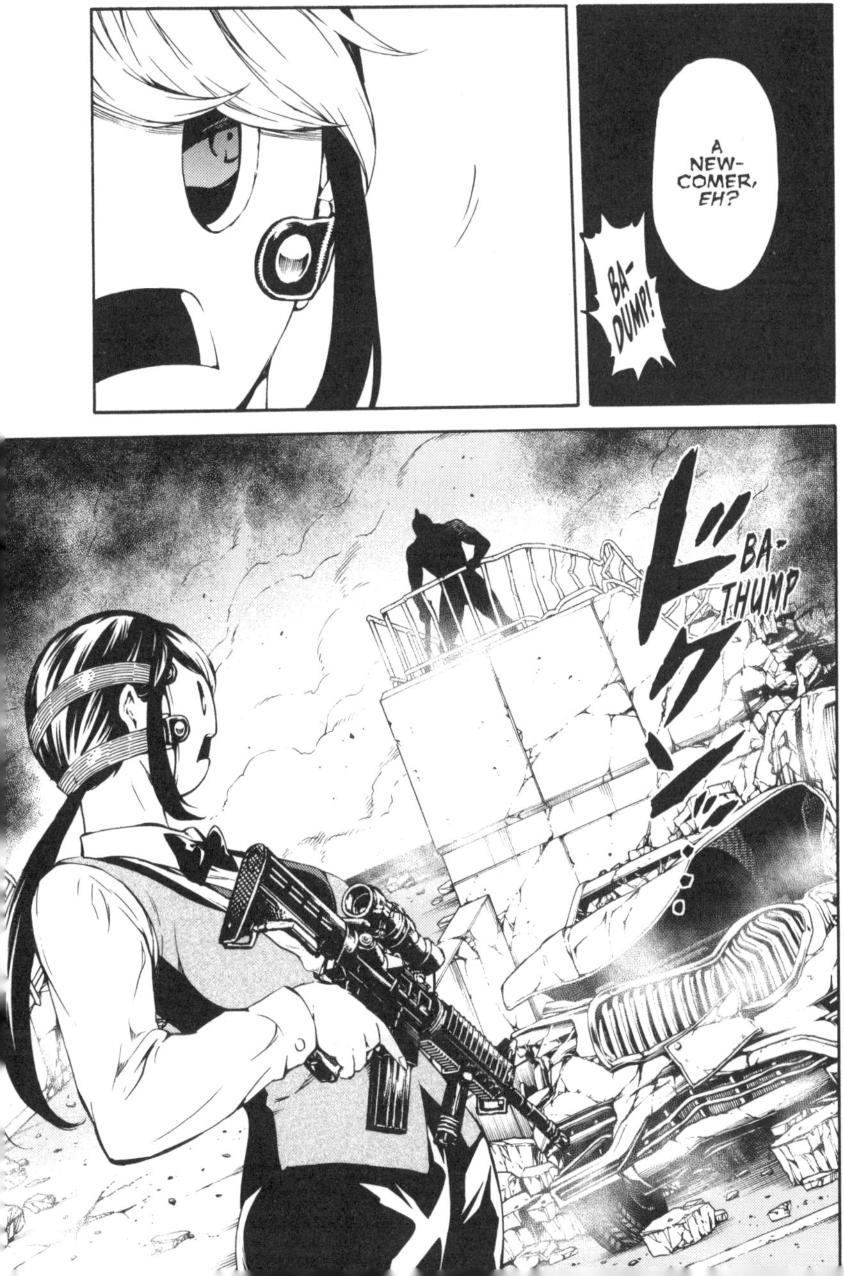
A NEW-COMER, EH?
BA-DUMP!
BA-THUMP

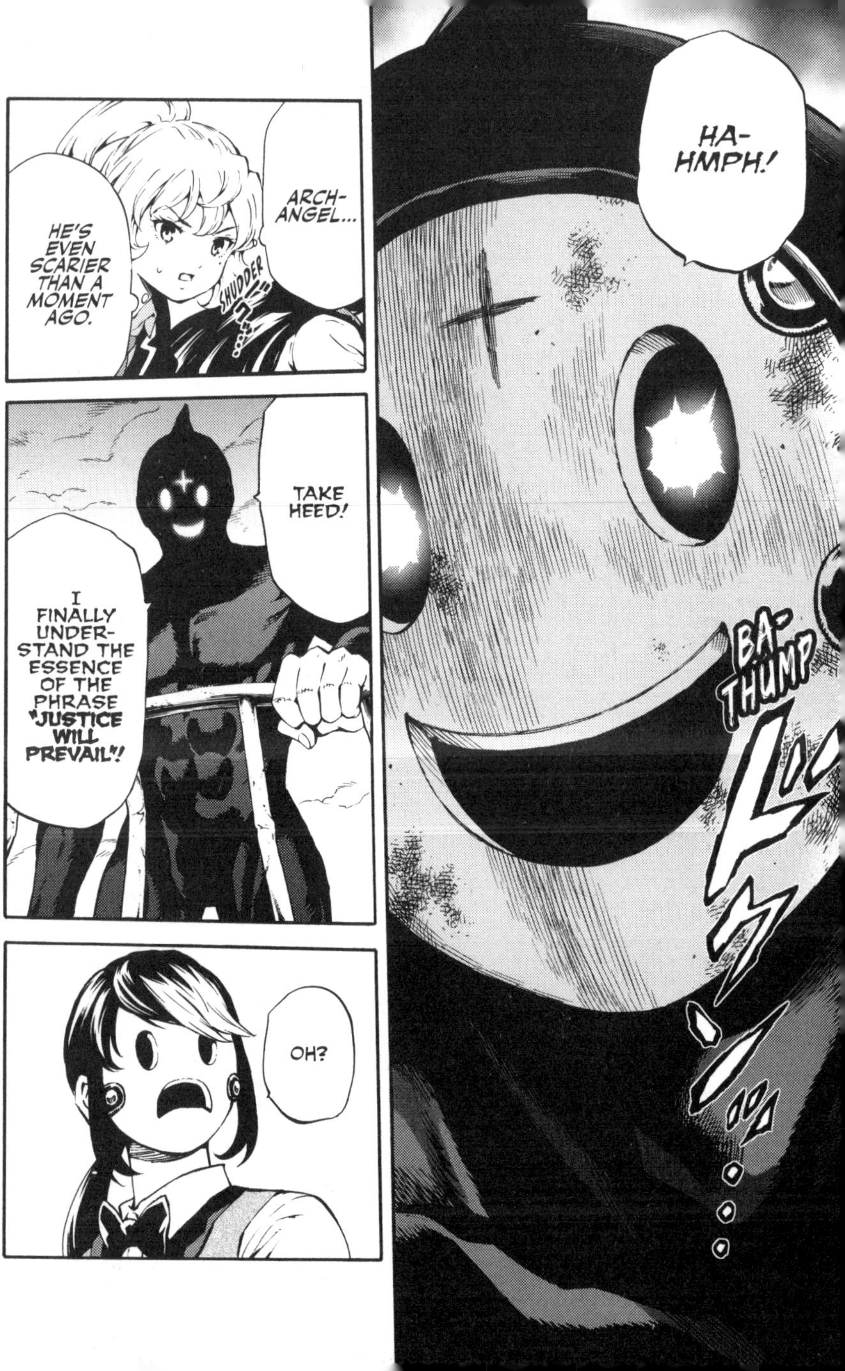

HA-HMPH!
BA-THUMP
ARCH-ANGEL...
SHUDDER
HE'S EVEN SCARIER THAN A MOMENT AGO.
TAKE HEED!
I FINALLY UNDERSTAND THE ESSENCE OF THE PHRASE "JUSTICE WILL PREVAIL"!
OH?

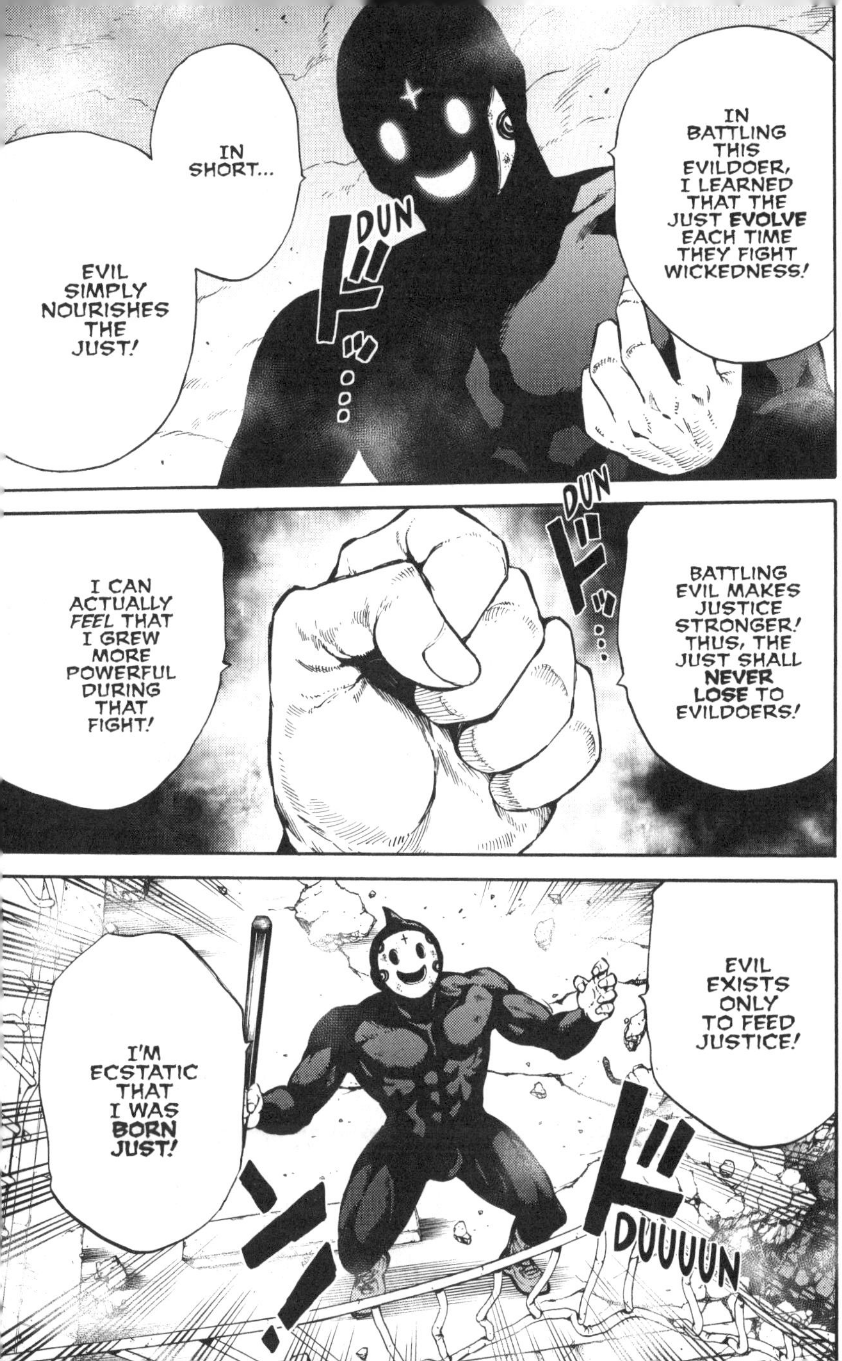

IN BATTLING THIS EVILDOER, I LEARNED THAT THE JUST **EVOLVE** EACH TIME THEY FIGHT WICKEDNESS!
DUN
IN SHORT...
EVIL SIMPLY NOURISHES THE JUST!
DUN
BATTLING EVIL MAKES JUSTICE STRONGER! THUS, THE JUST SHALL **NEVER LOSE** TO EVILDOERS!
I CAN ACTUALLY *FEEL* THAT I GREW MORE POWERFUL DURING THAT FIGHT!
EVIL EXISTS ONLY TO FEED JUSTICE!
I'M ECSTATIC THAT I WAS **BORN JUST**!
DUUUUN

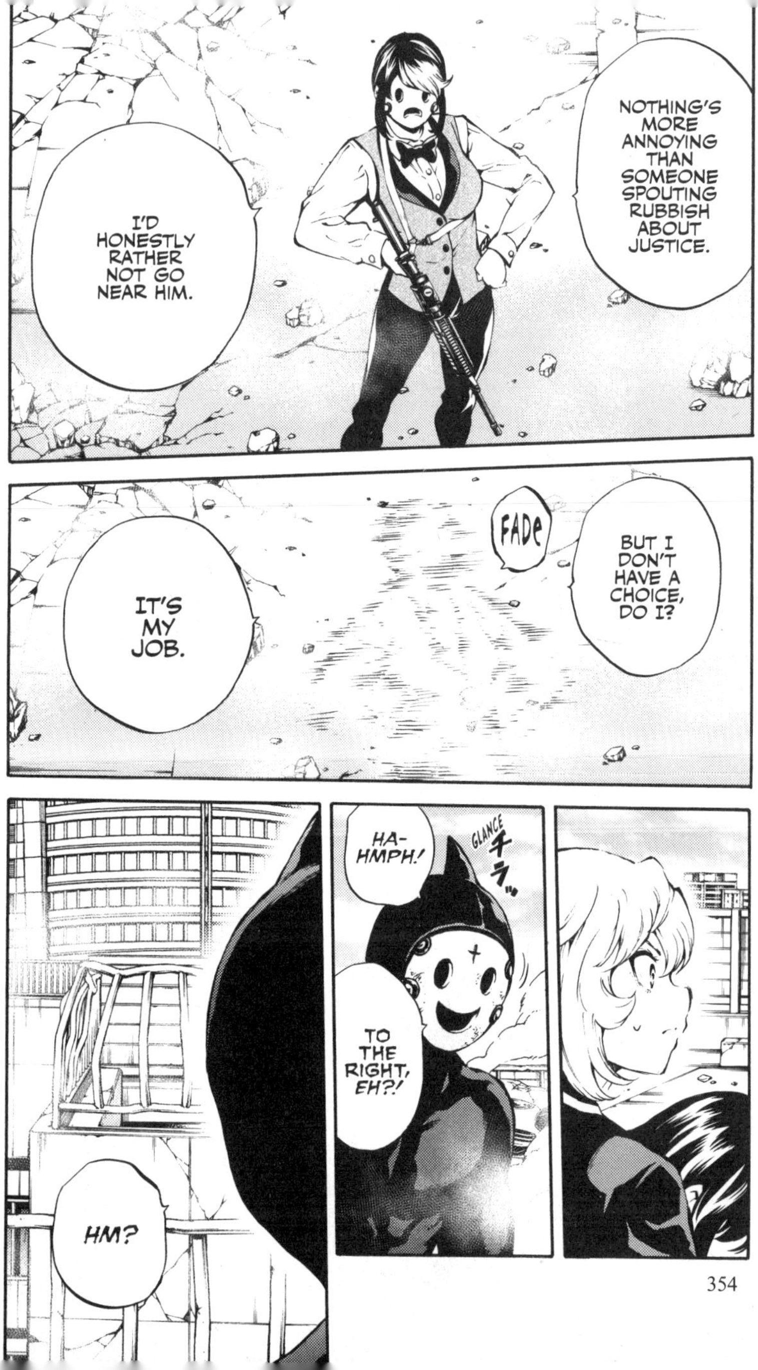
NOTHING'S MORE ANNOYING THAN SOMEONE SPOUTING RUBBISH ABOUT JUSTICE.
I'D HONESTLY RATHER NOT GO NEAR HIM.
FADE
BUT I DON'T HAVE A CHOICE, DO I?
IT'S MY JOB.
GLANCE
チラッ
HA-HMPH!
TO THE RIGHT, EH?!
HM?

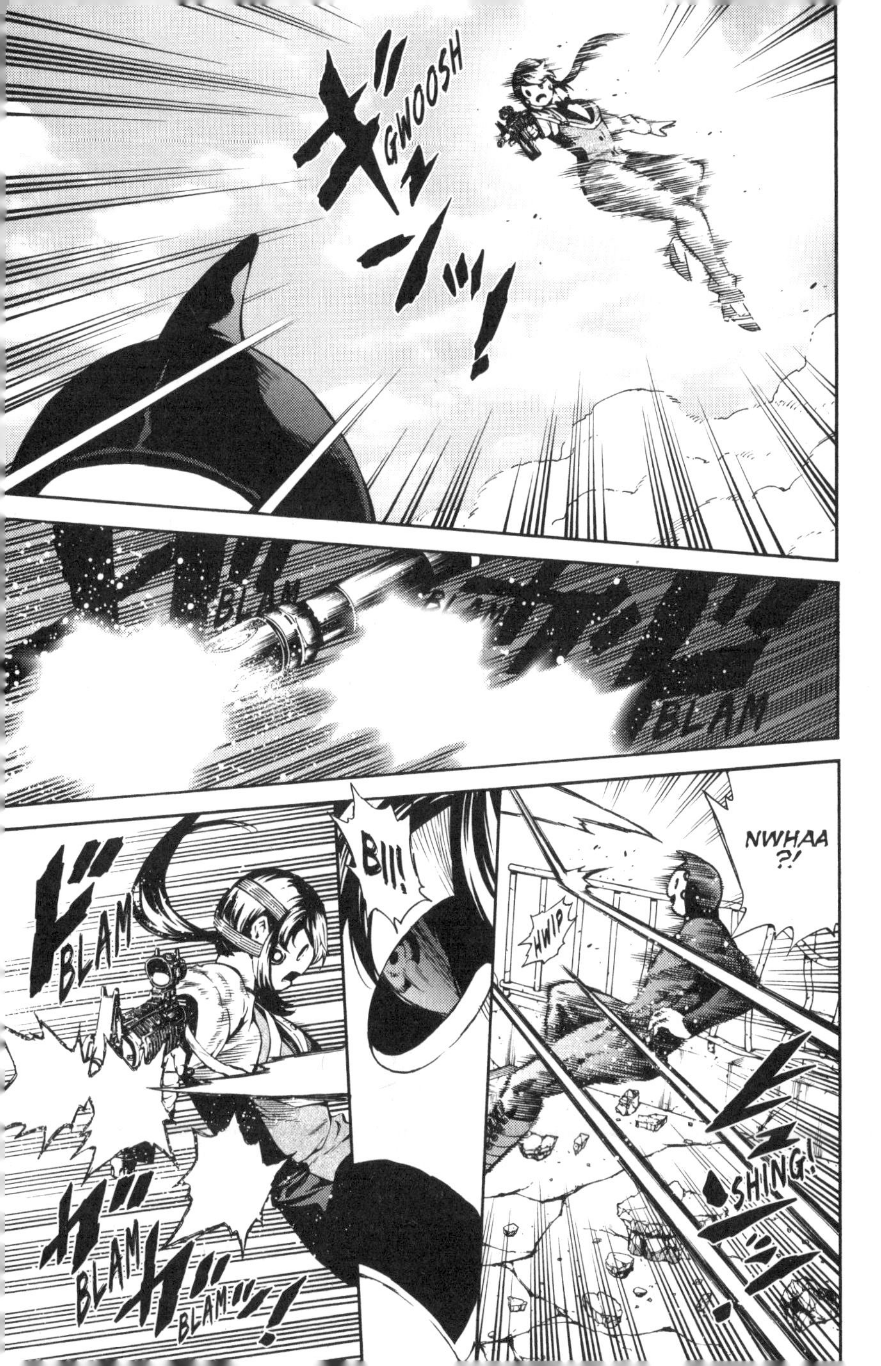
GWOOSH
BLAM
BLAM
NWHAA ?!
HWIP
SHING!
BII!
BLAM
BLAM
BLAM

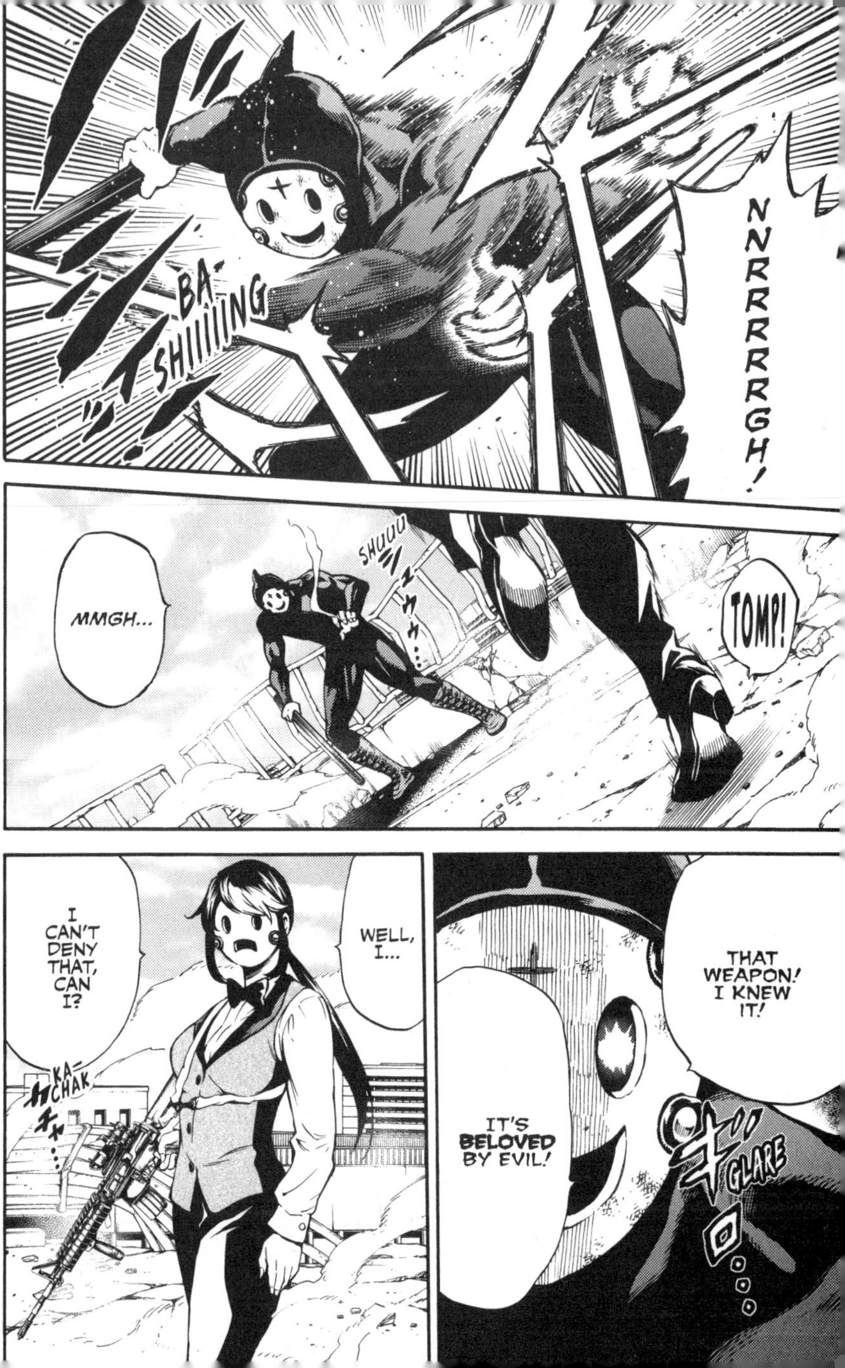
NNRRRRRGH!
BA SHIIIIING
TOMP!
SHUUU
MMGH...
THAT WEAPON! I KNEW IT!
IT'S BELOVED BY EVIL!
GLARE
WELL, I...
I CAN'T DENY THAT, CAN I?
KA CHAK

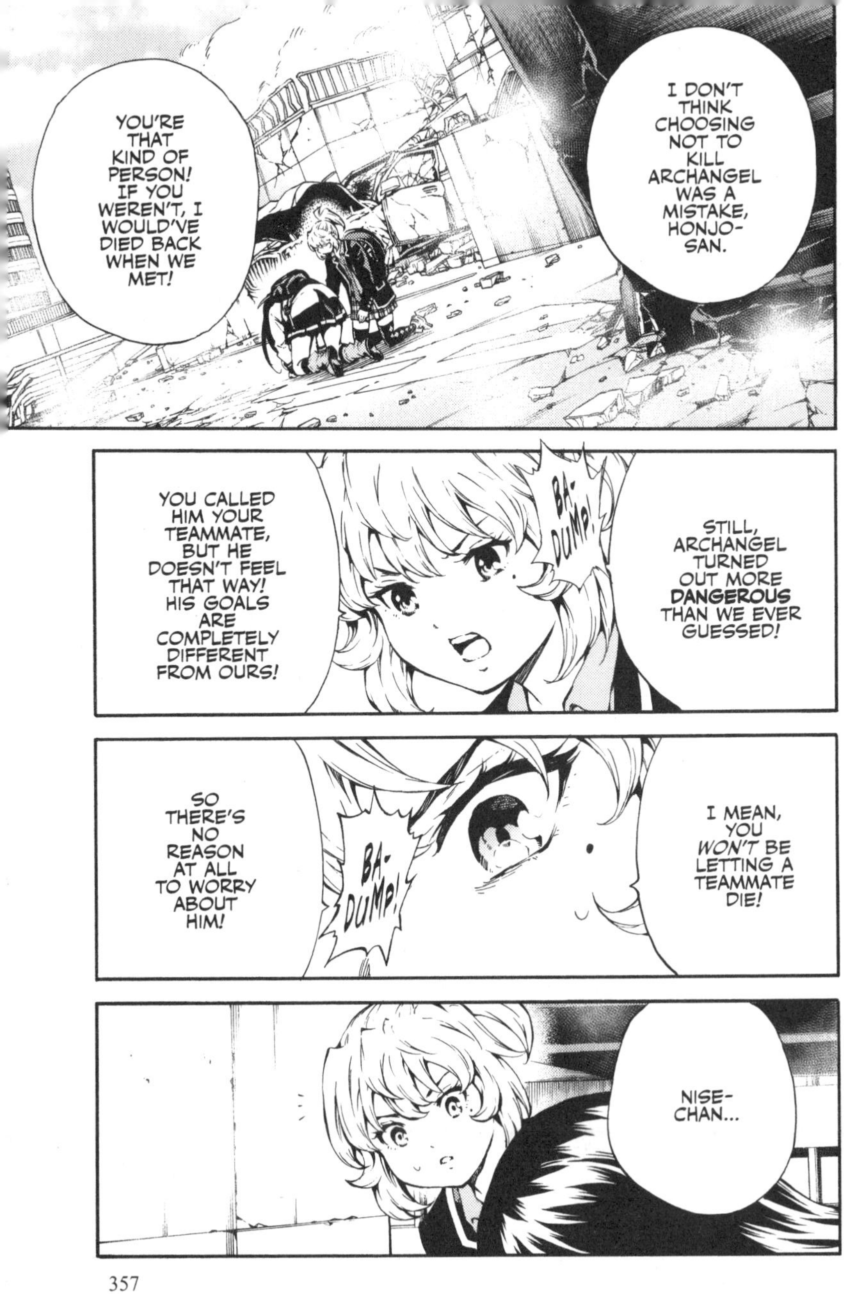
I DON'T THINK CHOOSING NOT TO KILL ARCHANGEL WAS A MISTAKE, HONJO-SAN.
YOU'RE THAT KIND OF PERSON! IF YOU WEREN'T, I WOULD'VE DIED BACK WHEN WE MET!
STILL, ARCHANGEL TURNED OUT MORE **DANGEROUS** THAN WE EVER GUESSED!
BA-DUMP!
YOU CALLED HIM YOUR TEAMMATE, BUT HE DOESN'T FEEL THAT WAY! HIS GOALS ARE COMPLETELY DIFFERENT FROM OURS!
I MEAN, YOU *WON'T* BE LETTING A TEAMMATE DIE!
BA-DUMP!
SO THERE'S NO REASON AT ALL TO WORRY ABOUT HIM!
NISE-CHAN...

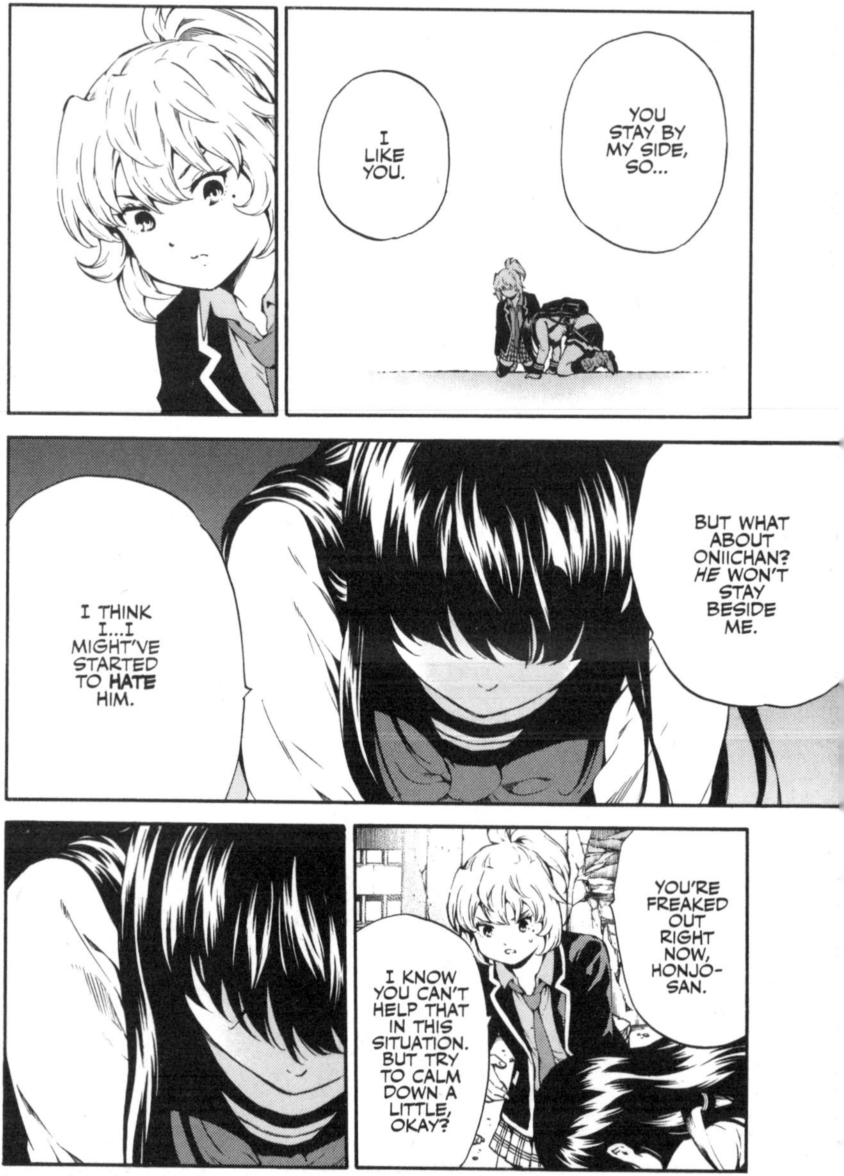
YOU STAY BY MY SIDE, SO...
I LIKE YOU.
BUT WHAT ABOUT ONIICHAN? *HE* WON'T STAY BESIDE ME.
I THINK I...I MIGHT'VE STARTED TO **HATE** HIM.
YOU'RE FREAKED OUT RIGHT NOW, HONJO-SAN.
I KNOW YOU CAN'T HELP THAT IN THIS SITUATION. BUT TRY TO CALM DOWN A LITTLE, OKAY?

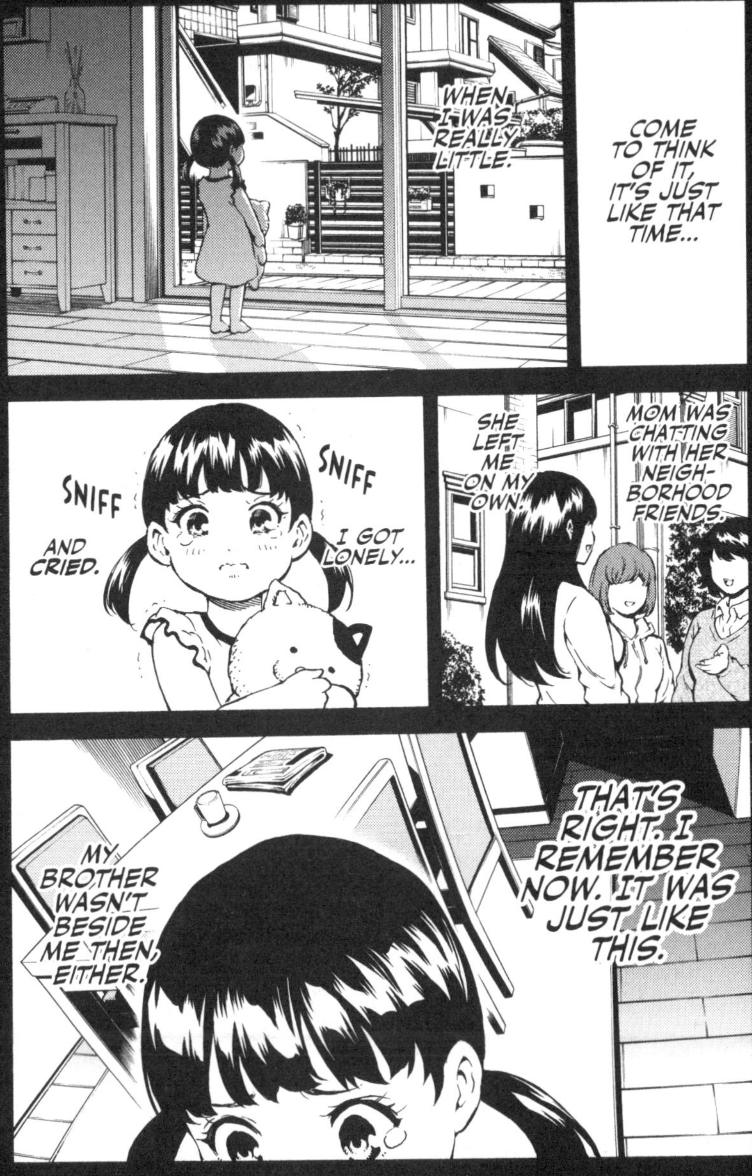
COME TO THINK OF IT, IT'S JUST LIKE THAT TIME...
WHEN I WAS REALLY LITTLE.
MOM WAS CHATTING WITH HER NEIGH-BORHOOD FRIENDS.
SHE LEFT ME ON MY OWN.
SNIFF
I GOT LONELY...
SNIFF
AND CRIED.
THAT'S RIGHT. I REMEMBER NOW. IT WAS JUST LIKE THIS.
MY BROTHER WASN'T BESIDE ME THEN, EITHER.

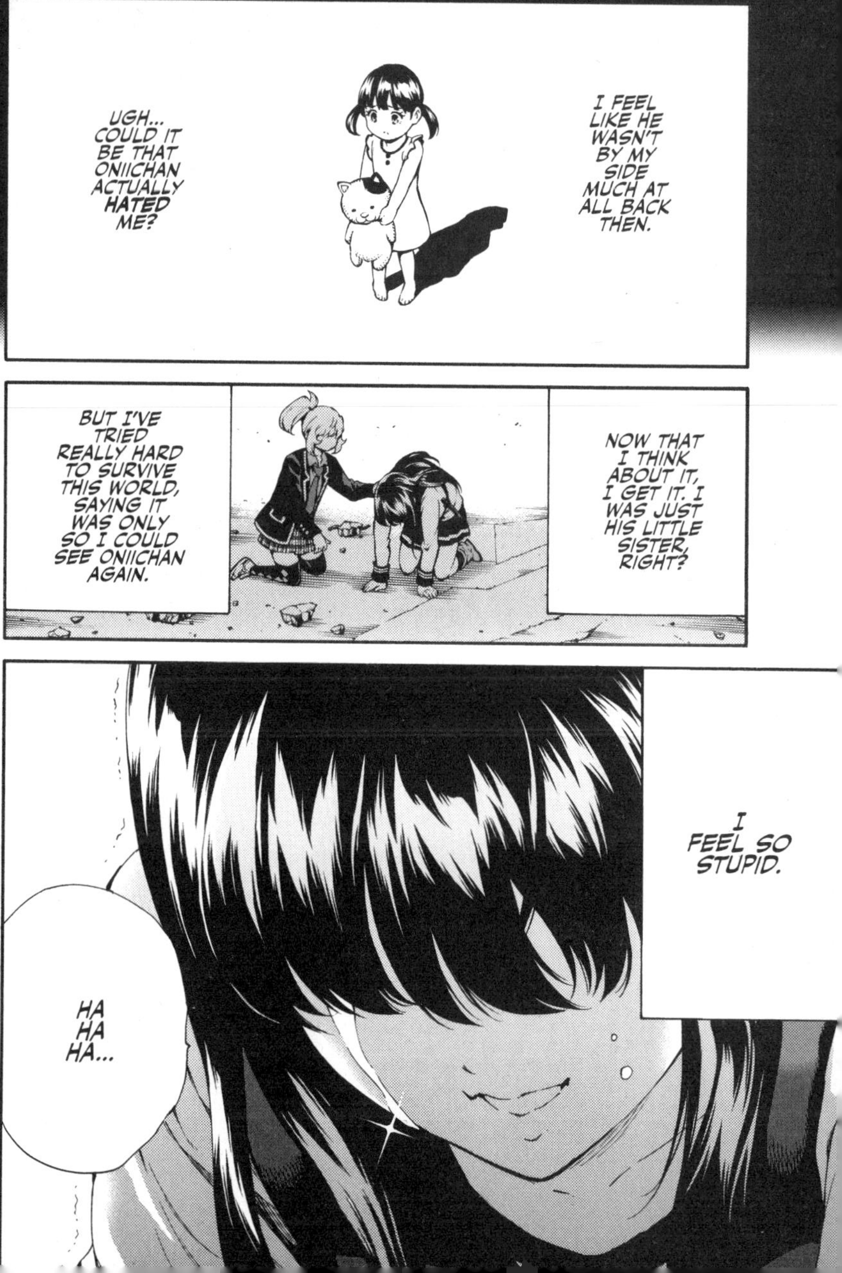
I FEEL LIKE HE WASN'T BY MY SIDE MUCH AT ALL BACK THEN.
UGH... COULD IT BE THAT ONIICHAN ACTUALLY **HATED** ME?
NOW THAT I THINK ABOUT IT, I GET IT. I WAS JUST HIS LITTLE SISTER, RIGHT?
BUT I'VE TRIED REALLY HARD TO SURVIVE THIS WORLD, SAYING IT WAS ONLY SO I COULD SEE ONIICHAN AGAIN.
I FEEL SO STUPID.
HA HA HA...

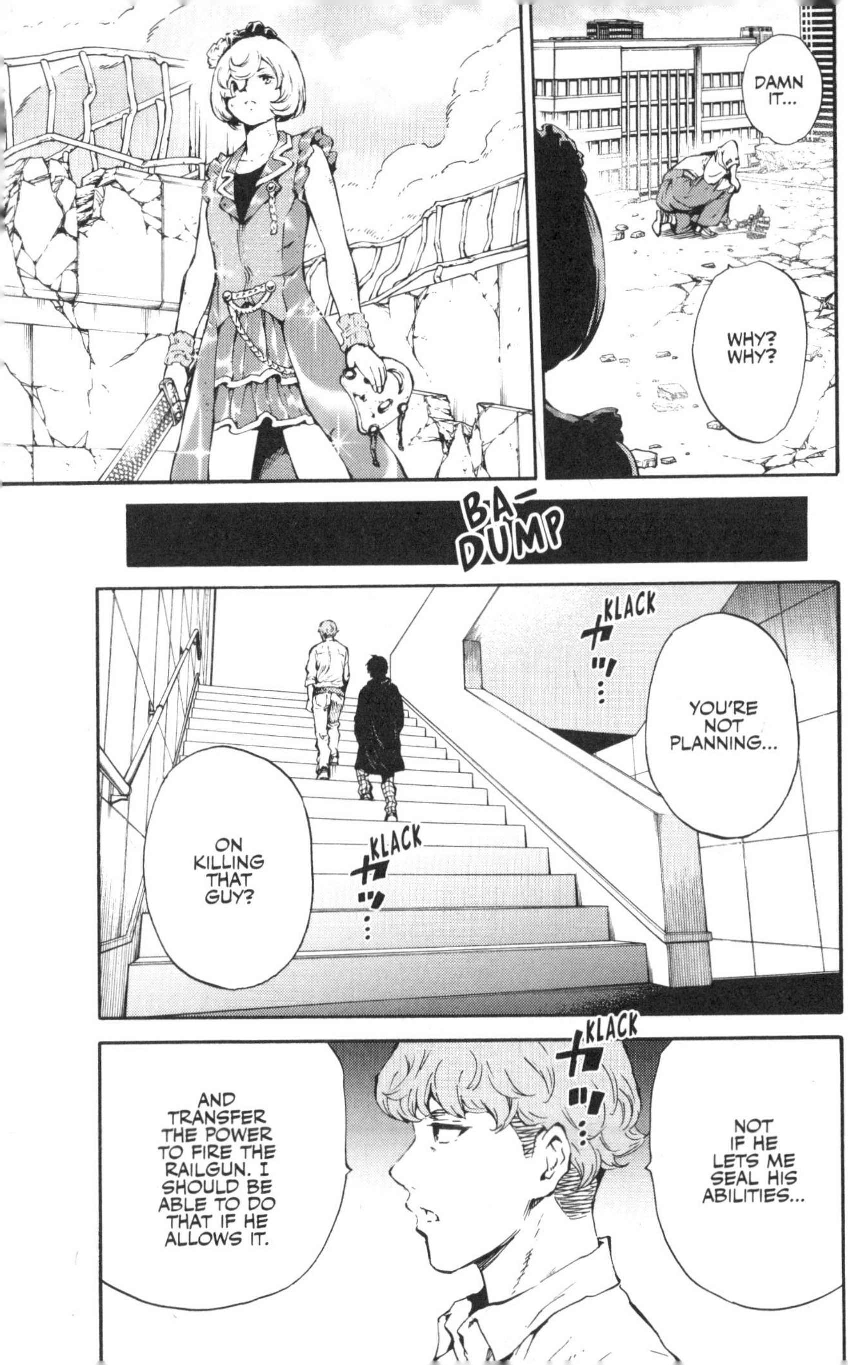
DAMN IT...
WHY? WHY?
BA-DUMP
KLACK
YOU'RE NOT PLANNING...
KLACK
ON KILLING THAT GUY?
KLACK
NOT IF HE LETS ME SEAL HIS ABILITIES...
AND TRANSFER THE POWER TO FIRE THE RAILGUN. I SHOULD BE ABLE TO DO THAT IF HE ALLOWS IT.

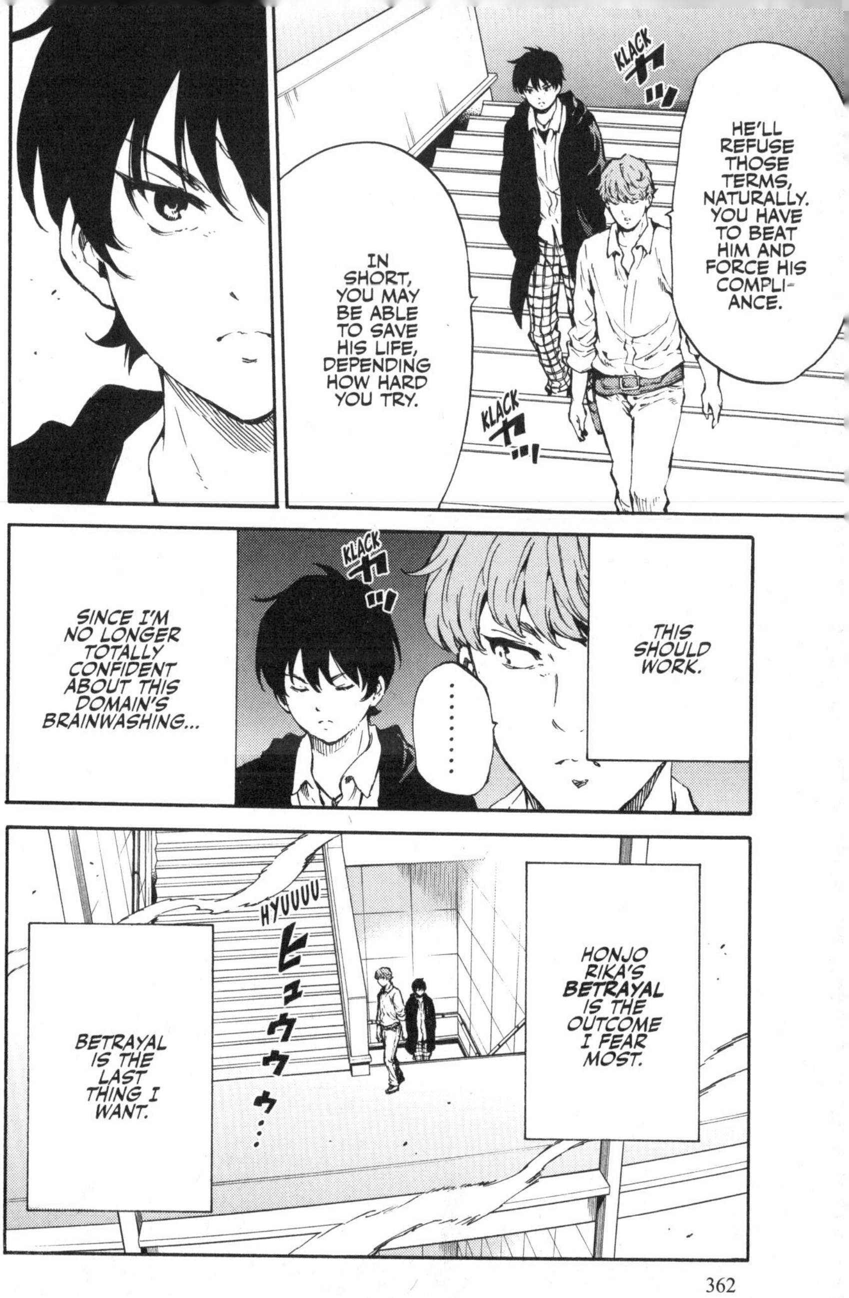
HE'LL REFUSE THOSE TERMS, NATURALLY. YOU HAVE TO BEAT HIM AND FORCE HIS COMPLI-ANCE.
KLACK
IN SHORT, YOU MAY BE ABLE TO SAVE HIS LIFE, DEPENDING HOW HARD YOU TRY.
KLACK
THIS SHOULD WORK.
KLACK
....
SINCE I'M NO LONGER TOTALLY CONFIDENT ABOUT THIS DOMAIN'S BRAINWASHING...
HONJO RIKA'S BETRAYAL IS THE OUTCOME I FEAR MOST.
HYUUUU
BETRAYAL IS THE LAST THING I WANT.

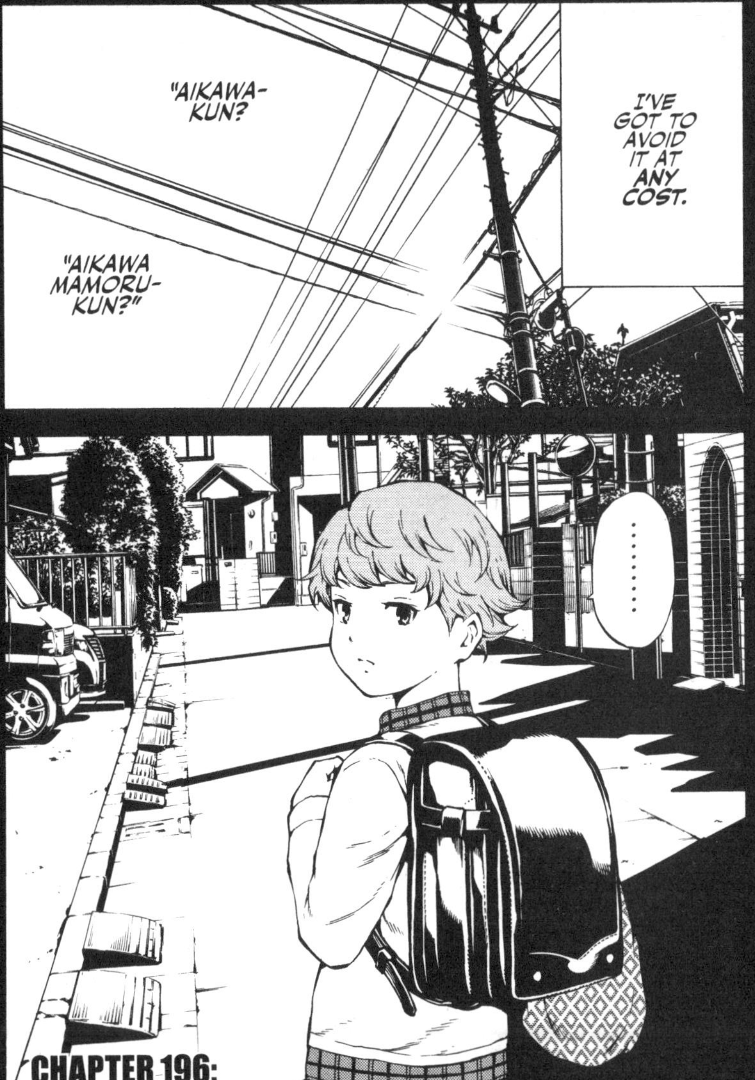
I'VE GOT TO AVOID IT AT ANY COST.
"AIKAWA-KUN?
"AIKAWA MAMORU-KUN?"
…………
CHAPTER 196: Memories

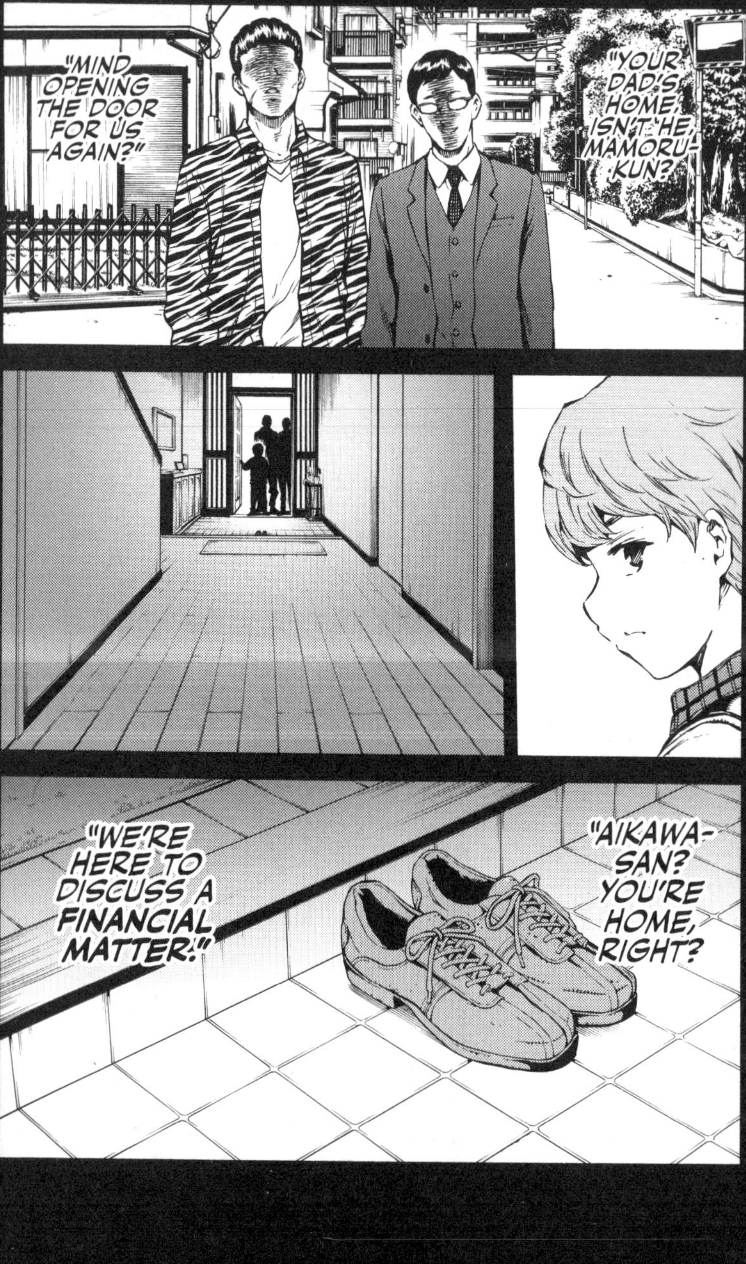
"YOUR DAD'S HOME, ISN'T HE, MAMORU-KUN?
"MIND OPENING THE DOOR FOR US AGAIN?"
"AIKAWA-SAN? YOU'RE HOME, RIGHT?
"WE'RE HERE TO DISCUSS A FINANCIAL MATTER."

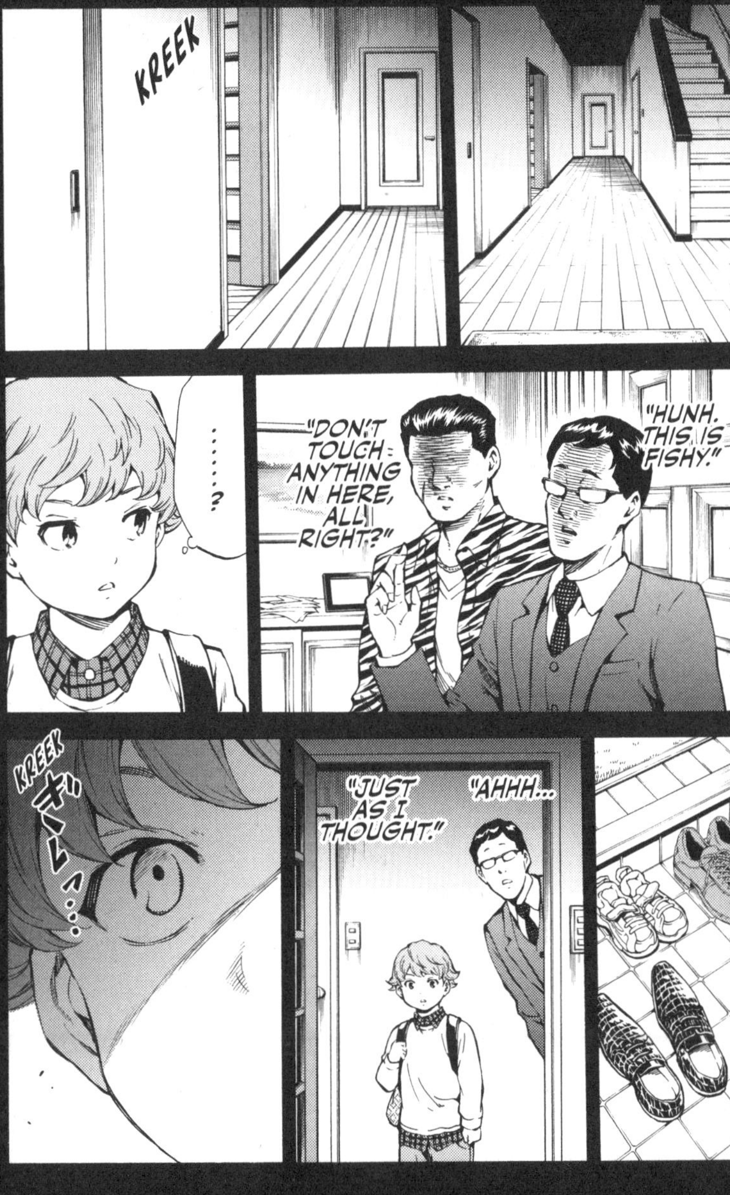
KREEK
"HUNH. THIS IS FISHY."
"DON'T TOUCH ANYTHING IN HERE, ALL RIGHT?"
......?
"AHHH...
"JUST AS I THOUGHT."
KREEK

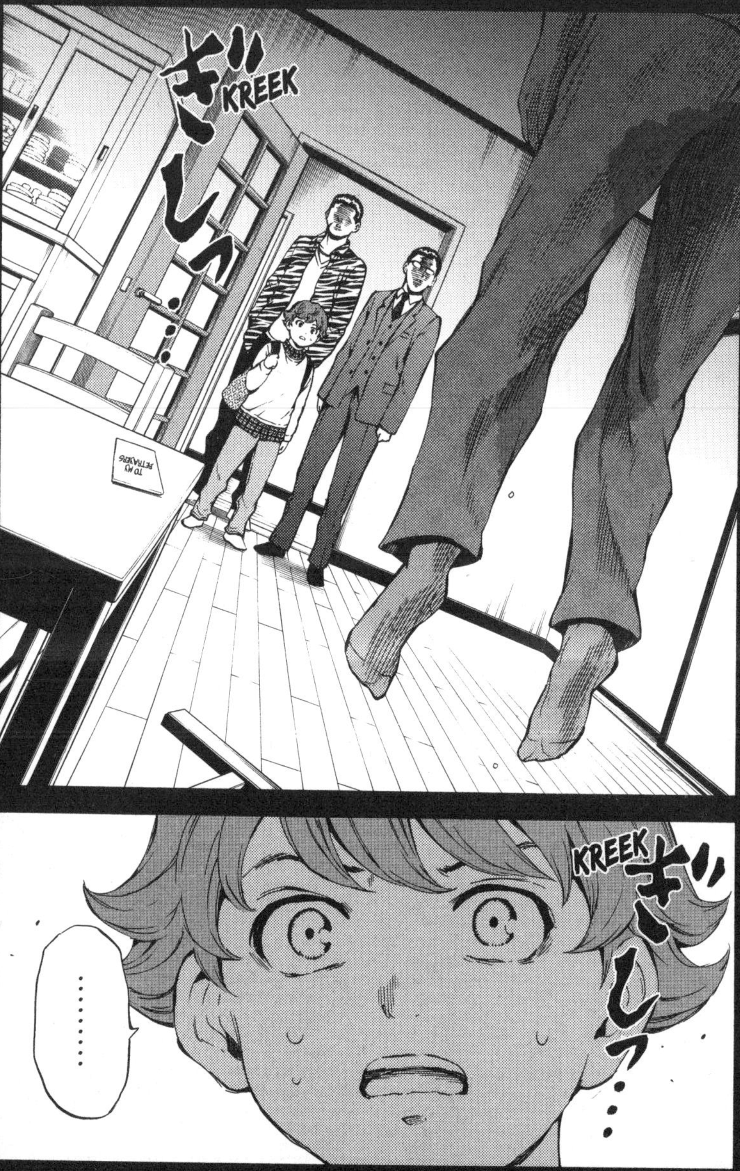
ぎしっ…
KREEK
TO MY BETRAYERS
KREEK
ぎしっ…
…………

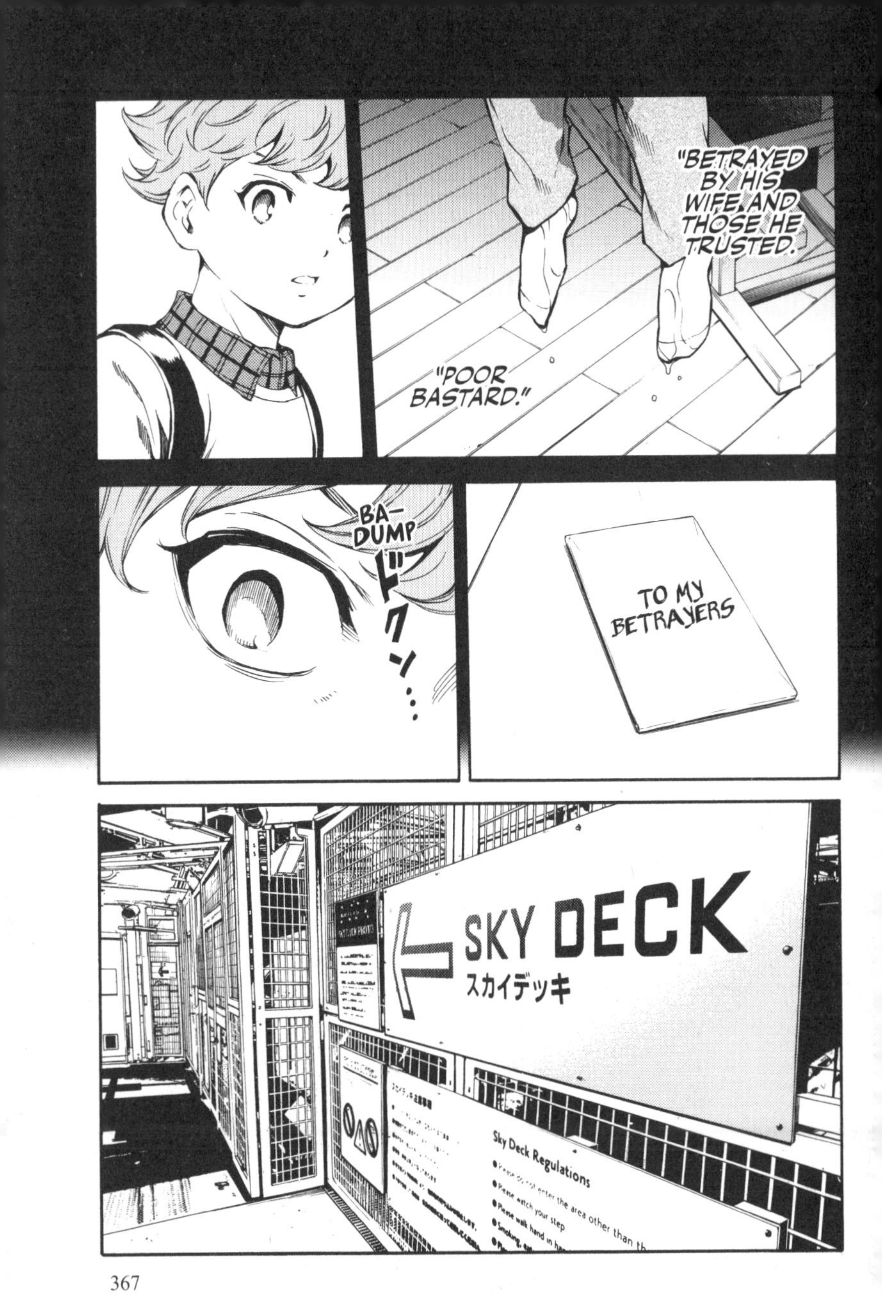
"BETRAYED BY HIS WIFE AND THOSE HE TRUSTED.
"POOR BASTARD."
TO MY BETRAYERS
BA-DUMP
ドクン…
SKY DECK
スカイデッキ
Sky Deck Regulations
Please watch your step

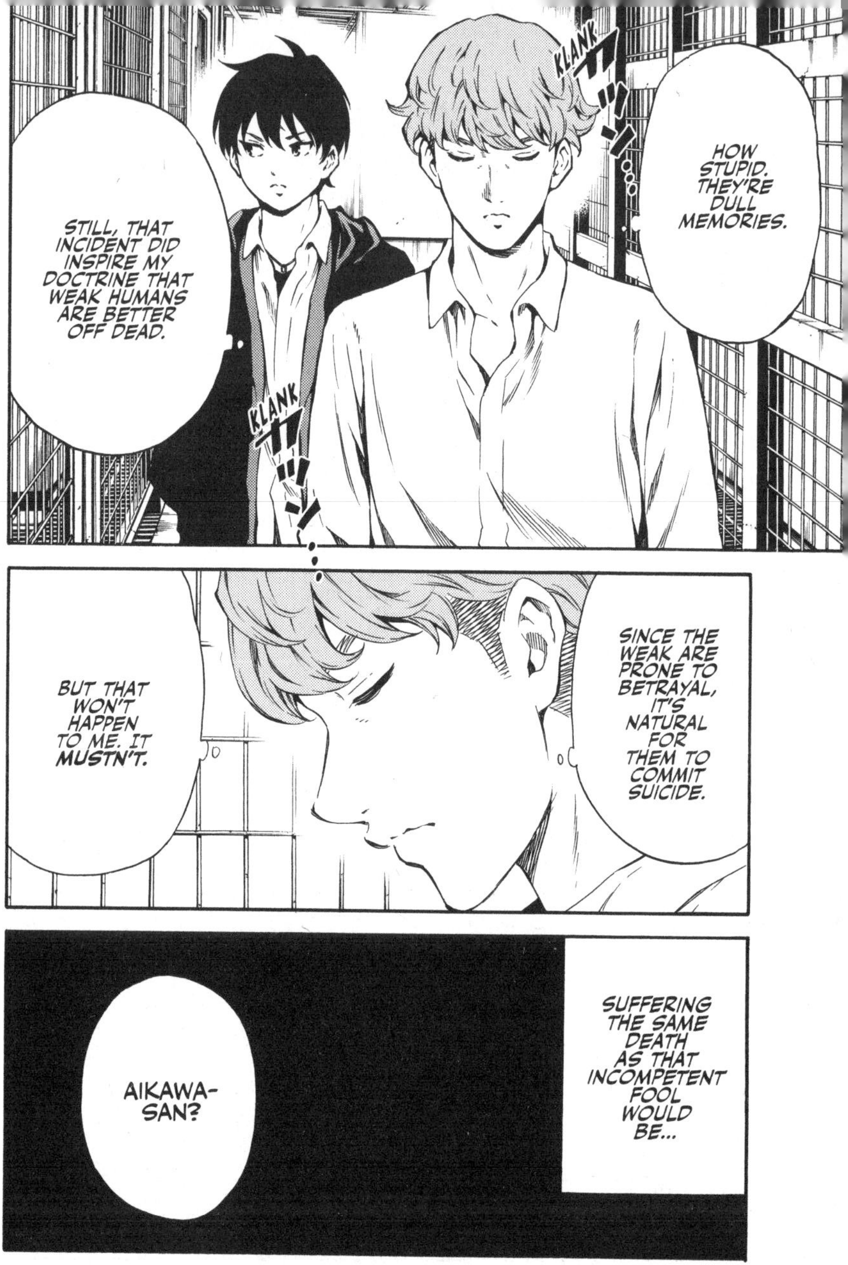

KLANK
HOW STUPID. THEY'RE DULL MEMORIES.
STILL, THAT INCIDENT DID INSPIRE MY DOCTRINE THAT WEAK HUMANS ARE BETTER OFF DEAD.
KLANK
SINCE THE WEAK ARE PRONE TO BETRAYAL, IT'S NATURAL FOR THEM TO COMMIT SUICIDE.
BUT THAT WON'T HAPPEN TO ME. IT MUSTN'T.
SUFFERING THE SAME DEATH AS THAT INCOMPETENT FOOL WOULD BE...
AIKAWA-SAN?

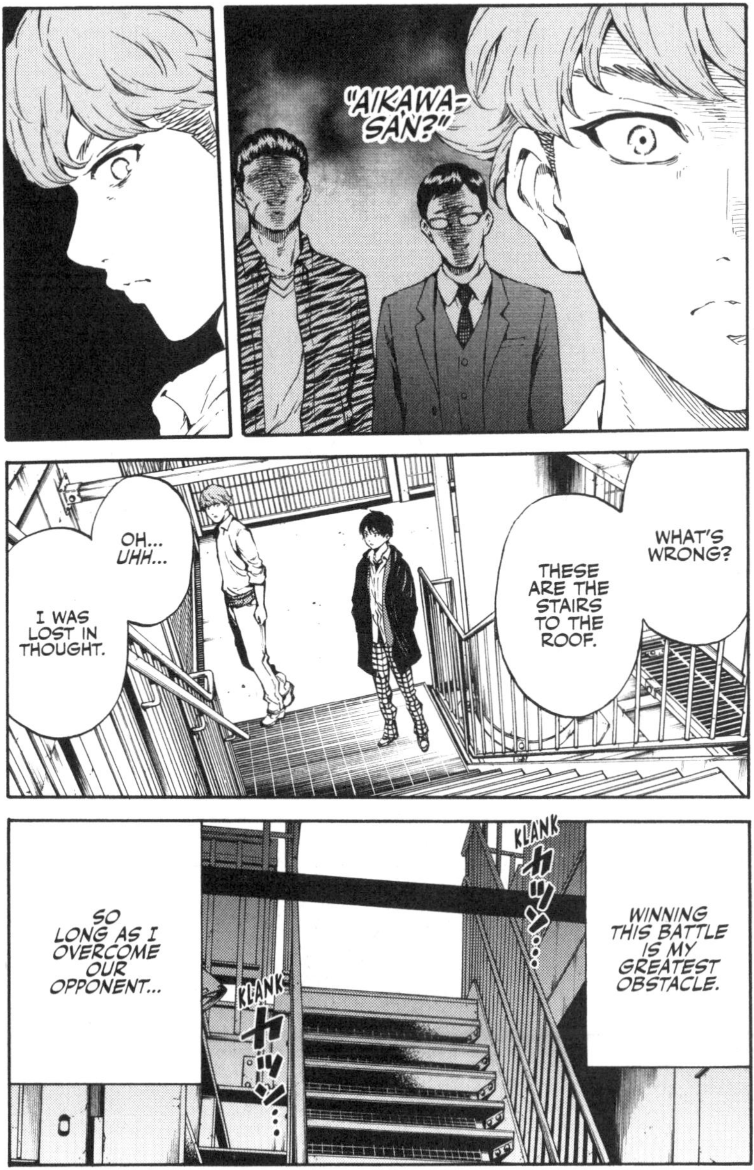
"AIKAWA-SAN?"
WHAT'S WRONG?
THESE ARE THE STAIRS TO THE ROOF.
OH... UHH...
I WAS LOST IN THOUGHT.
WINNING THIS BATTLE IS MY GREATEST OBSTACLE.
KLANK
KLANK
SO LONG AS I OVERCOME OUR OPPONENT...

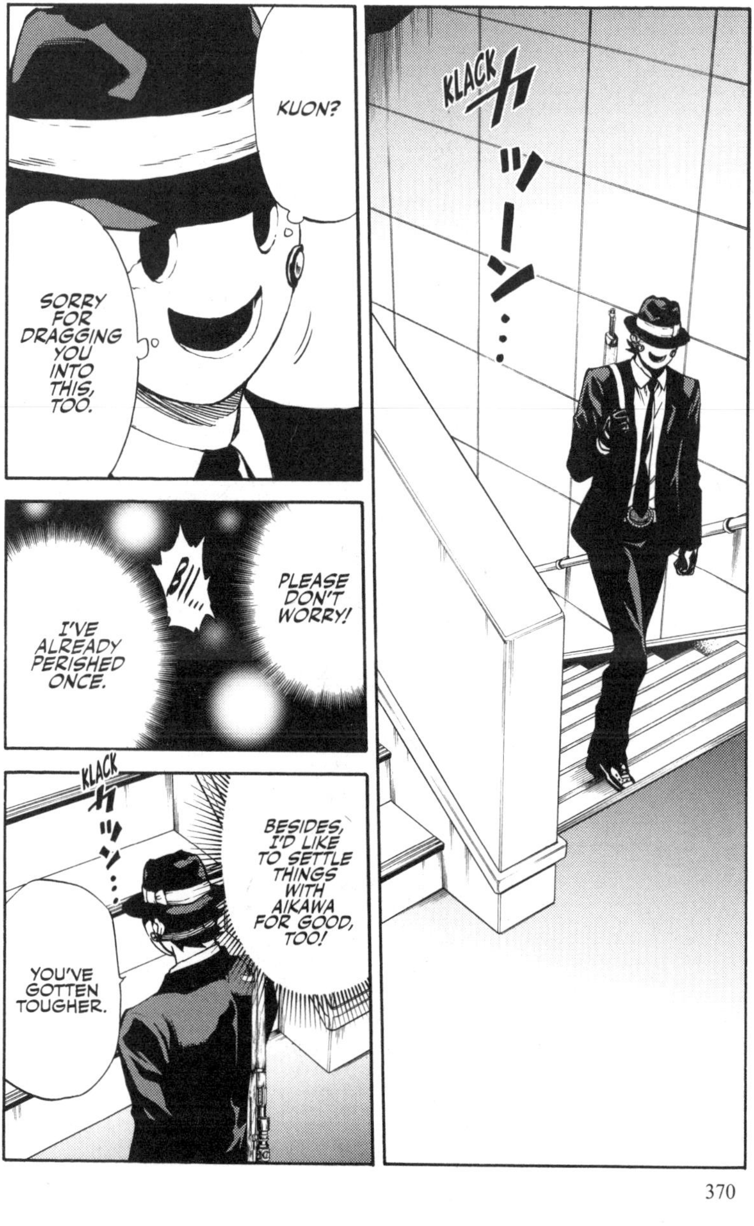
KLACK
KUON?
SORRY FOR DRAGGING YOU INTO THIS, TOO.
PLEASE DON'T WORRY!
BII...
I'VE ALREADY PERISHED ONCE.
KLACK
BESIDES, I'D LIKE TO SETTLE THINGS WITH AIKAWA FOR GOOD, TOO!
YOU'VE GOTTEN TOUGHER.

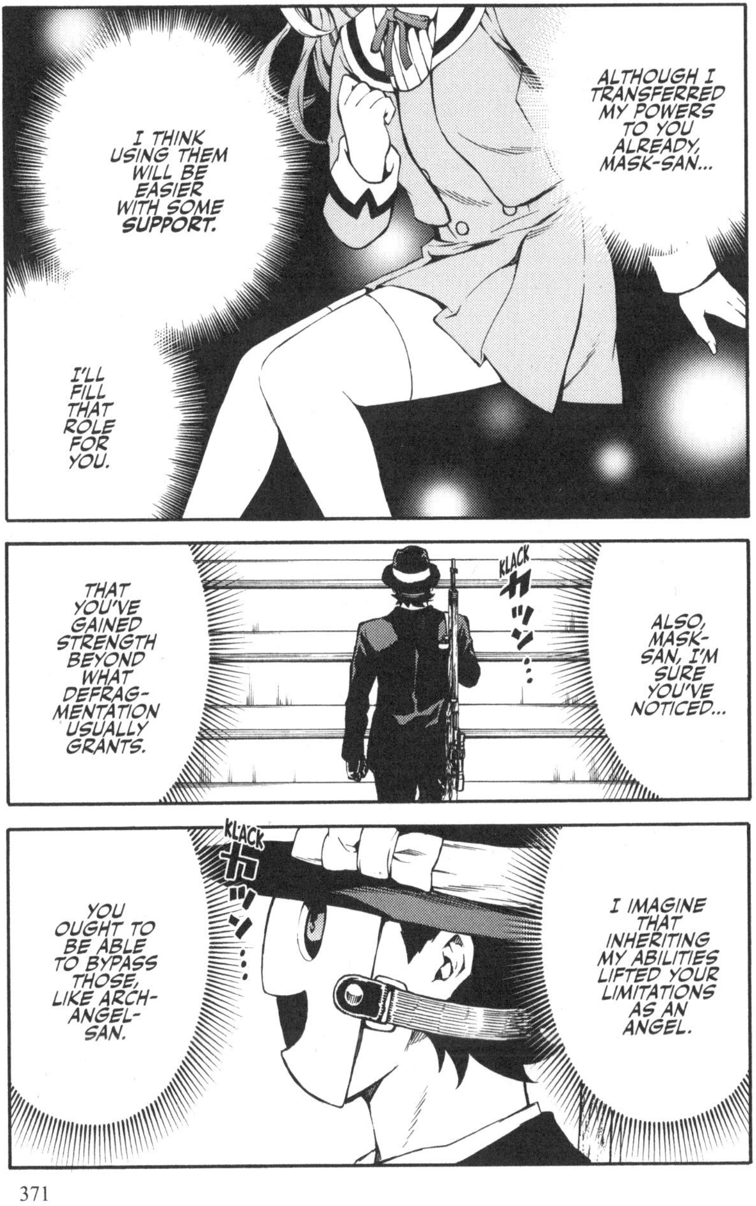

ALTHOUGH I TRANSFERRED MY POWERS TO YOU ALREADY, MASK-SAN...
I THINK USING THEM WILL BE EASIER WITH SOME SUPPORT.
I'LL FILL THAT ROLE FOR YOU.
KLACK
カッ…
ALSO, MASK-SAN, I'M SURE YOU'VE NOTICED...
THAT YOU'VE GAINED STRENGTH BEYOND WHAT DEFRAGMENTATION USUALLY GRANTS.
I IMAGINE THAT INHERITING MY ABILITIES LIFTED YOUR LIMITATIONS AS AN ANGEL.
KLACK
カッ…
YOU OUGHT TO BE ABLE TO BYPASS THOSE, LIKE ARCH-ANGEL-SAN.

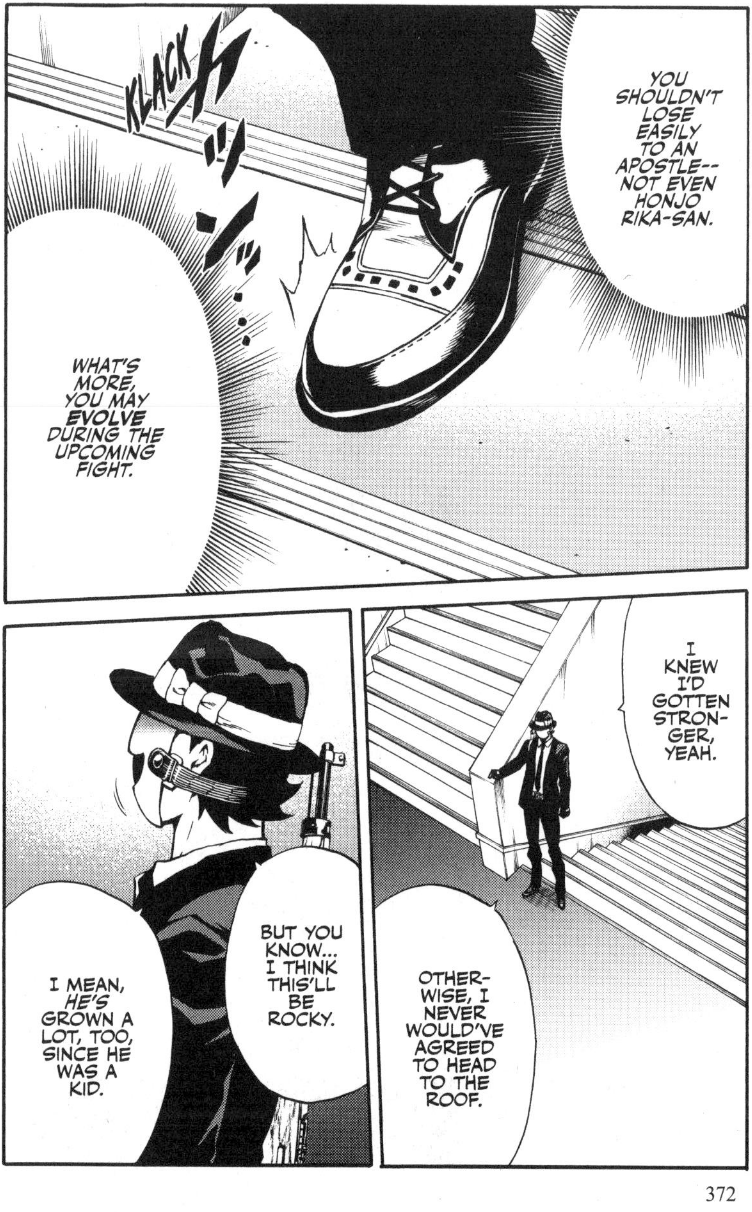
YOU SHOULDN'T LOSE EASILY TO AN APOSTLE--NOT EVEN HONJO RIKA-SAN.
KLACK
WHAT'S MORE, YOU MAY **EVOLVE** DURING THE UPCOMING FIGHT.
I KNEW I'D GOTTEN STRONGER, YEAH.
OTHERWISE, I NEVER WOULD'VE AGREED TO HEAD TO THE ROOF.
BUT YOU KNOW... I THINK THIS'LL BE ROCKY.
I MEAN, *HE'S* GROWN A LOT, TOO, SINCE HE WAS A KID.

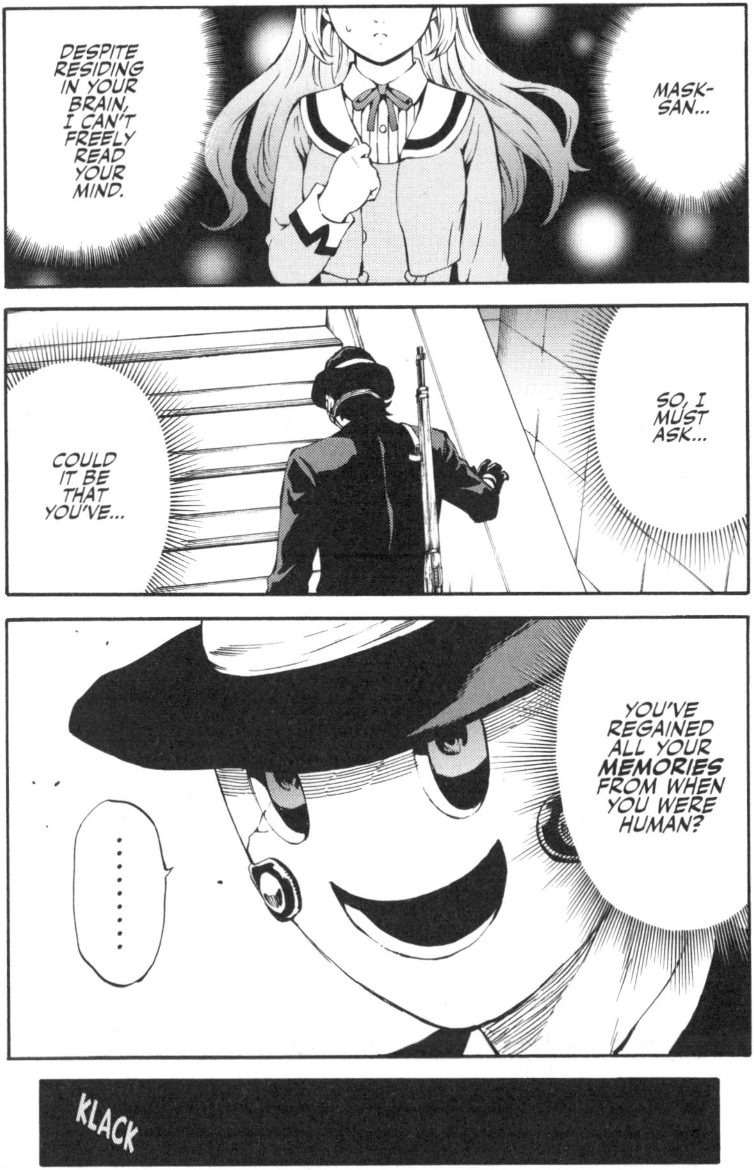
MASK-SAN...
DESPITE RESIDING IN YOUR BRAIN, I CAN'T FREELY READ YOUR MIND.
SO, I MUST ASK...
COULD IT BE THAT YOU'VE...
YOU'VE REGAINED ALL YOUR MEMORIES FROM WHEN YOU WERE HUMAN?
....
KLACK

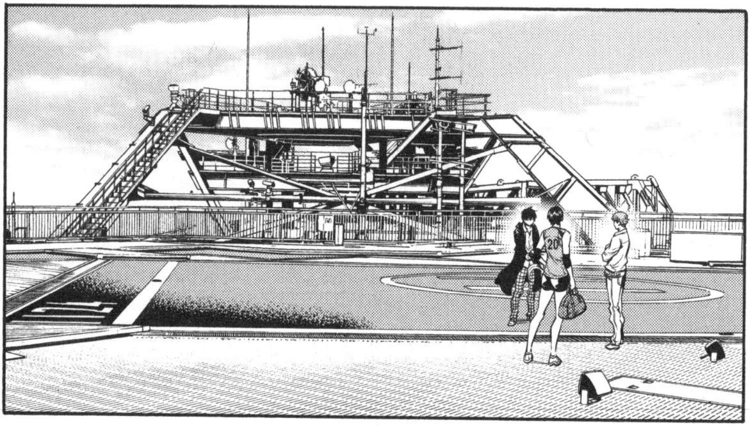

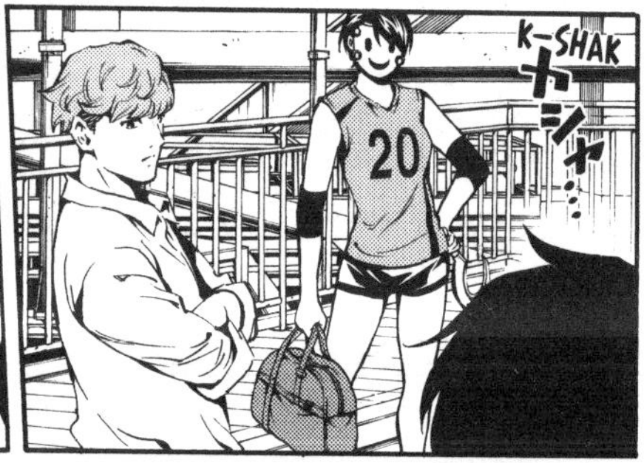
K-SHAK
カシャ

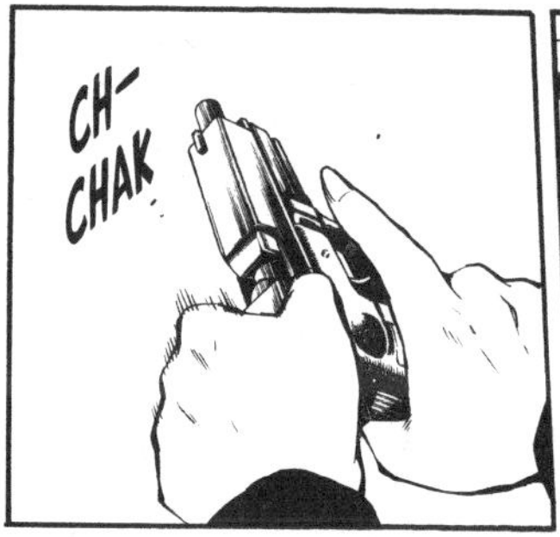
CH-CHAK

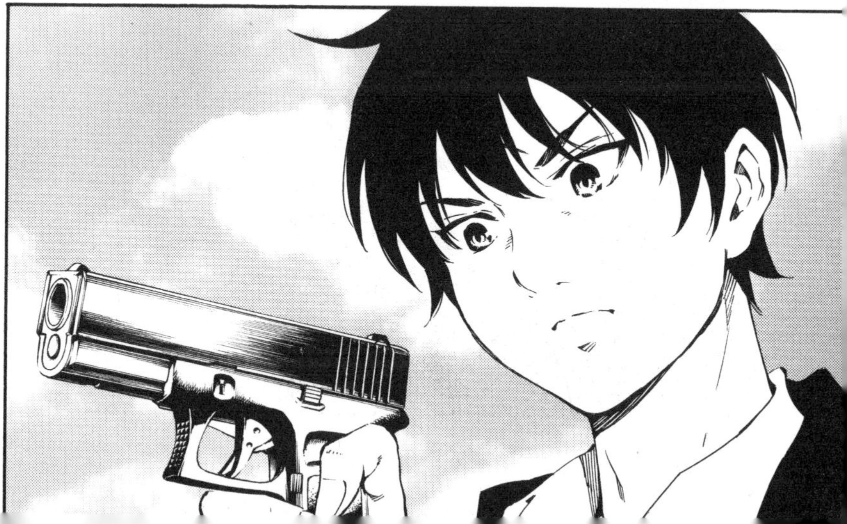

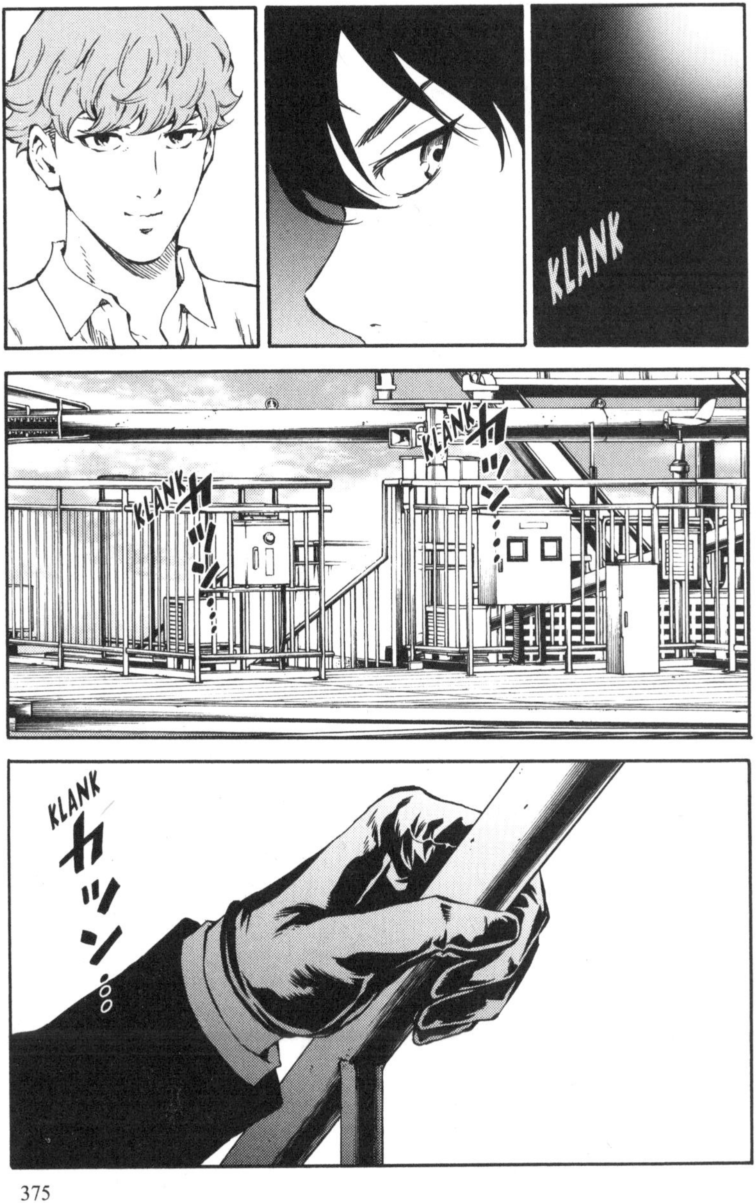
KLANK
KLANK
カッン…
KLANK
カッン…
KLANK
カッン…

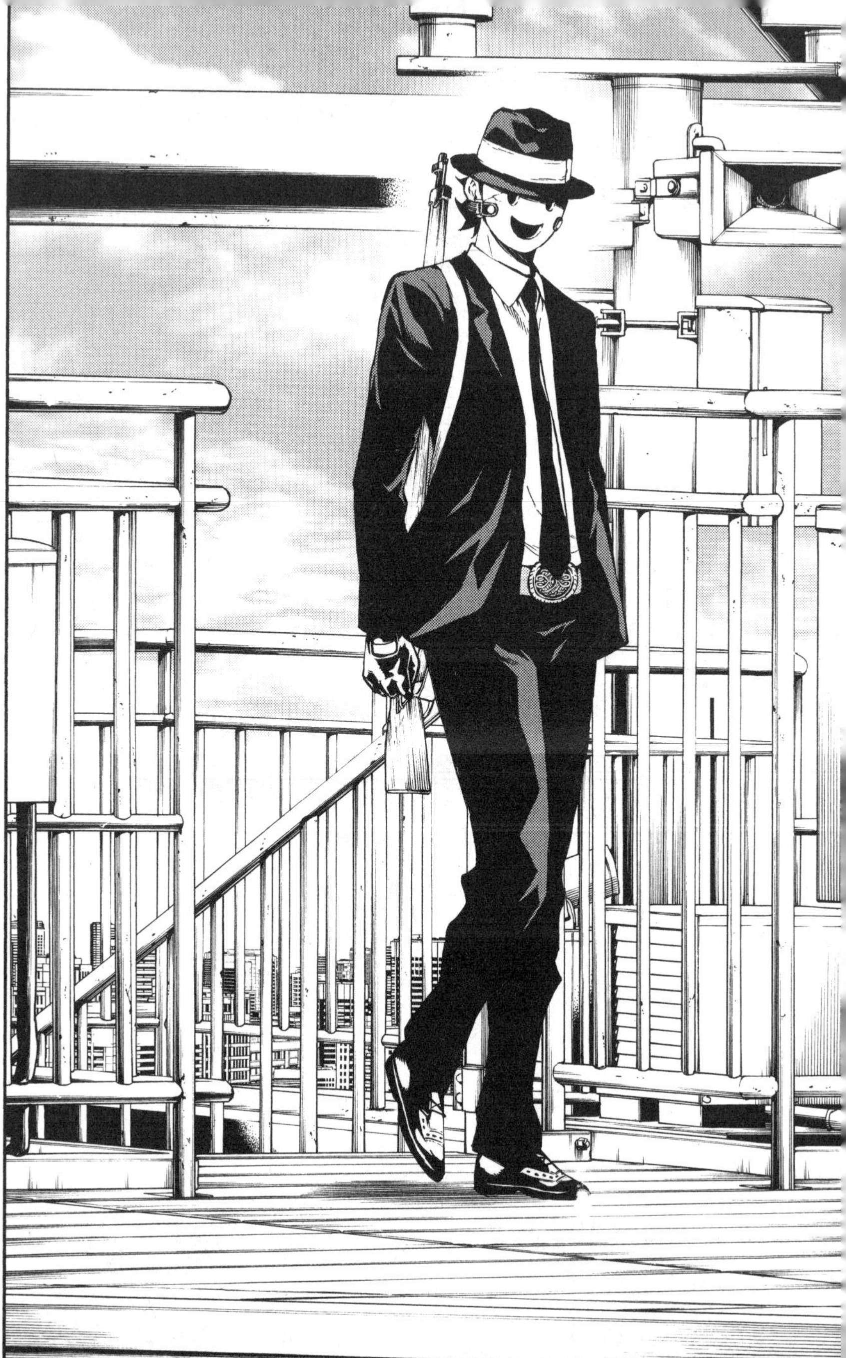

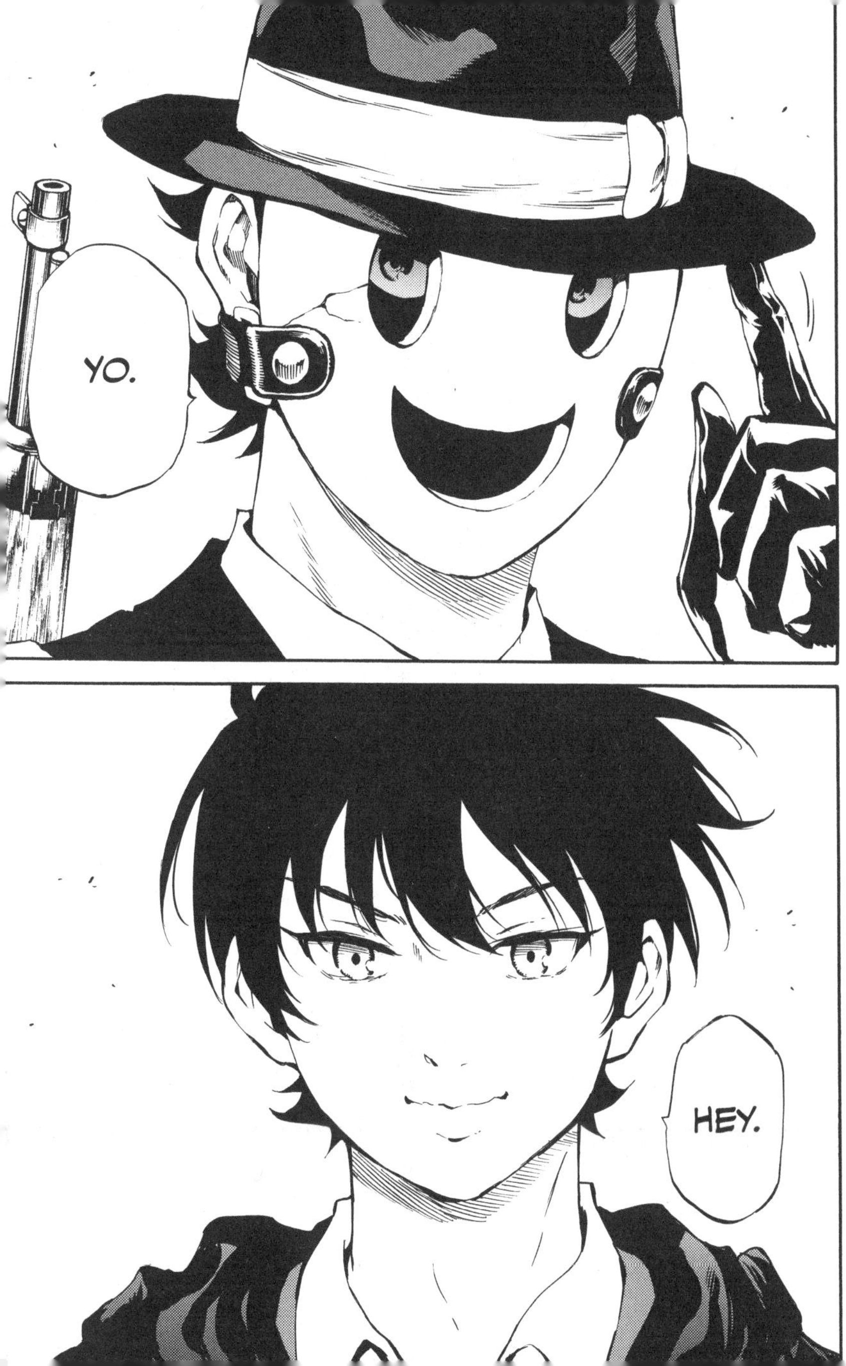
YO.
HEY.

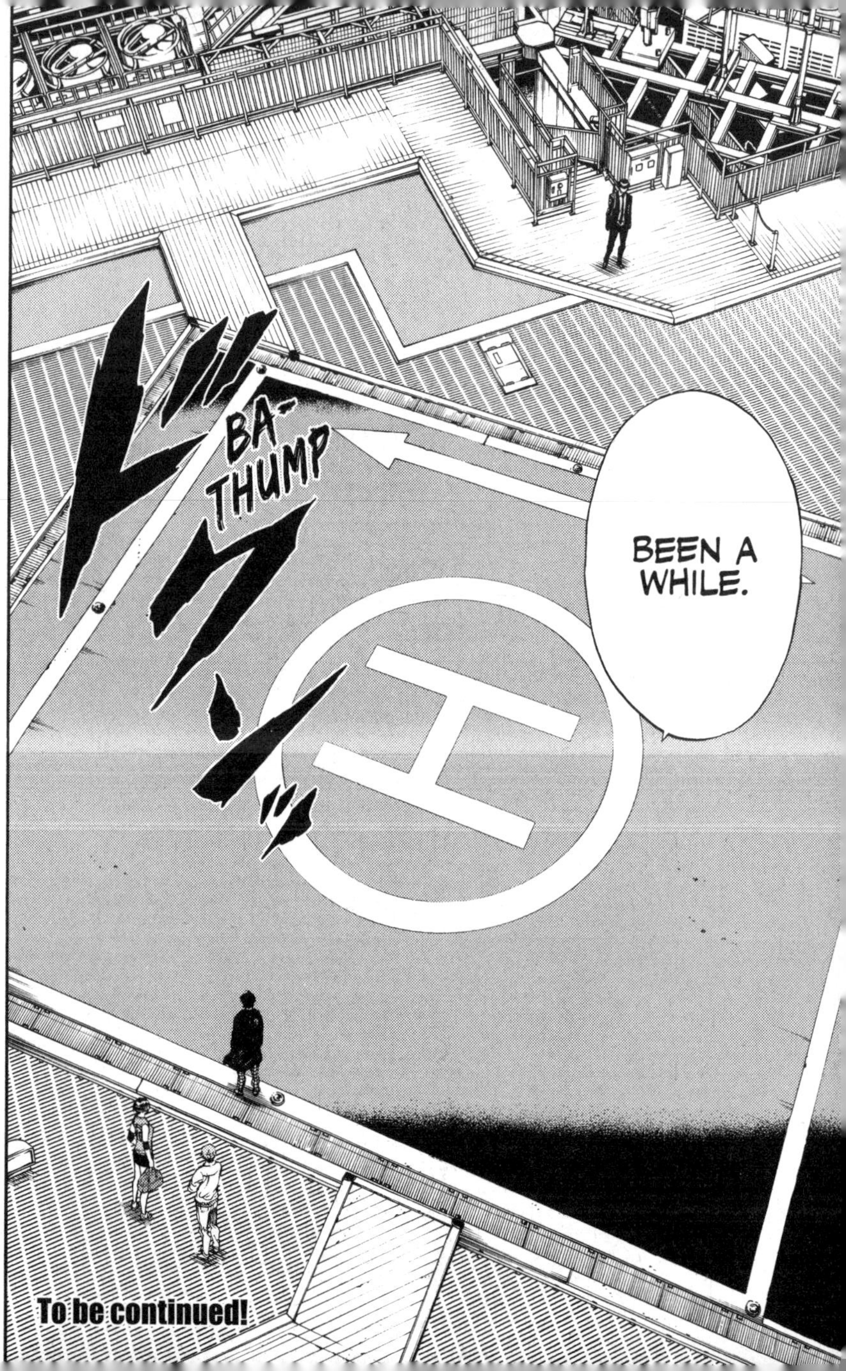
BA-THUMP
BEEN A WHILE.
To be continued!

HIGH-RISE INVASION

STORY
Tsuina Miura

ART
Takahiro Oba

STAFF
Fukuen Kanako
Sakurai Hiroshi
Igarashi Tae

EDITORS
Uchida Tomohiro
Kohori Ryuuichi

COMICS EDITOR
Nozawa Shinobu

COVER DESIGN
Inadome Ken

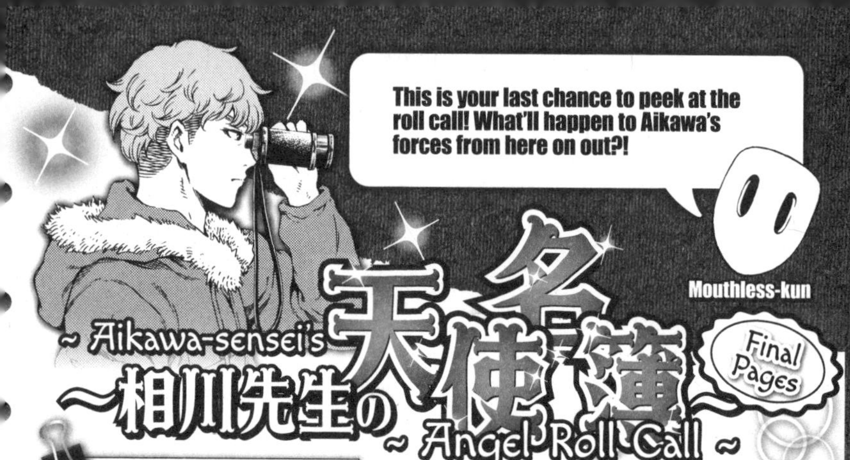
This is your last chance to peek at the roll call! What'll happen to Aikawa's forces from here on out?!
Mouthless-kun
~ Aikawa-sensei's
~相川先生の天使名簿~
~ Angel Roll Call ~
Final Pages

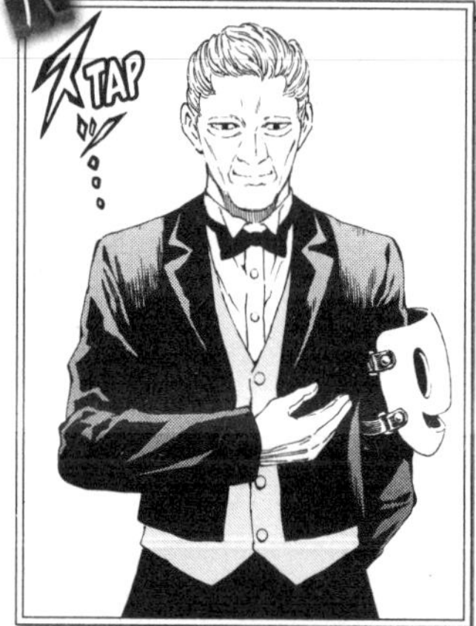
TAP

Follower #: 1 **Nickname:** Kijima

Outfit: Butler uniform

Age: 50s **Speech:** No ⟶ Yes

Weapon: Damascus steel dagger

Rating: 5 ⟶ 9

Notes: Since I control more Angels now, I'm listing them on a roll call, like I did in the old world. I named the very first Mask I drafted after a student from the class I led. Despite being an Angel, he's retained some intelligence. That might come in handy outside combat. **Update:** Smarter Angels can make the most of their physical abilities. Thus, as time's passed, Kijima's become unrecognizably strong. His ability to speak unlocked. He's now indistinguishable from a human. When Angels become more human, however, it may also undermine my control. Going forward, I'll have to be cautious about that.

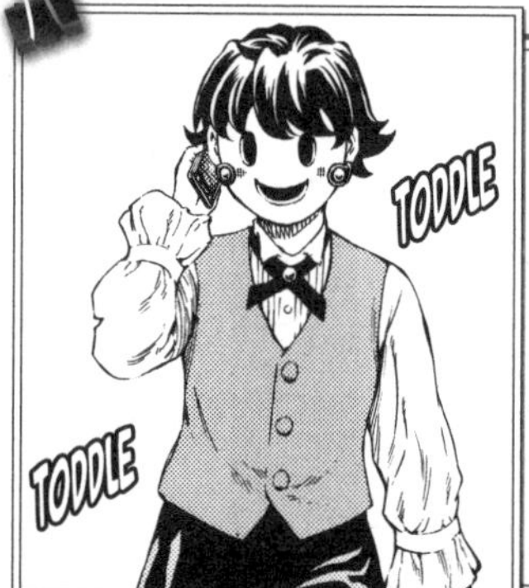
TODDLE
TODDLE

Follower #: 26 **Nickname:** Kaneda-kun

Outfit: Child's butler uniform? **Age:** Teens **Speech:** Yes

Weapon: Capoeira **Rating:** 3

Notes: Once I used my strength-measuring ability, I knew he was underpowered. Still, since our wavelengths matched, I drafted him for the sake of numbers. He could speak and so on from the get-go, so his intelligence proved high. He's an excellent point of contact. **Update:** His legs are short, so he's completely unable to use the capoeira skill he gained. He'll remain weak when it comes to combat, unfortunately.

Follower #: 17/18/19 **Nickname:**

Sword/Longsword/Spear, Idol Mask(s)

Outfit: Idol costumes (Red)

Age: 16 (Longsword, Spear)/17 (Sword) **Speech:** No

Weapon: Ancient Chinese bronze sword/Unique western longsword/Japanese Sengoku-period spear

Rating: TBD (Currently training for formation attacks)

Notes: I discovered these idols just after losing the Glock Sisters, while keeping an eye out for another cooperative team. Once we masked them, the wavelengths of all three matched mine, so I drafted the trio. Finding them was lucky. In our old world, they were apparently famous in their own right. My students discussed them, so I know a bit about them, too. As I recall, they were chosen to break off from a larger idol group and form a trio based on their talent. Their choreography was evidently well-known, although I'm not familiar with it personally. I'm not certain, but depending on how their training goes, they might end up capable of facing opponents at Archangel's level.

Re: All-Out Battle with the Railgun User

※ This memo just lists controlled Angels I can currently use. I'll strategize in more detail later.

- Football Mask
- Falchion Mask
- Electric Saw Mask
- Rake Mask
- Ball and Chain Mask
- Bandana Mask
- Knickerbocker Mask

※ Doubt they'd even slow the foe down.

- Gun Mask (Combat Magnum)
- Gun Mask (Walther P38)
- Ishida
- Inoue

※ Might do damage if they caught the foe at the right time.

- Santa Mask
- Reindeer Mask

※ Decently strong. Capable of speech. Could threaten the foe. Side note: Might've named "Reindeer Mask" too sloppily.

- Nunchaku Mask
- Volleyball Mask
- Student Mask

※ Strong themselves, but weak weapons. Not sure how to use them.

- White Feather

※ My strongest drafted Mask. The foe knows her abilities, though, which hamstrings her a bit.

- Grenade Launcher Mask Two

※ Use when the sniper's off guard.

- Kijima
- Idol Mask Trio

※ Leave them to Kijima.

- Maid Mask
- Kaneda-kun
- Medic Mask

※ Unusable.

- Racket Mask

※ Keep using to monitor Ikebukuro Building.

- Kusakabe

※ Whereabouts unknown. Don't expect her to return.

Bye-bye!

So, Aikawa-sensei turned out to like idols despite hating humans, huh? Well, I think that's fine!

Text/Tsuina Miura

This Volume's Extra Goodies!

The My-Staff-Made-Awesome-3D Models-I'm-Unveiling-Unapproved Corner!

Hey there! We're showing these off to you just 'cause we can! Turn your book, smartphone, or tablet to make this easier to read!

Mouthless-kun

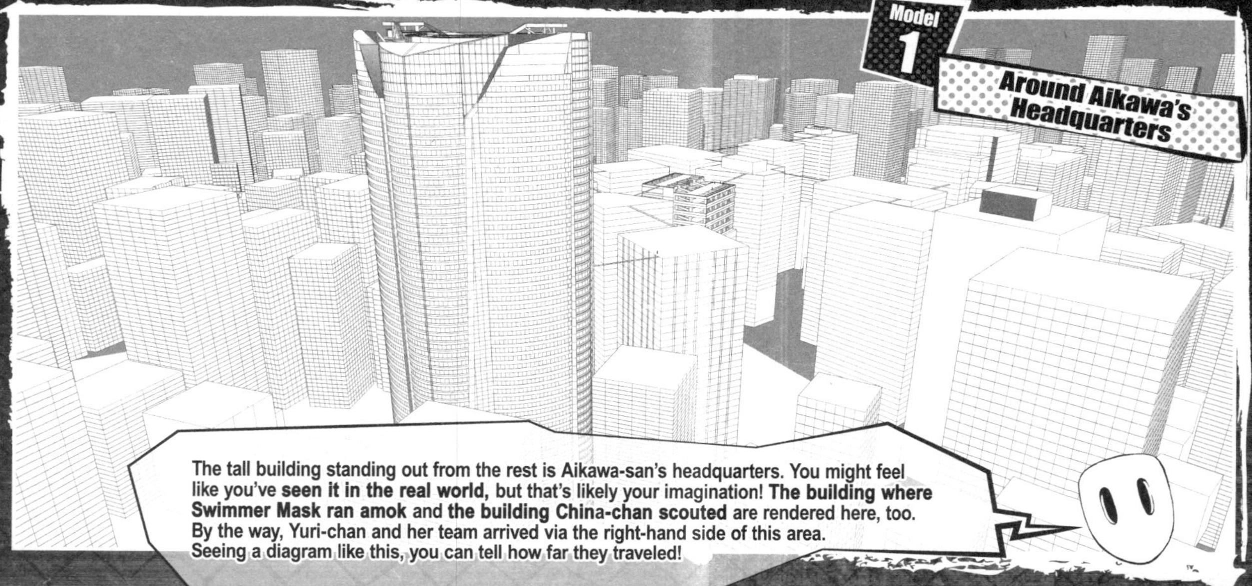
Model 1
Around Aikawa's Headquarters
The tall building standing out from the rest is Aikawa-san's headquarters. You might feel like you've **seen it in the real world,** but that's likely your imagination! **The building where Swimmer Mask ran amok** and **the building China-chan scouted** are rendered here, too. By the way, Yuri-chan and her team arrived via the right-hand side of this area. Seeing a diagram like this, you can tell how far they traveled!

Model 2 — Parking Garage

This nonsensical car park makes you wonder why something like it even exists in the high-rise world! Human models were included to provide scale. Man, the creators didn't half-ass this 3D model at all! Archangel-kun and Guardian Angel-san are battling spectacularly in here right now! This building housed numerous luxury cars for some reason…but they've all been thoughtlessly wrecked. FYI, though, they aren't car models that actually exist! After all, we have to consider things like that, or we could get in trouble!

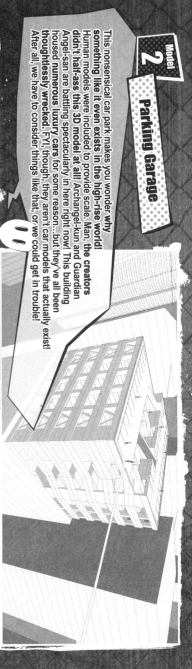

Model 3 — Aikawa's HQ Roof

Here's the rooftop where Rika-kun and Sniper-san reunited in this volume! I wonder what's gonna happen to those two? This area's appeared plenty of **times in the past.** A helicopter even flew by! This model's also quite intricate! I guess it was necessary so that an artist could draw it from an aerial perspective. To change the subject, I hear that the view from the Roppongi rooftop that looks like this one is amazing! Everyone should visit at least once!

Bye-bye!

If I get any more interesting models, I'll unveil them here again! Oh, and when I said "unapproved," I was kidding!

Text/Tsuina Miura / Model Production/Sakurai Hiroshi

SEVEN SEAS ENTERTAINMENT PRESENTS

HIGH-RISE INVASION Vol. 15-16

story by TSUINA MIURA / art by TAKAHIRO OBA

TRANSLATION
Nan Rymer

ADAPTATION
Rebecca Schneidereit

LETTERING AND RETOUCH
Meaghan Tucker

COVER DESIGN
Kris Aubin

PROOFREADER
Janet Houck

EDITOR
Peter Adrian Behravesh

PREPRESS TECHNICIAN
Rhiannon Rasmussen-Silverstein

PRODUCTION MANAGER
Lissa Pattillo

MANAGING EDITOR
Julie Davis

ASSOCIATE PUBLISHER
Adam Arnold

PUBLISHER
Jason DeAngelis

TENKUU SHINPAN VOLUME 15-16
© Tsuina Miura 2018, © Takahiro Oba 2018
All rights reserved.
First published in Japan in 2018 by Kodansha Ltd., Tokyo.
Publication rights for this English edition arranged through Kodansha Ltd.,
Tokyo.

Seven Seas press and purchase enquiries can be sent to Marketing Manager
Lianne Sentar at press@gomanga.com. Information regarding the distribution
and purchase of digital editions is available from Digital Manager CK Russell
at digital@gomanga.com.

Seven Seas and the Seven Seas logo are trademarks of
Seven Seas Entertainment. All rights reserved.

ISBN: 978-1-64505-756-7

Printed in Canada

First Printing: November 2020

10 9 8 7 6 5 4 3 2 1

FOLLOW US ONLINE: *www.sevenseasentertainment.com*

READING DIRECTIONS

This book reads from *right to left*, Japanese style. If this is your first time reading manga, you start reading from the top right panel on each page and take it from there. If you get lost, just follow the numbered diagram here. It may seem backwards at first, but you'll get the hang of it! Have fun!!

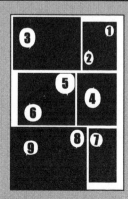